"RIGHT MAKES MIGHT"

"RIGHT MAKES MIGHT"

Proverbs and the American Worldview

Wolfgang Mieder

INDIANA UNIVERSITY PRESS

This book is a publication of

Indiana University Press
Office of Scholarly Publishing
Herman B Wells Library 350
1320 East 10th Street
Bloomington, Indiana 47405 USA

iupress.indiana.edu

© 2019 by Wolfgang Mieder

All rights reserved
No part of this book may be reproduced or utilized in any form or by any means, electronic or mechanical, including photocopying and recording, or by any information storage and retrieval system, without permission in writing from the publisher. The paper used in this publication meets the minimum requirements of the American National Standard for Information Sciences—Permanence of Paper for Printed Library Materials, ANSI Z39.48-1992.

Manufactured in the United States of America

Library of Congress Cataloging-in-Publication Data

Names: Mieder, Wolfgang, author.
Title: "Right makes might" : proverbs and the American worldview / Wolfgang Mieder.
Description: Bloomington, Indiana, USA : Indiana University Press, [2019] | Includes bibliographical references and index.
Identifiers: LCCN 2018049711 (print) | LCCN 2018061381 (ebook) | ISBN 9780253040367 (e-book) | ISBN 9780253040343 (cl : alk. paper) | ISBN 9780253040350 (pb : alk. paper)
Subjects: LCSH: United States—Politics and government—Miscellanea. | United States—Politics and government—Quotations, maxims, etc. | Proverbs, American—History and criticism. | Proverbs—Political aspects—United States. | Political oratory—United States—History. | Rhetoric—Political aspects—United States—History. | Politicians—United States—Language. | National characteristics, American.
Classification: LCC E183 (ebook) | LCC E183 .M543 2019 (print) | DDC 320.973—dc23
LC record available at https://lccn.loc.gov/2018049711

1 2 3 4 5   24 23 22 21 20 19

CONTENTS

Preface vii

Introduction: Ruminations on Authentically American Proverbs 1

1 "Let Us Have Faith That Right Makes Might": Proverbial Rhetoric in Decisive Moments of American Politics 34

2 "These Are the Times That Try Women's Souls": The Proverbial Rhetoric for Women's Rights by Elizabeth Cady Stanton and Susan B. Anthony 63

3 "The American People Rose to the Occasion": A Proverbial Retrospective of the Marshall Plan after Seventy Years 100

4 "Making a Way Out of No Way": Martin Luther King Jr.'s Proverbial Dream for Human Rights 123

5 "Keep Your Eyes on the Prize": Congressman John Lewis's Proverbial Odyssey for Civil Rights 145

6 "I'm Absolutely Sure About—the Golden Rule": Barack Obama's Proverbial Audacity of Hope 182

7 "Politics Is Not a Spectator Sport": Proverbs in the Personal and Political Writings of Hillary Rodham Clinton 200

8 "The Rich Get Richer, and the Poor Get Poorer": Bernie Sanders's Proverbial Rhetoric for an American Sociopolitical Revolution 230

9 "M(R)ight Makes R(M)ight": The Sociopolitical History of a Contradictory Proverb Pair 263

10 "All Men Are Created Equal": From Democratic Claim to Proverbial Game   287

11 "Laissez faire à Georges" and "Let George Do It": A Case of Paremiological Polygenesis   317

12 "To Be (All) Greek to Someone": Origin, History, and Meaning of an English Proverbial Expression   334

Index   353

PREFACE

IT IS WITH MUCH PLEASURE THAT I PRESENT this collection of twelve relatively recent studies under the umbrella title of *"Right Makes Might": Proverbs and the American Worldview*. I am delighted and honored that Indiana University Press is adding this book to its prestigious publications in folklore, giving me the opportunity to make especially those articles that appeared in Germany, Greece, Portugal, Russia, and Spain more accessible. Ten of them stem from the period between 2008 and 2015, with the additional three appearing here for the first time. Together they represent a multifaceted picture of the use and function of proverbs, some of them of unique American vintage, during the history of the United States from its early beginnings to the very modern time. The various chapters are connected by a sociopolitical theme that includes presidential politics, the early struggle for women's rights, the civil rights movement, and more recent attempts to revolutionize national politics. This preoccupation with social and political issues is also present in the final chapters, which take a close look at four proverbs and proverbial expressions, showing that one and the same traditional phrase can take on numerous expressive roles over time.

The proverbial red thread that ties these individual studies together is their concern with the significance of proverbial language as part of the communicative processes in the sociopolitical arena of the United States and beyond. After all, the proverbial rhetoric does not merely take place regionally and nationally but also on the international level, with this country being a major player on the world scene. That traditional proverbs or innovative antiproverbs have their impressive role to play in all of this is what this book is all about. Just one particular pair of proverbs makes this perfectly clear, to wit the aggressive proverb "might makes right" that has been traced back to 1311 in the English language and its humane antiproverb "right makes might" that established itself in 1381 but with less frequent use. By the time Abraham Lincoln employed the latter in 1860 in his famed Cooper Union address of February 27, 1860, in New York City, it had taken on an ethical and democratic connotation: "Let us have faith that right makes might, and in that faith, let us, to the end, dare to do our duty as we understand it." While this remarkable president did not originate the proverb "right makes might," as is so often maintained, it is his use of it in this very sentence that informs my studies and that should be the guidepost for American and global politics.

The introduction: "Ruminations on Authentically American Proverbs" serves as an overview to the nature of proverbs, with unique emphasis on American proverbs and not on the numerous proverbs of British origin. It is based on intensive diachronic research and treats the origin, the (inter) national distribution, and some German loan translations of truly American proverbs as an example of their global spread. By way of numerous examples, their structures and variants, aspects of antiproverbs, their known or attributed authors, and their origin from songs, films, advertisements, and the mass media in general are discussed. It is also shown that the world of sports, technology, and finance has led to proverb creations, with many of them stressing such themes as success, time, and life. There is also a discussion about values being expressed in these proverbs, something that should be taken cum grano salis, since proverbs as generalizations must not be understood as definite expressions of worldview. And yet, such proverbs as "paddle your own canoe," "this is a free country," "making a way out of no way," "freedom is not for sale," and "think outside the box" are blatantly American. The quintessential American proverb "different strokes for different folks," with its earliest recorded reference from 1945, was coined among the African American population and was popularized throughout the country by way of the song "Everyday People" (1968) by the group Sly and the Family Stone. Without any doubt, this proverb is the very embodiment of the sense of individual freedom in America, where people can develop freely, as long as those personal liberties do not interfere with the rights of others.

Sociopolitical issues come to the fore in the following eight chapters, starting with the first chapter entitled "'Let Us Have Faith That Right Makes Might': Proverbial Rhetoric in Decisive Moments of American Politics." It shows that there exists an obvious predominance of proverbs in American political discourse. This is a fact already in early colonial times with didactic proverbs in Benjamin Franklin's *Poor Richard's Almanacks* (1733–1758) and his famous proverbial essay *The Way to Wealth* (1758) whose 105 proverbs became the basis of the so-called Protestant work ethic. John and Abigail Adams used proverbs frequently in their various communications, and Abraham Lincoln made effective use of the Bible proverb "a house divided against itself cannot stand" (Mark 3:25) in his arguments for keeping the young Union together. Social reformers like Frederick Douglass, Elizabeth

Cady Stanton, and Susan B. Anthony, and in modern times Martin Luther King Jr. included the authority of biblical as well as folk proverbs in their eloquently delivered messages. The same is true for such presidents as Franklin D. Roosevelt, Harry S. Truman, John F. Kennedy, Ronald Reagan, and Barack Obama. As these well-known public figures addressed American citizens, they were well aware of the fact that they were speaking or writing to heterogeneous groups. Trying to find a common denominator, they quite frequently relied on proverbs and proverbial expressions to add authoritative and emotional strength to their political rhetoric. Proverbs in particular can underscore the value system and mentality of the people, and if used at the right moment in the right place, they can most certainly help to underscore an important sociopolitical message.

The second chapter, "'These Are the Times That Try Women's Souls': The Proverbial Rhetoric for Women's Rights by Elizabeth Cady Stanton and Susan B. Anthony" offers a detailed look at how proverbial language enhanced their untiring efforts to improve the status of women. While something is known about the proverbial rhetoric of well-known American male politicians, there has been no such interest in the proverbial speech of female public figures. And yet even a cursory glance at the letters, speeches, and essays of Elizabeth Cady Stanton and Susan B. Anthony clearly reveals that these two nineteenth-century feminists are the equals of the male political giants when it comes to the employment of proverbial language during the fifty years of their unceasing, emotive, and aggressive struggle for women's rights. Partial justification for referring to Stanton and Anthony as "rhetorical giants" is due to their incredibly effective use and innovative manipulation of proverbial wisdom and proverbial metaphors in the service of feminist rhetoric. Advocating and teaching go hand in hand to a certain degree, and it is no wonder that Stanton and Anthony often saw themselves in the role of educating women in demanding their self-evident rights as equals of men. Since proverbs, among other functions, often take on a didactic purpose, it should thus not be surprising that both women would call on them to add generational wisdom to their arguments. Of course, that is not to say that these forward-looking reformers did not also disagree with some of the traditional messages of proverbs! In other words, both Stanton and Anthony made use of proverbial language in whatever way it served their social reform purpose, with the proverbial Golden Rule (Matthew 7:12) serving as a strategic sign for gender equality.

With the third chapter on "'The American People Rose to the Occasion': A Proverbial Retrospective of the Marshall Plan After Seventy

Years," I pay personal tribute to General George Marshall, whose European Recovery Program after World War II helped Western Europe get back on its feet and assured the survival of many starving people, including youngsters like me in my native Germany. The untiring efforts of this American soldier-statesman made it possible to rebuild their economies on democratic principles, for which he was awarded the Nobel Peace Prize in 1953. In his numerous addresses, speeches, and testimonies for the sociopolitical Marshall Plan, named in his honor, he also stressed the necessity of humanitarian aid in the form of food, clothes, and other necessities to return life to normal in sixteen war-torn countries. While his rhetoric was, for the most part, straightforward and to the point, he did employ such proverbs as "a little knowledge is a dangerous thing," "the proof of the pudding is in the eating," "practice what you preach," and "man does not live by bread alone" (Deuteronomy 8:3, Matthew 4:4) to add metaphorical expressiveness to his deliberations. Proverbial expressions like "to sell the same horse twice," "to throw down the gauntlet," "to tighten one's belt," and "to hang in the balance" played their part in making Marshall's rhetoric more effective by supplying some colloquial color. While there is no plethora of proverbial language, George Marshall clearly helped his important cause by relying on at least some traditional folk speech and its emotional cadence.

The following fourth chapter with the encouraging title "'Making a Way Out of No Way': Martin Luther King Jr.'s Proverbial Dream for Human Rights" looks at America's greatest civil rights leader, who received the Nobel Peace Prize in 1964. In barely forty years of life, Martin Luther King Jr. distinguished himself as one of the most influential social reformers of modern times. A vast array of biographies and studies have celebrated him as a fighter for civil rights, a defender of nonviolence in the struggle for desegregation, a champion of the poor, an antiwar proponent, and a broadminded visionary of an interrelated world of free people. His large amount of verbal and written communications in the form of sermons, speeches, interviews, letters, essays, and several books are replete with such Bible proverbs as "love your enemies" (Matthew 5:44), "he who lives by the sword shall perish by the sword" (Matthew 26:52), and "man does not live by bread alone," (Deuteronomy 8:3; Matthew 4:4) as well as such folk proverbs as "time and tide wait for no man," "last hired, first fired," "no gain without pain," and "making a way out of no way." He also delighted in citing quotations that have long become proverbs, to wit "no man is an island," "all men are created equal," and "no lie can live forever." King recycled these bits of traditional wisdom in various contexts, varying his proverbial messages as he addressed the multifaceted issues of civil rights. His rhetorical prowess is thus informed to a considerable degree by his effective use of his repertoire of proverbs, which he frequently used as leitmotifs or amassed into set pieces of fixed phrases to be employed repeatedly. There is no doubt that he received his rhetorical training as a Baptist minister, whose verbal and written communications take on a sermonic character richly enhanced by proverbial messages.

It is well known that John Lewis was a close associate and friend of Martin Luther King Jr. who almost lost his life on March 7, 1965, during a civil rights march across the Edmund Pettus Bridge in Selma, Alabama. The fifth chapter, "'Keep Your Eyes on the Prize': Congressman John Lewis's Proverbial Odyssey for Civil Rights" is dedicated to this voice of conscience in the US House of Representatives. He is the last surviving member of the six major leaders of the American civil rights movement of the 1950s, 1960s, and 1970s. He was the chairman of the SNCC (Student Nonviolent Coordinating Committee) that played a significant role in getting students and others from the North and the South of the United States actively involved in the slow process of desegregation and the advancement of civil and human rights for African Americans and the population at large. His impressive sociopolitical rhetoric is informed by the traditional sermonic style of Baptist preachers and by the rhetorical prowess of his idol and friend Martin Luther King Jr.

Lewis's language is rich in proverbs from the Bible, proverbs from the American democratic tradition, and folk proverbs as well as proverbial expressions. This language is part and parcel of his highly informative and emotive style. In fact, his autobiography, *Walking with the Wind: A Memoir of the Movement* (1998), with its proverbial title and also his book *Across That Bridge: Life Lessons and a Vision for Change* (2012) are not only classic personal accounts of the experienced civil rights movement but also extremely well-written documents of the past and for the future, due in large part to their effective communicative and emotional use of numerous proverbial metaphors.

President Barack Obama stands very much in the tradition of not only Frederick Douglass and Abraham Lincoln but clearly also of Martin Luther King Jr. and John Lewis. Like George Marshall and King, he has been awarded the Nobel Peace Prize in 2009 for his efforts to create a world of peace and humanity. In somewhat of a sermonic and certainly ethical manner, proverbs of both the Bible and the people appear repeatedly in his speeches and writings. The sixth chapter, entitled "'I'm Absolutely Sure

About—the Golden Rule': Barack Obama's Proverbial Audacity of Hope" investigates his early proverbial prowess in his book *The Audacity of Hope: Thoughts on Reclaiming the American Dream* (2006). The book sets forth his political agenda, which is informed by a sincere commitment to fair play, equality, democracy, respect, and above all humanity. His frequent employment of proverbs and proverbial expressions helps him rhetorically and stylistically to find a common denominator of effective communication, where the proverbial metaphors add common sense to his sociopolitical rhetoric for everyone to understand. As he discusses the American constitution, political parties, opportunities, values, race, faith, and his vision for a better world, he underscores his points by a whole array of proverbs and proverbial expressions, including "war is hell," "talk is cheap," "a house divided against itself cannot stand," and "the rising tide lifts all boats." Not surprisingly, the deeply religious Obama relies also on Bible proverbs, making the Golden Rule "do unto others as you would have them do unto you" his basic sociopolitical principle that continues to guide his approach to safeguarding the American way of life and to ensure basic humanity throughout the world.

The seventh chapter is called "'Politics Is Not a Spectator Sport': Proverbs in the Personal and Political Writings of Hillary Rodham Clinton," who came very close to becoming the first female president of the United States. Hillary Clinton is a thoughtful proverbial stylist in her books *It Takes a Village and Other Lessons Children Teach Us* (1996), *Living History* (2003), and *Hard Choices* (2014). Just like other politicians, she too has attempted to formulate concise statements that have the possibility of becoming familiar quotations and perhaps even proverbs. Being a world traveler, she has picked up foreign proverbs that she incorporates into her communications with appropriate introductory formulas. But she also draws special attention to English language proverbs, changing some of them to expressive antiproverbs. She appreciates the fact that the complex interplay of proverbs and political language is of great importance as she writes to communicate her thoughts on American political history and the future role that the United States might play in the world. In doing so, she does not employ proverbs as an ideological instrument but rather as a linguistic tool to enhance her often quite factual prose with vivid metaphors. Looking at her instantiation of proverbs shows the fundamental polysituativity, polyfunctionality, and polysemanticity of proverbs in actual contexts. Each proverb occurrence offers new insights into her being, her reflections, and her aspirations for herself and for her country. Whatever one might think of her political agenda, she most certainly has proven herself to be an engaged and experienced leader in the United States and on the world stage. It is of interest that she is more proverbial in her written texts than in her oral expression. A little bit more proverbial language might have helped her to communicate more effectively during her two presidential campaigns.

Bernie Sanders, the independent senator from Vermont, gave Hillary Clinton an impressive run for her money during the 2016 presidential campaign, due in part to his more effective and forceful rhetoric. The eighth chapter cites his favorite proverb in its title: "'The Rich Get Richer, and the Poor Get Poorer': Bernie Sanders's Proverbial Rhetoric for an American Sociopolitical Revolution." The reasons for his good showing are many, but one of them is doubtless his engaging grassroots rhetoric that excited young people in particular to accept his revolutionary stance as a democratic socialist. His many speeches and books *Outsider in the House* (1997, updated in 2015) and *Our Revolution: A Future to Believe in* (2016) contain a steady reiteration of his progressive politics that swept the country like a fresh breeze. Since he is unwavering from his socialist agenda, his political message is steadfast and clear with a number of proverbial leitmotifs making up his sociopolitical agenda. The tautological proverb "enough is enough" is his often-repeated slogan for his dissatisfaction with the American political status quo in need of a truly revolutionary change as he attacks America's unfortunate move toward an oligarchy with the most inequitable distribution of wealth in the entire world. The proverb "the rich get richer, and the poor get poorer" is a perfect phrase to add emotive power to his steady warnings. Other proverbs serve Sanders as subversive instruments to bring about revolutionary social change in the United States. His rich proverbial repertoire also includes the Golden Rule (Matthew 7:12) that appears to be fallen by the wayside in the United States in an era poisoned by racism and supremacist ideology.

The final chapters look at the origin, history, and meaning of four individual proverbs and proverbial expressions and show what role they continue to play in American life. Chapter 9 looks at "'M(R)ight Makes R(M)ight': The Sociopolitical History of a Contradictory Proverb Pair." Beginning with a theoretical and historically documented discussion of the nature of so-called contradictory proverb pairs as "absence makes the heart grow fonder" and "out of sight, out of mind," it moves on to a survey of paremiographical, titular, and intertextual references of the proverb "might makes right" from 1311 to the present day. It had its start in classical times and was subsequently loan translated into English and other languages.

This is followed by a similar list of references for the opposite proverb "right makes might" from 1598 on, with Abraham Lincoln having played a major role in 1860 in getting this proverb solidly established in the American language and psyche. It is then shown that both proverbs actually appear together as a special contradictory proverb pair already in 1381. Other references of this proverbial doublet follow, with all of them showing that both proverbs are no absolute truths and that even their apparent truth value can only be understood properly in actual contexts. The individual proverbs as well as the proverb pair have been cited by such authors as William Shakespeare, James Fenimore Cooper, Henry Wadsworth Longfellow, Ralph Waldo Emerson, T. H. White, and others. Social reformers and politicians like Frederick Douglass, Elizabeth Cady Stanton, Harry S. Truman, Martin Luther King Jr., and Barack Obama have also made effective use of them, indicating that this sociopolitical proverb pair has proven itself to be a perfectly suitable metaphor for the dialectics of the human condition.

The tenth chapter, entitled "'All Men Are Created Equal': From Democratic Claim to Proverbial Game," takes a different approach, in that it begins with three bibliographical lists of major dictionaries and collections of quotations, proverbs, idioms, and to a lesser degree of slang: 1. publications including Anglo-American materials, 2. compilations of primarily British texts, and 3. works dedicated especially to American phrases. Many of these voluminous reference works are not known any longer or are unavailable in print. However, some are now accessible by way of the internet, if scholars know that they actually exist. They are invaluable for the historical study of individual fixed phrases, and it would certainly be a mistake if scholars were to ignore them by restricting their work ever more to database searches. To prove the point, the second part of the chapter presents the origin, dissemination, history, and meaning of the quotation turned proverb "all men are created equal." It is traced from Thomas Jefferson's Declaration of Independence (1776) to its sociopolitical employment by major American figures like Frederick Douglass, Abraham Lincoln, Elizabeth Cady Stanton, Susan B. Anthony, Harry S. Truman, Richard Nixon, Jimmy Carter, Bill Clinton, Hillary Rodham Clinton, Martin Luther King Jr., and Barack Obama. There are also references from literary works like George Orwell's *Animal Farm* (1945). Parodies in the form of modern antiproverbs and the proverb's use in advertisements are also discussed, showing that the proverb is well established as a serious statement about freedom and equality as well as in satirical, ironical, or humorous parodies expressing the imperfections of humankind.

The eleventh chapter deals with the doubtful relationship between an older French and a more modern American proverb as explained in its intriguing title: "'Laissez faire à Georges' and 'Let George Do It': A Case of Paremiological Polygenesis." While polygenesis appears to be a rare phenomenon with proverbs, the French proverb "laissez faire à Georges" from the end of the fifteenth century and the American proverb "let George do it" from the last quarter of the nineteenth century do in fact have two different origins. This is shown by numerous references from French and Anglo-American proverb collections and dictionaries. Even though some paremiographers and lexicographers continue to insist on a monogenetic relationship between the two proverbs, the argument for two separate origins has steadily gained acceptance. The two "Georges" of the proverbs have no relationship to each other, and it would have made little sense for the old French proverb with its relationship to Georges d'Amboise of the late fifteenth century to have been adopted by the Anglo-American world. Clearly the American proverb is based on another George, namely the generic name given to emancipated slaves who were employed as African American porters on the Pullman railroad cars during the second half of the nineteenth century and beyond. While the French proverb has long been out of circulation, the American proverb is still in occasional use today, with its racially motivated beginnings having been forgotten. Its history does, however, recall the stereotypical view of African Americans held by insensitive fellow citizens of the time.

Finally, then, the twelfth chapter considers the coinage, dissemination, and significance of a popular proverbial phrase and its variants: "'To Be (All) Greek to Someone': Origin, History, and Meaning of an English Proverbial Expression." While the medieval Latin proverb "graecum est, non potest legi" and its alternates can be found in English scholarly writings from time to time, it appeared as the English loan translation "to be Greek to someone" in literary works as early as 1566. This means that William Shakespeare did not originate the proverbial expression when he employed it in his play *Julius Caesar* (1599) to indicate that something is as incomprehensible or unintelligible as the difficult Greek language. By the beginning of the seventeenth century, it can be found in the plays of Thomas Middleton and Ben Jonson, indicating that it was well established in this wording with such variants as "to be heathen Greek to someone," "to be Hebrew Greek to someone," and "to be Latin and Greek to someone" existing with lesser frequency as well. All of this is illustrated by numerous Anglo American contextualized references from such well-known authors as Charles

Dickens, Sir Walter Scott, Herman Melville, Mark Twain, George Bernard Shaw, Washington Irving, and many others. Since the nineteenth century, the variant "to be all Greek to someone" is found as well, together with the older standard form "to be Greek to someone." Together they continue to be generally known and frequently occurring metaphors for all sorts of incomprehensible matters, without much thought about their beginnings.

Together these twelve chapters show that proverbs and proverbial expressions have occupied an important place in sociopolitical matters, and they certainly continue to inform the worldview of Americans as they strive toward a world order that reflects the proverbial ideal of "right makes might." Especially in the governmental arena, the proverb "politics is not a spectator sport" should be kept in mind, and the inclusive wisdom that "all men and women are created equal" should at all times be the guidepost for the humane and compassionate treatment of all people. The knowledge that I have gained from my work on these chapters has enriched my life by showing me that there is goodness, decency, compassion, and love in the way Americans try to be good citizens of this country and on a global scale. The serious commitment to the proverb of "making a way out of no way" and the adherence to the Golden Rule of "do unto others as you would have them do unto you" should give us hope for the future.

I would like to thank previous publishers of some of these chapters for their permission to present them in this cohesive compilation. My sincere thanks are also due to Janice Frisch, Kate Schramm, and their colleagues at Indiana University Press for taking on this project. Since ten of the thirteen chapters were originally prepared for various journals and volumes here and abroad, I had to use different stylistic conventions regarding notes and bibliographical references. I have adjusted them such that there are no notes and only lists of references at the end of each chapter, making it possible to copy individual chapters for possible class use. For that reason, there is no inclusive bibliography at the very end of the volume. Instead I have provided a key-word index of the many proverbs and proverbial expressions, making it possible to find individual proverbial texts in their communicative contexts. As I now look at this book as a collective sample of my recent labors in the field of proverb studies, I sense that it represents a composite picture of the significance and richness of proverbs as expressions of folk wisdom and as part of the American worldview.

It is out of respect, admiration, and appreciation that I dedicate this book to two friends who have shown tremendous leadership and sincere commitment to my beloved University of Vermont, where I have had the privilege and honor to be a professor of German and folklore for close to fifty years. President Thomas Sullivan, also professor of political science, and his wife Leslie Sullivan, first lady and graduate from this university, represent the best possible pair to guide a major institution of higher learning through the present time with its many challenges and concerns. They are committed to the teacher/scholar model on our campus, they enhance our insistence on excellence, and they foster a diverse and prejudice-free place of learning. Together they have hitched their wagon to a star, as Ralph Waldo Emerson would say, and the university community is honored and excited to travel with them into an ever more challenging but exciting academic future.

Wolfgang Mieder

"RIGHT MAKES MIGHT"

INTRODUCTION
Ruminations on Authentically American Proverbs

WHAT IS AN AUTHENTIC AMERICAN PROVERB? THIS QUESTION is easily asked, but the answer is tied to all sorts of difficulties. American English is based on the English language that is widely used beyond Great Britain, which in turn goes back to Indo-European origins and is particularly rich in classical, biblical, and medieval Latin language material (Mieder 2015). Many proverbs in this world language are loan translations from those old sources, but added, of course, is an abundance of indigenous proverbs that are familiar in English only. Immigrants have brought foreign-language proverbs to America that were sometimes translated into the local language, such as the German proverb "Man muß das Kind nicht mit dem Bade ausschütten" from the sixteenth century that is known in the United States since the nineteenth century as "do not throw the baby out with the bathwater" (Mieder 1993, 193–224). This proverb is appropriately listed in the *Dictionary of American Proverbs* (Mieder, Kingsbury, and Harder 1992, 33; Tóthné Litovkina 1996), but it is not a proverb that originated in America. This is true for a large number of the more than fifteen thousand proverbs in that collection, whose title should more aptly be *Dictionary of Proverbs Current in America*. This is a problem that can be found in almost all national proverb collections, because they also register with only a few exceptions proverbs borrowed from other languages that have gained currency in translation in the particular language.

Many of the English-language proverb collections (see list in the bibliography), at least since the 1950s, include more and more truly American proverbs, which have gained international circulation in English or in translation due to the significant linguistic and cultural influence of America. But if one looks at major collections such as *English Proverbs Explained* (Ridout and Witting 1967), *English Proverbs* (Mieder 1988), *Random House Dictionary of Popular Proverbs and Sayings: Over 1,500 Proverbs and Sayings with 10,000 Illustrative Citations* (Titelman 1996), *Dictionary of Proverbs and Their Origins* (Flavell and Flavell 1997), *Dictionary of Proverbs* (Pickering 1997), *The Facts on File Dictionary of Proverbs: Meanings and Origins of More Than 1,500 Popular Sayings* (Manser and Fergusson 2002), and *The Oxford Dictionary of Proverbs* (Speake 2008), they are always compilations in which American proverbs are underrepresented, even though they offer exquisite historical examples (Doyle 2007).

Promising collections such as *Dictionary of American Proverbs* (Kin 1955), *American Proverbs, Maxims & Folk Sayings* (Smith 1968), *101 American English Proverbs: Understanding Language and Culture Through Commonly Used Sayings* (Collis 1992), and *American Proverbs* (Reitman 2000) that use the word *American* in their title are largely unscientific compilations of English proverbs that lack any proof of American origin and simply string together British texts without further commentary. This picture looks significantly better in case of the substantial proverb collections by the American paremiologist Bartlett Jere Whiting, because his collections are based on historical texts taken from literature and other publications in America: *Early American Proverbs and Proverbial Phrases* (1977), *A Dictionary of American Proverbs and Proverbial Phrases, 1820–1880* (1958, co-authored with the renowned paremiologist Archer Taylor), and *Modern Proverbs and Proverbial Sayings* (1989).

Other dictionaries to mention here are *The Home Book of Proverbs, Maxims and Familiar Phrases* (Stevenson 1948), *A Dictionary of Anglo-American Proverbs and Proverbial Phrases Found in Literary Sources of the Nineteenth and Twentieth Centuries* (Bryan and Mieder 2005), and *The Dictionary of Modern Proverbs* (Doyle, Mieder, and Shapiro 2012; see Doyle 1996; Mieder 2014b, 80–130). Just like the massive collections of Bartlett Jere Whiting, these as well are scholarly compilations, but most of the material is "English," and "American" refers basically to proverbs that are frequently used in America without necessarily having originated in this country. The one exception is Wolfgang Mieder's new collection *"Different Strokes for Different Folks": 1250 authentisch amerikanische Sprichwörter* (2015). It is the first-ever attempt to list 1,250 proverbs based on considerable research to prove their American (in rare cases Canadian) origin. For each proverb, the date of the earliest written text has been identified with substantial effort, and for German-speaking readers (where appropriate), explanations for words and meanings are added. Despite this effort, however, it must be said that the historical dates do not always have to be the final answer, because with the help of ever-larger databases containing written texts of any kind, it will certainly be possible to push back some first references even further. But at least here now is a collection of 1,250 proverbs that deserves the label "American proverbs."

So, where do proverbs come from in general, and what are the sources for English proverbs overall and for American proverbs in particular? Each proverb has its origin with an individual who expresses a thought, an observation, or an experience in a particularly concise and catchy form for the first time. This individual utterance is then taken up by other speakers of the same language, which may lead to variants. Initially, the new orally transmitted proverb may be known only within a family, but then one hears it possibly in a whole village, in a city, a county, a state, a nation, and finally through loan translations in neighboring countries or nowadays even globally (Winick 1998; Honeck and Welge 2003; Mieder 2015, 28–48). Of course, proverbs have written origins as well, such as William Shakespeare's "brevity is the soul of wit" from *Hamlet* (1600). Originally, this was a literary quotation which, linked to Shakespeare, over time became a winged word that one cites in certain situations orally or in writing without reference to *Hamlet*. Eventually, even the connection to Shakespeare is lost, and the quotation has become a popular proverb. A person competent in literature may still associate the proverb with Shakespeare, but the general population regards it as an anonymous proverb.

As mentioned before, there are many proverbs in national languages that one can trace far back (see Mieder 2008b, 9–44 for the following four major areas of origin). Many sayings commonly known in Europe come from Greek and Roman antiquity and through the Latin lingua franca and the *Adagia* (1500 ff.) of Erasmus of Rotterdam have been spread all over Europe and beyond, where they have occurred for centuries until today as direct loan translations with significant frequency. For example, "big fish eat little fish," "one swallow does not make a summer," "one hand washes the other," and "love is blind." The Bible is the second major source of common European proverbs, with such familiar texts as "there is nothing new under the sun" (Proverbs 1:9), "man does not live by bread alone" (Deuteronomy 8:3; Matthew 4:4), "do unto others as you would have them do unto you" (Matthew 7:12), and "the prophet is not without honor, save in his own country" (Matthew 13:57). The third source of common European proverbs consists of many well-known texts that have their origin in medieval Latin, having been translated in parochial schools and by humanists into the developing national languages. For example, "strike while the iron is hot," "all that glitters is not gold," "the pitcher goes so often to the well that it is broken at last," and "new brooms sweep clean."

The popular proverb "all roads lead to Rome" belongs into this group, because it relates—perhaps surprisingly—not to the imperial but the papal

Rome. Although these three processes of derivation had a significant impact on the shared set of European proverbs, as evidenced in Gyula Paczolay's comparative collection *European Proverbs in 55 Languages with Equivalents in Arabic, Persian, Sanskrit, Chinese and Japanese* (1997), and other useful collections of this kind (Mieder 2011, 17–36), one must not forget that proverbs of later origin were also borrowed from one language to another, especially among linguistically related and geographically neighboring languages.

Because Europe is growing together more and more in modern times by general globalization (politics, mass media, business, internet, tourism, etc.), old and new proverbs will certainly continue to be disseminated through direct borrowing or loan translations (Mieder 2000a). Eventually, native speakers will no longer be aware that certain proverbs are not originally from within their own linguistic culture. These days, one often finds introductory phrases such as "a German proverb says" or "as the old German proverb goes," which are then followed only by recently translated proverbs such as "Der frühe Vogel fängt den Wurm" (the English proverb "the early bird catches the worm" is from 1636; Mieder 2010b, 285–96) or "Ein Apfel pro Tag hält den Arzt fern" (the American proverb originated in 1870; Mieder 2010b, 307–21). Nowadays, translated proverbs are relatively quickly absorbed into a language by the media and become folk wisdom. What previously took years or decades to occur can happen today in a flash.

This leads us to the fourth and most modern source of proverbs that are in use across linguistic and cultural borders. It is based on the fact that British English, as well as other "Englishes" of the world, have developed into today's international lingua franca, which obviously includes with great importance American English. It must be stressed that most of the proverbs that originated on British soil have not been translated into German, for example, but circulate in their original English version only. One of the exceptions is "don't put all your eggs into one basket" (1662, Mieder 2010b, 297–306) which is current since the early 1980s as "Man muß (soll) nicht alle Eier in einen Korb legen (tun)" with such frequency that it can be viewed as a new German proverb. But the following texts that originated in England are, in fact, circulating in English only: "he who sups with the devil should have a long spoon" (1390), "forewarned is forearmed" (1425), "birds of a feather flock together" (1545), "beggars can't be choosers" (1546), "cleanliness is next to godliness" (1605), "a penny saved is a penny earned" (1640), "it is no use crying over spilled milk" (1659), "appearances are deceptive"

(1666), "a hedge between keeps friendship green" (1707), "beauty is in the eye of the beholder" (1742), "any port in a storm" (1749), "waste not, want not" (1772), "accidents will happen in the best-regulated families" (1819), "a watched pot never boils" (1848), and "curiosity killed the cat" (1873).

As expected, these English proverbs and countless others are very common in America, but they are not original American proverbs. To carve truly American proverbs out from the plethora of English proverbs is indeed a laborious and vexing task. These authentic American texts have their origin during the past four centuries. They range from the oldest proverb, "it is harder to use victory than to get it" (1633) to the newest proverb, "there is an app for everything" (2010)—which refers to the modern arrival of "application software," where one can now find, in fact, practically everything. Another and very popular American proverb from the early computer age is "garbage in, garbage out" (1957) that can now also be found abbreviated as GIGO in verbal conversation.

Before distinctive characteristics of truly American proverbs are discussed, a few additional comments regarding the fourth group of proverbs with worldwide distribution should be added here, a group that nowadays includes besides English proverbs quite certainly also American proverbs. A particularly interesting example is the biblical saying "a house divided against itself cannot stand" (Mark 3:25). The proverb in the quoted wording is from the masterfully translated King James Bible (1611), and it appears for the first time in 1704 in America, where it became a popular proverb, just as in England, while Martin Luther's less successful translation, "Wenn ein Haus mit sich selbst uneins wird, kann es nicht bestehen," did not become proverbial in German. The circumstances in religious America, however, were quite different; there, the Bible text has gone through a process of secularization and appeared in the eighteenth century already as a metaphor for social and political conditions. Well-known Americans like Thomas Paine and Daniel Webster have used the proverb, and in his famous "House Divided" speech of June 18, 1858, in Springfield, Illinois, Abraham Lincoln raised it to the level of a national slogan. He repeatedly used it as a verbal leitmotif to argue against the dissolution of the young democracy, against the imminent Civil War, and especially against slavery. Since that time, Lincoln's name is associated with this Bible proverb, and most Americans consider him the original author! When Willy Brandt, then still mayor of Berlin, was invited to Springfield in 1959 to speak at a celebration of Abraham Lincoln's 150th birthday on April 12, he actually mentioned him in his English lecture as the man "[who] quoted the passage from the Bible about the house divided against itself," in obvious reference to his divided city of Berlin in a divided Germany.

Brandt kept using this proverb, and when he gave speeches in various cities in Germany at the time of reunification, he concluded these repeatedly with a reference to Lincoln by citing the English proverb "a house divided against itself cannot stand" along with his own successful German adaptation "Ein in sich gespaltenes Haus hat keinen Bestand." His use of this version has prevailed in the German language, because thousands of people followed his speeches on television and radio or read excerpts in newspapers and magazines. Mass media has spread his words to the entire population, and so his wording of the Bible text has become a German proverb by way of Abraham Lincoln (Mieder 2000c, 171–203; 2005, 90–117, 264–71). Today, many examples can be found that prove beyond doubt that this is a loan proverb derived from American English (and not so much from the Bible).

A second example of a proverb that is falsely attributed to Abraham Lincoln as well can also be mentioned, but in this case, extensive research has shown that it is an authentic American proverb. The American president had used this proverb on June 9, 1864, during his second campaign: "I have not permitted myself to conclude that I am the best one in the country, but I am reminded, in this connection, of a story of an old Dutch farmer, who remarked to a companion once that 'it was not best to swap horses when crossing streams.'" The earliest American example dates from 1834 and proves that Lincoln is not the author of this proverb, which nowadays is mostly used in the standard form "don't change horses in midstream" or as the variant "don't swap horses in the middle of the stream." Of course, Lincoln never alleged that the catchy proverb was his invention. Nevertheless, his name is still associated with this phrase, which is even the case for the use of the German translation "Mitten im Strom soll man die Pferde nicht wechseln" that appears in the media and in dictionaries of quotations and sayings with reference to Lincoln (see Mieder 2008b, 205–50; 2010, 323–40).

Since all good things come in threes, as we know, a somewhat recent example of how the American language and its proverbs are spread globally shall be mentioned here, because the following loan translation does not only occur in German. This time it was President Ronald Reagan who enabled the modern American proverb "it takes two to tango" to leap across the big pond. This proverb goes back to the popular song "Takes Two to Tango" (1952) with lyrics by Al Hoffman and music by Dick Manning and made very popular by the African American singer Pearl Bailey. Reagan knew the song and proverb, and when he was asked after Leonid Brezhnev's death whether or not the relationship between the United States and the Soviet Union under Yuri Andropov would improve, he said on November 11, 1982, quite spontaneously: "For ten years détente was based on words from them [the Russians] and not deeds to back those words up. And we need some action that they—it takes two to tango—that they want to tango too." About a week later, on November 19, 1982, German journalist Theo Sommer cited Reagan's statement in a convincingly translated headline for his front-page article of *Die Zeit*: "*Zum Tango gehören immer zwei*" (Mieder and Bryan 1983). In the meantime, this phrase has established itself slightly shortened as "Zum Tango gehören zwei" as a German loan proverb, and this is true for other European languages as well. In addition, the short American original is used every now and then in English—further proof that the Anglo-American language really is the lingua franca of Europe and around the world. This phenomenon has been described in more detail in "'Many Roads Lead to Globalization.' The Translation and Distribution of Anglo-American Proverbs in Europe" (Mieder 2014b, 55–79).

Other examples from Mieder's (2015) collection could be explained in more detail as well, but at this juncture, let us just list a few American proverbs with their German loan translations (they exist in other European languages as well) from the second half of the twentieth century. Only the proverb "time is money" (1719), used but not coined by Benjamin Franklin in 1748 (Damien and Mieder 2017), was already translated into German in the nineteenth century. (See the detailed analyses for this and other proverbs in the bibliography.)

Good fences make good neighbors. (1834; Mieder 2005, 210–43, 287–96)
Gute Zäune machen gute Nachbarn.

An apple a day keeps the doctor away. (1870; Mieder 1993, 152–72)
Ein Apfel pro Tag hält den Arzt fern.

The show must go on. (1879)
Die Show (Schau) muß weitergehen.

One picture is worth a thousand words. (1911; Mieder 1993, 135–51)
Ein Bild sagt mehr als tausend Worte.

You can't unscramble eggs. (1911)
Ein Rührei wird zu keinem Ei mehr.

The grass is always greener on the other side of the fence. (1913; Mieder 1994, 515–42)
Das Gras ist immer grüner auf der anderen Seite des Zaunes.

The glass is either half empty or half full. (1930)
Das Glas ist entweder halb leer oder halb voll.

Someday they will give a war and nobody will come. (1936)
Stell Dir vor, es ist Krieg und keiner geht hin.

There are no atheists in foxholes. (1942)
Es gibt keine Atheisten im Schützengraben.

Think globally, act locally. (1942)
Global denken, lokal handeln.

Diamonds are a girl's best friend. (1949)
Diamanten sind eines Mädchens beste Freunde.

You have to kiss a lot of frogs to find a (your handsome) prince. (1976)
Man muß viele Frösche küssen, bevor man einen Prinzen findet.

Unfortunately, America is also the source of a German loan proverb (translated into other languages as well) that should probably not have been borrowed. It is well known that there are proverbs that contain ethnic stereotypes or racial slurs. Minorities are regarded as troublemaking outsiders, foreigners are labeled as inferior, believers of other religions are demonized, and in extreme cases, such verbal aggression leads to genocide. In America, this kind of hatred and prejudice led to the misguided coinage of the proverb "the only good Indian is a dead Indian" (Mieder 1997, 138–59, 221–27). It was recorded first in 1868, at a time when the United States Army persecuted the Native Americans, drove them into reservations, or in worst cases killed them. This cruel wisdom caught on and became the stereotypical slogan against the country's native people, about whose proverbs in their tribal languages we know very little (Mieder 1989, 99–110).

So far, it is an unsolved linguistic and anthropological mystery why the Native Americans have only an extremely small number of proverbs, while African tribal languages, in comparison, have a plethora of proverbs, some of which were brought to North America by the slaves and loan translated into English (Barnes-Harden 1980; Brewer 1933; Daniel 1973; Daniel, Smitherman-Donaldson, and Jeremiah 1987; Mieder 1989, 111–28; Prahlad 1996). In the meantime, the terribly misguided proverb has become a standard metaphor by which one can react to unwanted people, animals, and objects. In principle, the proverbial attack was reduced to the structural formula "the only good X is a dead X," where the variable can easily be substituted with words like *nigger, Jew, German, Serb, teacher, rat*, and so on. (Mieder 1997). It is inexplicable that this terrible proverb circulates in its German translation since about 1980 as "Nur ein toter Indianer ist ein guter Indianer." There is no doubt that this loan proverb is established firmly in German use, and this is unfortunately also the case in other European languages. It should be noted that stereotypes, expressed in catchy proverbial structures, have always been existent in Europe and around the world (Mieder 2004, 137–39), as collections such as Otto von Reinsberg-Düringsfeld's *Internationale Titulaturen* (1863), Abraham Aaron Roback's *A Dictionary of International Slurs* (1944), and more recently José Esteban's *Refranero contra Europe* (1996) have proven more than sufficiently.

But most of the 1,250 American proverbs that Mieder has recorded do not circulate in German as translated loan proverbs. Rather, those are exceptions, but it is likely that more texts will be translated over time because the wisdom contained in them will be generally accepted far beyond America. On the other hand, some proverbs will immediately appear as limited to the United States, especially those that contain the name of the country: "see America first" (1910), "don't sell America short" (1922), and President Barack Obama's already proverbial statement "if you invest in America, America will invest in you" (2008). The same applies to proverbs with connections to baseball as the national sport that have a general significance, yet require some knowledge of the game: "three strikes and you're out" (1901), "you can't steal first base" (1915), "nobody bats a thousand" (1930), "you can't hit the ball if you don't swing" (1943), and "step up to the plate" (1965). Even specific proverbs such as "Boston folks are full of notions" (1788), "good Americans, when they die, go to Paris" (1858), "what is good for General Motors is good for America" (1953), "don't mess with Texas" (1985) and "what happens in Las Vegas stays in Las Vegas" (2002) are based on distinct American aspects and are not always immediately comprehensible.

Before we next talk about language, style, imagery, origin, tradition, and meaning of American proverbs, an important warning is in order. Repeatedly, studies have tried to draw conclusions about a certain national or group character based on a proverb collection of a specific language community. Studies about "the German" or "the Englishman" in his proverbs, or even "the gypsies" or "the Jews" in proverbs, need to be carried out with great caution, or better yet, not at all, because they can quickly lead to questionable generalizations on the basis of small volumes of text. Likewise, the

1,250 proverbs from several centuries of American history listed in Mieder do not allow for such conclusions. Nevertheless, some general statements can be made, of course, to describe the dominant trends in these proverbs. This occurs to some degree in Wolfgang Mieder's *American Proverbs: A Study of Texts and Contexts* (1989) and Stan Nussbaum's *American Cultural [and Proverbial] Baggage: How to Recognize and Deal with It* (2005), but it once again needs to be pointed out that the majority of recorded texts are not authentic American proverbs but rather proverbs of different origin and tradition that appear in American usage in oral and written communication.

The title of Wolfgang Mieder's in-depth contribution "American Proverbs as an International, National, and Global Phenomenon" (2005, 1–14, 244–48) condenses what has been said so far into a triadic formula: first, the English proverbs circulating in America originate from the international distribution of ancient, biblical, medieval, and English proverbs; secondly, there are homegrown nationally (even regionally) spread authentic American proverbs; and thirdly, there is the ever-increasing distribution of these truly American proverbs on a global scale, either in American English or as loan translations. The attached list of English proverb collections includes regional collections from different states like Vermont (Hughes 1960; Mieder 1986) or areas such as New England (Cole 1961; Mieder 1989), and also scientific studies such as "'Good Proverbs Make Good Vermonters': The Flavor of Regional Proverbs" (Mieder 1993, 173–92) and "Yankee Wisdom: American Proverbs and the Worldview of New England" (Mieder 2007). But it must be emphasized that the 1,250 American proverbs of Mieder's new collection (2015) present examples of folk wisdom that have found a nationwide distribution in their vast country of origin, with many of them belonging to the paremiological minimum of American English (Mieder 1993, 41–57; Lau 1996; Chlosta and Grzybek 2004; Haas 2008; Grzybek and Chlosta 2009; Čermák 2014, 225–34).

Just like English proverbs in general, American proverbs consist of on average of about seven words. The shortest texts have only two words, in which the first word indicates a certain topic and the following verb presents a commentary. For example:

Safety first. (1818)
Think big. (1907)
Manners matter. (1909)
Speed kills. (1939)
Everybody shits. (1968)

More common are proverbs that express a plausible folk wisdom in three short words. Here indeed the soul of wit is in brevity, as can be seen in the following selection.

Facts don't lie. (1748)
Talk is cheap. (1843)
Work before play. (1894)
Hurry and wait. (1930)
Can't never could. (1952)

Particularly frequent are proverbs that consist of four words, which often show a parallel structure to enhance the memorability of such short but concise wisdom.

Late children, early orphans. (1742)
Consistency is a jewel. (1867)
Crime does not pay. (1874)
You can't have everything. (1893)
Chicken today, feathers tomorrow. (1958)
All talk, no action. (1948)
Aim small, miss small. (2000)

A small special group is formed by those proverbs that follow the modern structural formula "My X, my Y." These may also lead to variants in which the personal pronoun *my* is replaced by *your*.

My game, my rules. (1963)
My money, my rules. (1975)
My house, my party. (1979)
My house, my rules. (1983)
My party, my rules. (2003)

Of course, there are also much longer proverbs, but they can make memorization difficult and do occur less frequently because they are too cumbersome, especially in rapid oral conversation. Not surprisingly, these complex proverbs generate variations. It is often sufficient for the more familiar lengthy texts to simply allude to them in a shortened way.

A lie can go around the world and back while the truth is lacing up its boots. (1885)
Variant: A lie can travel round the world while the truth is tying up its shoestrings.

It's not the size of the dog in the fight that matters; it's the size of the fight in the dog. (1911)

> If it looks like a duck, walks like a duck, and quacks like a duck, it's a duck. (1948)
>
> In order to get where you want to go, you have to start from where you are now. (1965)
>
> When you're up to your ass in alligators, it's hard to remember you're there to drain the swamp. (1971)
> Variant: When you're up to your ass in alligators, it's too late to start figuring out how to drain the swamp.

Proverbial variants are by no means limited to longer proverbs. On the contrary, particularly orally transmitted proverbs develop into fixed standard texts only over time, and often one or even two variants continue to exist on the side. Here are a few examples.

> Shoot for the stars. (1847)
>   Variant: Aim for the stars.
> Don't judge someone till you have walked a mile in his shoes. (1930)
>   Variant: Don't criticize a man till you have walked a mile in his moccasins.
> A messy desk is a sign of a messy mind. (1974)
>   Variant: A cluttered desk is a sign of a messy person.
> God doesn't make junk. (1975)
>   Variant: God doesn't make trash.
> Never bring a knife to a gunfight. (1988)
>   Variant: You don't take a knife to a gunfight.

Of course, decency sometimes creates euphemistic variants, as for example in the case of these two offensive proverbs.

> Fuck them and forget them. (1922)
>   Variant: Fool them and forget them.
> Shit happens. (1944)
>   Variant: Stuff happens.

We have now arrived at the topic of scatology and sexuality in proverbs, which is suppressed in most proverb collections to date. However, it is a fact that such proverbs exist and that they occur in oral use and in literary works (just think of William Shakespeare or a number of modern writers), movies, songs, and so on with considerable frequency. They should not be omitted because of prudishness, and so Mieder's collection (2015) contains a significant number of scatological and sexual texts for keywords like *fuck*, *piss*, *sex*, *shit*, and so on. Here are two groups of selected texts.

Scatology:
Shit or get off the pot. (1935)
Shit in one hand and hope in the other; see which one fills up first. (1941)
The one who smelt it dealt it. (1971)
You can't kill shit. (1997)

Sexuality:
Situation normal—all fucked up. (1941)
If you've got it, flaunt it. (1968)
Bad sex is better than no sex. (1969)
Old enough to bleed, old enough to breed. (1971)

For some proverbs that express sexuality only indirectly, explanations of words and metaphors are necessary to clarify the meaning, for example:

The blacker [skin color] the berry, the sweeter the juice. (1929)
It's not the meat [penis], it's the motion. (1951)
It's not what you've got [penis size], it's what you do with it. (1934)
If there is grass [female pubic hair] on the field, you can play ball. (1998)

In contrast to such often not only offensive but also brutally aggressive proverbs, the following metaphorical proverb shall be mentioned: "no glove, no love" (1982). Here "glove" stands for condom, and the proverb has the very important message of "safe sex" in light of the AIDS epidemic.

As one would expect, certain structural patterns form the syntactic basis for a considerable number of proverbs. While many proverbs are simple words of wisdom, such as "a true friend is the best possession" (1744), "great minds think alike" (1856), "children are our future" (1920), and "it's not easy to be green" (1970), others are sentences of negation or imperatives utilizing the following structures:

You can't . . .
You can't ever tell what a lousy calf will come to be. (1836)
You can't fight city hall. (1933)
You can't be a little pregnant. (1942)
You can't make chicken salad out of chicken shit. (1980)

Don't . . .
Don't kick a fellow when he is down. (1809)
Don't bite off more than you can chew. (1895)
Don't rock the boat. (1920)
Don't rearrange the deck chairs on the *Titanic*. (1991)

Never...
Never say die. (1814)
Never give a sucker an even break. (1923)
Never try to teach a pig to sing; it wastes your time, and it annoys the pig. (1973)
Never play leapfrog with a unicorn. (1977)

Then there are such proverbs that occur as interrogatives that might need an explanatory comment.

Why buy milk when you've got a cow at home? (1957)
A bird may love a fish, but where would they live? (1964)
Why go out for hamburger when you can eat steak at home? (1971)
Where's the beef? (1984; Barrick 1986)

But there are also structural formulas that are well-suited to express modern wisdom (Mieder 2014c). Some particularly productive base structures include the following.

No X, no Y
No guts, no glory. (1945)
No body, no crime. (1947)
No dough, no go. (1952)
No harm, no foul. (1956)

X is (are) X
Facts are facts. (1760)
A bet is a bet. (1857)
Bosses are bosses. (1907)
A deadline is a deadline. (1933)

X is better than Y
A friend nearby is better than a brother far off. (1682)
The chase is better than the kill. (1904)
A live trout is better than a dead whale. (1941)
A long shot is better than no shot. (1947)

X is a journey, not a destination.
Success is a journey, not a destination. (1933)
Education is a journey, not a destination. (1936)
Happiness is a journey, not a destination. (1937)
Marriage is a journey, not a destination. (1943)

If you can't X, Y
If you can't beat them, join them. (1882)
If you can't be good, be careful. (1902)

If you can't dazzle them with brilliance, baffle them with bullshit. (1972)
If you can't run with the big dogs, stay on the porch. (1985)

There are no X, only (just) Y
There are no dull subjects, just dull writers. (1922)
There are no problems, only opportunities. (1948)
There are no bad dogs, only bad owners. (1949)
There are no bad students, only bad teachers. (1958)

There's more than one way to X
There's more than one way to beat the devil around the bush. (1776)
There's more than one way to skin a cat. (1843)
There's more than one way to cook a goose. (1941)
There's more than one way to peel an orange. (1954)

Yet new proverbs are not only based on such structural formulas; they also arise from disagreement with traditional words of wisdom when they become questionable. Proverbs are not philosophical constructions built on logic but contain and reflect the contradictions of life. Therefore, there are proverbs that rephrase an existing proverb into its opposite. Charles Clay Doyle has coined the term "counter proverb" (Doyle, Mieder, and Shapiro 2012, xi–xii). A few examples of this phenomenon are:

Size doesn't matter. (1903)
   Counter proverb: Size does matter. (1964)
   (the size of a penis)
Good enough is not good enough. (1907)
   Counter proverb: Good enough is good enough. (1910)
Not all publicity is good publicity. (1915)
   Counter proverb: All publicity is good publicity. (1925)
Flattery will get you everywhere. (1926)
   Counter proverb: Flattery will get you nowhere. (1938)

More prevalent are those reactions to common proverbs that Wolfgang Mieder has called "Antisprichwörter" (antiproverbs), which are humorous, ironic, or satirical modifications that contain new insights and generalizations, with the possibility of becoming new proverbs (Mieder 2004, 150–53). Here are a few examples.

Beauty is only skin deep. (1615)
   Anti-proverb: Beauty is only skin. (1963)
Experience is the best teacher. (1617)
   Anti-proverb: Expedience is the best teacher. (1966)

Nobody is perfect. (1763)
  Anti-proverb: No body is perfect. 1958)
If at first you don't succeed, try, try (, try) again. (1838)
  Anti-proverb: If at first you don't succeed, try reading the instructions. (1962)
Absence makes the heart grow fonder. (1944)
  Anti-proverb: Absence makes the heart grow wander. (1908)

Even ancient proverbs like "tempus fugit" or "time flies" may lead to new insights through antiproverbs: "time flies when you are having fun" (1939). The same is true for Bible proverbs: "love thy neighbor" (Galatians 5:14) turns into "love thy neighbor, but do not get caught" (1967), and the biblical Golden Rule, "do unto others as you would have them do unto you" (Matthew 7:12) competes for a hundred years now with the pitiful wisdom "do unto others before they do unto you" (1915).

For most proverbs, the author is obviously unknown, but Mieder's collection (2015) contains a considerable number of proverbs that go back to well-known public personalities and specific dates of American politics (Mieder 2003, 325–66; 2005, 147–86, 278–83; 2014, 198–229).

Give me liberty, or give me death. (1775)
  (revolutionary slogan of Patrick Henry)
All men are created equal. (1776)
  (President Thomas Jefferson, Declaration of Independence)
These are the times that try men's souls. (1776)
  (publisher and revolutionary Thomas Paine)
Sounds often terrify more than realities. (1796)
  (President George Washington)
Happy is the country which has no history. (1807)
  (President Thomas Jefferson)
Eternal vigilance is the price of liberty. (1837)
  (President Andrew Jackson)
My country, right or wrong. (1847)
  (President John Quincy Adams)
All men and women are created equal. (1848)
  (feminist Elizabeth Cady Stanton; Mieder 2014a)
The arc of the moral universe is long, but it bends toward justice. (1853)
  (abolitionist and preacher Theodore Parker; Kraller 2016)
If there is no struggle, there is no progress. (1857)
  (escaped slave and abolitionist Frederick Douglass; Mieder 2001)
Broken eggs cannot be mended. (1860)
  (President Abraham Lincoln; Mieder 2000b)
Equal pay for equal work. (1869)
  (feminist Susan B. Anthony; Mieder 2014a)

Honor lies in honest toil. (1884)
  (President Grover Cleveland)
Speak softly and carry a big stick. (1900)
  (President Theodore Roosevelt)
The business of America is business. (1925)
  (President Calvin Coolidge)
The only thing we have to fear is fear itself. (1933)
  (President Franklin Delano Roosevelt)
Injustice anywhere is a threat to justice everywhere. (1958)
  (civil rights leader Martin Luther King Jr.)
Ask not what your country can do for you, ask what you can do for your country. (1961)
  (President John F. Kennedy)
The time is always right to do what is right. (1965)
Freedom is not given, it is won. (1967)
The line of progress is never straight. (1967)
  (civil rights leader Martin Luther King Jr.; Mieder 2010)
What is good for Main Street is good for Wall Street. (2007)
  (President Barack Obama; Mieder 2009)

Revolutionaries, presidents, and social reformers have contributed to the richness of American proverbs, and that is especially true for the diplomat, inventor, scientist, businessman, politician, journalist, revolutionary, and early American par excellence Benjamin Franklin. Between 1733 and 1758 he published his *Poor Richard's Almanack* for the enlightenment and entertainment of his compatriots, which contained about forty proverbs as didactic stopgaps in each annual edition (Franklin 1964; Barbour 1974). In 1758, he added the essay "The Way to Wealth" to the last edition, which basically consisted of a selection of 105 proverbs that were intended to show readers the way to a healthy, busy, and decent life. This article has become a kind of bible for "puritan ethics" and was translated into many languages. Some ten thousand copies of the almanac were printed each year, and with its many proverbs, they became sort of a secular bible. The proverbs, however, were largely copied from older English proverb collections (Franklin eventually admitted to this in 1788). But the *Almanack* also included texts that he created, and these have long become popular proverbs (Gallacher 1949; Gallagher 1973; Meister 1952; Mieder 1989, 129–42; 1993, 98–134; 2004, 171–80, Newcomb 1957). Without doubt, Franklin has to be regarded as the greatest known author of American proverbs. A few of these are mentioned below, and more are found in Mieder's (2015) collection.

By diligence and patience the mouse bit in two the cable. (1735)
Some are weatherwise, some are otherwise. (1735)
Industry need not wish. (1739)
There will be sleeping enough in the grave. (1741)
Experience keeps a dear school, but fools learn in no other. (1743)
Drive thy business, or it will drive thee. (1744)
If passion drives, let reason hold the reins. (1749)
Laziness travels so slowly, that poverty soon overtakes it. (1756)
Sloth makes all things difficult, but industry all easy. (1758)
Three removes is as bad as a fire. (1758)

Nobody can compete with this master of proverbs, but here are some well-known authors whose proverbs circulate mostly anonymously today:

Stoop low and it will save you many a bump through life. (1724)
   (preacher and writer Cotton Mather)
Hear before you blame. (1798)
   (Abigail Adams, wife of President John Adams)
Be sure you are right, then go ahead. (1812)
   (patriot and folk hero David Crockett)
It is a poor rule that will not work both ways. (1837)
   (writer James Fenimore Cooper)
Behind the clouds the sun is shining. (1841)
   (writer Henry Wadsworth Longfellow)
The houses hope builds are castles in the air. (1853)
   (writer Thomas Chandler Haliburton)
Hitch your wagon to a star. (1862)
   (transcendentalist and writer Ralph Waldo Emerson; Mieder 2014b, 261–83)
It is not the trumpeters that fight the battles. (1887)
   (preacher and writer Henry Ward Beecher)
It is difference of opinion that makes horseraces. (1894)
   (writer Mark Twain)
Genius is 1 percent inspiration and 99 percent perspiration. (1898)
   (inventor and businessman Thomas Alva Edison)
The bigger they are, the harder they fall. (1905)
   (boxer Robert Fitzsimmons)
History is bunk. (1916)
   (carmaker Henry Ford)
It's not over till it's over. (1921)
   (baseball player Yogi Berra)
Gentlemen prefer blondes. (1925)
   (writer Anita Loos)
There must be pioneers, and some of them get killed. (1928)
   (aviator Charles A. Lindbergh)

Candy is dandy, but liquor is quicker. (1931)
   (writer Ogden Nash)
War will cease when men refuse to fight. (1933)
   (physician Albert Einstein)
You can't go home again. (1940)
   (writer Thomas Wolfe)
You can run, but you can't hide. (1946)
   (boxer Joe Louis)
Each generation is better than the last. (1954)
   (Eleanor Roosevelt, wife of President Franklin D. Roosevelt)
Everybody will be famous for fifteen minutes. (1968)
   (artist Andy Warhol)

Sometimes proverbs are attributed to famous individuals without providing any evidence. For example, in Germany the saying "Wer nicht liebt Wein, Weib und Gesang, der bleibt ein Narr sein Leben lang" is accredited to Martin Luther, although the first written document was discovered only in 1775 in a short poem possibly written by Johann Heinrich Voss (Mieder 1993, 80–89). Such unproven attributions often remain in place even if there are solid scholarly refutations. President Harry Truman has publicly stated that the two immensely popular proverbs "if you can't stand the heat, get out of the kitchen" (1931) and "the buck stops here" (1942) were not coined by him. However, because he used them often, both proverbs are still quoted with a reference to him (Mieder and Bryan 1997). A special phenomenon is the origin of the well-known proverb "you can fool all of the people some of the time; you can fool some of the people all of the time; but you can't fool all of the people all of the time" (1877). It has been repeatedly asserted that Abraham Lincoln used this phrase on May 29, 1856, in a speech that is not documented. Although the proverb cannot be found in Lincoln's writings, on August 27, 1887, the otherwise-reliable *New York Times* attributed it to him. This claim has remained in popular opinion to this day, and it will probably not change anymore (Mieder 2000b). A number of such doubtful attributions follow, where primary documents discovered so far often do not match the biographical dates of the alleged author.

Taxation without representation is tyranny. (1761)
   (revolutionary patriot James Otis?)
Good fences make good neighbors. (1834)
   (poet Robert Frost?; Mieder 2005, 210–43, 287–96)
There is room enough at the top. (1867)
   (statesman Daniel Webster?)

From shirtsleeves to shirtsleeves in three generations. (1874)
   (industrialist and philanthropist Andrew Carnegie?)
War is hell. (1880)
   (General William Tecumseh Sherman?)
Build a better mousetrap, and the world will beat a path to your door. (1871)
   (transcendentalist and writer Ralph Waldo Emerson?)
No one ever went bankrupt taking a profit. (1902)
   (banker J. P. Morgan?)
Winning isn't everything; it's the only thing. (1950)
   (football coach Vince Lombardi?)
When the going gets tough, the tough get going. (1954)
   (Joseph P. Kennedy?, father of President John F. Kennedy)
Trust but verify. (1966)
   (President Ronald Reagan?)
Old age is not for sissies. (1969)
   (actress Bette Davis?)
In the middle of difficulty lies opportunity. (1975)
   (physicist Albert Einstein?)
A woman without a man is like a fish without a bicycle. (1976)
   (feminist Gloria Steinem?)

In regard to the identification of an exact origin for certain proverbs, it should be mentioned that the world of music, film, and especially advertising spread many new proverbs using the enormous influence of the media (Mieder 1993, 135–51; Winick 2011, 2013; Konstantinova 2015). Here are a few examples.

Songs
Everybody wants to go to heaven, but nobody wants to die. (1950)
   (song title)
For every drop of rain that falls, a flower grows. (1953)
   (line from the song "I Believe")
The world is a place. (1976)
   (song title and chorus)

Films
There are no rules in a knife fight. (1969)
   (line from the movie *Butch Cassidy and the Sundance Kid*)
No glove, no love. (1982)
   (line from the movie *The World According to Garp*)
Life is like a box of chocolates. (1994)
   (line from the movie *Forrest Gump*; Winick 2013)

Advertising
When it rains, it pours. (1914)
   (advertising slogan by Morton Salt company)
Reach out and touch someone. (1970)
   (advertising slogan by AT&T phone company)
Shop till you drop. (1984)
   (advertising slogan by Volkswagen in Los Angeles)

An indication of the enormous influence of American advertising agencies are the two early proverbs "It pays to advertise" (1868) and "Do not advertise what you can't fulfill" (1919), whose message obviously holds true today, where advertising of any kind appears in all media. It is not surprising, then, that short advertising slogans claiming a general validity become new proverbs.

Of course, the world of sports, which plays a dominating role in all kinds of media, has contributed many proverbs to the repertoire of American folk wisdom. It should be noted, however, that their use is not limited to sports alone, because their imagery and message usually have an indirect correlation to life itself. Of the many examples in Mieder's (2015) collection, only a few striking samples are given here, which, as mentioned before, do not necessarily have to refer to a competition or a game in the linguistic context.

You can't win them all. (1918)
Play to win or don't play at all. (1938)
Every game has a winner and a loser. (1943)
There is no "I" in team. (1960)
You can't score if you don't shoot. (1965)

It has to be surprising that the modern world of technology, by comparison, plays a very small role in proverbs. However, there are several proverbs that refer to the automobile. About ten years after the appearance of the American proverb "you can't judge a book by its cover" (1897), the new proverb "you can't judge a car by its paint job" (1908) became popular, representing the same idea using a different metaphor. Also in America, the land of the automobile, the following piece of wisdom was created: "nobody washes a rental car" (1985). And then there is the proverb "dogs do not bark at parked cars," which has nothing to do with automobiles; the general meaning is that people don't show a reaction until something moves or changes. Finally, the car contributes the metaphorical image to a variant of the proverb "trust in God, but lock your door": "trust in God, but lock your car" (1991).

The world of finance in the land of capitalism, on the other hand, plays a considerable role in proverbs. Money, stocks, trade, etc. have led to general rules and insights that have found their way into the proverbial language, such as:

> Money is power. (1741)
> Competition is the life of trade. (1816)
> Banks have no heart. (1853)
> Buy low, sell high. (1895)
> The customer is always right. (1905; Taylor 1958)
> Another day, another dollar. (1907)
> Business goes where it is invited and stays where it is treated well. (1910)
> If you have to ask the price, you can't afford it. (1926)
> You never accumulate if you don't speculate. (1941)
> Money has no memory. (1991)

Of course, success plays a significant role in American proverbs, because accomplishments in all aspects of life are undoubtedly an important objective, be it in college, at work, or in sports (White 1987; Arthurs 2003). As the following examples make clear, it does require proper commitment to achieve and to secure success.

> Nothing succeeds like success. (1867)
> Success comes in *cans*, failure in *can'ts*. (1910)
> Success is never final. (1920)
> Success is a journey, not a destination. (1933)
> The only place where success comes before work is in a dictionary. (1955)
> Success is always preceded by preparation. (1981)

As expected, there are also many proverbs that deal with time, because the element of time governs human life continually.

> Time and chance happen to all men. (1677)
> Lost time is never found again. (1748)
> Nothing is more precious than time, yet nothing is less valued. (1775)
> Time wasted is time lost. (1865)
> The best way to kill time is to work it to death. (1914)
> The time to shoot bears is when they are out. (1914)

And what can generally be derived from proverbs about life? They ultimately reflect a certain philosophy of life: as generalizations of human existence and also as a guide to a dedicated life. Mieder's (2015) collection contains thirty-five proverbs with *life* as the key word, a clear sign of the preoccupation with the meaning, value, and purpose of life.

Life has its ups and downs. (1853)
You get out of life what you put into it. (1901)
If life hands you lemons, make lemonade. (1910)
Life is a bowl of cherries. (1931)
Life is too short to waste sleeping. (1944)
Life is not a spectator sport. (1958)
Nobody ever said life is easy. (1965)
Life is a bitch, and then you die. (1982)
If life gives you a bag of hammers, build something. (2000)
Life comes at you fast. (2004)

At this juncture, the proverbial triad "life, liberty, and the pursuit of happiness" (1776) from Thomas Jefferson's Declaration of Independence must be mentioned, as it includes the basic rights of all people (Mieder 2014b, 133–71). This phrase is considered self-evident for all Americans, as well as the triadic definition of democracy: "government of the people, by the people, and for the people" (1850) that has become proverbial by Abraham Lincoln's famous Gettysburg Address on November 19, 1863. However, these two proverbs are, of course, to be understood only as desirable ideals (Mieder 2005, 15–55, 248–58). But here now are some characteristic proverbs from America that refer in a very concise way to independence, individualism, initiative, freedom, and unlimited opportunities. These values are not limited to the American people (Nussbaum 2005), but the following proverbs that all originated in the United States may contribute somewhat to an understanding of the worldview in this large and differentiated country that is generally associated with freedom and liberty.

Paddle your own canoe. (1802)
Hoe your own row. (1844)
This is a free country. (1848)
You have to pull your own wagon. (1907)
The sky is the limit. (1909)
Making a way out of no way. (1922)
Freedom is not for sale. (1949)
Go with the flow. (1962)
Follow your own bliss. (1971)
Think outside the box. (1971)
Our choices define us. (1985)

Last but not least, the anonymous proverb "different strokes for different folks" (1945) that was coined among the African American population must be mentioned. It is well known at least since 1968 because of the song

"Everyday People" by the group Sly and the Family Stone (Mieder 1989, 317–32; 2006a; McKenzie 2003, 311–24). The verses contain the wisdom of the proverb "all men are created equal" (1776) and its extension to "all men and women are created equal" (1848), by drawing attention to equality and equal rights for all people, no matter how different they may be.

Undoubtedly, the proverb "different strokes for different folks" has to be considered the embodiment of the sense of individual freedom in America, where the people of this melting pot can develop more or less freely, as long as the personal liberties allow for the ethical coexistence with others. In principle, it is all about the human, all too human, and this is not just the case for American proverbs but the proverbial folk wisdom all over the world.

References

Secondary Literature

This list includes only Anglo-American proverb publications that deal primarily or at least in part with proverbs that originated in North America. For further references, see Wolfgang Mieder (2009). *International Bibliography of Paremiology and Phraseology.* 2 vols. Berlin: Walter de Gruyter.

Arthurs, Jeffrey D. 2003. "Proverbs in Inspirational Literature: Sanctioning the American Dream." In *Cognition, Comprehension, and Communication: A Decade of North American Proverb Studies (1990–2000)*, edited by Wolfgang Mieder, 37–52. Baltmannsweiler: Schneider Verlag Hohengehren.
Barrick, Mac E. 1986. "'Where's the Beef?'" *Midwestern Journal of Language and Folklore* 12: 43–46.
Browne, Ray B. 1968. "'The Wisdom of Many': Proverbs and Proverbial Expressions." In *Our Living Traditions: An Introduction to American Folklore*, edited by Tristam Potter Coffin, 192–203. New York: Basic Books.
Brunvand, Jan Harold. 1968. "Proverbs and Proverbial Phrases." In *The Study of American Folklore: An Introduction*, edited by J. H. Brunvand, 38–47. New York: W. W. Norton.
Bryan, George B., and Wolfgang Mieder. 1995. *The Proverbial Eugene O'Neill: An Index to Proverbs in the Works of Eugene Gladstone O'Neill*. Westport, CT: Greenwood Press.
Bryant, Margaret M. 1945. *Proverbs and How to Collect Them*. Greensboro, NC: American Dialect Society.
———. 1951. "Proverbial Lore in American Life and Speech." *Western Folklore* 10: 134–42.
Čermák, František. 2014. *Proverbs: Their Lexical and Semantic Features*. Burlington: University of Vermont.
Chlosta, Christoph, and Peter Grzybek. 2004. "Was heißt eigentlich 'Bekanntheit' von Sprichwörtern? Methodologische Bemerkungen anhand einer Fallstudie zur Bekanntheit anglo-amerikanischer Sprichwörter in Kanada und in den USA." In *Res humanae proverbiorum et sententiarum: Ad honorem Wolfgangi Mieder*, edited by Csaba Földes, 37–57. Tübingen: Gunter Narr.

Daniel, Jack L. 1973. "Towards an Ethnography of Afroamerican Proverbial Usage." *Black Lines* 2: 3–12.
Daniel, Jack L., Geneva Smitherman-Donaldson, and Milford A. Jeremiah. 1987. "Makin' a Way outa No Way: The Proverb Tradition in the Black Experience." *Journal of Black Studies* 17: 482–508.
de Caro, Francis (Frank) A. 1987. "Talk Is Cheap: The Nature of Speech According to American Proverbs." *Proverbium* 4:17–37.
de Caro, Francis (Frank) A., and William K. McNeil. 1971. *American Proverb Literature: A Bibliography*. Bloomington: Folklore Forum, Indiana University.
Doyle, Charles Clay. 1996. "On 'New' Proverbs and the Conservativeness of Proverb Dictionaries." *Proverbium* 13: 69–84. Also in *Cognition, Comprehension, and Communication: A Decade of North American Proverb Studies (1990–2000)*, edited by Wolfgang Mieder, 85–98. Baltmannsweiler: Schneider Verlag Hohengehren, 2003.
———. 2007. "Collections of Proverbs and Proverb Dictionaries: Some Historical Observations on What's in Them and What's Not (With a Note on Current 'Gendered' Proverbs)." In *Phraseology and Culture in English*, edited by Paul Skandera, 181–203. Berlin: Walter de Gruyter.
———. 2012. *Doing Proverbs and Other Kinds of Folklore*. Burlington: University of Vermont.
———. 2015. "Proverbs in Literature." In *Introduction to Paremiology: A Comprehensive Guide to Proverb Studies*, edited by Hrisztalina Hrisztova-Gotthardt and Melita Aleksa Varga, 262–75. Berlin: Walter de Gruyter.
Fiedler, Sabine. 2007. *English Phraseology: A Coursebook*. Tübingen: Gunter Narr.
Gallacher, Stuart A. 1949. "Franklin's *Way to Wealth*: A Florilegium of Proverbs and Wise Sayings." *Journal of English and Germanic Philology* 48: 229–51.
Gallagher, Edward J. 1973. "The Rhetorical Strategy of Franklin's *Way to Wealth*." *Eighteenth Century Studies* 6: 475–85.
Gläser, Rosemarie. 1986. *Phraseologie der englischen Sprache*. Leipzig: VEB Verlag Enzyklopädie.
Grzybek, Peter, and Christoph Chlosta. 2009. "Some Essentials on the Popularity of (American) Proverbs." In *The Proverbial "Pied Piper": A Festschrift Volume of Essays in Honor of Wolfgang Mieder on the Occasion of His Sixty-Fifth Birthday*, edited by Kevin J. McKenna, 95–110. New York: Peter Lang.
Haas, Heather A. 2008. "Proverb Familiarity in the United States: Cross-Regional Comparisons of the Paremiological Minimum." *Journal of American Folklore* 212: 319–47.
Harder, Kelsie B. 1983. "Proverbs and Proverbial Sayings." *Publications of the American Dialect Society* no volume given, no. 71: 60–66.
Higbee, Kenneth L., and Richard J. Millard. 1983. "Visual Imagery and Familiarity Ratings for 203 Sayings." *American Journal of Psychology* 96: 211–22.
Hirsch, E. D. 1987. *Cultural Literacy: What Every American Needs to Know*. With an Appendix "What Literate Americans Know" by E. D. Hirsch, Joseph Kett, and James Trefil. Boston: Houghton Mifflin.
Honeck, Richard P., and Jeffrey Welge. 2003. "Creation of Proverbial Wisdom in the Laboratory." In *Cognition, Comprehension, and Communication: A Decade of North American Proverb Studies (1990–2000)*, edited by Wolfgang Mieder, 205–30. Baltmannsweiler: Schneider Verlag Hohengehren.
Hrisztova-Gotthardt, Hrisztalina, and Melita Aleksa Varga, eds. 2015. *Introduction to Paremiology: A Comprehensive Guide to Proverb Studies*. Berlin: Walter de Gruyter.

Jente, Richard. 1931–1932. "The American Proverb." *American Speech* 7: 342–48.
Kerschen, Lois. 1998. *American Proverbs about Women: A Reference Guide*. Westport, CT: Greenwood Press.
Konstantinova, Anna. 2015. "Proverbs in Mass Media." In *Introduction to Paremiology: A Comprehensive Guide to Proverb Studies*, edited by Hrisztalina Hrisztova-Gotthardt and Melita Aleksa Varga. Berlin: Walter de Gruyter. 276–93.
Kraller, Anna-Lisa. 2016. *"Resistance to Tyrants Is Obedience to God": Theodore Parker's Proverbial Fight for the Ideal American Society*. Burlington: University of Vermont.
Lau, Kimberly J. 1996. "'It's about Time': The Ten Proverbs Most Frequently Used in Newspapers and Their Relation to American Values." *Proverbium* 13:135–59. Also in *Cognition, Comprehension, and Communication: A Decade of North American Proverb Studies (1990-2000)*, edited by Wolfgang Mieder, 231–54. Baltmannsweiler: Schneider Verlag Hohengehren, 2003.
McKenzie, Alyce M. 2003. "'Different Strokes for Different Folks': America's Quintessential Postmodern Proverb." In *Cognition, Comprehension, and Communication: A Decade of North American Proverb Studies (1990-2000)*, edited by Wolfgang Mieder, 311–24. Baltmannsweiler: Schneider Verlag Hohengehren.
Meister, Charles W. 1952–1953. "Franklin as a Proverb Stylist." *American Literature* 24: 157–66.
Mieder, Wolfgang. 1989. *American Proverbs: A Study of Texts and Contexts*. Bern: Peter Lang.
———. 1993. *Proverbs Are Never Out of Season: Popular Wisdom in the Modern Age*. New York: Oxford University Press; reprinted 2012, New York: Peter Lang.
———, ed. 1994. *Wise Words: Essays on the Proverb*. New York: Garland Publishing, 1994.
———. 1996. "Proverbs." In *American Folklore: An Encyclopedia*, edited by Jan Harold Brunvand, 597–601. New York: Garland Publishing.
———. 1997. *The Politics of Proverbs: From Traditional Wisdom to Proverbial Stereotypes*. Madison: University of Wisconsin Press.
———. 2000a. "The History and Future of Common Proverbs in Europe." In *Folklore in 2000: Voces amicorum Guilhelmo Voigt sexagenario*, edited by Ilona Nagy and Kincsö Verebélyi, 300–14. Budapest: Universitas Scientiarium de Rolando Eötvös nominata.
———. 2000b. *The Proverbial Abraham Lincoln: An Index to Proverbs in the Works of Abraham Lincoln*. New York: Peter Lang.
———. 2000c. *Strategies of Wisdom: Anglo-American and German Proverb Studies*. Baltmannsweiler: Schneider Verlag Hohengehren.
———. 2001. *"No Struggle, No Progress": Frederick Douglass and His Proverbial Rhetoric for Civil Rights*. New York: Peter Lang.
———, ed. 2003. *Cognition, Comprehension, and Communication: A Decade of North American Proverb Studies (1990-2000)*. Baltmannsweiler: Schneider Verlag Hohengehren.
———. 2004. *Proverbs: A Handbook*. Westport, CT: Greenwood Press, 2004; reprinted 2012, New York: Peter Lang.
———. 2005. *Proverbs Are the Best Policy: Folk Wisdom and American Politics*. Logan: Utah State University Press, 2005.
———. 2006a. "'Different Strokes for Different Folks.'" In *Encyclopedia of African American Folklore*, edited by Anand Prahlad, 1:324–27. 3 vols. Westport, CT: Greenwood Press.
———. 2006b. "Proverbs and Sayings." In *Encyclopedia of American Folklife*, edited by Simon J. Bronner, 3:996–99. 4 vols. Armonk, NY: M. E. Sharpe.
———. 2007. "Yankee Wisdom: American Proverbs and the Worldview of New England." In *Phraseology and Culture in English*, edited by Paul Skandera, 205–34. Berlin: Walter de Gruyter.

———. 2008a. "'Let Us Have Faith That Right Makes Might'. Proverbial Rhetoric in Decisive Moments of American Politics." *Proverbium* 25:319–52.
———. 2008b. *"Proverbs Speak Louder Than Words": Folk Wisdom in Art, Culture, Folklore, History, Literature, and Mass Media*. New York: Peter Lang.
———. 2009. *"Yes We Can": Barack Obama's Proverbial Rhetoric*. New York: Peter Lang.
———. 2010a. *"Making a Way Out of No Way": Martin Luther King's Sermonic Proverbial Rhetoric*. New York: Peter Lang.
———. 2010b. *"Spruchschlösser (ab)bauen": Sprichwörter, Antisprichwörter und Lehnsprichwörter in Literatur und Medien*. Vienna: Praesens Verlag.
———. 2011. *International Bibliography of Paremiography: Collections of Proverbs, Proverbial Expressions and Comparisons, Quotations, Graffiti, Slang, and Wellerisms*. Burlington: The University of Vermont.
———. 2014a. *"All Men and Women Are Created Equal": Elizabeth Cady Stanton's and Susan B. Anthony's Proverbial Rhetoric Promoting Women's Rights*. New York: Peter Lang.
———. 2014b. *Behold the Proverbs of a People: Proverbial Wisdom in Culture, Literature, and Politics*. Jackson: University Press of Mississippi.
———. 2014c. "Futuristic Paremiography and Paremiology. A Plea for the Collection and Study of Modern Proverbs." *Folklore Fellows' Network*, no volume given, no. 44: 13–17, 20–24.
———. 2015. "Origin of Proverbs." In *Introduction to Paremiology: A Comprehensive Guide to Proverb Studies*, edited by Hrisztalina Hrisztova-Gotthardt and Melita Aleksa Varga, 28–48. Berlin: Walter de Gruyter.
Mieder, Wolfgang, and George B. Bryan. 1983. "'Zum Tango gehören zwei.'" *Der Sprachdienst* 27: 100–102, 181. Also in W. Mieder. 1985. *Sprichwort, Redensart, Zitat: Tradierte Formelsprache in der Moderne*. Bern: Peter Lang.
———. 1997. *The Proverbial Harry S. Truman: An Index to Proverbs in the Works of Harry S. Truman*. New York: Peter Lang.
Monteiro, George. 1972. "'Good Fences Make Good Neighbors.' A Proverb and a Poem." *Revista de Etnografia* 16:83–88.
Newcomb, Robert. 1957. *The Sources of Benjamin Franklin's Sayings of Poor Richard*. PhD dissertation, University of Maryland.
Nierenberg, Jess. 1994. "Proverbs in Graffiti: Taunting Traditional Wisdom." In *Wise Words: Essays on the Proverb*, edited by Wolfgang Mieder, 543–61. New York: Garland Publishing.
Nussbaum, Stan. 2005. *American Cultural [and Proverbial] Baggage: How to Recognize and Deal with It*. Maryknoll, NY: Orbis Books.
Prahlad, Sw. Anand (Dennis Folly). 1996. *African-American Proverbs in Context*. Jackson: University of Mississippi Press.
———. 2006. "Proverbs." In *Encyclopedia of African American Folklore*. Hrsg. A. Prahlad. 3 vols. Westport, CT: Greenwood Press. 2:1022–27.
Skandera, Paul, ed. 2007. *Phraseology and Culture in English*. Berlin: Walter de Gruyter.
Taylor, Archer. 1931. *The Proverb*. Cambridge, MA: Harvard University Press; reprinted as *The Proverb and an Index to The Proverb*. 1962. Hatboro, PA: Folklore Associates, 1962. Copenhagen: Rosenkilde and Bagger; reprinted again with an introduction and bibliography by Wolfgang Mieder. 1985. Bern: Peter Lang.
———. 1958. "'The Customer Is Always Right'." *Western Folklore* 17:54–55.
———. 1994. "The Most Powerful Markers of Proverbiality: Perception of Proverbs and Familiarity with Them among 40 Americans." *Semiotische Berichte*, no volume given, nos. 1–4: 327–53.

———. 1996. "A Few Aspects of a Semiotic Approach to Proverbs, with Special Reference to Two Important American Publications [Wolfgang Mieder, *American Proverbs: A Study of Texts and Contexts* (1989) and Wolfgang Mieder, Stewart A. Kingsbury, and Kelsie B. Harder, eds., *A Dictionary of American Proverbs* (1992)]." *Semiotica* 108:307–80.

———. 1998. "An Analysis of Popular American Proverbs and Their Use in Language Teaching." In *Die heutige Bedeutung oraler Tradition: Ihre Archivierung, Publikation und Index-Erschließung*, edited by Walther Heissig and Rüdiger Schott, 131–58. Opladen: Westdeutscher Verlag.

———. 2000. *A Proverb a Day Keeps Boredom Away*. Szekszárd: IPF-Könyvek.

Villers, Damien, and Wolfgang Mieder. 2017. "'Time Is Money': Benjamin Franklin and the Vexing Problem of Proverb Origins." *Proverbium* 34:391–404.

White, Geoffrey M. 1987. "Proverbs and Cultural Models: An American Psychology of Problem Solving." In *Cultural Models in Language and Thought*, edited by Dorothy Holland and Naomi Quinn, 151–72. Cambridge: Cambridge University Press.

Whiting, Bartlett Jere. 1994. *"When Evensong and Morrowsong Accord": Three Essays on the Proverb*, edited by Joseph Harris and Wolfgang Mieder. Cambridge, MA: Department of English and American Literature and Language, Harvard University.

Winick, Stephen D. 1998. *The Proverb Process: Intertextuality and Proverbial Innovation in Popular Culture*. PhD dissertation, University of Pennsylvania.

———. 2011. "Fall into the (Intertextual) Gap: Proverbs, Advertisements and Intertextual Strategies." *Proverbium* 28:339–80.

———. 2013. "Proverb Is as Proverb Does: Forrest Gump, the Catchphrase, and the Proverb." *Proverbium* 30:377–428.

Collections

The following list presents the most important Anglo American collections of proverbs, proverbial expressions, and slang. None of them deals exclusively with American proverbs. For additional references, see Wolfgang Mieder. 2011. *International Bibliography of Paremiography: Collections of Proverbs, Proverbial Expressions and Comparisons, Quotations, Graffiti, Slang, and Wellerisms*. Burlington: University of Vermont.

Adams, Owen S. 1947–48. "Traditional Proverbs and Sayings from California." *Western Folklore* 6:59–64 and 7:136–44.

Adams, Ramon F. 1968. *Western Words: A Dictionary of the American West*. Norman: University of Oklahoma Press.

Apperson, G. L. 1929. *English Proverbs and Proverbial Phrases: A Historical Dictionary*. London: J. M. Dent; reprinted Detroit: Gale Research Company, 1969.

———. 2006. *The Wordsworth Dictionary of Proverbs*. Edited by Stephen J. Curtis and Martin H. Manser. Ware, Hertfordshire: Wordsworth Editions (expanded edition).

Aron, Paul. 2008. *We Hold These Truths . . . And Other Words That Made America*. Lanham, MD: Rowman & Littlefield.

Barbour, Frances M. 1965. *Proverbs and Proverbial Phrases of Illinois*. Carbondale: Southern Illinois University Press.

———. 1974. *A Concordance to the Sayings in Franklin's "Poor Richard."* Detroit: Gale Research Company.

Barrick, Mac E. 1963. "Proverbs and Sayings from Cumberland County [Pennsylvania]." *Keystone Folklore Quarterly* 8:139–203.

Bartlett, John. 2012. *Familiar Quotations: A Collection of Passages, Phrases, and Proverbs Traced to Their Sources in Ancient and Modern Literature*. Edited by Geoffrey O'Brien. 18th ed. Boston: Little, Brown and Company (1st ed. 1855).
Bartlett, John Russell. 1849. *The Dictionary of Americanisms*. New York: Bartlett & Welford, 1849; reprinted New York: Crescent Books, 1989.
Berrey, Lester V., and Melvin van den Bark. 1942. *The American Thesaurus of Slang: A Complete Reference Book of Colloquial Speech*. New York: Thomas Y. Crowell.
Boatner, Maxine Tull, and John E. Gates. 1975. *A Dictionary of American Idioms*. Woodbury, NY: Barron's Educational Series.
Bohle, Bruce, ed. 1967. *The Home Book of American Quotations*. New York: Dodd, Mead & Company; reprinted New York: Gramercy Publishing Company, 1986.
Bradley, F. W. 1937. "South Carolina Proverbs." *Southern Folklore Quarterly* 1:57–101.
Brewer, Ebenezer Cobham. 1870. *Dictionary of Phrase and Fable*. London: Cassell. Expanded edition edited by Ivor H. Evans. New York: Harper & Row, 1970 (14th ed. 1989).
———. 1992. *Brewer's Dictionary of 20th-Century Phrase and Fable*. Edited by David Pickering, Alan Isaacs, and Elizabeth Martin. Boston: Houghton Mifflin.
———. 2000. *Brewer's Dictionary of Modern Phrase & Fable*. Edited by Adrian Room. London: Cassell.
Brunvand, Jan Harold. 1961. *A Dictionary of Proverbs and Proverbial Phrases from Books Published by Indiana Authors before 1890*. Bloomington: Indiana University Press.
Bryan, George B., and Wolfgang Mieder. 2005. *A Dictionary of Anglo-American Proverbs and Proverbial Phrases Found in Literary Sources of the Nineteenth and Twentieth Centuries*. New York: Peter Lang.
Burrell, Brian. 1997. *The Words We Live By: The Creeds, Mottoes, and Pledges That Have Shaped America*. New York: The Free Press.
Carruth, Gorton, and Eugene Ehrlich. 1988. *The Harper Book of American Quotations*. New York: Harper & Row.
Cassidy, Frederic G., and Joan Houston Hall. 1985–2013. *Dictionary of American Regional English*. 5 vols. Cambridge, MA: Harvard University Press.
Chapman, Robert L. 1989. *Thesaurus of American Slang*. New York: Harper & Row.
Cole, Arthur H. 1961. *The Charming Idioms of New England: An Essay upon Their Significance, Together with a Compilation of Those Current in the Region Around 1900*. Freeport, ME: The Bond Wheelwright Company.
Collis, Harry. 1992. *101 American English Proverbs: Understanding Language and Culture through Commonly Used Sayings*. Lincolnwood, IL: Passport Books.
Conlin, Joseph R. 1984. *The Morrow Book of Quotations in American History*. New York: William Morrow.
Costello, Robert B., ed. 1981. *American Expressions: A Thesaurus of Effective and Colorful Speech*. New York: McGraw-Hill Book Company.
Dalzell, Tom, ed. 2009. *The Routledge Dictionary of Modern American Slang and Unconventional English*. New York: Routledge.
Dickson, Paul. 2006. *Slang: The Topical Dictionary of Americanisms*. New York: Walker.
Donadio, Stephen, Joan Smith, Susan Mesner, and Rebecca Davison, eds. 1992. *The New York Public Library Book of Twentieth-Century American Quotations*. New York: Warner.
Doyle, Charles Clay, Wolfgang Mieder, and Fred R. Shapiro. 2012. *The Dictionary of Modern Proverbs*. New Haven, CT: Yale University Press.
Elizabeth, Mary. 2009. *American Slang Dictionary and Thesaurus*. New York: Barron's Educational Series.

Farkas, Anna. 2002. *The Oxford Dictionary of Catchphrases*. Oxford: Oxford University Press.
Flavell, Linda, and Roger Flavell. 1993. *Dictionary of Proverbs and Their Origins*. London: Kyle Cathie; reprinted New York: Barnes & Noble, 1997.
Flexner, Stuart Berg. 1976. *I Hear America Talking: An Illustrated Treasury of American Words and Phrases*. New York: Van Nostrand Reinhold.
———. 1982. *Listening to America: An Illustrated History of Words and Phrases from Our Lively and Splendid Past*. New York: Simon and Schuster.
Flexner, Stuart Berg, and Doris Flexner. 1993. *Wise Words and Wives' Tales: The Origins, Meanings, and Time-Honored Wisdom of Proverbs and Folk Sayings, Olde and New*. New York: Avon Books.
Flexner, Stuart Berg, and Anne H. Soukhanov. 1997. *Speaking Freely: A Guided Tour of American English from Plymouth Rock to Silicon Valley*. New York: Oxford University Press.
Franklin, Benjamin. 1964. *Poor Richard: The Almanacks for the Years 1733–1758. By Richard Saunders*. Edited by Van Wyck Brooks. Illustrations by Norman Rockwell. New York: Limited Editions Club; reprinted New York: Bonanza Books, 1979.
Frost, Elizabeth. 1988. *The Bully Pulpit: Quotations from America's Presidents*. New York: Facts on File.
Green, Jonathon. 1998. *The Cassell Dictionary of Slang*. London: Cassell.
———. 2010. *Green's Dictionary of Slang*. 3 vols. London: Chambers.
Hardie, Margaret. 1929. "Proverbs and Proverbial Expressions Current in the United States East of the Missouri and North of the Ohio Rivers." *American Speech* 4:461–72.
Harnsberger, Caroline Thomas. 1964. *Treasury of Presidential Quotations*. Chicago: Follett.
Haywood, Charles F. 1963. *Yankee Dictionary: A Compendium of Useful and Entertaining Expressions Indigenous to New England*. Lynn, MA: Jackson & Phillips.
Hendrickson, Robert. 1987. *The Facts on File Encyclopedia of Word and Phrase Origins*. New York: Facts on File Publications. Expanded edition New York: Facts on File Publications, 1997.
———. 1992. *Whistlin' Dixie: A Dictionary of Southern Expressions*. New York: Facts on File.
———. 1994. *Happy Trails: A Dictionary of Western Expressions*. New York: Facts on File.
———. 1996. *Yankee Talk: A Dictionary of New England Expressions*. New York: Facts on File.
———. 1997. *Mountain Range: A Dictionary of Expressions from Appalachia to the Ozarks*. New York: Facts on File.
———. 1998. *New Yawk Tawk A Dictionary of New York City Expressions*. New York: Facts on File.
———. 2000. *American Regionalisms: Local Expressions from Coast to Coast*. New York: Facts on File.
Hirsch, E. D., Joseph Kett, and James Trefil. 1988. *The Dictionary of Cultural Literacy: What Every American Needs to Know*. Boston: Houghton Mifflin (proverb, S. 46–57; idioms, S. 58–80).
Holder, R. W. 1987. *A Dictionary of American and British Euphemisms*. Bath: Bath University Press, 1987.
Hughes, Muriel J. 1960. "Vermont Proverbs and Proverbial Sayings." *Vermont History* 28:113–42, 200–230.
Hurd, Charles. 1964. *A Treasury of Great American Quotations*. New York: Hawthorn.
Kieffer, Jarold. 1989. *What Are Those Crazy Americans Saying? An Easy Way to Understand Thousands of American Expressions*. Fairfax, VA: Kieffer.
Kin, David (pseud. David George Plotkin). 1955. *Dictionary of American Proverbs*. New York: Philosophical Library.

Knowles, Elizabeth, ed. 1997. *The Oxford Dictionary of Phrase, Saying, and Quotation*. Oxford: Oxford University Press.
———. 1999. *The Oxford Dictionary of Quotations*. 5th ed. Oxford: Oxford University Press (1st ed. 1941).
———. 2009. *Little Oxford Dictionary of Proverbs*. Oxford: Oxford University Press.
Lighter, Jonathan E., ed. 1994–1997. *Random House Historical Dictionary of American Slang*. 2 vols. New York: Random House (3rd. vol. was not published).
Maitland, James. 1891. *The American Slang Dictionary: Embodying All American and English Slang Phrases in Current Use, with Their Derivation and Philology*. Chicago: R. J. Kittredge.
Makkai, Adam. 1984. *Handbook of Commonly Used American Idioms*. Woodbury, NY: Barron's Educational Series.
———. 1987. *A Dictionary of American Idioms*. New York: Barron's Educational Series.
Manser, Martin H., and Rosalind Fergusson. 2002. *The Facts on File Dictionary of Proverbs: Meanings, and Origins of More Than 1,500 Popular Sayings*. New York: Checkmark Books.
Mathews, Mitford M. 1951. *A Dictionary of Americanisms on Historical Principles*. Chicago: University of Chicago Press.
———. 1966. *Americanisms: A Dictionary of Selected Americanisms on Historical Principles*. Chicago: University of Chicago Press.
Melton, Buckner F., ed. 2004. *The Quotable Founding Fathers: A Treasury of 2,500 Wise and Witty Quotations from the Men and Women Who Created America*. Washington, DC: Potomac Books.
Mieder, Wolfgang. 1986. *Talk Less and Say More: Vermont Proverbs*. Shelburne, VT: The New England Press.
———. 1988. *English Proverbs*. Stuttgart: Philipp Reclam.
———. 1989. *Yankee Wisdom: New England Proverbs*. Shelburne, VT: The New England Press.
———. 2015. *"Different Strokes for Different Folks": 1250 authentisch amerikanische Sprichwörter*. Bochum: Norbert Brockmeyer.
Mieder, Wolfgang, Stewart A. Kingsbury, and Kelsie B. Harder, eds. 1992. *A Dictionary of American Proverbs*. New York: Oxford University Press.
Miller, Donald L. 1989. *From George . . . to George: 200 Years of Presidential Quotations*. Washington, DC: Braddock Communications.
Partridge, Eric. 1937. *A Dictionary of Slang and Unconventional English*. New York: Macmillan (7th ed. 1970).
———. 1977. *A Dictionary of Catch Phrases: British and American, from the Sixteenth Century to the Present Day*. New York: Stein and Day. Expanded edition by Paul Beale. Lanham, MD: Scarborough House, 1992.
Pickering, David. 1997. *Dictionary of Proverbs*. London: Cassell.
Platt, Suzy. 1992. *Respectfully Quoted: A Dictionary of Quotations from the Library of Congress*. Washington, DC: Congressional Quarterly.
Rawson, Hugh, and Margaret Miner. 2006. *The Oxford Dictionary of American Quotations*. New York: Oxford University Press.
Rees, Nigel. 1984. *Sayings of the Century: The Stories Behind the Twentieth Century's Quotable Sayings*. London: George Allen and Unwin.
———. 1995. *Phrases and Sayings*. London: Bloomsbury.
———. 2006. *A Word in Your Shell-Like: 6,000 Curious & Everyday Phrases Explained*. London: HarperCollins.
Reitman, Judith, ed. 2000. *American Proverbs*. New York: Hippocrene Books.

Ridout, Ronald, and Clifford Witting. 1967. *English Proverbs Explained.* London: Pan Books.
Shankle, George Earlie. 1941. *American Mottoes and Slogans.* New York: H. W. Wilson.
Shapiro, Fred R. 2006. *The Yale Book of Quotations.* New Haven, CT: Yale University Press.
Shelton, Ferne, ed. 1971. *Pioneer Proverbs. Wit and Wisdom from Early America.* Collected by Mary Turner. High Point, NC: Hutcraft.
Smith, Elmer L., ed. 1968. *American Proverbs, Maxims & Folk Sayings.* Lebanon, PA: Applied Arts Publishers.
Snapp. Emma Louise. 1933. "Proverbial Lore in Nebraska." *University of Nebraska Studies in Language, Literature, and Criticism* 13:51–112.
Speake, Jennifer, ed. 2008. *The Oxford Dictionary of Proverbs.* 5th ed. Oxford: Oxford University Press. 1st ed. by John A. Simpson with the title *The Concise Oxford Dictionary of Proverbs* (1982).
Spears, Richard A. 1989. *NTC's Dictionary of American Slang and Colloquial Expressions.* Lincolnwood, IL: National Textbook Company (3rd. ed. 2000).
———. 1990a. *Essential American Idioms.* Lincolnwood, IL: National Textbook Company.
———. 1990b. *Forbidden American English: A Serious Compilation of Taboo American English.* Lincolnwood, IL: National Textbook Company.
———. 1995. *NTC's Dictionary of American English Phrases.* Lincolnwood, IL: National Textbook Company.
———. 1998. *Hip and Hot! A Dictionary of 10,000 American Slang Expressions.* New York: Gramercy Books.
Spears, Richard A., and Linda Schinke-Llano, eds. 1987. *NTC's American Idioms Dictionary.* Lincolnwood, IL: National Textbook Company.
Sperber, Hans, and Travis Trittschuh. 1962. *American Political Terms: An Historical Dictionary.* Detroit, Michigan: Wayne State University Press.
Stevenson, Burton Egbert. 1948. *The Home Book of Proverbs, Maxims and Familiar Phrases.* New York: Macmillan; reprinted as *The Macmillan Book of Proverbs, Maxims, and Familiar Phrases.* New York: Macmillan, 1968.
Taylor, Archer, and Bartlett Jere Whiting. 1958. *A Dictionary of American Proverbs and Proverbial Phrases, 1820–1880.* Cambridge, MA: Harvard University Press.
Titelman, Gregory Y. 1996. *Random House Dictionary of Popular Proverbs and Sayings: Over 1,500 Proverbs and Sayings with 10,000 Illustrative Citations.* New York: Random House.
Urdang, Laurence, Walter W. Hunsinger, and Nancy LaRoche. 1985. *Picturesque Expressions: A Thematic Dictionary.* Detroit: Gale Research Company.
Van Meter, Jan R. 2008. *Tippecanoe and Tyler Too: Famous Slogans and Catchphrases in American History.* Chicago: University of Chicago Press.
Wentworth, Harold, and Stuart Berg Flexner. 1960. *Dictionary of American Slang.* New York: Thomas Y. Crowell. Expanded edition New York: Thomas Y. Crowell, 1975.
———. 1968. *The Pocket Dictionary of American Slang.* New York: Pocket Books.
Whiting, Bartlett Jere. 1952. "Proverbs and Proverbial Sayings [from North Carolina]." *The Frank C. Brown Collection of North Carolina Folklore.* Edited by Newman Ivey White. 7 vols. Durham, NC: Duke University Press. 1:329–501.
———. 1977. *Early American Proverbs and Proverbial Phrases.* Cambridge, MA: Harvard University Press.
———. 1989. *Modern Proverbs and Proverbial Sayings.* Cambridge, MA: Harvard University Press.

Wilkinson, P. R. 1993. *Thesaurus of Traditional English Metaphors*. London: George Routledge.
Wilson, F. P. 1970. *The Oxford Dictionary of English Proverbs*. 3rd ed. Oxford: Clarendon Press (1st ed. 1935 by William George Smith).
Woods, Henry F. 1945. *American Sayings: Famous Phrases, Slogans, and Aphorisms*. New York: Duell, Sloan and Pearce. Expanded edition New York: Perma Giants, 1950.
Yates, Irene. 1947. "A Collection of Proverbs and Proverbial Sayings from South Carolina Literature." *Southern Folklore Quarterly* 11:187–99.

1

"LET US HAVE FAITH THAT RIGHT MAKES MIGHT"

Proverbial Rhetoric in Decisive Moments of American Politics

THE FASCINATION WITH PROVERBS CAN BE TRACED BACK to the earliest written records. Proverbs have been collected throughout the world, with literally thousands of collections attesting to the ubiquity of this traditional wisdom literature couched in short metaphorical and easy-to-remember sentences. Scholars of diverse fields, but notably folklorists, linguists, and cultural historians, have long shown that these traditional bits of wisdom play a major role in everyday oral and written communication. To explain their rhetorical value and meaning, they have investigated the appearance of proverbs in literary works dating from classical texts and the Bible to their frequent employment in medieval literature and that of later centuries. Much is known, for example, about the use and function of proverbs in the works of such well-known authors as Geoffrey Chaucer, François Rabelais, William Shakespeare, Miguel de Cervantes Saavedra, Johann Wolfgang von Goethe, Benjamin Franklin, Charles Dickens, Mark Twain, Agatha Christie, and many others (Mieder and Bryan 1996). In the past four decades, scholars have also made impressive advances in analyzing proverbs in the mass media, ranging from studies on their appearance in newspapers and magazines to their inclusion in cartoons, comic strips, and advertisements.

One realm, however, that has received less attention is the employment of proverbs in the political arena. Cicero, one of the greatest Roman orators, used proverbs as effective rhetorical weapons, and humanists and reformers like Erasmus of Rotterdam and Martin Luther practiced the shrewd and manipulative use of proverbs to fight their intellectual and theological battles. The politics of the nineteenth century saw Abraham Lincoln and Otto von Bismarck employing proverbs in important speeches, and, in the early part of the twentieth century, Theodore Roosevelt and Vladimir I. Lenin appreciated proverbs as ready-made tools to effect political change. In more modern times, Winston S. Churchill, Adolf Hitler, Franklin D. Roosevelt, Harry S. Truman, Nikita Khrushchev, and John F. Kennedy serve as examples of politicians who flavored their utterances with didactic and commonly accepted wisdom. As you might have noticed, President Barack Obama also relies quite heavily on proverbial speech in his oral and written communications.

Basing the following remarks to a considerable extent on my books *The Politics of Proverbs: From Traditional Wisdom to Proverbial Stereotypes* (Mieder 1997) and *Proverbs Are the Best Policy: Folk Wisdom and American Politics* (Mieder 2005) and additional materials, I would like to show by some poignant contextualized examples from the past three centuries that there exists an obvious predominance of proverbs in American political discourse. Many examples could be cited, of course, where proverbs or proverbial expressions are simply part of normal language use without any particular significance, save that of using metaphorical language. But I will concentrate instead on truly remarkable proverbial utterances to illustrate the incredible significance they can attain in political rhetoric, far beyond the almost subconscious use of a seemingly mundane proverb. What will become clear from these remarks is that traditional proverbs are indeed a living part of all political discourse. They play a significant role in the speeches and writings of major politicians, who employ them both positively and negatively to reach their political goals. Normally proverbs fulfill a useful communicative role, but when employed in a manipulative or discriminatory fashion, these expressions and images can become aggressive and harmful tools, strengthened by the claim of proverbial authority behind them. Proverbs in the political arena are thus speech patterns that should be understood with care and caution. In the hands of demagogues, bigots, and racists, proverbs can become dangerous verbal weapons. Clearly, proverbs are ambivalent bits of wisdom, adding both positive and negative elements to communicative processes.

Turning now to a selective historical survey of the use of proverbs by a few American public figures, it would be tempting indeed to start with Benjamin Franklin (1706–1790), who literally bombarded his fellow prerevolutionary compatriots with proverbs in twenty-five volumes of his *Poor Richard's Almanack* that he published from 1733 to 1758 (Barbour 1974). But this impressive collection of proverbs and Franklin's famous essay on *The Way to Wealth* (1758), which amassed more than a hundred of these proverbs into a didactic manifest on Protestant work ethics, have little to do with rhetoric. In these works the proverbs are simply presented as guideposts for a productive and moral life, including making a bit of good money for your efforts.

> Let us hearken to good advice, and something may be done for us; *God helps them that help themselves*, as Poor Richard says. . . . *Sloth, like rust, consumes faster than labor wears, while the used key is always bright*, as Poor Richard says. *But dost thou love life, then do not squander life, for that is the stuff life is made of*, as Poor Richard says. How much more than is necessary do we spend in sleep, forgetting, that *The sleeping fox catches no poultry*, and that *There will be sleeping enough in the grave*, as Poor Richard says. . . . *If time be of all things the most precious, wasting time must be*, as Poor Richard says, *the greatest prodigality*; since, as he elsewhere tells us, *Lost time is never found again; and what we call time enough, always proves little enough*. Let us then up and be doing, and doing to the purpose; so by diligence shall we do more with less perplexity. *Sloth makes all things difficult, but industry all easy*, and *He that riseth late must trot all day, and shall scarce overtake his business at night*; while *Laziness travels so slowly, that Poverty soon overtakes him*. *Drive thy business, let not that drive thee*, and *Early to bed, and early to rise, makes a man healthy, wealthy, and wise*, as Poor Richard says. (Sparks 1840, 2:94, with italics in the original; Gallacher 1949; Mieder 2004)

That is all fine and good, and this proverbial sermon had a lasting effect on the American worldview that life should be a steady progression of hard work connected with a bit of deserved success. Ultimately this philosophy leads to a materialistic attitude that ignores such social concerns as compassion and understanding for less fortunate people.

But let me turn to two contemporaries of Benjamin Franklin who employed numerous proverbs in their social and political communications. Both John Adams (1735–1826), second president of the United States, and his wife, Abigail Adams (1744–1818), made much use of proverbial rhetoric in their voluminous correspondence with each other and the major political figures of their time. In particular, Abigail Adams's predilection to proverbial wisdom indicates her resolve, her eagerness to give advice, her debating abilities, her role as an independent matriarch, her struggle for the proper treatment of women, her unbending morality, her skill as a political strategist, her insightful observations on human nature, and her incredible optimism regarding the future of her new country. Her favorite proverb was the internationally disseminated "God helps them who help themselves" that has been traced back to classical antiquity (Paczolay 1997,

150–54). Abigail used it as a leitmotif of resolve and determination several times, as for example in a letter of September 16, 1775: "God helps them that help themselves . . . and if we can obtain the divine aid [for the revolutionary cause] by our own virtue, fortitude and perseverance we may be sure of relief" (Butterfield 1963–93, 1:280), with John Adams quoting it back to her on October 1, 1775, accepting it as a principle of taking fate into one's own hands: "As to Politicks, We have nothing to expect but the Whole Wrath and Force of G. Britain. But your Words are as true as an oracle 'God helps them, who help them selves" (1:290).

Throughout her massive correspondence, Abigail shows herself as a sociopsychological analyst, reflecting on common traits of human nature (Bernstein 2002, 42–63). When one considers that proverbs are in fact generalized truths of the human condition that have been appropriately defined as "monumenta humana" (Kuusi 1957, 52), it is not surprising that the more philosophical passages of Abigail's epistles abound with proverbs from the Bible or traditional folk proverbs. Thus, in a letter of February 27, 1774, she turned to the Bible proverb "Love thy neighbor as thyself" (Leviticus 19:18; Matthew 19:19) to reflect upon the ambivalent value of human ambition that, in its negative effects, has factionalized the country and has undermined the moral values of its people.

> When I consider the Spirit which at present prevails throughout this continent I really detest that restless ambition of those artful and designing men which has thus broken this people into factions—and I every day see more and more cause to deprecate the growing Evil. This party Spirit ruins good Neighbourhood, eradicates all the Seeds of good nature and humanity—it sours the temper and has a fatal tendency upon the Morals and understanding and is contrary to that precept of christianity thou shallt Love thy Neighbour as thy self. (Butterfield 1963–93, 1:98)

But it is her letter to John of November 27, 1775, that contains one of her most powerful statements about human nature, written at the time of American revolutionary reactions against the British abuse of power. The proverb "Big fish eat little fish" has served to describe human power struggles since classical times (Mieder 1987), and it most assuredly is also a befitting metaphor for eighteenth-century politics, showing that human nature in the Age of Reason and Enlightenment has barely evolved from that of the fish world.

> I am more and more convinced that Man is a dangerous creature, and that power whether vested in many or a few is ever grasping, and like the grave cries give, give. The great fish swallow up the small, and he who is most

strenuous for the Rights of the people, when vested with power, is as eager after the prerogatives of Government. You tell me of degrees of perfection to which Humane Nature is capable of arriving, and I believe it, but at the same time lament that our admiration should arise from the scarcity of the instances. (Butterfield 1963–93, 1:329)

This is a devastating indictment of humanity, bordering on a fatalistic worldview regarding the corruptness of power and government.

As matriarch of the Adams family, Abigail cared deeply for her children, loved and supported her husband, and was forever involved in the extended family, but she also never lost sight of the well-being and future of the United States that she, in her own way, helped to establish. At the time of the War of 1812, she wrote thoughts to her friend Mercy Otis Warren on December 30, 1812, that are of universal application long beyond their inception.

> So long as we are inhabitants of this earth and possess any of our faculties, we cannot be indifferent to the state of our country, our posterity and our friends.... We have passed through one revolution and have happily arrived at the goal, but the ambition, injustice and plunder of foreign powers have again involved us in war, the termination of which is not given us to see....
>
> Our native State [of Massachusetts] has had much to complain of as it respected a refusal of naval protection, yet that cannot justify her in paralyzing the arm of government when raised for her defence and that of the nation. A house divided against itself—and upon that foundation do our enemies build their hopes of subduing us. May it prover a sandy one to them. (Adams 1848, 412–13)

There was no need for Abigail to cite the Bible proverb "A house divided against itself cannot stand" (Mark 3:25) in its entirety. Her friends and her contemporaries knew it only too well. The proverb has been used repeatedly with the intent of placing national unity above the interests of individual states, certain groups of people, and policies or actions that might tear the nation apart.

The house-divided proverb will forever be most closely connected in the American psyche with Abraham Lincoln (1809–1865), who famously used it as an authoritative leitmotif before the Civil War in his arguments for maintaining the Union at all costs (Mieder 1998; Mieder 2000, 10–18). The proverb has played a major role in American politics both before and after Lincoln's time, however, starting with its use in Thomas Paine's remarkable essay on *Common Sense; Addressed to the Inhabitants of America* (1776) and followed by its employment by such major political figures as Sam Houston and Daniel Webster (Paine 1989, 6–7; Houston 1850, 102; Webster 1903,

243–45, 258). By the time Abraham Lincoln gave his famous "house divided" speech on June 16, 1858, the proverb had long been a metaphor for the division in the American nation over the issue of slavery. The idea developed into a proverbial slogan during the famous Lincoln-Douglas debates of that same year, and it electrified the audience of the Republican Convention in Springfield, Illinois, on that evening in June. Here is what he said:

> If we could first know *where* we are, and *whither* we are tending, we could then better judge *what* to do, and *how* to do it.
> We are now far into the *fifth* year, since a policy was initiated, with the *avowed* object, and *confident* promise, of putting an end to slavery agitation.
> Under the operation of that policy, that agitation has not only, *not ceased*, but has *constantly augmented*.
> In *my* opinion, it *will* not cease, until a *crisis* shall have been reached, and passed.
> "A house divided against itself cannot stand."
> I believe this government cannot endure, permanently half *slave* and half *free*.
> I do not expect the Union to be *dissolved*—I do not expect the house to *fall*—but I *do* expect it will cease to be divided.
> It will become *all* one thing, or *all* the other.
> Either the *opponents* of slavery, will arrest the further spread of it, and place it where the public mind shall rest in the belief that it is in course of ultimate extinction; or its *advocates* will push it forward, till it shall become alike lawful in *all* the States, *old* as well as *new*—*North* as well as *South*. (Basler 1953, 2:461–62)

Carl Sandburg, in the first part of his celebrated 1926 biography of Abraham Lincoln, states quite appropriately: "This was so plain that two farmers fixing fences on a rainy morning could talk it over.... What interested the country most, as many newspapers published the speech in full, was its opening paragraph. It became known as the 'House Divided' speech. It went far" (Sandburg [1926] 1954, 138). The speech did not prevent the Civil War, but it brought the slavery issue to a head and eventually led to the Emancipation Proclamation on January 1, 1863.

There is a second example of Lincoln's powerful use of proverbs that I would like to cite from the many examples I have assembled in my book *The Proverbial Abraham Lincoln: An Index to Proverbs in the Works of Abraham Lincoln* (2000). Interestingly enough, it is also one of many proverbial texts that have escaped the attention of scholars. The proverb appears in the last paragraph of Lincoln's famous Cooper Union speech delivered on February 27, 1860, in New York City. In this speech, Lincoln outlined in very clear and logical terms his solid commitment to maintaining the Union and to keeping slavery from spreading. As he moved toward the final two paragraphs of his speech, the president rose to an oratorical height that must have moved his audience then just as it does readers today. One can sense here the tension and anxiety in yet one more pitch to prevent the country from entering a devastating civil war:

> Wrong as we think slavery is, we can yet afford to let it alone where it is, because that much is due to the necessity arising from its actual presence in the nation; but can we, while our votes will prevent it, allow it to spread into the National Territories, and to overrun us here in these Free States? If our sense of duty forbids this, then let us stand by our duty, fearlessly and effectively. Let us be diverted by none of those sophistical contrivances wherewith we are so industriously plied and belabored—contrivances such as groping for some middle ground between the right and the wrong. . . .
>
> Neither let us be slandered from our duty by false accusations against us, nor frightened from it by menaces of destruction to the Government nor of dungeons to ourselves. *Let us have faith that right makes might, and in that faith, let us, to the end, dare to do our duty as we understand it.* (Basler 1953, 3:550, italics in original; see also 3:554 and 4:8, 30)

In an otherwise superb essay on "Lincoln's Development as a Writer," Roy P. Basler, one of the most knowledgeable Lincoln scholars, introduces his quotation of the last short paragraph of this speech with the observation that Lincoln's "peroration is one of his most effective and memorable conclusions" (1946, 33). But his readers would want to know why this is the case. Note the following observation, once again citing that one "unique" sentence: "Then comes the last sentence and its note of grand, imperial music, rising from the heart of the poet who was to be: 'Let us have faith that right makes might, and in that faith, let us, to the end, dare to do our duty as we understand it.' In this sentence, with its magnificent rhythm rising spontaneously and naturally from deep emotion, Lincoln strikingly had revealed in the written word the heart of a poet" (Edwards and Hankins 1962, 60). What these authors have said is, of course, true and correct, but might it not have helped for a better understanding of Lincoln's rhetorical power to point out that by claiming that "right makes might" he is employing a proverb that dates back at least to the fourteenth century? To be sure, its antipode "might makes right" is just so old (Mieder, Kingsbury, and Harder 1992, 410, 510).

Surely it must be agreed by all interpreters of the last sentence of this significant speech that it is the wisdom of the proverb "right makes might" that adds authority and conviction to Lincoln's argument. It summarizes everything he had just argued about, namely that the preservation of the Union and the control of slavery are just and "right" goals. This being the case, people believing in these principles will have the "might" to keep matters under control.

Frederick Douglass (1818–1895), former slave and abolitionist spokesman, shared the proverbial prowess of his friend Abraham Lincoln. As a deeply religious person, Douglass relied heavily on biblical proverbs to strengthen the social and moral statements in his debates, lectures, and writings. But while this wisdom from the Bible provided religious authority to Douglass's rhetoric, he was also very much aware of the social significance of folk proverbs in his fights against slavery and for civil rights. He employs proverbs as collective wisdom not only in the struggle for his own race after the Civil War but also in his work to expand women's rights. Douglass fought with words and deeds for his egalitarian beliefs, with his own proverbial motto, "if there is no struggle, there is no progress," expressing his moral commitment.

Morality and religion were one and the same for Frederick Douglass, and it should come as no surprise that the "Golden Rule" of Christianity, in the form of the proverb "do unto others as you would have them do unto you" (Matthew 7:12), would become the perfect expression of human equality for him. It appears again and again for over fifty years in his speeches and writings, and it must be considered one of Douglass's most important rhetorical and philosophical leitmotifs. Being thoroughly entrenched in the abolitionist movement for personal and humanitarian reasons, Douglass gave the noble cause a solid endorsement in his speech on March 30, 1847, in London, placing abolitionism on the basic truth of the Golden Rule.

> When the history of the emancipation movement shall have been fairly written, it will be found that the abolitionists of the nineteenth century were the only men who dared to defend the Bible from the blasphemous charge of sanctioning and sanctifying Negro slavery. . . . It will then be seen that they were the men who planted themselves on the immutable, eternal, and all-comprehensive principle of the sacred New Testament—"All things whatsoever ye would that men should do unto you, do ye even so unto them"—that, acting on this principle, and feeling that if the fetters were on their limbs, the chain upon their own persons, the lash falling quick and hard upon their own quivering bodies, they would desire their fellow men about them to be faithful to their cause; and, therefore, carrying out this principle, they have dared to risk their lives, fortunes, nay, their all, for the purpose of rescuing from the tyrannous grasp of the slaveholder these 3,000,000 of trampled-down children of men. (Blassingame 1985–92, 2:32)

But Douglass is certain that the slaveholders will pay for their sins in due time (as expressed on April 13, 1854), and even if the law cannot touch them, they will be haunted by their own guilty consciences.

> Verily there is a God to bring to nought the counsels of wicked men. They seek peace for the Slaveholder, but to the Slaveholder there can be no peace; his is a bad business; to him, while a Slaveholder, there can be neither peace of mind nor peace of conscience. If they could close up all Anti-Slavery Conventions, take all our Publications, *Uncle Tom's Cabin*, and the portions of the Bible which teach that men should do to others as they should wish to be done by, place them in the District of Columbia, set a match to them until the flames reached the sky; if they could have every abolitionist's tongue cut out, thus to procure their silence, they will not have obtained their object, for deep down in the secret corners of the Slaveholder's soul, God Almighty has planted an abolition sentinel in his monitor, the conscience. (Blassingame 1985–92, 2:465)

That is a true fire-and-brimstone sermon by a skilled orator and preacher. If only the slaveholders had heard Douglass—but they didn't attend the abolition conventions, of course. Nevertheless, if there was any decency left in them, their guilty consciences must have tormented them at night and on their deathbeds. The Golden Rule proverb "do unto others as you would have them do unto you" served Frederick Douglass and his various causes extremely well, and there is no reason why this most humane wisdom should not continue to be the guiding light for civil rights in this country and throughout the world.

As is well known, Frederick Douglass also became an extremely important champion of women's rights, vigorously supporting the efforts of two early social reformers and feminists, Elizabeth Cady Stanton (1815–1902) and Susan B. Anthony (1820–1906). In a speech entitled "Is It a Crime for a US Citizen to Vote?" that Susan B. Anthony delivered on January 16, 1873, in Washington, DC, at the National Woman Suffrage Association meeting, Anthony made effective use of a well-established American proverb from revolutionary times.

> *One-half* of the people of this nation, to-day, are utterly powerless to blot from the statute-books an *unjust* law, or write there a *new and just one*. The *women*, dissatisfied as they are with *this* form of government that enforces "taxation without representation"—that compels them to obey laws to which they have never given their consent—that imprisons and hangs them without a trial by a jury of their peers—that robs them, in *marriage*, of the custody of their own persons, wages, and children, are—this half of the people—left wholly at the mercy of the other half, in direct violation of the spirit and letter of the declarations of the framers of this government, every one of which was based on the immutable principles of *"equal rights to all."* (Gordon 1997–2013, 2:555, italics in original)

That is quite strong rhetorical medicine, despite the fact that Anthony does not cite the entire proverb, "taxation without representation is tyranny," something that nevertheless is clear from her forceful statement. In a related speech entitled "The Subjection of Woman" written in May 1873 (no occasion of its actual delivery has been discovered), her friend Elizabeth Cady Stanton is equally chilling in her attacks against male dominance, characterizing men's misogynous and aggressive behavior by the negative proverb "might makes right."

> As I read history old and new the subjection of woman may be clearly traced to the same cause that subjugated different races and nations to one another, the law of force, that made might right, and the weak the slaves of the strong. Men mistake all the time their reverence for an ideal womanhood, for a sense of injustice towards the actual being, that shares with them the toils of life. Man's love and tenderness to one particular woman for a time is no criterion for his general feeling for the whole sex for all time. The same man that would die for one woman, would make an annual holocaust of others, if his appetites or pecuniary interests required it. Kind husbands and Fathers that would tax every nerve and muscle to the uttermost to give their wives and daughters every luxury, would grind multitudes of women to powder in the world of work for the same purpose. (Gordon 1997–2013, 2:626–27)

With women rallying to each other's support, it is not surprising to find Susan B. Anthony made the following statement in a letter of August 9, 1878, arguing strongly for female solidarity with a well-placed authoritative proverb at the end of a paragraph.

> If all "The Suffragists" of all the States could but see eye to eye on this point [that they are the political equals of men], and stand shoulder to shoulder against any and every party and politician not fully and unequivocally committed to "Equal Rights for Woman," we should, at once, become a balance of power that could not fail to compel the party of the highest intelligence to proclaim Woman Suffrage the chief plank of its platform. "In union there is strength." (Gordon 1997–2013, 3:405–6)

With much hope for the younger generation, Elizabeth Cady Stanton went on the lecture circuit in 1880 with one of her most popular speeches, entitled "Our Girls." It contains several proverbial messages for young women (Mieder 2014a), including one with the well-known classical proverb "Mens sana in corpore sano," translated into English: "The coming girl is to have health. One of the first needs for every girl who is to be trained for some life work, some trade or profession, is good health. As a sound body is the first step towards a sound mind, food, clothes, exercise, all the conditions of daily life, are important in training girls either for high scholarship, or practical work" (Gordon 1997–2013, 3:492). She even cites a German proverb that acknowledges the plight of young women, who now are on the move to forge ahead in finding independence, equality, and recognition in all aspects of life.

> An old German proverb says that every girl is born into the world with a stone on her head. This is just as true now as the day it was first uttered.
> Your [men's] creeds, codes, and conventionalisms have indeed fallen with crushing weight on the head of woman in all ages, but nature is mightier than law and custom, and in spite of the stone on her head, behold her to-day close upon the heels of man in the whole world of thought, in art, literature and government. (Gordon 1997–2013, 3:504)

But compare this type of sociopolitical rhetoric with a statement that the boisterous Theodore Roosevelt (1858–1919) made in a speech in January 1886, just fifteen years before he became president.

> I suppose I should be ashamed to say that I take the Western view of the Indian. I don't go so far as to think that the only good Indians are dead Indians, but I believe nine out of every ten are, and I shouldn't like to inquire too closely into the case of the tenth. The most vicious cowboy has more moral principle than the average Indian. Turn three hundred low families of New York into New Jersey, support them for fifty years in vicious idleness, and you will have some idea of what the Indians are. Reckless, revengeful, fiendishly cruel, they rob and murder, not the cowboys, who can take care of themselves, but the defenseless, lone settlers of the plains. (Hagedorn 1921, 355; Dyer 1980, 86)

As I have shown in my detailed study on "'The Only Good Indian Is a Dead Indian': History and Meaning of a Proverbial Stereotype" (Mieder 1993a), this proverb unfortunately became popular in the United States shortly after 1850, and by now it has become the structural formula "The only good X is a dead X." The variable has been replaced by such terms as *Jew, nigger, German,* or *Serb*, and an alarming internationalization of this proverbial pattern has taken place in more recent years. At the same time, the original proverbial stereotype against Native Americans continues to survive, together with other slurs. Fortunately, we remember Theodore Roosevelt today for his creation of the proverb "speak softly and carry a big stick" that he used in an address at the Minnesota State Fair on September 2, 1901, barely two weeks before becoming president after President William McKinley's assassination on September 14: "There is a homely old adage which runs: 'Speak softly and carry a big stick; you will go far.' If the American nation will speak softly and yet build and keep at a pitch of the highest training a thoroughly efficient navy, the Monroe Doctrine will go far" (Titelman 1996, 306; Shapiro 2006, 648). Its usage today can be quite harmless, but of course it has also been employed as a motto of the imperialistic policies of the United States. Be that as it may, such proverbs and their ill-advised quotation by public figures show the danger that proverbs can present in spreading stereotypes and political threats.

As expected, Woodrow Wilson (1856–1924), the intellectually inclined former president of Princeton University, would strike quite a different tone a dozen years later in his first inaugural address on March 4, 1913. While he begins his speech by mentioning the great past of this country, he cautions of "the evil that has come with the good." Then follow two paragraphs that amass such proverbial expressions as "to see the bad with the good," "to have fair play," and "to make up one's mind." He clearly wants to confront the citizens with what we would call today a "reality check," and he adds quite a bite to his jeremiad by satirically reducing the prevailing American philosophy of life to the proverb "every man for himself." The fact that he cites two variations of the proverb that indicate the all-pervasiveness of this worldview from one generation to another makes his statement especially powerful.

> At last a vision has been vouchsafed us of our life as a whole. We see the bad with the good, the debased and decadent with the sound and vital. With this vision we approach new affairs. Our duty is to cleanse, to reconsider, to restore, to correct the evil without impairing the good, to purify and humanize every process of our common life without weakening or sentimentalizing it. There has been something crude and heartless and unfeeling in our haste to succeed and be great. Our thought has been "Let every man look out for himself," while we reared giant machinery which made it impossible that any but those who stood at the levers of control should have a chance to look out for themselves. We had not forgotten our morals. We remembered well enough that we had set up a policy which was meant to serve the humblest as well as the most powerful, with an eye single to the standards of justice and fair play, and remembered it with pride. But we were heedless and in a hurry to be great.
>
> We have come now to the sober second thought. The scales of heedlessness have fallen from our eyes. We have made up our minds to square every process of our national life again with the standards we so proudly set up at the beginning and have always carried at our hearts. Our work is a work of restoration. (Hunt 1997, 324–25)

That is quite a proverbial wake-up call for the nation. But this is not a boisterous president who speaks only of the greatness of the United States. Instead, one senses the sincerity and humility of Abraham Lincoln in these remarks. Little did Woodrow Wilson know that the next year World War I would break out in Europe!

Never again will there be a president of the United States who will have the opportunity of delivering four inaugural addresses, but Franklin Delano Roosevelt (1882–1945), as the thirty-second president, did exactly that, and he did so with much pervasive rhetorical power. The beginning paragraph of his speech at the first inauguration on March 4, 1933, is a telling example of his oratorical abilities that were to dominate American politics during the next twelve years, while Winston Churchill soared to rhetorical heights in Great Britain and Adolf Hitler manipulated the German language to bring about World War II and the Holocaust. All three political leaders made ample use of proverbial language to convince their respective people of their plans and intentions (Mieder 1993b; Mieder and Bryan 1995; Mieder 1997, 9–38 [Hitler], 9–38 [Churchill]). Roosevelt began his speech with a statement that included the three proverbial texts "to speak the truth, the whole truth, and nothing but the truth," "the only thing we have to fear is fear itself," and "to be a dark hour."

> I am certain that my fellow Americans expect that on my induction into the presidency I will address them with a candor and a decision which the present situation of our nation impels. This is preeminently the time to speak the truth, the whole truth, frankly and boldly. Nor need we shrink from honestly facing conditions in our country today. This great nation will endure as it has endured, will revive and will prosper. So, first of all, let me assert my firm belief that the only thing we have to fear is fear itself—nameless, unreasoning, unjustified terror which paralyzes needed efforts to convert retreat into advance. In every dark hour of our national life a leadership of frankness and vigor has met with that understanding and support of the people themselves which is essential to victory. I am convinced that you will again give that support to leadership in these critical days. (Hunt 1997, 377–78)

As Roosevelt promised the country a New Deal after the devastating depression, he chose his words well when he proclaimed with much optimism that "the only thing we have to fear is fear itself." This statement has long found its way into quotation dictionaries and even into the *Dictionary of American Proverbs* (Mieder, Kingsbury, and Harder 1992, 203–4). However, the editors of these collections of quotations and proverbs are quick to point out that Roosevelt based his sententious remark on a number of possible sources (Stevenson 1948, 783–84; Reaver 1967; Bartlett 1992, 648).

> Whenever conscience commands anything, there is only one thing to fear, and that is fear (c. 1575)
> (St. Theresa of Avila)
>
> The thing I fear most is fear (1580)
> (Michel Eyquem de Montaigne)
>
> Nothing is terrible except fear itself (1623)
> (Francis Bacon)

The only thing I am afraid of is fear (1831)
(Arthur Wellesley, Duke of Wellington)

Nothing is so much to be feared as fear (1851)
(Henry David Thoreau)

Perhaps Roosevelt alone or with the help of speechwriters coined this variant of the formulaic theme of fearing fear, but it might also have been formulated in knowledge of some of these earlier statements. In any case, in its unique wording it has correctly become associated with Franklin D. Roosevelt (Taylor and Parks 1965), and in the minds of most Americans, he did in fact invent it.

At the height of World War II, the country elected Roosevelt to a fourth term, but due to the tense situation, Roosevelt's inaugural address on January 20, 1945, spanned barely a page and a half. Yet, at this somber moment, President Roosevelt cited two proverbial expressions and a proverb to remind people of the necessity to find peace in the world by being a player on the world scene. Isolationism is clearly not a choice for a world power like the United States.

> Today, in this year of war, 1945, we have learned lessons—at a fearful cost—and we shall profit from them. We have learned that we cannot live alone, at peace; that our own well-being is dependent on the well-being of other nations far away. We have learned that we must live as men, not as ostriches, nor as dogs in the manger. We have learned the simple truth, as Emerson said, that "the only way to have a friend is to be one." We can gain no lasting peace if we approach it with suspicion and mistrust or with fear. We can gain it only if we proceed with the understanding, the confidence, and the courage which flow from conviction. (Hunt 1997, 396)

The metaphors of the proverbial expressions "to be an ostrich" and "to be a dog in the manger" serve Roosevelt well to express the two ideas that America cannot afford to be blind to the events in the world and that it cannot retreat selfishly on its own territory, leaving the rest of the world to its own devices. Instead, the United States needs to be a friend to all other free nations, as Roosevelt explains by quoting a line from Ralph Waldo Emerson's essay *Friendship* (1841), a line that had long since become a proverb (Stevenson 1948, 896; La Rosa 1976; Mieder 1989, 143–69; Mieder, Kingsbury, and Harder 1992, 239).

President Harry S. Truman (1884–1972) continued Roosevelt's policies, but he himself deserves the credit for the Marshall Plan, the North Atlantic Treaty Organization, and the start of the United Nations. Truman delighted in using proverbial expressions in his speeches, news conferences, and many books (Mieder and Bryan 1997). In fact, he was proud of his plain speaking, and he might well have been the most proverbial American president ever. There are numerous textual examples of Truman's integration of complete proverbs into his speeches and writings. When cited in their traditional wording, these proverbs usually take on the function of supporting an argument, proving a point, and teaching a simple lesson. It is the latter use that plays a major role in Truman's verbal communication. He quite likes himself in the role of teacher, if not preacher, and obviously exact proverbs are suitable to spread pithy wisdom among the common people. There is, however, also a remarkable example from 1945 of Truman's taking a traditional three-word proverb and simply altering the word order to express a better idea, one that would be appropriate for a democracy: "we will be forced to accept the fundamental concept of our enemies, namely, that 'Might makes right.' . . . We must, once and for all, reverse the order, and prove by our acts conclusively, that Right Has Might" (Truman 1961, 23). This is certainly reminiscent of Abraham Lincoln's effective use of the proverb "right makes might" some eighty-five years earlier.

But there is also a proverb that has undeniably become associated with Truman. As many Americans know, Truman had a sign on his desk in the White House that stated with proverbial precision, "the buck stops here." This piece of wisdom has entered the general language. It is found in phraseological dictionaries (Rees 1984, 70; Bartlett 1992, 655); the mass media employ it in advertisements, cartoons, and caricatures; and it has also been used as chapter headings in books on Truman (Phillips 1966, 329–50; McCullough 1992, 467–524). While the phrase is used by many, it is not clear that they actually understand its finer linguistic and cultural points. Some probably think of "buck" in terms of money, recalling this as a slang expression for a one-dollar bill. However, in this semantic connotation, the phrase makes little sense. Actually the "buck" is part of the poker players' expression "to pass the buck" or simply "passing the buck," which refers to a marker that can be passed on to another player by someone who does not wish to deal the cards. In its figurative sense, the proverbial phrase has taken on the meaning of passing on a problem or responsibility (Wentworth and Flexner 1975, 67). The expression has been known since the nineteenth century, Mark Twain having used it in 1871 in *Roughing It*: "I reckon I can't call that hand. Ante and pass the buck" (Lighter 1994, 1:282). In view of Truman's appreciation of Twain, it should not surprise us that he might have picked up the phrase from this American author.

In any case, Truman refers to the sign on his desk twice in his many speeches. On January 31, 1951, at a dinner of the Democratic National Congressional Committee in Washington, DC, he talked about the basic duties of a president which, reduced to the lowest common denominator, are that decisions must be made and actions must be taken: "And never a day goes by that . . . I don't have to act. And there's a sign on my desk which says, 'The Buck Stops Here'" (Truman 1965, 132). The same theme was picked up by Truman during an address at the National War College on December 19, 1952.

> You know, it's easy enough for the Monday morning quarterback to say what the coach should have done, after the game is over. But when the decision is up before you—and on my desk I have a motto which says "The buck stops here"—the decision has to be made. That decision may be right. It may be wrong. If it is wrong, and it has been shown that it is wrong, I have no desire to cover it up. I admit it, and try to make another decision that will meet the situation. And that is what any President of the United States has to do. Just bear that in mind. (Truman 1966, 1094–95)

Another use of the buck-passing phrase is particularly important, since Truman employs it to answer that omnipresent question of why he decided to drop the atomic bomb at the end of World War II. Truman seldom entered into philosophical deliberations, and instead of talking about an existential or ethical dilemma, he chose a plain proverbial expression to answer that haunting question in an address on October 14, 1948, in Milwaukee, Wisconsin.

> As President of the United States, I had the fateful responsibility of deciding whether or not to use this weapon [the atomic bomb] for the first time. It was the hardest decision I ever had to make. But the President cannot duck hard problems—he cannot pass the buck. I made the decision after discussions with ablest men in our Government [Churchill agreed as well], and after long and prayerful consideration.
> I decided that the bomb should be used in order to end the war quickly and save countless lives—Japanese as well as American.
> But I resolved then and there to do everything I could to see that this awesome discovery was turned into a force for peace and the advancement of mankind.
> Since then, it has been my constant aim to prevent its use for war and to hasten its use for peace. (Truman 1964, 788)

It should not be a surprise, then, to see Truman return to this significant proverbial phrase in his "Farewell Address to the American People," which was broadcast from his office in the White House on January 15, 1953.

While speaking, he probably glanced across his desk to the sign with the motto "The Buck Stops Here."

> The greatest part of the President's job is to make decisions—big ones and small ones, dozens of them almost every day. The papers may circulate around the Government for a while but they finally reach his desk. And then, there's no place else for them to go. The President—whoever he is—has to decide. He can't pass the buck to anybody. No one else can do the deciding for him. That's his job. (Truman 1966, 1197)

Naturally, Truman had his faults, and he certainly committed plenty of errors that precipitated numerous crises. The classical proverb "to err is human" could just as well be changed to "to act is Truman," or even more appropriately, to the apposite "to speak plainly is Truman." Would that every president communicated with the American people as President Harry S. Truman did throughout his political life.

When the youthful and vigorous John F. Kennedy (1917–1963) was sworn in on January 20, 1961, as the thirty-fifth president (Corbett 1965), he included two memorable and quotable statements in his refreshing inaugural address. Clearly, Kennedy and his sophisticated speechwriters (primarily Theodore C. Sorenson) formulated them by adopting the parallel structure of many proverbs (Meyer 1982, 240–41). Speaking of the danger of the Cold War with its arms race, Kennedy calls upon both sides to remember "that civility is not a sign of weakness, and sincerity is always subject to proof. *Let us never negotiate out of fear. But let us never fear to negotiate*" (Hunt 1997, 430, italics in the original). The last sentence has found its way into John Bartlett's *Familiar Quotations* (Bartlett 1992, 741; see also Lewis and Rhodes 1967), but it would probably go too far to assign a proverbial character to it.

This leads us to the antithetical phrase, "ask not what your country can do for you; ask what you can do for your country" (Corbett 1965, 512) toward the end of the speech.

> In the long history of the world, only a few generations have been granted the role of defending freedom in its hour of maximum danger. I do not shrink from this responsibility—I welcome it. I do not believe that any of us would exchange places with any other people or any other generation. The energy, the faith, the devotion which we bring to this endeavor will light our country and all who serve it—and the glow from that fire can truly light the world. *And so, my fellow Americans, ask not what your country can do for you; ask what you can do for your country. My fellow citizens of the world: Ask not what America will do for you, but what together we can do for the freedom of man.* (Hunt 1997, 431, italics in the original)

This reliable resource cites the following statement from an address delivered on May 30, 1884, by Oliver Wendell Holmes as a possible source: "For, stripped of the temporary associations which gave rise to it, it is now the moment when by common consent we pause to become conscious of our national life and to rejoice in it, to recall what our country has done for each of us, and to ask ourselves what we can do for our country in return" (Bartlett 1992, 741). It is hard to imagine that Kennedy's famous civic slogan was not taken from this speech by Oliver Wendell Holmes. Be that as it may, it has now, in the precise wording by John F. Kennedy, become a sententious remark and is well along to become an American proverb as well.

Kennedy's presidency and the following years were also the time of the civil rights movements that brought the rhetorical prowess of Martin Luther King Jr. (1929–1968) as its leader to the foreground. As was the case with his predecessor, Frederick Douglass, King also relies on proverbs and proverbial expressions to bring across his message of equal rights and opportunities in a most effective way. In his programmatic "Letter from a Birmingham Jail" (1963), King used a well-known proverb to put the injustice done to African Americans into a precise formula.

> This "Wait" has almost always meant "Never." It has been a tranquilizing thalidomide, relieving the emotional stress for a moment, only to give birth to an ill-formed infant of frustration. We must come to see with the distinguished jurist of yesterday that "justice too long delayed is justice denied." We have waited for more than 340 years for our constitutional and God-given rights. The nations of Asia and Africa are moving with jet-like speed toward the goal of political independence, and we still creep at horse and buggy pace toward the gaining of a cup of coffee at a lunch counter. (King 1992, 88)

And, of course, in his famous "I Have a Dream" (1963) speech that King delivered before the Lincoln Memorial on August 28, 1963, as the keynote address of the March on Washington, DC, for civil rights, he utilized naturally and effectively two of America's most well-known proverbial mottoes, as Abraham Lincoln and Frederick Douglass and other great public figures of good will had done before.

> So we've come here today to dramatize a shameful condition. In a sense we've come to our nation's capital to cash a check. When the architects of our republic wrote the magnificent words of the Constitution and the Declaration of Independence, they were signing a promissory note to which every American was to fall heir. This note was the promise that all men, yes, black men as well as white men, would be guaranteed the unalienable rights of life, liberty, and the pursuit of happiness.

> So I say to you, my friends, that even though we must face the difficulties of today and tomorrow, I still have a dream. It is a dream deeply rooted in the American dream that one day this nation will rise up and live out the true meaning of its creed—we hold these truths to be self-evident, that all men are created equal. (King 1992, 102, 104)

Despite the passage of the Civil Rights Act of 1964, African Americans were still denied their voting rights in some parts of the South. Following yet another protest march—this time from Selma to Montgomery, Alabama—King gave his powerful "Our God Is Marching On!" speech on March 25, 1965, concluding it with a triad of proverbs lifting the civil rights agenda into the religious sphere.

> I know you are asking today, "How long will it take?" I come to say to you this afternoon however difficult the moment, however frustrating the hour, it will not be long, because truth pressed to earth will rise again.
> How long? Not long, because no lie can live forever.
> How long? Not long, because you still reap what you sow.
> How long? Not long. Because the arm [arc] of the moral universe is long but it bends toward justice.
> How long? Not long, 'cause mine eyes have seen the glory of the coming of the Lord, trampling out the vintage where the grapes of wrath are stored. He has loosed the fateful lightning of his terrible sword. The truth is marching on.
> He has sounded forth the trumpets that shall never call retreat. He is lifting up the hearts of man before His judgment seat. Oh, be swift, my soul, to answer Him. Be jubilant, my feet. Our God is marching on. (King 1992, 124)

Again and again, like Frederick Douglass before him, Reverend King employed biblical proverbs, especially at the end of his spiritually poetic and dramatically forceful speeches, as evidenced in the concluding remarks of his address "Where Do We Go from Here?" delivered on August 16, 1967, at the Ebenezer Baptist Church in Atlanta, Georgia: "Let us go out realizing that the Bible is right: 'Be not deceived, God is not mocked. Whatever a man soweth, that shall he reap' (Galatians 6:7). This is for hope for the future, and with this faith we will be able to sing in some not too distant tomorrow with a cosmic past tense, 'We have overcome, we have overcome, deep in my heart, I did believe we would overcome'" (King 1992, 179).

What some of the political leaders have uttered since such memorable oratory by Martin Luther King Jr. is, for the most part, rather disappointing. Sure, with Ronald Reagan (1911–2004) as the fortieth president, the nation had found a "great communicator" (Phifer 1983, 385) to guide it through an increased military buildup and the implementation of supply-side economics in the form of spending cuts and tax cuts (Cassell 1984; Adler 1996). Reagan has been criticized and satirized for his inclination toward sound-bite rhetoric, with his infamous one-liners usually appearing during supposedly spontaneous remarks. But I do recall a memorable utterance where he helped to make a relatively young American proverb become internationally known. When Leonid Brezhnev died on November 10, 1982, Reagan found himself having to deal with a series of new Kremlin leaders during the heights of the Cold War. Yet old warriors die hard, and when asked whether he had hopes that relationships between the United States and the Soviet Union might improve with the new leader Yuri V. Andropov, Reagan responded with a short statement on November 11 that included a proverbial quip: "For ten years détente was based on words from [the Russians] and not any deeds to back those words up. And we need some action that they—it takes two to tango—that they want to tango also" (Weekly Compilation 1982, 1459).

It is well known that Reagan was avoiding the dance floor just as much as the Soviets at that time, but his statement popularized the proverb "it takes two to tango" throughout the world in the mass media. The expression, which actually started as a variant of the older proverb "it takes two to quarrel," dates from a 1952 song written and composed by Al Hoffman and Dick Manning called "Takes Two to Tango" and sung by Pearl Bailey. Since that time, the tango metaphor has often appeared in headlines in the international press, and it has gained currency as a proverb in loan translation in other languages as well.

President George W. Bush (1946–) is certainly not known for any particular linguistic prowess. But to his credit, he did say on December 13, 2000, after the Supreme Court had made him the forty-third president: "Our nation must rise above a house divided" (Fournier 2000, 1). The allusion to the Bible proverb "A house divided against itself cannot stand," echoing Abraham Lincoln's use of it in his struggle to keep the Union together, was well chosen for this momentous occasion. It had been my conjecture that Bush would incorporate this fitting piece of traditional wisdom into this inaugural speech on January 20, 2001, but he and his speechwriter Michael Gersen decided against it (Bush 2001, 12–13). Bush's years as president have certainly not been marked by verbal eloquence.

Many of our modern presidents have not distinguished themselves as great orators, and the same appears to be true for various presidential contenders of recent years. It seems that they and their speechwriters have abandoned colorful and metaphorical language based on proverbial wisdom. Instead they deliver speeches full of empty sentences and facts and figures, always on the watch to be politically correct and not "folksy."

While I was not a supporter of Ross Perot's (1930–) bid for the presidency in 1992 or 1996, I do admit that his campaign speeches as well as his programmatic book with its shrewd proverbial title *United We Stand: How We Can Take Back Our Country* (1992) brought back the honest and plain-speaking rhetoric of Harry Truman and others. In the chapter "A National Commitment on Race," for example, he writes and at other times talked in proverbs that have a long tradition in American politics.

> "A house divided against itself cannot stand." Many people know Abraham Lincoln said that just before the Civil War. Fewer people recall that he was quoting scripture. What a timeless message and simple truth.
>
> We are divided by racial strife. We're a divided team in worldwide competition against united teams.
>
> We must reunite. I break this down into three approaches. First, we ought to love one another. That takes care of most of us. Second, for those who can't lift themselves up to that level, we have to get along with one another so we can team up and win. Third, for the hard-core haters, we're stuck with one another. Nobody is going anywhere. We're here, side by side. You might as well move up to category two so we can win, not lose, as a nation.
> ...
> I am not closing my eyes to the real world. I realize that some groups have advantages and that others have disadvantages, but we don't pull anyone up by pulling somebody else down. We're all in the same boat, and we will sink or sail together. (Perot 1992, 94–95; Livengood 1997)

Some people might well say that this is all quite simple in its proverbial language, but I might add that Perot, by using the proverbial phrase "to be in the same boat" as an expression of a unified fate is, in fact, doing the same that the famous orator Cicero did when he used the classical Latin phrase "in eadem es navi" in 53 BC (Mieder 1995, 140–59). And I might also point out that this very expression is also the basis of the most important proverbial exchange, and there were many, between the two great orators and world leaders Winston S. Churchill (1874–1965) and Franklin Delano Roosevelt. It took place on December 7, 1941, the very day the Japanese had attacked the American naval base at Pearl Harbor. Roosevelt called Churchill to tell him of the event and to inform him that he would ask Congress for a declaration of war against Japan on the next day, with Churchill pledging to do the same. Five years later, Churchill recalled the short conversation as follows: "In two or three minutes Mr. Roosevelt came through. 'Mr. President, what's this about Japan?' 'It's quite true,' he replied. 'They have attacked us at Pearl Harbor. We are all in the same boat now . . .' I got on again and said, 'This certainly simplifies things. God be with you,' or words of that effect" (Kimball 1984, 1:281).

This recollection of the use of the classical proverbial expression "to be in the same boat" is substantiated by a short exchange between the president and the prime minister on the two subsequent days. Having delivered his "war message" to Congress on December 8, 1941 (Stelzner 1966), referring at the beginning to the attack as "a date which will live in infamy," Roosevelt wrote this short telegram to Churchill: "The Senate passed the all-out declaration of war eighty-two to nothing, and the House has passed it three hundred eighty-eight to one. Today all of us are in the same boat with you and the people of the Empire and it is a ship which will not and cannot be sunk" (Kimball 1984, 1:283).

Churchill telegraphed back on December 9, using the proverbial phrase once again to express their common fate and struggle in a most fitting naval metaphor.

> I am grateful for your telegram of December 8. Now that we are as you say "in the same boat" would it not be wise for us to have another conference. We could review the whole war plan in the light of reality and new facts, as well as the problems of production and distribution. I feel all these matters, some of which are causing me concern, can best be settled on the highest executive level. It would also be a very great pleasure to me to meet you again, and the sooner the better. (Kimball 1984, 1:283–84)

It is questionable whether Roosevelt or Churchill was aware of the fact that their "boat" metaphor is an English translation of Cicero's Latin proverbial expression "in eadem es navi," but they most assuredly were in the same boat now, and their large and powerful vessel with its massive war machinery moved forward "full blast" (as Churchill wrote on September 6, 1942) toward final victory (Kimball 1984, 1:592). The proverbial expression "to be in the same boat," uttered at one of the deciding moments in world history, served Roosevelt and Churchill well as a metaphor for their joint struggle, and as such is convincing proof that proverbial language does indeed run the whole gamut from banal cliché to sublime wisdom.

Finally, consider President Barack Obama's rhetoric. He has most certainly rekindled the flame for eloquent speechmaking during his stump speeches, his formal addresses here in this country, and his extremely well-received speeches abroad (Mieder 2009b). There are so many examples I could cite, but let me begin with the unforgettable speech that he delivered on July 24, 2008—still as a presidential candidate—in Berlin, Germany, that earned him the respect and goodwill not only of Europeans but of citizens worldwide. Who could forget the excitement that his opening statement, "I speak to you not as a candidate for president, but as a citizen—a proud citizen of the United States, and a fellow citizen of the world," had on his large audience in Berlin and the millions of people who watched this dramatic event on television?

Being in Berlin clearly reminded Obama of the Berlin Wall that for many years had served as the symbol of a divided Germany but metaphorically also of the world. Mindful of "the burdens of global citizenship [that] bind us together" now that this wall has ceased to exist, Obama said:

> Partnership and cooperation among nations is not a choice; it is the one way, the only way, to protect our common security and advance our common humanity.
> That is why the greatest danger of all is to allow new walls to divide us from one another. The walls between old allies on either side of the Atlantic cannot stand. The walls between the countries with the most and those with the least cannot stand. The walls between races and tribes; natives and immigrants; Christian and Muslim and Jew cannot stand. These now are the walls we must tear down. (Obama 2002–2009; Mieder 2010, 29)

There is no doubt that this rhetorical high point is modeled on the Bible proverb "a house divided against itself cannot stand" (Mark 3:25) that Abraham Lincoln used repeatedly as he tried to preserve the American Union before and during the Civil War. After all, Obama has stated repeatedly that he turns to such great American leaders as Abraham Lincoln, Frederick Douglass, and Martin Luther King Jr. for philosophical and rhetorical inspiration.

Having made his views as possible peacemaker and humble servant of humankind known at his inaugural event that was broadcast to every corner of the world (Mieder 2009a), Obama got to work and soon realized that his refreshing idealism and courageous hope for a better world would face considerable obstacles at home and abroad. But the youthful and energetic president appears to be unshakable in his vision of carving out a better America and an improved world order. He certainly never tires of repeating his call for steady improvement, ever mindful that progress will only take place by way of struggle. He took the opportunity to repeat this fundamental belief when he traveled to Egypt, where on June 4, 2009, in front of five thousand students at Cairo University, he gave a major address reaching out to the Muslim world as no modern American president had done before. Arguing for a better understanding among people of different religions, he cited proverbial wisdom from the Koran, with the audience applauding his willingness to quote from this holy book.

> There must be sustained effort to listen to each other; to learn from each other; to respect one another; and to seek common ground. As the Holy Koran tells us, "Be conscious of God and speak always the truth." [Applause.] That is what I will try to do today—to speak the truth as best I can, humbled by the task before us, and firm in my belief that the interests we share as human beings are far more powerful than the forces that drive us apart.

> The Holy Koran teaches that whoever kills an innocent is as—it is as if he has killed all mankind [Applause.] And the Holy Koran also says whoever saves a person, it is as if he has saved all mankind. [Applause.] The enduring faith of over a billion people is so much bigger than the narrow hatred of a few. Islam is not part of the problem in combating violent extremism—it is an important part of promoting peace. (Obama 2002–2009; Mieder 2010, 32)

Throughout the speech, Obama stressed "our common humanity," claiming the "simple truth: that violence is a dead end." I have not been able to establish the proverbiality of this statement, but certainly the idea that "violence is a dead end" could well advance from the status of a pseudo-proverb to an actual proverb.

During this speech, Obama argued forcefully "against negative stereotypes of Islam," but he was quick to point out that eradicating the world of stereotypes must involve people everywhere, who, after all, were all created equal, as Obama never ceases to point out proverbially.

> Just as Muslims do not fit a crude stereotype, America is not the crude stereotype of a self-interested empire. The United States has been one of the greatest sources of progress that the world has ever known. We were born out of revolution against an empire. We were founded upon the ideal that all are created equal, and we have shed blood and struggled for centuries to give meaning to those words—within our borders, and around the world. We are shaped by every culture, drawn from every end of the Earth, and dedicated to a simple concept: E pluribus unum—"Out of many, one." (Obama 2002–2009; Mieder 2010, 32)

The old classical proverb "e pluribus unum," which is part of the American seal, embodies Obama's vision of a world in which people emphasize their similarities rather than stress their differences. This view includes a democratic form of government, of course, as Obama stresses by citing part of the proverbial triad of a "government of the people, by the people, for the people" that was popularized as the shortest definition of democracy by way of Abraham Lincoln's Gettysburg Address of November 19, 1863, when he had said at the end of his oration: "that this nation, under God, shall have a new birth of freedom—and that government of the people, by the people, for the people, shall not perish from the earth." But here is what Obama said about democracy during a speech in Cairo:

> There are some who advocate for democracy only when they're out of power; once in power, they are ruthless in suppressing the rights of others. [Applause.] So no matter where it takes hold, government of the people and by the people sets a single standard for all who would hold power: You must maintain your power through consent, not coercion; you must respect the rights of minorities, and participate with a spirit of tolerance and compromise; you must place the interests of your people and the legitimate workings of the political process

above your party. Without these ingredients, elections alone do not make a true democracy. (Obama 2002–2009; Mieder 2010, 33)

It is unclear why Obama does not cite the third element, "for the people," of this proverbial definition, but what he does say surely refers to the fact that the government is there for the people whom it serves. Then, very close to the end of this moving and inspiring speech to thousands of Arabic students, he asked them "to reimagine the world, to remake this world." Little wonder there was repeated applause and calls such as "Barack Obama, we love you!" during the speech. The climax of the speech was reached when the president called for a new world of brother- and sisterhood informed by empathy and mutual respect, with the center of his powerful statement being occupied by the proverbial Golden Rule.

> All of us share this world for but a brief moment in time. The question is whether we spend that time focused on what pushes us apart, or whether we commit ourselves to an effort—a sustained effort—to find common ground, to focus on the future we seek for our children, and to respect the dignity of all human beings.
>
> It's easier to start wars than to end them. It's easier to blame others than to look inward. It's easier to see what is different about someone than to find the things we share. But we should choose the right path, not just the easy path. There's one rule that lies at the heart of every religion—that we do unto others as we would have them do unto us. [Applause.] This truth transcends nations and peoples—a belief that isn't new; that isn't black or white or brown; that isn't Christian or Muslim or Jew. It's a belief that pulsed in the cradle of civilization, and that still beats in the hearts of billions around the world. It's a faith in other people, and it's what brought me here today. (Obama 2002–2009; Mieder 2010, 32; Mieder 2014b, 514–15)

That is rational and emotional rhetoric, coming both from the mind and the heart, as it calls for a new world based on ethical values that bind humankind together. One certainly can hear echoes of Abraham Lincoln, Frederick Douglass, and Martin Luther King Jr. in this deeply moral worldview.

All political leaders are faced with addressing heterogeneous audiences, and they must find a common denominator in their rhetoric that will be grasped and appreciated by the largest possible number of people, both here in the United States and throughout the world. In an enlightening article on "Maxims, 'Practical Wisdom,' and the Language of Action: Beyond Grand Theory" (1996) in the renowned journal *Political Theory*, political scientist Ray Nichols argued convincingly that political rhetoric must be characterized by "'practical wisdom,' 'practical knowledge,' 'practical reason,' [and] 'practical judgment" (1996, 687). The common sense of such practical wisdom expressed in quotable phrases or proverbs definitely adds to the communicative and emotional quality of political rhetoric. A memorable phrase or a traditional proverb represents a preformulated and commonly known bit of wisdom that underscores the value system and mentality of the people. All of this must be understood with an obvious caveat, of course. As with everything in life, the proverbs "everything in moderation" and "nothing in excess" also hold true for the use of proverbs in political discourse. But now and then a solid statement of timeless folk wisdom in the form of a proverb will clearly do no harm, as some of the very best American political speeches make abundantly clear. An occasional proverb at the right moment will not hinder the call for eloquence in political rhetoric. Proverbs permeate our sociopolitical life everywhere and at all times, and they are significant signs of the wisdom and worldview of an entire nation trying to uphold the inalienable rights of life, liberty, and the pursuit of happiness for all its citizens, and—with the help of the United Nations—for all humankind. There can be no doubt that proverbs as strategically used folk wisdom continue to be important communicative devices that deserve close scrutiny.

References

This chapter was first published in *Proverbium* 25 (2008): 319–52.

Adams, Charles Francis, ed. 1848. *Letters of Mrs. Adams, Wife of John Adams*. Boston: Wilkins, Carter, and Company.
Adler, Bill, ed. 1996. *The Uncommon Wisdom of Ronald Reagan: A Portrait in His Own Words*. Boston: Little, Brown and Company.
Barbour, Frances M. 1974. *A Concordance to the Sayings in Franklin's "Poor Richard."* Detroit: Gale Research Company.
Bartlett, John. 1992. *Familiar Quotations*. Edited by Justin Kaplan. 16th ed. Boston: Little, Brown and Company.
Basler, Roy P. 1946. "Lincoln's Development as a Writer." In *Abraham Lincoln: His Speeches and Writings*, edited by Roy P. Basler, 1–49. Cleveland: World Publishing Company.
———, ed. 1953. *The Collected Works of Abraham Lincoln*. 8 vols. New Brunswick, NJ: Rutgers University Press.
Bernstein, R. B., ed. 2002. *The Wisdom of John and Abigail Adams*. New York: MetroBooks.
Blassingame, John, ed. 1985–92. *The Frederick Douglass Papers*. 5 vols. New Haven, CT: Yale University Press.
Bush, George W. 2001. "President: 'I Ask You to Be Citizens.'" *New York Times*, January 21, 12–13.
Butterfield, L. H., ed. 1963–93. *Adams Family Correspondence (1761–1785)*. 13 vols. Cambridge, MA: Harvard University Press.

Cassel, Clark, ed. 1984. *President Reagan's Quotations*. Washington, DC: Braddock Publications.
Corbett, Edward. 1965. "Analysis of the Style of John F. Kennedy's Inaugural Address." In *Classical Rhetoric for the Modern Student*, edited by E. Corbett, 508–18. New York: Oxford University Press.
Dyer, Thomas G. 1980. *Theodore Roosevelt and the Idea of Race*. Baton Rouge: Louisiana State University Press.
Edwards, Herbert Joseph, and John Erskine Hankins. 1962. *Lincoln the Writer: The Development of His Literary Style*. Orono: University of Maine.
Fournier, Ron. 2000. "Bush Pledges Reconciliation: Gore Concedes Race; Transition Period Begins." *Burlington (VT) Free Press*, December 14, 1.
Gallacher, Stuart A. 1949. "Franklin's *Way to Wealth*: A Florilegium of Proverbs and Wise Sayings." *Journal of English and Germanic Philology* 48:229–51.
Gordon, Ann D., ed. 1997–2013. *The Selected Papers of Elizabeth Cady Stanton and Susan B. Anthony*. 6 vols. New Brunswick, NJ: Rutgers University Press.
Hagedorn, Hermann. 1921. *Roosevelt in the Bad Lands*. Boston: Houghton Mifflin.
Houston, Sam. 1850. "Speech of Mr. Houston of Texas, in the Senate of the United States, Friday, February 8, 1850." In *Appendix to the Congressional Globe for the First Session, Thirty-First Congress: Containing Speeches and Important State Papers* 22, part 1: 97–102. Washington, DC: John C. Rives.
Hunt, John Gabriel, ed. 1997. *The Inaugural Addresses of the Presidents*. New York: Gramercy Books.
Kimball, Warren F. 1984. *Roosevelt & Churchill: The Complete Correspondence*. 3 vols. Princeton, NJ: Princeton University Press.
King, Martin Luther, Jr. 1992. *I Have a Dream: Writings and Speeches that Changed the World*. Edited by James Melvin Washington. New York: HarperCollins.
Kuusi, Matti. 1957. *Parömiologische Betrachtungen*. Helsinki: Suomalainen Tiedeakatemia.
La Rosa, Ralph Charles. 1976. "Necessary Truths: The Poetics of Emerson's Proverbs." In *George Eliot, De Quincey, and Emerson*, edited by Eric Rothstein, 129–92. Madison: University of Wisconsin Press.
Lewis, Edward, and Richard Rhodes, ed. 1967. *John F. Kennedy: Words to Remember*. Kansas City, MO: Hallmark Cards.
Lighter, J. E., ed. 1994. *Random House Historical Dictionary of American Slang*. 2 vols. New York: Random House.
Livengood, R. Mark. 1997. "Pitching Politics for the People: An Analysis of the Metaphoric Speech of H. Ross Perot." *Western Folklore* 56:259–65.
McCullough, David. 1992. *Truman*. New York: Simon & Schuster.
Meyer, Sam. 1982. "The John F. Kennedy Inauguration Speech: Function and Importance of Its 'Address System.'" *Rhetoric Society Quarterly* 12:239–50.
Mieder, Wolfgang. 1987. "History and Interpretation of a Proverb about Human Nature: 'Big Fish Eat Little Fish.'" In *Tradition and Innovation in Folk Literature*, edited by W. Mieder, 178–228, 259–68 (notes). Hanover, NH: University Press of New England.
———. 1989. *American Proverbs: A Study of Texts and Contexts*. Bern: Peter Lang.
———. 1993a. "'The Only Good Indian Is a Dead Indian': History and Meaning of a Proverbial Stereotype." *Journal of American Folklore* 106:38–60.
———. 1993b. "Proverbs in Nazi Germany: The Promulgation of Anti-Semitism and Stereotypes Through Folklore." In *Proverbs Are Never Out of Season: Popular Wisdom in the Modern Age*, edited by W. Mieder, 225–55. New York: Oxford University Press.

———. 1995. *Deutsche Redensarten, Sprichwörter und Zitate: Studien zu ihrer Herkunft, Überlieferung und Verwendung.* Vienna: Edition Praesens.

———. 1997. *The Politics of Proverbs: From Traditional Wisdom to Proverbial Stereotypes.* Madison: University of Wisconsin Press.

———. 1998. *"A House Divided": From Biblical Proverb to Lincoln and Beyond.* Burlington: University of Vermont.

———. 2000. *The Proverbial Abraham Lincoln: An Index to Proverbs in the Works of Abraham Lincoln.* New York: Peter Lang.

———. 2004. "Benjamin Franklin's 'The Way to Wealth.'" In *Proverbs: A Handbook*, edited by W. Mieder, 216–24. Westport, CT: Greenwood Press.

———. 2005. *Proverbs Are the Best Policy: Folk Wisdom and American Politics.* Logan: Utah State University Press.

———. 2009a. "'We Must Pick Ourselves Up, Dust Ourselves Off': President Barack Obama's Proverbial Inaugural Address." *Paremia* 18:31–42.

———. 2009b. *"Yes We Can": Barack Obama's Proverbial Rhetoric.* New York: Peter Lang.

———. 2010. "The Golden Rule as a Political Imperative for the World: President Barack Obama's Proverbial Messages Abroad." *Milli Folklor* 85:26–35.

———. 2014a. *"All Men and Women Are Created Equal": Elizabeth Cady Stanton's and Susan B. Anthony's Proverbial Rhetoric Promoting Women's Rights.* New York: Peter Lang.

———. 2014b. "'I'm Absolutely Sure About—the Golden Rule': Barack Obama's Proverbial Audacity of Hope." In *Narratives Across Space and Time: Transmissions and Adaptations; Proceedings of the 15th Congress of the International Society for Folk Narrative Research (June 2009, Athens)*, edited by Aikaterini Polymerou-Kamilaki, Evangelos Karamanes, and Ioannis Plemmenos, 2:509–28. Athens: Academy of Athens, Hellenic Folklore Research Center.

Mieder, Wolfgang, and George B. Bryan. 1995. *The Proverbial Winston S. Churchill: An Index to Proverbs in the Works of Sir Winston Churchill.* Westport, CT: Greenwood Press.

———. 1996. *Proverbs in World Literature: A Bibliography.* New York: Peter Lang.

———. 1997. *The Proverbial Harry S. Truman: An Index to Proverbs in the Works of Harry S. Truman.* New York: Peter Lang.

Mieder, Wolfgang, Stewart A. Kingsbury, and Kelsie B. Harder. 1992. *A Dictionary of American Proverbs.* New York: Oxford University Press.

Nichols, Ray. 1996. "Maxims, 'Practical Wisdom,' and the Language of Action." *Political Theory* 24: 687–705.

Obama, Barack. 2002–2009. *Speeches.* http://www.obamaspeeches.com/.

Paczolay, Gyula. 1997. *European Proverbs in 55 Languages with Equivalents in Arabic, Persian, Sanskrit, Chinese and Japanese.* Veszprém: Veszprémi Nyomda.

Paine, Thomas. 1989. *Political Writings.* Edited by Bruce Kuklick. Cambridge: Cambridge University Press.

Perot, Ross. 1992. *United We Stand: How We Can Take Back Our Country.* New York: Hyperion.

Phifer, Gregg. 1983. "Two Inaugurals [Jefferson and Reagan]: A Second Look." *Southern Speech Communication Journal* 48:378–85.

Phillips, Cabell. 1966. *The Truman Presidency: The History of a Triumphant Succession.* New York: Macmillan Company.

Reaver, J. Russell. 1967. "Thoreau's Ways with Proverbs." *American Transcendental Quarterly* 1:2–7.

Rees, Nigel. 1984. *Sayings of the Century.* London: George Allen and Unwin.

Sandburg, Carl. 1954. *Abraham Lincoln: The Prairie Years and the War Years.* New York: Harcourt, Brace and Company (first published 1926).
Shapiro, Fred R. 2006. *The Yale Book of Quotations.* New Haven, CT: Yale University Press.
Sparks, Jared. 1840. *The Works of Benjamin Franklin.* 10 vols. Philadelphia: Childs & Peterson, 1840.
Stelzner, Herman G. 1966. "'War Message [by President Roosevelt],' December 8, 1941: An Approach to Language." *Speech Monographs* 33:419–37.
Stevenson, Burton. 1948. *Home Book of Proverbs, Maxims, and Famous Phrases.* New York: Macmillan.
Taylor, E., and Lois F. Parks, ed. 1965. *Memorable Quotations of Franklin D. Roosevelt.* New York: Thomas Y. Crowell.
Titelman, Gregory Y. 1996. *Dictionary of Popular Proverbs and Sayings.* New York: Random House.
Truman, Harry S. 1961. *Public Papers of the Presidents of the United States: Harry S. Truman.* April 12 to December 31, 1945. Washington, DC: US Government Printing Office.
———. 1964. *Public Papers of the Presidents of the United States: Harry S. Truman.* January 1 to December 31, 1948. Washington, DC: US Government Printing Office.
———. 1965. *Public Papers of the Presidents of the United States: Harry S. Truman.* January 1 to December 31, 1951. Washington, DC: US Government Printing Office.
———. 1966. *Public Papers of the Presidents of the United States: Harry S. Truman.* January 1, 1952, to January 20, 1953. Washington, DC: US Government Printing Office.
Webster, Daniel. 1903. "Reception at Buffalo [May 22, 1851]." *The Writings and Speeches of Daniel Webster* 4:242–62. Boston: Little, Brown, & Company.
Weekly Compilation of Presidential Documents. 1982. Edited by the Office of the Federal Register, National Archives and Records Service, General Services Administration, Washington, DC, 18, no. 45 (November 15).
Wentworth, Harold, and Stuart Berg Flexner, ed. 1975. *Dictionary of American Slang.* New York: Thomas Y. Crowell.

2

"THESE ARE THE TIMES THAT TRY WOMEN'S SOULS"

The Proverbial Rhetoric for Women's Rights by Elizabeth Cady Stanton and Susan B. Anthony

WHILE MUCH IS KNOWN ABOUT THE PROVERBIAL RHETORIC of such well-known American male politicians and social reformers as John Adams, Frederick Douglass, Abraham Lincoln, Franklin D. Roosevelt, Harry S. Truman, Martin Luther King Jr., and Barack Obama (Mieder 2000, 2001, 2005, 2009, 2010a; Mieder and Bryan 1997), there has been no such interest in the proverbial speech of female public figures. And yet even a cursory glance at the letters, speeches, and essays of Elizabeth Cady Stanton (1815–1902) and Susan B. Anthony (1820–1906) clearly reveals that these two nineteenth-century feminists are the equals of male political giants when it comes to the employment of proverbial language during the fifty years of their unceasing, emotive, and aggressive struggle for women's rights. Of course, they have been praised for their masterful use of the multifaceted English language, but their rather obvious reliance on folk speech in general and proverbs and proverbial expressions in particular has, with but one exception, received no attention by linguists, cultural historians, folklorists, and paremiologists (Mieder 2013).

The many biographies and studies about both Stanton and Anthony go into great detail about their fascinating lives and their progressive sociopolitical causes as they relate to women, but for the most part they fail in analyzing how their fight for abolition, temperance, gender equality, and women's suffrage in particular was verbalized and proverbialized in such a way that their messages effected social change over time (O'Connor 1954; Lutz 1959; Clarke 1972; Griffith 1984; Barry 1988; Ward 1999; Gornick 2005;

Ridarksy and Huth 2012). In other words, it is one thing to scrutinize what these two effective orators and essayists said in the cause of civil and women's rights, but it is also significant to analyze how they used what aspects of language to bring their message across. Just as Abigail Adams (1744–1818)—an early American feminist without a political voice—employed proverbs and proverbial phrases to argue for women's rights in her plethora of letters to her family and many friends (Mieder 2005, 56–89), so did Stanton and Anthony also rely on biblical and folk proverbs to make their relentless case for the equality of men and women before the law and in social interaction.

This lack of attention to the proverbial nature of Stanton's and Anthony's language is also apparent in Karlyn Kohrs Campbell's otherwise superb two-volume study, *Man Cannot Speak for Her* (1989a-b), that presents and analyzes nineteenth-century female rhetoric as it was practiced by Stanton and Anthony and some of their significant contemporaries in the struggle for women's rights. In her informative introduction, Campbell points out that "men have an ancient and honorable rhetorical history" dating back to ancient Greece and classical Rome, while "women have no parallel rhetorical history" since "for much of their history women have been prohibited from speaking" especially in the public arena (Campbell 1989a, 1:1). She defines rhetoric as "the study of the means by which symbols can be used to appeal to others, to persuade. The potential for persuasion exists in the shared symbolic and socioeconomic experience of persuaders (rhetors) and audiences [as well as readers]; specific rhetorical acts attempt to exploit that shared experience and channel it in certain directions" (1:2). And she goes on to state that rhetorical analysis has focused on "the rhetor's skill in selecting and adapting those resources available in language, in cultural values, and in shared experience in order to influence others" (1:2).

This makes perfect sense, but those linguistic resources available to women are exactly the aspects that have not been looked at in detail by scholars interested in the feminist movement over time. Campbell even speaks of a "feminine style" of the suffragists, whose "discourse will be personal in tone, relying heavily on personal experience, anecdotes, and other examples. It will tend to be structured inductively (crafts are learned bit by bit, instance by instance, from which generalizations emerge).... The goal of such rhetoric is empowerment, a term contemporary feminists have used to refer to the process of persuading listeners [or readers] that they can act effectively in the world, that they can be agents of change" (1:13). As will be seen, proverbs as generalizations of human behavior and expressions of social norms will add considerable weight to the "rhetorical creativity" (1:15) of feminists, and it is surprising that the vast scholarship on Elizabeth Cady Stanton and Susan B. Anthony in particular has not stressed this invaluable aspect of the rhetoric of the women's rights movement (see Fuss 1989; Waggenspack 1989, 91; Strange 1998, 18; DuBois and Smith 2007). As will be shown, the partial justification of referring to Stanton and Anthony as "rhetorical giants" (Campbell 1989b, 212) is due to their incredibly effective use and innovative manipulation of proverbial wisdom and proverbial metaphors in the service of feminist rhetoric.

Advocating and teaching go hand in hand to a certain degree, and it is no wonder that Stanton and Anthony often saw themselves in the role of teaching women to demand their self-evident rights as equals of men. Since proverbs often take on a didactic function, among other functions, it should thus not be surprising that Stanton and Anthony would call on them to add generational wisdom to their arguments. Of course, that is not to say that these forward-looking reformers did not also disagree with some of the traditional messages of proverbs! In other words, both Stanton and Anthony made use of proverbial language for social reform in whatever way it served their purpose. There is no doubt that "proverbs are strategies for dealing with situations" (Burke 1941, 256), and it is thus a natural consequence that for these two feminists they became verbal signs for recurrent social situations that needed to be questioned and changed as far as the role of women is concerned.

Stanton and Anthony were skilled rhetoricians and employed all registers of the English language, just as that great British orator Winston S. Churchill did in the following century. When Churchill was made an honorary citizen of the United States on April 9, 1963, President John F. Kennedy described Churchill's rhetorical grandeur with the following words: "In the dark days and darker nights when England stood alone—and most men save Englishmen despaired of England's life—he mobilized the English language and sent it into battle" (Mieder 1997, 66). The same could be said about these two untiring advocates of women's rights. They mobilized the English language to battle social ills, with Susan B. Anthony on two occasions brilliantly describing her fifty years of fighting for the women's cause with the antiproverb "these are the times that try women's souls" (Anthony, January 14, 1856; cited from Harper 1898–1908, 2:138–39; and Anthony, June 7, 1876, in Gordon 1997–2013, 3:228). By simply replacing the word "men" in Thomas Paine's proverbial statement "these are the times that try men's souls" from 1776 with "women" (Shapiro 2006, 576), Anthony was able to encompass the trials and tribulations of half of the population! Elisabeth

Cady Stanton performed a similar linguistic trick at the beginning of the women's rights movement when she changed the proverb "all men are created equal" to the inclusive "all men and women are created equal" (Stanton in Gordon 1997–2013, 1:78, July 19–20, 1848; see Aron 2008, 89–96). That revolutionary declaration served as the proverbial motto in Stanton and Anthony's dedicated struggle for equality of the sexes, and as will be seen throughout the pages of this book, proverbs and proverbial expressions played a major role in their constant struggle and lasting success.

Once Elizabeth Cady Stanton and Susan B. Anthony met in 1851, they formed a very close friendship that lasted for five decades until Stanton's death in 1902. They met numerous times at home and at conferences, and they were in constant epistolary contact with each other. With such a cooperative and trustworthy spirit informing their work, it should not be surprising that their personal correspondence is a touching testimony to their heartfelt friendship. In their letters to each other, they could let their guard down, so to speak. They include honest statements about life's small or large problems, its successes and failures, and its joys and sorrows. Both women rely on proverbial expressions in particular to add color and emotion to their epistles to each other. Six years after their first meeting, Elizabeth Cady Stanton made the following quite cocky comment to her friend, prophesying with the two proverbial phrases "shaking in their boots" and "turning over in their graves" the results of their fight for women's rights: "You [Susan B. Anthony] and I [Stanton] have a prospect of a good long life[;] we shall not be in our prime before fifty & after that we shall be good for twenty years at least[.] If we do not make old [Charles] Davies shake in his boots or turn in his grave I am mistaken" (Stanton in Gordon 1997–2013, 1:351–52, August 20, 1857).

In order to advance their agenda, it was of utmost importance for Anthony and Stanton to stay focused, something that Stanton expressed in two sentences to her friend that declare that they should follow the proverb's advice "let the past be the past" and that they should not waste their proverbial powder on temperance issues because they have much bigger fish to fry, as the proverbial phrase has it, and those "fish" represent the fight for women's rights: "Now, Susan, I do beg of you to let the past be past, and to waste no powder on the Woman's State Temperance Society. We have other and bigger fish to fry" (Stanton, June 20, 1853; cited from DuBois 1981, 57; see also O'Connor 1954, 79–83).

Self-doubt, as far as the women's rights movement was concerned, only seldom entered the picture, even if certain friends appeared to disagree with some of their views. The proverb "time will tell" served Anthony well in this note intended to put her friend Susan's mind at rest: "All the old friends, with scarce an exception, are sure we are wrong. Only time can tell, but I believe we are right and hence bound to succeed" (Anthony, January 1, 1868, in Gordon 1997–2013, 1:295). Anthony urged her friend to think positively and plow ahead, and when things looked tough and Stanton appeared to be faltering, then Anthony cited the biblical proverb "sour grapes will set teeth on edge" (Jeremiah 31:29) and the classical proverb "nature abhors a vacuum" to convince her friend to push ahead, putting her on a bit of a guilt trip in addition to it all by stating that she owed it to herself and her friend: "'Sour Grapes will set teeth on edge' still it seems—Now you [Stanton] [know] *nature abhors a vacuum*—& if you at head of our National Committee [*don't*] step boldly to the front at Washington—such a *truckling growlers* will—*Somebody* surely will be there—& you *owe it* to *yourself* & the cause to be there first—I was almost going to say—to *me too*—for *our obligations* to the *movement are one*—that is to *hold the helm* & keep the ship from running on to shoals & quicksands" (Anthony, September 10, 1871, in Gordon 1997–2013, 2:449).

Susan B. Anthony could get on quite a proverbial role when she wanted to convince Stanton of a certain idea or plan of action. In a letter of July 10, 1872, she first alluded to the classical proverb "the mountain labored and brought forth a mouse" (see Harder 1925–26) and subsequently cited the two proverbial phrases "to keep the pot boiling" and "to put something in a nutshell" to add some metaphorical expressiveness to her pleading for continued action in the cause.

> The mountain has brought forth its mole, and we are left to comfort ourselves with the Philadelphia splinter as best we may, and [Isabella] Hooker and Anthony propose to make it as large as possible. Hooker and self go to Philadelphia at 7 this eve, and in A.M. she to New Haven and I to Rochester.
>
> Now we must keep the pot boiling by every possible means. First by issuing an appeal to the women of the U.S. to take hold of the *promise* of the Republicans and hold them to it, and demand more and more. . . . Now do you [Stanton] at once, put in a nut-shell what you think *more* or different. (Anthony, July 10, 1872, in Gordon 1997–2013, 2:516)

But action also meant traveling hundreds of miles under difficult circumstances, and here is a telling excerpt from March 26, 1879, by Stanton to Anthony, indicating by the descriptive proverbial comparison "to be (feel) like a squeezed sponge" that she is utterly worn out by her constant traveling and lecturing. Surely her long trips with little sleep and many lectures, as well as writing speeches and essays, must have taken their toll.

> I [Stanton] have been wandering, wandering ever since we parted; up early and late, sleepy and disgusted with my profession, as there is not rest from the time the [lecturing] season begins until it ends. Two months more containing sixty-one days still stretch their long length before me. I must pack and unpack my trunk sixty-one times, pull out the black silk trail and don it, curl my hair, and pin on the illusion puffing round my spacious throat, sixty-one more times, rehearse "Our Boys," "Our Girls," or "Home Life," sixty-one times, eat 183 more miserable meals, sleep in cotton sheets with these detestable things called "comforters" (tormentors would be a more fitting name) over me sixty-one more nights, shake hands with sixty-one more committees, smile, look intelligent and interested in every one who approaches me, while I feel like a squeezed sponge, affect a little spring and briskness in my gait on landing in each new town to avoid making an impression that I am seventy, when in reality I feel more like crawling than walking. With her best foot forward, Yours. (Stanton in Gordon 1997–2013, 3:440, March 26, 1879)

Notice, however, that the overtired Stanton nevertheless closes her letter with a literal interpretation of the proverbial phrase "to put one's best foot forward." No matter how worn out, she would march on doing her best for the women's rights movement.

Of course, both women constantly wish that they could "put their heads together" to get their massive workloads done, but the unmarried Anthony also is perfectly capable of writing charming lines regarding love, marriage, and family as she knows them from her friend.

> I wish you [Stanton] were to be with us also—It is too cruel that you must be settled—fastened—so far away—so that I cant [sic] get to you without spending so much time & money—We ought to have our heads together for lots of the work before us now—Love to Maggie & Bob—& Congratulations to Kitt [Henry B. Stanton]—It must be fun to see him petting a lovely little girl!! Well—a fellow is pretty sure to get hit [get married]—at last—even if he does escape for so many years—Lovingly yours[,] *Susan B Anthony* (Anthony, November 27, 1892, in Gordon 1997–2013, 5:500)

However, references to work abound, and it is Susan B. Anthony who turns the proverb "you cannot have two bites at (of) a cherry" into its opposite in order to express that she will have to manage her busy schedule somehow. This proverb is no longer very popular, but it gives a wonderful bittersweet taste of what Anthony is facing: "Then I have a letter—giving me until *November 20th* to complete the Cyclopedia article—so that to get any time at all to be with you [Stanton]—I shall have to make two bites of a cherry—Then there is another home attraction—and that is that the last of September Miss [Frances] Willard & Miss [Anna] Gordon are to bring Lady Henry Somerset—Lady "Isabel"—I like better—to visit me—and I must not miss this chance" (Anthony, August 19, 1894, in Gordon 1997–2013, 5:642).

And here is Susan B. Anthony's last letter to Elizabeth Cady Stanton, her dear friend of over fifty years, who was to pass away on October 26, 1902. It summarizes one more time their unique and eventful partnership in the cause of women's rights and their very special friendship.

> We little dreamed when we began this contest, optimistic with the hope and buoyancy of youth, that half a century later we would be compelled to leave the finish of the battle to another generation of women. But our hearts are filled with joy to know that they enter upon this task equipped with a college education, with business experience, with the fully admitted right to speak in public—all of which were denied to women fifty years ago. They have practically but one point to gain—the suffrage; we had all. These strong, courageous, capable young women will take our place and complete our work. There is an army of them, where we were but a handful; ancient prejudice has become so softened, public sentiment so liberalized, and women have so thoroughly demonstrated their ability, as to leave not a shadow of doubt that they will carry our cause to victory. (Anthony, before October 26, 1902, in Gordon 1997–2013, 6:451)

Sensing the end of her friend's life, Anthony appears to summarize their joint accomplishments, emphasizing that their "hearts are filled with joy" about their valiant strides toward women's rights. To be sure, woman suffrage had not been reached, but Stanton could rest assured that there was not a proverbial shadow of doubt that the final victory would eventually be won. This final epistle must have meant the world to the dying Elizabeth Cady Stanton, knowing that Susan B. Anthony would carry on the torch with the younger generation of feminists. Unfortunately, she, too, would not see the Nineteenth Amendment passed in 1920 that finally gave women the right to vote. It is often referred to as the Susan B. Anthony amendment, but there is also no shadow of doubt that she would have wanted it to carry the names of both yoke-fellows!

Elizabeth Cady Stanton and Susan B. Anthony not only wrote numerous letters to each other but also corresponded with a multitude of contemporaries, including both women and men and high-ranking government employees all the way to the president of the United States. More than their talks and essays, these letters reveal the private lives of the two feminists, as they cover family life, their own anxieties, and, of course, also their constant struggle for women's rights. The epistles are filled with honest feelings, worries, and sociopolitical comments, especially regarding their work for various temperance and suffrage organizations. No matter how insurmountable the obstacles might have appeared, they carried on to make their dream of equal rights for women become a reality. There was nothing that could destroy the optimism of these two feminists.

Turning to folk speech, Stanton cites the proverbial expression "to play cat and mouse with someone" and the proverbial comparison "to jump like parched peas on a hot shovel" to formulate a colorful invective.

> Our legislative assemblies are simply playing with us [as] a cat does with a mouse. They agree among themselves to give us a good vote to keep us quiet, & they came so close to doing the thing outright in New York recently that two men in hot haste changed their votes at the last moment. We have had hearings before Congress for eighteen years steadily, good reports good votes, but no action. I am discouraged & disgusted, & feel like making an attack on some new quarter of the enemies' domain. Our politicians are calm & complacent under our fire, but the clergy jump round the moment you aim a pop gun at them like parched peas on a hot shovel. (Stanton in Gordon 1997–2013, 4:504–5; April 27, 1886)

But speaking of the hope for women reaching the ballot box and voting, here are two segments from letters that indicate Stanton's preoccupation with suffrage. The first example is of special interest, since it uses the proverbial expression "to burn one's bridges" in a positive rather than its traditionally negative connotation. The second text again uses the proverbial phrase "to shake in one's boots" as a satirical prophecy that men had better watch out, in light of the fact that women will come on ever stronger in their demands for equal treatment.

> Dear Mrs [Isabella Beecher] Hooker
> Well I am glad you have burned all your bridges & feel ready to work with all the daughters of Eve, no matter if some have blundered. I am with you for the last long strong pull until we reach the ballot box. I would like to see your call [to join a suffrage organization] when you get one that suits you *before it goes to print*, because I want to be sure that it is worthy the occasion. (Stanton in Gordon 1997–2013, 2:452; October 15, 1871)
>
> With prayers, & songs treating questions of finance, the inviolable homestead, Labor & Capital & woman's suffrage, we could soon create such a furor as would make these scoffing republicans tremble in their boots. (Stanton in Gordon 1997–2013, 2:478; February 2, 1872)

In one of her letters, Susan B. Anthony characterizes opponents as "dead as doornails" (see Barrick 1978) and alludes to the Bible proverb "let the dead bury their dead" (Matthew 8:22), while at the same time stressing that she is full of vigor and hope that women will be enfranchised in due time.

> Mrs. [Mary] Livermore, in her speech here in this city, said: "Some able lawyers have said"—not Victoria C. Woodhull had petitioned, and all Congress and the National Woman Suffrage Committee had chimed in with an amen—"that the fourteenth and fifteenth amendments enfranchised women; but she preferred the surer process of education to this short cut. She could afford to

wait." I wish I had the report. I sent it to the Revolution. But all of them are "dead as doornails" to this new and living gospel, and we live fellers must leave them to be buried by the dead. I have never in the whole twenty years' good fight felt so full of life and hope. (Anthony, February 4, 1871, in Gordon 1997–2013, 2:415)

In yet another letter, she calls on the proverb "in union (there) is strength" to add weight to her argument for a united effort on behalf of women, strengthening her argument even further by the two somatic proverbial phrases "to see eye to eye" and "to stand shoulder to shoulder": "If all 'the Suffragists' of all the States could but see eye to eye on this point, and stand shoulder to shoulder against any and every party and politician not fully and unequivocally committed to 'Equal Rights for Woman,' we should, at once, become a balance of power that could not fail to compel the party of highest intelligence to proclaim Woman Suffrage the chief plank of its platform. 'In union there is strength'" (Anthony, August 9, 1878, in Gordon 1997–2013, 3:405–6).

Major changes would have to be accomplished before this fight would be won, as Stanton had remarked at the beginning of the women's rights movement: "I should be a jewel in an Association for they say I am good natured, generous, & always well & happy. Oh what bliss is yet in store for us. All our talk about womans [sic] rights is mere *moonshine*, so long as we are bound by the present social system" (Stanton in Gordon 1997–2013, 1:215; December 6, 1852). Their talk, writings, and actions proved to be no moonshine, as the proverbial phrase would have it. In fact, while the suffrage movement started with the basics of equal rights, somewhat ironically expressed by way of the "a, b, c" phrase, the march progressed slowly but surely into a powerful demand for elevating women out of their bondage: "In petitioning Congress for an act of emancipation [of women], we began with the a, b, c. of human rights, and have thus made ourselves a power of freedom with the people and their representatives" (Stanton in Gordon 1997–2013, 1:519; May 7, 1864). And to indicate that she really meant business, Stanton declared that she could never wash her hands of the emancipation of women. By changing the proverbial phrase "to wash one's hands of something" from the Bible (see Matthew 27:24) into the negative, she declares emphatically that she is in the fight to the end and that there is nothing that would turn her into a Pontius Pilate! "Anything that is outward, all forms and ceremonies, faiths and symbols, policies and institutions, may be washed away, but that which is of the very being must stand forever. Nothing, nobody could abate the all-absorbing, agonizing interest

I feel in the redemption of woman. I could not wash my hands of woman's rights, for they are dyed clear through to the marrow of the bone" (Stanton in Gordon 1997–2013, 1:436; July 12, 1860).

Perhaps not surprisingly, both Stanton and Anthony repeatedly drew on animal metaphors in the form of proverbs, proverbial expressions, and proverbial comparisons to strengthen their arguments against the inhumanity of treating women as second-class citizens or to show that women are perfectly capable of advancing their cause by whatever means available to them. The following examples may well show how such phraseologisms as "the rats are leaving the sinking ship" and "every pig will burn its nose in the hot swill" helped Anthony bring their points across with accessible folk speech.

> I see your [Anna Dickinson's] speech is not [in] *The New Republic*—is *not woman*—but only the *black man*—whom, as I told you they would—The republicans *have thrown overboard*—I tell you *Anna rats*—that is *female rats* ought to know enough to leave a sinking ship—I just told this to Mr. Train—he says you ought to write that *stinking ship*—he says with ten minutes talk he could convince you that *woman* is *your* mission. (Anthony, November 28, 1867, in Gordon 1997–2013, 2:114)
>
> Mrs [Elizabeth] Harbert—to day—tells me of her plan to get out her "*New Era*["]—as a *Quarterly*!! and asks my opinion—and I have "*sat down*["] on the prop[os]al *heavy*—telling her if any of us had money or brains to invest in the newspaper line—we ought to concentrate both upon the *one paper now in existence*—It does seem a *craze* to start papers—Mrs [Lillie] Blake writes as if she expected me personally to set about working for *The Question*—Well, "every pig will burn its nose in the hot swill." (Anthony, March 23, 1887, in Gordon 1997–2013, 4:15–16)

Of special interest is what Susan B. Anthony does with the proverbial expression "to be a dog in the manger" that is part of an old fable tradition (Mieder 2011). It is a most fitting animal metaphor for human behavior that far too often is informed by envy, selfishness, and meanness. This figurative phrase is perfectly suited to express the inhumane disregard for the needs of others, and it served Anthony well to vent her frustration about people acting like a dog in the manger. Here are two references that include the phrase, with the first one adding the proverbial expressions "to be (get) between two millstones" and "to throw overboard" for good measure.

> I'll tell you a little *private opinion* of mine—"I think the Bureaus are *real humbugs*"—that is, my dealings with them doesn't give me much faith—"The dog in the manger" principle—The "rule or ruin" idea is their basis of action—If there were a cooperative Bureau it might greatly help—But as now Boston against both New York & Brooklyn & they against each other—each & all

> trying to defeat the success of every lecturer in the hands of any but self—viz you see the poor things are ground to powder between the mill stones—I'll tell you what I've done *thrown* each & all overboard—until I see them in brighter light than now—I like my *own self—no business mannagement* [sic] best (Anthony, December 23, 1870, in Gordon 1997–2013, 2:389)
>
> How I do wish it could be as in the olden time—that the *Ex. Committees* of the state & New England societies would be called together—& we all together study *how* to *press* on the good work—I have made no engagement for Monday the 4th—& if you [Caroline Dall] can see any way to help me to meet some of the *real workers*—not "*dogs in the manger*" sort of people—I should love to see them (Anthony, November 24, 1876, in Gordon 1997–2013, 3:273)

There were frustrations and obstacles enough, both human and pecuniary. But resignation simply was not an option for either Stanton or Anthony, even though the problem of raising money for the cause appeared insurmountable at times. In this regard, there is a fascinating use of the biblical proverbial phrase "to adore (worship) the golden calf" (Exodus 32:4) by Stanton. In fact, she calls for a "golden calf" so that there would be money enough to support the ongoing feminist struggle. Upon careful reading of this paragraph, it should also be noted that "the sinews of war" is an allusion to the proverb "money is the sinews of love and war." Stanton's audience would doubtless not have missed this mere "kernel" (Norrick 1985, 45) of the proverb.

> I think we are making some progress, but it is a sore tax on human patience to be forty years going through this moral wilderness with no one to give us manna, & no pillar of light to lead the way, & no Moses in direct communication with the ruler of the universe[.] But all this could be endured if we only had a golden calf whose ears & tail & legs could be thrown into the United states [sic] mint by piecemeal to supply us with the sinews of war. But alas on the distant horizon we see no coming calf, to say nothing of rich women who will share their abundance with us instead of giving bequests to Harvard Yale & Princeton, to educate theological striplings for the ministry. (Stanton in Gordon 1997–2013, 4:147; January 29, 1882)

Despite being plagued by money worries, the two friends moved on, with Anthony frequently comparing their commitment to "herculean labor," a proverbial phrase from classical mythology. The image of Hercules performing his many seemingly insurmountable tasks is a perfect fit, since it implies that the suffragists will succeed with their work, just as the strong Hercules did. Here is but one of several references to the "herculean labor"—this time toward the waning years of their careers, linking the need of finding money to their determination to support the incredible work that was left to be done by the next generation of feminists.

> I am perfectly willing to bequeath to the young women who are today taking up the suffrage work all of the labor, but I am not willing that they shall have to do the begging to pay for that work, which I have been compelled to do for the last fifty years. I verily believe that more than half of my spiritual, intellectual and physical strength has been expended in the anxiety over getting the money to pay for the Herculean work that has been done in our movement. The strain, of course, has not been so perfectly intense and immense as was your [Jane Stanford's] strain while the suit against your estate was pending, but nevertheless it has been so great that I am not willing that the next generation of women shall be compelled to endure it. (Anthony, April 25, 1898, in Gordon 1997–2013, 6:211)

But Anthony never gave up, declaring in one of her letters proverbially: "I shall keep pegging away so long as there is any hope to making ends meet" (Anthony, March 5, 1871, in Gordon 1997–2013, 2:421–22). In another letter she simply chose a proverb to declare that the fight must go on: "'Don't give up the Ship'—shall be our motto" (Anthony, December 15, 1883, in Gordon 1997–2013, 4:318), and there is also this one-liner from 1886: "Well—the world jogs on slowly—*too slowly*—for me—Still it jogs!!" (Anthony, March 16, 1886, in Gordon 1997–2013, 4:495). Citing the proverb "time flies," she had earlier characterized her ceaseless fight for women's right as "How time flies when head, heart & hands are full to brim with work—Who would have believed I should not have written you a line since the Kansas victory" (Anthony, January 1, 1868, in Gordon 1997–2013, 2:121).

Both Elizabeth Cady Stanton and Susan B. Anthony delivered innumerable speeches during the fifty years of their vigorous involvement in the women's rights movement. Especially between the years 1869 and 1881, they logged thousands of miles crisscrossing the country on their suffrage mission. They had signed up with various lyceum booking agencies that arranged their popular lecture tours that for twelve years gave them the opportunity to speak before local audiences, with their speeches receiving even broader distribution by way of newspaper reports (Banner 1980, 110–11, 121–24; Waggenspack 1989, 31–32). As Ann D. Gordon signifies with her essay appropriately entitled "Taking Possession of the Country" (1999), the two women on the lecture circuit were indeed taking a hold of the nation.

> No reformers—indeed, no politicians—rivaled the miles logged by Stanton and Anthony as they crisscrossed the country in the decade after 1869 to take their case for woman suffrage to the people. Leaving home in October or November, with trunk, portmanteau, and several lectures ready for the season, they stayed on the road until spring. With their lives centered somewhere in the Midwest, they adapted to the discomforts of strange beds, dirt, sleeping on trains, and schedules that conceded nothing to ill health. When Anthony

boarded the Michigan South Railroad one evening in Ohio, "there sat Mrs. Stanton all curled up—gray curls sticking out—fast asleep—." The travelers talked until the time came to change trains for their next destinations. . . . This was grueling work. As fast as the railroads extended their reach, Stanton and Anthony traveled new lines, reaching California just two years after the transcontinental line opened. Stanton lectured in Texas in 1870, and in 1871 Anthony toured the Pacific Northwest and went into British Columbia. At the termini of rail traffic, they hopped aboard sleighs, boats, stages, and horses to journey farther into the country. They made an enormous sweep across the continent and returned time and again to many towns throughout the decade. (Gordon 1999, 163–64)

The stamina of both women is beyond belief, with Stanton having born seven children to boot. While traveling, they would constantly edit their repertoire of lectures when tiredness would not keep them from working. At the foundation of their struggle lay the call for equal rights for women, an agenda that both women pursued with absolutism that bordered on fanaticism, arguing "that the rights and responsibilities of individual citizenship be granted to women on the same terms that they were granted to men, and [demanding] that state, church, and family adapt to that truth" (Ginzberg 2009, 193). They fought for equal rights by whatever means possible, with powerful words being their most effective weapon. They bombarded their listeners with facts, arguments, and stories that also included humor, irony, satire, and cynicism. Their oratory could reach eloquent heights but also did not shy away from everyday "plain English and plenty of it" (see Sherr 1995, 132) characterized by their inclusion of folk speech in the form of proverbs and proverbial expressions. In fact, Stanton emphasized this need to use "plain English" in their communications on several occasions (see the index of proverbs and proverbial phrases). Stanton and Anthony frequently employed such designations as adage, axiom, maxim, motto, principle, proverb, and saying to signal their intentional use of proverbial wisdom. Their proverbially informed rhetoric obviously meant something to them, and there is no doubt that it added much colloquial and metaphorical expressiveness to their speeches.

Elizabeth Cady Stanton's speech on "Woman's Rights," considered by her to be her first full-fledged public speech, was delivered several times in September and October of 1848 after the successful Woman's Rights Convention held July 19–20, 1848, in Seneca Falls, New York (see Wellman 2004). It was her manifesto on the topic, and to be sure, it is replete with proverbial language that set the tone for the dozens of speeches that were to follow. The following paragraphs speak for themselves, but their arguments are most certainly strengthened by the enclosed proverbs and proverbial expressions (here cited for easy identification before Stanton's statements).

> *Give an inch, take an ell.*
> Let us now consider man's claims to physical superiority. Methinks I hear some say, surely you will not contend for equality here. Yes, we must not give an inch lest you claim an ell, we cannot accord to man even this much and he has no right to claim it until the fact be fully demonstrated, until the physical education of the boy and the girl shall have been the same for many years. If you claim the advantage of size merely, why it may be that under any course of training in ever so perfect a developement [*sic*] of the physique in woman, man might still be the larger of the two, tho' we do not grant even this. (Stanton in Gordon 1997–2013, 1:101; September ?, 1848)

> *To set the wolf to keep (care for) the sheep (lamb).*
> In nothing is woman's true happiness consulted, men like to call her an angel—to feed her with what they think sweet food nourishing her vanity, to induce her to believe her organization is so much finer [and] more delicate than theirs, that she is not fitted to struggle with the tempests of public life but needs their care and protection. Care and protection? such as the wolf gives the lamb—such as the eagle the hare he carries to his eyrie. Most cunningly he entraps her and then takes from her all those rights which are dearer to him than life itself, rights which have been baptized in blood and the maintenance of which is even now rocking to their foundations the kingdoms of the old world. (Stanton, September ?, 1848, in Gordon 1997–2013, 1:106)

> *Woman is the weaker vessel.* (1 Peter 3:7)
> I think a man who under the present state of things has the moral hardihood to take an education at the hands of woman and at such an expense to her, ought as soon as he graduates with all his honours thick upon him take the first ship for Turkey and there pass his days in earnest efforts to rouse the inmates of the Harems to a true sense of their present debasement and not as is his custom immediately enter our pulpits to tell us of his superiority to us "weaker vessels" his prerogative to command, ours to obey—his duty to preach, ours to keep silence. (Stanton in Gordon 1997–2013, 1:109; September ?, 1848)

> *Judge not from appearances.*
> Many men who are well known for their philanthropy, who hate oppression on a southern plantation, can play the tyrant right well at home. It is a much easier matter to denounce all the crying sins of the day most eloquently too, than to endure for one hour the peevish moanings of a sick child. To know whether a man is truly great and good, you must not judge by his appearance in the great world, but follow him to his home—where all restraints are laid aside—there we see the true man his virtues and his vices too. (Stanton in Gordon 1997–2013, 1:111; September ?, 1848)

> *To pull a string.*
> There seems now to be a kind of moral stagnation in our midst. Philanthropists have pulled every string. War, slavery, drunkeness [*sic*], licentiousness

and gluttony have been dragged naked before the people and all their abominations fully brought to light. Yet with idiotic laugh we hug these monsters to our arms and rush on. Our churches are multiplying on all sides, our Sunday schools and prayer meetings are still kept up, our missionary and tract societies have long laboured and now the labourers begin to faint—they feel they cannot resist this rushing tide of vice, they feel that the battlements of righteousness are weak against the mighty wicked, most are ready to raise the siege. (Stanton in Gordon 1997–2013, 1:114; September ?, 1848)

Body and (or) soul.
To throw to the wind(s).
The earth has never yet seen a truly great and virtuous nation, for woman has never yet stood the equal with man. As with nations so with families. It is the wise mother who has the wise son, and it requires but little thought to decide that as long as the women of this nation remain but half developed in mind and body, so long shall we have a succession of men decrepit in body and soul, so long as your women are mere slaves, you may throw your colleges to the wind, there is no material to work upon, it is in vain to look for silver and gold from mines of copper and brass. (Stanton in Gordon 1997–2013, 1:114; September ?, 1848)

These folk and Bible proverbs, proverbial expressions and twin formulas together with five more similar sections appear on twenty-two pages of text (Stanton in Gordon 1997–2013, 1:95–116) and add up to about one phraseological unit per two pages. Anthony's speeches in comparison are less proverbial, but she too relies on metaphorical folk speech, as can be seen from her important speech "Is It a Crime for a U.S. Citizen to Vote?" that she delivered on January 16, 1873, in Washington, DC. In this politically charged speech, she cites a number of revolutionary quotations turned proverbs, but, as Stanton did, she also knows how to make effective use of the proverbial expression "to throw to the winds" in the first paragraph of the address.

To throw to the wind(s).
Our democratic-republican government is based on the idea of the natural right of every individual member thereof to a voice and a vote in making and executing the laws. We assert the province of government to be to secure the people in the enjoyment of their inalienable rights. We throw to the winds the old dogma that government can give rights. No one denies that before governments were organized each individual possessed the right to protect his own life, liberty and property. When 100 to 1,000,000 people enter into a free government, they do not barter away their natural rights; they simply pledge themselves to protect each other in the enjoyment of them through prescribed judicial and legislative tribunals. They agree to abandon the methods of brute force in the adjustment of their differences and adopt those of civilization. (Anthony, January 16, 1873, in Gordon 1997–2013, 2:554)

> *Taxation without representation is tyranny.*
> *One-half* of the people of this nation, to-day, are utterly powerless to blot from the statute-books an *unjust* law, or write there a *new and just one*. The *women*, dissatisfied as they are with *this* form of government that enforces "taxation without representation"—that compels them to obey laws to which they have never given their consent—that imprisons and hangs them without a trial by a jury of their peers—that robs them, in *marriage*, of the custody of their own persons, wages, and children, are—this half of the people—left wholly at the mercy of the other half, in direct violation of the spirit and letter of the declarations of the framers of this government, every one of which was based on the immutable principles of *"equal rights to all."* (Anthony, January 16, 1873, in Gordon 1997–2013, 2:555)

> *To not give (change, yield) an iota.*
> Miss Sarah E. Wall, of Worcester, Mass., twenty years ago, took this position [of not paying taxes]. For several years the officers of the law distrained [sic] her property and sold it to meet the necessary amount; still she persisted, and would not yield an iota, though every foot of her lands should be struck off under the hammer. And now, for several years the assessor has left her name off the tax-list, and the collector passed her by without a call. (Anthony, January 16, 1873, in Gordon 1997–2013, 2:561)

> *A rose would smell just as sweet by any other name.*
> There is an old saying that "A rose by any other name would smell as sweet." And I submit if the deprivation by law of the right of ownership of one's own person, wages, property, children; the denial of the right of an individual to sue and be sued in the courts is not a condition of servitude most bitter and absolute, though under the sacred name of marriage. (Anthony, January 16, 1873, in Gordon 1997–2013, 2:571)

This speech is also about twenty-two pages long, but it includes only seven phraseologisms, about one per every three pages. This discrepancy between the frequency of proverb use is found throughout the speeches and writings of both women, with Stanton being clearly more proverbial than her friend.

This is not to say that Susan B. Anthony shied away from folk proverbs when they could strengthen an observation or argument. At times they might not immediately be obvious, since she integrated them into the syntax of her sentences, to wit the expansion of the proverb "money is power" in her description of constant financial woes: "Money being the vital power of all movements—the wood and water of the engine—and, as our work through the past winter has been limited only by the want of it, there is no difficulty in reporting on finance" (Anthony, May 9, 1867, in Gordon 1997–2013, 2:61). This free use of supposedly fixed proverbs can also be seen in her break-up of the structure of the proverb "the last straw breaks the camel's back" in a couple of letters where she replaces the standard *straw* with *ounce* to boot.

> How I wish you [Rachel Foster] were made of *iron*—so you couldn't tire out—I fear all the time—you will put on that *added ounce* [straw]—that breaks even the Camel's back—You understand *just how* to make agitation—& that is the *secret* of successful work— (Anthony, April 5, 1882, in Gordon 1997–2013, 4:163)

> The palm which the University [of Rochester] women sent is flourishing finely. I am glad they selected a palm, because it is a lasting reminder of that day when you [Fannie Bigelow] took me the rounds to get the money and pledges that proved the open sessame [sic] to the University. I shall never regret that day's labor. It was the added ounce [straw] that broke the camel's back in more senses than one. In the largest sense, the back of the superstition, bigotry, and selfishness that held those old doors shut tight against the women. (Anthony, March 8, 1901, in Gordon 1997–2013, 6:389)

Of course, she also cites proverbs in their traditional wording as she recalls having heard and learned them in her younger years.

> I told them, when I arrived there [in Kansas], that I had been told in my youth that two wrongs will not make a right, and Kansas politicians were, to-day, trying to teach their people that two rights would make a wrong. These very men, who would cast their votes for enfranchising the black man, said that enfranchising the woman would be ruinous—that it would kill negro suffrage, and be an unjust thing. They were trying to prove that it would not be politically expedient to vote for woman's suffrage or advocate it in the State. (Anthony, November 25, 1867, in Gordon 1997–2013, 2:106)

Again and again Anthony relies on proverbs to argue the point that the women's rights movement must work to get the Congress of the United States to adopt a constitutional amendment. There is no use in working outside of the established political system, and if women were not to pursue this road, then other pressure groups would dominate Congress with their agendas. All of this is splendidly summarized with the proverb "nature abhors a vacuum" that dates back to classical Latin times: "Our organization is for the purpose of working upon Congress to enfranchise half of the people and it is something we cannot secure in any other way but through Congress, and I believe in continuity. Nature abhors a vacuum and if this National Association deserts Washington some other body will come in and possess Washington and do the work" (Anthony, January 16, 1893, in Gordon 1997–2013, 5:504).

With her incredible enthusiasm and optimism for the cause of the right of women to vote, she is simply unwilling to accept setbacks or actual defeat. And folk wisdom like "it is an ill wind that blows nobody good" is of good help in rationalizing political disappointments.

> I am not so disappointed in the result with the Constitution Convention as I might be. It is an ill-wind that blows nobody good. This is not a Waterloo, but a Bunker Hill defeat. It only means that we will take a breath, renew and double our forces and renew our attack. Had the Constitution Convention consented to submit the question of woman suffrage to the voters this fall, I doubt if we could have carried our point. The people at large are not educated up to it, and we should have had insufficient time to have enlightened them. (Anthony, August 22, 1894, in Gordon 1997–2013, 5:646)

At all times, Anthony remained focused on securing the ballot for women, arguing that in a way, all women's organizations had this right to vote as their ultimate goal. And it is certainly understandable that both Anthony and Stanton tired of the constitutional arguments that were ceaselessly leveled against granting women the right to vote. Thus, in 1860, Stanton employed the three proverbial expressions "to sit on the fence," "to hang like (have) a millstone around one's neck," and "to sink or swim" in a powerful and satirical paragraph stating that women should free themselves from their subjugation by men (see Campbell 1989a, 1:101).

> The Great Father has endowed all his creatures with the necessary powers for self-support, self-defence and protection. We do not ask man to represent us, it is hard enough in times like these for man to carry back-bone enough to represent himself. So long as the mass of men spend most of their time on the fence, not knowing which way to jump, they are surely in no condition to tell us [women] where we had better stand. In pity for man, we would no longer hang like a millstone round his neck. Undo what man did for us in the dark ages, and strike out all special legislation for us; strike out the name, *woman*, from all your constitutions, and then, with fair sailing, let us sink or swim, live or die, survive or perish together. (Stanton, March 20, 1860; cited from Campbell 1989a, 1:183)

Little wonder that a few months later, Stanton, in a moment of utter frustration, turned to the utterly appropriate proverb "a burnt child dreads the fire" to vent her dismay. "I am actually nauseated with the word constitution[.] It is used as a cover for such base fraud & hypocracy [sic]. I remember [Seymour Boughton] Treadwell, witnessed his vain efforts to get up meetings in Boston & have been bored with him by the hour. My soul has literally groaned under constitutional logic so long that I dread the subject as a 'burnt child does the fire'" (Stanton in Gordon 1997–2013, 1:471; December 16, 1860).

But here is one more telling example of how Stanton never tires of finding popular phrases from folk speech to supplement her arguments with ever-different metaphors. Her listeners must have been thrilled to hear her utter the proverb "two dogs over one bone seldom agree," since that animal metaphor made her spirited lecture come alive with everyday imagery.

> There is no danger that women will corrupt politics or that politics will corrupt them. But when the women vote they will be pretty sure to demand better and cleanlier [sic] places for voting. Law should be a holy thing and the ballot box the holy of holies. It is claimed that the ballot for women will divide the family, or merely duplicate the voting. But it produces unpleasantness in the family now. Give two dogs a bone and they will fight over it. But give them two bones and there is peace immediately. Woman would not be so bothered and perplexed over the finance question as men are. (Stanton in Gordon 1997–2013, 3:83; May 30, 1874)

And yet, like her friend Anthony, she is not only concerned about women's rights. As a mother, she is especially interested in the proper upbringing of children. Thus, citing the proverb "the hand that rocks the cradle is the hand that moves the world" as folk wisdom regarding the importance of women in child raising, she wrote:

> In common parlance we have much fine-spun theorizing on the exalted office of the mother, her immense influence in moulding the character of her sons; "the hand that rocks the cradle moves the world," etc, but in creeds and codes, in constitutions and Scriptures, in prose and verse, we do not see these lofty paeans recorded or verified in living facts. As a class, women were treated among the Jews as an inferior order of beings, just as they are to-day in all civilized nations. And now, as then, men claim to be guided by the will of God. (Stanton 1895–98, 1:102)

Ten years later, Anthony followed suit in a satirical comment during an interview, stressing that mothers do not have absolute control over what becomes of their boys once they leave the cradle, become young men, and come under the influence of misguided males who prove to be bad role models.

> What does Grover Cleveland know about "sanctity of the home" and "woman's sphere," I should like to know? Why isn't the woman herself the best judge of what woman's sphere should be? The men have been trying to tell us for years. We have no desire to vote if the men would do their duty. Why are not the laws enforced in regard to saloons, gambling places and houses of ill repute? The women want a chance to see what they can do in making present laws effective. Mr. Cleveland remarks that the "hand that rocks the cradle is the hand that rules the world." That would be all right if you could keep the boys in the cradle always. (Anthony, April 25, 1905, in Gordon 1997–2013, 6:549)

But to return to Stanton and switch from boys to girls, one of her most successful lectures that she delivered many times on her speaking tours was

"Our Girls," with plenty of advice for keeping young women in good health. Even though she does not cite the two proverbs "early to bed and early to rise, makes a man healthy, wealthy, and wise" (see Gallacher 1949; Barbour 1974, 12; Mieder 1993, 98–134) and "a healthy mind in a healthy body" directly in the following excerpts from that speech, there can be no doubt that her listeners recognized their wisdom.

> The coming girl is to be healthy, wealthy, and wise. She is to hold an equal place with her brother in the world of work, in the colleges, in the state, the church and the home. Her sphere is to be no longer bounded by the prejudices of a dead past, but by her capacity to go wherever she can stand. The coming girl is to be an independent, self-supporting being, not as to-day a helpless victim of fashion, superstition, and absurd conventionalisms. (Stanton in Gordon 1997–2013, 3:489; winter 1880)

> The coming girl is to have health. One of the first needs for every girl who is to be trained for some life work, some trade or profession, is good health. As a sound body is the first step towards a sound mind, food, clothes, exercise, all the conditions of daily life, are important in training girls either for high scholarship, or practical work. Hence, girls, in all your gettings get health, it is the foundation of success in every undertaking. Sick men and women always take sickly views of everything and fail in the very hour they are most needed. One of the essential elements of health is freedom of thought and action, a right to individual life, opinion, ambition. (Stanton in Gordon 1997–2013, 3:492; winter 1880)

One thing is for certain: whatever cause Stanton might be championing, proverbs as rhetorical metaphors with the wisdom of generations behind them are bound to come into play. When she expresses her disappointment with the way Reconstruction is handled after the Civil War, she quickly adapts the proverb "charity begins at home" to "Reconstruction begins at home," and when she presses the State of New York to push for universal suffrage as part of the Reconstruction effort, the proverb "example is better than precept" is well chosen to argue for serious action.

> Reconstruction [Charity] begins at home. The President [Andrew Johnson] of the United States, in his veto of the District of the Columbia Suffrage bill, says: "It hardly seems consistent with the principles of right and justice for Representatives from States where the colored man is denied the right of suffrage, or holds it on property or educational qualifications, to press on the people of the District an experiment their own constituents have thus far been unwilling to try for themselves." (Stanton in Gordon 1997–2013, 2:25; February 19, 1867)

> Is there anything more rasping to a proud spirit than to be rebuked for short comings by those who are themselves guilty of the grossest violations of right and justice? Does the North consider it absurd for its women to vote and hold office? So views the South her negroes. Does the North consider its women a

part of the family to be represented by the white male citizen? So views the South her negroes. Example is better than precept. Would New-York, now that she has the opportunity to amend her own Constitution, take the lead by making herself a genuine Republic, with what a new and added power our representatives could press universal suffrage on the Southern states. The work of this hour is a broader one than the reconstruction of the Rebel States! It is the lifting of the entire nation into higher ideas of right and justice. It is the realization of what the world has never yet seen, a genuine Republic. (Stanton in Gordon 1997–2013, 2:26; February 19, 1867)

These are serious issues, but the main drive for Stanton as for Anthony is women's suffrage, and whoever joined the cause was advised not to do so half-heartedly, since any procrastination or unnecessary delay would be, proverbially speaking, dangerous to the cause. "The men and women who are dabbling with the suffrage movement for women should be at once therefore and emphatically warned that what they mean logically if not consciously in all they say, is next social equality and next Freedom or in a word Free Love, and if they wish to get out of the boat they should for safety get out now, for delays are dangerous" (Stanton in Gordon 1997–2013, 2:396; c. 1871). In the long run, it is not surprising that Stanton also turned to the fourteenth-century proverb "might makes right" (Mieder, Kingsbury, and Harder 1992, 410) to characterize men's willful dominance over women. When she used it for the first time, she integrated it syntactically in such a way that the normal structure of the proverb was lost, but her listeners will probably have recognized the proverb. The second time she introduced the proverb by calling it a "principle" with the intent of getting her audience to see the evil of this attitude.

> As I read history old and new the subjection of woman may be clearly traced to the same cause that subjugated different races and nations to one another, the law of force, that made might right, and the weak the slaves of the strong. Men mistake all the time their reverence for an ideal womanhood, for a sense of justice towards the actual being, that shares with them the toils of life. Man's love and tenderness to one particular woman for a time is no criterion for his general feeling for the whole sex for all time. The same man that would die for one woman, would make an annual holocaust of others, if his appetites or pecuniary interests required it. Kind husbands and Fathers [sic] that would tax every nerve and muscle to the uttermost to give their wives and daughters every luxury, would grind multitudes of women to powder in the world of work for the same purpose. (Stanton in Gordon 1997–2013, 2:626–27; August ?, 1873)

Society at large, based on the principle that might makes right has in a measure excluded women from the profitable industries of the world, and where she has gained a foothold her labor is at a discount. Man occupies the ground and holds the key to the situation. As employer, he plays off the cheap labor of a disfranchised class against the employee, and thus in a measure undermines his independence, making wife and sister in the world of work the rivals of husband and father. (Stanton in Gordon 1997–2013, 5:366; February 26, 1891)

Finally, befitting an optimistic sociopolitical reformer, there is Stanton's allusion to the proverb "hope springs eternal" in her remarkable speech on "The Pleasures of Age" on her seventieth birthday on November 12, 1885. Arguing that the hopeful building of proverbial castles in the air is better left to young people (see Gallacher 1963), she maintains that the older generation is justified in being hopeful because of the positive social changes that have taken place.

> The young have no youthful memories with which to gild their lives, none of the pleasures of retrospection. Neither has youth a monopoly of the illusions of hope, for that is eternal, to the end we have something still to hope. And here age has the advantage in basing its hopes on something rational and attainable. Instead of building castles in the air we clear off the mortgages from our earthly habitations. Instead of waiting for the winds of good fortune to waft us to elysian fields and heights sublime, we plant and gather our own harvests and climb step by step on ladders of our own making. After many experiences on life's tempestuous seas we learn to use the chart and compass, to take soundings, to measure distances, to shun the dangerous coasts, to prepare for winds and weather, to reef our sails, and when it is wise to stay in safe harbor. From experience we understand the situation, we have a knowledge of human nature, we learn how to control ourselves, to manage children with tenderness, servants with consideration, and our equals with proper respect. Years bring wisdom and charity, pity, rather than criticism, sympathy, rather than condemnation, for the most unfortunate. (Stanton in Gordon 1997–2013, 4:456–57; November 12, 1885)

Lest it be missed, this statement by the grand lady of women's rights concludes with yet another proverb. "Years bring wisdom" is certainly a truism that fits both Elizabeth Cady Stanton and Susan B. Anthony as wise champions for women, with their rhetorical use of folk proverbs serving them well to bring their message across to both women and men.

If "all men and women are created equal," as Elizabeth Cady Stanton proclaimed on July 19–20, 1848, at Seneca Falls, New York, then it follows logically that women deserve equality on all sociopolitical fronts beyond the obvious right to vote as US citizens. First among some of the issues beyond equal suffrage was equal education. Obviously, Elizabeth Cady Stanton was extremely well qualified to comment on raising and educating children, since she did so with vigorous commitment for her five boys and two girls. Little wonder that she developed two popular lectures simply called "Our

Girls" and "Our Boys" that she began to deliver in 1869 and 1875 respectively and which she repeated during her speaking engagements throughout the country (see Waggenspack 1989, 74–75). Regarding the female gender, "she pleaded for a free and independent life for every girl, for clothes that would give her freedom of action, for an education which would enable her to support herself, for an equal opportunity in business and the professions" (Lutz 1940, 194). Regarding young males, she argued that they should be educated "to both embrace feminine as well as masculine virtues and cultivate practical as well as abstract knowledge" (Strange 1998, 145). As a pair of influential lectures, they struck "at the root of sexism in the socialization and education of young children and portended the deep and abiding concern of twentieth-century feminists with expanding educational opportunities of girls and young women" (145). Both lectures "challenged traditional sex-role stereotypes" and "emphasized practical wisdom [and knowledge] over abstract knowledge" (Hogan and Hogan 2003, 423, 426). Much of the advice given in these lectures is based on the common sense of Stanton as an experienced mother, but that is exactly what touched a nerve among her many listeners, made up predominantly of parents in this case. Leaving the "boys" aside at this point, here is a bit of sapiential advice by mother Stanton to "girls" preoccupied with beauty, as it were (see Strange 1998, 134). It is solid advice, of course, but what a shame that in this case she did not cite the proverb "beauty is only skin deep."

> Remember [you girls] that beauty works from within, it cannot be put on and off like a garment, and it depends far more on the culture of the intellect, the tastes, sentiments, and affections of the soul, on an earnest unselfish life purpose to leave the world better than you find it, than the color of the hair, eyes or complexion. Be kind, noble, generous, magnanimous, be true to yourselves and your friends, and the soft lines of these tender graces and noble virtues, will reveal themselves in the face, in a halo of glory about the head, in a personal atmosphere of goodness, and greatness that none can mistake. To make your beauty lasting when old age with the wrinkles and grey hairs come and the eyes grow dim and the ears heavy, you must cultivate those immortal powers that gradually unfold and grasp the invisible as from day to day the visible ceases to absorb the soul. (Stanton in Gordon 1997–2013, 3:497; winter 1880)

But she also makes use of the biblical proverb "eat, drink, and be merry" (Ecclesiastes 8:15, Luke 12:19) to stress to the young girls that life is not only fun and games, marriage, and motherhood.

> Your life work dear girls is not simply to eat, drink, dress, be merry, be married and be mothers, but to mould yourselves into a perfect womanhood. Choose then those conditions in life that shall best secure a full symmetrical

> developement [sic]. We cannot be one thing and look another. There are indelible marks in every face showing the real life within. One cannot lead a narrow, mean, selfish life and hide its traces with dye, cosmetics, paint and balm. Regard yourselves precisely as the artist does his painting or statue, ever stretching forward to some grand ideal. Remember that your daily, hourly lives, every impulse, passion, feeling of your soul, every good action, high resolve and lofty conception of the good and true, are delicate touches here and there gradually rounding out and perfecting in yourselves a true womanhood. Oh! do not mar the pure white canvas or marble statue with dark shadows, coarse lines, and hasty chiseling. (Stanton in Gordon 1997–2013, 3:497; winter 1880)

As has been observed by Lisa Strange, "Stanton's feminist vision stressed the importance of personal responsibility, complete self-sovereignty and self-sufficiency" (Strange 1998, 209).

Of course, just like her friend Stanton, Susan B. Anthony also maintained that women should not automatically feel that their only roles in life are wife and motherhood: "She must first be a woman—free, trained, above old ideas and prejudices, and afterwards the wife and mother. The old theory of wife and mother needing only the capacity to cook and scrub is rapidly going to the dark ages" (Anthony, January 31, 1896, in Gordon 1997–2013, 6:35). And surely Stanton spoke for Anthony as well when she called for the best possible education of all the people in the land.

> If, as a nation, we hope to celebrate the second centennial of our national life, we must give new thought to thorough education of our whole people. We should demand in our schools and colleges a knowledge of those practical branches of learning that self-government involves. Surely an intelligent understanding of the great principles of Finance, Land Monopoly, Taxes and Tariffs, the relations of Labor and Capital and the laws of Commerce are far more important in a republic than a knowledge of Homer and Virgil, their descriptions of the heroes of a forgotten age, or the speculations of Dante and Milton as to the sufferings of lost souls in the Inferno. The one vital necessity to the success of our experiment of self-government is the education of our people, and in the sciences rather than foreign languages and the classics. (Stanton in Gordon 1997–2013, 3:309–10; May 24, 1877)

This is a rather one-sided and pragmatic approach to education that most assuredly flies in the face of the modern ideal of a liberal education, but the key issue is that both Stanton and Anthony recognized that women needed to be granted equal access to education in order to become self-sufficient individuals ready to compete with the male part of the population in the many tasks that confronted the American society.

There was work enough to do for men and women alike. They themselves were both educated "work-horses" in the same yoke, steadily moving forward in the service of the women's rights movement. As the sixty-three-year-old Anthony observed in an interview on February 22, 1883, in Philadelphia before departing on a trip to Europe, "I am in perfect health and intend to occupy my time in the saloon [of the ship] writing and preparing for my future work, for I do not intend to be idle. Although I am going for recreation I shall combine some work with it, and shall probably deliver several addresses and lectures in different European cities before returning to America" (Anthony, February 22, 1883, in Gordon 1997–2013, 4:223). About two years later, she said in Pennsylvania, "I don't know what religion is. I only know what work is, and that is all I can speak on, this side of Jordan. I can then on this morning talk simply of work" (Anthony, June 6, 1885, in Gordon 1997–2013, 4:421). This statement includes a splendid allusion to the proverbial expression "to cross the Jordan" that is a classical euphemism for dying (see Reid 1983). And there is also this short description of her life's story: "The world is full of work & in so many places at the same time—that I do not [know] which thing to do first" (Anthony, August 19, 1894, in Gordon 1997–2013, 5:642) followed by her delightful employment of the folk proverb "all work and no play makes Jack a dull boy": "To barely go to Washington and hold a convention, and hurry out of it immediately afterwards, does not and cannot accomplish much. Of course, as all work and no play makes Jack a dull boy and all play and no work makes him a mere toy, so all work before Congress and none in the States, or all work in the States and none before Congress, would result poorly" (Anthony, May 27, 1898, in Gordon 1997–2013, 6:226).

Surely Susan B. Anthony was anything but dull as she pressed her women's rights agenda forward. Driven by her motto that "failure is impossible" (Partnow 1992, 842; Sherr 1995), she plowed forward with enthusiastic strength that at times also gave her a chance to let her guard down for enjoyable moments with family members, friends, and her soul mate, Elizabeth Cady Stanton.

Obsessed by work themselves, both Stanton and Anthony had much to say regarding the role of women in the workforce, where they traditionally have been treated as second-class citizens. And as the latter explains by way of the negation of the proverb "father knows best," the proverbial expression "to know where the shoe pinches," and the proverb "the mother is the queen of the home," wives and mothers cannot develop their full potential if husbands continue to play first fiddle at home and in the workplace.

> Woman's work commences early and ends late. To her is committed the chief care of the children, laboring more hours than man and gets no credit for anything. The property is supposed to be all earned by the husband, and the woman owned and supported by him too. If woman used the ballot, think you

this false condition of things would continue? She must care for the children in almost every regard, and yet they early learn that mother's opinions and authority are worthy of little respect, as "father knows best." (Anthony, April 15, 1870, in Gordon 1997–2013, 2:327)

The mother may have toiled over the same old and rickety cook-stove for many years, and repeatedly received a lecture for poor cooking or poor baking, but she must continue on in the same fatiguing and unhappy way for half a score of years more, while the father secures to himself all the modern improvements in machinery wherewith to accomplish his work. She can't see "where the shoe pinches" unless she wears it. (Anthony, April 15, 1870, in Gordon 1997–2013, 2:327–28)

You are looking at the matter of sterilizing milk, which is a good thing, and of guiding children at pivotal times in their lives, which is also a good thing. But of all things, mothers need aid to shape the conditions that should surround the child outside as well as inside the home. The mother is said to be the queen of the home, but you all know that she is often the victim of circumstances and that she cannot have absolute sway in her own home. (Anthony, February 27, 1902, in Gordon 1997–2013, 6:426)

This unconditional emancipation of women from all types of subjection is something that Anthony preached throughout her long life, her goal being their total liberation from servitude and the absolute equality with men. To describe this assertion of their individuality as women, she turned to the Bible proverb "in the sweat of thy brow shalt thou eat bread" (Genesis 3:19).

To be esteemed worthy to speak for woman, for the slave, for humanity, is ever grateful to me, and I regret that I can not be with you at your annual gathering to get myself a fresh baptism, a new and deeper faith. I would exhort all women to be discontented with their present condition and to assert their individuality of thought, word and action by the energetic doing of noble deeds. Idle wishes, vain repinings [sic], loud-sounding declamations never can bring freedom to any human soul. What woman most needs is a true appreciation of her womanhood, a self-respect which shall scorn to eat the bread of dependence. Whoever consents to live by "the sweat of the brow" of another human being inevitably humiliates and degrades herself. (Anthony, January ?, 1859; cited from Harper 1898–1908, 1:169)

No more dependency or subjection but only independence and equality is the message, but this self-assertion meant, as Stanton and especially Anthony well realized, also a change in the attitude toward work outside of the home. Playing off the proverb "a drowning man will clutch at a straw," Stanton found a fitting metaphor to explain that the newly emancipated women need no longer think that marriage, with its pitfalls, is their predestined role in life. They certainly should not feel compelled to hold on to a straw offered to them by irresponsible future husbands.

> It is said that the 10,000 libertines, letchers [sic] and egotists would take a new wife every Christmas if they could legally and reputably rid themselves in season of the old one. . . . [This] objection is based on the idea that woman will always remain the penniless, helpless, resistless victim of every man she meets, that she is to-day. But in the new regime, when she holds her place in the world of work, educated to self-support, with land under her feet and a shelter over her head, the results of her own toil, the social, civil and political equal of the man by her side, she will not clutch at every offer of marriage, like the drowning man at the floating straw. Though men should remain just what they are, the entire revolution in woman's position now inaugurated forces a new moral code in social life. (Stanton, c. 1875; cited from DuBois 1981, 135)

The new position of women in the social order included for Stanton and Anthony also a new understanding of the role women could play in the workforce outside of the home. Far too long had women been forced into a subservient corner in the home, where their demands of life were reduced to accept the status quo that was well expressed by the proverb "beggars must not be choosers." Quoting this wisdom and also playing off the Bible proverb "there is no new thing under the sun" (Ecclesiastes 1:9), Anthony argues strongly that this must not remain the attitude as ever more women searched for gainful employment.

> You remember the old adage, "Beggars must not be choosers;" they must take what they can get or nothing! That is exactly the position of women in the world of work today; they can not choose. If they could, do you for a moment believe they would take the subordinate places and the inferior pay? Nor it is a "new thing under the sun" for the disfranchised, the inferior classes weighed down with wrongs, to declare they "do not want to vote." The rank and file are not philosophers, they are not educated to think for themselves, but simply to accept, unquestioned, whatever comes. (Anthony, c. 1875; cited from Sherr, 138)

In fact, Anthony argued strongly for women entering various professions without being discriminated against because of their gender. Proverbially speaking, they should not have to run the gauntlet when looking for work, being sent from one place to another and turned down for most jobs. Anthony understood that this situation would best be changed if more women could advance so far in a given workplace that they would be the ones in charge of hiring new employees.

> And it is precisely such a gauntlet that every girl who comes to St. Louis, Chicago or New York has to run when she goes to solicit work in the shops or offices of our great cities. Now, what we must have everywhere is women employers as well as employes [sic]. We must have women employers, women superintendents, committees and legislators everywhere, ere a poor girl who is compelled to seek the means of subsistence, shall always find good, noble

> women. Nay, more than that, we must have women ministers, lawyers and doctors; that wherever women go to seek spiritual or legal counsel they will be sure to find the best and noblest of their own sex to minister to them. (Anthony, April 12, 1875, in Gordon 1997–2013, 3:163)

She continued this line of thought by looking into the future, arguing that the proverb "the laborer is worthy of his hire" does not hold for women at the turn of the century, since they for the most part would have to be classified as unskilled laborers. She foresaw that this would definitely change in the twentieth century, and yet she would be surprised to learn that well into the second decade of the twenty-first century, women are still trying to break through the glass ceilings of some professional hierarchies.

> We women must be up and doing. I can hardly sit still when I think of the great work waiting to be done. Above all, women must be in earnest, we must be thorough, and fit ourselves for every emergency; we must be trained, and carefully prepare ourselves for the place we wish to hold in this world. The time is passed when the unskilled laborer is worthy of his hire. More and more does the world demand specialists, and women must rise to her opportunities as never before. I shall not be here to see it, but the twentieth century will see as great a change in the position and progress of woman in the world as has been accomplished in this century, but it will have ceased to cause comment, and will be accepted as a matter of course. There will be nothing in the realm of ethics in which woman will not have her own recognized place, and all political questions, and all the laws which govern us will have a feminine side, for woman and her influence, in making and shaping of affairs, will have to be reckoned with. (Anthony, January 1, 1901, in Gordon 1997–2013, 6:376)

But breaking through glass ceilings is only one side of the employment coin, with the other side being the appalling salary gap between the genders for the same work that is also still an issue today. Remarkably so, the ever-agitating Anthony was on to this discrepancy as early as October 8, 1869, when she wrote in *The Revolution*: "Join the union, girls, and together say, 'Equal Pay for Equal Work'" (Dorr 1928, 87; Rees 1995, 146–47; Shapiro 2006, 23). Some thirty years later, with the move of women into the workforce having become much more widespread, Anthony returned to her sententious remark turned proverb by then and became—how could it be otherwise—an outspoken champion of its significant message: "What I have been working for all these years is just this. . . . Equal pay for equal work. There isn't a woman in the sound of my voice, who does not want this justice. There never was one—there never will be one who does not want justice and equality. But they have not yet learned that equal work and equal wages can come only through the political equality, represented by the ballot" (Anthony, July 29, 1897, in Gordon 1997–2013, 6:155).

It is of interest to note that in 1897, Anthony had no choice but to argue that the demand of "equal pay for equal work" would have no way of becoming law as long as women did not have the right to cast their vote. More than a hundred years later, the struggle for equal pay for equal work is still going on, but great progress has indeed been made, and it behooves modern women to give considerable credit for these advances to Susan B. Anthony in particular.

This cause obviously was dear to Anthony's heart, but it must be remembered that both she and Elizabeth Cady Stanton always mustered up enough energy and willpower to take on ever new tasks, and it must not be forgotten that they were also aware of the fact that many sociopolitical problems could best be addressed and hopefully solved by women and men working together as equal partners. As Stanton observes with a fitting quotation from Alfred, Lord Tennyson's *The Princess* (1847), it is this supportive partnership that could conquer the work that lay ahead.

> Yes, the spheres of man and woman are the same, with different duties according to the capacity of the individual. Woman, like all created things, lives, moves, and has her being obedient to law, exploring with man the mysteries of the universe and speculating on the glories of the hereafter. . . .
> The question is no longer the sphere of a whole sex but of each individual. Women are now in the trades and professions, everywhere in the world of work. They have shown their capacity as students in the sciences, their skill as mariners before the mast, their courage as rescuers in lifeboats. They are close on the heels of man in the arts, sciences and literature; in their knowledge and understanding of the vital questions of the hour, and in the every day practical duties of life. Like man, woman's sphere is in the whole universe of matter and mind, to do whatever she can, and thus prove "the intentions of the Creator." (Stanton in Gordon 1997–2013, 5:724; November 12, 1895)

How pleased both Stanton and Anthony would have been to know that there are now also modern proverbs that encapsulate through folk speech what they had fought for. Thus, the traditional proverb "a woman's place is in the home" has been countered by the antiproverb "a woman's place is any place she wants to be" (earliest reference 1918; see Litovkina and Mieder 2006), and modern feminists have coined the proverb "a woman without a man is like a fish without a bicycle" (Mieder 1982; Stibbs 1992, 224; Doyle, Mieder, and Shapiro 2012, 279–80) in 1976 to counteract the many antifeministic proverbs from earlier times (see Kerschen 1998; Schipper 2003). No doubt, the proverbial fight for women's rights in the workplace is in very good hands and continues to make good progress.

Finally, on a more philosophical level, it should not be surprising that Elizabeth Cady Stanton and Susan B. Anthony, just as social reformers before and after them have done, turned to the so-called Golden Rule which, in the Christian faith, is found in the New Testament as "do unto others as you would have them do unto you" (Matthew 7:12; see Hertzler 1933–34; Burrell 1997, 13–27; Templeton 1997, 8–12). It represents the ultimate proverbial law of life that calls for equal and treatment of all people. Already in July 1848, right at the beginning of the crusade for women's rights, Stanton and Elizabeth W. McClintock wrote a lengthy letter to the editor of the *Seneca County Courier* in which they accuse "religionists" of having forgotten the golden rule in their support of the unjust treatment of people.

> Now, it seems to us, the time has fully come for this much abused book [the Bible] to change hands. Let the people no longer trust to their blind guides, but read and reason for themselves—even though they thus call down on themselves the opprobrious epithet of "infidel," than which no word in our language is more misunderstood and misapplied. We throw back the charge of infidelity on the religionists of the present day, for though they assert their belief in the Divinity of Christ, they deny, in theory and practice, his Divine commands. Do they not rally around and support all the great sins of this guilty nation? What say they to the golden rule, and the injunction, "Resist not evil"? Why, the self-styled christians of our day have fought in and supported the unjust and cruel Mexican war, and have long held men, women, and children in bondage. (Stanton in Gordon 1997–2013, 1:89; July 23, 1848)

About six years later, Stanton returned to the Golden Rule in her widely acknowledged address to the legislature of New York of February 14, 1854. Here "she pointed to the misogyny lurking behind the statutes defining the legal position of married women, and the tone of her speech revealed the intensity of women's dissatisfaction with their current condition. . . . She linked logic, legal and historical evidence, and the Judeo-Christian tradition to make a case for women's rights" (Campbell 1989a, 1:94–96). Various commentators have cited the following paragraph from this speech, stating that by referring to the Golden Rule and actually citing it verbatim, Stanton invoked "God's *rule of justice (a truth)*" (Waggenspack 1986, 176), that "justice suggested that all women want is the same protection the laws grant men" (Waggenspack 1989, 54), and that "women felt the same love of freedom and had the same 'clear perception of justice,' as any man" (Pellauer 1991, 52).

> But if, gentlemen [the legislators], you take the ground that the sexes are alike, and, therefore, you are our faithful representatives—then why all these special laws for woman? Would not one code answer for all of like needs and wants? Christ's golden rule is better than all the special legislation that the ingenuity of man can devise: "Do unto others as you would have others do unto you." This, men and brethren, is all we ask at your hands. We ask no better laws than

those you have made for yourselves. We need no other protection than that which your present laws secure to you. (Stanton in Gordon 1997–2013, 1:254; February 14, 1854)

As stated, scholars are well aware of this important passage arguing for women's equality under the law by offering the Golden Rule as authoritative support of this demand. However, they apparently have completely ignored several very informative statements by Stanton in which she returned to the Golden Rule both as a religious but even more so as a secular law of humanity. Thus, she argued vehemently against the misinterpretation of the Bible by the clergy, legislators, and others as an authority that supports such injustices as slavery and the subjugation of women.

> "Servants obey your masters" outweighed the Golden Rule with the teachers of the people. When the Fugitive Slave Law was passed in 1850, the Northern pulpit made haste to teach that it was the duty of Christian men and women to catch "Onesimus" [a slave sent back to his owner by the apostle Paul] wherever they found him, and send him back to the house of bondage. The effort to abolish capital punishment is stoutly resisted by the same class of minds, for the same reason, though not one text of Scripture can be found in favor of our barbarous system. (Stanton in Gordon 1997–2013, 3:447–48; May 11, 1879)

As one would expect, Susan B. Anthony also turned to the Golden Rule proverb, and it is her convention speech of May 14, 1863, during the middle of the Civil War, that deserves special attention (see Brigance 2005, 2). Accusing the country of having had nothing but war, with the war between slave and slaveholder being one of the worst, she argues that there must be no return to this despicable status quo after the war at hand. Above all, slavery must once and for all be eradicated and the Bible proverb "do unto others as you would have them do unto you" must be the guiding principle of a new beginning.

> We talk about returning to "the Union as it was" and "the Constitution as it is"—about "restoring our country to peace and prosperity—to the blessed conditions which existed before the war!" I ask you what sort of peace, what sort of prosperity, have we had? Since the first slave ship sailed up the James river with its human cargo and there, on the soil of the Old Dominion, it was sold to the highest bidder, we have had nothing but war. When that pirate captain landed on the shores of Africa and there kidnapped the first stalwart negro and fastened the first manacle, the struggle between that captain and that negro was the commencement of the terrible war in the midst of which we are today. Between the slave and the master there has been war, and war only. This is but a new form of it. No, no; we ask for no return to the old conditions. We ask for something better. We want a Union which is a Union in fact, a Union in spirit, not a sham. By the Constitution as it is, the North has stood

> pledged to protect slavery in the States where it existed. We have been bound, in case of insurrections, to go to the aid, not of those struggling for liberty but of the oppressors. It was politicians who made this pledge at the beginning, and who have renewed it from year to year. These same men have had control of the churches, the Sabbath-schools and all religious institutions, and the women have been a party in complicity with slavery. They have made the large majority in all the churches throughout the country and have, without protest, fellowshipped the slaveholder as a Christian; accepted proslavery preaching from their pulpits; suffered the words "slavery a crime" to be expurgated from all the lessons taught their children, in defiance of the Golden Rule, "Do unto others as you would that others should do unto you." They have meekly accepted whatever morals and religion the selfish interest of politics and trade dictated. (Anthony, May 14, 1863; cited from Harper 1898–1908, 1:228)

This statement echoes the use of the Golden Rule proverb by her fellow crusaders against slavery. Here is what her friend Frederick Douglass, who cited the Golden Rule numerous times as an argument against slavery and the ultimate wisdom for equality (Mieder 2001, 95–103, 184–92; Mieder 2004b, 141–46), said at approximately the same time:

> The progress of our nation downward has been rapid as all steps downward are apt to be. 1st. We found the Golden Rule impracticable. 2nd. We found the Declaration of Independence very broadly impracticable. 3rd. We found the Constitution of the United States, requiring that the majority shall rule, is impracticable. 4th. We found that the union was impracticable. The golden rule did not hold the slave tight enough. The Constitution did not hold the slave tight enough. The Declaration of Independence did not hold the slave at all; and the union was a loose affair and altogether impracticable. (May 15, 1863; Blassingame 1985–1992, 3:573; Mieder 2001, 190)

Not a year later, still during the Civil War, Abraham Lincoln also turned to the Golden Rule, attacking in particular the established church of the South for condoning slavery.

> When, a year or two ago, those professedly holy men of the South, met in the semblance of prayer and devotion, and, in the name of Him who said "As ye would all men should do unto you, do ye even so unto them" appealed to the christian world to aid them in doing to a whole race of men, as they would have no man do unto themselves, to my thinking, they contemned and insulted God and His church, far more than did Satan when he tempted the Saviour with the Kingdoms of the earth. (May 30, 1864; Basler 1953, 7:368; Mieder 2000, 80–81)

One hundred years later, Martin Luther King Jr. preached a sermon in which he said that "the acceptable year of the Lord is that year when men will do unto others as they will have others do unto themselves [Matthew 7:12].

The acceptable year of the Lord is that year when men will love their enemies, bless them that curse them, pray for them that despitefully use them [Matthew 5:44]" (cited from Mieder 2010b, 268). For these social reformers the Golden Rule proverb serves as a beacon of hope for what the world could be if humankind were to adhere to this simple law of life.

But to return to Elizabeth Cady Stanton's reliance on this Bible proverb, here is yet another unique passage with the Golden Rule where she shows herself as quite the scholar of comparative religion. She is absolutely correct in stating that the world's religions all have the Golden Rule in one form or another, as has been shown by Albert Griffin in his *Religious Proverbs: Over 1600 Adages from 18 Faiths Worldwide* (1991, 67–69). Even though there are differences in these faiths, the common Golden Rule as the supreme moral guidepost should enable people everywhere to live in peace and enjoy their human rights of life, liberty, and the pursuit of happiness.

> "Every race," says a recent writer [Octavius Frothingham in his *The Religion of Humanity* (1873)], "above the savage has its Bible. Each of the great religions of mankind has its Bible. The Chinese pay homage to the wise words of Confucius, the Brahmans prize their Vedas, the Buddhists venerate their Pitikas, the Zoroastrians cherish their Avesta, the Scandinavians their Eddas, the Greeks their Oracles and the songs of their bards," the Christians believe the New Testament to be divinely inspired, the Hebrews of our day accept with equal reverence the Old Testament, and thus all along each nation has had its own idea of God, religion, revelation; and each alike has believed its own ideas the absolute and ultimate. Much as these 'Bibles' differ in all that is transient and local, the texture of sentiment, the moral and religious principles are the same, showing a responsive chord in every human soul, in all ages and latitudes. All Bibles contain something like the decalogue; the 'Golden Rule,' written in the soul of man, has been chanted round the globe by the lips of sages in every tongue and clime. This is enough to assure us that what is permanent in morals and religion can safely bear discussion and the successive shocks of every new discovery and reform. (Stanton in Gordon 1997–2013, 3:456–57; May 11, 1879)

More than a century later, presidential candidate Senator Barack Obama said something quite similar in his remarkable speech "A More Perfect Union" on March 18, 2008, in Philadelphia: "In the end then, what is called for is nothing more, and nothing less, than what all the world's great religions demand—that we do unto others as we would have them do unto us. Let us be our brother's keeper; Scripture tells us. Let us be our sister's keeper. Let us find that common stake we all have in one another, and let our politics reflect that spirit as well" (March 18, 2008; cited from Mieder 2009, 201; Mieder 2010a).

Complete adherence to the Golden Rule is by no means a reality in the modern age, and both Stanton and Anthony were well aware of the fact that it represents but an ideal state of humanity that all people can do no more than strive toward. They both did this with their souls and minds, and there is no doubt that their social reform activism was informed to a considerable degree by their effective proverbial rhetoric.

References

This chapter was first published in *Proverbium* 32 (2015): 261–330.

Aron, Paul. 2008. *We Hold These Truths . . . And Other Words That Made America*. Lanham, MD: Rowman & Littlefield.
Banner, Lois W. 1980. *Elizabeth Cady Stanton: A Radical for Woman's Rights*. Boston: Little, Brown and Company.
Barbour, Frances M. 1974. *A Concordance to Proverbs in Franklin's "Poor Richard."* Detroit: Gale Research Company.
Barrick, Mac E. 1978. "'As Dead as a Doornail.'" In *Studies in English and American Literature*, edited by John L. Cutler and Lawrence S. Thompson, 332–35. New York: Whitston Publishing Company.
Barry, Kathleen. 1988. *Susan B. Anthony: A Biography of a Singular Feminist*. New York: New York University Press.
Bartlett, John. 2012. *Familiar Quotations*. 18th ed. Edited by Geoffrey O'Brien. New York: Little, Brown and Company.
Basler, Roy P., ed. 1953. *The Collected Works of Abraham Lincoln*. 8 vols. New Brunswick, NJ: Rutgers University Press.
Blassingame, John, ed. 1985–92. *The Frederick Douglass Papers*. 5 vols. New Haven, CT: Yale University Press.
Brigance, Linda Czuba. 2005. "Ballots and Bullets: Adapting Women's Rights Arguments to the Conditions of War." *Women and Language* 28:1–7.
Burke, Kenneth. 1941. "Literature [i.e., Proverbs] as Equipment for Living." In *The Philosophy of Literary Form: Studies in Symbolic Action*, edited by K. Burke, 253–62. Baton Rouge: Louisiana University Press.
Burrell, Brian. 1997. *The Words We Live By: The Creeds, Mottoes, and Pledges That Have Shaped America*. New York: Free Press.
Campbell, Karlyn Kohrs. 1989a. *Man Cannot Speak for Her*. Vol. 1, *A Critical Study of Early Feminist Rhetoric*. Vol. 2, *Key Texts of the Early Feminists*. Westport, CT: Greenwood Press.
———. 1989b. "The Sound of Women's Voices." *Quarterly Journal of Speech* 75:212–58.
Clarke, Mary Stetson. 1972. *Bloomers and Ballots: Elizabeth Cady Stanton and Women's Rights*. New York: Viking Press.
Davis, Sue. 2008. *The Political Thought of Elizabeth Cady Stanton: Women's Rights and the American Political Traditions*. New York: New York University Press.
Dolby, Sandra K. 2005. *Self-Help Books: Why Americans Keep Reading Them*. Urbana: University of Illinois Press.

Dorr, Rheta Childe. 1928. *Susan B. Anthony: The Woman Who Changed the Mind of a Nation*. New York: Frederick A. Stokes.
Doyle, Charles Clay, Wolfgang Mieder, and Fred R. Shapiro, eds. 2012. *The Dictionary of Modern Proverbs*. New Haven, CT: Yale University Press.
DuBois, Ellen Carol, ed. 1981. *Elizabeth Cady Stanton/Susan B. Anthony: Correspondence, Writings, Speeches*. New York: Schocken Books.
DuBois, Ellen Carol, and Richard Cándida Smith, eds. 2007. *Elizabeth Cady Stanton, Feminist as Thinker: A Reader in Documents and Essays*. New York: New York University Press.
Engbers, Susanna Kelly. 2007. "With Great Sympathy: Elizabeth Cady Stanton's Innovative Appeals to Emotion." *Rhetoric Society Quarterly* 37:307–32.
Eret, Dylan. 2001. "'The Past Does Not Equal the Future': Anthony Robbins Self-Help Maxims as Therapeutic Forms of Proverbial Rhetoric." *Proverbium* 18:77–103.
Fuss, Diana. 1989. *Essentially Speaking: Feminism, Nature & Difference*. New York: Routledge.
Gallacher, Stuart A. 1949. "Franklin's *Way to Wealth*: A Florilegium of Proverbs and Wise Sayings." *Journal of English and Germanic Philology* 48:229–51.
———. 1963. "Castles in Spain." *Journal of American Folklore* 76:324–29.
Ginzberg, Lori D. 2009. *Elizabeth Cady Stanton: An American Life*. New York: Hill and Wang.
Gordon, Ann D., ed. 1997–2013. *The Selected Papers of Elizabeth Cady Stanton and Susan B. Anthony*. 6 vols. New Brunswick, NJ: Rutgers University Press.
———. 1999. "Taking Possession of the Country." In *Not for Ourselves Alone: The Story of Elizabeth Cady Stanton and Susan B. Anthony: An Illustrated History*, edited by Geoffrey C. Ward, 163–69. New York: Alfred A. Knopf.
Gornick, Vivian. 2005. *The Solitude of Self: Thinking about Elizabeth Cady Stanton*. New York: Farrar, Straus and Giroux.
Griffin, Albert Kirby. 1991. *Religious Proverbs: Over 1600 Adages from 18 Faiths Worldwide*. Jefferson, NC: McFarland & Company.
Griffith, Elisabeth. 1984. *In Her Own Right: The Life of Elizabeth Cady Stanton*. New York: Oxford University Press.
Harder, Franz. 1925–26. "'Parturient [sic] montes, nascetur ridiculus mus.'" *Zeitschrift des Vereins für Volkskunde* 35–36:278–80.
Harper, Ida Husted. 1898–1908. *The Life and Work of Susan B. Anthony, Including Public Addresses, Her Own Letters and Many from Her Contemporaries During Fifty Years: A Story of the Evolution of the Status of Woman*. 3 vols. Indianapolis: Hollenbeck Press.
Hertzler, Joyce O. 1933–34. "On Golden Rules." *International Journal of Ethics* 44:418–36.
Hirsch, E. D., Joseph F. Kett, and James Trefil. 2002. *The New Dictionary of Cultural Literacy*. 3rd ed. Boston: Houghton Mifflin Company.
Hogan, Lisa H., and J. Michael Hogan. 2003. "Feminine Virtue and Practical Wisdom: Elizabeth Cady Stanton's 'Our Boys.'" *Rhetoric and Public Affairs* 6:415–36.
Huxman, Susan Schultz. 2000. "Perfecting the Rhetorical Vision of Woman's Rights: Elizabeth Cady Stanton, Anna Howard Shaw, and Carrie Chapman Catt." *Women's Studies in Communication* 23:307–36.
Kerschen, Lois. 1998. *American Proverbs about Women: A Reference Guide*. Westport, CT: Greenwood Press.
Krikmann, Arvo. 2009. *Proverb Semantics: Studies in Structure, Logic, and Metaphor*. Edited by Wolfgang Mieder. Burlington: University of Vermont.
Litovkina, Anna T., and Wolfgang Mieder. 2006. *Old Proverbs Never Die, They Just Diversify: A Collection of Anti-Proverbs*. Burlington: University of Vermont.

Lutz, Alma. 1940. *Created Equal: A Biography of Elizabeth Cady Stanton*. New York: Octagon Books.
———. 1959. *Susan B. Anthony: Rebel, Crusader, Humanitarian*. Boston: Beacon Press.
Mieder, Wolfgang. 1982. "'Eine Frau ohne Mann ist wie ein Fisch ohne Velo!'" *Sprachspiegel* 38: 141–42.
———. 1993. *Proverbs Are Never Out of Season: Popular Wisdom, in the Modern Age*. New York: Oxford University Press.
———. 1997. *The Politics of Proverbs: From Traditional Wisdom to Proverbial Stereotypes*. Madison: University of Wisconsin Press.
———. 2000. *The Proverbial Abraham Lincoln: An Index to Proverbs in the Works of Abraham Lincoln*. New York: Peter Lang.
———. 2001. *"No Struggle, No Progress": Frederick Douglass and His Proverbial Rhetoric for Civil Rights*. New York: Peter Lang.
———. 2004. *Proverbs: A Handbook*. Westport, CT: Greenwood Press.
———. 2005. *Proverbs Are the Best Policy: Folk Wisdom and American Politics*. Logan: Utah State University Press.
———. 2009. *"Yes We Can": Barack Obama's Proverbial Rhetoric*. New York: Peter Lang.
———. 2010a. "The Golden Rule as a Political Imperative for the World: President Barack Obama's Proverbial Messages Abroad." *Milli Folklor* 85:26–35.
———. 2010b. *"Making a Way Out of No Way": Martin Luther King's Sermonic Proverbial Rhetoric*. New York: Peter Lang.
———. 2011. "'The Dog in the Manger': The Rise and Decline in Popularity of a Proverb and a Fable." *Midwestern Folklore* 37:3–44.
———. 2013a. *"Neues von Sisyphus": Sprichwörtliche Mythen der Antike in Moderner Literatur, Medien und Karikaturen*. Vienna: Praesens Verlag.
———. 2013b. "'What's Sauce for the Goose Is Sauce for the Gander.' The Proverbial Fight for Women's Rights by Elizabeth Cady Stanton and Susan B. Anthony." In *Frazeologiia v mogoiazychnom obshchestve*, edited by Elena Arsentyeva, 21–38. Kazan': Kazanskii Federal'nyi Universitet.
Mieder, Wolfgang, and George B. Bryan. 1997. *The Proverbial Harry S. Truman: An Index to Proverbs in the Works of Harry S. Truman*. New York: Peter Lang.
Mieder, Wolfgang, Stewart A. Kingsbury, and Kelsie B. Harder, eds. 1992. *A Dictionary of American Proverbs*. New York: Oxford University Press.
Norrick, Neal R. 1985. *How Proverbs Mean. Semantic Studies in English Proverbs*. Amsterdam: Mouton.
O'Connor, Lillian. 1954. *Pioneer Women Orators: Rhetoric in the Ante-Bellum Reform Movement*. New York: Columbia University Press.
Partnow, Elaine. 1992. *The New Quotable Women*. New York: Facts on File.
Pellauer, Mary D. 1991. *Toward a Tradition of Feminist Theology: The Religious Social Thought of Elizabeth Cady Stanton, Susan B. Anthony, and Anna Howard Shaw*. Brooklyn, NY: Carlson Publishing.
Rees, Nigel. 1995. *Phrases & Sayings*. London: Bloomsbury.
Reid, J. H. 1983. "'Über den Jordan gehen.' A Note on the History of a Metaphor." *New German Studies* 11: 155–69.
Ridarsky, Christine L., and Mary M. Huth, eds. 2012. *Susan B. Anthony and the Struggle for Equal Rights*. Rochester, NY: University of Rochester Press.
Röhrich, Lutz. 1991–92. *Das große Lexikon der sprichwörtlichen Redensarten*. 3 vols. Freiburg: Herder Verlag.

Schipper, Mineke. 2003. *"Never Marry a Woman with Big Feet": Women in Proverbs from around the World*. New Haven, CT: Yale University Press.
Shapiro, Fred R. 2006. *The Yale Book of Quotations*. New Haven, CT: Yale University Press.
Sherr, Lynn. 1995. *Failure Is Impossible: Susan B. Anthony in Her Own Words*. New York: Times Books.
Stanton, Elizabeth Cady, et al. 1895–98. *The Woman's Bible*. 2 vols. New York: European Publishing Company.
Stanton, Elizabeth Cady, Susan B. Anthony, Matilda J. Gage, and Ida H. Harper, eds. 1887–1922. *History of Woman Suffrage*. 6 vols. New York: National American Woman Suffrage Association.
Stibbs, Anne, ed. 1992. *Like a Fish Needs a Bicycle . . . And Over 3,000 Quotations by and about Women*. London: Bloomsbury.
Strange, Lisa S. 1998. *Pragmatism and Radicalism in Elizabeth Cady Stanton's Feminist Advocacy: A Rhetorical Biography*. Bloomington: Indiana University Press.
Taylor, Archer. 1975. *Selected Writings on Proverbs*. Edited by Wolfgang Mieder. Helsinki: Suomalainen Tiedeakatemia.
Templeton, John Marks. 1997. *Worldwide Laws of Life: 200 Eternal Spiritual Principles*. Philadelphia: Templeton Foundation Press.
Waggenspack, Beth M. 1989. *The Search for Self-Sovereignty: The Oratory of Elizabeth Cady Stanton*. Westport, CT: Greenwood Press.
Wander, Karl Friedrich Wilhelm. 1867–80. *Deutsches Sprichwörter-Lexikon*. 5 vols. Leipzig: F. A. Brockhaus,
Ward, Geoffrey C. 1999. *Not for Ourselves Alone: The Story of Elizabeth Cady Stanton and Susan B. Anthony; An Illustrated History*. New York: Alfred A. Knopf.
Wellman, Judith. 2004. *The Road to Seneca Falls: Elizabeth Cady Stanton and the First Woman's Rights Convention*. Urbana: University of Illinois Press.
Zimmer, Benjamin. 2005. "'Pull Oneself up by One's Bootstraps': A Now Serious Expression Originally Expressed an Absurdly Impossible Task." *Comments on Etymology* 35:5–10.

3

"THE AMERICAN PEOPLE ROSE TO THE OCCASION"

A Proverbial Retrospective of the Marshall Plan after Seventy Years

SERENDIPITY IS OFTEN A PART OF SCHOLARSHIP, AS the following deliberations will illustrate. My distinguished colleague and friend Mark A. Stoler from the history department of the University of Vermont delighted me twenty years ago with an inscribed copy of his acclaimed biography, *George C. Marshall. Soldier-Statesman of the American Century* (1989). I still remember vividly how I hurried home in great expectation to read what he had to say about the Marshall Plan or the European Recovery Program (ERP) that was designed to help Western Europe back on its sustainable feet after the devastations of World War II, with its nutritional and economic hardships.

At the end of his six-page discussion of this humanitarian and sociopolitical plan, I learned that George Catlett Marshall (1880–1959) for his visionary engagement "clearly deserved his second Man of the Year selection from *Time* magazine in January 1948 and the Nobel Prize he would receive in 1953. As *Time* noted in explaining its selection, Marshall was 'the man who offered hope to those who desperately needed it,' as well as the symbol of the U.S. decision to assume world leadership" (Stoler 1989, 167). I had not known that George Marshall had been honored with the Nobel Peace Prize for his role as the fifteenth United States Army chief of staff from 1939 to 1945, the fiftieth United States secretary of state from 1947 to 1949, and the tenth president of the American Red Cross from 1949 to 1950, to name but a few of the achievements of this estimable soldier-statesman.

All of this brought back memories of my childhood that I spent in Germany between 1944 and 1960 before leaving on my own as a sixteen-year-old student to find my way in America with such personal heroes as Abraham Lincoln and George Marshall on my mind. About Lincoln I had learned something in school, but the name Marshall I had heard from my parents numerous times between 1948 and 1952, when the Marshall Plan helped to rebuild Europe and made it possible for children like me to survive deprivation and hunger. I expressed my thankfulness for the humanitarian side of the Marshall Plan in an invited plenary address by the American Folklore Society Fellows on October 23, 2009, in Boise, Idaho, that was entitled "'It Takes a Village to Change the World': Proverbial Politics and Ethics of Place." Commenting on President Harry S. Truman's inaugural address on January 20, 1949, that included a call for a democratic and peaceful world order, I stated the following:

> Truman meant what he said, to wit the creation of the humanitarian Marshall Plan that helped undernourished youngsters like me to get fed. I was but five years old at the time, but my earliest childhood memories are my mother mixing powdered milk (perhaps from my beloved Vermont) with water or making scrambled eggs from dried eggs for me, and my father adding a bit of sugar to condensed milk so that I could enjoy something sweet. All of this came from America, including my favorite shoes, jacket, and pants. And then there were those little care packages. You should have seen my little legs carrying me to the small grocery store at the corner of the street to get one of them when a new shipment from America had arrived. A small treasure of peanut butter crackers, candied fruit, chewing gum (which we were not allowed to chew at school and did nevertheless), a candy bar, of course, and many other things. Perhaps this is why I longed to come to America from my childhood on, and at the age of sixteen, only fifteen years after America defeated the menace and horrors of Nazi Germany, I had the opportunity of a lifetime. I will always be thankful to President Truman and General Marshall for what they did for us kids and to the hundreds of Americans who helped me to find the ethics of place in my village of Williston, the state of Vermont, the United States, and other parts of the world. (Mieder 2011, 18–19)

A few years later, my friend Mark Stoler together with Larry I. Bland edited the massive sixth volume of *The Papers of George Catlett Marshall* with its proverbial title *"The Whole World Hangs in the Balance": January 8, 1947–September 30, 1949* (2013). I knew he was involved with this enormous scholarly undertaking, of which he edited the seventh and final volume in 2016. During one of our numerous historical discussions, I congratulated him on the conclusion of this significant project and in passing asked him which volume dealt in particular with the Marshall Plan. As I should have known and remembered, the definitive answer was volume 6, showing me by a raised eyebrow and a smiling face that I surely must be aware of that. A few days later, I went to the library, checked out the 805-page volume, and started reading it at night in bed, with my wife loving to tell the story that her husband always has a heavy book of people like Otto von Bismarck, Martin Luther King Jr., Willy Brandt, Barack Obama, and lately George Marshall on his chest. But the Marshall volume that has been my most recent late-evening reading was a special experience, since it deepened my understanding and appreciation of this giant of a man whose sincere, precise, and well-thought-out rhetoric resulted in effective action that made the world a better place.

Speaking of the world, George Marshall, in his role as the United States Army chief of staff, had become only too aware that the world is an interconnected place and that the United States as a major player during World War II needed to think and act globally. This recognition deepened as he took on the position of secretary of state during the aftermath of the war from 1947 through 1949. Even though the phrase "the world is a small place" had not yet been registered as an obvious proverb, Marshall in his "Speech to the Congress of Industrial Organizations [CIO]" on October 15, 1947, in Boston, made good use of it: "It is rather trite to say that the world is now a small place but that is a fact and what happens in distant places affects our affairs and our lives inevitably, often very quickly, and sometimes most seriously. The present situation in Europe is definitely of the last-mentioned character" (226; unless otherwise noted, all page references are from Bland and Stoler 2013).

Citing the fact of a small world once again at the Annual Meeting of the National Farm Institute on February 13, 1948, in Knoxville, Tennessee, Marshall repeated the wisdom and elaborated on it by pointing out that the proverb "mind your own business" should not lead to an isolationist world view by Americans. The following excerpt includes a rather rare but touching subjective reference to a meeting that he had two days earlier with a group of Cub Scouts at the State Department that clearly moved him (he again recalled this memorable encounter in his "Commencement Address at the Pennsylvania College for Women" on June 12, 1950, in Pittsburgh (Stoler 2016, 102–4).

> A few days ago a group of seven little cub scouts came to see me in the State Department. They had started a Junior Marshall Plan and were engaged in raising funds to take care of some little children in Europe. They made a great impression on me by their alert appearance, their active, practical interest in doing something for children thousands of miles away. I thought of my boyhood, what I knew and felt about the world when I was nine years old, and it

moved me to make some comments on the great changes which had taken place in this country in my lifetime.

[... In the short period of my lifetime, we are now recognized everywhere as being the most powerful Nation in the world and being the acknowledged leader in the world.

Therefore, I think it is all the more impressive and all the finer for a group of boys your age to undertake what you are now trying to do. That is a generous and fine action on your part for the children of Europe who are so much in need of your help. And it is of great international importance in establishing relations of friendship and good will and trust that are so important to our Government, to our people and to the world and to peace. (355)]

All of which means that the world is now a very small place. We cannot live apart and aloof from what is taking place across the seas. The future for a family in Iowa is not limited to conditions in the Mississippi valley, however far that may be from the sea coast, or from Berlin or Cairo, New Delhi or Nanking. I acknowledge that it is a good rule to mind your own business, but that should not be taken to mean that we should ignore starvation in the next block. (360)

As Marshall in his role as secretary of state was helping President Truman to give Germany a chance to rejoin the international community, he did well to remind the Russians in his "Statement on Reconstruction of Germany on a Democratic Basis" on March 14, 1947, in Moscow, what democracy means. In fact, he was, albeit indirectly, lecturing Stalin on democratic principles as the Soviet leader was strengthening his control over Eastern European countries behind the Iron Curtain. He was, after all, only too aware of what his wartime friend Winston Churchill had stated on March 5, 1946, at Westminster College in Fulton, Missouri: "From Stettin in the Baltic to Trieste in the Adriatic, an iron curtain has descended across the Continent. Behind that line lie all the capitals of the ancient states of Central and Eastern Europe, Warsaw, Berlin, Prague, Vienna, Budapest, Belgrade, Bucharest, Sofia, all these famous cities and the populations around them lie in what I must call the Soviet sphere, and all are subject in one form or another, not only to Soviet influence, but to a very high, and in many cases, increasing measure of control from Moscow" (James 1974, 7:7290; Mieder 1997, 56).

Here then is Marshall's definition of democracy that includes the well-known and often repeated proverbial triad of "life, liberty, and the pursuit of happiness" from the Declaration of Independence (Aron 2008, 89–96):

I realize that the word *democracy* is given many interpretations. To the American Government and citizen it has a basic meaning. We believe that human beings have certain inalienable rights, that is, rights which may not be given or taken away. They include the right of every individual to develop his mind and his soul in ways of his own choice, free of fear or coercion—provided only he does not interfere with the like right of others. To us a society is not democratic if men who respect the rights of their fellow men are not free to express their own beliefs and convictions without fear that they may be snatched away from their home and family. To us a society is not free if law-abiding citizens live in fear of being denied the right to work or deprived of life, liberty, and the pursuit of happiness. (77–78)

It is a bit surprising to me personally that Marshall did not cite the proverb "all men are created equal" that usually precedes the triad (Mieder 2015a), and I also think he missed the opportunity here to quote the most succinct proverbial definition of democracy that has its beginnings in the late eighteenth century and was popularized by way of Abraham Lincoln's closing sentence of the Gettysburg Address of November 19, 1863: "government of the people, by the people, for the people" (Mieder 2003). These two proverbial statements are part and parcel of America's sociopolitical history, and they have been cited repeatedly by the presidents (Mieder and Bryan 1997; Mieder 2000, 2009) and other famous leaders like Frederick Douglass, Elisabeth Cady Stanton and Susan B. Anthony, Martin Luther King Jr., and Hillary Rodham Clinton (Mieder 2001, 2010, 2014, 2015b).

The dealings with the Soviets, especially with his Russian counterpart Vyacheslav Molotov, could indeed be frustrating, especially regarding the fate of Germany (Mayer 1969; Gimbel 1976, 247–66; Maier 1991). This becomes clear from Marshall's "Statement to the Eighteenth Meeting of the Council of Foreign Ministers" on March 31, 1947, in Moscow, where he employed the proverbial phrase "to sell the same horse twice" to add considerable metaphorical expressiveness to his description of the Russian double talk during negotiations.

> We must make certain, however, that when we reach agreement, the agreement means the same thing to all of us. . . . We regret that the Soviet Delegation found it necessary to state "the acceptance of reparations from current production is an absolute condition of the Soviet Delegation's acceptance of the principle of economic unity." The Potsdam agreement for economic unity [of Germany] was not conditioned on the acceptance of reparation from current production. The United States categorically rejects the imposition of such a condition. It looks very much to us as though the Soviet Union is trying to sell the same horse twice. (86–87)

Separating fact from fiction was always on Marshall's mind as he negotiated the troubled waters of diplomacy as secretary of state. This involved the press as well, whose responsibility he saw as presenting not only the facts but also the underlying truth of these very facts. To drive this point across, he cited the proverb "a little knowledge is a dangerous thing" in a "Speech to Business Organizations Representatives" on June 4, 1947, in Washington.

> You will remember the conclusion reached by a recent, privately sponsored study of the American press [Commission on the Freedom of the Press], that "No longer is it enough to report the fact truthfully. It is now necessary to report the truth about the fact." This distinction applies with particular force in matters of foreign policy. Merely to report truthfully the day-to-day fact of our foreign relations is to leave the task of informing the public less than half done—and in a democracy a little knowledge of foreign affairs can be a truly dangerous thing. The balance of an over-all perspective, of "the truth about the fact," is indispensable to the public understanding. (146, see note 4)

In order to increase the knowledge of the complex and challenging foreign affairs of postwar America, Marshall frequently saw himself in the position of having to educate the powers that be as well as the general public about the status of the world outside of the United States, with a special concern for the developments in Europe. Together with such highly qualified advisors as Dean Acheson, Charles Bohlen, Will Clayton, and George F. Kennan, he oversaw in a period of merely two years at the helm of the State Department "some of the most important and revolutionary developments in the history of U.S. foreign relations. Under the impact of its growing conflict with the Soviet Union, the United States during these years articulated an activist, global foreign policy highlighted by the Truman Doctrine, the Marshall Plan, the containment policy, and moves that would culminate in the creation of West Germany and the North Atlantic Treaty Organization (NATO)" (Stoler 1989, 152). As these highly qualified government officials with the blessing of President Truman developed the idea of the European Recovery Program that became known as the Marshall Plan, George Marshall needed a public forum to explain its underlying rationale and intent. The occasion presented itself when he was recognized with a "doctor honoris causa" from Harvard University on June 5, 1947. In his "Speech to the Harvard University Alumni," drafted with the help of Bohlen and Kennan, he outlined this plan to aid and rebuild Europe, and this communication is considered to be the beginning of what has become known throughout the world as the Marshall Plan. It was above all a plan for economic recovery, but it most certainly had a humanitarian side to it, as becomes ever clearer in later statements by Marshall.

In considering the requirements for the rehabilitation of Europe, the physical loss of life, the visible destruction of cities, factories, mines and railroads was correctly estimated, but it has become obvious during recent months that this visible destruction was probably less serious than the dislocation of the entire fabric of European economy.... The rehabilitation of the economic structure of Europe quite evidently will require a much longer time and greater effort than had been foreseen....

The truth of the matter is that Europe's requirement for the next three or four years of foreign food and other essential products—principally from America—are so much greater than her present ability to pay that she must have substantial additional help, or face economic, social and political deterioration of a very grave character....

It is logical that the United States should do whatever it is able to do to assist in the return of normal economic health in the world, without which there can be no political stability and no assured peace. Our policy is directed not against any country [notably the Soviet Union] or doctrine [i.e., Communism] but against hunger, poverty, desperation and chaos. Its purpose should be the revival of a working economy in the world so as to permit the emergence of political and social conditions in which free institutions can exist. Such assistance, I am convinced, must not be on a piece-meal basis as various crises develop. Any assistance that this Government may render for the future should provide a cure rather than a mere palliative. (147–48)

It should be noted here that Marshall and his colleagues envisioned an aid plan for all of Europe that unfortunately was boycotted by the Soviet Union as Stalin established his iron grip over Eastern Europe. In his retrospective "Remarks at Meeting, Hunter College" on November 29, 1949, in New York City, Marshall expressed his disappointment about these developments that ushered in the Cold War: "I have always regretted that we could not have proceeded on the Recovery Plan on a Europe-wide basis as was originally suggested, regretted that suspicions for which there was no basis—or Communistic intentions, as seems to have been the case, caused the gauntlet to be flung down by others along the line of the iron curtain" (Stoler 2016, 36).

It is interesting to note that Marshall does not go into much detail but rather chooses to employ the fitting proverbial expression "to fling (throw) down the gauntlet" to refer to the antagonistic Soviet policy in an indirect way.

In any case, the relatively short but consequential Harvard speech of just three printed pages (147–49) got the proverbial ball rolling. Someone else might have carried on for a much longer time, but Marshall was a strong believer in clear and concise communications that hopefully would not be open to all types of different interpretations. He explained this modus operandi in a splendid paragraph in his short (barely more than two printed pages) "Speech to the Graduates of the National War College" on June 20, 1947, in Washington. Surely the eager graduates must have enjoyed his use of the truncated proverb "the proof of the pudding is in the eating."

> I recall that in dealing with President Roosevelt I found it advantageous not only to make my requests as brief as possible, but actually to reduce them to a piece of paper about one-third the length of an ordinary sheet, if I could concentrate the essence of the problem in that restricted space. I had a letterhead prepared that was close to the top of the paper so that when the unused portion of the paper was cut off immediately below my signature the entire paper was often no more than five or six inches in length. Now, as a matter of interest and as the proof of the pudding, I usually got an "OK, FDR", and what was important I got an immediate decision. My previous experience had been that the technical General Staff document was seldom read beyond the first few paragraphs and usually provoked an irritating response. I found that the same proposal boiled down to the fewest possible paragraphs generally got favorable and immediate action. And this is only logical when you consider the tremendous pressures on a Chief Executive, particularly in time of war. My experiences with the Committees of Congress were somewhat similar, exactly similar so far as condensation of statements was concerned and the use of terminology and illustrations easily understandable to the civilian. (158)

And yet, despite Marshall's attempt at honest, open, and direct communication regarding the European Recovery Program, he saw himself again and again in a position to have to defend its basic intent, which he reiterated in a "Speech to the Women's National Press Club" on July 1, 1947, in Washington, by employing the emotionally loaded proverbial expression "to lend a helping hand."

> Historical records clearly show that no people have ever acted more generously and more unselfishly than the American people in tendering assistance to alleviate distress and suffering. The history of past decades records numerous examples of readiness to lend a helping hand in situations where there could not possibly have been other compensation than the satisfaction that comes from assisting those in need.
> But it would not be entirely accurate to say that the efforts of this Government to contribute to the restoration of world economy since the termination of the recent war have been motivated solely by considerations of charity. Our people do realize, I feel sure, that a stable and prosperous world is important to their own well-being. (166)

Just like President Truman, Marshall was a straight shooter who didn't mince words, as can be seen from these words from the same speech with which he countered reactions from some quarters that the recovery plan was nothing but an imperialistic venture by the United States: "There could be no more fantastic misrepresentation, no more malicious distortion of the truth than the frequent propaganda assertions of implications that the United States has imperialist aims or that American aid has been offered in order to fasten upon the recipients some form of political and economic domination" (166).

At the heart of the matter, as far as Marshall was concerned, was always the wish of "restoring hope and confidence among the people concerned that the world will know peace and security in the future" (167). But it is amazing how aware Marshall was of the importance of language in communicating his diplomatic endeavors to people at home. "Marshall believed that language used in organizational communication [and also in his many speeches] should be brief and concise, employ the plainest words capable of conveying intended meaning, and be appropriate to the audience" (Pops 2009, 193). He explained this convincingly in his "Speech to the Governors' Conference" on July 14, 1947, in Salt Lake City: "State papers and state pronouncements must be couched in diplomatic, at least dignified phraseology, and unless one is a master of the English language, such as Mr. Churchill for example, it is very difficult to combine these requirements with the urgent necessity of making impressively clear to the ordinary citizen the matter under discussion" (173).

There was deep respect and admiration between Churchill and Marshall, and the latter must have been touched by Churchill's handwritten note to him of September 24, 1947, that concludes, "It gives me confidence in these days of anxiety—in some ways more painful than war time ordeals—to know that you are at the helm of the most powerful of nations, and to feel myself in such complete accord with what you say and do" (223n2). It is interesting to observe that Churchill, as a former first lord of the admiralty, uses the maritime proverbial expression "to be at the helm" to acknowledge Marshall's effective leadership as the United States secretary of state (see Mieder and Bryan 1995).

There is no doubt that a proverb or a proverbial expression now and then—there is certainly no abundance of them in Marshall's papers—add a bit of colloquial color to his quite serious messages. This is certainly the case in his "Testimony on Admitting Displaced Persons to the United States" on July 16, 1947, at a congressional hearing in Washington. In his argument that the United States should accept displaced persons from Europe just as this country had been telling Western European countries to do, he cited the proverb "practice what you preach" twice by adding the pronoun "we" to it, thus bringing his point home to the American citizens.

In our discussions with other countries we are constantly met with the question, "What is the United States, which is urging others to accept these people as useful and desirable immigrants, doing about accepting a part of them itself?" If we practice what we preach, if we admit a substantial number of these people as immigrants, then with what others are already doing and will do we can actually bring an end to this tragic situation. In so doing, we will also confirm our moral leadership and demonstrate that we are not retreating behind the Atlantic Ocean.

If we practice what we preach, if we admit a substantial number of these people as immigrants, then with what others are already doing and will do we can actually bring an end to this tragic situation. In so doing, we will also confirm our moral leadership and demonstrate that we are not retreating behind the Atlantic Ocean.

I repeated that because it is the kernel of the whole business. You cannot assert leadership and then not exercise it.

Although we have left it to other countries to take the lead in active measures to alleviate this tragic situation, yet we are actually in a better position to receive a substantial number of these people than any other nation. We have numbers of the stock already in this country who know their language and who have the resources and interest to assume the task of fitting a relatively small number of their kinsmen into our vast economy, without expense to this Nation in their resettlement, and with a reasonable assurance that they will not become public charges. (180)

The fact that George Marshall repeats his proverbial call for action is indicative of his sincere commitment to have this country fully engaged in this humanitarian crisis. His words should well be recalled as the United States deals with refugee problems from various countries throughout the globe today. But I would also add a small personal comment here. My father, Horst Mieder, was placed in charge by the British of a large displaced persons camp at this time in Lübeck, Germany. I remember well going with him and meeting many wonderful people from the Baltic countries, Poland, Hungary, and other Eastern European countries. My dad helped many of them to immigrate to the United States, who, once they resettled, wrote touching letters to him (see some selections in Pletzing 2007, 102–6). I am wondering at times if all of this planted the seed in me to find my own way to America some ten years later.

Of course, to continue with these personal reflections, I was only three and a half years old when George Marshall gave his "NBC Radio Speech" on August 15, 1947, in Washington, and yet in an indirect way, he was talking to me as one of the children who were dependent on American aid, especially in the form of food and clothing. In this speech, Marshall was still trying to convince Congress to approve the European Recovery Program, and one can sense the sincerity and urgency that he felt for its eventual passage that hopefully would get the people and their countries, proverbially speaking, "back on their feet."

> Two years ago the last shot sounded in the most destructive war in history. In the peace and plenty of America this may seem a long time—time enough to forget. But to millions of people of Europe and Asia the destructive effect of the war is still today a living and present and terrible thing. They live in a region of depopulated villages, demolished factories and homes, unfertile fields, destroyed herds, wrecked railroads, inflated economics, and demoralized people.—And of all these war-born troubles the worst is the evil of the empty plate. Hundreds of millions of men, women and children will go to bed hungry tonight, as they have for an endless procession of nights—some of them for eight long years.
>
> Americans want a prosperous world. We want to see a world economy restored from the destruction of war and moving forward towards the higher levels of prosperity which science today makes possible. We know that the sooner the countries of Europe and Asia can get back on their feet, the sooner the need for special relief from the United States will cease. We must realize that the United Nations cannot hope to retain even the present level of prosperity in a degenerate world.
>
> Rehabilitation demands intensive work over a long period on the part of every able-bodied person in war-torn countries. It is physically impossible for this work to be performed with a deficiency of food. Food is the basis of all reconstruction. It is psychologically impossible for a hungry person to work with the drive, the vision and the cooperative spirit that will be necessary. (195; see Price 1955, 87–111)

Uncharacteristically for Marshall, he concluded his short address with a proverbial line from the Lord's Prayer that must have moved his religiously grounded American audience: "Let us, as Americans, be truly grateful to a bountiful providence which has blessed us with plenty for ourselves and given us the means of helping others. Let us never forget that all over the world today millions of our fellow men will be praying with desperate appeal—'Give us this day our daily bread . . .'" (196).

A few months later, in his "Radio Speech on the Food Conservation Program" on October 5, 1947, in New York City, Marshall spoke with even greater urgency to convince American citizens to help starving people abroad by "tightening their belts," with the proverbial expression adding a drastic image to his plea: "European economy might well break down under the intolerable strain of another winter of hunger, cold, and want. . . . And the evil consequences of a European collapse would spread in ever-widening circles until we too would be seriously affected.

Food from America can prevent this chain of events. The American people can meet the shortage by an all-out, united effort to avoid waste of food and economize in food consumption. We can tighten our belts—clean our plates—push ourselves away from the table" (222).

Three weeks later, in his "Speech to the Herald-Tribune Forum" on October 22, 1947, in New York City, Marshall stated that the time for getting the idea of a European recovery program on solid footing by way of governmental approval had come after several months of discussions. With him as its major champion, people were already referring to the European Recovery Program (as it was officially called) as the Marshall Plan, with the humble Marshall finding that designation somewhat out of place.

> I do not believe any project of our Government has ever received more careful study and preparation than has this problem of the reconstruction of Europe. And I am certain that no governmental effort has ever enjoyed such complete cooperation on the part of all the agencies concerned. When it is completed it will truly be a program of the United States Government and not of any department or agency....
>
> There has been constant reference to a Marshall Plan. The reference to me personally was unfortunate, but the reference to a plan was definitely misleading. There was no plan. There was a suggestion. Now we are in the process of drafting a plan as a proposal to the Congress of the United States. That is the situation at the moment.
>
> The period of study and preparation is thus drawing to a close. The time of action is at hand. (232)

Not quite three weeks later, on November 10, 1947, George Marshall gave his lengthy "Statement to a Joint Meeting of the Senate Foreign Relations and House Foreign Affairs Committees" that includes the following passionate plea for approval based in part on a restatement of such proverbs as "help others as they help you," "you always help yourself by helping others," and "God helps those who help themselves" (Mieder, Kingsbury, and Harder 1992, 255, 297).

> The automatic success of the program cannot be guaranteed. The imponderables are many. The risks are real. They are, however, risks which have been carefully calculated, and I believe the chances of success are good. There is convincing evidence that the peoples of Western Europe want to preserve their free society and the heritage we share with them. To make that choice conclusive they need our assistance. It is in the American tradition to help. In helping them we will be helping ourselves—because in the larger sense our national interests coincide with those of a free and prosperous Europe.
>
> We must not fail to meet this inspiring challenge. We must not permit the free community of Europe to be extinguished. Should this occur it would

be a tragedy for the world. It would impose incalculable burdens upon this country and force serious readjustments in our traditional way of life. One of our important freedoms—freedom for choice in domestic and foreign affairs would be drastically curtailed.

Whether we like it or not, we find ourselves, our Nation, in a world position of vast responsibility. We can act for our own good by acting for the world's good. (254–55)

About two weeks later, during his "Speech to the American Society of London" on November 27, 1947, Marshall told his British audience something quite similar, but this time working the proverb "nobody is perfect" into his concluding paragraph, expressing humility, as America by necessity must play the leadership role in rebuilding Europe. Great Britain rightfully received the largest share of the Marshall Plan in due time; (the other fifteen countries were Austria, Belgium, Denmark, France, Germany, Greece, Iceland, Ireland, Italy, Luxembourg, Netherlands, Norway, Portugal, Sweden, and Turkey (756–57; Wilson 1977, 26–28): "I have confidence that the American people will not be deterred by criticism, name calling or any form or degree of misrepresentation from doing their invariable generous best to help the other fellow. That's the American tradition. It's the finest trait of our people. We may humanly err in our procedure at times. The Lord knows, and we are well advised, that we are far from perfect. But we do our best, I think, in every important test and the American people can be depended upon to do their very best in the present great emergency" (276).

It might well be that Marshall also had the proverb "man proposes, God disposes" in mind when he formulated this heartfelt statement about the necessary and worthwhile American commitment to the greater good of humankind during the hard years after World War II.

At this time, it had already become clear that Germany would be a divided country at the insistence of the Soviet Union. Marshall spoke directly of this unfortunate fact in his "Address on the London Conference of Foreign Ministers" on December 19, 1947, in Washington.

> It was clearly evident that for many years Germany would be involved in a desperate struggle to build up sufficient foreign trade to pay for the food and other items on which she will be dependent from outside sources. The best example of this phase of the situation that I can give is the present necessity for Great Britain and the United States to pay out some 700 millions a year to provide the food and other items to prevent starvation and rather complete disintegration of that portion of Germany occupied by our forces. . . .
>
> We cannot look forward to a unified Germany at this time. We must do the best we can in the area where our influence can be felt. (300–301)

Of course, large sums of money were needed, and understandably it took a great effort to sell Americans on making sacrifices after having done so much to bring the war to an end. It goes to Marshall's richly deserved credit that he soldiered on in advocating for the recovery program in Europe while the United States was itself in the process of getting back to normalcy. He made the following fitting comments in his "Statement to the Senate Committee on Foreign Relations" of January 8, 1948.

> We have engaged in a great war. We poured out our resources to win that war. We fought it to make real peace possible. Though the war has ended the peace has not commenced. We must not fail to complete that which we commenced.
> The peoples of Western Europe have demonstrated their will to achieve a genuine recovery by entering into a great cooperative effort. Within the limits of their resources they formally undertake to establish the basis for the peace which we all seek, but they cannot succeed without American assistance. Dollars will not save the world, but the world today cannot be saved without dollars....
> We are dealing with democratic governments. One of the major justifications of asking the American people to make the sacrifice necessary under this [recovery] program is the vital stake that the United States has in helping to preserve democracy in Europe. As democratic governments they are responsive, like our own, to the peoples of their countries—and we would not have it otherwise. (310–11, 315)

The common proverbial expression "to have a stake in something" is of paramount significance in this powerful endorsement of democratic governments, and it shows that it was definitely in the self-interest of the United States to support the democratic aspirations in Western Europe. But of importance is also the statement "dollars will not save the world, but the world today cannot be saved without dollars." It certainly has a proverbial ring to it, and its first half has in fact reached somewhat of a proverbial status if several thousand Google hits can be trusted.

But there is another powerful proverbial metaphor in this speech which, with its ten pages of text (309–19), is one of Marshall's longer official presentations. The seemingly simple proverbial expression "to be (hang) in the balance" with the basic meaning of "to be in a position where an outcome of something is not known—as though one is waiting for a balance to be tipped one way or the other" (Rees 2006, 287) appears first in a very short paragraph toward the end of the speech: "To be quite clear, this unprecedented endeavor of the New World to help the Old is neither sure nor easy. It is a calculated risk. But there can be no doubts as to the alternatives. The way of life that we have known is literally in balance" (319).

As if this image were not already drastic enough, he repeated the proverbial expression in his very last paragraph of this long address, this time citing a more explicit variant of "hanging in the balance" to bring the urgency of the acceptance and implementation of the Marshall Plan into inescapable focus.

> I would like to close by saying that this is a complex program. It is a difficult program. And you know, far better than I do, the political difficulties involved in this program [in reference to the Soviet Union and its own Molotov Plan]. But there is no doubt whatever in my mind that if we decide to do this thing we can do it successfully, and there is no doubt in my mind that the whole world hangs in the balance, as to what it is to be, in connection with what we are endeavoring to put forward here. (319)

Here is yet another serendipitous matter: When I reached this statement in my reading of this fascinating historical and sociopolitical volume, I made a note to myself that "the whole world hangs in the balance" could very well serve as the proverbial title of my paper. But then, when I typed its bibliographical information, I realized that Larry Bland and Mark Stoler had chosen the phrase as the title of this particular volume of *The Papers of George Catlett Marshall*. Not wanting to repeat this ingenious choice, I looked for another proverbial expression used by George Marshall for my title and came across "to rise to the occasion," as will become clear in due time.

On the same day, January 8, 1948, Marshall gave an additional *five hours* of "Senate Testimony on the European Recovery Program," employing the four proverbial expressions "to get (back) on one's feet," "to get down to business," "to get the ball rolling," and "to break the bottleneck"—an amassment of metaphors that is rather uncharacteristic of Marshall's normal speech. Even without citing their context, it becomes clear that Marshall is growing frustrated with all of this continued testimony, talk, questioning, etc. without getting closer to the so-much-needed actual action on behalf of the suffering people in Europe. There exists the wonderful proverb "the mills of the gods grind slowly, but they grind exceedingly fine" with several variants (Mieder, Kingsbury, Harder 1992, 411), and I am sure that Marshall in his mind must have substituted for the ancient gods "government" in general or "the Senate" in particular. At least he knew that he had the definite support from President Truman, for whom George Marshall was a hero par excellence, all along the way. But here is what the secretary of state said.

> My concern in the matter [of integration among the European nations], to state it very frankly, is to get this affair going in such a way that the cooperation, the

commitments, which bring those countries closer together will increase rather than remain as they are at the time they begin to get more or less on their feet. [See Hogan 1987, 88–134.]

I feel certain that if we had not had a tragic dilemma of vast proportions we never could have gotten these agreements [of cooperation] out of the western nations at all. It could have been talked about and would for many, many years [Marshall would be surprised if he could see the European Union today], but, like unity of command, all will agree with you in principle but they won't agree with you when you get down to business, unless it is their man that is in command, unless it is their business that is to be protected.

The $6.8 billion European Recovery Program request which is a very sizable amount for us [the Senate] to consider for the American taxpayer, is yet a very small percentage of the whole requirement, but it is the important portion needed to start the ball rolling. You might say it fulminates the charge. It will begin to break the bottlenecks. (323)

A crude scatological proverb comes to mind which Marshall could have uttered here at the end of five hours of testimony, but frustrated as the secretary of state might have been after this grueling event, he would never have lowered himself to such a level as a soldier-diplomat trained in proper social etiquette.

It would still take three more months before President Truman would sign the bill for the European Recovery Program. In the meantime, the untiring Marshall gave one speech or testimony after another to advocate for it, such as his "Speech to the National Cotton Council" on January 22, 1948, in Atlanta. Stressing that economic aid might well be the most important part of this aid package, he quoted the biblical proverb "man does not live by bread alone" (Deuteronomy 8:3, Matthew 4:4) to underscore this claim without wanting to downplay the ever-present need for food.

> Never was it more true than it is today in Europe that "man does not live by bread alone." The war, with its legacy of hardships and suffering, has placed cruel strains on the people of that continent. It has caused them to question in many cases the basic principles on which their society—and ours—has developed.
>
> Today, they are troubled not only about their economic problems but also about some of the most profound questions of political philosophy [i.e., between democracy and communism]. And, they are extremely sensitive to the impulses which come to them from outside, and to the degree of support which they feel they have from this country.
>
> What is at stake here is not only the economic basis of European society. It is the confidence of the Europeans in themselves and in this western civilization to which they and we belong. There are powerful forces which are urging them to part with this faith, and to entrust themselves to a political system which involved the abandonment of their liberties. (339–40)

Proverbially speaking, there was indeed much at stake, and one senses that the Marshall Plan had a political side to it in keeping at least Western Europe safe for democracy. In his "Speech Delivered at the Mid-Point Anniversary of ECA [Economic Cooperation Act, passed by Congress to administer the ERP]" on April 3, 1950, in Washington, Marshall delved deeper into the political split between East and West that prevented the Marshall Plan from supplying aid to Eastern Europe. Here the experienced general and former secretary of state reflects on the relationship between the Marshall Plan and the buildup of the Cold War and warns in no uncertain terms that this struggle is of greatest importance. The statement "Make no mistake about it, the chips are down," with its intensifying phrase, followed by the proverbial expression underscoring the crucial state of the political situation, serves as a metaphorical wake-up call to face these political developments head-on.

> We are now engaged in a great struggle. You here may not be in the same sort of physical danger as troops on the battlefield, but you are engaged in a contest with a foe who has designs no less deadly than those we have ever faced. Make no mistake about it, the chips are down. Winning this struggle is as vital to peace and prosperity of the world as any military campaign in history. I think it is important these critical days to have constantly in mind that the original suggestion of the European Recovery Program applied to all of Europe. The present division between the East and the West was drawn by Mr. Molotov for the Kremlin. Indeed, unless we achieve victory our great military and financial sacrifices may have been largely in vain, I fear. (Stoler 2016, 74–75)

But, always the pragmatic optimist, Marshall argued for the continuation of the European Recovery Program for two more years until its planned cessation on June 30, 1952, so that at least Western Europe could "get its house in order," as the proverbial expression would have it.

> It is true that for Western Europe to get its economic house in such order that it can survive and prosper in this competitive modern world requires a tremendous effort over the next two years. The erasing of old trade barriers and the construction of new channels, such as a clearing union for Europe's varied moneys, may require a miracle of cooperation.
>
> But, looking again at the conditions prevalent in the spring of 1947, and again considering the situation at this moment, I can only feel that one near miracle has been accomplished. We must work for, and expect, another miracle. (Stoler 2016, 75–76)

One would not necessarily expect a former general to speak of miracles, but this prophetic statement has been proven amazingly correct. The Marshall Plan was a secular miracle in rebuilding Western Europe;

the struggle between East and West was eventually ended, with the principles of democracy establishing themselves in large parts of Eastern Europe as well, and Marshall's hints at a united Europe have also come true.

And yes, politics and economics played a major role in pushing the European Recovery Program along, with some revisionist cynics claiming that the entire aid package was nothing more than America spreading its imperialistic hegemony over Western Europe as the Kremlin leaders did over Eastern Europe. Be that as it may, democracy was at stake, and lest we forget, lives had to be saved, lives of children who were starving and with whom rested the future of a new Europe. It was this threat of the severe shortage of food that never left Marshall's concerned mind and humanitarian drive. In his "Remarks Before the National Garden Institute" on February 2, 1948, in Washington, he stated this with the utmost urgency: "I have said or pointed out on a number of occasions since I became Secretary of State a year ago the tremendous importance of food. Because when hunger and illness invade the home men will accept almost any cure that is proposed at the moment. Anything is better than the existing circumstance and you have the ripest possible field for demagogic, audacious or calculated propaganda and planning and scheming. Therefore, the food has great importance" (347).

In his "Remarks to the National Farm Institute Annual Meeting" on February 13, 1948, in Knoxville, Tennessee, he continued his crusade to get the European Recovery Program accepted by Congress. His use of the proverbial comparison "clear as crystal" underscores his efforts to explain this complex program as straightforwardly as possible to the American people, while his employment of the proverbial expression "to be at the crossroads" emphasizes the fact that the European crisis needs immediate and resolute action.

> The European Recovery Program is far more than a mere economic transaction. It represents a tremendous effort of constructive leadership. If adopted, it will rank, I think, as one of the great historic undertakings in the annals of world civilizations....
>
> What I wish to make clear as crystal is the great objective of the program and its relationship to the future of the world and this country of ours. Make no mistake, the consequences of its success or failure will determine the survival of the kind of a world in which democracy, individual liberty, economic stability and peace can be maintained....
>
> In my opinion, we are quite literally at the crossroads. The decision we must make will set the course of history for a long time to come and our own destiny for a distant future. (357–58)

Marshall was realist enough to admit that the program might well have its flaws, for as the proverb says, "nothing is perfect." And even though the program had bipartisan support in the end, there were plenty of proverbial "pulls and tugs" while American politics were preoccupied by the presidential campaign of Harry S. Truman. By pointing to the strengths of the program while also admitting its imperfections, Marshall employed effective proverbial rhetoric to argue his important cause.

> I do not think ever before in our history has such intensive work been done and so many people of recognized talent and experience been consulted or employed as in the preparation of the European Recovery Program. I know that never before have various departments of the government so closely coordinated their efforts to a single end. Even so, of course, it is not perfect. Nothing ever is perfect, particularly when it must be exposed to all the political tugs and pulls of a Presidential campaign. But I think in its general framework and conception it will stand the strains and justify the forethought and wisdom of those who gave so much time and thought to its preparation. (361)

After prolonged analysis, countless hearings, and much back-and-forth in Congress and elsewhere, the European Recovery Program was finally approved and signed by President Truman on April 3, 1948, who, by insisting that it be called the Marshall Plan, honored George Marshall as its primary champion. Marshall did not falter in his commitment to the program in the ensuing months and years until the Marshall Plan came to its highly successful termination in 1952. This can be seen especially in his "Speech on Behalf of American Overseas Aid and the UN Appeal for Children" on May 25, 1948, in New York City. Since I was one of those children, I am deeply touched by these historic remarks: "I am sure that there is no one listening tonight who does not recognize that children whose bodies have been starved and warped are likely to develop, if they survive, into a generation of embittered adults. Our national interest, as well as our humanitarian instinct, demands that we do not permit this to happen. If we fail to do our part for the nourishment and care and normal development today of the children with whom our children will have to live tomorrow, we shall have failed in statesmanship as well as in humanity" (462).

Due in large part to the Marshall Plan, Americans played their part and stepped forth to help nourish children in particular. I know this only too well, and instead of growing up embittered, I was able to eat and develop normally, thanks in part to the Marshall Plan. I am well aware that the fate of European children was only part of this magnanimous aid package by the United States, but George Marshall's kindness and special interest in children add a wonderful human touch to this great soldier-statesman. Millions of people benefitted from the Marshall Plan, which gave them the opportunity to rebuild their countries with democratic governments, get their economies back on track, and by working together begin the process of the modern united Europe.

Of course, President Truman was also deeply appreciative of his secretary of state, and when George Marshall retired, primarily for health reasons, from this post on January 3, 1949, the thankful president wrote to him on January 7.

> As Chief of Staff of the United States Army you were the guide and counselor of two Commanders in Chief [Franklin D. Roosevelt and Harry S. Truman]. You brought to the performance of your task abilities and qualifications which inspired the armies of the Democratic nations to victory in a war unparalleled in magnitude and in the vastness of the issues involved.
>
> When the great office of Secretary of State became vacant it seemed to me fortunate that you were available for the position, although you had richly earned retirement. As it turned out, your previous training and experience were a preparation for the onerous duties which befell you in directing our foreign affairs—particularly in the formulation and execution of the Marshall Plan. (648)

Surely George Marshall must have appreciated the fact that the president did not use the official title of European Recovery Program but rather the designation "Marshall Plan" that had quickly become the preferred name. In fact, it has become somewhat proverbial to speak of a large-scale rescue plan as being "equivalent to the Marshall Plan."

Of course, it was not George Marshall alone who made the European Recovery Program possible. The president, members of Congress, high-level advisors, government officials, and dedicated bureaucrats all helped in their own ways. The titles of three comprehensive books summarize the enormous accomplishments of this undertaking, and since I always tell my students that they must work carefully on the titles of their papers so that they signal the crux of the matter, let me cite them here with their authors: Charles L. Mee, *The Marshall Plan: The Launching of the Pax Americana* (1984), Greg Behrman, *The Most Noble Adventure: The Marshall Plan and the Time When America Helped Save Europe* (2007), and Gerald M. Pops, *Ethical Leadership in Turbulent Times: Modeling the Public Career of George C. Marshall* (2009). There can be no doubt that George Marshall, steeped in ethical convictions, brought about a sea change with his peaceful reconstruction of Europe.

It was George Marshall as the most positive Pied Piper who rose to the occasion to make a giant difference, and by his showing the way, the American people of all ages and walks of life followed suit. In his "Remarks at Marshall Plan Anniversary Dinner" on June 5, 1949, in Washington—two years after his speech at Harvard University—he gave eloquent and appreciative credit to the American people who rose to the occasion and lent a helping hand.

> To me, the impressive fact is that these people of the United States made an overwhelming and unhesitating decision to do their best to bring Western Europe back to peace and prosperity. There were, of course, speeches pro and con, but the American people rose to the occasion, to that world crisis, and declared themselves partners in the stupendous effort to restore Europe to a level of continuing peace. All participated—cities, towns, women's clubs, and the young people. Even little children played a valuable part. That was, and continues to be, an impressive demonstration of the heart of America. (716)

Looking back on the accomplishments of the European Recovery Program after the first half of its four-year duration, George Marshall observed on April 3, 1950, in Washington: "Let me sum up: We are engaged in a perilous struggle with an implacable foe: we must carry this battle to the finish; we must avoid the temptation to imperil the whole investment—and it is just that, an investment in saving all those precious articles of faith and ways of life we call democracy. It is an investment in preserving the freedom of men in a clean and decent world" (Stoler 2016, 76; see Hoffmann and Maier 1984).

Indeed, the Marshall Plan was a multifaceted investment in the future of humankind, planned and executed by a remarkable humanitarian who, despite his military, economic, and political actions on the world's stage, never forgot the little children. Caring for their survival played a role in the lasting success of George Marshall's visionary involvement of rebuilding Europe. He was what the Germans call a *Gutmensch*—a good man—and true to the proverb that "goodness is the only investment that never fails," he is remembered as an exemplary soldier-statesman of democracy who made a giant difference for millions of thankful people.

References

This chapter was first published in *Western Folklore* 76 (2017): 261–92.

Aron, Paul. 2008. *We Hold These Truths . . . And Other Words that Made America*. Lanham, MD: Rowman & Littlefield.

Behrman, Greg. 2007. *The Most Noble Adventure: The Marshall Plan and the Time When America Helped Save Europe.* New York: Free Press.
Bland, Larry I., and Mark A. Stoler, eds. 2013. *The Papers of George Catlett Marshall.* Volume 6. "The Whole World Hangs in the Balance." January 8, 1947–September 30, 1949. Baltimore: Johns Hopkins University Press.
Gimbel, John. 1976. *The Origins of the Marshall Plan.* Stanford, CA: Stanford University Press.
Hoffmann, Stanley, and Charles Maier, eds. 1984. *The Marshall Plan: A Retrospective.* Boulder, CO: Westview Press.
Hogan, Michael J. 1987. The *Marshall Plan: America, Britain, and the Reconstruction of Western Europe, 1947–1952.* Cambridge: Cambridge University Press.
James, Robert Rhodes, ed. 1974. *Winston S. Churchill: His Complete Speeches, 1897–1963.* 8 vols. London: Chelsea House.
Maier, Charles S., ed. 1991. *The Marshall Plan and Germany: West German Development within the Framework of the European Recovery Program.* Oxford: Berg.
Mayer, Herbert Carleton. 1969. *German Recovery and the Marshall Plan, 1948–1952.* New York: Edition Atlantic Forum.
Mee, Charles L. 1984. *The Marshall Plan: The Launching of the Pax Americana.* New York: Simon and Schuster.
Mieder, Wolfgang. 1997. *The Politics of Proverbs: From Traditional Wisdom to Proverbial Stereotypes.* Madison: University of Wisconsin Press.
———. 2000. *The Proverbial Abraham Lincoln: An Index to Proverbs in the Works of Abraham Lincoln.* New York: Peter Lang.
———. 2001. *"No Struggle, No Progress": Frederick Douglass and His Proverbial Rhetoric for Civil Rights.* New York: Peter Lang.
———. 2003. "'Government of the People, by the People, for the People': The Making and Meaning of an American Proverb." *Proverbium* 20:259–308. Also in Wolfgang Mieder, 2005. *"Proverbs Are the Best Policy": Folk Wisdom and American Politics,* 15–55, 248–58 (notes). Logan: Utah State University Press.
———. 2009. *"Yes We Can": Barack Obama's Proverbial Rhetoric.* New York: Peter Lang,
———. 2010. *"Making a Way Out of No Way": Martin Luther King's Sermonic Proverbial Rhetoric.* New York: Peter Lang.
———. 2011. "'It Takes a Village to Change the World.' Proverbial Politics and Ethics of Place." *Journal of American Folklore* 124:4–28. Also in Wolfgang Mieder, 2014. *"Behold the Proverbs of a People": Proverbial Wisdom in Culture, Literature, and Politics,* 198–229 (here 216–17). Jackson: University Press of Mississippi.
———. 2014. *"All Men and Women Are Created Equal": Elizabeth Cady Stanton's and Susan B. Anthony's Proverbial Rhetoric Promoting Women's Rights.* New York: Peter Lang.
———. 2015a. "'All Men Are Created Equal': From Democratic Claim to Proverbial Game." *Scientific Newsletter: Series: Modern Linguistic and Methodical-and-Didactic Researches (Voronezh State University of Architecture and Civil Engineering, Voronezh, Russia),* no volume given, no. 1: 10–37.
———. 2015b. "'Politics Is Not a Spectator Sport.' Proverbs in the Personal and Political Writings of Hillary Rodham Clinton." *Tautosakos Darbai/Folklore Studies* (Vilnius) 50: 43–74.
Mieder, Wolfgang, and George B. Bryan. 1995. *The Proverbial Winston S. Churchill: An Index to Proverbs in the Works of Sir Winston Churchill.* Westport, CT: Greenwood Press.

———. 1997. *The Proverbial Harry S. Truman: An Index to Proverbs in the Works of Harry S. Truman*. New York: Peter Lang.
Mieder, Wolfgang, Stewart A. Kingsbury, and Kelsie B. Harder, eds. 1992. *A Dictionary of American Proverbs*. New York: Oxford University Press.
Pletzing, Christian. 2007. "'Stadt der Displaced Persons.' DPs aus den baltischen Staaten in Lübeck." In *Displaced Persons: Flüchtlinge aus den baltischen Staaten in Deutschland*, edited by Christian and Marianne Pletzing, 85–106. München: Martin Meidenbauer.
Pops, Gerald M. 2009. *Ethical Leadership in Turbulent Times: Modeling the Public Career of George C. Marshall*. Lanham, MD: Lexington Books.
Price, Harry Bayard. 1955. *The Marshall Plan and Its Meaning*. Ithaca, NY: Cornell University Press.
Rees, Nigel. 2006. *A Word in Your Shell-Like: 6,000 Curious & Everyday Phrases Explained*. London: Collins.
Stoler, Mark A. 1989. *George C. Marshall: Soldier-Statesman of the American Century*. Boston: Twayne Publishers.
———, ed. 2016. *The Papers of George Catlett Marshall*. Vol. 7, *"The Man of the Age": October 1, 1949–October 16, 1959*. Baltimore, MD: Johns Hopkins University Press.
Wilson, Theodore A. 1977. *The Marshall Plan, 1947–1951 [1952]*. New York: Foreign Policy Association.

4

"MAKING A WAY OUT OF NO WAY"

*Martin Luther King Jr.'s Proverbial
Dream for Human Rights*

A VAST ARRAY OF BIOGRAPHIES AND STUDIES HAVE celebrated Martin Luther King Jr. (1929–1968) as a civil rights leader, a defender of nonviolence in the struggle for desegregation, a champion for the poor, an antiwar proponent, and a broad-minded visionary of an interrelated world of free people. The proverbial truths expressed in the beginning of the Declaration of Independence that "all men are created equal" and that they have the right to "life, liberty, and the pursuit of happiness" form the basis of his engaged and heartfelt fight for freedom, universal suffrage, antiracism, and socioeconomic improvements for minorities. As a communicator par excellence, he made ample use of fixed phrases as leitmotifs in his effective oral and written rhetoric in the service of a plethora of topics and causes. Even though the term *proverb* does not belong to King's active vocabulary, he most certainly delights in using folk and Bible proverbs, famous quotations (some of which have taken on a definite claim to proverbiality), and a wealth of proverbial phrases.

It is incomprehensible that the vast scholarship on King's magisterial use of the English language has hardly commented on the proverbial nature of his multifaceted communications. It is as if the study of rhetoric as a discipline by not stressing phraseological matters has prevented any attention being paid to such preformulated language. As the massive two-volume collection of recent essays entitled *Phraseology: An International Handbook of Contemporary Research* (Burger et al. 2007) shows, this picture is slowly changing, since rhetorical scholars are now more eager to include the disciplines of phraseology in general and paremiology (the study of proverbs) in particular (Mieder 2009a). Nevertheless, regarding the proverbial language of Martin Luther King Jr., the studies dedicated to his highly expressive and emotive language have almost completely ignored his reliance on proverbs and proverbial expressions, with my former student Dženeta Karabegović's revealing short essay "'No Lie Can Live Forever': Zur sprichwörtlichen Rhetorik von Martin Luther King" (2007) being the exception.

Having surveyed the extant secondary literature on King's sermonic and sociopolitical language, there is little to report. Mervyn A. Warren deals with the "vividness and imagery" as well as the "figures of speech" (Warren 1966, 201) in King's style, but no mention is made of proverbial matters in the discussion of alliteration, anaphora, comparison, metaphor, repetition, and simile (see Warren 1966, 201–8). Other scholars speak of King's "figures of speech—similes, metaphors, allegories, and personifications" (Boulware 1969, 254), his "metaphoricality" (Spillers 1971, 17 [1989, 879]), and his stylistic preoccupation with metaphors, repetition, parallelism, and antithesis (Ensslin 1990, 120–22), with Lewis V. Baldwin at least referring in passing to "King's eloquence and brilliant use of imagery and the folk idiom [that] help explain the ease with which he found a route to the hearts and eventually to the heads of his people" (Baldwin 1991, 296). Jonathan Rieder makes the keen observation that "A King [sermonic or rhetorical] performance was a collective act . . . his . . . sermons and speeches were collage compositions. . . . If he was able to provoke assorted audiences, it was because his life lay at the junction of diverse lines of affiliation that taught him to speak in many tongues. Those networks formed a transmission belt through which the raw materials of song, argument, homily, citation, inflection, philosophy, sermon, rhythm, examples, authors, theology, and ideas flowed" (Rieder 2008, 10–11). All of these remarks are perfectly fitting, but why are proverbs and proverbial phrases missing in these enumerations of King's elements of style?

Keith D. Miller, as the undeniable expert on King's differentiated rhetoric, has characterized his discursive use of formulaic language as "shared treasure, voice merging, and self-making" (Miller 1990, 77; see also Farrell 1991; Miller 1991b). Miller also observed that "In the folk pulpit, one gains an authoritative voice by adopting the persona of previous speakers as one adapts the sermons and formulaic expressions of a sanctified tradition. Like generations of folk preachers before him, King often borrowed, modified, and synthesized themes, analogies, metaphors, quotations, illustrations, arrangements, and forms of argument used by other preachers. Like other folk preachers, King typically ended his oral sermons (and almost every major speech) by merging his voice with the lyrics of a spiritual, hymn, or gospel song" (Miller 1991a, 121; see also Rosenberg 1970; McKenzie 1996). In other words, while many of his powerful formulaic statements are not his own, it is the "blending" (Rieder 2008, 160) of them with his own voice that assures the discursive powers of Martin Luther King Jr. as a speaker and writer.

David Fleer has spoken in this regard of King's impressive and innovative "reformation" of his vast number of sources. Reminding scholars and others that by 1957, King gave at least two hundred sermons and speeches a year (in later years one or two a day), it should not be surprising that he had to rely on voice merging and certain sets of materials that he could easily intersperse into his sermons and speeches. This voice merging is part and parcel of his compelling and persuasive oral and written rhetoric, with his creative transformation or reformation of his sources making King a rhetorical artist (see Fleer 1995, 158–60). Similar thoughts and arguments were also presented by Keith D. Miller, arguing that King borrowed from many sources, of which a considerable amount "are highly familiar—the modern equivalents of the commonplaces of classical rhetoric" (Miller 1986, 249 [1989, 643]).

Even though King is not prone to use the term *proverb*, he certainly based a number of sermonic outlines and actual sermons on the explication of proverbs, citing them at times as leitmotifs but not explicitly referring to them as Bible or folk proverbs. Always being the preacher and teacher, it is not surprising that he would call on such proverbial wisdom as a base of his religious and social messages. An early example can be seen from a minuscule sermon introduction with the proverb "Life is what you make it" as a title.

Life Is What You Make It
INTRODUCTION
Many people wander into the world, and they pick up everything they can get their hands upon looking for life. They never get it. What they get is existence. Existence is what you find; life is what you create. Therefore, if life ever seems worth while to you, it is not because you found it that way, but because you made it so. (6:83–84; November 30, 1948–February 16, 1949; all volume numbers refer to the six volumes of Clayborne Carson et al., eds., *The Papers of Martin Luther King, Jr.* [1992–2007])

Always having another sermon in mind, King also wrote down short sermon conclusions that might come in handy when another text needed to be composed in a hurry. These introductions and conclusions were kept in folders for ready reference. The following example is once again of special interest, since King uses the introductory formula "there is an old saying" to indicate that he is citing a folk proverb. The "saying" designation implies a proverb, of course, but even this term appears very seldom in King's communications:

> *Success in Life*
> There is an old saying, "If wishes were horses beggars would ride." Friends, the great highroad of success lies along the old high-way of steadfast well-doing; and they who are the most industrious and the most persistent, and work in the truest spirit, will invariably be the most successful. Success treads on the heels of every right effort. (6:85; November 30, 1948–February 16, 1949)

While such paragraphs are mere rudiments, King also has left us with complete sermons with a proverbial title and an ensuing explication of that very text. The quintessential example is King's preoccupation with the Bible proverb "love your enemies" (Matthew 5:44), which he explicated in a number of related "Loving Your Enemies" sermons. In fact, King used the proverb "love your enemies" a total of fifty-three times, and it will be no surprise to anyone that it is Martin Luther King Jr.'s favorite proverb as an expression of his Christian-based "fundamental concept of nonviolence" (Hedgepeth 1984, 81 [1989, 543]). This pervasive proverb illustrates the many mutations of King's basic argument that love is the key element in a world of nonviolence. Adding the folk proverb "hate begets hate" as a warning to his emphasis on the Bible proverb "love your enemies," he makes the following strong statement in one of the restatements of this sermon in his book *Strength to Love* (1963).

> *Why should we love our enemies?* The first reason is fairly obvious. Returning hate for hate multiplies hate, adding deeper darkness to a night already devoid of stars. Darkness cannot drive out darkness; only light can do that. Hate cannot drive out hate; only love can do that. Hate multiplies hate, violence multiplies violence, and toughness multiplies toughness in a descending spiral of destruction. So when Jesus says "Love your enemies" [Matthew 5:44], he is setting forth a profound and ultimately inescapable admonition. Have we not come to such an impasse in the modern world that we must love our enemies—or else? The chain reaction of evil—hate begetting hate, wars producing more wars—must be broken, or we shall be plunged into the dark abyss of annihilation. (King 1963, 37)

This paragraph becomes a proverbial cautionary tale, as in fact many of King's sermons might well be classified. Of course, despite all of this anxiety, gloom, and despair, King always has the audacity of hope for a better world. The purpose of his sermonic explications of proverbs is thus an uplifting attempt at finding a better way for humankind to struggle for freedom and peace throughout the world. His favorite Bible proverb, "love your enemies," is without doubt the wisdom that can lead us there.

Martin Luther King Jr. was, above all, a preacher whose "rhetoric was of the *Biblical vernacular*" (Marbury 1971, 4 [1989, 626]). He knew his Bible, and he spoke and wrote with the holy book always on his mind. He could cite entire passages from the Bible, and he used its well-known passages to add authority to his views and arguments (Calloway-Thomas and Lucaites 1993). The scriptures were always with him, but as he quoted them, he also was perfectly capable of applying them to the sociopolitical issues of his time. While he was steeped in the Bible and believed in the Word of God, he most certainly used its language and wisdom to help the cause of desegregation and civil rights along. There is thus hardly a page in King's oeuvre that does not at least contain a reference to the Bible (Stevenson 1949; Mieder 1990; Griffin 1991). A fine example involves the widely known proverb "man does not live by bread alone" (Deuteronomy 8:3; Matthew 4:4) that appears in both the Old and New Testament. King used it in a sermon, "The Christian Doctrine of Man," on March 12, 1958, at the Council of Churches' Noon Lenten Services in Detroit, stating that he as a minister has a moral and social obligation to his parishioners and the world at large. But there is also an extremely important interpretive twist of the proverb in this text when King states that the word *alone* in the proverb implies that Jesus was very well aware that man cannot live without bread nor by it alone (Turner 1977, 52 [1989, 1,000]; Rieder 2008, 289). This in turn gives King the proverbial argument that poverty must be combated in the United States and throughout the world.

> And so in Christianity the body is sacred. The body is significant. This means that in any Christian doctrine of man we must forever be concerned about man's physical well-being. Jesus was concerned about that. He realized that men had to have certain physical necessities. One day he said, "Man cannot live by bread alone" [Deuteronomy 8:3, Matthew 4:4]. [*Yeah*] But the mere fact that the "alone" was added means that Jesus realized that man could not live without bread. [*Yes*] So as a minister of the gospel, I must not only preach to men and women to be good, but I must be concerned about the social conditions that often make them bad. [*Yeah*] It's not enough for me to tell men to be honest, but I must be concerned about the economic conditions that make them dishonest. [*Amen*] I must be concerned about the poverty in the world. I must be concerned about the ignorance in the world. I must be concerned about the slums in the world. (6:332; March 12, 1958)

Usually relying on the proverbial wisdom of Jesus (Winton 1990), King found the perfect metaphor for his social agenda in the New Testament proverb "he who lives by the sword shall perish by the sword" (Matthew 26:52). It became *the* symbolic argument against all the ills of violent mistreatment of others. In his address on "The Montgomery Story" at the Annual NAACP Convention on June 27, 1956, in San Francisco, he cited the Bible proverb as a metaphorical sign of violence that must be overcome by a philosophy of nonviolence.

> From the beginning there has been a basic philosophy undergirding our movement. It is a philosophy of nonviolent resistance. It is a philosophy which simply says we will refuse on a nonviolent basis, to cooperate with the evil of segregation. In our struggle in America we cannot fret with the idea of retaliatory violence. To use the method of violence would be both impractical and immoral. We have neither the instruments nor the techniques of violence, and even if we had it, it would be morally wrong. There is the voice crying [*applause*], there is a voice crying through the vista of time, saying: "He who lives by the sword will perish by the sword" [Matthew 26:52]. [*applause*] History is replete with the bleached bones of nations who failed to hear these words of truth, and so we decided to use the method of nonviolence, feeling that violence would not do the job. (3:305; June 27, 1956)

While Martin Luther King Jr. has numerous favorite Bible proverbs and literary quotations that he cites on numerous occasions as rhetorical leitmotifs, he does not show this great fascination with any particular folk proverb. This does not mean he shies away from using such folk wisdom when it suits him, but as a preacher he is clearly more steeped in biblical truths. As has been pointed out already, King does not even use the term *proverb* when citing proverbs from traditional folk speech. If he uses introductory formulas at all, he prefers such designations as *truism* or *saying*, but usually he simply integrates folk proverbs without calling special attention to them. He might well have thought that they are so well known that they need no label. After all, he assumes the same with many of the Bible proverbs that he also often does not identify as such. Even though King does not overemphasize folk proverbs by using them as sapiential leitmotifs, he uses numerous proverbs with great rhetorical skill. Actually, just as Abraham Lincoln and Frederick Douglass have done before him and as Barack Obama is doing now, it is the combined emphasis on Bible and folk proverbs that makes their sociopolitical statements so effective (Mieder 2000; 2001; 2009c; 2011). People then and now could easily identify with this wisdom (see Mieder 1993) and subsequently marched along with their champions in the struggle for equality and freedom. There certainly is no doubt that proverbs have played a significant role in political discourse over the centuries, and they continue to be of considerable effectiveness in national and international politics today (see Nichols 1996; Mieder 1997, 2005; Louis 2000).

King certainly utilizes various proverbs and proverbial expressions in his depictions of segregation and the necessary fight against it. There is, in fact, a most fitting proverb that King found to describe how African Americans have fought segregation in a nonviolent way by, proverbially speaking, straightening up their backs and thereby validating the proverb "you can't ride a man's back unless it is bent." The passage that includes both the proverbial phrase and the proverb in tandem appears in the published version of an interview in the January 1965 issue of *Playboy*. In this statement, King is also reflecting on the best way of protesting against segregation, arguing that more specific approaches in certain locales are better than general arguments against segregation as a whole.

> The mistake I made there [at Albany, Georgia] was to protest against segregation generally rather than against a single and distinct facet of it. Our protest was so vague that we got nothing, and the people were left very depressed and in despair. It would have been much better to have concentrated upon integrating the buses or the lunch counters. One victory of this kind would have been symbolic, would have galvanized support and boosted morale. But I don't mean that our work in Albany ended in failure. The Negro people there straightened up their bent backs; you can't ride a man's back unless it's bent. Also, thousands of Negroes registered to vote who never had voted before, and because of the expanded Negro vote in the next election for governor of Georgia—which pitted a moderate candidate against a rabid segregationist—Georgia elected its first governor who had pledged to respect and enforce the law impartially. And what we learned from our mistakes in Albany helped our later campaigns in other cities to be more effective. We have never since scattered our efforts in a general attack on segregation, but have focused upon specific, symbolic objectives. (Washington 1986, 344; January 1965)

In his stirring address of June 23, 1963, at the Freedom Rally in Cobo Hall in Detroit, King cites the modern proverb "last hired, first fired" as an unfortunate truism, especially regarding the employment injustice that African Americans face in light of racial discrimination.

> We've been pushed around so long; we've been the victims of lynching mobs so long; we've been the victims of economic injustice so long—still the last hired and the first fired all over this nation. And I know the temptation. I can understand from a psychological point of view why some caught up in the clutches of the injustices surrounding them almost respond with bitterness and come to the conclusion that the problem can't be solved within, and they talk about getting away from it in terms of racial separation. But even though I can understand it psychologically, I must say to you this afternoon that this isn't the way. Black supremacy is as dangerous as white supremacy. [*Applause*] And oh, I hope you will allow me to say to you this afternoon that God is not interested merely in the freedom of black men and brown men and yellow men. God is interested in the freedom of the whole human race. [*Applause*]

> And I believe that with this philosophy and this determined struggle we will be able to go on in the days ahead and transform the jangling discords of our nation into a beautiful symphony of brotherhood. (Carson and Shepard 2001, 68–69; June 23, 1963)

The element of time in eradicating such racial injustice wore heavily on Martin Luther King Jr.'s mind. In his chapter on "The Dilemma of Negro Americans" in his book *Where Do We Go from Here: Chaos or Community?* (1967), he alludes negatively to the two folk proverbs "time heals all wounds" and "time and tide wait for no man," with the first alteration implying that the evils of segregation will not be forgotten and the second variation stating that the time has surely come to rid the country of this racial injustice once and for all.

> The challenge we face is to unite around powerful action programs to eradicate the last vestiges of racial injustice. We will be greatly misled if we feel that the problem will work itself out. Structures of evil do not crumble by passive waiting. If history teaches anything, it is that evil is recalcitrant and determined, and never voluntarily relinquishes its hold short of an almost fanatical resistance. Evil must be attacked by a counteracting persistence, by the day-to-day assault of the battering rams of justice.
>   We must get rid of the false notion that there is some miraculous quality in the flow of time that inevitably heals all evils. There is only one thing certain about time, and that is that it waits for no one. If it is not used constructively, it passes you by. (King 1967, 128)

In his constant concern for the progress in the fight for civil rights, King found another proverb to express that there is no easy way or quick fix, namely "no pain, no gain." King cites the less common variant "no gain without pain" in his already-mentioned address at the Freedom Rally in Cobo Hall (1963) to explain that there is a heavy price to pay (an additional proverbial phrase) for social advancement.

> And I do not want to give you the impression that it's going to be easy [to get civil rights]. There can be no great social gain without individual pain. And before the victory for brotherhood is won, some will have to get scarred up a bit. Before the victory is won, some more will be thrown into jail. Before the victory is won, some, like Medgar Evers, may have to face physical death. But if physical death is the price that some must pay to free their children and their white brothers from an eternal psychological death, then nothing can be more redemptive. Before the victory is won, some will be misunderstood and called bad names, but we must go on with a determination and with a faith that this problem can be solved. [*Yeah*] [*Applause*] (Carson and Shepard 2001, 70–71; June 23, 1963)

Also of much use to King was "John Donne's famous dictum 'No man is an island' [from his poem of 1624] to reinforce his argument about

America's interrelationship with the rest of the world and therefore its need to be concerned about all citizens not just its own" (Sharman 1999, 98). This proverbial quotation appears in numerous sermons and speeches (Boesak 1976, 28 [1989, 86]); Lischer 1995, 43) with the last one being included in his sermon "Remaining Awake Through a Great Revolution" at the National Cathedral (Episcopal) on March 31, 1968, in Washington, DC.

> Through our scientific and technological genius, we have made of this world a neighborhood and yet . . . we have not had the ethical commitment to make of it a brotherhood. But somehow, and in some way, we have got to do this. We must all learn to live together as brothers. Or we will all perish together as fools. We are tied together in the single garment of destiny, caught in an inescapable network of mutuality. And whatever affects one directly affects all indirectly. For some strange reason I can never be what I ought to be until you are what you ought to be. And you can never be what you ought to be until I am what I ought to be. This is the way God's universe is made; this is the way it is structured.
>
> John Donne caught it years ago and placed it in graphic terms—"No man is an island entire of itself. Every man is a piece of the continent—a part of the main." And he goes on toward the end to say, "Any man's death diminishes me because I am involved in mankind. Therefore never send to know for whom the bell tolls; it tolls for thee." We must see this, believe this, and live by it . . . if we are to remain awake through a great revolution. (Washington 1986, 269–70; March 31, 1968)

In his book *Where Do We Go from Here: Chaos or Community?* (1967), King included a chapter titled "The World House," arguing that "we have inherited a large house, a great 'world house' in which we have to live together—black and white, Easterner and Westerner, Gentile and Jews, Catholic and Protestant, Moslem and Hindu—a family unduly separated in ideas, culture and interest, who, because we can never again live apart, must learn somehow to live with each other in peace" (167). And here, in this uplifting passage from his sermon, he speaks of a brotherhood (sisterhood implied) that is poetically "tied together in the single garment of destiny, caught in an inescapable network of mutuality." As we speak today of globalization and an interconnected world, it behooves us to remember such passages from Martin Luther King Jr. to appreciate what great visionary he really was, not only for civil rights in the United States but for justice, equality, and freedom all over the globe.

There is one more quotation turned proverb that needs to be mentioned, namely the historian Charles A. Beard's insight based on the natural phenomenon that "when it gets dark enough you can see the stars" that King cites for the last time in his sermon "I See the Promised Land" on April 3, 1968, just one day before his assassination in Memphis, Tennessee. "I know, somehow, that only when it is dark enough, can you see the stars. And I see God working in this period of the twentieth century in a way that men, in some strange way, are responding—something is happening in our world. The masses of people are rising up. And wherever they are assembled today, whether they are in Johannesburg, South Africa; Nairobi, Kenya; Accra, Ghana; New York City; Atlanta, Georgia; Jackson, Mississippi; or Memphis, Tennessee—the cry is always the same—'We want to be free'" (Washington 1986, 279–80; April 3, 1968). Stars of hope were everywhere when Martin Luther King Jr. spoke of freedom with his typical eloquence that was at least in part informed by his perfect utilization of quotations with a certain claim of proverbiality.

It should not be surprising that someone so inclined to use proverbial quotations and proverbs would not also amass them into paragraphs of utmost rhetorical authority. Once King found a certain combination of quotations and proverbs that he liked as "set pieces," he usually kept them in the same order when making use of these ready-made collages in his sermons and speeches (Miller 1992, 153–55; Lischer 1995, 104–5). Whenever appropriate, he could simply call on this impressive repertoire that he basically had memorized and employ them to add biblical, literary, or folkloric authority to his often quite spontaneous remarks.

His preference of stringing together two or more quotations and proverbs to express a certain belief or conviction can clearly be seen by his frequent reliance on two famous statements from the Declaration of Independence. By citing the proverb "all men are created equal" and the proverbial triad "life, liberty, and the pursuit of happiness" in tandem as they appear originally in this American creed (Aron 2008, 91–96), King knows that his listeners and readers will identify positively with the fundamental ideas of equality and freedom expressed in them. But as can be imagined, Martin Luther King Jr. was not always satisfied with just citing his favorite proverb "all men are created equal" and "life, liberty, and the pursuit of happiness." To add even more rhetorical credence to his arguments, he expanded this double dose of authority by one, two, or even three additional quotations or proverbs in the same paragraph. And in order to add a somewhat satirical twist to these phrase collages, he constructed them around the idea of a responsible person having to be "maladjusted." Employing the anaphora "as maladjusted as" and other uses of the word *maladjusted*, King claims that it takes maladjusted people to bring about equality, justice, and freedom. In his speech of September 2, 1957, in Monteagle, Tennessee, on "A Look to the Future," King the stylistic tinkerer and "mix-master, blending and layering different elements of talk" (Rieder 2008, 104), augments Jefferson's proverbial words with three Bible proverbs, namely "let judgment run down like waters and righteousness like a mighty stream" (Amos 5:24), "he who lives by the sword will perish by the sword" (Matthew 26:52) and "love your enemies" (Matthew 5:44). With that anaphoral tour de force, he has indeed found an authoritative statement for the future in which people will be courageously "maladjusted" to bring about social change.

> But there are some things in our social system to which I am proud to be maladjusted and to which I suggest that you too ought to be maladjusted. I never intend to adjust myself to the viciousness of mob rule. I never intend to adjust myself to the evils of segregation and the crippling effects of discrimination. I never intend to adjust myself to the tragic inequalities of an economic system which takes necessities from the masses to give luxuries to the classes. I never intend to become adjusted to the madness of militarism and the self-defeating method of physical violence. I call upon you to be maladjusted. Well you see, it may be that the salvation of the world lies in the hands of the maladjusted. The challenge to you this morning as I leave you is to be maladjusted—as maladjusted as the prophet Amos, who in the midst of the injustices of his day, could cry out in terms that echo across the centuries, "Let judgment run down like waters and righteousness like a mighty stream" [Amos 5:24]; as maladjusted as Lincoln, who had the vision to see that this nation could not survive half slave and half free; as maladjusted as Jefferson, who in the midst of an age amazingly adjusted to slavery could cry out in words lifted to cosmic proportions, "All men are created equal, and are endowed by their creator with certain inalienable rights, that among these are life, liberty and the pursuit of happiness." Yes, as maladjusted as Jesus of Nazareth who dared to dream a dream of the fatherhood of God and the brotherhood of man. He looked at men amid the intricate and fascinating military machinery of the Roman Empire, and could say to them, "He who lives by the sword will perish by the sword" [Matthew 26:52]. Jesus, who could look at men in the midst of their tendencies for tragic hate and say to them, "Love thy enemies. Bless them that curse you. Pray for them that despitefully use you" [Matthew 5:44]. The world is in desperate need of such maladjustment. Through such maladjustment we will be able to emerge from the bleak and desolate midnight of man's inhumanity to man into the bright and glittering daybreak of freedom and justice. (4:276; September 2, 1957)

While this rhetorical set piece in its various mutations can be found several times in King's sermons, speeches, and books, mention should also be made of a similar often-repeated and reformulated paragraph that also appears in his emotionally charged speech "Our God Is Marching On!" on March 25, 1965, in Montgomery. It amasses three quotational proverbs and a Bible proverb into a set piece of "messianic discourse" (Charteris-Black 2005, 64).

> Our aim must never be to defeat or humiliate the white man but to win his friendship and understanding. We must come to see that the end we seek is a society at peace with itself, a society that can live with its conscience. That will be a day not of the white man, not of the black man. That will be the day of man as man.
> I know you are asking today, "How long will it take?" I come to say to you this afternoon however difficult the moment, however frustrating the hour, it will not be long, because truth pressed to earth will rise again [William Cullen Bryant].
> How long? Not long, because no lie can live forever [Thomas Carlyle].
> How long? Not long, because you still reap what you sow [Galatians 6:7].
> How long? Not long. Because the arm [sic, arc] of the moral universe is long but it bends toward justice [Theodore Parker].
> How long? Not long, 'cause mine eyes have seen the glory of the coming of the Lord, trampling out the vintage where the grapes of wrath are stored. He has loosed the fateful lightning of his terrible swift sword. His truth is marching on.
> He has sounded forth the trumpets that shall never call retreat. He is lifting up the hearts of man before His judgment seat. Oh, be swift, my soul, to answer Him. Be jubilant, my feet. Our God is marching on. (Washington 1986, 230; March 25, 1965)

According to fellow civil rights advocate and now US Representative John Lewis, "this is poetry" (Carson and Shepard 2001, 116), and it would have been absolutely ridiculous if King had in fact included the names of Bryant, Carlyle, and Parker or the precise Bible reference in his powerful anaphora "How long? Not long, because . . ." (Lischer 1995, 128; see Carter 1996, 128, 141, who mistakenly thinks Parker's statement to be King's "own metaphor"). Jonathan Rieder, referring to this set piece, very appropriately speaks of King's "theology of hope" (Rieder 2008, 322) that it expresses, calling to mind Barack Obama's more secularly stated "audacity of hope" (2006) for humankind.

Martin Luther King Jr.'s struggle for freedom and equality moved forward in many different ways, and as he spoke about the various paths taken, he frequently used proverbs and proverbial phrases that have the noun *way* in them. They are by their very nature usually future oriented and are thus perfectly suited as metaphors to describe and reflect upon the way to progress. There is no doubt that King himself never tired of going out of his way for the civil and human rights movement, giving his energy and time for the cause of justice and equality in the United States and far beyond. With all the setbacks and defeats, he never faltered, citing the proverbial phrase "to have come a long way" to emphasize the progress that had been made, while at the same time stressing with the proverbial phrase "to have a long way to go" that much work still lies ahead. He connects these two phrases for the first time in his philosophically informed article on "The 'New Negro' of the South" that appeared in the June 1956 journal the *Socialist Call*: "Like the synthesis of Hegelian philosophy, the realistic attitude seeks to reconcile the truths of two opposites and avoid the extremes of both. So the realist in race relations would agree with the optimist in saying, we have come a long way, but he would balance that by agreeing with the pessimist that we have a long long way to go. It is this realistic position that I would like to set forth: We have come a long long way, and we have a long long way to go" (3:282; June 1956).

There is one speech with the title "A Long Way to Go" that wins the proverbial prize, so to speak. King delivered it on April 27, 1965, on the campus of the University of California at Los Angeles, and it was published six years later in Arthur L. Smith and Stephen Robb's edited volume, *The Voice of Black Rhetoric: Selections* (1971), with the editors commenting very briefly that "'A Long Way to Go' demonstrates King's mastery of the classical canons of style and arrangement. Clearly delineating introduction, body and conclusion in this speech, King's rhetorical organization is presented at its best. While there is little that is creative about the two-section arrangement (it has been used by many speakers), King's content allows suspense to be a key factor in this speech" (183).

Agreed, but what would have been wrong in also saying that the speech has a proverbial title and that both the proverbial expressions "to have come a long way" and "to have a long way to go" as individual and combined leitmotifs (always with the emphatic double use of *long*) inform the structural and rhetorical mastery of this address? As it is, the two folk metaphors are part of the dual structure of the lecture, and it cannot possibly be a surprise to learn that this rhetorical genius does begin his speech with a juxtaposition of them to set the stage.

> Many of you want to know, are we making any progress? That is the desperate question, a poignant question on the lips of millions of people all over our nation and all over the world. I get it almost every day. It is a question of whether we are making any real progress in the area of race relations. And so I'm going to try to answer that question and deal with many of the issues involved using as a subject from which to speak, the future of integration.
>
> Now there are some people who feel that we aren't making any progress; there are some people who feel that we're making overwhelming progress. I would like to take what I consider a realistic position and say that we have come a long, long way in the struggle to make justice and freedom a reality in our nation, but we still have a long, long way to go. And it is this realistic position that I would like to use as a basis for our thinking together. (Smith and Robb 1971, 188–89; April 27, 1965)

Having said this, the realistic King is ready to present a short history lesson regarding the progress in racial relations, couching this optimistic view into the proverbial "to have come a long way." In the second half of the speech, King gives an overview of what remains to be done, now using the proverbial phrase "to have a long, long way to go" as his hopeful leitmotif. Altogether, the speech becomes a prophetic vision of the future.

But in addition to these proverbial expressions commenting on the "long way" of the civil rights movement, there is also Martin Luther King Jr.'s ingenious use of the spiritual (faith) and secular (hope) proverb "God can (will) make a way out of no way." It grew out of the African American experience of searching to carve out a life of equality and dignity. Strange as it might seem, very little is known about the actual origin, history, and dissemination of this hopeful piece of folk wisdom. It does not appear in any of the standard proverb collections that are notoriously slow in registering new proverbs (Doyle 1996; Mieder 2009b; Mieder, Shapiro, and Doyle 2011). But there is no doubt that it is indeed a folk proverb with considerable amounts of recorded references. Its original version, "God can (will) make a way out of no way," yields 2,950 Google hits, with its truncated and secular variant, "making a way out of no way" easily reaching 84,300 references on Google. The proverb does not appear to have been registered in print before 1900, which does not mean that it might not have been in spoken use prior to that date. Certainly, Jack L. Daniel, Geneva Smitherman-Donaldson, and Milford A. Jeremiah, who have studied the rich proverb lore of African Americans, know this text, as can be seen from the title of their article "Makin' a Way out of No Way: The Proverb Tradition in the Black Experience" (1987). However, strangely enough, they do not present the proverb in their list of fifty proverbs collected from African Americans. All their article does include is the statement "that the essence of the Black Experience is: to make a way out of no way" (Daniel, Smitherman-Donaldson, and Jeremiah 1987, 494; see also Daniel 1973, 1979; Smitherman 1977, 245–46; Barnes-Harden 1980, 57–80; Folly 1982; Mieder 1989, 111–28; Smitherman 1994; Prahlad 1996; Rieder 2008, 152–57). This, however, is proof positive that these scholars consider this proverb to be reflecting the African American worldview of trying to cope and advance with God's help in a world that is not exactly supportive of their efforts.

With this background, we can turn to Martin Luther King Jr.'s obvious knowledge and multiple use of this proverb. For example, during his interview with the *Playboy* editors that appeared in the January 1965 issue, he recounted what he had said to the people involved in the Montgomery bus boycott. And while his memory is quite correct, he now states the proverb with God as its clear subject: "God will make a way for us when there seems no way." By expanding its text slightly, King does explicate its meaning to the editors, who, most likely as whites, might not have known the African American proverb at that time.

> There was one dark moment when we doubted it [to be successful with the bus boycott]. We had been struggling to make the boycott a success when the city of Montgomery successfully obtained an injunction from the court to stop our car pool. I didn't know what to say to our people. They had backed us up, and we had let them down. It was a desolate moment. I saw, all of us saw, that the court was leaning against us. I remember telling a group of those working closest with me to spread in the Negro community the message, "We must have the faith that things will work out somehow, that God will make a way for us when there seems no way." It was about noontime, I remember, when Rex Thomas of the Associated Press rushed over to where I was sitting and told me of the news flash that the U.S. Supreme Court had declared that bus segregation in Montgomery was unconstitutional. It had literally been the darkest hour before the dawn. (Washington 1986, 343–44; January 1965)

On August 16, 1967, King cited the proverb once again in his last address as president of the Southern Christian Leadership Conference, entitling his remarks with the question "Where Do We Go from Here?" Almost as expected by now, the proverb is to be found in the last paragraph of the entire speech, in which King looks with much hope to a better future. While the two quotational proverbs "the arc of the moral universe is long, but it bends towards justice" and "truth crushed to earth will rise again" together with the Bible proverb "as you sow, so shall you reap" (Galatians 6:7) imply that morality, honesty, and diligence will be rewarded, it is also made clear that there is "a power [i.e., God] that is able to make a way out of no way" for the African American people.

> When our days become dreary with low-hovering clouds of despair, and when our nights become darker than a thousand midnights, let us remember that there is a creative force in this universe, working to pull down the gigantic mountains of evil, a power that is able to make a way out of no way and transform dark yesterdays into bright tomorrows. Let us realize the arc of the moral universe is long but it bends toward justice [Theodore Parker].
> Let us realize that William Cullen Bryant is right: "Truth crushed to earth will rise again." Let us go out realizing that the Bible is right: "Be not deceived, God is not mocked. Whatsoever a man soweth, that shall he also reap" [Galatians 6:7]. This is for [sic] hope for the future, and with this faith we will be able to sing in some not too distant tomorrow with a cosmic past tense, "We have overcome, we have overcome, deep in my heart, I did believe we would overcome." (Washington 1986, 252; August 16, 1967)

The fact that Dr. King quotes the proverb in these variants is an indication that he could rely on his audience knowing it in its basic wording. More importantly, its encouraging wisdom and orientation to the future made it the perfect proverb for King's religious and secular messages filled with faith, hope, and love for a world of peace and freedom. Against all odds and obstacles, Martin Luther King Jr., as a servant of God and humanity, was indeed a man who believed in and succeeded in "making a way out of no way" in words and deeds. There is no doubt that this proverb epitomizes the entire civil and human rights movement in the United States and throughout the world, and as such, it is the perfect verbal sign for unwavering hope and courageous action. But there is one more fact that deserves to be registered at this point: Martin Luther King Jr.'s oral and written rhetoric would perhaps not have held people's attention to the degree it did without its proverbial language adding life, spice, and wisdom to it by way of traditional and innovative metaphors.

Finally, there is one more metaphor that needs to be addressed that goes hand in hand with the proverb "making a way out of no way." In order to look for the ways of social improvements, humankind needs to have a visionary and prophetic dream that promises that a solid faith and unwavering hope in the struggle for civil and human rights will eventually lead to progress. King himself adhered to this dream of equality and justice for all during his entire life. He and the many participants in the civil rights movement fortunately had the audacity to dream of making a way out of no way, and it should thus not be surprising that dreams of an interconnected new world house for all of humanity are a leitmotif in many of King's sermons and speeches, with the very word *dream* repeatedly appearing in their titles. To a certain degree, these "dream" speeches foreshadow King's famous "I Have a Dream" oration of August 28, 1963 (Carson and Holloran 1998, xvi–xvii).

By the time King delivered his "I Have a Dream" speech, with its set of quotational and proverbial statements, at the Lincoln Memorial on August 28, 1963, it was billed as the keynote address of the March on Washington, DC, for Civil Rights. The press from here and abroad was present, a quarter million people had assembled, and Dr. King found himself at the largest public event of the civil rights movement. It gave him and his idea of nonviolent struggle for equality, justice, and freedom a national and subsequently an international forum, never to be forgotten by those who were fortunate enough to be present at this momentous occasion, who witnessed the speech on television or listened to it on the radio, read it in the papers the following day, or have come across it on film or in print ever since. Not surprisingly, much scholarly attention has been directed to this very speech (see Patton 1993; Solomon 1993; Vail 2006), including two invaluable books by Drew D. Hansen, *The Dream: Martin Luther King Jr., and the Speech That Inspired a Nation* (2003), and very recently by Eric J. Sundquist, *King's Dream* (2009).

Here then is the slightly shortened "I Have a Dream" peroration with its three proverbial statements: "all men are created equal" and the proverbial phrases "to be judged by the content of one's character and not by the color of one's skin" and "to join hands with someone," with the latter being cited twice as a verbal sign of true brother- and sisterhood in an America of equality, justice, and freedom.

> So I say to you, my friends, that even though we must face the difficulties of today and tomorrow, I still have a dream. It is a dream deeply rooted in the American dream that one day this nation will rise up and live out the true meaning of its creed—we hold these truths to be self-evident, that all men are created equal.
>
> I have a dream that one day on the red hills of Georgia, sons of former slaves and sons of former slave-owners will be able to sit down together at the table of brotherhood.
>
> I have a dream that one day, even the state of Mississippi, a state sweltering with the heat of injustice, sweltering with the heat of oppression, will be transformed into an oasis of freedom and justice.
>
> I have a dream my four little children will one day live in a nation where they will not be judged by the color of their skin but by content of their character. I have a dream today!
>
> I have a dream that one day, down in Alabama, with its vicious racists, with its governor having his lips dripping with the words of interposition and nullification, that one day, right there in Alabama, little black boys and black girls will be able to join hands with the little white boys and white girls as sisters and brothers. I have a dream today!
>
> . . .
>
> With this faith we will be able to hear [*sic*, i.e. hew] out of the mountain of despair a stone of hope. With this faith we will be able to transform the jangling discords of our nation into a beautiful symphony of brotherhood.
>
> With this faith we will be able to work together, to pray together, to struggle together, to go to jail together, to stand up for freedom together, knowing that we will be free one day. This will be the day when all of God's children will be able to sing with new meaning—"my country 'tis of thee: sweet land of liberty; of thee I sing; land where my fathers died, land of the pilgrim's pride; from every mountain side, let freedom ring"—and if America is to be a great nation, this must become true.
>
> So let freedom ring . . .
>
> And when we allow freedom to ring, when we let it ring from every village and hamlet, from every state and city, we will be able to speed up that day when all of God's children—black men and white men, Jews and Gentiles,

Catholics and Protestants—will be able to join hands and to sing in the words of the old Negro spiritual, "Free at last, free at last; thank God Almighty, we are free at last."
(Washington 1986, 219–20; August 28, 1963)

It goes to Eric J. Sundquist's credit that he draws attention to King's formulaic "Not by the Color of Their Skin" statement at the beginning of his long chapter with that title in his book *King's Dream* (2009, 194–228).

> Even though it does not provide the Dream speech's most famous phrase, one sentence stands alone for the philosophy it appeared to announce and the contentious use to which it has since been put: "I have a dream that my four little children will one day live in a nation where they will not be judged by the color of their skin but by the content of their character." If King's dream began to be realized with passage of the Civil Rights Act of 1964, his apparently clear elevation of character over color proved central to subsequent arguments about the reach and consequences of that landmark legislation. Those thirty-five spontaneous words have done more than any politician's polemic, any sociologist's theory, or any court's ruling to frame public discussion of affirmative action over the past four decades. (Sundquist 2009, 194)

Regarding the "spontaneous" use of the "phrase"—Sundquist comes close to calling it a proverbial phrase—it must be observed that King had used it two months earlier in his similar "Dream" speech on June 23, 1963 (see Carson and Shepard 2001, 71–73), in Detroit. In fact, he liked its metaphor and meaning, citing it three more times in sermons and speeches during 1967, thereby effectively helping his very own formulation along the path of becoming a proverbial expression. (For other King statements that have become quotational or even proverbial, see Hoskins 1968; Ayres 1993.)

By the end of 1967, the "I have a dream" anaphora, modified to "I still have a dream" after its international exposure at the Lincoln Memorial on August 28, 1963, had doubtlessly become King's rhetorical signature phrase. Of course, it represents but one of his quotational and proverbial leitmotifs that made his sermons, speeches, letters, essays, and books into such effective and memorable statements in the cause of civil and human rights. Quotations turned proverbs, Bible proverbs, folk proverbs, and a plethora of proverbial expressions are an intrinsic part of King's rhetorical prowess, providing his messages with colorful metaphors and authoritative strength. His noble dream of an America and a world interconnected by equality, justice, freedom, love, and hope had to be expressed through language so that the nonviolent movement for civil and human rights could march forward. Individual words and sentences were needed to bring these dignified ideals across, and there can be no doubt that proverbs and proverbial phrases as ready-made expressions served King extremely well in adding imagery and expressiveness to his numerous oral and written communications. His dream needed words and deeds, and being a master of both, Martin Luther King Jr. was and remains the visionary champion of making a way out of no way for all of humanity that, thanks to him, has come a long way but still has a long way to go. Moving on with an adherence to the biblical triad of "faith, hope, and love" and the acceptance of the African American proverb "making a way out of no way" will keep Dr. King's proverbial dream alive for future generations as they confront their fate in the world house of brotherly and sisterly mutuality.

References

This chapter was first published in *Aspekte der historischen Phraseologie und Phraseographie*, edited by Natalia Filatkina, Ane Kleine-Engel, Marcel Dräger, and Harald Burger, 147–66. Heidelberg: Carl Winter, 2012.

Aron, Paul. 2008. *We Hold These Truths . . . And Other Words That Made America*. Lanham, MD: Rowman & Littlefield.
Ayres, Alex, ed. 1993. *The Wisdom of Martin Luther King, Jr*. New York: Meridian.
Baldwin, Lewis V. 1991. *There Is a Balm in Gilead: The Cultural Roots of Martin Luther King, Jr*. Minneapolis: Augsburg Fortress.
Barnes-Harden, Alene L. 1980. "Proverbs, Folk Expressions, and Superstitions." In *African American Verbal Arts: Their Nature and Communicative Interpretation (A Thematic Analysis)*, edited by A. L. Barnes Harden, 57–80. PhD dissertation, State University of New York at Buffalo.
Boesak, Allan. 1976 (1989). *Coming in out of the Wilderness: A Comparative Interpretation of the Ethics of Martin Luther King, Jr. and Malcolm X*. Kampen, Nederland: Theologische Hogeschool der Gereformeerde Kerken. Also in *Martin Luther King, Jr.: Civil Rights Leader, Theologian, Orator*, edited by David J. Garrow, 1:59–126. 3 vols. Brooklyn, NY: Carlson Publishing.
Boulware, Marcus H. 1969. *The Oratory of Negro Leaders: 1900–1968*. Westport, CT: Negro Universities Press.
Burger, Harald, Dmitrij Dobrovol'skij, Peter Kühn, and Neal R. Norrick, eds. 2007. *Phraseology: An International Handbook of Contemporary Research*. 2 vols. Berlin: Walter de Gruyter.
Calloway-Thomas, Carolyn, and John Louis Lucaites. 1993. *Martin Luther King, Jr., and the Sermonic Power of Public Discourse*, edited by Carolyn Calloway-Thomas and John Louis Lucaites. Tuscaloosa: The University of Alabama Press.
Carson, Clayborne, Peter Holloran, Ralph E. Luker, and Penny A. Russell, eds. 1992–2007. *The Papers of Martin Luther King, Jr*. 6 vols. Berkeley: University of California Press.
Carson, Clayborne, and Peter Holloran, eds. 1998. *A Knock at Midnight: Inspiration from the Great Sermons of Reverend Martin Luther King, Jr*. New York: Warner Books.
Carson, Clayborne, and Kris Shepard, eds. 2001. *A Call to Conscience: The Landmark Speeches of Dr. Martin Luther King, Jr*. New York: Grand Central Publishing.
Carter, Dale. 1996. "Bending Towards Justice: Martin Luther King, Jr. and the Assessment of History." *American Studies in Scandinavia* 29: 128–41.

Charteris-Black, Jonathan. 2005. "Martin Luther King: Messianic Myth." In *Politicians and Rhetoric: The Persuasive Power of Metaphor*, edited by J. Charteris-Black, 58–85, 214–17 (appendix). New York: Palgrave Macmillan.

Daniel, Jack L. 1973. "Towards an Ethnography of Afroamerican Proverbial Usage." *Black Lines* 2:3–12.

———. 1979. *The Wisdom of Sixth Mount Zion [Church] from The Members of the Sixth Mount Zion and Those Who Begot Them*. Pittsburgh: University of Pittsburgh, College of Arts and Sciences.

Daniel, Jack L., Geneva Smitherman-Donaldson, and Milford A. Jeremiah. 1987. "Makin' a Way out of No Way: The Proverb Tradition in the Black Experience." *Journal of Black Studies* 17:482–508.

Doyle, Charles Clay. 1996. "On 'New' Proverbs and the Conservativeness of Proverb Dictionaries." *Proverbium: Yearbook of International Proverb Scholarship* 13:69–84.

Ensslin, Birgit. 1990. "'I Have a Dream'—Martin Luther King und die Bürgerrechtsbewegung in den USA. Eine rhetorische Analyse ausgewählter Texte von Martin Luther King." *Lebende Sprachen* 35:118–23.

Farrell, Thomas J. 1991. "The Antecedents of King's Message." *Publications of the Modern Language Association* 106:529–30.

Fleer, David. 1995. *Martin Luther King, Jr.'s Reformation of Sources: A Close Rhetorical Reading of His Compositional Strategies and Arrangement*. PhD dissertation, University of Washington.

Folly, Dennis Wilson (Sw. Anand Prahlad). 1982. "'Getting the Butter from the Duck': Proverbs and Proverbial Expressions in an Afro-American Family." In *A Celebration of American Family Folklore: Tales and Traditions from the Smithsonian Collection*, edited by Steven J. Zeitlin, Amy J. Kotkin, and Holly Cutting Baker, 232–41 and 290–91 (notes). New York: Pantheon.

Garrow, David J., ed. 1989. *Martin Luther King, Jr.: Civil Rights Leader, Theologian, Orator*. 3 vols. Brooklyn, NY: Carlson Publishing.

Griffin, Albert Kirby. 1991. *Religious Proverbs: Over 1,600 Adages from 18 Faiths Worldwide*. Jefferson, NC: McFarland.

Hansen, Drew D. 2003. *The Dream: Martin Luther King, Jr., and the Speech That Inspired a Nation*. New York: HarperCollins.

Hedgepeth, Chester M. 1984 (1989). "Philosophical Eclecticism in the Writings of Martin Luther King, Jr." *Western Journal of Black Studies* 8:79–86. Also in *Martin Luther King, Jr.: Civil Rights Leader, Theologian, Orator*, edited by David J. Garrow, 2:541–48. 3 vols. Brooklyn, NY: Carlson Publishing.

Hoskins, Lotte, ed. 1968. *"I Have a Dream": The Quotations of Martin Luther King Jr.* New York: Grosset & Dunlap.

Karabegović, Dženeta. 2007. "'No Lie Can Live Forever': Zur sprichwörtlichen Rhetorik von Martin Luther King." In *Sprichwörter sind Goldes wert: Parömiologische Studien zu Kultur, Literatur und Medien*, edited by Wolfgang Mieder, 223–40. Burlington: University of Vermont.

King, Martin Luther, Jr. 1963. *Strength to Love*. New York: Harper & Row.

———. 1967. *Where Do We Go from Here: Chaos or Community?* New York: Harper & Row.

Lischer, Richard. 1995. *The Preacher King: Martin Luther King, Jr. and the Word That Moved America*. New York: Oxford University Press.

Louis, Cameron. 2000. "Proverbs and the Politics of Language." *Proverbium: Yearbook of International Proverb Scholarship* 17:173–94.

Marbury, Carl H. 1971 (1989). "An Excursus on the Biblical and Theological Rhetoric of Martin Luther King." In *Essays in Honor of Martin Luther King, Jr.*, edited by John H. Cartwright, 14–28. Evanston, IL: Garrett Evangelical Theological Seminary. Also in *Martin Luther King Jr.: Civil Rights Leader, Theologian, Orator*, edited by David J. Garrow, 3:623–34. 3 vols. Brooklyn, NY: Carlson Publishing, 1989.

McKenzie, Alyce M. 1996. *Preaching Proverbs: Wisdom for the Pulpit*. Louisville, KY: Westminster John Knox Press.

Mieder, Wolfgang. 1989. *American Proverbs: A Study of Texts and Contexts*. Bern: Peter Lang.

———. 1990. *Not By Bread Alone: Proverbs of the Bible*. Shelburne, VT: New England Press.

———. 1993. *Proverbs Are Never Out of Season: Popular Wisdom in the Modern Ages*. New York: Oxford University Press.

———. 1997. *The Politics of Proverbs: From Traditional Wisdom to Proverbial Stereotypes*. Madison: University of Wisconsin Press.

———. 2000. *The Proverbial Abraham Lincoln: An Index to Proverbs in the Works of Abraham Lincoln*. New York: Peter Lang.

———. 2001. *"No Struggle, No Progress": Frederick Douglass and His Proverbial Rhetoric for Civil Rights*. New York: Peter Lang.

———. 2005. *Proverbs Are the Best Policy: Folk Wisdom and American Politics*. Logan: Utah State University Press.

———. 2009a. *International Bibliography of Paremiology and Phraseology*. 2 vols. Berlin: Walter de Gruyter.

———. 2009b. "'New Proverbs Run Deep': Prolegomena to a Dictionary of Modern Anglo-American Proverbs." *Proverbium: Yearbook of International Proverb Scholarship* 26:237–74.

———. 2009c. *"Yes We Can": Barack Obama's Proverbial Rhetoric*. New York: Peter Lang.

———. 2011. *"Making a Way out of No Way": Martin Luther King's Sermonic Proverbial Rhetoric*. New York: Peter Lang.

Mieder, Wolfgang, Stewart A. Kingsbury, and Kelsie B. Harder, eds. 1992. *A Dictionary of American Proverbs*. New York: Oxford University Press.

Mieder, Wolfgang, Fred Shapiro, and Charles C. Doyle, eds. 2011. *Yale Dictionary of Modern Proverbs*. New Haven, CT: Yale University Press.

Miller, Keith D. 1986 (1989). "Martin Luther King Jr. Borrows a Revolution: Argument, Audience, and Implications of a Secondhand Universe." *College English* 48:249–65. Also in *Martin Luther King Jr.: Civil Rights Leader, Theologian, Orator*, edited by David J. Garrow, 3:643–59. 3 vols. Brooklyn, NY: Carlson Publishing.

———. 1990. "Composing Martin Luther King Jr." *Publications of the Modern Language Association* 105:70–82.

———. 1991a. "Martin Luther King Jr., and the Black Folk Pulpit." *Journal of American History* 78:120–23.

———. 1991b. "Reply [to Thomas J. Farrell, 'The Antecedents of King's Message']." *Publications of the Modern Language Association* 106:530–31.

———. 1992. *Voice of Deliverance: The Language of Martin Luther King Jr. and Its Sources*. New York: Free Press.

Nichols, Ray. 1996. "Maxims, 'Practical Wisdom,' and the Language of Action." *Political Theory* 24:687–705.

Obama, Barack. 2006. *The Audacity of Hope: Thoughts on Reclaiming the American Dream*. New York: Three Rivers Press.

Patton, John H. 1993. "'I Have a Dream': The Performance of Theology Fused with the Power of Orality." In *Martin Luther King Jr., and the Sermonic Power of Public Discourse*, edited by Carolyn Calloway-Thomas and John Louis Lucaites, 104–26. Tuscaloosa: University of Alabama Press.

Prahlad, Sw. Anand. 1996. *African-American Proverbs in Context*. Jackson: University Press of Mississippi.

Rieder, Jonathan. 2008. *The Word of the Lord Is Upon Me: The Righteous Performance of Martin Luther King Jr*. Cambridge, MA: Harvard University Press.

Rosenberg, Bruce. 1970. *The Art of the American Folk Preacher*. New York: Oxford University Press.

Sharman, Nick. 1999. "'Remaining Awake through a Great Revolution': The Rhetorical Strategies of Martin Luther King Jr." *Social Semiotics* 9:85–105.

Smith, Arthur L., and Stephen Robb, eds. 1971. *The Voice of Black Rhetoric: Selections*. Boston: Allyn and Bacon.

Smitherman, Geneva. 1977. *Talkin' and Testifyin': The Language of Black America*. Detroit: Wayne State University Press.

———. 1994. *Black Talk: Words and Phrases from the Hood to the Amen Corner*. Boston: Houghton Mifflin Company.

Solomon, Martha. 1993. "Covenanted Rights: The Metaphoric Matrix of 'I Have a Dream.'" In *Martin Luther King Jr., and the Sermonic Power of Public Discourse*, edited by Carolyn Calloway-Thomas and John Louis Lucaites, 68–84. Tuscaloosa: University of Alabama Press.

Spillers, Hortense J. 1971 (1989). "Martin Luther King and the Style of the Black Sermon." *Black Scholar* 3:14–27. Also in *Martin Luther King Jr.: Civil Rights Leader, Theologian, Orator*, edited by David J. Garrow, 3:876–89. 3 vols. Brooklyn, NY: Carlson Publishing.

Stevenson, Burton. 1949. *The Home Book of Bible Quotations*. New York: Harpers & Brothers.

Sundquist, Eric J. 2009. *King's Dream*. New Haven, CT: Yale University Press.

Turner, Otis. 1977 (1989). "Nonviolence and the Politics of Liberation." *Journal of the Interdenominational Theological Center* 4:49–60. Also in *Martin Luther King Jr.: Civil Rights Leader, Theologian, Orator*, edited by David J. Garrow, 3: 997–1008. 3 vols. Brooklyn, New York: Carlson Publishing.

Vail, Mark. 2006. "The 'Integrative' Rhetoric of Martin Luther King Jr.'s 'I Have a Dream' Speech." *Rhetoric & Public Affairs* 9:51–78.

Warren, Mervyn A. 1966. *A Rhetorical Study of the Preaching of Doctor Martin Luther King Jr., Pastor and Pulpit Orator*. PhD dissertation, Michigan State University.

Washington, James M., ed. 1986. *A Testament of Hope: The Essential Writings of Martin Luther King Jr*. San Francisco: Harper & Row.

Winton, Alan P. 1990. *The Proverbs of Jesus: Issues of History and Rhetoric*. Sheffield, UK: Sheffield Academic Press.

5

"KEEP YOUR EYES ON THE PRIZE"

Congressman John Lewis's Proverbial Odyssey for Civil Rights

There is an old American folk song called "Gospel Plow" with the alternative titles of "Hold On" and "Keep Your Hands on that Plow," with the latter being an allusion to the Bible passage "And Jesus said unto him [a man], No man, having put his hand to the plow, and looking back, is fit for the kingdom of God" (Luke 9:62). Variants of the song have been registered in John and Alan Lomax's famous collection, *Our Singing Country* (1941), in Cecil James Sharp and Olive Campbell's *English Folk Songs from the Southern Appalachians* (1917, 2:292), and in Newman Ivey White's *American Negro Folk-Songs* (1928, 115). It is generally assumed that the song had its origin in the African American diaspora, with part of the lyrics stating:

> Got my hands on the gospel plow,
> Wouldn't take nothin' for my journey now.
> Keep your hands on that plow, hold on.
>
> Hold on, hold on
> Keep your hands on that plow, hold on
> (Lomax 1941, 44–45)

The song probably originated from the African American gospel tradition, and it is thus not surprising that an adaptation of this popular song of hopeful struggle by African Americans toward equal human rights became a battle hymn of the civil rights movement during the middle of the twentieth century. In fact, Alice Wine is usually credited with having changed the lyrics during the early 1950s to express in an even stronger way that the fight for equality must go on despite strong opposition. There might have been others at work on creating the lyrics of the modern adaptation, but

Wine changed the title of the old song to "Keep Your Eyes on the Prize" that perhaps is an allusion to the Bible passages "I press toward the mark for the prize of the high calling of God in Jesus Christ" (Philippians 3:14) and "keep your eyes on those who live as we do" (Philippians 3:17). The names of Paul and Silas in the song calling for the continuation of the struggle for equality and liberty are also an allusion to their survival in the face of adversaries in the Bible (Acts 16:19–16). But here is the song from the civil rights movement that helped to keep its participants focused on the ultimate goal of equal civil rights:

Keep Your Eyes on the Prize
Paul and Silas, bound in jail
Had no money for to go their bail
Keep your eyes on the prize, hold on

Hold on (hold on), hold on (hold on)
Keep your eyes on the prize, hold on
Hold on (hold on), hold on (hold on)
Keep your eyes on the prize, hold on

Paul and Silas began to shout
Doors popped open, and all walked out
Keep your eyes on the prize, hold on
Hold on (hold on), hold on (hold on)

Well, the only chains we can stand
Are the chains of hand in hand
Keep your eyes on the prize, hold on

Got my hand on the freedom plow
Wouldn't take nothing for my journey now
Keep your eyes on the prize, hold on

Hold on (hold on), hold on (hold on)
Keep your eyes on the prize, hold on
Hold on (hold on), hold on (hold on)
Keep your eyes on the prize, darling

Hold on (hold on), hold on (hold on)
Keep your eyes on the prize, hold on

> Hold on (hold on), hold on (hold on)
> Keep your eyes on the prize, hold on
> (Carawan and Carawan 1963: 111–12)

With the song being an inspirational battle hymn of sorts to keep "plowing" along toward the ultimate "prize" of liberation and freedom, it is little wonder that its leitmotif of "keep your eyes on the prize" became a proverbial slogan for the civil rights movement (Williams 1987). As John Lewis recalls in his book *Across That Bridge: Life Lessons and a Vision of Change* (2012), this song kept him and other civil rights proponents going as they found themselves jailed, as Paul and Silas had been centuries ago.

> Soon, the cells all around me were full of [freedom] riders, and we began to sing songs of freedom to remind us of our purpose and keep our spirits high. We sang: "Keep your eyes on the prize, hold on," and "This little light of mine, I'm going to let it shine." We sang "Woke up this morning with my mind stayed on freedom," and many other songs that reminded us of our faith. The songs seemed to aggravate prison officials who ultimately took away our Bibles, our toothbrushes, and even our mattresses and bedding, leaving us to sleep on steel cots, all to snuff out the joy in our hearts. (B36; all references from this book will be cited with the letter B followed by the page numbers)

Later in this book, John Lewis returns to the proverb "keep your eyes on the prize," which can also be employed as the proverbial expression "to keep your eyes on the prize," in a telling paragraph about the nonviolent civil rights struggle of which he was one of the great leaders.

> Even though we had been rejected by society, we believed that all people had the capacity to be good. We believed not only we, but the perpetrators of violence, were victims as well, who began their lives in innocence but were taught to hate, abuse, and draw distinctions between themselves and others. We held no malice toward them and believed in the power of the truth to penetrate that negative conditioning and remind people of their innocence once again. We focused on the end we hoped to see and kept our eyes on that prize. We could not waste time harboring bitterness or resentment. We knew that our focus had to be on what we hoped to create, not the indignities we were pressing to leave behind. Hating our aggressors was like looking back when we wanted to move forward. We had to use our energy to manifest our dreams, and entertaining animosity would have given more power to the status quo. (B105–6)

But who then is this John Lewis who has made the nonviolent struggle for civil and human rights his mission as a fellow citizen and as a longtime congressman of the United States of America? And how does this modest, courageous, and forceful small man tower above others in simple language and benevolent deeds? As will become clear, his humanitarian philosophy is deeply grounded in his religious faith and his simple and poor upbringing that is void of any signs of grandstanding or intellectual snobbism. In fact, he expresses his thoughts and opinions in ordinary language that is accessible to all, and he enhances his rhetoric like other great civic leaders before him, with plenty of proverbs and proverbial expressions from the Bible and folk speech.

Three relatively short biographies for juvenile readers have appeared: Christine Hill's *John Lewis: From Freedom Rider to Congressman* (2002), Ann Bausum's *Freedom Riders: John Lewis and Jim Zwerg on the Front Lines of the Civil Rights Movement* (2006), and Jim Haskins and Kathleen Benson's *John Lewis in the Lead: A Story of the Civil Rights Movement* (2006). While these books present a vivid account of John Lewis as a poor sharecropper's son in rural Alabama who became a leading activist in the civil rights movement and who since 1987 serves as a member of the US House of Representatives from the state of Georgia, they cannot possibly measure up to the informed authenticity of John Lewis's detailed autobiography *Walking with the Wind: A Memoir of the Movement* (1998). This is not the place to trace the fascinating life of John Lewis in the detail that such an account would deserve. Suffice it to say that he was born on February 21, 1940, in Troy, Alabama, into a family of sharecroppers with ten children. After high school, he attended the American Baptist Theological Seminary in the hope of becoming a preacher. He subsequently attended Fisk University, also located in Nashville, Tennessee, where he majored in philosophy and religion. Already as a student, he became very interested in the philosophy of nonviolence as he participated in sit-ins at Nashville that brought about the desegregation of lunch counters in that city. In 1961 he became one of the first Freedom Riders (six blacks and seven whites) who rode a bus from Washington, DC, to New Orleans to uphold the new law that forbade segregation on interstate bus travel. Together with others, he was beaten and jailed, but he continued to push forward on his nonviolent mission for civil rights. From 1963 to 1966, he was the influential chairman of the SNCC (Student Nonviolent Coordinating Committee), and at the age of just twenty-three, he was one of the speakers on August 28, 1963, at the Lincoln Memorial in Washington, DC, where his hero Dr. Martin Luther King Jr. delivered his unforgettable "I Have a Dream" speech. In fact, Lewis's speech was quite aggressive compared to those of the older civil rights icons. Using the proverbial expression "to pay the price for something," he declared that the civil rights revolution must move forward no matter how high the price might be.

> To those who have said, "Be patient and wait," we have long said that we cannot be patient. We do not want our freedom gradually, but we want to be free now! We are tired. We are tired of being beaten by policemen. We are tired of seeing our people locked up in jail over and over again. And then you holler, "Be patient." How long can we be patient? We want our freedom and we want it now. We do not want to go to jail. But we will go to jail if this is the price we must pay for love, brotherhood, and true peace.
>
> I appeal to all of you to get into this great revolution that is sweeping this nation. Get in and stay in the streets of every city, every village and hamlet of this nation until true freedom comes, until the revolution of 1776 is complete. We must get in this revolution and complete the revolution....
>
> We will not stop.... We will march with the spirit of love and with the spirit of dignity that we have shown here today. By the force of our demands, our determination, and our numbers, we shall splinter the segregated South into a thousand pieces and put them together in the image of God and democracy. We must say: "Wake up America! Wake up!" For we cannot stop, and we will not and cannot be patient. (Lewis 1963)

Lewis marched with thousands of others, gaining even more prominence as one of the most eminent civil rights advocates when on March 7, 1965, he led hundreds of marchers across the Edmund Pettus Bridge in Selma, Alabama, on the march to Montgomery. As they reached the end of the bridge, they were brutally beaten by Alabama state troopers, making this day the "Bloody Sunday" of the civil rights movement. Even though Lewis's skull was fractured, he continued on his nonviolent crusade with Martin Luther King Jr. as his guidepost. King has remained his idol to this day, as can be seen from remarks he made on November 13, 2006, at the King Memorial groundbreaking ceremony in Washington, DC. He used the proverbial expressions "to get in the way of something," the proverb "all men are created equal," and Dr. King's own proverbial quotations "we must learn to live together as brothers and sisters or perish together as fools" and "a threat to justice anywhere is a threat to justice everywhere" to express the need to continue the work of the civil rights movement.

> Martin Luther King Jr. inspired me and thousands of other Americans to get in the way. He inspired us to get in trouble, but it was good trouble, necessary trouble.
>
> It seems it was only a few years ago that I stood with Martin Luther King Jr. and eight other leaders of the Civil Rights Movement as he spoke just a short distance from here on the steps of the Lincoln Memorial. And in that now historic speech, that included the words, "I have a dream that one day this nation will rise up and live out the true meaning of its creed: We hold these truths to be self-evident that all men are created equal."

> In that speech when he said, "I have a dream today, a dream deeply rooted in the American dream," Martin Luther King Jr., the moral leader of the nation, transformed those marble steps into a modern day pulpit. He spoke to the conscience of us all telling us that the way of peace, the way of love, the way of non-violence is a better way, a more excellent way.
> He spoke to the noble idea that we must learn to live together as brothers and sisters or perish together as fools. Through his life and through his actions, he moved the mountains of our faith by declaring that a threat to justice anywhere is a threat to justice everywhere.
> ... this monument will inspire generations yet unborn to get in the way. It will help them see that one human being can make a difference.
> ("Rep. John Lewis's Speech at King Memorial Groundbreaking" 2006)

John Lewis is one of those human beings who has been making a difference his whole life. After he left SNCC, he had various jobs until he was elected to the Atlanta city council in 1981. Five years later, he made the jump into national politics by becoming a member of the US House of Representatives, an elected position that he began on January 3, 1987 and has maintained ever since. While he has been called the "conscience of Congress" (Kemper 2006), he also acts as an esteemed and acclaimed voice of the struggle for worldwide human rights in front of young people. In speeches on university campuses, he often makes use of his repertoire of proverbs and proverbial expressions to bring his views across effectively, as evidenced in the following remarks of August 26, 2005, to the students of the College of William and Mary in Williamsburg, Virginia. With the power of proverbial rhetoric, he advises the students "to get in the way," and he tells them that he kept his eyes on the prize throughout his life, and then he adds the two proverbs "keep your eyes on the prize" and "walk with the wind" as wisdom of an engaged life. The message is that the students should focus on achieving a positive end result in their pursuits and that they should move with the wind of change for a better world.

> So I say to you students, lead us into the 21st century. Find a way to get in the way. Find a way to get in trouble. Find a way to make some noise, to make our country and our world a better place....
> When I got in trouble, I began to accept nonviolence as a way of life, as a way of living. I got arrested a few times and went to jail, was beaten and left bloody and unconscious at the Greyhound bus station in Montgomery in May of 1961, got a concussion at the bridge in Selma 40 years ago, March 7, 1965. But I didn't give up. I didn't give in. I kept the faith. I kept my eyes on the prize.
> And I say to you, never give up. Never, ever, consider giving in. Keep your eyes on the prize, keep the faith and walk with the wind.
> (http://web.wm.edu/news/archive/?id-5125, website no longer available, accessed September 2013)

It has been my good fortune to have been present at one of these incredible speeches that Congressman John Lewis has delivered on numerous campuses and elsewhere. He was our special commencement speaker on May 20, 2007, at the University of Vermont in Burlington. After receiving an honorary doctoral degree, he spoke to a spellbound audience of students, faculty, staff, parents, relatives, and friends, and I recall vividly that he touched me so deeply with his wise words that I had tears in my eyes. Once again, he employs several proverbial phrases to encourage the graduates to embark on a life of civic engagement.

> The most pressing challenge in our society today is defined by the methods we use to defend the dignity of humankind. But too often we are focused on accumulating the trappings of a comfortable life—the big house, some new clothes, and a shiny, new car. But, if you want a better, more just, more fair society then you have to get in the way. You cannot wait for someone else to create change....
> What it is you care about—whether it's getting to the truth about the war in Iraq, global warming, shrinking economic opportunities for the middle class, or the injustice of poverty—you have to find your passion and make your contribution....
> The journey through life is difficult, but it is more meaningful when it is fueled by a vision, a dream, a determination to make life better for someone other than yourself. You have the power to change the social, political, and economic structures around you. You have the power to lead. Just find a way to get in the way and make your voices heard. So with that I say to you walk with the wind, and let the Spirit of History be your guide. (Lewis 2007)

When I finished my book *"Making a Way Out of No Way": Martin Luther King's Sermonic Proverbial Rhetoric* (2010) three years later, I included part of this address in my preface (x–xi) and then went on to say that it is a great honor to dedicate my study to this special person who has told thousands of people to find a way to get in the way of injustice and inequality.

> Just as his friend Martin Luther King had before him, John Lewis explained to us [at the University of Vermont] what is meant by the African American proverb "Making a way out of no way" [Doyle, Mieder, and Shapiro 2012, 102] standing in front of us as the epitome of dedicated and unselfish service in the cause of others.
> It is, then, my distinct honor to dedicate this book to John Lewis in recognition and admiration of his commitment and dedication to create a better world based on civil and human rights. He is a model of courage and dignity for us all, and it is my sincere hope that John Lewis will help guide humanity for many years to come by his exemplary insights and actions. (Mieder 2010, xi–xii)

One of my great personal treasures is a letter of June 10, 2011, from Congressman John Lewis that has left a lasting impression on me as I continue my scholarly work on proverbial rhetoric. I have reread his kind words many times, and they have become a guiding light in my small contributions to a kinder world.

> Dear Professor Mieder:
> First and foremost, I was deeply touched that you dedicated your most recent book, *"Making a Way Out of No Way": Martin Luther King's Sermonic Proverbial Rhetoric* to me. I was surprised and delighted to see that you also included parts of my 2007 commencement speech at the University of Vermont in the text.
> You have researched the phenomenon that is ingrained in African American culture, especially in the pulpit. I will never forget sitting in the congregation when Dr. King was preaching at Ebenezer Baptist Church in Atlanta. His father, who co-pastored the church with him at that time, would be sitting in the audience, and when the spirit began to move, Daddy King would say, "Make it plain, son. Make it plain." The way he, and other Baptist ministers did that, was by telling the stories, using the sayings and language that people used everyday to discuss religious principles and ideas. The proverbs you have so lovingly researched help us even today to make it plain.
> Besides our love of good public speaking, you and I also have something else in common. You began as a visitor to this country, and I actually visited your homeland last year just about this time. I had a chance to meet some activists there [in Germany], and I was deeply moved by their devotion to Civil Rights history. They knew so much about the movement. I was very impressed and deeply moved.
> Thank you, Professor Mieder for the signed copy of your book and for keeping the language of freedom and justice alive. I wish you all the best with your future academic endeavors and literary publications.
>
> Keep the faith!
> John Lewis
> Member of Congress

Taking out the time from his busy schedule as a congressman to write such a kind and meaningful letter to a professor in Vermont shows that John Lewis is indeed a considerate and compassionate person who knows how to bring his message across in plain words filled with emotional strength.

This can best be seen in his inspirational autobiography, *Walking with the Wind: A Memoir of the Movement* (1998), in which he tells two stories. One recounts his personal odyssey from childhood in the segregated South of the United States to respected and admired congressman, and the other represents the experienced account of the civil rights movement. When I read this moving personal and historical biography, I was immediately struck by its accessible and plain language, informed by a richness of proverbs and proverbial expressions. But while the book received much-deserved praise in numerous journalistic and scholarly reviews, this colorful metaphorical language is hardly ever mentioned. At least Jon Meacham remarked in *Newsweek* that "the strength of Lewis's powerful new book is not only the witness he bears but also the simplicity of his voice" (1998, 69); Mary McGrory called the book "a literary event, for sure" (1998, C1) in the *Washington Post*; William Chafe of the *New York Times* declared that Lewis had written a "powerful memoir [and] compelling account" (1998, 14); Zachary Dowdy paid Lewis the compliment that his autobiography "is superbly written, with Lewis's searing honesty showing through" (1998, D4) in the *Boston Globe*; and Joseph Dolman considered the book "beautifully written" (1998, 20) in *The New Leader*. Jack Nelson of the *Los Angeles Times* even prophesied that this book would become a "classic in civil rights literature" (1998, 8), and it has in fact reached this status. But what do these general accolades from the mass media mean as far as John Lewis's expressive rhetoric is concerned?

The more scholarly reviews from journals also do not go beyond superficial statements, if they mention the language or style of the memoir at all. Thus, Garry Wills (1998), Kathryn Nasstrom (1999), and Bill Whit (2000) say nothing about the language of the book in their reviews. Mike Miller speaks at least of a "powerful narrative" and acknowledges Lewis's "strength of character and conviction as he tells this tale" (1998, 46) but says nothing about how the tale is told. John Salmond calls the book an "at times intensely moving and always lively memoir" (2000, 167), and Enrique Rigsby ends his insightful review with the following paragraph: "As a witness of history, Lewis reminds the reader that the civil rights movement was rhetorical. Scholars of public affairs should drink deeply from his book. John Lewis is an American treasure; and few such treasures remain who can offer a rich personal perspective on some of the most important years in United States history" (2000, 681). Indeed, John Lewis by now is the only surviving major leader of the civil rights movement, but since Enrique Rigsby published his review in the *Rhetoric & Public Affairs* journal, it would have been welcome if he had commented on the sociopolitical rhetoric and ethical rhetoric that distinguishes John Lewis as a reformer whose political language is informed by proverbs and proverbial expressions. (For proverbs in politics in general see Louis 2000; Mieder 1997, 2004, 137–39; 2005, 2008; Nichols 1996). As will be shown, he is part of a tradition of African American politicians who have used proverbial speech to enhance their expressive and at times sermonic rhetoric, to wit the well-documented linguistic prowess of Frederick Douglass, Martin Luther King Jr., and Barack Obama (Mieder 2001, 2009, 2010). With the respect and admiration that John Lewis feels for Dr. King, with whom he also shares his religiously informed language, it should not be surprising that he echoes his friend's proverbial rhetoric in particular.

It is not possible to comment in detail on all the proverbs, proverbial expressions, proverbial comparisons, and other types of phraseologisms contained in John Lewis's three books—his voluminous autobiography, *Walking with the Wind: A Memoir of the Movement* (1998), his small philosophical book, *Across That Bridge: Life Lessons and a Vision for Change* (2012), and his graphic novel for juvenile readers, *March: Book One* (2013; two more volumes are planned). While his first book contains 654 proverbial texts on 503 pages (one per 0.8 pages), the second book includes only 71 on 180 pages (one per 2.5 pages), and the third book features but 17 texts on 121 pages (one per 7.1 pages), due to its graphic nature with little text. Clearly, Lewis's autobiography is of special interest as far as his proverbial rhetoric is concerned. In fact, the phraseologisms included in the graphic novel for the most part are repetitions from the memoir. However, there are some proverbs and proverbial expressions that appear only in his small philosophical treatise, and some of these will be included in the following discussion that deals primarily with the rich proverbial rhetoric of John Lewis's autobiography. While most proverbial texts occur only once or twice, some have multiple occurrences, as for example "to get down to business," "to throw down the gauntlet," "to be in the middle of nowhere," "to get (see) the big picture," "to roll up one's sleeves," "to be a team player" (all three times), "to strike a chord," "to be dead set against somebody or something," "to take into one's own hands," "to play by the rules," "to be the last straw" (four times), "to hold (stand) one's ground," "in the long run" (five times), "to be in the air," "the rank and file," "to take someone to task," "to rub someone the wrong way" (six times), "to open someone's eyes" (seven times), "to draw the line" (eight times), "to work behind the scene" (nine times), and "to put on the line" (eleven times). In the following analysis, especially relevant Bible proverbs, folk proverbs, and proverbial expressions will be discussed in their context, showing that this proverbial rhetoric plays a major role in the books and speeches about civil and human rights by Congressman John Lewis.

Before John Lewis became involved in the civil rights movement as a student, he had envisioned himself becoming a preacher. He certainly went to church with his parents, he preached to his flock of chickens, he delivered a sermon as a youngster, he studied religion and philosophy at college, and he has remained to this day a deeply religious person with a social conscience that led the preacher into politics. It should not be surprising that he is well versed in the Bible and that he relies on its proverbial wisdom to express basic human issues. He does so without becoming overly didactic but rather compassionate, like when he explains why his parents were not at all pleased about his turn toward revolutionary social changes. The following paragraph merely alludes to the Bible proverb "straight is the gate, and narrow is the way which leadeth unto life" (Matthew 7:14) to describe the simple but poor existence of his sharecropper parents, who were filled with anxiety about their young son's intent to turn the world upside down, as Lewis comments proverbially.

> Change, as I learned back when I was growing up, was not something my parents were ever very comfortable with. And who could blame them? They, like hundreds of thousands—no, *millions*—of black men and women of their generation, worked harder than seemed humanly possible, under circumstances more difficult than most Americans today could possibly imagine, to carve out a life for themselves and their children in a society that saw them as less than fully human. Theirs was, as the Bible says, a straight and narrow way. There was little room for change in the world my parents knew, and what change there was was usually for the worse. It's not hard to understand at all the mixture of fear and concern they both felt as they watched me walk out into the world as a young man to join a movement aimed, in essence, at turning the world they knew upside down. (9)

In his book *Across That Bridge*, Lewis includes a similar paragraph in which he describes how he somewhat deviously pursued his strong desire to get an education, with his parents being caught between the proverbial rock and a hard place in trying to understand his drive while needing his labor in the field. The proverbial phrase certainly adds much metaphorical emphasis to their ambivalent situation.

> Sometimes when I was needed in the fields to help my parents pick cotton, peanuts, or corn, I would get up very early. I would get dressed and then hide under the front porch until the school bus stopped at my house. Then I would hop on the bus without my parents knowing. They were always angry when they discovered I was gone, as most parents would be, but they never punished me for going to school. We were all victims of the narrow limitations our society had proscribed for us. They were trapped too, between a rock and a hard place that required them to pit their survival as sharecroppers against the education of their children. (B129)

In yet another telling passage replete with proverbial language, Lewis explains that while he understood his parents' resigned attitude of not actively fighting against the injustice of segregation, he could not accept that many of the Baptist ministers did nothing to fight against this social evil. As so often in his autobiography, he amasses proverbial language to add metaphorical color to his discourse, including the twin formula "right and left," the Bible proverb "an eye for an eye, a tooth for a tooth" (Exodus 21:24), and the proverbial expressions "pie in the sky" and "between the cradle and the grave."

> My parents' attitude toward injustice didn't bother me nearly as much as the attitude I saw among the ministers at church. Our minister at Macedonia Baptist lived in Montgomery and traveled out to preach to us once a month. It always bothered me that he knew, as we all did, how sharecroppers were cheated by our landlords right and left, underpaid and overcharged every year, but not once did he ever speak about this in his sermons. Sunday after Sunday he'd talk about an eye for an eye, a tooth for a tooth, how the soul must be saved by and by for that pie in the sky after you die, but hardly a word about *this* life, about *this* world, about some sense of salvation and righteousness right *here*, between the cradle and the grave. It also did not escape my notice that that minister arrived and departed in a pretty nice automobile, and that he went back to a very comfortable home in Montgomery, more comfortable than the homes any of us lived in. (44)

Regarding the famous proverb from Exodus, it expresses a vindictive philosophy that John Lewis, with his uncompromising commitment to nonviolence, could not possibly agree with. In fact, when the peaceful civil rights movement came under attack by more aggressive forces led by Malcolm X, Lewis cites the Bible proverb to voice his strong opposition to militant action.

> I respected Malcolm. I saw him as a very articulate, very forceful spokesperson for what he believed in. But I never accepted his ideas. I didn't—and I don't—have any sympathy with black nationalism, separatism, the attitude of an eye for an eye or violence of any sort. I can respect a person and understand what he's saying and still not be sympathetic to it. As far as I was concerned, Malcolm was not a civil rights leader. Malcolm was not part of the movement. The movement had a goal of an integrated society, an interracial democracy, a Beloved Community. What Malcolm X represented were the seeds of something different, something that would eventually creep into the movement itself and split it apart. He was not about integration, not about an interracial community, and he was not nonviolent. To his credit, he preached personal independence and responsibility, self-discipline and self-reliance. But he also urged the black man to fight back in self-defense—"by any means necessary," as he famously put it. And I just could not accept that. (205–6)

Later in the autobiography, Lewis returns to the more militant advocates of the civil rights movement, notably H. (for Hubert) "Rap" Brown, who in 1967 "grabbed headlines with quotes like 'Violence is as American as cherry pie'" (395). He varied the standard proverbial comparison "as American as apple pie" during a SNCC press conference on July 27, 1967 (Shapiro 2006, 107), perhaps changing the apples to cherries since the red color fits well to the violence (blood) that he was talking about. It is interesting to note that Lewis quotes this proverbial "slogan," having no choice but to agree with this unfortunate characterization of American society.

> I would actually agree with this statement. Violence has always been endemic to American culture. Dr. King said the same thing. We are, and have always been, a very violent society. But that doesn't mean we have to accept it. It doesn't mean that we have to respond to the worst of America with the worst of ourselves. We have something better to offer. I have always believed that. I have always believed it is possible to show ourselves a different way, a better way to solve our problems. This is what Gandhi tried to do in India. It is what Dr. King tried to do here, and it goes far beyond civil rights alone. It extends to all of the conflicts we face among ourselves and among other nations. There are simply other and better ways to solve our differences than through violence. (395)

No wonder Lewis's disapproval of the Old Testament "eye for an eye" proverb of forceful retribution becomes a leitmotif in his nonviolent struggle for equal rights, as can be seen from yet another powerful paragraph in which he argues against the ills of uncontrolled riots by also questioning the proverbial claim "anything goes" and the equally proverbial insistence "to let it all out."

> That's what a riot is—just letting it out. Nothing is held back. Anything goes. Burning. Looting. Killing. Even one another. Part of the movement was to tame the madness of men, to take the beast that lives in all of us and turn it toward love, to show humankind a different way, to teach the way of compassion, of connection and community, of peace and nonviolence. Yes, we are human, and yes, there is a savage side in all of us. The first impulse of man has always been to react like an animal, to respond to attack in like manner. If someone hits you, strike back. If someone bombs you, bomb back. But there have been teachers, men and women throughout history, who have stood and said, No, you can't take an eye for an eye. If you do, we will all be blind. At some point we have to lift ourselves to a higher plane. And it is possible. Men have shown throughout history that it is possible. (409)

Lewis is consistent in his view against this ill-conceived wisdom from the Old Testament, as can be seen from its dual appearance in his more recent book *Across That Bridge: Life Lessons and a Vision for Change*.

> For those who could not find their dignity in the actions of nonviolent resistance, especially after the assassination of leaders like Dr. Martin Luther King

> Jr. . . ., black power or the ideas of self-defense grew in popularity. They were advocated as quicker paths to self-respect and an appreciation of one's self-worth through retaliating against the wrongs brought against us. It may have worked for some people. I would never question the value of affirming oneself, or recognizing and utilizing collective strength to make our voices heard. However, I would say that the danger of matching threat for threat, violence with violence, resistance with force, is that it has the potential to create the same spiritual deficit the victim is struggling against within him or herself. The notion of an eye for an eye, though biblical, only lowers an individual to the level of his or her attacker. (B155–56)

In his final condemnation of this Bible proverb, Lewis even adds the related proverb "blood asks (for) blood" (Genesis 9:6) to it, scolding all those "who want to spill blood for blood, ravage an eye for an eye, or rip out a tooth for a tooth" (B176).

It is obvious that a nonviolent person would argue against these biblical proverbs, but Lewis also feels forced to cite positive Bible proverbs to show that their humane messages are unfortunately not adhered to by those who preach them in the segregated South. A good example are his thoughts about the proverb "love thy neighbor as thyself (Matthew 22:39) that he had studied as a student of religion and philosophy at American Baptist Theological Seminary and Fisk University in Nashville.

> I had never heard anything like this [the enlightening lectures]. Except for Dr. King's speeches. I had never been exposed to religion beyond the bounds of the Good Book. Now my brain was crackling as it strained to assess and absorb these new ideas [of Plato, Socrates, St. Augustine, Kant, Hegel, etc.]. Now I saw philosophical and theological underpinnings for what I'd sensed and deeply felt all my life—that there was a contradiction between what was and what ought to be. This contradiction extended even to training people to preach the Gospel. For the most part, white Southern Baptist churches didn't even want black people to step inside their buildings. Yet within these very institutions, people were being taught that Jesus Christ says to love thy neighbor as thyself. How could that be? How could people reconcile that belief with the way they lived? It was illogical. It was contradictory. I was more convinced than ever that Dr. King was right and the white South was wrong. (63–64)

Again and again in his writings and speeches, Lewis returns to his mentor and friend Martin Luther King Jr., whom he met in 1957 at the young age of seventeen. In 1955, the young John Lewis had heard a sermon by King on the radio that "set him on fire" proverbially speaking and influenced him from then to now: "This was the first time I had ever heard something I would learn was called the social gospel—taking the teachings of the Bible and applying them to the earthbound problems and issues confronting a community and a society. I was on fire with the words I was hearing. I felt that this man—his name was Martin Luther King Jr.—was speaking directly to me. This young preacher was giving voice to everything I'd been feeling and fighting to figure out for years" (45–46).

Later in his autobiography, Lewis writes this touching testimonial about King and uses the proverbial expression "to open someone's eyes" to indicate that King showed him the way of the social gospel. The short paragraph is a touching indication of how two of the greatest Americans of the modern age were soulmates in their struggles.

> Dr. King was my friend, my brother, my leader. He was the man, the one who opened my eyes to the world. From the time I was fifteen until the day he died—for almost half my life—he was the person who, more than any other, continued to influence my life, who made me who I was. He made me who I *am*. To this day I owe more of myself to him than to anyone else I have ever known. It's difficult to express in words. I have never believed in any man as much as I believed in Martin Luther King. When he was killed I really felt I'd lost a part of myself. (412–13)

King, just like Mohandas Gandhi, is for Lewis the epitome of nonviolence. Giving hope for a better life to disadvantaged people by turning the social gospel of the New Testament into nonviolent action is always present, as can be seen in the following comments with that hopeful proverb "Blessed are the meek, for they shall inherit the earth" (Matthew 5:5).

> Dr. King would often say that we've got to love people no matter what. Most of all, he would say, we must love the unlovable. Love the *hell* out of them, he would say. And he meant that literally. If there is hell in someone, if there is meanness and anger and hatred in him, we've got to *love* it out.
> I had no doubt that this could be done. Gandhi showed it could be done. This one little man [like John Lewis], armed with nothing but the truth and a fundamental faith in the response of human society to redemptive suffering, was able to reshape an entire nation without raising so much as a fist. And he did it not by aiming high, at the people in power, but by aiming low, at the downtrodden, the poor, the men and women and children who inhabited the streets and the fields of his country. It is an ancient theme, as old as the Christian Bible: "Blessed are the meek; for they shall inherit the earth. . . . Blessed are they who are persecuted for righteousness' sake; for theirs is the kingdom of heaven." (78)

It is perhaps somewhat surprising that John Lewis does not cite the Golden Rule of the proverb "do unto others as you would have them do unto you" (Matthew 7:12) that is part and parcel of all the major religions of the world (Hertzler 1933–34; Griffin 1991, 67–69; Burrell 1997, 13–27;

Templeton 1997, 8–12). Other social reformers like Abraham Lincoln, Frederick Douglass, Elizabeth Cady Stanton and Susan B. Anthony, Martin Luther King, and Barack Obama all made use of it as the most basic law of human life. But Lewis does at least refer to it in a rather intriguing way when he recounts the story of the first thirteen Freedom Riders of 1961, of whom he was one: "There was [also] Albert Bigelow, a big, rugged-looking guy from New England who looked as if he belonged on a sailing ship a century ago. In fact, he *had* been a sailor, a Navy captain during World War II, and that experience had turned him into a committed pacifist—so committed that he was arrested in 1958 for steering a skiff he called *The Golden Rule* into a nuclear testing zone in the South Pacific as a protest against the use of the atomic bomb" (131).

In any case, Lewis certainly employs the proverbial triad "faith, hope, and love (1 Corinthians 13:13) as yet another underlying biblical principle of the civil rights movement, altering it slightly to indicate that courage was a major component for its participants as they confronted brutal force.

> Faith, hope and courage—these were all essential ingredients for the work SNCC was doing in the Deep South in those early years. And anger, too. Yes, there was anger among us in SNCC, but it was good anger, a healthy anger, at least in that early stage. It was a positive, constructive type of anger. We were rebels, absolutely. We were all about rebellion, but it was a rebellion against an evil thing, the whole system and structure of segregation and racial discrimination. If the old guard leadership of our own black community was holding us back, then we were rebelling against them, too. (188)

Lewis also cites the biblical proverbial phrase "to be a thorn in the flesh" (2 Corinthians 12:7) to describe the positively rebellious SNCC, which he expanded into a massive organization of young blacks and whites pushing for desegregation. "We were created, in a way, to be a thorn in the flesh of the American body politic and of the established, traditional civil rights movement" (284).

Being not only a preacher by nature but also a natural teacher, Lewis is quick to call on biblical phrases in support of his inspirational "Life Lessons and Vision for Change" (Arthurs 2003). In the introduction to the book that carries this statement as its subtitle, he cites the expression "to have the scales fall from one's eyes" (Acts 9:18) to stress the importance for people of all walks of life to be wide awake and keep their eyes open at all times so that the social revolution never ceases.

> This book is for the people. It is for the grassroots leaders who will emerge not for the sake of fame or fortune, but with a burning desire to do good. It

is for all those willing to join in the human spirit's age-old struggle to break free from the bondage of concepts and structures that have lost their use. It is for the masses of people who with each new day have the chance to peel the scales from their eyes and remember it is they alone who are the most powerful agents of change. It is for anyone who wants to reform his or her existence or to fashion a better life for the children. It's for those who want to improve their community or to make their mark in history. This book is a collection of a few of the truths that I have learned as one who dreamed, worked, and struggled in America's last revolution. (B2–3)

Finally, he draws on the biblical phrase "to be a voice crying in the wilderness" (Matthew 3:3) to warn people that standing up for social change can be a lonely business, but it must be faced in a courageous, informed, and nonviolent way with faith, hope, and love for all people.

> It is only through examining history that you [people] become aware of where you stand within the continuum of change. you may find you are the "voice crying in the wilderness" who will have to walk alone. Or you may find only a few devotees who will join you throughout the whole period of your activism. This does not mean your work is not important. It means the part you must play is simply different than those leaders who stand at the front lines of a mass movement. Every contribution is important to the work of change, and it is only when you study the history of activism that you can perceive what your role may be and how others managed in the same kind of position years and decades before. It is through study and preparation that you can increase the power of your work. (B70)

Indeed, much can be learned through study as the highly educated Martin Luther King Jr. in particular showed in his sermons, speeches, writings, and actions. This can be seen from his integration of the three proverbial quotations "truth crushed to the earth will rise again" (William Cullen Bryant), "no lie can live forever (Thomas Carlyle), and "the arc (arm) of the moral universe is long, but it bends toward justice" (Theodore Parker); the Bible proverb "as you sow, so shall you reap" (Galatians 6:7); as well as the folk proverb "the truth is marching on" into one powerful paragraph in one of his most important speeches on March 25, 1965 in Montgomery, Alabama. It was a high point of civil rights rhetoric at the time, and its repetition by Lewis in his autobiography is not only a tribute to King but also a central message that he wants to give to his readers.

> I [Dr. King] know some of you are asking today, "How long will it take?" I come to say to you this afternoon however difficult the moment, however frustrating the hour, it will not be long, because truth pressed to the earth will rise again.
> How long? Not long, because no lie can live forever.

> How long? Not long, because you will reap what you sow.
> How long? Not long, because the arm [sic: arc] of the moral universe is long but it bends toward justice.
> How long? Not long, because mine eyes have seen the glory of the coming of the Lord, trampling out the vintage where the grapes of wrath are stored. He has loosed the faithful lightning of his terrible swift sword. His truth is marching on.
> Glory hallelujah! *Glory hallelujah!* (360; the entire speech in Washington 1986: 230)

In the final chapter of his book *Across That Bridge*, John Lewis reminds his readers that the proverb "all men are created equal" and the proverbial triad "life, liberty, and the pursuit of happiness" from the Declaration of Independence should forever be the social compass with its message deeply ingrained in the minds and hearts of citizens (see Aron 2008, 91–96): "The Declaration of Independence expresses the purposes of human community by affirming this [basic freedoms] as a fundamental root of our founding: 'We hold these truths to be self-evident, that all men are created equal, that they are endowed by their Creator with certain inalienable rights, among these are life, liberty, and the pursuit of happiness.' Inalienable means that no law, no man, no woman, no child, no power can separate us from this divine quest" (B170).

Toward the end of his autobiography, Lewis says something quite similar, stressing that the country must pay special attention to instill in its young, poor black people the belief in a better existence for all. As he continues, he broadens his uplifting little "sermon" to include the disadvantaged of all age groups, urging them proverbially that they must think about how their lives can improve "in the long run."

> I truly believe that if we don't invest more in our young people, we are headed for disaster. And this is where the [modern] revolution must begin. A revolution of values. A revolution of attitude. A revolution that instills the sense of *possibility* in these young people's minds and hearts, a belief that this nation does indeed offer to them the opportunities of life, liberty, and the pursuit of happiness.
> The people, young and old alike, in these [poor and largely black] communities need to organize, to form a movement, a movement fueled not just by anger and rage, but by moral *authority*, by a sense of human righteousness fueled by the spirit. First, however, that spirit must be kindled within and among these communities—in these homes, in these neighborhoods, among the poor and the outcast themselves. I have been poor. I know what it is like. And I know that it is possible to pool our interests, to gather our resources, as cant as they might seem. And I am not talking just about money. I am talking about courage and strength of character, about stepping back and deciding

what is important and valuable about life in the long run, not just how to make ourselves happy today, or maybe tomorrow. . . .

Replace them [elected officials] with people who will do what is demanded, what is needed. People are too quiet, too patient. In the great words of a nineteenth-century civil rights fighter, Fredrick Douglass, we need to "agitate, agitate, agitate." (488)

I am surprised that John Lewis does not cite Douglass's other dictum here, namely "if there is no struggle, there is no progress" that he stated in a powerful abolitionist speech of August 3, 1857.

> Let me give you a word of philosophy of reform. The whole history of the progress of human liberty shows that all concessions yet made to her august claims, have been born of earnest struggle. The conflict has been exciting, agitating, all-absorbing, and for the time being, putting all the tumults to silence. It must do this or it does nothing. If there is no struggle, there is no progress. Those who profess to favor freedom and yet depreciate agitation, are men who want crops without plowing up the ground, they want rain without thunder and lightning. They want the ocean without the awful roar of its many waters. This struggle may be a moral one, or it may be a physical one, and it may be both moral and physical, but it must be a struggle. Power concedes nothing without a demand. It never did and it never will. (Blassingame 1985–92, 3:204; Mieder 2001, 456–57)

I took the liberty of shortening Douglass's proverbial quotation to "No Struggle, No Progress" for the title of my book *Frederick Douglass and His Proverbial Rhetoric for Civil Rights* (2001), hoping that it might catch on as a new proverb in time.

But to return to our proverbial muttons, it should be noted that at the beginning of his book *Across That Bridge*, John Lewis also refers to the lesser-known quotation that follows the triad of "life, liberty, and the pursuit of happiness," namely "no just government can be formed without the consent of the governed." He might have done well to point out that this truth was penned by Thomas Jefferson as well in the Declaration of Independence, but be that as it may, Lewis as the humanitarian politician did well with the following statement, echoing the repeated use of it by Elizabeth Cady Stanton and Susan B. Anthony in their struggle for women's rights in the nineteenth century (see Mieder 2013).

> Nothing can stop the power of a committed and determined people to make a difference in our society. Why? Because human beings are the most dynamic link to the divine on this planet. Governments and corporations do not live. They have no power, no capacity in and of themselves. They are given life and derive all their authority from their ability to assist, benefit, and transform the lives of the people they touch. All authority emanates from the consent of the

governed and the satisfaction of the customer. Somehow it seems leaders have forgotten this fundamental principle, and we must right ourselves before the people withdraw their support. (B6–7)

In a later chapter called "Truth" in this book, Lewis appears to be creating a string of pseudo-proverbs based on the fourteenth-century proverb "familiarity breeds contempt" (Mieder, Kingsbury, and Harder 1992, 198). They all maintain the simple structure of "X breeds Y," giving Lewis a multitude of ways to show how people get drawn into a downward spiral of disrespect and hate.

> What will it take for each of us to learn from the lessons of segregation and separation and apply them liberally to our own lives? If we are truly to learn the lessons of the Civil Rights Movement, the Holocaust, or the conflict in Northern Ireland, we must concede that discomfort breeds dislike, dislike breeds disdain, disdain breeds contempt, and contempt breeds hate. We cannot afford to relegate the victories in the struggle between love and hate to one group or another, whether they happen on American shores or not. The truth is, as long as we see life in terms of its duality, instead of its commonality, our lives will always demand we overcome. (B101)

John Lewis is well aware of the fact that the United States, like any other country, has its problems and faults, but there is hope for improvement, as is implied by his quotation of Bill Clinton's dictum "mend it, don't end it" that causes Lewis to also employ the proverbial expression "to throw the baby out with the bathwater." That expression first appeared in a satirical literary work in Germany in 1512 and was subsequently translated into English in the late nineteenth century, to express the idea of getting rid of the good together with the bad (Mieder 1993, 224): "To all these determined critics of affirmative action [and other important civil rights legislation, for that matter]: I agree with President Clinton. I say, 'Mend it, don't end it.' Yes, there are problems with some aspects of affirmative action programs. Adjustments can be made. Solutions can be found. But we should not end affirmative action simply because the system has problems. Its principles are sound. They are healthy. We should not throw the baby out with the bathwater" (492).

Lewis also cites Mother Teresa's "to keep a lamp burning, we have to keep putting oil in it" (501) to keep people's spirits up and to take care of those less fortunate: "Talk is fine. Discussion is fine. But we must respond. We must act. Mother Teresa acted. She reached out to those who were left behind—the forsaken, the poorest of the poor, the sickest of the sick. And where did she find her strength, her focus, her fuel? She was asked that question back in 1975, for that *Time* magazine story on 'living saints' [of whom John Lewis was one!]. Her answer was succinct. The fuel, she explained, is prayer. 'To keep a lamp burning,' she said, 'we have to keep putting oil in it.' Prayer" (501).

Of course, this type of prayer does not imply only a *vita contemplativa* but rather a *vita activa*, filled with words turned into action, or, as the folk proverb going back to the early seventeenth century has it, "actions speak louder than words" (Mieder, Kingsbury, and Harder 1992, 7). Actually, John Lewis says all of this much better in the very last paragraph of his classic autobiography, citing a piece of traditional African wisdom: "There is an old African proverb: 'When you pray, move your feet.' As a nation, if we care for the Beloved Community, we must move our feet, our hands, our hearts, our resources to build and not to tear town, to reconcile and not to divide, to love and not to hate, to heal and not to kill. In the final analysis, we are one people, one family, one house—the American house, the American family" (503).

The proverb is also cited as a separate piece of wisdom at the end of the chapter called "Faith" in *Across That Bridge*: "*When you pray, move your feet.*—African Proverb" (B39). It should be observed, however, that the African origin of this proverb has not been established. The earliest printed reference found thus far is from 1936, indicating a probable Quaker source, even though "in recent times, it is regularly referred to as an African or an African American proverb" (Doyle, Mieder, and Shapiro 2012, 84–85).

Clearly, all people have their responsible roles to play on the world's stage, as John Lewis states by borrowing the proverbial wisdom of William Shakespeare in his treasure of personal life lessons.

> What Shakespeare wrote in *As You Like It* is not only poetic and beautiful, it also expresses a profound truth: "All the world's a stage," he says, "and all the men and women merely players." Life is like a drama, and any person who is truly committed to an ideal must believe in the authority of a divine plan. Not a rigid, micromanagement of human behavior that predicts every step of every individual, but a set of divine boundaries that governs the present, the past, and the future—a set of principles humankind does not have the capacity to override, no matter how far we attempt to stray from its dictates. (B20–21)

To add even more proverbiality at the end of this discussion of Bible proverbs and a few quotational proverbs as well, it can be stated that all people need to keep their eyes on the prize and struggle toward it with optimism and hope while keeping the Golden Rule ever in mind.

This next section too can start with a reference to John Lewis's family. He is well aware that he broke away from his parents and siblings who remained in the rural South, but he assures his readers that he remains humble despite his political successes that have brought him into close contact with members of Congress, the presidents and vice presidents since John F. Kennedy, other American politicians, and also foreign dignitaries. He returns to his native Troy, Alabama, as often as he can when he is home from Washington, DC, in Atlanta, Georgia. He loves these large family gatherings, valuing all of his relatives as they try to deal with his accomplishments and fame. The proverb "there is nothing like family" amply describes his allegiance.

> It's quite a crowd when we all get together, along with our spouses and children. The energy, the closeness, the comfort—there really is nothing in the world like family. When I come home like this, I'm not a congressman anymore making speeches on national television. Nor am I a civil rights warrior quoted in history books. Or a "living saint," as *Time* magazine once called me years ago, to the unending amusement of my closest friends. No, by the time I step onto my mother's front porch, all those labels have faded away and I'm just plain Robert [his middle name] again, third oldest of Eddie and Willie Mae Lewis's ten children. (8–9)

As he explains the hardships that his poor family as sharecroppers endured working in the hot sun with the proverbial comparison "the air as still as death" adding colloquial expressiveness to the misery, he mentions that they lacked almost all modern amenities but were happy just the same. After all, as the proverb says, "it is hard to miss what you have never had (known)."

> There is really no way to describe how hot and heavy the summer months get in a place like south Alabama. You work all day, outside, under that broiling sun, the air as still as death, then you come home to a house that is hardly cooler inside than out, even with the shade, even at nighttime. We had no fans; we had no electricity. Air-conditioning would have sounded like something out of science fiction—if we had even heard of it, which we had not. Still, again, it's hard to miss what you have never known. What might sound like hardship today still holds a happy, sentimental place in my memory. (20)

Once John Lewis left his home for the American Baptist Theological Seminary in 1957, he became involved in a string of sit-ins that succeeded in desegregating the city of Nashville. In his memoir, he describes a visit at that school almost forty years later, where an older student pays Lewis a compliment by using the relatively new African American proverb "if you want to talk the talk, you've got to walk the walk," whose earliest written record comes from 1967 (Doyle, Mieder, and Shapiro 2012, 250): "He [the student, Mike Flippin] admitted he didn't recognize my name at first, but he knew about the movement that had begun here four decades before. 'I don't know if we today would *have* that kind of courage,' he said. 'We might talk the talk, but people like you all, you walked the *walk*'" (60).

Recalling his first reluctant and then unsuccessful attempt to run for a seat in the U.S. House of Representatives in 1977, Lewis in a bit of self-analysis returns to this proverb:

> I still had several reservations [about running for national office], several reasons to wonder if I was really ready for this. First, I had no background or experience whatsoever in politics at any level, not at a school board, not on a county commission, not on a city council—nothing. And I was not charming or charismatic.... I always preferred to walk the walk rather than talk the talk. But politics is about walking and talking. Give me the room to talk, to actually spend some time with people—whether it's making a speech or having a real conversation—and I can make the points and have the effect I desire. But the same qualities that can come through so strongly in that kind of setting—earnestness, sincerity, substance—can come across in ten-second sound bites on the evening news as just plain dull. And as everyone knows, modern political campaigns are, unfortunately, steered largely by sound bites. (441)

John Lewis has walked the walk, determined to make a difference for many decades, but by staying away from opportune sound bites, his voice has become recognized as one of compassionate reason, stressing "the essence of the nonviolent way of life—the capacity to forgive" (77). Perhaps recalling Martin Luther King Jr.'s warning, "hate begets hate, violence begets violence, and toughness begets a greater toughness" (King 1958, 87; Mieder 2010, 337–38) that King might well have based on the structure of the common proverb "money begets money," Lewis talks of the evil of violence, hate, and anger with words that are anything but mundane or "just plain dull."

> And it [nonviolence] is a way of life.... It is not something you turn on or off like a faucet. This sense of love, this sense of peace, the capacity of compassion, is something you carry inside yourself every waking minute of the day. It shapes your response to a curt cashier in the grocery store or to a driver cutting you off in traffic just as surely as it keeps you from striking back at a state trooper who might be kicking you in the ribs because you dared to march in protest against an oppressive government. If you want to create an open society, your means of doing so must be consistent with the society you want to create. Means and ends are absolutely inseparable. Violence begets violence. Hatred begets hatred. Anger begets anger, every minute of the day, in the smallest of moments as well as the largest. (77–78)

Lewis returns to the proverbial wisdom "violence begets violence" when he describes how nonviolent behavior eventually had positive results during the confrontational sit-ins in Nashville. The phrase "to egg someone on" adds a colloquial element to this description, and one almost wishes that Lewis would have added the proverbial expression "to have egg on one's face" to it, to describe how the violent segregationists lost out in this situation: "I got back on my stool [at the lunch counter] and sat there, not saying a word. The others did the same. Violence does beget violence, but the opposite is just as true. Hitting someone who does not hit back can last only so long. Fury spends itself pretty quickly when there's no fury facing it. . . . They continued trying to egg us on, but the beating subsides" (99–100). It is of interest to note here that Lewis has kept parts of this proverbial paragraph in his graphic novel, *March: Book One* that, by its nature, uses only minimalistic prose with its illustrations. "Violence does beget violence, but the opposite is just as true. Fury spends itself pretty quickly when there's no fury facing it" (M100–101).

The nonviolent students of Nashville had every reason to be proud of their accomplishment, but as Ella Baker from the SCLC (Southern Christian Leadership Conference) told them, this really was only the beginning of a much larger struggle to desegregate the South. As Lewis describes her caveats, he seems to quote her as stating that the young people should stay focused on the prize, that is, "keep it pure" and "keep it real." If in fact Baker did say "keep it real" in 1960, this proverb would be fifteen years older than the first documented use of it in the *Dictionary of Modern Proverbs* (Doyle, Mieder, and Shapiro 2012, 132)—or is Lewis's linguistic memory playing a trick with him here? Of course, "keep it real" could well have been in oral use by 1960. Here is the actual account from the memoir.

> [Ella] Baker herself, in a speech titled "More Than a Hamburger," praised our success so far but warned that our work had just begun. Integrating lunch counters in stores already patronized mostly by blacks was one thing. Breaking down barriers in areas as racially and culturally entrenched as voting rights, education and the workplace was going to be much tougher than what we had faced so far. She had another warning as well. . . . Don't let anyone else, especially the older folks, tell you what to do. Think and act for yourselves. Hold onto your energy and your vision. Keep it pure. Keep it real. (108)

She might just as well have added "keep your eyes on the prize," and that is, of course, exactly what John Lewis and students did in the years to come. It should also be noted that John Lewis has a good ear and memory for proverbs used by others. Thus, he recalls one of the SNCC members of having used the proverb "a bird needs two wings to fly" (180) as a fitting metaphor for the two sections of that organization, the one going primarily after voter registration, the other sticking with the drive for desegregation.

Lewis agreed to this two-pronged approach as a compromise, even though he firmly believed that they "needed to push and push and not stop pushing" (180). His political pragmatism is indeed impressive, but so is his nonflamboyant leadership style in the civil rights movement. He never minded taking a back seat, he did not push himself into the glaring limelight, and he didn't care about getting credit. These three proverbial expressions plus the proverb "here today and gone tomorrow" and the phrase "to be a flash in the pan" used to characterize those who do things only for the sake of getting attention without having staying power are a clear indication of the rich proverbial rhetoric of Lewis's autobiography. The following five paragraphs certainly exemplify his lively and authentic style that makes his account such an invaluable experience for the readers.

> From the beginning, people were coming at me from all sides, trying to force me into a more politically active role, to be more conscious and forceful in dealing with other civil rights organizations. [Jim] Forman and Marion Barry kept pushing and saying, "Take on this person, take on that organization." Infighting and one-upmanship was the game, they told me. "Don't take a back seat," they'd say.
>
> When I returned from that July meeting in New York, Forman took me aside and pointed at a newspaper photo where I'm at the end of the group, almost out of the frame. "You've got to get out *front*," he said. "Don't let King get all the credit. Don't stand back like that. Get out *front*."
>
> I just never thought that way. Trying to get out front and worry about who's getting the credit, that's just never been my concern. Let's get the job done—that's how I feel. That's how I've always felt. Don't worry about the limelight. Get the job done, and there will be plenty of credit to get around.
>
> I realize that attitude has sometimes—some would say often—resulted in my being overlooked now and then through the course of my life. I've never been the kind of person who naturally attracts the limelight. I'm not a handsome guy. I'm not flamboyant. I'm not what you would call elegant. I'm short and stocky. My skin is dark, not fair—a feature that was still considered a drawback by many black people in the early '60s. For some or all of these reasons, I simply have never been the kind of guy who draws attention.
>
> And I'm thankful for that. It's always seemed to me that the people who are fed by and who focus on visibility and notoriety and getting the credit don't have what you might call staying power. They rise and fall in the public eye, here today and gone tomorrow. Too often they become flashes in the pan, winding up in those "Where Are They Now?" columns. It's sad. Dr. King used to talk about this. He said individuals who fall in love with public attention are not worthy of it. People who hunger for fame don't realize that if they're in the spotlight today, somebody else will be tomorrow. Fame never lasts. The work you do, the things you accomplish—that's what endures. That's what really means something. (211)

I wish that such humility could be found in more public figures. If as a paremiologist I ever have the honor of meeting John Lewis in person, I would tell him that his speeches and writings win the prize when it comes to the political rhetoric of today.

There are other such paragraphs in this moving book, one more of which must be cited here. In it, Lewis draws on the proverbial expression "to stand on the shoulders of giants" that goes back to Isaac Newton (Deutscher 2006; Mieder 2011, 4–5) to express with sincere humility that every new generation is indebted to the accomplishments of the previous one and that there are many unsung heroes who paid their dues to bring about positive social change.

> We have problems. We will always have problems. A free and open society—a democracy—is by definition an eternal work-in-progress. . . . Each generation stands on the shoulders of the previous one. This is the way we move ahead, as individuals, as families and as a nation. Without the years of struggle of the civil rights movement, without people like Dr. King, without the unsung heroes of the movement, without the people who came before them and the people who came after, we would not be where we are today. The barriers that have fallen down would still be up. (494–95)

Yes, there will always be problems, and there were plenty of them, even among and within the various civil rights organizations. As with most organizations, SNCC had its share of infighting, causing John Lewis plenty of anguish and anxiety, especially when he returned from a trip to Africa in the fall of 1964. Members of the inner circle accused him of having been away too long in his role as the chairman. Lewis remembers the pain of management meetings and the accusatory use of the folk proverb "while the cat's away, the mice will play" by some of the top SNCC members.

> As soon as I got back [from Africa], my friends—people like Charles Sherrod, Bill Hansen, Bob Mants, Laverne Baker and Julian [Bond]—rushed to let me know what had happened while I was gone. They chastised me, telling me I had stayed away too long. I should have been more savvy, they said, more politically astute. "While the cat's away, the mice will play"—all that. I shouldn't have been so naive, they said. I shouldn't have been so trusting. But there was no other way I could be. There is no other way I can be. I always begin with an attitude of trust. I assume that your word is good until you show me otherwise. I refuse to be suspicious until I have *reason* to be. Yes, this sets me up to be burned now and then, but the alternative is to be constantly skeptical and distanced. I'd rather be occasionally burned but able to connect than always safe but always distant. "A circle of trust"—that's what it is all about. (308)

As the civil rights movement faded in the 1970s, old SNCC friendships also faltered over time. This certainly happened between Julian Bond and

John Lewis, with the latter citing the proverb "out of sight, out of mind" to explain their drifting apart that eventually led to them vying for the same seat in the US House of Representatives in the election of 1986.

> And Julian? He was different now, too. Our relationship was different. During the time I was in Washington, something of a gap grew between us. Part of that was the geographic separation—out of sight, out of mind. But we had grown apart in other ways as well. We had always been different in our lifestyles and personalities, but that had never affected our friendship. In fact, our differences were part of what we appreciated in each other, part of what attracted each of us to the other. Now that we were in the same line of work, however—politics—the differences in how we saw our own roles as elected officials—how we approached our *jobs*—could not be ignored. (461)

The campaign between the two friends became rather unpleasant, with Lewis, while trying to take the high road, also being drawn into aggressive rhetoric as he tried to differentiate himself from Bond. It got especially confrontational during a televised debate between them, with Bond accusing Lewis of having accepted two small campaign contributions that supposedly represented a conflict of interest. As the latter recalls in his memoir, Bond employed the modern proverb "if it looks like a duck, walks like a duck, and quacks like a duck, it's a duck," with the year 1948 being its earliest written recording thus far (Doyle, Mieder, and Shapiro 2012, 64), in an accusatory fashion. It was a decisive moment during the event, as can also be seen from Lewis's use of the proverbial phrase "you could have cut it with a knife."

> "If it looks like a duck," he deadpanned, "and quacks like a duck and waddles like a duck, then it must be a duck."
> I [John Lewis] was stunned. I could not believe he [Julian Bond] was questioning my integrity, of all things. And he *knew*, he *knew* this was not true. . . .
> It's not in my nature to let my emotions rise up. It's not in my nature to strike out. But this was a time when it happened. This was the time when I hit back.
> "Mr. Bond," I said. "My friend. My brother. We were asked to take a drug test not long ago, and five of us went and took that test. Why don't we step out and go to the men's room and take another test?"
> The room was dead silent. You could have cut the tension with a knife.
> "It seems," I went on, "like *you're* the one doing the ducking."
> Julian was flabbergasted. (477)

What an incredible comeback by Lewis in the heat of an emotionally charged debate. It is difficult to retort to a proverb well placed, but he succeeded in doing so splendidly by turning the duck metaphor around and accusing his opponent of "ducking" a drug test. A bit of linguistic mudslinging, yes, but it gave Lewis the upper hand in this case, and there was no way to stop him from winning the election to Congress in due time.

On a higher note, Lewis includes a paragraph from a campaign speech that deserves to be cited here, not only because of its important message but also because of the inclusion of the two proverbial phrases "to have come a long way" and "to have a long way to go." I would conjecture here once again that Lewis is remembering a great speech from his hero, Martin Luther King Jr. Actually, King used both expressions numerous times (Mieder 2010, 527–33), but it was in his speech with the title "A Long Way to Go" that he delivered on April 27, 1965, on the campus of the University of California at Los Angeles, that stands out. Not only does the speech have a proverbial title, but the two phrases as individual and combined leitmotifs (always with the emphatic double use of "long") inform the structural and rhetorical mastery of this address. The two folk metaphors are part of the dual structure of the lecture that talks about how far the civil rights struggle had come but how far it also still had to go. As expected from this rhetorical genius, King began his memorable speech with a skillful juxtaposition of the proverbial phrases to set the stage for their repeated use to make his dual point of successes obtained and challenges to face.

> Many of you want to know, are we making any progress? That is the desperate question, a poignant question on the lips of millions of people all over our nation and all over the world. I get it almost every day. It is a question of whether we are making a real progress in the area of race relations. And so I'm going to try to answer that question and deal with many of the issues involved using as a subject from which to speak, the future of integration.
>
> Now there are some people who feel that we aren't making any progress; there are some people who feel that we're making overwhelming progress. I would like to take what I consider a realistic position and say that we have come a long, long way in the struggle to make justice and freedom a reality in our nation, but we still have a long, long way to go. And it is this realistic position that I would like to use as a basis for our thinking together. (For the text of the speech, see Smith and Robb 1971, 183–204; for its interpretation, see Mieder 2010, 175–80.)

What follows here is John Lewis's profound and inclusive statement made during his first congressional campaign that includes his unshakable belief in the "Beloved Community" that Dr. King used to speak about and which Lewis defines in his book *Across That Bridge* as "a society based on simple justice that values the dignity and the worth of every human being" (B11).

> We have come a long way in recent decades in terms of our treatment of blacks and women and gays in America—and Hispanics, and Native Americans, and the poor. But we still have a good way to go. And we must not tolerate

the kind of backlash that has gathered in recent years against each of these movements—the attempts to repeal affirmative action, the hard-heartedness of wholesale welfare reform, the rising complaints of that newly emerging "oppressed" class of Americans, white males. Those complaints might well be, to a certain extent, justified. But there is a difference between fixing something and throwing it out. We must never lose sight of the distance we have traveled in recent decades in pursuit of a just, fair and inclusive Beloved Community, and we must not let the kinks in the programs we have created along the way blind us to the worthiness of what those programs aim to achieve. (468)

It is noteworthy that Lewis changes "a long way to go" to "a good way to go," even though it might be argued that they mean pretty much the same thing. Nevertheless, I would argue that it fits John Lewis's entire being and philosophy of life to employ the "good" adjective because the necessary way ahead is a good one, a humane one, a compassionate one, and an ethical one. Lewis is willing to walk the whole way; he even literally declined to climb into a long, white limousine that was supposed to take him to his election celebration, saying, "We needed to *walk*.... This was the best. I was walking with the wind" (479).

The last chapter of the autobiography is appropriately entitled "Onward," as it describes Lewis's work ever since beginning his dedicated service in the US House of Representatives in early 1987. As he describes his beliefs and activities, he again and again relies on proverbs and proverbial expressions to add metaphorical power to his statements. To describe the beginning of his regimen as "at least a twelve-hour day" (480) of concentrated work for his Georgian constituents, he turns to the proverbial phrase "to hit the ground running."

> [When I arrived at Washington, D.C. as a newly elected Congressman] I hit the ground running, attending every caucus meeting and every briefing session, accepting every invitation to speak, and never, not once, missing a vote during that first term. I was one of only twelve out of the 435 members of the House to compile a perfect voting record that session, and I've continued close to that pace during the ensuing decade, casting my vote more than 95 percent of the time. My constituents might not agree with every vote I make, but I make them. I'm there. And they appreciate that fact. (481)

On a more philosophical level, stressing that Americans represent one giant whole, he relies on the phrase "to be all together in something" to express this important claim: "The struggle for such [human] rights is a global one, and we must approach it that way. Just as we must recognize that as Americans we are all part of a connected community, so must we see that America is inextricably linked to the rest of the world as part of a global community. Simply put, we are all in this together. The principles we apply to ourselves we must apply to others—including the principles of nonviolence" (482).

In yet another telling paragraph, he repeats this positive expression at the very end after he cites the proverb "every man for himself" as well as the proverbial phrases "to have a stake in something," "to turn one's back on somebody or something," and "to circle the wagons" to explain the challenges on the way toward broader human rights.

> The poor, the sick, the disenfranchised. We cannot run away from them. We're all living in this house. When we move away from community and connection and live instead in a climate of "every man for himself" we are sowing the seeds that will lead to the destruction of American society as we know it. If we are not going to become divided and balkanized, like Northern Ireland or Lebanon or Rwanda or so much of Eastern Europe, we must push and advocate and make real the policies and decisions that can pull us together, that recognize our dependence on one another as members of a family. If we continue to allow hundreds of thousands of young people—black, Hispanic, Asian, Native American, white—to grow up without a feeling that they have a stake in this society. if we let them come into young adulthood without ever holding a meaningful job, without any sense of hope, I think we are asking for trouble. We can't retreat from them. We can't turn our backs on them. We can't circle the wagons in suburban developments with armed guards at the gates and believe that we are safe. The people, the masses, will eventually arrive at those gates, angry and upset, and then it will be too late. We must reach out to one another *now*. We must realize that we are all in this together. Not as black or white. Not as rich or poor. Not even as Americans or "non"-Americans. But as human beings. (486)

Surely this is proverbial rhetoric at its best, and if Lewis had wanted to avoid his second use of "to be all together in something," he might well have chosen the classical expression "to be in the same boat" that goes back to Cicero's "in eadem es navi" from 53 BC (Mieder 2005, 199–200). After all, he used it twice as an expression of solidarity at the beginning of his autobiography as "we were all in the same boat" (14, 34). Also, since Lewis refers to the "house" metaphor, it is somewhat surprising that he does not quote the Bible proverb "a house divided against itself cannot stand" (Mark 3:25) here that became Abraham Lincoln's proverbial leitmotif as he struggled to keep the young nation from drifting into the Civil War, in his famous "A House Divided" speech of June 16, 1858, in Springfield, Illinois.

> If we could first know *where* we are, and *whither* we are tending, we could then better judge *what* to do, and *how* to do it.
> We are now far into the *fifth* year, since a policy was initiated, with the *avowed* object, and *confident* promise, of putting an end to slavery agitation.

> Under the operation of that policy, that agitation has not only, *not ceased*, but has *constantly augmented*.
> In *my* opinion, it *will* not cease, until a *crisis* shall have been reached, and passed.
> "A house divided against itself cannot stand."
> I believe this government cannot endure, permanently half *slave* and half *free*.
> I do not expect the Union to be *dissolved*—I do not expect the house to *fall*—but I *do* expect it will cease to be divided.
> It will become *all* one thing, or *all* the other.
> (Basler 1953, 2:461–62; for an interpretation, see Mieder 1998, 63–74 and Mieder 2000, 10–18)

Besides Lincoln, such political figures as Frederick Douglass, Barack Obama, and others made repeated use of this secularized Bible proverb (Mieder 2001, 287–88; Mieder 2005, 90–117; Mieder 2009, 245), and it seems strange that it does not appear to belong to John Lewis's active proverb repertoire. It also does not play a part in King's rhetoric either, even though both civil rights leaders were steeped in biblical metaphors.

Just like Martin Luther King Jr., John Lewis believes with all his heart and might in the African American proverb "God will make a way out of no way" and its secular variant "making a way out of no way." Its earliest appearance in print is in Coe Hayne's *Race Grit: Adventures on the Borderland of Liberty* from 1922: "God can make a way out of no way. Pray to him, and he will open a way" (109). It has predominantly been found in the sermonic literature and secular speech of African Americans (Daniel 1973; Daniel, Smitherman-Donaldson, and Jeremiah 1987; Prahlad 1996), and it might possibly have started as an allusion to the biblical passage "I [God] will even make a way in the wilderness, and rivers in the desert (Isaiah 43:19; Doyle, Mieder, and Shapiro 2012, 102).

Interestingly, it is Barack Obama, in his book *The Audacity of Hope: Thoughts on Reclaiming the American Dream* (2006), who offers convincing proof of this proverb playing a significant role in African American church services.

> I was drawn to the power of the African American religious tradition to spur social change. Out of necessity, the black church had to minister to the whole person. Out of necessity, the black church rarely had the luxury of separating individual salvation from collective salvation. It had to serve as the center of the community's political, economic, and social as well as spiritual life; it understood in an intimate way the biblical call to feed the hungry and clothe the naked and challenge powers and principalities. In the history of these struggles, I was able to see faith as more than just a comfort to the weary or

a hedge against death; rather, it was an active, palpable agent in the world. In the day-to-day work of the men and women I met in church each day, in their ability to "make a way out of no way" and maintain hope and dignity in the direst of circumstances, I could see the Word made manifest. (Obama 2006, 207; Mieder 2009, 337)

To be sure, King's predilection toward this proverb helped to establish it beyond African American parlance. Here is but one example from a chapter on "Desegregation at Last" from his acclaimed book *Stride toward Freedom: The Montgomery Story* (1958) that Lewis has doubtless read. King speaks here of God being part of the struggle during the bus boycott at Montgomery and that it is the faith in God's omnipotence that will give participants the strength to carry on. So, when King writes "We must believe that a way will be made out of no way," the hidden subject of this sentence in the passive mode is, in fact, God Almighty, who can find a way out of no way, as the proverb has it.

> The evening came, and I mustered up enough courage to tell them [the boycotters] the truth. I tried, however, to end on a note of hope. "This may well be," I said, "the darkest hour just before dawn. We have moved all of these months with the daring faith that God was with us in the struggle. The many experiences of days gone by have vindicated that faith in a most unexpected manner. We must go out with the same faith, the same conviction. We must believe that a way will be made out of no way." But in spite of these words, I could feel the cold breeze of pessimism passing through the audience. It was a dark night—darker than a thousand midnights. It was a night in which the light of hope was about to fade away and the lamp of faith about to flicker. We went home with nothing before us but a cloud of uncertainty. (King 1988, 158–59)

This statement bears witness to how King's proverbial rhetoric gave hope to thousands, with his typically optimistic message being enhanced by the allusion to the folk proverb "the darkest hour is just before dawn." (For a discussion of King's other uses of the "way" proverb, see Mieder 2010, 181–86.)

John Lewis's rhetoric is, of course, equally footed in the sermonic art of Baptist preachers with their rhetorical use of biblical passages, proverbs, leitmotifs, and anaphora (see McKenzie 1996; Rosenberg 1970). Even though the proverb "making a way out of no way" surprisingly does not appear in *Walking with the Wind*, it is present in his *Across That Bridge: Life Lessons and a Vision for Change* that was published six years after Barack Obama's *The Audacity of Hope*. I can imagine that Obama's book might well have influenced Lewis in writing his small volume, but no matter what, these two treatises bear wonderful witness to their continuation of Dr. King's dream of an America and a world based on human rights in which "the better angels of our nature" (Basler 1953, 4:271; last words of Abraham Lincoln's first inaugural address of March 4, 1861) make us live together in peace as brothers and sisters.

In the introduction to his book of hopeful wisdom, Lewis writes with compassion and empathy about people who have not been as fortunate as he has been. As he does so, he remembers his own impoverished and underprivileged youth in the segregated South, declaring proverbially "we made a way out of no way to free ourselves."

> I understand the sense of helplessness and hopelessness that can surround a people who feel thwarted at every turn. I could not have been further away from the halls of Congress or the chambers of the Supreme Court as a small boy in Alabama. Back then I could not choose my seat on a bus or sit down at a lunch counter to eat, and blacks certainly didn't have the access to vote. No provision had been made for me and others like me to communicate the dictates of our conscience to the leadership of a nation. We had to build that road ourselves. We made a way out of no way to free ourselves from oppression and bring an American society one step closer to realizing its pledge: "one nation, indivisible, with liberty and justice for all." (B12)

Not surprisingly, the proverb "making a way out of no way" becomes a threefold repeated leitmotif in his chapter on "Faith" that has as its motto the Bible passage "faith is the substance of things hoped for, the evidence of things not seen" (Hebrews 11:1). It appears twice in a paragraph in which Lewis explains how he and other young students broke away from the status quo of their suppressed parents, with the proverb becoming their verbal compass for the absolutely necessary and long-overdue struggle against segregation and all the ills that came with it.

> In the [civil rights] movement, we had very little money, no political influence, no military force, and very few in the society around us believed in our capacity to contribute even the most basic of human gifts—to think with any clarity, to learn new things, to invent or create, to understand the world around us, or even to stand up to defend ourselves. We had no safety net, no one to turn to. We were born into the unfair circumstances that most people find themselves facing only temporarily at some point in their lives. We began stripped down to the bare minimum. We started out our lives dangling by a tenuous thread, so many of us came to the work of change already deeply experienced in the transformative power of faith. Our mothers and fathers had prayed us through the dire circumstances of living in the Deep South—poverty, hunger, grinding debt, a system of sharecropping stacked against us, illiteracy, limited educational opportunity, not to mention the terrorism of the nightriders and mob violence. So many of our parents stayed on their knees and made sure we leaned to pray that we were already familiar with the power of the divine

grace that would meet us in our darkest hour and somehow, someway seemed to stretch the span of our universe to make two short ends meet. This was so much part of our everyday lives that we had a name for it. We called it "making a way out of no way." So when we were standing in protest facing police dogs and fire hoses, we knew without any doubt that somebody who was greater than us all would make a way out of no way and protect the defenders of the truth. (B30–31)

The two proverbial expressions, "to hang on a thin thread" and "to make ends meet," do indeed help to underscore the tenuous situation the young protestors found themselves in as they moved forward with the faith that God would help to make a way out of no way. The deeply religious John Lewis believes in the transformative power of the faith in God (see B38), but he realizes on a more secular level that people must pray by moving their feet; that is to say, they must actively work on making a way out of no way with faith, hope, and love giving them strength. The old folk proverb "God helps them who help themselves" comes to mind here. But the last proverbial word belongs to the secular saint John Lewis, as he addresses his readers directly in his last paragraph on "faith"—not just religious faith but a belief in the goodness of humankind as it strives to continue its walk toward universal civil and human rights.

> You will discover that no government, no teacher, no abusive parent or spouse, not even torture or terror has the power to define you. Once you find within you the true ability to define yourself according to the dictates of your conscience and your faith, you have come a long way down the path that can lead to social transformation. Faith will be the lifeblood of all your activism, and it has the power to make a way out of no way. You may be in your darkest hour, it may be darker than ten thousand nights on your path to lasting change, but there is something in you that keeps you moving, feeling your way through the night until you can see a glimmer of light. That is the power of faith. (B39)

References

This chapter was first published in *Proverbium* 31 (2014): 331–93.

Aron, Paul. 2008. *We Hold These Truths . . . and Other Words that Made America*. Lanham, MD: Rowman & Littlefield.

Arthurs, Jeffrey D. 2003. "Proverbs in Inspirational Literature: Sanctioning the American Dream." In *Cognition, Comprehension, and Communication: A Decade of North American Proverb Studies (1990–2000)*, edited by Wolfgang Mieder, 37–52. Baltmannsweiler: Schneider Verlag Hohengehren.

Basler, Roy P., ed. 1953. *The Collected Works of Abraham Lincoln*. 8 vols. New Brunswick, NJ: Rutgers University Press.

Bausum, Ann. 2006. *Freedom Riders: John Lewis and Jim Zwerg on the Front Lines of the Civil Rights Movement*. Washington, DC: National Geographic Society.
Blassingame, John, ed. 1985–92. *The Frederick Douglass Papers*. 5 vols. New Haven, CT: Yale University Press.
Burrell, Brian. 1997. *The Words We Live By: The Creeds, Mottoes, and Pledges That Have Shaped America*. New York: The Free Press.
Carawan, Guy, and Candie Carawan, eds. 1963. *We Shall Overcome: Songs of the Southern Freedom Movement*. New York: Oak.
Chafe, William H. 1998. "Keeping Faith." *New York Times*, June 28, 14.
Daniel, Jack L. 1973. "Towards an Ethnography of Afroamerican Proverbial Usage." *Black Lines* 2:3–12.
Daniel, Jack L., Geneva Smitherman-Donaldson, and Milford M. Jeremiah. 1987. "Makin' a Way Out of No Way: The Proverb Tradition in the Black Community." *Journal of Black Studies* 17:482–508.
Deutscher, Guy. 2006. "Standing on the Shoulders of Clichés: A Key Milestone on the Way to Ordinary Language." In *"Gold Nuggets or Fool's Gold?" Magazine and Newspaper Articles on the (Ir)relevance of Proverbs and Proverbial Phrases*, edited by Wolfgang Mieder and Janet Sobieski, 223–24. Burlington: University of Vermont.
Dolman, Joseph. 1998. "Walking with the Wind: A Memoir of the Movement." *New Leader*, June 29: 20.
Dowdy, Zachary. 1998. "Civil Rights Memoir Details the Simple Acts of Courage." *Boston Globe*, September 4, D4.
Doyle, Charles Clay, Wolfgang Mieder, and Fred R. Shapiro. 2012. *The Dictionary of Modern Proverbs*. New Haven, CT: Yale University Press.
Griffin, Albert Kirby. 1991. *Religious Proverbs: Over 1,600 Adages from 18 Faiths Worldwide*. Jefferson, NC: McFarland.
Haskins, Jim, and Kathleen Benson. 2006. *John Lewis in the Lead: A Story of the Civil Rights Movement*. New York: Lee & Low Books.
Hayne, Coe. 1922. *Race Grit: Adventures on the Border-Land of Liberty*. Philadelphia: Judson.
Hertzler, Joyce O. 1933–34. "On Golden Rules." *International Journal of Ethics* 44:418–36.
Hill. Christine M. 2002. *John Lewis: From Freedom Rider to Congressman*. Berkeley Heights, NJ: Enslow Publishers.
John Lewis (Civil Rights Leader). Accessed June 28, 2018. https://en.wikipedia.org/wiki/John_Lewis_(civil_rights_leader).
Kemper, Bob. 2006. "John Lewis: 'Conscience' Carries Clout. Civil Rights Icon's Moral Authority Enhanced." *Atlanta Journal-Constitution*, May 21, 1.
King, Martin Luther, Jr. 1958. *Stride Toward Freedom: The Montgomery Story*. New York: Harper & Row.
Lewis, John. 1963. "Speech at the March on Washington." August 28. Speech text provided by Voices of Democracy: US Oratory Project. Department of Communication, University of Maryland. http://voicesofdemocracy.umd.edu/lewis-speech-at-the-march-on-washington-textual-authentication/.
———. 1998. *Walking with the Wind: A Memoir of the Movement*. New York: Simon & Schuster. New York: Harvest Book, 1999 (paperback edition). Written with the assistance of Michael D'Orso.
———. 2007. Commencement address, University of Vermont. http://www.uvm.edu/president/ceremonies/commencement2007/?Page=commencementaddress_lewis.html
———. 2012. *Across That Bridge: Life Lessons and a Vision for Change*. New York: Hyperion. Written with the help of Brenda Jones.

———. 2013. *March: Book One*. Marietta, GA: Top Shelf Production. A graphic novel produced together with Andrew Aydin and Nate Powell.
Lomax, John A., and Alan Lomax. 1941. *Our Singing Country: A Second Volume of American Ballads and Folk Songs*. New York: Macmillan.
Louis, Cameron. 2000. "Proverbs and the Politics of Language." *Proverbium: Yearbook of International Proverb Scholarship* 17:173–94.
McGrory, Mary. 1998. "A Man of Consequence." *Washington Post*, June 14, C1.
McKenzie, Alyce M. 1996. *Preaching Proverbs: Wisdom for the Pulpit*. Louisville, KY: Westminster John Knox Press.
Meacham, Jon. 1998. "A Storm in the Streets." *Newsweek*, June 1, 69.
Mieder, Wolfgang. 1993. *Proverbs Are Never Out of Season: Popular Wisdom in the Modern Age*. New York: Oxford University Press.
———. 1997. *The Politics of Proverbs: From Traditional Wisdom to Proverbial Stereotypes*. Madison: University of Wisconsin Press.
———. 1998. *"A House Divided": From Biblical Proverb to Lincoln and Beyond*. Burlington: University of Vermont.
———. 2000. *The Proverbial Abraham Lincoln: An Index to Proverbs in the Works of Abraham Lincoln*. New York: Peter Lang.
———. 2001. *"No Struggle, No Progress": Frederick Douglass and His Proverbial Rhetoric for Civil Rights*. New York: Peter Lang.
———. 2004. *Proverbs: A Handbook*. Westport, CT: Greenwood Press.
———. 2005. *Proverbs Are the Best Policy: Folk Wisdom and American Politics*. Logan: Utah State University Press.
———. 2008. "'Let Us Have Faith That Right Makes Might': Proverbial Rhetoric in Decisive Moments of American Politics." *Proverbium: Yearbook of International Proverb Scholarship* 25:319–52.
———. 2009. *"Yes We Can": Barack Obama's Proverbial Rhetoric*. New York: Peter Lang.
———. 2010. *"Making a Way Out of No Way": Martin Luther King's Sermonic Proverbial Rhetoric*. New York: Peter Lang.
———. 2011. "'It Takes a Village to Change the World': Proverbial Politics and the Ethics of Place." *Journal of American Folklore* 124:4–28.
———. 2013. "'What's Sauce for the Goose Is Sauce for the Gander': The Proverbial Fight for Women's Rights by Elizabeth Cady Stanton and Susan B. Anthony." In *Frazeologiia v mnogoiazychnom obshchestve*, edited by Elena Arsentyeva, 21–38. Kazan': Kazanskii Federal'nyi Universitet.
Mieder, Wolfgang, Stewart A. Kingsbury, and Kelsie B. Harder. 1992. *A Dictionary of American Proverbs*. New York: Oxford University Press.
Miller, Mike. 1998. "Walking with the Wind: A Memoir of the Movement." *Social Policy* 29:46–47.
Nasstrom, Kathryn L. 1999. "Walking with the Wind. A Memoir of the Movement." *Journal of American History* 86:849–51.
Nelson, Jack. 1998. "A Hero of Our Time." *Los Angeles Times*, June 14, 8.
Nichols, Ray. 1996. "Maxims, 'Practical Wisdom,' and the Language of Action." *Political Theory* 24:687–705.
Obama, Barack. 2006. *The Audacity of Hope: Thoughts on Reclaiming the American Dream*. New York: Three Rivers Press.
Prahlad, Sw. Anand. 1996. *African American Proverbs in Context*. Jackson: University of Mississippi Press.

"Rep. John Lewis's Speech at King Memorial Groundbreaking." 2006. Congressman John Lewis website. Media Center press release, November 13. https://johnlewis.house.gov/media-center/press-releases/rep-john-lewiss-speech-king-memorial-groundbreaking.

Rigsby, Enrique D. "Walking with the Wind: A Memoir of the Movement." *Rhetoric & Public Affairs* 3:679–81.

Rosenberg, Bruce. 1970. *The Art of the American Folk Preacher.* New York: Oxford University Press.

Salmond, John. 2000. "Walking with the Wind: A Memoir of the Movement." *Journal of Southern History* 66:167–68.

Shapiro, Fred R. 2006. *The Yale Book of Quotations.* New Haven, CT: Yale University Press.

Sharp, Cecil James, and Olive Campbell. 1917. *English Folk Songs from the Southern Appalachians.* New York: G. P. Putnam's Sons.

Smith, Arthur L., and Stephen Robb, eds. 1971. *The Voice of Black Rhetoric: Selections.* Boston: Allyn and Bacon.

Templeton, John Marks. 1997. *Worldwide Laws of Life: 200 Eternal Spiritual Principles.* Philadelphia: Templeton Foundation Press.

Washington, James Melvin, ed. 1986. *A Testament of Hope: The Essential Writings of Martin Luther King Jr.* San Francisco: Harper & Row.

Whit, Bill. 2000. "Walking with the Wind: A Memoir of the Movement." *Michigan Sociological Review* 14:124–26.

White, Newman Ivey. 1928. *American Negro Folk-Songs.* Cambridge, MA: Harvard University Press.

Williams, Juan. 1987. *Eyes on the Prize: America's Civil Rights Years, 1954–1965.* New York: Viking.

Wills, Garry. 1998. "Those Were the Days." *New York Review of Books*, June 25, 27.

6

"I'M ABSOLUTELY SURE ABOUT— THE GOLDEN RULE"

Barack Obama's Proverbial Audacity of Hope

Proverbs, proverbial expressions, and other types of phraseologisms have always played an important role in the world of politics (Mieder 1997; Louis 2000), with their effective employment by such varied twentieth-century politicians as Willy Brandt (Eggert 1998; Mieder and Nolte 2015), Winston S. Churchill (Mieder and Bryan 1995), Adolf Hitler (Mieder 1997, 9–38, 193–200), Nikita Khrushchev, Vladimir Ilich Lenin (Breuillard 1984; Viellard 2001), Mao Tse-tung (Schäfer 1983), Franklin D. Roosevelt (Mieder 2005, 187–209, 284–87), Harry S. Truman (Mieder and Bryan 1997), and others. In American politics, proverbial language has long been part of the discourse (Mieder 2005), with former presidents like John Adams (Mieder 2008b, 169–204), Abraham Lincoln (Mieder 2000), and Theodore Roosevelt standing out as particularly proverbial in their rhetoric. Of course, there were also such proverbial giants as Benjamin Franklin (Newcomb 1957; Barbour 1974; Mieder 2004, 171–80, 216–18), Daniel Webster, Frederick Douglass (Mieder 2001), Susan B. Anthony, Elizabeth Cady Stanton (Mieder 2008a, 328–30; Mieder 2014), and Dr. Martin Luther King Jr. (Karabegović 2007; Mieder 2010), who relied heavily on traditional metaphors and folk wisdom in their oral and written communication with the American people. Modern politicians clearly would do well in taking a look at their reliance on proverbs and proverbial phrases to add some commonsense appeal to their own political messages.

Barack Obama, as a major figure on today's American political scene, has clearly heeded this advice, as is readily apparent from his two bestselling books, *Dreams from My Father: A Story of Race and Inheritance* (1995) and *The Audacity of Hope: Thoughts on Reclaiming the American*

Dream (2006), as well as his major national addresses and regional speeches (Mieder 2009). As one reads his prose or listens to his speeches, it is evident that this extremely well-educated individual is deeply rooted in American political history, with his three heroes being Abraham Lincoln, Frederick Douglass, and Martin Luther King Jr.

What is fascinating to the folklorist in general and the paremiologist in particular is the fact that Obama shares a certain predilection to proverbial language with Lincoln, Douglass, and King. He has certainly read them, and he must have been impressed and at times moved by some of their deeply felt statements that were quite often couched in proverbial language. Abraham Lincoln's use of the biblical proverb "a house divided against itself cannot stand" (Mark 3:25), Frederick Douglass's use of Jefferson's declaration turned proverb "all men are created equal," and Dr. King's insistence on the Golden Rule, "do unto others as you would have them do unto you" (also used by Lincoln and Douglass) readily come to mind. There is doubtless some direct or indirect rhetorical influence here, which is by no means to say that Obama does not have "a certain talent for rhetoric," as he justifiably points out in *The Audacity of Hope* (67; sole page numbers in parentheses refer to Barack Obama's *The Audacity of Hope*). And right he is! In this book of 364 pages, a total of 391 phraseologisms have been located, basically one idiom, proverbial phrase, or proverb for every page of text. Just twenty-two of these are actual proverbs, an indication that Obama, as opposed to Lincoln, Douglass, and King, is much less the didactic or sermonic rhetorician.

This is probably a wise move, since modern readers and audiences would tire quickly from a cannonade of proverbial wisdom. In fact, even when he cites proverbs, they are often used as allusions, as for example when he speaks of a "'winner-take-all' economy, in which a rising tide doesn't necessarily lift all boats" (146). Being a modern politician, he does not only use such old standbys as "father knows best" (31) and "look before you leap" (310), but also such modern texts as "better is not good enough" (233) or "been there, done that" (312). Sometimes he doesn't quote the fitting piece of folk wisdom at all and instead adds a bit of indirect proverbial wisdom to a statement by claiming that "conventional wisdom" (see 16, 124, etc.) holds it to be true.

Most of Obama's use of folk speech comes in the form of proverbial phrases without any claim to wisdom or truth. He uses these metaphorical phrases to add a certain expressiveness, emotion, color, imagery, and colloquialism to his writings and speeches. It is here that he shows himself to be part of the general population. He prides himself on listening to and thinking about "the voices of all the people" (356), and consequently he mixes their conventional and proverbial language into his utterances. As an impressive intellectual, he does well to follow in the footsteps of a Woodrow Wilson or John F. Kennedy, who also took to heart the folk speech patterns of their constituents. A few telling examples of Obama's folk speech prowess with very little context are: "I had gotten some taste of how the game had come to be played" (16), "We might've fought like cats and dogs" (35), "It would have been typical of toady's politics for each side to draw a line in the sand" (58), "Simply put, they have an ax to grind" (116), "America's schools are not holding up their end of the bargain" (159), "But over the long haul" (213), "racial discrimination stays on the front burner" (248), "the instinct to throw their weight around" (306), etc.

Of course, various reviews of Barack Obama's personal and political manifesto with its intriguing title of *The Audacity of Hope* have praised him for his writing and rhetorical skills. Michiko Kakutani wrote in the *New York Times* of October 17, 2006, that "Barack Obama . . . is that rare politician who can actually write—and write movingly and genuinely about himself," and he also observed that "Mr. Obama strives in these pages to ground his policy thinking in simple common sense, while articulating these ideas in level-headed, nonpartisan prose" (2006). Michael Klein followed suit in the *Washington Post* of October 22, 2006: "Obama's knack for mixing stirring rhetoric about good and evil with practical policy ideas is rare in the modern history of U.S. politics. . . . In our lowdown, dispiriting era, Obama's talent for proposing humane, sensible solutions with uplifting, elegant prose does fill one with hope" (2006). Christopher Hitchens in the *Times* of May 6, 2007, mentioned that "Obama's open and engaging style can be found on almost every page" (2007), leaving the reader to wonder what exactly that means.

None of the reviewers ever refers to the rather obvious fact that Barack Obama's books and speeches are replete with proverbial folk speech. This is also not the case in David Olive's "A Note on Barack Obama's Oratorical Style and Its Impact," which does not go beyond the general observation that "Obama proved words do matter" (2008, 87–90, here p. 88). In fact, they really say very little or nothing about his style that combines folk language with a superb literary style, proverbs with quotations, and common sense with intellectualism into a most effective sociopolitical discourse based on a deep sense of humanity and morality (see Rogak 2007). In trying to understand how Obama manages to bring about the considerable convergence of at times diametrically opposed viewpoints and standpoints, I will argue that at least in part it is through his proverbial language that he stylistically finds a common denominator of effective communication. The metaphors of the proverbial phrases add commonality and common sense for everybody to understand to his sociopolitical rhetoric. He is doubtless a most skillful communicator (see Obama 2008a, b), having learned much from Lincoln, Douglass, King, and others and also finding his own way to communicate regionally, nationally, and globally with people of very different backgrounds.

"So, make no mistake about it," to use one of Barack Obama's favorite phrases from his speeches (for example on July 10, 2008, and on August 4, 2008), his book *The Audacity of Hope* is, in addition to all of its other claims to fame, also a testimony to the value of proverbial phrases in modern political rhetoric. On page two of the prologue, Obama uses one of his favorite proverbial expressions to state how he used to argue against the cynicism that is often voiced against a life dedicated to politics and public issues: "I understood the skepticism, but there was—and always had been—another tradition to politics, a tradition that stretched from the days of the country's founding to the glory of the civil rights movement, a tradition based on the simple idea that we have a stake in one another, and that what binds us together is greater than what drives us apart, and that if enough people believe in the truth of that proposition and act on it, then we might not solve every problem, but we can get something meaningful done" (2). He then continues in relatively simple terms to talk proverbially about the "cutthroat politics and unremitting culture wars" (8), the fact that "we feel in our guts the lack of honesty, rigor, and common sense in our policy debates" (9), and that "if we don't change course soon, we may be the first generation in a very long time that leaves behind a weaker and more fractured America than the one we inherited" (9). Of course, "changing course" is one of Obama's major metaphors for having gotten involved in politics in the first place.

Republicans and Democrats

The first chapter on "Republicans and Democrats" indicates that Barack Obama has a clear understanding of these feuding parties that ever more looked at the political divide as "a menu of either-or, for-or-against, sound-bite-ready choices. No longer was economic policy a matter of weighing trade-offs between competing goals of productivity and distributional justice, of growing the pie and slicing the pie. You were for either tax cuts or tax hikes, small government or big government. . . . You were with us or against us. You had to choose sides" (33–34). In addition to the proverbial phrase of "slicing the pie," Obama even alludes to the biblical proverb "he that is not with me is against me" (Matthew 12:30) to add extra authority to his correct claim. The remaining pages of this chapter continue in this vein, underscoring the ills of this "ideological deadlock" (34), where "deficit reduction can't take place on the backs of the poor" (37), where "hardball tactics" (39) prevail, and where some "seek to chip away at the very idea of government" (40). Of special interest on these pages is the following statement with its two allusions to the proverbs "war is hell" and "the best-laid plans of mice and men often go astray" (see Mieder, Kingsbury, and Harder 1992, 467, 640): "When I ponder the work of a George Kennan or a George Marshall, when I read the speeches of Bob Kennedy or an Everett Dirksen, I can't help feeling that the politics of today suffers from a case of arrested development. For these men, the issues America faced were never abstract and hence never simple. War might be hell and still the right thing to do. Economies could collapse despite the best-laid plans. People could work hard all their lives and still lose everything" (36).

The proverb allusions help Obama to bring his point across that life is full of contradictions and complexities, and "What's needed is a broad majority of Americans—Democrats, Republicans, and independents of goodwill—who are reengaged in the project of national renewal, and who see their own self-interest as inextricably linked to the interests of others" (40). And thus, almost predictably by now for Barack Obama, who shows himself in this book as the grand unifier of opposite views, he concludes his concise review of American government with the following comment.

> Maybe the critics are right. Maybe there's no escaping our great political divide, an endless clash of armies, and any attempts to alter the rules of engagement are futile. Or maybe the trivialization of politics has reached a point of no return, so that most people see it as just one more diversion, a sport, with politicians our paunch-bellied gladiators and those who bother to pay attention just fans on the sidelines: We paint our faces red or blue and cheer our side and boo their side, and if it takes a late hit or cheap shot to beat the other team, so be it, for winning is all that matters.
>
> But I don't think so. They are out there, I think to myself, those ordinary citizens who have grown up in the midst of all the political and cultural battles, but who have found a way—in their own lives, at least—to make peace with their neighbors and themselves. (41–42)

Every reader can relate to these comments and certainly to the phrase of something being a cheap shot and the intentional play with the proverb "winning isn't everything" with which Obama adds some colloquial spice to his satirical description of those who will not come together for the common good. They believe in the antiproverb "winning is all that matters" and its variant "winning isn't everything, it's the only thing." The message is clear in its simple proverbiality. In politics, winning is not everything, but compromise, fairness, and the work toward the common good would perhaps create a win-win situation.

Values

With these comments Obama has found a natural bridge to his second chapter, "Values," in which he raises the important question, "What are the core values that we, as Americans, hold in common?" (52). After all, he continues, the "shared values—the standards and principles that the majority of Americans deem important in their lives, and in the life of the country—should be the heart of our politics, the cornerstone of any meaningful debate about budgets and projects, regulations and policies" (52–53). Perhaps not surprisingly, he begins with the first few lines of the Declaration of Independence, with its two proverbial truths that contain the most basic wisdom: "We hold these truths to be self-evident, that all men are created equal, that they are endowed by their Creator with certain unalienable Rights, that among these are Life, Liberty and the pursuit of Happiness" (53). Obama then discusses such virtues as competence and authenticity, but it is when he talks about the moral value of empathy that he reaches one of the stylistic, proverbial, and ethical high points of his *Audacity of Hope* by combining philosophical thought with subjective experience.

> It [empathy] is at the heart of my moral code, and it is how I understand the Golden Rule—not simply as a call to sympathy and charity, but as something more demanding, a call to stand in somebody else's shoes and see through their eyes.
> Like most of my values, I learned about empathy from my mother. She disdained any kind of cruelty or thoughtlessness or abuse of power, whether it expressed itself in the form of racial prejudice or bullying in the schoolyard or workers being underpaid. Whenever she saw even a hint of such behavior in me she would look me square in the eyes and ask, "How do you think that would make you feel?" (66)

Four proverbial expressions—"to be at the heart of something," "to stand in somebody else's shoes," "to see something through someone else's eyes," and "to look someone square in the eyes"—form the folk speech underpinning of this short exegesis on the value of empathy, with the actual proverb that has become known as the Golden Rule not being stated explicitly: "Do unto others as you would have them do unto you" (Matthew 7:12).

Why not? I would assume that Obama believes that all of his readers will know what the Golden Rule is, and it might be added here that it is not just wisdom from Jesus's Sermon on the Mount in the New Testament, but that its idea is similarly expressed in other religions and also in Immanuel Kant's categorical imperative (see Hertzler 1933–34; Burrell 1997, 235–40). Let us hope that Obama's readers do know the actual text of the Golden Rule, but with cultural literacy being on a decline, he might just assume a bit too much. Abraham Lincoln and Frederick Douglass, who also used the Golden Rule several times, usually quoted the proverb as well, even though they could at their time count more on their audience knowing the wisdom from their Bible (see Mieder 1990).

At the conclusion of his elaboration on a humane value system (see Templeton 1997), Obama argues that "in the end a sense of mutual understanding isn't enough. After all, talk is cheap; like any value, empathy must be acted upon. . . . If we aren't willing to pay the price for our values, if we aren't willing to make some sacrifices in order to realize them, then we should ask ourselves whether we really believe in them at all" (68). And as if the proverb "talk is cheap" and the proverbial expression of "having to pay the price" were not enough, he drives his point home with yet one more concluding proverb: "Although we recognize that they [our values] are subject to challenge, can be poked and prodded and debunked and turned inside out by intellectuals and cultural critics, they have proven to be both surprisingly durable and surprisingly constant across classes, and races, and faiths, and generations. We can make claims on their behalf, so long as we understand that our values must be tested against fact and experience, so long as we recall that they demand deeds not just words. To do otherwise would be to relinquish our best selves" (69). It might be of interest that the Nobel Prize laureate Winston S. Churchill chose the proverb "deeds, not words" as a rallying battle cry in his relentless fight against Nazi Germany, and in due time, he won his military and moral victory against the evil Third Reich with the help of the Allies (see Mieder and Bryan 1995, 192–93). Obama is not fighting such a menace, but his two proverbs of "Do unto others as you would have them do unto you" and "deeds, not words" certainly qualify as beacons in the rekindling of the basic values of human decency, respect, and compassion.

Our Constitution

Just as the somewhat didactic second chapter ends with a proverb, the third more erudite chapter on the Constitution by Barack Obama, the Harvard-educated lawyer, begins with a proverbial comparison coined among US senators: "There's a saying that senators frequently use when asked to describe their first year on Capitol Hill: 'It's like drinking from a fire hose'" (71). This reference represents a wonderful example of Obama as a folkloristic field researcher who records various proverbial phrases, folk narratives, and other traditional matters. In fact, he proves himself to be quite the ethnographer in his *Dreams from My Father* autobiography that is filled with folk speech, anecdotes, stories, etc.

As Obama reflects on the Constitution, his thoughts turn quite naturally to Abraham Lincoln, who grounded his presidency in the most difficult times on pragmatism, compromise, and an adherence to the Constitution, repeatedly basing his arguments on the Bible proverb "a house divided against itself cannot stand" (see Mieder 1998).

> I'm left then with Lincoln, who like no man before or since understood both the deliberative function of our democracy and the limits of such deliberation. We remember him for the firmness and depth of his convictions—his unyielding opposition to slavery and his determination that a house divided could not stand. But his presidency was guided by a practicality that would distress us today, a practicality that led him to test various bargains with the South in order to maintain the Union without war; to appoint and discard general after general, strategy after strategy, once war broke out; to stretch the Constitution to the breaking point in order to see the war through to a successful conclusion. (97–98)

Almost predictably, Obama returned to the proverb during his historical speech of February 10, 2007, in Springfield, Illinois: "It was here, in Springfield, where North, South, East and West come together that I was reminded of the essential decency of the American people—where I came to believe that through this decency, we can build a more hopeful America. And that is why, in the shadow of the Old State Capitol, where Lincoln once called on a divided house to stand together, where common hopes and common dreams still exist, I stand before you today to announce my candidacy for President of the United States."

Obama's clear preoccupation with Lincoln has led Morgan Meis to the overstated claim that "Obama thinks of himself as Lincoln," beginning her article with the statement that "If platitudes had weight, Barack Obama's *The Audacity of Hope* would be impossible to lift off the table. Still, it's a good book. By the standards of 'writings by politicians' it's in the top percentile. You read it and you like the man" (Meis 2008). This is a strange mixture of innuendo, criticism, and praise, to say the least. Obama is way too humble, just as Lincoln was, to think of himself as the much-admired former president (see Obama 2005). He looks at him as a hero, and he wants to emulate him the best he can in modern times, and that is a noble cause. As far as platitudes are concerned, there are certainly some (at times perhaps even expressed by elements of folk speech), but Obama's style is too sophisticated to suffer from it. To be sure, it is good writing, and not just as far as the writings by politicians are concerned. Obama can well stand his own, just as his three admired precursors Abraham Lincoln, Frederick Douglass, and Martin Luther King Jr. could before him.

Opportunity

While it is interesting to note that the chapter primarily addressing economic "Opportunity," with its more than fifty pages, is the longest of the book, it should not be too surprising that this is the case. After all, opportunity has much to do with Barack Obama's basic theme of hope for a better world. As always, he makes use of a number of very general preformulated phrases that enter automatically into his books and speeches, as for example "but over the long term" (148), "getting their money's worth" (157), "not holding up their end of the bargain" (159), "the heavy-handed approach" (169), "the bottom line is" (170), "would go a long way" (171, 180), "when all is said and done" (173), and "the public debate has been deadlocked" (183). But in the excitement of argumentation, Obama is quick in choosing more elaborate proverbial phrases to add some metaphorical spice to his comments, to wit "anyone who would challenge it [laissez-faire economics] swims against the prevailing tide" (150), "Democratic policy makers [were] more obsessed with slicing the economic pie than with growing the pie" (157), "it was Clinton who put the nation's fiscal house in order even while lessening poverty" (158, 175), and "If we're serious about avoiding such a future [with a large national debt], then we'll have to start digging ourselves out of this hole" (188).

In fact, Obama goes into considerable detail explaining the ills of the socioeconomic situation, couching all of it into a remarkable summary made up of a proverbial expression and an allusion to a proverb. According to his interpretation, we have "what some call a 'winner-take-all' economy, in which a rising tide doesn't necessarily lift all boats" (146). The proverbial phrase "winner-take-all" refers to an economic policy where the rich get richer and the poor get poorer, and the added proverb "the rising tide lifts all boats" is negated in light of the fact that only the wealthy rise, while leaving the poor stranded. Obama likes this proverb, as can be seen from a positive use of its wisdom in a major speech on "Our Common Stake in

America's Prosperity" delivered on September 17, 2007, in New York City. While he praises the American economic system in this address, he also is aware that we need "in FDR's words, a re-appraisal of our values as a nation."

> I believe that America's free market has been the engine of America's great progress. . . . But I also know that in this country, our grand experiment has only worked because we have guided the market's invisible hand with a higher principle. It's the idea that we are all in this together. From CEOs to shareholders, from financiers to factory workers, we all have a stake in each other's success because the more Americans prosper, the more America prospers. . . . Our economy has . . . been the tide that has lifted the boats of the largest middle-class in history. . . . [But] in recent years, we have seen a dangerous erosion of the rules and principles that have made our market to work and our economy to thrive. Instead of thinking about what's good for America or what's good for business, a mentality has crept into certain corners of Washington and the business world that says, "what's good for me is good enough."

The catastrophic result of this deplorable change can be seen from the economic world crisis that started in the United States. Playing off the two proverbial expressions "to be in something together" and "to be on one's own," both of which are leitmotifs in his speeches as well, he summarizes the mess we are in as follows: "If the guiding philosophy behind the traditional system of social insurance could be described as 'We're all in it together,' the philosophy behind the Ownership Society seems to be 'You're on your own'" (178–79). He is, of course, right in concluding that "we rise and fall together" (193), and that we need a new "balancing act between self-interest and community [while we] affirm our bonds with one another" (193). At this point, Obama might well have chosen the proverb "united we stand, divided we fall" as a final word of wisdom, obvious as it might be in its simplicity.

Faith

There is another proverb that Barack Obama, somewhat surprisingly perhaps, has not used in his books and speeches, namely the biblical claim that "Faith can remove mountains" (1 Corinthians 13:2). But not to worry, he certainly makes biblical wisdom as expressed in folk proverbs the center part of this chapter. There is no doubt that Obama is well versed in religious rhetoric, and while he is aware from his own background that "we are no longer just a Christian nation; we are also a Jewish nation, a Muslim nation, a Buddhist nation, a Hindu nation, and a nation of nonbelievers" (218), he understandably relies primarily on words and passages from the New Testament, notably from "the Sermon on the Mount—a passage so radical that it's doubtful that our Defense Department would survive its application" (218). What incredible irony here, but again, is this mere mentioning of the Sermon on the Mount (Matthew, chapters 5–7) enough information to understand what Obama is striving at? Simple allusions are not always effective, and Obama must be careful that he will not be one of those politicians who, in his own chastising words, "sprinkles in a few biblical citations to spice up a thoroughly dry policy speech" (216). For a lesson on how to be even more engaging with his biblical rhetoric, he might well look in particular at his three heroes, Frederick Douglass, Abraham Lincoln, and Martin Luther King Jr., who, like "the majority of great reformers in American history—not only were motivated by faith but repeatedly used religious language to argue their causes" (218).

Then follows a barely four-line paragraph toward the end of this chapter on faith that is a personal testimony but also a summary of the entire book, whose central message serves as the title of my discussion. Having in his usual fair way looked at various issues of faith, including some of his own doubts and his unwillingness to interpret the Bible literally, he states: "This is not to say that I'm unanchored in my faith. There are some things that I'm absolutely sure about—the Golden Rule, the need to battle cruelty in all its forms, the value of love and charity, humility and grace" (224).

This reminds me of my study on "'Do Unto Others as You Would Have Them Do Unto You': Frederick Douglass's Proverbial Struggle for Civil Rights" (Mieder 2005, 118–46), and a comforting realization how deeply Barack Obama is grounded in the religious, secular, and yes, proverbial wisdom of Douglass, Lincoln, and King, the remarkable triad of truly great Americans.

Race

These civil rights champions and many others like Rosa Parks, Jesse Jackson, and John Lewis (see p. 226) have had great influence on Obama's thoughts on race, which are, of course, also based on his personal experiences. His own summary says it all.

> When I meet people for the first time, they sometimes quote back to me a line in my speech at the 2004 Democratic National Convention that seemed to strike a chord: "There is not a black America and white America and Latino America and Asian America—there's the United States of America." For them, it seems to capture a vision of America finally freed from the past of

Jim Crow and slavery, Japanese internment camps and Mexican braceros, workplace tensions and cultural conflict—an America that fulfils Dr. King's promise that we be judged not by the color of our skin but by the content of our character. (231)

Yet with all the progress that has been made over the years, Obama is quick to point out that this does not mean "that we have arrived at a 'postracial politics' or that we already live in a color-blind society" (232). In fact, "to suggest that our racial attitudes play not part in these [socioeconomic] disparities is to turn a blind eye to both our history and our experience—and to relieve ourselves of the responsibility to make things right" (233). These two expressive "blind" metaphors are followed up with a forcefully stated proverb that acts as a rallying slogan to keep going with the struggle against racially based inequality: "As much as I insist that things have gotten better, I am mindful of this truth as well: Better isn't good enough" (233). There are still plenty of proverbial "hard-nosed" (235) people and "roadblocks" (241) left that keep the steady "pattern of a rising tide lifting minority boats" (246) from moving ahead more swiftly. But Obama warns against concentrating solely on proposals that would benefit only minorities while alienating the white majority. Instead, he stresses the search for "universal appeals around strategies that help all Americans, along with measures that ensure our laws apply equally to everyone and hence uphold broadly held American ideals" (248). In other Obama words, here surprisingly not used, we are all in this struggle together. This paradigm change is certainly not an easy matter, as Obama explains with a series of proverbial metaphors that add much emotional expressiveness to his comments. He even begins with a very basic proverb underlining the fact that there is much social and political inertia still to overcome on the road to greater equality: "Such a shift in emphasis is not easy: Old habits die hard, and there is always fear on the part of many minorities that unless racial discrimination, past and present, stays on the front burner, white America will be left off the hook and hard-fought gains may be reversed. I understand these fears—nowhere is it ordained that history moves in a straight line, and during difficult economic times it is possible that the imperatives of racial equality get shunted aside" (248).

Being the eternal optimist filled with unwavering hope, Obama pushes these understandable reservations and doubts aside, arguing that we should be cognizant of the achievements that at least have been made thus far. "What's remarkable is not the number of minorities who have failed to climb into the middle class but the number who succeeded against the odds; not the anger and bitterness that parents of color have transmitted to their children but the degree to which such emotions have ebbed. That knowledge gives us something to build on. It tells us that progress can be made" (249).

About two years after this statement, on March 18, 2008, Obama presented his incredible speech on race in Philadelphia (see Garry Wills 2008), basing his title "A More Perfect Union" on the short preamble to the Constitution of the United States: "We, the People of the United States, in order to form a more perfect union, establish justice, insure domestic tranquility, provide for the common defense, promote the general welfare, and secure the blessings of liberty to ourselves and our posterity, do ordain and establish this Constitution for the United States of America." This time, following the upheaval and ramifications of Reverend Jeremiah Wright's racially charged and ill-conceived comments, Obama added much emotional rhetorical power to his argumentation. I would think that his biblically informed proclamation based on the proverb of the Golden Rule and the slightly changed but wonderfully expanded proverbial interrogative "am I my brother's keeper" (Genesis 4,9) in the form of a moral imperative explicitly including women will go down in the annals of famous quotations: "In the end, then, what is called for is nothing less, than what all the world's great religions demand—that we do unto others as we would have them do unto us. Let us be our brother's keeper, Scripture tells us. Let us be our sister's keeper. Let us find that common stake we all have in one another, and let our politics reflect that spirit as well."

I wish Obama had already included this fundamental wisdom in *The Audacity of Hope*, but clearly there is a difference in confronting racial issues intellectually in a book and reacting to it in the heat of political debate with the whole nation listening to every word that comes from a candidate campaigning for the presidency of the United States. For the record, it should also be noted that the "brother's/sister's keeper" dyad already appeared in several speeches in 2008 before and after this major address, but without the "Golden Rule" proverb (see January 20, March 4, April 4, July 8, and August 28, 2008). In fact, it had its debut in the 2004 Democratic Convention speech of July 27, 2004: "Alongside our famous individualism, there's another ingredient in the American sage. . . . A belief that we are connected as one people. . . . It's that fundamental belief—I am my brother's keeper, I am my sister's keeper—that makes this country work. It's what allows us to pursue our individual dreams, yet still come together as a single American family. 'E pluribus unum.' Out of many, one" (see Aron 2008, 23–25). To be sure, it is at such moments that proverbs, if chosen well and perhaps even modified to be more inclusive, can make a great difference. This also means that each "generation will surely be tested" (269), and as Obama says at the end of this chapter on race, "we are all tested by those voices that would divide us and have us turn on each other" (269). This being said, Barack Obama writes his last sentence on this subject by talking about all Americans, including his two daughters: "America is big enough to accommodate all their dreams" (269).

The World Beyond Our Borders

Barack Obama most certainly would agree that this chapter is but a quick overview or lesson on international diplomacy and world affairs as they relate to the American dream.

Turning to more modern times, Obama writes: "Then came September 11—and Americans felt their world turned upside down" (290). The consequence was America's misguided war against Iraq, with Obama making the following comments regarding his visit with the American troops and the hope that, proverbially speaking, "at the end of the day our actions would result in a better life for a nation of people we barely knew" (297): "And yet, three conversations during the course of my visit would remind me of just how quixotic our efforts in Iraq still seemed—how, with all the American blood, treasure, and the best of intentions, the house we were building might be resting on quicksand" (297–98). Yet true to his controlled and diplomatic approach to serious issues of world politics, Obama is quick to state proverbially and thus convincingly: "I don't presume to have this grand strategy [for a revised foreign policy framework] in my hip pocket. But I know what I believe" (303). After outlining some of his foreign policy beliefs, he talks of the proverbial "rules of the road" that are part of international cooperation, and this phraseologism has become a major linguistic leitmotif in his speeches (see August 28, September 16 and 30, 2008) as well: "The growing threat, then, comes primarily from those parts of the world on the margins of the global economy where the international 'rules of the road' have not taken hold—the realm of weak or failing states, arbitrary rule, corruption, and chronic violence; lands in which an overwhelming majority of the population is poor, uneducated, and cut off from the global information grid; places where the rulers fear globalization will loosen their hold on power, undermine traditional cultures, or displace indigenous institutions" (305).

Later on, he returns to the necessity of following some basic political concepts that he refers to proverbially as the "rules of the road" of international relations: "Why conduct ourselves in this way? Because nobody benefits more than we do from the observance of international 'rules of the road.' We can't win converts to those rules if we act as if they apply to everyone but us. When the world's sole superpower willingly restrains its power and abides by internationally agreed-upon standards of conduct, it sends a message that these are rules worth following. and robs terrorists and dictators of the argument that these rules are simply tools of American imperialism" (309).

He then couches his advice of careful adherence to international diplomatic rules of the road into a well-formulated statement that is based on the wisdom of a straightforwardly expressed proverb: "The painstaking process of building coalitions forces us to listen to other points of view and therefore look before we leap" (310).

Epilogue

It is well known that Obama was asked as a very junior politician to speak at the 2004 Democratic Convention at Boston that was to elevate him to national prominence. As he prepared his unforgettable speech, he "thought about the voices of all the people" (356) he had met during his small political campaign for state office, somewhat like the way Illinois poet Carl Sandburg expressed them in his epic poem *The People, Yes* (1931) and in his earlier poem "Good Morning, America" (1928), which includes the lines: "A code arrives; language; lingo; slang; / behold the proverbs of a people, a nation" (Sandburg 1970, 328–30; see also Bryan and Mieder 2003; Mieder 1971,1973, 1989, 184–87). Of course, these voices of the people also bring to mind the classical Latin proverb "vox populi, vox dei" or its English translation "the voice of the people is the voice of God" with its basic democratic meaning that people's opinions expressed in words should count (see Gallacher 1945; Boas 1969, 3–38). Barack Obama might well have used this internationally disseminated proverb here or elsewhere in his sociopolitical rhetoric as he reflects on the trials and tribulations of citizens of all walks of life throughout the country. Be that as it may, he follows his thoughts about the voices of the people with a deeply moving comment that describes his hopeful fight for a better body politic of the land.

> It wasn't just the struggle of these men and women that had moved me. Rather, it was their determination, their self-reliance, a relentless optimism in the face of hardship.
>
> The audacity of hope.
>
> That was the best of the American spirit, I thought—having the audacity to believe despite all the evidence to the contrary that we could restore a sense of community to a nation torn by conflict; the gall to believe that despite

personal setbacks, the loss of a job or an illness in the family or a childhood mired in poverty, we had some control—and therefore responsibility—over our own fate.

It was that audacity, I thought, that joined us as one people. It was that pervasive spirit of hope that tied my own family's story to the larger American story, and my own story to those of the voters I sought to represent. (356–57)

Such thoughts concerning humankind inform all of Obama's speeches and writings, and while the common woman and man inspire him in his rhetoric, he clearly draws on the wisdom of some of the great American leaders, mentioning especially Abraham Lincoln and Martin Luther King Jr. once again at the end of *The Audacity of Hope*: "I think about America and those who built it. This nation's founders, who somehow rose above petty ambitions and narrow calculations to imagine a nation unfurling across a continent. And those like Lincoln and King, who ultimately laid down their lives in the service of perfecting an imperfect union. And all the faceless, nameless men and women, slaves and soldiers and tailors and butchers, constructing lives for themselves and their children and grandchildren, brick by brick, rail by rail, calloused hand by calloused hand, to fill in the landscape of our collective dreams" (361–63).

There are no proverbs or proverbial phrases here at the end of Obama's emotionally expressed thoughts. That would perhaps have been too didactic or clichéd. But this folk speech nevertheless serves Obama well throughout the pages of *The Audacity of Hope*, whose message is effectively expressed through proverbial language that everyone can understand, relate to, identify with, and descant on.

References

This chapter was first published in *Narratives across Space and Time: Transmissions and Adaptations: Proceedings of the 15th Congress of the International Society for Folk Narrative Research (June 2009, Athens)*, edited by Aikaterini Polymerou-Kamilaki, Evangelos Karamanes, and Ioannis Plemmenos, 2:509–28. Athens: Academy of Athens, Hellenic Folklore Research Center, 2014.

Aron, Paul. 2008. *We Hold These Truths . . . And Other Words that Made America*. Lanham, MD: Rowman & Littlefield.
Barbour, Frances M. 1974. *A Concordance to the Sayings in Franklin's "Poor Richard."* Detroit: Gale Research Company.
Boas, George. 1969. *Vox Populi: Essays in the History of an Idea*. Baltimore: Johns Hopkins University Press.
Breuillard, Jean. 1984. "Proverbes et pouvoir politique: Le cas de l'U.R.S.S." In *Richesse du proverbe*, edited by François Suard and Claude Buridant, 2:155–66. Lille: Université de Lille.

Bryan, George B., and Wolfgang Mieder. 2003. "The Proverbial Carl Sandburg (1878–1967). An Index of Folk Speech in His American Poetry." *Proverbium* 20: 15–49.
Burrell, Brian. 1997. *The Words We Live By: The Creeds, Mottoes, and Pledges that Have Shaped America.* New York: Free Press.
Eggert, Sonja B. (1998) *"Kleine Schritte sind besser als keine Schritte": Willy Brandts sprichwörtliche Rhetorik.* Honors thesis, University of Vermont.
Gallacher, Stuart A. 1945. "'Vox Populi, Vox Dei.'" *Philological Quarterly* 24:12–19.
Harrison, Maureen, and Steve Gilbert, eds. 2007. *Barack Obama: Speeches 2002–2006.* Carlsbad, CA: Excellent Books.
Hertzler, Joyce O. 1933–34. "On Golden Rules." *International Journal of Ethics* 44:418–36.
Hitchens, Christopher. 2007. "The Audacity of Hope." *Times*, May 6, online. http://entertainment.timesonline.co.uk/tol/arts_and_entertainment/books/non-fiction/article.
Kakutani, Michiko. 2006. "Obama's Foursquare Politics, With a Dab of Dijon." *New York Times*, October 17, online. http://www.nytimes.com/2006/10/1/17/books/17kaku.html.
Karabegovic, Dženeta. 2007 "'No Lie Can Live Forever': Zur sprichwörtlichen Rhetorik von Martin Luther King." In *Sprichwörter sind Goldes wert: Parömiologische Studien zu Kultur, Literatur und Medien*, edited by Wolfgang Mieder, 223–40. Burlington: University of Vermont.
Klein, Joe. 2006. "Rising Star: A Dashing Young Senator Lays Out His Vision for His Party and His Country." *Washington Post*, October 22, online. http://www.time.com/time/magazine/article/0,9171,1546362-3,00.html.
Louis, Cameron. 2000. "Proverbs and the Politics of Language." *Proverbium* 17: 173–94.
Meis, Morgan. 2008. "Idle Chatter. Barack Obama: *The Audacity of Hope.*" *The Smart Set: From Drexel University*, February 14, online. http://www.thesmartset.com/article/article02140801.aspx.
Mieder, Wolfgang. 1971. "'Behold the Proverbs of a People': A Florilegium of Proverbs in Carl Sandburg's Poem 'Good Morning, America.'" *Southern Folklore Quarterly* 35: 160–68.
———. 1973. "Proverbs in Carl Sandburg's *The People, Yes*." *Southern Folklore Quarterly* 37:15–36.
———. 1989. *American Proverbs: A Study of Texts and Contexts.* Bern: Peter Lang.
———. 1990. *Not by Bread Alone: Proverbs of the Bible.* Shelburne, VT: New England Press.
———. 1997. *The Politics of Proverbs.* Madison: University of Wisconsin Press.
———. 1998. *"A House Divided": From Biblical Proverb to Lincoln and Beyond.* Burlington: University of Vermont.
———. 2000. *The Proverbial Abraham Lincoln: An Index to Proverbs in the Works of Abraham Lincoln.* New York: Peter Lang.
———. 2001. *"No Struggle, No Progress": Frederick Douglass and His Proverbial Rhetoric for Civil Rights.* New York: Peter Lang.
———. 2004. *Proverbs. A Handbook.* Westport, CT: Greenwood Press.
———. 2005. *Proverbs Are the Best Policy: Folk Wisdom and American Politics.* Logan: Utah State University Press.
———. 2008a. "'Let Us Have Faith That Right Makes Might': Proverbial Rhetoric in Decisive Moments of American Politics." *Proverbium* 25:319–52.
———. 2008b. *"Proverbs Speak Louder than Words": Folk Wisdom in Art, Culture, Folklore, History, Literature, and Mass Media.* New York: Peter Lang.
———. 2009. *"Yes We Can": Barack Obama's Proverbial Rhetoric.* New York: Peter Lang.
———. 2010. *"Making a Way Out of No Way": Martin Luther King's Sermonic Proverbial Rhetoric.* New York: Peter Lang.

———. 2014. *"All Men and Women Are Created Equal": Elizabeth Cady Stanton's and Susan B. Anthony's Proverbial Rhetoric Promoting Women's Rights.* New York: Peter Lang.
Mieder, Wolfgang, and George B. Bryan. 1995. *The Proverbial Winston S. Churchill: An Index to Proverbs in the Works of Sir Winston Churchill.* Westport, CT: Greenwood Press.
———. 1997. *The Proverbial Harry S. Truman: An Index to Proverbs in the Works of Harry S. Truman.* New York: Peter Lang.
Mieder, Wolfgang, Stuart A. Kingsbury, and Kelsie B. Harder, eds. 1992. *A Dictionary of American Proverbs.* New York: Oxford University Press.
Mieder, Wolfgang, and Andreas Nolte. 2015. *"Kleine Schritte sind besser als große Worte": Willy Brandts politische Sprichwortrhetorik.* New York: Peter Lang.
Newcomb, Robert. 1957. *The Sources of Benjamin Franklin's Sayings of Poor Richard.* PhD dissertation, University of Maryland.
Obama, Barack. *Obama News & Speeches.* Accessed July 19, 2018. http://www.barackobama.com.
———. 2004. *Dreams from My Father: A Story of Race and Inheritance.* New York: Three Rivers Press (originally published 1995).
———. 2005. "What I See in Lincoln's Eyes." *Time* magazine, June 27, 74.
———. 2006. *The Audacity of Hope: Thoughts on Reclaiming the American Dream.* New York: Three Rivers Press.
———. 2008a. *Barack Obama: What He Believes in from His Own Words; Resolutions and Bills Sponsored & Co-Sponsored by Senator Barack Obama During the 110th Session (First Half) of the US Congress January 4, 2007 to December 19, 2007.* Rockville, MD: Arc Manor.
———. 2008b. *Change We Can Believe In: Barack Obama's Plan to Renew America's Promise.* New York: Three Rivers Press (with seven speeches on pp. 193–271).
Olive, David, ed. 2008. *An American Story: The Speeches of Barack Obama.* Toronto: ECW Press.
Prahlad, Sw. Anand. 1996. *African-American Proverbs in Context.* Jackson: University Press of Mississippi.
Rogak, Lisa, ed. 2007. *Barack Obama in His Own Words.* New York: Carroll & Graf.
Sandburg, Carl. 1970. *The Complete Poems of Carl Sandburg.* New York: Harcourt, Brace, Jovanovich.
Schäfer, Ingo. 1983. *Populäre Sprachformen und politische Argumentation: Zur Funktion der Idiomatik in den Schriften Mao Zedongs.* Frankfurt am Main: Haag & Herchen.
Templeton, John M. 1997. *Worldwide Laws of Life.* Philadelphia: Templeton Foundation Press.
Viellard, Stéphane. 2001. "Le statut du proverbe dans le discours soviétique de la première moitié du XX-ème siècle." In *Russkii iazyk: Peresekaia granitsy*, edited by Marguerite Guiraud-Weber and I. B. Shatunovskii, 54–65. Dubna: Mezhdunarodnyi Universitet.
Wills, Garry. 2008. "Two Speeches [by Lincoln and Obama] on Race." *New York Review of Books*, May 1: 4, 6, 8.

7

"POLITICS IS NOT A SPECTATOR SPORT"

*Proverbs in the Personal and Political
Writings of Hillary Rodham Clinton*

The well-known American proverb "politics make strange bedfellows" (1832) and such modern proverbs as "politics is a contact sport" (1960; Mieder, Kingsbury, Harder 1992, 472; Shapiro 2006, 618) and "in politics, perception is reality" (1961) from the United States can all serve to describe the sociopolitical endeavors of Hillary Rodham Clinton (born October 26, 1947), who has dedicated her life since her student years to government service of various types. If there was one person in North America who definitely had the experience and qualifications to become president of the United States, then Hillary Clinton would have been the one. But politics is a fickle business, with constant changes and surprises, as characterized by yet another relatively new American proverb: "a week is a long time in politics" (1961; Doyle, Mieder, Shapiro 2012, 203, 274). Her campaign to become the first female president of the nation was riddled with ups and downs, and it was indeed a wide-open question who might have been elected president of the United States in November 2016.

Certainly, Hillary Clinton has earned her stripes to be a highly qualified candidate. This is not the place to analyze her endless list of accomplishments. It must suffice to mention but a few highlights from an impressive career as a public servant. She was educated at Wellesley College in Massachusetts, where she received her bachelor of arts degree in political science in 1969. She went on to study law at Yale University and started her successful career as a lawyer in 1973. She married her fellow law student, Bill Clinton, in 1975 and became the first lady of Arkansas from 1979 to 1981 and 1983 to 1992 while her husband was governor of that state. From 1993 to 2001, she was the first lady of the United States, while Bill Clinton served his two terms as president. From 2001 to 2009, she was the first female United States senator from the state of New York. After having lost her first presidential bid to President Barack Obama, he chose her as the sixty-seventh United States secretary of state, a clear indication of the high esteem that he has for this formidable woman. After having served in this significant position from 2009 to 2013 during Obama's first term, she resigned in order to begin preparing for her second attempt to become president of the United States in her own right.

In the spirit of Eleanor Roosevelt, the socially engaged and strong-willed wife of President Franklin Delano Roosevelt, Hillary Clinton has proven herself to be an outspoken, independent, powerful, and at times aggressive proponent of healthcare; an empathetic advocate for children and families; and above all a dedicated champion of women throughout the world.

A public figure of her stature and strength could, of course, not avoid controversies, of which at least some have been the result of scandals brought about by the questionable behavior of her husband. But she too has had her personal crises stemming from financial dealings, the questions remaining about the attack on the American Embassy at Benghazi, and lately her inappropriate use of a personal email account to conduct the sometimes-confidential business of the State Department. During investigations of issues like these, she has at times given the impression of not being cooperative or forthcoming, and her flippant or even sarcastic responses have not endeared her to considerable segments of the population. Once, when her professional ethics as a lawyer were questioned, she fired back on March 16, 1992, "I could have stayed home, baked cookies and had teas, but what I decided was to fulfill my profession, which I entered before my husband was in public life" (Brock 1996, 265; Knowles 1999, 221; Burrell 2001, 31; Shapiro 2006, 159). While she was asserting the right for herself and for all women to have a professional career, she was at the same time offending those women who were proud of being homemakers caring for large families. Without wanting to antagonize certain segments of the population, her remarks often polarize her listeners or readers because of her strained "perseverance rhetoric," with "endurance having always been a key component of Clinton's fighting style" (Spiker 2009, 109).

Speaking of rhetorical style (see Bowers and Ochs 1971; Burgchardt 1995; Elspaß 2002, 2007), it must be said that the numerous books and articles written about the successes and failures of this unique public figure say basically nothing about her effective use of language, with Julia A. Spiker's essay "It Takes a Village to Win: A Theoretical Analysis of 'Hillary for President'"

(2009) being a valuable exception. She points out that Hillary Clinton uses "literal language almost exclusively" in her various speeches for the sake of precision and correctness at the expense of emotional vividness (102). In fact, "her rhetoric demonstrates competence, knowledge of the complex nature of serious issues, a clear and consistent message ('I am a problem-solver'), and direct, strong language with few embellishments or emotional entanglements" (102). All of this means that Clinton employs only "the rare metaphor" (103) in her speeches, and it thus should not come as a surprise that she uses proverbial language only sparingly in her addresses, a fact that distinguishes her greatly from the proverbial rhetoric by Frederick Douglass, Abraham Lincoln, Elizabeth Cady Stanton, Susan B. Anthony, Harry S. Truman, Martin Luther King Jr., and her friend Barack Obama (Mieder 2000, 2001, 2009, 2010, 2014a; Mieder and Bryan 1997). The lack of proverbial metaphors in her speeches appears to be a conscious choice by Hillary Clinton, who has stated that she wants her speeches to be "accessible to the broadest possible audience" and "simple and direct" (Clinton 2014, 579). Especially in her role as secretary of state, it was important for Clinton to be precise when dealing with foreign leaders for whom English is a foreign language. Proverbial expressions could easily be misunderstood or not understood at all, and thus it might be best to speak in straightforward English. "It's easy to get lost in semantics, but words constitute much of a diplomat's work, and I knew they would shape how the rest of the world received our agreement and how it was understood on the ground in Syria" (Clinton 2014, 458). In any case, Clinton is well aware of the importance of language in sensitive political communications: "Words matter, and words from an American President [Bill Clinton] carry great weight around the world" (Clinton 2003, 457). Not surprisingly then, she spends much time on writing and editing her speeches with the help of speechwriters. "The speech team still had work to do. We were on our fifth or sixth draft" (302). Here is how she recalls getting ready for her speech on August 28, 2008, at the Democratic National Convention in Denver, Colorado, nominating Barack Obama to be the democratic candidate for the presidency of the United States.

> For as many speeches as I'd given, this was a big one, in front of a huge audience in the arena and millions more watching on TV. I have to admit I was nervous. I tinkered with the speech right up until the very last minute, so that when my motorcade arrived one of my aides had to leap out of the van and sprint ahead to hand the thumb drive to the teleprompter operator. The Obama campaign had asked to see it much earlier, and when I didn't share it,

some of his advisors worried I must be hiding something they wouldn't want me to say. But I was simply using every second I had to get it right. (Clinton 2014, 9)

"Getting it right" can stand for Hillary Clinton's obsession with perfection, but as my own analysis of several of her major addresses has corroborated, this aspect of her oral rhetoric prevents her from emoting naturally. Interestingly but not surprisingly then, her speeches are lacking in the vividness and expressiveness that a more conscious reliance on proverbial metaphors would add to her intelligent and well-intended messages.

Things are completely different when it comes to the passionate and certainly emotional yet natural style of her books. The "cool" or "icy" and certainly intellectual Hillary Clinton is perfectly capable of letting her official hair down, to put it proverbially. And yes, her books show Clinton to be quite the proverbialist. Her first book, *It Takes a Village and Other Lessons Children Teach Us* (1996), written with the help of Georgetown journalism professor Barbara Feinman (Olson 1999, 277–79; Andersen 2004, 145–46), made the bestseller list of the *New York Times*, and it shows Clinton's concern for and commitment to all aspects of child raising, especially the matters of health care, proper treatment, and education.

Her next two books are of less consequence to this investigation of her proverbial language. There is the splendidly documented children's book *Dear Socks, Dear Buddy: Kids' Letters to the First Pets* (1998) about the cat and dog of the Clinton family in the White House, followed by her richly illustrated coffee-table book, *An Invitation to the White House: At Home with History* (2000). Then came her autobiography, *Living History* (2003), on whose pages Clinton found her personal voice filled with facts, stories, dreams, anxieties, joys, emotion, passion, and much more. The book was favorably received and translated into twelve languages and provided a telling glimpse into the life of one of America's leading women politicians. When her book *Hard Choices* (2014) appeared some eleven years later, the reaction was not as positive to this account of her work as the secretary of state. To some readers and critics, it was too self-serving in its prose, although it must be admitted that it too is written in a lucid, informed, and vivid style. From a proverbial point of view, the three major books are deserving of a closer look, especially since the reviewers and critics of the books pay no attention to paremiological matters that are part of their personal and historical significance.

As can be seen from comments that Hillary Clinton has made in her books and speeches about the influence of her parents on her own outlook on life, they definitely instilled proverbial wisdom in her during the formative years as a young girl that she adheres to with fond and appreciative memory of them to this day. Her father, Hugh Ellsworth Rodham (1911–1993), was a conservative Republican and built a successful small textile business, with her more liberal mother, Dorothy Emma Howell (1919–2011), being an efficient homemaker who took care of the family that includes Hillary's brothers Hugh and Tony. As churchgoing Methodists, they instilled solid Puritan ethics in their children that included proverbs cited as signs and strategies for a successful and responsible life (Burke 1941; Seitel 1969; Arthurs 1994). As Hillary Clinton recalls in her first book: "My parents drilled into my brothers and me that familiar refrain 'Sticks and stones may break my bones, but words will never hurt me' and the advice to 'take a deep breath and count to ten' to give us ways to avoid hostile confrontation" (*It Takes a Village* (hereafter cited simply as V, 178). In her autobiography, she recalls: "I think if my father and mother said anything to me more than a million times, it was: 'Don't listen to what other people say. Don't be guided by other people's opinions. You know, you have to live with yourself.' And I think that is good advice" (*Living History*, hereafter cited simply as L, 226). Indeed, the American proverb "You have to live with yourself" (1902) has been a guiding principle for Clinton as she maneuvers her private life, that of her family, and her public persona through the political waters that often find her between the proverbial rock and a hard place.

Her father played the traditional patriarchal role in the family, as she explains with the obvious proverb to describe the situation: "I grew up in a cautious, conformist era in American history. But in the midst of our *Father Knows Best* upbringing, I was taught to resist peer pressure. My mother never wanted to hear about what my friends were wearing or what they thought about me or anything else. 'You're unique,' she would say. 'You can think for yourself. I don't care if everybody's doing it. We're not everybody. You're not everybody'" (L, 14). And here is yet another proverbial string by her practical mother: "Mom measured her own life by how much she was able to help us and serve others. I knew if she was still with us, she would be urging us to do the same. Never rest on your laurels. Never quit. Never stop working to make the world a better place. That's our unfinished business" (*Hard Choices*, hereafter cited simply as H, 589). Even in her all-important campaign launch speech of June 13, 2015, she remembered her mother fondly, crediting her for her own strength of character and will power: "I certainly haven't won every battle I've fought. But leadership means perseverance and hard choices. You have to push through the setbacks and disappointments and keep at it. I think you know by now that I've been called many things by many people—'quitter' is not one of them. Like so much in my life, I got this from my mother. . . . I can still hear her saying: 'Life's not about what happens to you, it's about what you do with what happens to you—so get back out there'" (Clinton 2015a).

Little wonder that the thankful daughter also writes that "Sometimes Mother knows best too!" (V, 14). It is doubtful that the knowledgeable Hillary Clinton knew that the proverb "Mother knows best" (1871) was formed as an antiproverb to the American proverb "Father knows best" that was coined in 1870, originally meant ironically, by the admired feminist Susan B. Anthony (Mieder 2014a, 172; Mieder 2015, 104, 171).

Her father also "bombarded" his children with proverbial insights, often telling them "'When you work, work hard. When you play, play hard. And don't confuse the two'" (V, 15). As with her mother's teachings, she remembers her father's proverbial advice with the wisdom of experienced hindsight: "I'm sure I inherited my [monetary] concerns from my notoriously frugal father, who made smart investments, put his kids through college and retired comfortably. My dad taught me how to follow the stock market when I was still in grade school and frequently reminded me that 'money doesn't grow on trees.' Only through hard work, savings and prudent investing could you become financially independent" (L, 86).

But the most impressive testimony to her dad's proverbial prowess is the chapter title "The Best Tool You Can Give a Child Is a Shovel" (V, 135) in her book *It Takes a Village*. It is a Rodham family proverb of sorts, as Hillary Clinton points out in the introduction to her book: "It is about giving our children the skills they need to overcome adversity and to 'shovel their way out from under whatever life piles on.' It's my father's metaphor. Whenever I got stuck, he would say, 'Hillary, how are you going to dig yourself out of this one?'" (V, xvii). In the chapter itself, she writes: "My father's approach [to character building] was vintage Hugh Rodham. When I was facing a problem, he would look me straight in the eyes and ask, 'Hillary, how are you going to dig yourself out of this one?' His query always brought to mind a shovel. That image stayed with me, and over the course of my life I have reached for mental, emotional, and spiritual shovels of various sizes and shapes—even a backhoe or two" (V, 136–37).

With such proverbial preoccupation it can hardly be surprising to find the following folkloric observation in this very book: "The lessons men and women have learned over thousands of years are available to anyone, in the form of fables, stories, poems, plays, proverbs, and scriptures that have stood the test of time" (V, 137). Clinton is even somewhat of a phraseographer, cutting out passages, quotations, and other memorable statements and putting them "in a little book of sayings and Scriptures that I keep" (V, 166). It would be good to see the entries of that book one of these days, but it can be assumed that some of the familiar quotations and proverbs to be discussed here might well be included in this personal treasure.

Speaking of Scriptures, it is clear that Hillary Clinton is a religious person solidly informed by the Bible. "I had read my Bible and other books about religion and spirituality" (L, 267). She is a churchgoing Methodist, she takes part in prayer meetings, and she remembers "an old saying from Sunday school: Faith is like stepping off a cliff and expecting one of two outcomes—you will either land on solid ground or you will be taught to fly" (L, 494). She also remembers the proverbial exaggerations and biblical phrases employed by her sixth-grade teacher to get her young pupils motivated: "If we were sluggish in responding to her questions, she said, 'You're slower than molasses running uphill in winter.' She often paraphrased the verse from Matthew [5:15]: 'Don't put your lamp under a bushel basket, but use it to light up the world'" (L, 15). The biblical call for love of other human beings has touched her deeply, as can be seen from the following two statements based on the Bible proverbs "love your neighbor as yourself" (Galatians 5:14) and "love your enemies" (Matthew 5:44): "Learning to live affirmatively begins with the way we feel about ourselves. Children who grow up thinking of their own lives in positive terms are more likely to value the lives of others as well. Religious teachings remind us that we are to love others as we love ourselves. Loving oneself is not a matter of narcissism or egocentrism; it means respecting yourself and feeling affirmed in your identity" (L, 172).

She added, "It is not always easy to live what we believe, however. For example, while I believe there is no greater gift that God has given any of us than to be loved and to love, I find it difficult to love people who clearly don't love me. I wrestle nearly every day with the biblical admonition to forgive and love my enemies" (L, 166).

But it is the "Golden Rule" imperative that informs Hillary Clinton's personal and political ethics, just as it has been a guidepost for President Barack Obama's worldview (Mieder 2014b, 172–97). Both of them know that the proverb "do unto others as you would have them do unto you" (Matthew 7:12) is known in variants in all the major religions of the world (Hertzler 1933–34; Griffin 1991, 67–69; Burrell 1997, 235–40; Templeton 1997, 8–12). It continues to encapsulate the most basic ethical law for the modern age of globalization (Mieder 2014b, 204, 222). Always interested in the children of the world, Clinton writes: "I wish more churches—and parents—took seriously the teachings of every major religion that we treat one another as each of us would want to be treated. If that happened, we could make significant inroads on the social problems we confront" (L, 164; Kengor 2007, 111–12). So that people really get the message, she chose Barbara Reynold's aphorism "the Golden Rule does not mean that gold shall rule" (L, 265) as a motto for a chapter on "Every Business Is a Family Business" (L, 265–79). After all, it is the humanitarian engagement rather than the mercantile successes that make the world a better place for humankind.

As evidenced by these examples of Bible proverbs, Hillary Clinton does not necessarily cite them verbatim, perhaps in order to avoid an overemphasis of religious didacticism. After all, most of her listeners and readers will recognize the underlying proverbial message in these allusions. This is also the case when she simply alludes to folk proverbs, but in her two employments of the classical proverb "nature passes nurture," she might have gone a bit too far away from its recognizable wording: "It is increasingly apparent that the nature-nurture question is not an 'either/or' debate so much as a 'both/and' proposition" (V, 50) and "Cream will rise to the top no matter what we do, so let nature take its course and forget about nurture" (L, 227). Notice that the second example includes the proverb "cream will rise to the top," making this statement a powerful claim. But here are a few more contextualized examples where Clinton does not cite the proverbs in their standard wordings or structures, which are cited in italics.

> *Children are our future.*
> It is often said that children are our last and best hope for the future, and that if we want society to evolve, we must teach the next generation the importance of active citizenship. Teaching children how to become good citizens and giving them an appreciation of governance is another way to elicit their natural empathy, compassion, idealism, and thirst for service. (V, 183–84)

> *You can't go home again.*
> A month after school [Wellesley College] started, I called home collect and told my parents I didn't think I was smart enough to be there. My father told me to come on home and my mother told me she didn't want me to be a quitter. After a shaky start, the doubts faded, and I realized that I really couldn't go home again, so I might as well make a go of it. (L, 27–28)

> *Don't kick a fellow when he is down.*
> Bill [Clinton] was raised by his mother to believe that you don't hit people when they're down, that you treat your adversaries in life or politics with decency. (L, 211)

> *Every cloud has a silver lining.*
> With his skeptical views about politics and people, [Dick] Morris served as a counterweight to the ever optimistic Bill Clinton. Where Bill saw a silver lining in every cloud, Morris saw thunderstorms. (L, 251)
>
> *If life hands you lemons, make lemonade.*
> I told the President [Barack Obama] that if the votes for action against Syria were not winnable in Congress, he should make lemonade out of lemons and welcome the unexpected overture from Moscow. (H, 468)
>
> *The perfect is the enemy of the good.*
> The Chinese weren't giving an inch; neither were the Indians and Brazilians. Some of the Europeans were letting the perfect be the enemy of the good—and the possible. We emerged, frustrated and tired, sometime around 2:00 in the morning, still without an agreement. (H, 498)
>
> *What is good for Main Street is good for Wall Street.*
> As a former senator from New York, I know firsthand the role that Wall Street can and should play in our economy, helping main street grow and prosper, and boosting new companies that make America more competitive. (Clinton 2015b, speech on "Economic Vision" on July 13, 2015, at the New School in New York City)

The last example is of special interest, since this socioeconomic proverb originated only in 1995, based on the proverb "what is good for General Motors is good for America" from 1953. It was subsequently popularized by President Barack Obama in various speeches, and perhaps Hillary Clinton picked it up from him. In any case, as this reference and also such proverbs as "children are our future" (1920), "you can't go home again" (1940), and "if life hands you lemons, make lemonade" (1910) indicate, this astute woman is perfectly attuned to the world of modern proverbs (see Doyle, Mieder, Shapiro 2012, 38, 123, 140).

Hillary Clinton did not refer to her former boss in this speech on her "Economic Vision," since she obviously wants to campaign for the presidency on her own terms and not by way of a lame-duck president with plenty of problems, primarily due to the uncooperative Republican-controlled Congress. However, she does enjoy citing familiar quotations from well-known figures, with some of them having gained a proverbial status by now (Boller 1967). It might perhaps again be surmised that some of these "proverbial quotations" are to be found in that "little book of sayings."

> James Carville (1992; U.S. political consultant)
> I don't think Bill [Clinton] expected that health care reform would become a cornerstone of his campaign. After all, James Carville's famous war room slogan was "It's the economy, stupid." (L, 115, see also p. 379; Shapiro 2006, 138)

Samuel Johnson (1763; English man of letters)
There's a similar thought attributed to Dr. Samuel Johnson by [James] Boswell: "Sir, a woman preaching is like a dog's walking on its hind legs. It is not done well; but you are surprised to find it done at all." (L, 190; Shapiro 2006, 402)

Harry S. Truman (no date; US president)
It's often said that the President has the loneliest job in the world. Harry Truman once referred to the White House as "the crown jewel in the American penal system." (L, 223)

Mark Twain (1903; US writer)
One day, I was persuaded to try a round of golf with Bill [Clinton], whose leg had healed enough to permit a return to his favorite pastime. Frankly, I don't like golf. And I'm a terrible player. I side with Mark Twain: "Golf is a good walk spoiled." (L, 415; Shapiro 2006, 782, attributed to Mark Twain)

Nelson Mandela (no date; South African president)
"But if our expectations, if our fondest prayers and dreams are not realized," he [Mandela] said, "then we should all bear in mind that the greatest glory of living lies not in never falling, but in rising every time you fall." (L, 480)

John F. Kennedy (1961; US president)
Diplomacy would be easy if we had to talk only to our friends. That's not how peace is made. Presidents throughout the Cold War understood that when they negotiated arms control agreements with the Soviets. As President Kennedy put it, "Let us never negotiate out of fear. But let us never fear to negotiate." (H, 163–64; Shapiro 2006, 421)

Yitzhak Rabin (no date; Israeli prime minister)
I hope that one day the constituencies for peace among both peoples [Palestinians and Israelis] would grow so strong and loud that their leaders would be forced to compromise. In my head I heard the deep and steady voice of my slain friend Yitzhak Rabin: "The coldest peace is better than the warmest war." (H, 330; for proverbs on war and peace see Mieder 2014b, 230–58)

Hafez Ibrahim (no date; Egyptian poet)
I quoted the Egyptian poet Hafez Ibrahim, who wrote, "A mother is a school. Empower her and you empower a nation," and I talked about my own experiences with all-women's education at Wellesley [College]. (H, 354)

Barack Obama (2009; US president)
In his first inaugural address, President Obama had told Iran and other pariah states that we would "extend a hand if you are willing to unclench your fist." (H; 434, see also 54; Mieder 2009, 143)

The most interesting proverbial quotation is the well-known feminist claim that "A woman is like a teabag. You never know how strong she is until she's in hot water." Together with many others, Hillary Clinton strongly believes that it originated with Eleanor Roosevelt—humanitarian and diplomat as well as wife of President Franklin Delano Roosevelt—as can be seen from these comments in her autobiography, *Living History*, and her later book *Hard Choices*.

> One dreary November morning, I stopped by my office after a meeting with Bill [Clinton] in the Oval Office and glanced at the framed photograph of Eleanor Roosevelt displayed on a table. I am a huge fan of Mrs. Roosevelt, and I have long collected portraits and mementos from her career. Seeing her calm, determined visage brought to mind some of her wise words: "A woman is like a teabag," Mrs. Roosevelt said. "You never know how strong she is until she's in hot water." It was time for another talk with Eleanor. (L, 258)

> At times when I felt daunted by the scope of challenges we were trying to overcome, I often found myself looking for comfort to a portrait of Eleanor Roosevelt that I kept in my office. The examples she set as a fearless First Lady and a courageous fighter for human rights inspired and fortified me. . . . Eleanor's language of "full participation [of women]" . . . has always resonated with me. So have many of her other words. "A woman is like a teabag," she once observed wryly. "You never know how strong she is until she's in hot water." I love that and, in my experience, it's spot on. (H, 564)

As her short book chapter on "Conversations with Eleanor" (L, 258–67) illustrates, Hillary Clinton does indeed have somewhat of a mystical relationship to this exemplary woman with whom she carries on short imaginary conversations to gain strength and courage in moments of anxiety and disappointment (Sheehy 1999, 261–62; Bernstein 2007, 239–40; Gerth and van Natta 2007, 148). There is no doubt that these two strong women are kindred spirits and that they were the two most actively involved first ladies who also had to deal with the infidelity of their presidential husbands. But alas, Eleanor Roosevelt did not originate this proverbial quotation, and neither did the unlikely Nancy Reagan, the trim and proper wife of President Ronald Reagan (Shapiro 2006, 629). It has simply become attached to Eleanor Roosevelt's name, as is the case with many other proverbs that have been attributed to historical persons without any proof (Taylor 1931, 34–43). In fact, the earliest evidence of the possible origin of the phrase is from the 1915 *Times-Picayune* newspaper in Seattle, Washington, referring only to tea and surprisingly to men:

> "Men are like tea."
> "How so?"
> "Their real strength is not drawn out until they get into hot water."

In 1958, a reference with "tea bags" appeared, referring to both men and women: "People are like tea bags. They never know their strength until they get into hot water." Finally, in 1963, a variant with "women" appeared: "Women are like tea-bags—they don't know their strength until they are in hot water." But as phrase sleuth Ralph Keyes had to conclude after tracing the expression by way of numerous historical references, there is absolutely no evidence that Eleanor Roosevelt ever used it at all (Keyes 2013; I also acknowledge the help of my friend Charles Clay Doyle with this matter).

This quite naturally leads these deliberations to memorable quotations by Hillary Clinton herself. Just like all politicians, she too has attempted to formulate concise statements that have the possibility of becoming familiar quotations and perhaps even proverbs. For now, they might be considered pseudoproverbs.

> Service is not a one-way street. (Foss 1999, 228; comment during a White House ceremony on National Youth Service Day on April 20, 1993)
>
> If women and girls don't flourish, families won't flourish. And if families don't flourish, communities and nations won't flourish. (Foss 1999, 274; remark celebrating the seventy-fifth anniversary of the ratification of the Nineteenth Amendment to the US Constitution on August 26, 1995, at Grand Teton National Park, Wyoming)
>
> There is no such thing as other peoples' children. (Rawson and Miner 2006, 109; Clinton in *Newsweek*, January 15, 1996)
>
> Every child needs a champion. (V, 25, chapter title; see also V, 41)
>
> Security takes more than a blanket. (V, 117, chapter title)
>
> Every business is a family business. (V, 265, chapter title)
>
> Where women prosper, countries prosper. (Foss 1999, 209; speech on March 27, 1996, at Istanbul, Turkey)
>
> In other words: Aid is a bridge to trade. (Clinton 1997, 46)
>
> Honor the past, imagine the future. (Clinton 1998, 195, 201; L, 461)
>
> Silence is not spoken here. (L, 268, chapter title; see also L, 286)

Yet the most famous remark that has become quotational if not proverbial is certainly "Human rights are women's rights and women's rights are human rights" (H, 585). By now it has been entered without context in books of famous quotations (Foss 1999, 124; Bartlett 2012, 864), but here is what Hillary Rodham Clinton, as an effective advocate for women's rights worldwide, actually said at the end of a powerful anaphora during a major address at the United Nations Fourth World Conference on Women on September 5, 1995, in Beijing, China:

> It is a violation of *human* rights when babies are denied food, or drowned, or suffocated, or their spines broken, simply because they are born girls.
> It is a violation of *human* rights when women and girls are sold into the slavery of prostitution.
> It is a violation of *human* rights when women are doused with gasoline, set on fire and burned to death because their marriage dowries are deemed too small.
> It is a violation of *human* rights when individual women are raped in their own communities and when thousands of women are subjected to rape as a tactic or prize of war.
> It is a violation of *human* rights when a leading cause of death worldwide among women ages 14 to 44 is the violence they are subjected to in their own homes.
> It is a violation of *human* rights when young girls are brutalized by the painful and degrading practice of genital mutilation.
> It is a violation of *human* rights when women are denied the right to plan their own families, and that includes being forced to have abortions or being sterilized against their will.
> If there is one message that echoes forth from this conference, it is that human rights are women's rights—and women's rights are human rights. Let us not forget that among those rights are the right to speak freely—and the right to be heard.
> Women must enjoy the right to participate fully in the social and political lives of their countries if we want freedom and democracy to thrive and endure....
> Let this Conference be our—and the world's—call to action.
> (Clinton 1995, 5–7)

This important speech "meant the world"—to put it proverbially—to Hillary Clinton, as can be seen from remarks in her book *Hard Choices* some twenty years later.

> I wanted to push the envelope as far as I could on behalf of women and girls. I wanted my speech to be simple, vivid, and strong in its message that women's rights are not separate from or a subsidiary of the human rights every person is entitled to enjoy....
> The heart of the speech was a statement that was both obvious and undeniable but nonetheless too long unsaid on the world stage. "If there is one message that echoes forth from this conference," I declared, "let it be that human rights are women's rights and women's rights are human rights, once and for all."...
> My speech ended with a call for all of us to return to our countries and renew our efforts to improve educational, health, legal, economic, and political opportunities for women. When the last words left my lips, the delegates leaped from their seats to give me a standing ovation. As I exited the hall, women hung over the banisters and raced down escalators to shake my hand.

> My message had resonated with the women in Beijing, but I could never have predicted how far and wide the impact of this twenty-one-minute speech would stretch. For nearly twenty years women around the world have quoted my words back to me, or asked me to sign a copy of my speech, or shared personal stories about how it inspired them to work for change. (H, 560–61)

Indeed, especially the statement about human rights also being women's rights deserves to be quoted, remembered, and adhered to as a piece of quintessential wisdom. The entire speech showed Clinton's fighting spirit which, on a personal level, could also be seen in her first attempt to become the first woman president during the presidential campaign of 2008. She did lose that hard-fought political battle to Barack Obama, but even as the loser, she rose to the occasion of endorsing Obama to be the next president in her speech of June 7, 2008, which ended her own presidential campaign. Clearly this was a difficult and emotional speech for her, but the fighter in her was not lost, and she took the opportunity to make a powerful statement on behalf of women by making use of the proverbial expression "to break through the glass ceiling," with the metaphor of the glass ceiling referring to "an invisible barrier on the career ladder that some employees, in particular women and members of minority groups, find they can see through but which they cannot surmount" (Room 2000, 282). In this speech, "Clinton's rhetoric transcended her standard issue-listing, problem-solving structure.... It soared above her previous rhetoric in that it incorporated the powerful metaphor of 'light shining through,' offering hope. She redefined her efforts and those efforts of her supporters as putting 'eighteen million cracks' in the glass ceiling, the ultimate metaphor signaling the societal limitations on women with power" (Spiker 2009, 111–12; see also Kornblut 2009, 11).

> Although we [primarily her women supporters] weren't able to shatter the highest, hardest glass ceiling this time, thanks to you, it's got about 18 million cracks in it. And the light is shining through like never before, filling us all with the hope and the sure knowledge that the path will be a little easier next time. That has always been the history of progress in America. You will always find me on the front line of democracy—fighting for the future. The way to continue our fight now, to accomplish the goals for which we stand, is to take our energy, our passion, our strength and do all we can to help elect Barack Obama the next President of the United States. (H, 6; see also the picture and caption H, 174a)

Not surprisingly, Theodore Sheckels chose the title *Cracked but Not Shattered: Hillary Rodham Clinton's Unsuccessful Campaign for the Presidency* (2009) for his book analyzing what went wrong with Clinton's attempt to become the first woman president. In the meantime, she is continuing her fight for women's rights, working "on a digital 'global review' of the status of women and girls in time for the twentieth anniversary of Beijing in September 2015" (H, 584). Describing this effort, she has returned to the "glass ceiling" metaphor: "Eventually we started calling our initiative No Ceiling: The Full Participation Project. The name was a playful echo of the '18 million cracks in the glass ceiling' that became famous at the end of my Presidential campaign, but it meant much more than that. You didn't have to be at the highest levels of politics or business; women and girls everywhere still faced all sorts of ceilings that held back their ambition and aspirations and made it harder, if not impossible, for them to pursue their dreams" (H, 585; see also Schnoebelen, Carlin, Warner 2009: 45).

In any case, it remains to be seen whether Hillary Clinton will be able to break through the "last glass ceiling" (Allen and Parnes 2013, 379), as the title of a recent book chapter suggests. Whether it will be she in 2016 or another deserving woman, the time has surely come to elect a woman president of the United States. "Decades ago, Hillary's heroine Eleanor Roosevelt offered the following wisdom: 'Some day, a woman may be president. . . . I hope it will only become a reality when she is elected as an individual because of her capacity and the trust which the majority of the people have in her integrity and ability as a person.' Eleanor Roosevelt is waiting" (Gerth and van Natta 2007, 346).

Hillary Clinton has learned well from her soulmate, Eleanor Roosevelt, declaring already in a speech on February 23, 2007, at San Francisco: "Although I'm proud to be a woman, I'm not running as a woman candidate" (Gerth and van Natta 2007, 343). This also holds true as she is in the middle of her second attempt to reach the highest political office of the United States. Of course, she wants and needs the support of women, but she clearly wants to be the president of many men as well.

Leaving the glass ceiling issue aside, there is a second proverbial metaphor that has served Hillary Clinton well on her long and engaged political and social journey. It all has to do with the proverbial title of her extremely successful first book, *It Takes a Village and Other Lessons Children Teach Us* (1996) that begins with a chapter also entitled "It Takes a Village" (V, 1–11). A few pages into it, she makes the following comments around the proverb "it takes a village to raise a child" that encapsulates the entire thrust of this book on the raising and educating of children. As can be seen from her remarks, she very astutely incorporates the village with its familial and social structures, traditions, and values as a small place into the nation as a whole, and beyond that into the world. After all, the child of today is a citizen not only of a particular village or country but of the interconnected world.

> Children exist in the world as well as in the family. From the moment they are born, they depend on a host of other "grown-ups"—grandparents, neighbors, teachers, ministers, employers, political leaders, and untold others who touch their lives directly and indirectly. Adults police their streets, monitor the quality of their food, air, and water, produce the programs that appear on their television, run the businesses that employ their parents, and write the laws that protect them. Each of us plays a part in every child's life: It takes a village to raise a child.
> I chose that old African proverb to title this book because it offers a timeless reminder that children will thrive only if their families thrive and if the whole of society cares enough to provide for them. . . .
> In earlier times and places—and until recently in our own country—the "village" meant an actual geographic place where individuals and families lived and worked together. . . . For most of us, though, the village doesn't look like that anymore. . . . The horizons of the contemporary village extend well beyond the town line. From the moment we are born, we are exposed to vast numbers of other people and influences through radio, television, newspapers, books, movies, computers, compact discs, cellular phones, and fax machines. Technology connects us to the impersonal global village it has created. . . .
> The sage who first offered that proverb would undoubtedly be bewildered by what constitutes the modern village. . . . The village can no longer be defined as a place on a map, or a list of people or organizations, but its essence remains the same: it is a network of values and relationships that support and affect our lives. (V, 5–7; see also V, 11)

The supposedly African proverb caught on quickly in the United States and beyond by way of Clinton's book, as she herself describes it in the tenth-anniversary edition of her book in 2006.

> This small book with the bright, whimsical jacket provided endless opportunities for headline writers, who have come up with such variations as "It Takes a Village to Have a Parade!," "It Takes a Village to Build a Zero Waste Community," and, my all-time favorite, "It Takes a Village to Raise a Pig." More significantly, the book helped to initiate conversations about how parents and the greater community—the village—all shape the lives of children. People took its message to heart. During my travels as First Lady, several people told me that their PTA [Parent-Teacher Association] had adopted "It takes a village" as a slogan to encourage more community involvement. At a children's hospital, I saw staff wearing buttons that said: "This is the village that takes care of children." I got off a plane in Asmara, Eritrea, on an official trip to Africa and was greeted by a large group of women with a colorful painted sign: YES, IT REALLY DOES TAKE A VILLAGE. (V, xiii; the sign is also mentioned in L, 405)

Clinton shows herself as a folklorist or paremiologist here, noting how a proverb can be changed into effective antiproverbs and slogans. Above all, of course, she sees deep wisdom in the proverb: "The African proverb 'It takes a village to raise a child' summed up for me the commonsense conclusion that, like it or not, we are living in an interdependent world where what our children hear, see, feel, and learn will affect how they grow up and who they turn out to be. The five years since 9/11 have reinforced one of my main points: How children are raised anywhere can impact our lives and our children's futures" (V, xii). Owing to her celebrity status, the proverb has become attached to her name by now (Rawson and Miner 2006, 109; Bartlett 2012, 864), but alas, as she herself states, it was not coined by her, but neither is it an African proverb, even though a somewhat similar Swahili proverb, "one hand (person) cannot bring up (nurse) a child" has been located (Nnaemeka 2000, 1; Shapiro 2006, 529; Mieder 2014b, 201). Rather:

> It probably is of American coinage, with Toni Morrison's related statement during a 1981 interview hardly qualifying as the first use of the actual proverb: "I don't think one parent can raise a child. I don't think two parents can raise a child. You really need the whole village." It is, however, of interest that the next appearance of the proverb in 1984 relates back to this very interview: As author Toni Morrison has said, "it takes a village to raise a child, not one parent, not two parents, but the whole village." It was popularized by way of Jane Cowen Fletcher's young adult novel It *Takes a Village* (1993), where Yemi tries to watch her little brother Kokou on market day in a small village in Benin and finds that the entire village is watching out for him as well. (Mieder 2014b, 202; see also Shapiro 2006, 529; Speake 2008, 336).

Be that as it may, all of this, as well as the fact that Toni Morrison is a well-known African American writer, might have led Hillary Clinton erroneously to conclude that she was using an African proverb. Clinton cites the proverb numerous times in *Living History* (see L, 263, 291, 311, 320, 330, 375), with one reference in particular standing out that relates to her own family, their beloved daughter, Chelsea, and to children in general. It was the crescendo of her major address at the Democratic National Convention on August 27, 1996, in Chicago that handed Bill Clinton the nomination for his second term as the president of the United States.

> For Bill and me, there has been no experience more challenging, more rewarding and more humbling than raising our daughter. And we have learned that to raise a happy, healthy, and hopeful child, it takes a family. It takes teachers. It takes clergy. It takes businesspeople. It takes community leaders. It takes those who protect our health and safety. It takes all of us.
> Yes, it takes a village.

> And it takes a President.
> It takes a President who believes not only in the potential of his own child, but of all children, who believes not only in the strength of his own family, but of the American family.
> It takes Bill Clinton. (L, 376)

Clinton obviously likes the proverb, as can also be seen from the first sentence of the acknowledgments (L, 533–38) at the end of her autobiography, *Living History*: "This book may not have taken a village to write, but it certainly took a superb team, and I am grateful to everyone who helped" (L, 533). Politics, books, and speeches aside, the proverb is a guidepost for her personal life as a mother and now as a proud grandmother. She refers to this close family bond often, and she is definitely justified in merely citing the first half of the proverb that has become so well known in a relatively short time due to her belief in its universal wisdom.

When she used this proverb the first time in 1996 in her book *It Takes a Village*, she employed it with the introductory formula "that old African proverb" (V, 5), thereby adding authoritative expressiveness to the proverb, even though she is wrong about its origin. Being the world traveler that she has been as first lady and secretary of state, she has picked up foreign proverbs, which she enjoys incorporating into her communications with appropriate introductory formulas. While she obviously cites them in English translation, these proverbs add considerable cultural and historical value to her statements. Naturally, she has friends, colleagues, speechwriters, and others to help her with these proverbial bits of wisdom, but her effort in this regard, especially during her four years as secretary of state, were most certainly appreciated. But as the first two examples show, she also uses proverbs from other languages to reflect on her own life and thoughts:

> Let Us Build a Village Worthy of Our Children. (chapter title)
>
> A civilization flourishes when people plant trees under whose shade they will never sit. Greek proverb (motto for this chapter) (V, 295)
>
> "What you don't learn from your mother, you learn from the world" is a saying I once heard from the Masai tribe in Kenya. By the fall of 1960, my world was expanding and so were my political sensibilities. (L, 16)
>
> The Chinese have an ancient saying, that women hold up half the sky, but in most of the world, it's really more than half. Women handle a large share of responsibility for the welfare of their families. Yet their work often goes unrecognized and unrewarded inside the family or by the formal economy. These inequities are starkly visible in South Asia, where more than half a

billion people live in grinding poverty—the majority of them women and children. (L, 269; see also L, 460)

A week later I went to the Asia Society in New York to deliver my first major address as Secretary on our approach to the Asia-Pacific. Orville Schell, the Asia Society's silver-haired China scholar, suggested that I use an ancient proverb from Sun Tzu's *The Art of War* about soldiers from two warring feudal states who find themselves on a boat together crossing a wide river in a storm. Instead of fighting, they work together to survive. In English the proverb roughly translates as, "When you are in a common boat, cross the river peacefully together." For the United States and China, with our economic destinies bound up together in the middle of a global financial storm, this was good advice. My use of the proverb was not lost on Beijing. Premier Wen Jiabao and other leaders referenced it in later discussions with me. (H, 46–47; see also H, 70)

If I had seen the worst of humanity on this trip [to Africa], I had also seen the best, especially those women who, after they had recovered from being raped and beaten, went back to the forest to rescue other women left to die. During my trip to the DRC [Democratic Republic of Congo], I heard of an old African proverb: "No matter how long the night, the day is sure to come." These people were doing their best to make that day come faster, and I wanted to do all I could to help. (H, 282)

I knew that flickers of progress [in Burma] could easily be extinguished. There is an old Burmese proverb: "When it rains, collect water." This was the time to consolidate reforms and lock them in for the future, so that they would become ingrained and irreversible. (H, 117)

Of course, well educated as Hillary Clinton is, she felt at ease to cite a well-known classical Latin proverb in its original tongue, adding the English version of the proverb just to make sure that the wisdom was not lost: "All children, especially in today's stressful world, need the joyful release of free play as well as healthful exercise. *Mens sana in corpore sano*, the ancients advised, and it still holds true—a strong mind in a strong body" (V, 108). Not surprisingly, she also enjoys referring to English proverbs abroad to bring alive her own culture, as in this comment with its "inspiration" anaphora during her visit to South Africa during her extended trip to Africa in 1997.

Today, we Americans find inspiration in the generous and forgiving spirit that has won you this democracy. We find inspiration in the democratic institutions that have come to light here in just a few years. We find inspiration in your progressive new constitution, which is being distributed around the country this week, and especially in the rights it enshrines for women and children. We find inspiration in the work you are undertaking in every sector of society to build your new nation. We have an old saying in America that "idle hands are the devil's work[shop]." From what I have seen in just a few short days, the devil will have no help here. South Africa is a country that is too busy to hate. (Clinton 1997, 8)

Clearly, Hillary Clinton is tuned in to proverbs, recalling even those she picked up during the years that Bill Clinton was governor of Arkansas. Here she is showing herself as somewhat of an ethnographer, folklorist, and paremiologist: "Sure enough, the 'vast conspiracy' line got [Kenneth] Starr's attention. He took the unusual step of firing off a statement complaining that I had cast aspersions on his motives. He called the notion of a conspiracy 'nonsense.' As they say in Arkansas, 'It's the hit dog that howls.' My comment seemed to have touched a nerve" (L, 446).

Below are a few more references in which Clinton employs English language proverbs by directly calling attention to them with introductory formulas that help to strengthen the proverbial point she wishes to make. In the first example, she even declares her "love" for a particular proverb. No proverb scholar could ask for more.

> There's an old saying I love: You can't roll up your sleeves and get to work if you're still wringing your hands. So, if you, like me, are worrying about our kids; if you, like me, have wondered how we can match our actions to our words, I'd like to share with you some of my convictions I've developed over a lifetime—not only as an advocate and a citizen but as a mother, daughter, sister, and wife—about what children need from us and what we owe to them. (V, 10)

> But we have also tried to teach her [daughter Chelsea], as we were taught, that service is a part of daily life—as the saying goes, the rent we pay for life. There is no shortage of needs waiting to be met. (V, 182)

> I will never forget the mother of the boys as she testified on their behalf. Fierce as a lioness defending her cubs, she denied—in the face of overwhelming evidence—that her sons were the vandals. They couldn't be, she explained, because she had quit work and stayed home to raise them. (That was the first time I really understood the meaning of the saying "Denial ain't just a river in Egypt"!) (V, 196)

> There used to be this old saying that the lie can be halfway around the world before the truth gets its boots on. Well, today, the lie can be twice around the world before the truth gets out of bed to find its boots. (Foss 1999, 153; comment at a press conference on February 11, 1998, at the White House)

> Both Rabins [Yitzhak and Leah] were realistic about the challenges that lay ahead for Israel. They believed they had no choice but try to achieve a secure future for their nation through negotiations with their sworn enemies. Their

attitude called to mind the old saying "Hope for the best, plan for the worst." That was also Bill's and my assessment. (L, 184–85)

You have to do the research and run the numbers; that's how we minimize risk and maximize impact. And these days we keep statistics on everything we care about from RBIs [runs batted in] in baseball to ROI [returns on investment] in business. There's a saying in management circles: "What gets measured gets done." So if we were serious about helping more girls and women achieve their full potential, then we had to get serious about gathering and analyzing the data about the conditions they faced and the contributions they made. (H, 570)

Here is a splendid account of how the English proverb "the proof of the pudding is in the eating" was used in a diplomatic exchange between Hillary Clinton as secretary of state and two foreign ministers regarding sanctions for Iran.

When we spoke afterward, the Foreign Ministers of Brazil and Turkey both tried to sell me on the merits of the deal. They reported on their tough eighteen-hour negotiations and tried to convince me that they had succeeded. I think they were surprised that their triumph was being greeted with such skepticism. But I wanted to see action from Iran, not more words. "We have a saying that the proof is in the pudding," I told [Celso] Amorim [from Brazil]. "I agree that the tasting of the pudding is key, but there must be time to get the spoon out and have time to try it," he replied. To that I replied, "This pudding has been in for over a year now!" (H, 431)

If proof were needed that proverbs continue to play an important role in the modern age—that proverbs are indeed never out of season (Mieder 1993)—then this exchange can serve as such. But that the strategic and indirect use of the metaphorical proverb succeeded is in large part due to Minister Amorim's solid knowledge of the proverb, since Hillary Clinton truncated it by leaving out the "eating" or "tasting" part, as added by Amorim. Clearly though, the proverb gave the diplomats an opportunity to communicate by way of indirection, one of the major functions of proverbs in actual communicative contexts.

However, proverbs don't necessarily need statements to introduce them, and Hillary Clinton is perfectly aware of that. Following the pseudo-proverbial chapter title "Security Takes More Than a Blanket" (V, 117) that is based on a child's security blanket, she simply adds a well-known proverb stated twice, remembering it from a line in *The Wizard of Oz*: "There's no place like home . . . there's no place like home" (L, 117; see also V, 118). She also uses the proverb "Seeing Is Believing" (L, 249) as yet another straightforward chapter heading. And here is an example where she actually cites a scientist using the proverb "use it or lose it" that at first glance appears to be a modern proverb but that actually dates back to 1838: "As neuroscientist Bob Jacobs says, the bottom line is: 'You have to use it or you lose it.' If we think of the brain as our most important muscle, we can appreciate that it requires activity in order to develop. Just as babies need to flex their arms and legs, they also need regular, varied stimulation to exercise all the parts of their brains" (V, 48).

There is also a fascinating paragraph that concludes with the nondescript proverb "easier said than done." But in its context, it becomes a very honest conclusion to comments and reflections by Hillary Clinton regarding the many attacks and the considerable criticism that she has had to bear during decades of political service: "Some of the attacks, whether demonizing me as a woman, mother and wife or distorting my words and positions on issues, were politically motivated and designed to rein me in. Others may have reflected the extent to which our society was still adjusting to the changing roles of women. I adopted my own mantra: Take criticism seriously, but not personally. If there is truth or merit in the criticism, try to learn from it. Otherwise, let it roll right off you. Easier said than done" (L, 110; see also H, 95).

Of course, as one would expect, she also cites the proverb "all men are created equal" and the proverbial triad "life, liberty, and the pursuit of happiness" from the Declaration of Independence (1776), something that is literally expected and followed by all American politicians reaching her level of national achievement (Fields 1996, 3–4; Burrell 1997, 249; Aron 2008, 91–96; Melton 2008, 64–65). While she does not quote them in customary unison, she places the well-known proverbial claims into two separate paragraphs dealing with different issues. In the first case, she reports on Eleanor Roosevelt's greatest achievement in helping to draft the Universal Declaration of Human Rights that was finally adopted by the UN General Assembly on December 10, 1948, after close to two years of intense negotiations in her international committee.

> They discussed, they wrote, they revisited, revised, and rewrote. They incorporated suggestions and revisions from governments, organizations, and individuals around the world. It is telling that even in the drafting of the Universal Declaration there was a debate about women's rights. The initial version of the first article stated, "All men are created equal." It took women members of the Commission, led by Hansa Mehta of India, to point out "all men" might be interpreted to exclude women. Only after long debate was the language changed to say, "All human beings are born free and equal in dignity and rights." (H, 565)

That expanded gender-free formulation is most appropriate, but it is noteworthy that the American feminist Elizabeth Cady Stanton had already stated in the "Declaration of Sentiments" at the start of the women's rights movement on July 19, 1848, in Seneca Falls, New York, that "all men and women are created equal" (Mieder 2014a, 65–74). One wonders whether Eleanor Roosevelt and the other members of the commission were aware of this. The same is true for Hillary Clinton, who unfortunately mentions Stanton and her feminist friend Susan B. Anthony only in passing as she recalls her visit to the Women's Rights National Historical Park in Seneca Falls and her speech there in July 1999 (see H, 462–63). Had Hillary Clinton known about the significant change to Jefferson's male-oriented proverbial claim of equality, she would almost certainly have mentioned it at Seneca Falls or in conjunction with her statement just cited.

The second reference is less complex, but Clinton's comments on the three basic rights of all human beings is a proverbial reminder of the important role that government must play in making certain that they are achieved and maintained: "When we're reminded of the bounty and protection we enjoy, most of us are grateful. Our gratitude has its roots in a view of government that dates back to the Pilgrims and to the successive waves of immigrants who came to the country seeking religious and political freedom and better economic opportunities. In this view, government is an instrument both to promote the common good and to protect individuals' rights to life, liberty, and the pursuit of happiness" (V, 284).

All of this brings to mind a second important proverbial triad from American political history, namely the ultimate short definition of democracy: "government of the people, by the people, [and] for the people". It originated in the late eighteenth century and became established by its occurrence in the speeches and writings of President John Adams, Chief Justice John Marshall, Daniel Webster, and the abolitionist preacher Theodore Parker in the first half of the nineteenth century. Then Abraham Lincoln immortalized it in the American psyche by concluding his famous Gettysburg Address of November 19, 1863 with these words: "that this nation, under God, shall have a new birth of freedom—and that government of the people, by the people, for the people, shall not perish from the earth" (Mieder 2005, 15–55). There are still high school students in America today who memorize the entire address, as it was quite common in earlier times (Safire 1978, 256–57). Perhaps Hillary Clinton was one of them, but the governmental triad does not appear in her own prose of her five books. However, in her book *An Invitation to the White House: At Home with*

History, she recalls that in 1997 and 1998, President Bill Clinton and she as the first lady welcomed leaders from China to the White House as an attempt to improve relations between the two countries: "I will never forget Premier Zhu Ronji of China recalling in his toast that he had memorized the Gettysburg Address as a schoolboy. He recited a section from memory, including the phrase 'of the people, by the people, for the people'—a hope we hold for the Chinese people" (Clinton 2000, 61). There can be no doubt that this event touched a nerve among the diplomatic and governmental dignitaries at the White House, and it is yet another proof that proverbs uttered at the right moment can be a most effective tool for international relations and understanding (Raymond 1956; Pei 1969, 101–10).

The proverbial wisdom from the Declaration of Independence and also most of the proverbs used by Hillary Clinton are of considerable age. In fact, she herself quite often uses the adjective "old" in her introductory formulas to add a traditional and authoritative claim to them. But this is not to say that she is not thoroughly aware and ingrained in modern proverbs (twentieth century) as well. Here is a selection of contextualized references with the proverbs' dates of origin in parentheses (see Doyle, Mieder, Shapiro 2012 for more information).

> *Three strikes and you're out.* (1901)
> The 1994 Violent Crime Control and Law Enforcement Act banned nineteen types of military-style assault weapons whose only purpose is to kill people and it stopped the revolving door of career criminals with its "three strikes and you're out" provision. (V, 126)
>
> *A candle loses nothing of its light by lighting another candle.* (1918)
> Childhood Can Be a Service Academy. (chapter title)
> A candle loses nothing of its light by lighting another candle. James Keller. (motto for this chapter) (V, 171)
> [Clinton assumes that the proverb stems from the American priest and broadcaster James Keller (1900–1977), but the proverb predates him.]
>
> *Don't ask, don't tell.* (1993)
> After both the House and Senate expressed their opposition by veto-proof margins, Bill [Clinton] agreed to a compromise: the 'Don't Ask, Don't Tell' policy. Under the policy, a superior is forbidden to ask a service member if he or she is homosexual. If a question is asked, there is no obligation to answer. But the policy has not worked well. (L, 241)
>
> *The devil is in the details.* (1963)
> Of course, in politics, as in life, the devil is in the details. The details of welfare reform or budget negotiations were hard fought and difficult and sometimes

resembled a Rubik's Cube more than an isosceles triangle. (L, 290; see also L, 323)

The buck stops here. (1942)
But as I knew from history and my own experience, the sign on Harry Truman's desk in the Oval Office was correct: the buck did stop with the President. (H, 22; Mieder 1997, 96–98)

Don't worry, be happy. (1908)
But it was George Shultz who gave me the best gift of all: a teddy bear that sang "Don't Worry, Be Happy" when its paw was squeezed. I kept it in my office, first as a joke, but every so often it really did help to squeeze the bear and hear that song. (H, 31)
[Clinton is referring to the 1988 hit song "Don't Worry, Be Happy" by Bobby McFerrin. (Doyle, Mieder, Shapiro 2012, 282)]

Trust but verify. (1966)
I called key Senate Republicans, who told me they didn't trust the Russians and worried the United States would not be able to verify compliance [to the New Strategic Arms Reduction Treaty]. I explained that the treaty gave us mechanisms to do just that and if the Russians didn't live up to their word, we could always withdraw. I reminded them that even President Reagan, with his philosophy of "trust but verify," had signed disarmament agreements with the Soviets. And I stressed that time was of the essence. (H, 234)
[The proverb is often attributed to Ronald Reagan, even though he stated that he had learned it as a Russian proverb from Mikhail Gorbachev. (Doyle, Mieder, Shapiro 2012, 264; for such political maxims see Titus 1945)]

These examples, like others before them, show the polyfunctionality of proverbs. For example, the second-to-last reference about the teddy bear and the proverb "don't worry, be happy" shows the supposedly cool, reserved, and tense Hillary Clinton from a more humane and emotive side. She definitely also has a sense of humor, as can be seen in her use of the modern proverb "life is like a box of chocolates" in a skit that she prerecorded for fun to entertain Washington journalists and politicians at the annual Gridiron Dinner, at which she could not be present because she was traveling in South Asia. The proverb originated in the popular film *Forrest Gump* (1994), where it appears as "Life is a box of chocolates, Forrest. You never know what you're going to get" (Doyle, Mieder, Shapiro 2012, 143): "As the tape rolled, a white feather drifted out of a blue sky and landed in front of the White House near a park bench, where I, Hillary Gump, sat with a box of candy on my lap. 'My mama always told me the White House is like a box of chocolates,' I said in my best Tom Hanks imitation. 'It's pretty on the outside, but inside there's lots of nuts'" (L, 287).

The humor of the dialogue results from the double meaning of the word "nut" as a fruit kernel and as a fool or even crazy person. Surely the guests enjoyed this humorous self-characterization of the White House, including Bill and Hillary Clinton, as ridiculous people. This yearly event of humor and satire is a splendid opportunity to release tension, stress, and at times ill will among the various constituencies in Washington, DC.

But speaking of a sense of free expression by way of proverbial humor, it should also be noted that Hillary Clinton understands the communicative value of antiproverbs (Mieder 2004, 28). In her acclaimed book *It Takes a Village*, she begins three chapters with antiproverbial titles. Her antiproverb "No Family Is an Island" (V, 13) is based on the proverb "no man is an island" that appears first in 1624 in John Donne's works. "An Ounce of Prevention Is Worth a Pound of Intense Care" (V, 99) connects Benjamin Franklin's proverb "an ounce of prevention is worth a pound of cure" from 1735, based on the shorter English proverb "prevention is better than cure" from 1732, with America's concern about national health care; and Clinton's "Child Care Is not a Spectator Sport" (V, 207) clearly has its connection to the modern proverb "life is not a spectator sport" from 1958. Things are not so obvious with her statement "High expectations begin at home" (V, 228), but she might have had the proverb "charity begins at home" from the fourteenth century in mind. There is also the following humorous account relating to Hillary Clinton's difficulties with appropriate hairdos.

> We [Bill and Hillary Clinton and traveling companions] also scheduled some necessary R&R [rest and recreation]. We visited the Great Barrier Reef while we were in Australia after stops in Sydney and Canberra. At Port Douglas, Bill announced American support for the International Coral Reef Initiative, to stem the erosion of reefs around the world, and then we took a boat out to the reef in the Coral Sea. I was anxious to get into the water. "C'mon you guys!" I said to my staff. "Life is too short to worry about getting your hair wet!" (L, 386)

The underlying structure of such modern proverbs as "life is too short to waste it sleeping" (1944), "life is too short to wait for someday" (1969), and "life is too short to drink bad wine" (1985) might well have been the basis for her playful remark (Doyle, Mieder, Shapiro 2012, 144–45). In any case, her manipulations of proverbs add an innovative aspect to her prose style, and there is no reason why an antiproverb like "no family is an island" should not become a proverb in its own right.

In conclusion, it can be said that while Hillary Clinton is perhaps not as proverbial in her verbal political rhetoric as such major sociopolitical American figures as Abraham Lincoln, Frederick Douglass, Elizabeth Cady

Stanton, Susan B. Anthony, Harry S. Truman, Martin Luther King Jr., and Barack Obama, she certainly relies on proverbs (and more so on proverbial expressions) in her three major books, *It Takes A Village*, *Living History*, and *Hard Choices*. As is the case with the other Americans just mentioned, she is aware of the fact that the "practical wisdom, practical knowledge, practical reason, [and] practical judgment" (Nichols 1996, 687) expressed in proverbs is of definite use in bringing across her personal and political agenda. She also seems to appreciate the fact that the complex interplay of proverbs and political language (see Louis 2000) is of great importance as she writes to communicate her thoughts on American political history and the future role that the United States might play in the world. In doing so, she does not employ proverbs as an ideological instrument but rather as a linguistic tool to enhance her often quite factual prose with vivid metaphors. Looking at her instantiation of proverbs shows once again the fundamental polysituativity, polyfunctionality, and polysemanticity of proverbs in actual contexts (Mieder 2004, 9). Each proverb occurrence offers new insights into her being, her reflections, and her aspirations for herself and for her country. Whatever one might think of her political agenda, she most certainly has proven herself to be an engaged and experienced leader in the United States and on the world stage. The modern proverb "life is not a spectator sport" from 1958 holds absolutely true for her, but so does the antiproverb "politics is not a spectator sport" from 1963 that encourages citizens everywhere to play an active and responsible role in supporting democracies as Hillary Rodham Clinton has done throughout her lifetime.

References

This chapter was first published in *Tautosakos Darbai/Folklore Studies* (Vilnius) 50 (2015): 43–74.

Allen, Jonathan, and Amie Parnes. 2013. *HRC: State Secrets and the Rebirth of Hillary Clinton*. New York: Crown Publishers.

Andersen, Christopher. 2004. *American Evita: Hillary Clinton's Path to Power*. New York: HarperCollins.

Aron, Paul. 2008. *"We Hold These Truths . . ." And Other Words that Made America*. Lanham, MD: Rowman & Littlefield.

Arthurs, Jeffrey. D. 1994. "Proverbs in Inspirational Literature: Sanctioning the American Dream." *Journal of Communication and Religion* 17: 1–15. Also in *Cognition, Comprehension, and Communication: A Decade of North American Proverb Studies (1990–2000)*, edited by Wolfgang Mieder, 37–52. Baltmannsweiler: Schneider Verlag Hohengehren, 2003.

Bartlett, John. 2012. *Familiar Quotations*. 18th ed. Edited by Geoffrey O'Brien. New York: Little, Brown and Company.
Bernstein, Carl. 2007. *A Woman in Charge: The Life of Hillary Rodham Clinton*. New York: Alfred A. Knopf.
Boller, Paul F. 1967. *Quotemanship: The Use and Abuse of Quotations for Polemical and Other Purposes*. Dallas: Southern Methodist University Press.
Bowers, John Waite, and Donovan J. Ochs. 1971. *The Rhetoric of Agitation and Control*. Reading, MA: Addison-Wesley.
Brock, David. 1996. *The Seduction of Hillary Rodham [Clinton]*. New York: Free Press.
Burgchardt, Carl. 1995. *Readings in Rhetorical Criticism*. State College, PA: Strata Publishing.
Burke, Kenneth. 1941. "Literature [i.e., Proverbs] as Equipment for Living." In *The Philosophy of Literary Form: Studies in Symbolic Action*, edited by Kenneth Burke, 253–62. Baton Rouge: Louisiana University Press.
Burrell, Barbara. 2001. *Public Opinion, the First Ladyship, and Hillary Rodham Clinton*. New York: Routledge.
Burrell, Brian. 1997. *The Words We Live By: The Creeds, Mottoes, and Pledges That Have Shaped America*. New York: Free Press.
Clinton, Hillary Rodham. 1995: *Remarks by First Lady Hillary Rodham Clinton: United Nations Fourth World Conference on Women: September 5–6, 1995; China*. Washington, DC: Executive Office of the President.
———. 1996. *It Takes a Village and Other Lessons Children Teach Us*. 10th anniversary edition with a new introduction, 2006. New York: Simon & Schuster (the page numbers refer to the anniversary edition).
———. 1997. *Remarks and Commentary by First Lady Hillary Rodham Clinton: Africa, March 1997*. Washington, DC: US Government Printing Office.
———. 1998. *Dear Socks, Dear Buddy: Kids' Letters to the First Pets*. New York: Simon & Schuster.
———. 2000. *An Invitation to the White House: At Home with History*. New York: Simon & Schuster.
———. 2003. *Living History*. New York: Simon & Schuster.
———. 2014. *Hard Choices*. New York: Simon & Schuster.
———. 2015a. "Campaign Launch Speech." *Time* magazine online. http://time.com/3920332/transcript-full-text-hillary-clinton-campaign-launch/.
———. 2015b. "Economic Vision Speech." *Wall Street Journal* online. http://blogs.wsj.com/washwire/2015/07/13/hillary-clinton-campaign-speech-transcript-118973.html.
Doyle, Charles Clay, Wolfgang Mieder, and Fred R. Shapiro. 2012. *The Dictionary of Modern Proverbs*. New Haven, CT: Yale University Press.
Elspaß, Stephan. 2002. "Phraseological Units in Parliamentary Discourse." In *Politics as Text and Talk: Analytic Approaches to Political Discourse*, edited by Paul Chilton and Christina Schäffner, 81–110. Amsterdam: Benjamins.
———. 2007. "Phrasemes in Political Speech." In *Phraseology: An International Handbook of Contemporary Research*, edited by Harald Burger, Dmitrij Dobrovol'skij, Peter Kühn, and Neal R. Norrick, 1:284–92. 2 vols. Berlin: Walter de Gruyter.
Fields, Wayne. 1996. *Union of Words: A History of Presidential Eloquence*. New York: Free Press.
Foss, William O. 1999. *First Ladies Quotation Book: A Compendium of Provocative, Tender, Witty, and Important Words from the Presidents' Wives*. New York: Barricade Books.
Gerth, Jeff, and Don van Natta. 2007. *Her Way: The Hopes and Ambitions of Hillary Rodham Clinton*. New York: Little, Brown and Company.

Griffin, Albert Kirby. 1991. *Religious Proverbs: Over 1,600 Adages from 18 Faiths Worldwide*. Jefferson, NC: McFarland.
Hertzler, Joyce O. 1933–34. "On Golden Rules." *International Journal of Ethics* 44:418–36.
Jay, Antony. 1996. *The Oxford Dictionary of Political Quotations*. Oxford: Oxford University Press.
Kengor, Paul. 2007. *God and Hillary Clinton: A Spiritual Life*. New York: HarperCollins.
Keyes, Ralph. 2013. "A Woman Is Like a Teabag: You Never Know How Strong She Is until She's in Hot Water." Quote Investigator. http://quoteinvestigator.com/2013/03hot-water.
Knowles, Elizabeth. 1999. *The Oxford Dictionary of Quotations*. 5th ed. Oxford: Oxford University Press.
Kornblut, Anne E. 2009. *Notes from the Cracked Ceiling: Hillary Clinton, Sarah Palin, and What It Will Take for a Woman to Win*. New York: Crown Publishers.
Louis, Cameron. 2000. "Proverbs and the Politics of Language." *Proverbium* 17:173–94. Also in *Cognition, Comprehension, and Communication: A Decade of North American Proverb Studies (1990–2000)*, edited by Wolfgang Mieder, 271–92. Baltmannsweiler: Schneider Verlag Hohengehren, 2003.
Melton, Buckner F. 2008. *The Quotable Founding Fathers: A Treasury of 2,500 Wise and Witty Quotations from the Men and Women Who Created America*. New York: Fall River Press.
Mieder, Wolfgang. 1993. *Proverbs Are Never Out of Season: Popular Wisdom in the Modern Age*. New York: Oxford University Press; reprinted New York: Peter Lang, 2012.
———. 1997. *The Politics of Proverbs: From Traditional Wisdom to Proverbial Stereotypes*. Madison: University of Wisconsin Press.
———. 2000. *The Proverbial Abraham Lincoln: An Index of Proverbs in the Works of Abraham Lincoln*. New York: Peter Lang.
———. 2001. *"No Struggle, No Progress": Frederick Douglass and His Proverbial Rhetoric for Civil Rights*. New York: Peter Lang.
———. 2004. *Proverbs: A Handbook*. Westport, CT: Greenwood Press; reprinted New York: Peter Lang, 2012.
———. 2005. *Proverbs Are the Best Policy: Folk Wisdom and American Politics*. Logan: Utah State University Press.
———. 2009. *"Yes We Can": Barack Obama's Proverbial Rhetoric*. New York: Peter Lang.
———. 2010. *"Making a Way out of No Way": Martin Luther King's Sermonic Proverbial Rhetoric*. New York: Peter Lang.
———. 2014a. *"All Men and Women Are Created Equal": Elizabeth Cady Stanton's and Susan B. Anthony's Proverbial Rhetoric Promoting Women's Rights*. New York: Peter Lang.
———. 2014b. *"Behold the Proverbs of a People": Proverbial Wisdom in Culture, Literature, and Politics*. Jackson: University Press of Mississippi.
———. 2015. *"Different Strokes for Different Folks": 1,250 authentisch amerikanische Sprichwörter*. Bochum: Norbert Brockmeyer.
Mieder, Wolfgang, and George B. Bryan. 1997. *The Proverbial Harry S. Truman: An Index to Proverbs in the Works of Harry S. Truman*. New York: Peter Lang.
Mieder, Wolfgang, Stewart A. Kingsbury, and Kelsie B. Harder. 1992. *A Dictionary of American Proverbs*. New York: Oxford University Press.
Nichols, Ray. 1996. "Maxims, 'Practical Wisdom,' and the Language of Action: Beyond Grand Theory." *Political Theory* 24:687–705.
Nnaemeka, Obiama. 2000. "The Clinton Controversies and the African (Igbo) World." *West Africa Review* 2, no. 1, 5 pp. (electronic journal).

Olson, Barbara. 1999. *Hell to Pay: The Unfolding Story of Hillary Rodham Clinton.* Washington, DC: Regnery Publishing.
Partnow, Elaine. 1992. *The New Quotable Woman.* New York: Facts on File.
Pei, Mario. 1969. *Words in Sheep's Clothing: How People Manipulate Opinion by Distorting Word Meanings.* New York: Hawthorn Books.
Rawson, Hugh, and Margaret Miner. 2006. *The Oxford Dictionary of American Quotations.* Oxford: Oxford University Press.
Raymond, Joseph. 1956. "Tensions in Proverbs: More Light on International Understanding." *Western Folklore* 15:153–58. Also in *The Wisdom of Many: Essays on the Proverb*, edited by Wolfgang Mieder and Alan Dundes, 300–308. New York: Garland Publishing, 1981; reprinted Madison: University of Wisconsin Press, 1994.
Room, Adrian. 2000. *Brewer's Dictionary of Modern Phrase and Fable.* London: Cassell.
Safire, William. 1978. *Political Dictionary.* New York: Random House.
Schnoebelen, James M., Diana B. Carlin, and Benjamin R. Warner. 2009. "Hillary, You Can't Go Home Again: The Entrapment of the First Lady Role." In *Cracked but Not Shattered: Hillary Rodham Clinton's Unsuccessful Campaign for the Presidency*, edited by Theodore F. Sheckels, 45–67. Lanham, MD: Lexington Books.
Seitel, Peter. 1969. "Proverbs: A Social Use of Metaphor." *Genre* 2:143–61. Also in *The Wisdom of Many: Essays on the Proverb*, edited by Wolfgang Mieder and Alan Dundes, 122–39. New York: Garland Publishing, 1981; reprinted Madison: University of Wisconsin Press, 1994.
Shapiro, Fred. R. 2006. *The Yale Book of Quotations.* New Haven, CT: Yale University Press.
Sheckels, Theodore F., ed. 2009. *Cracked but Not Shattered: Hillary Rodham Clinton's Unsuccessful Campaign for the Presidency.* Lanham, MD: Lexington Books.
Sheehy, Gail. 1999. *Hillary's Choice.* New York: Random House.
Speake, Jennifer. 2008. *The Oxford Dictionary of Proverbs.* 5th ed. Oxford: Oxford University Press.
Spiker, Julia A. 2009. "It Takes a Village to Win: A Rhetorical Analysis of 'Hillary for President.'" In *Cracked but Not Shattered: Hillary Rodham Clinton's Unsuccessful Campaign for the Presidency*, edited by Theodore F. Sheckels, 99–124. Lanham, MD: Lexington Books.
Taylor, Archer. 1931. *The Proverb.* Cambridge, MA: Harvard University Press; reprinted as *The Proverb and An Index to "The Proverb."* Hatboro, PA: Folklore Associates, 1962; reprinted again with an introduction and bibliography by Wolfgang Mieder. Bern: Peter Lang, 1985.
Templeton, John Marks. 1997. *Worldwide Laws of Life.* Philadelphia: Templeton Foundation Press.
Titus, Charles H. 1945. "Political Maxims." *California Folklore Quarterly* 4:377–89.

8

"THE RICH GET RICHER, AND THE POOR GET POORER"

Bernie Sanders's Proverbial Rhetoric for an American Sociopolitical Revolution

BERNIE SANDERS IS A SOCIOPOLITICAL PHENOMENON THE LIKES of which the United States has not known before. He was born on September 8, 1941, in Brooklyn, New York, into a Polish Jewish immigrant family. Despite his working-class background, he was able to study political science at the renowned University of Chicago, where in 1962 he began his political activism during a civil rights sit-in in the city of Chicago. In 1968, he moved to Burlington, Vermont, building a small business in educational filmstrips. In 1981, he became its mayor as an independent progressive politician, and after having been reelected as mayor three times, he was elected to the US House of Representatives in 1990, where he served as an independent for sixteen years. In 2006, he ran for the US Senate and has represented Vermont ever since as a senator with the longest record of any independent politician in the Congress of the United States.

He has been an incredibly important voice in Washington and, by his own admission, a proverbial "thorn in their [members of Congress] side for some time" (*Outsider in the House*, hereafter abbreviated as H, 3), but his influence on both the Democratic and Republican parties has been truly remarkable in light of the fact that he is a declared democratic socialist. In fact, there are politicians and political scientists who "would label 2016 Sanders a social democrat rather than a democratic socialist" (Conroy 1990, preface to 2016 edition, x). Notwithstanding this "splitting hairs over terminology" (Elliott 2016, 32), the word *socialism* is highly suspect if not taboo in the United States. It has thus been an uphill struggle for Sanders, but he has stuck to his proverbial guns and consistently championed his fight for democratic socialism, by which he means "a mixed economy that offers more robust social programs such as universal health care, free college education, increased Social Security benefits, and a great investment in services like public transportation. He does not mean the centralized control of the economy or nationalization of natural resources" (Elliott 2016, 34). Undoing the myth that America is, without exception, always the best, he challenges this exceptionalist and hubristic view with several self-critical questions: "Let's take a hard look, at what's going on in the rest of the world. My Republican colleagues in the Senate often talk about 'American exceptionalism.' Well, they're right, but not for the reasons they think. It turns out that the United States is exceptional in being far, far behind many other nations in addressing basic needs of working families. Why is the United States the only major country on earth not to guarantee health care to all people as a right? If the United Kingdom, France, Germany, Scandinavia and Canada can do it, why can't we?" (*Our Revolution*, hereafter abbreviated as R, 89)

The vexing problem of universal health care is one of Sanders's major struggles, as he feels strongly that the national government must be involved in this matter. He recognizes once and for all that "Health care is a right, not a privilege. The United States must join the rest of the industrialized world and guarantee health care to every man, woman, and child through a Medicare for All single-payer system" (R, 318). On the same page of his book *Our Revolution* (2016a), Sanders repeats his very own proverbial slogan: "I have, for as far back as I can remember, always believed that health care is a *right* of all people, not a privilege" (R, 318). Not following his lead by properly financing a health care system for the nation, the entire social welfare system will continue to decline and validate the proverb "penny wise, pound foolish": "Over the last several decades we have made a bad situation even worse by cutting back on the programs and support systems that mentally ill people need in order to survive and improve. Once again, we are being penny-wise and pound-foolish. We save money by cutting back on housing and treatment for the mentally ill. We spend far, far more by having vulnerable people end up in jail" (R, 381).

The unresolved health care situation is only one of the shortcomings, and Sanders goes on to ask why Americans have longer work days, shorter vacation time, no paid family and medical leave, no effective child care system, more people in jail than other countries have, an exorbitantly expensive higher education system, etc. (see R, 89).

For half a century, Sanders has "preached" his social message with a sincere consistency and an honest authenticity (Tasini 2015, ix–xi; Conroy

2016, xii) that gains in rhetorical effectiveness at least in part because of its proverbial language as has been shown to be the case in political discourse in general (Raymond 1956; Nichols 1996; Mieder 1997, 2004, 137–39; Meider 2008; Louis 2000; Manders 2006). The image of a tenacious wordsmith with a powerful hammer comes to mind, as he uses the political bully pulpit (Davis 2015, iii) to broaden his grassroots movement for change in an America ruled by an oligarchy of wealthy people and big business, with little regard for the middle class and driving ever more people into poverty.

The ever-widening gap between rich and poor with its slow disappearance of the middle class is always on his mind. During his successful yet failed presidential campaign in 2015–16, his hoarse voice brought forth his belief in a fairer and more humane America: "Every speech, every appearance he hammered away on the economic and political forces that were killing America's middle class" (Jaffe 2015, xiii). With plenty of idealism and pragmatic realism, Sanders continues to fight for revolutionary sociopolitical change, even after losing his bid for the presidency. But perhaps even more importantly, his voice continues to be heard, and his repeated call for *Our Revolution*, as he entitled his recent book summarizing his political life and his socially responsible view of America's future, is catching on as more and more Americans realize that democratic socialism could put their country back on the right track.

The "hammer" image with its steady blows is indeed a fitting metaphor for Sanders's powerful rhetoric that is marked by a number of proverbial leitmotifs that drive home his revolutionary calls for change. Here is what he said on May 26, 2015, in his hometown of Burlington, Vermont, when he announced his candidacy for the presidency of the United States:

> Today, here in our small state—a state that has led the nation in so many ways—I am proud to announce my candidacy for President of the United States of America.
>
> Today, with your support and the support of millions of people throughout this country, we begin a political revolution to transform our country economically, politically, socially and environmentally.
>
> Today, we stand here and say loudly and clearly that: "Enough is enough. This great nation and its government belong to all of the people, and not a handful of billionaires, their Super-PACs [Political Action Committees] and their lobbyists." (R, 117)

The nonmetaphorical tautological proverb "enough is enough" from the sixteenth century (Mieder, Kingsbury, Harder 1992: 181) in its simplicity is nevertheless a statement that expresses that the American people are fed up with politics as usual, or as Sanders is prone to say with one of his favorite proverbial twin formulas, they are "sick and tired" (R, 134, 153, 160, 205, 228; Holschuh 2015, 66) of the status quo, where people feel that their government does not deal effectively with such important issues as health care, wealth distribution, taxes, economy, justice, education, immigration, climate change, environment, etc. The importance of this proverb—one of the most frequently used proverbs in America (Lau 1996, 137; see also Mieder 1992)—for Sanders as an expression of the need for change is clear from this statement:

> When we declare, "Enough is enough," we are demanding a country and a future that meets the needs of the vast majority of Americans: a country and a future where it is hard to buy elections and easy to vote in them; a country and a future where tax dollars are invested in jobs and infrastructure instead of jails and incarcerations; a country and a future where we have the best-educated workforce and the widest range of opportunities for every child and every adult; a country and a future where we take steps necessary to ending systemic racism; a country and a future where we assure once and for all that no one who works forty hours a week will live in poverty. (H, xviii)

The proverb became a rallying cry in his eight-and-a-half-hour-long Senate speech of December 10, 2010, that was published soon after as *The Speech: A Historic Filibuster on Corporate Greed and the Decline of the Middle Class* (2011). In it Sanders argued against a tax deal that President Barack Obama, whom he otherwise greatly respects, had struck with Republicans that clearly favored the rich. It was a filibuster, of course, but instead of just reading from the telephone book or any such irrelevant publication, he actually delivered a revolutionary speech that castigated America's move from a government of the people, by the people, and for the people to one that approaches an oligarchy. The proverb "enough is enough" became a five-times-cited theme for his informed, emotional argument that things have gone far enough.

> The American people must stand up and work with us. They must get on their phones and call their Senators and call their Congressmen and Congresswomen. They must make their voices heard and say: Enough is enough. The rich have it all right now. (*The Speech*, hereafter abbreviated as S, 48)

> America now has a situation where the CEOs of large corporations make over 260 times more than the average American worker: In many other countries, everybody wants to be rich, but there is a limit. You can't become a billionaire stepping over children sleeping on the street. That is not what this country is supposed to be about. Enough should be enough. (S, 123)

> The point that needs to be made is, when is enough enough? That is the essence of what we are talking about. Greed, in my view, is like a sickness. It is like an addiction. We know people who are on heroin. They can't stop. (S, 125)

> When is enough enough? How much do they [wealthy people] need? (S, 160)

> So we are giving money [by way of tax breaks] to [rich] people who, in some cases [Bill Gates and Warren Buffett], don't even want it. I do know there are others out there who do want it. I think if there is one issue that we as a Congress and a government have to address, it is the extraordinary level of greed in this country. We have to stand tall and draw a line in the sand and simply say: Enough is enough. How much do you want? How much do you need? (S, 249–50)

Of course, things can get a bit repetitive with this rather nondescript proverb and with other often-stated claims and demands, but by adding the proverbial expression "to draw a line in the sand" in the last reference, Sanders adds considerable urgency to his statement. He is well aware of this, as he stated at the end of this marathon speech on the floor of the Senate: "I know I have been, to say the least, a bit repetitious" (S, 254). Sanders is perfectly capable of a bit of self-irony, and by all seriousness of his agenda, he is also not lacking in a good sense of humor. The repetitive nature of his speeches come to the fore especially in his campaign rhetoric. But this is the case for most politicians who deliver, at times, two or three speeches a day on campaign stops. Here are two examples from April 30, 2015, and June 6, 2016, of this modus operandi, necessitated by the grueling schedule of a presidential campaign.

> The campaign is not about Bernie Sanders. It's about a grassroots movement of Americans standing up and saying: "Enough is enough. This country and our government belong to all of us, not just a handful of billionaires." (Holschuh 2015, 8)

> This campaign is not about Bernie Sanders. You can have the best president in the history of the world, but that person will not be able to address the problems that we face unless there is a mass movement, a political revolution in this country. Right now, the only pieces of legislation that get to the floor of the House and Senate are sanctioned by big money, Wall Street, the pharmaceutical industry, et cetera. The only way we win and transform America is when millions of people stand up, as you are doing today, and say, "Enough is enough." The country belongs to all of us and not just a handful of billionaires. (R, 136)

As can be seen from some of these excerpts, Bernie Sanders is no friend of big money. As a declared democratic socialist, he is against the influence that the wealthy have on elections and the government, he is opposed to giant corporate banks, he objects to giving tax breaks to the rich, and he is deeply concerned about the growing gap between the rich and the poor that is destroying the solid middle class. For this economic part of his sociopolitical crusade, he has relied on the proverb "the rich get richer, and the poor get poorer" that says in a concise and oppositional way that America is splitting itself into two extreme halves. This American proverb is relatively young, with the earliest reference found thus far appearing in a short untitled "jotting" by author and journalist Nathaniel Parker Willis (1806–1867) in *The New Mirror* of August 5, 1843. He presents an argument that New York City needs an exclusive park for the rich, as could be found in other major cities (Central Park was established 1857–58) at the time.

> As a metropolis of wealth and fashion, New York has one great deficiency—that of a *driving park*. Rome has its Pincian Hill, Florence its Cascine, Paris its Bois de Bologne, and London its Hyde Park; and most other capitals have places of resort-on-wheels, where fresh air and congenial society may be met in the afternoon hours. Such a place is only *not* considered indispensable in New York, because it has never been enjoyed. It is, for the rich, the highest of luxuries. . . . There is enough room for such a park in the neighborhood of Union square, or on the East or North river. . . . I think it possible such an exclusive resort might be at first a little unpopular (remembering that some three years ago a millionaire was stoned for riding through Broadway with a mounted servant in livery behind him), but, as one of the hand-to-mouth class, I do not care how soon the rich get richer and the poor get poorer—leaving a comfortable middle class, in which ambition might stop to breathe. (287; also in Willis 1846, 605)

Surely Sanders would be interested in this early appearance of one of his favorite proverbs, obviously noting that Central Park today is rightfully open to all strata of society and not just the rich! The proverb was popularized by way of its appearance in the song "Ain't We Got Fun" (1921):

> There's nothing surer,
> The rich get richer and the poor get poorer,
> In the meantime, in between time,
> Ain't we got fun.

The song also includes the antiproverb "the rich get richer, and the poor get (have) children" as a humorous variant that has gained currency, but certainly not always as a lighthearted comment on social issues (Mieder, Kingsbury, Harder 1992, 508; Titelman 1996, 290).

In his early book *Outsider in the House* (1997, updated 2015), Sanders cites the proverb three times, albeit not always completely and with an indication that his preferred variant is "the rich get richer, and everyone else gets poorer." As he talks about the influence that rich people have on the American electoral process, he also emphasizes all the ills of the society that make an independent progressive politician as himself look ever more appealing as an alternative to the two major political parties that are at loggerheads and do nothing to stop the dichotomy between rich and poor.

> If you have no influence over your own work conditions, what kind of power can you have over the economics and politics of the entire country? Why bother to vote? Why bother to pay attention to politics? And millions don't. In Vermont and throughout the country, the rich ante up $500 or $5,000 at a fundraising event to support the candidate who will represent their interests. Meanwhile, the majority of the poor and working people don't even vote. No wonder the rich get richer and everyone else gets poorer. Are we really living in a democracy? (H, 31)

> The political climate in Vermont and America was changing. The excesses of the 1980s were becoming more and more apparent, and it wasn't just the savings and loan scandal. The rich were getting richer, the middle class was shrinking, the new jobs being created were low-wage jobs, and the people of Vermont were increasingly dissatisfied with status quo politics. The idea of going outside of the two-party system became more and more appealing. In this context, an Independent candidate began to look attractive. (H, 107)

> Let's take a hard look at some of America's major problems: While the Rich Get Richer, Almost Everyone Else Gets Poorer; the Standard of Living of Most Americans Is in Decline; Democracy Is in Crisis, and Oligarchy Looms; What We Know Is Determined by the Corporate Media; Our Health Care System Is in Shambles; Our Educational System Is Facing a Crisis. (H, 273–74)

Below are nine references just from his above-mentioned long Senate speech that illustrate how the proverb becomes a leitmotif in the true sense of that word, that is, it appears in various forms without ever losing its effective message that underlies Sanders's call for a political revolution.

> People are coming out because the very, very rich are getting richer, while the rest of us are getting poorer—they feel the rigged economy every day. (S, ix; 2015 ed.)

> The richer people become much richer, the middle class shrinks. Millions of Americans fall out of the middle class and into poverty. (S, 21)

> The rich get richer. The middle class shrinks. Poverty increases. Apparently, good is not good enough yet for some of the richest people. (S, 22)

> The rich get richer. The middle class shrinks. Not enough. Not enough. The very rich seem to want more and more and more, and they are prepared to dismantle the existing political and social order in order to get it. (S, 23)
>
> The rich get richer, and they don't sit on this money. What they then do is to use it to elect people who support them and to unelect people who oppose their agenda. (S, 23–24)
>
> The rich and large corporations get richer, the CEOs earn huge compensation packages, and when things get bad, don't worry; Uncle Sam and the American taxpayers are here to bail you out. But when you are in trouble, well, we just can't afford to help you, if you are in the working class or the middle class of this country. (S, 47)
>
> There is something more important in life than the richest people becoming richer when we have the highest rate of childhood poverty in the industrialized world. (S, 125)
>
> What worries me so much about the growing concentration of wealth and income in this country is that when the rich get richer, they don't just simply put that money under the mattress. They don't simply go out and buy yachts and planes and 18 homes and all the things rich people do. They do that, but they do something else. They say: I am not rich enough. I need to be richer. What motivates some of these people is greed and greed and more greed. There is no end to it. (S, 219)
>
> So that is what this debate is about. It is about fundamentally whether we continue the process by which the richest people in this country become richer, at a time when we have the most unequal distribution of income and wealth of any major country on Earth. (S, 246)

Of course, there is considerable truth to what Sanders was saying in what many of his fellow members of Congress considered his inflammatory and certainly revolutionary statements. Nevertheless, he does paint his attacks on the wealthy with a very wide brush and borders on being somewhat unfair to those wealthy people who are not driven by greed alone and who are responsible citizens committed to social improvements by word and deed. Sanders knows that, and he usually singles the billionaires Warren Buffet and Bill Gates out as representatives of philanthropically minded rich people. What Sanders is most upset about is those people of wealth who influence elections by way of large sums of money. In his already-mentioned speech opening his presidential campaign, he said on May 25, 2015, in Burlington, "American democracy is not about billionaires being able to buy candidates and elections. It is not about the Koch brothers [Charles and David], Sheldon Adelson, and other incredibly wealthy individuals spending billions of dollars to elect candidates who will make the rich richer and everyone else poorer" (R, 121).

Things can get quite heated during a campaign, and here is a tweet from August 6, 2015, that shows that Sanders can be quite aggressive in such a spontaneous message: "The very rich get richer, everyone else poorer. And Republicans who take campaign money from billionaires have nothing significant to say" (Holschuh 2015, 62). It would doubtless be best if politicians, and certainly presidents, would refrain from using Twitter altogether. Such hastily composed sound bites do not add to the civil communication necessary to make sociopolitical progress.

But there is no doubt that Bernie Sanders made and continues to make a most effective use of this proverb that stands as a summary of his major argument about the ill-fated discrepancy between the rich and the poor in the United States. Little wonder that the proverb in various reiterations appears ten times in his book *Our Revolution*. They represent a clear picture of capitalism having gone astray when money is in such overwhelming control that it undermines the democratic foundations of the country.

> Republicans have cultivated, into a fine art, the ability to divide people up by race, gender, nationality, or sexual orientation. That's what they do. That is the essence of their politics. They get one group to fight another group while their wealthy friends and campaign contributors get richer and laugh all the way to the bank. (R, 59)

> In the real world, the very rich are getting richer and most everyone else is getting poorer. Is Congress listening? Whose interests is Congress representing? Certainly not those of working families struggling to get by. (R, 191)

> The fact is, the wealthiest people and largest corporations in this country have never had it so good. While most Americans are hurting financially and deeply frightened about the future, the very rich are getting richer, as the majority of new income is now going to the top 1 percent. (R, 206)

> That's the race to the bottom. That's a nation where our people are becoming poorer and poorer. That's something we must not allow to happen. (R, 214)

> Even when the jobs remain in this country, it is harder and harder for workers to earn a living wage that affords a middle-class lifestyle. Just another example of workers getting squeezed more and more by corporate greed. Just another example of the rich getting richer while everyone else gets poorer. (R, 217)

> The rich have gotten much richer in recent years. It's time for low-wage workers to get a pay raise, too. (R, 220)

> And the Rich Get Richer. (R, 302—section title)

> Instead of turning the middle class against those in pain, we need to develop a sense of solidarity and stand together against wealthy special interests who get richer and richer while most everybody else gets poorer. (R, 410)

> We need to stop payday lenders from exploiting millions of Americans and making the poor even poorer. (R, 315; *Guide to Political* Revolution, hereafter abbreviated as G, 72–73)

Sanders expands this last reference when he moves from greedy payday lenders on to the practice of usury that is, as he says, condemned in all religions. He chooses the proverb "you can't get blood out of a stone" to add a twofold metaphorical claim that this practice of driving people to ruin must stop on moral grounds.

> We know every major religion on Earth—Christianity, Judaism, Islam, you name it—has always felt that usury is immoral. What we mean by usury is that when someone doesn't have a lot of money and you loan them money, you don't get blood out of a stone. You can't ask for outrageously high interest rates when somebody is hurting. That is immoral. Every major religion, all great philosophers have written about this. Yet today we have millions of people in our country—and I hear from Vermonters every week on this issue—who are paying 25 percent or 30 percent and in some cases even higher interest rates on their credit cards—20 percent, 30 percent interest rates. That is getting blood out of a stone. (S, 37)

There is one striking final reference that needs to be mentioned, as it combines the "rich-poor" proverb with the folkloric adventures of that folk hero Robin Hood. In his long filibuster speech of December 10, 2010, Sanders had already used this image in order to describe the absurdity of giving tax breaks to the wealthy: "It makes no sense to us to be giving huge tax breaks to the richest people in this country—literally millionaires and billionaires—and driving up the national debt so our kids can pay more in taxes in order to pay off that debt. This is a transfer of wealth. It is Robin Hood in reverse. We are taking from the middle class and working families and we are giving it to the wealthiest people in this country" (S, 48).

Six years later, he returned to his description of "Robin Hood in reverse," but this time he added the proverb "it takes money to make money" for good measure, to add even more folkloric proof to the wisdom that wealthy people continue to add money to their financial holdings: "The old adage 'It takes money to make money' is alive and well. The tax code is helping the very rich get insanely richer, while the middle class is disappearing and the poor are getting poorer. It is the Robin Hood principle in reverse" (R, 266).

People will doubtless remember how Robin Hood took from the rich to help the poor, making this proverbial statement a rhetorical masterpiece to convince them that the reversal of this benevolent action is simply not fair or acceptable.

But it is not only the amassing of wealth in the hands of the top 1 percent of the American population that Sanders is attacking. He also accuses these greedy oligarchs of buying votes and elections by their large donations to political campaigns and unfairly influencing Congress and other governmental agencies. Once again Sanders has found a proverbial slogan that has served him well in his fight against this misuse of pecuniary power by rich individuals, corporations, and large banks. While the gender-specific slogan "one man, one vote" was first registered in Alexander Paul's British *History of Reform: A Record of the Struggle for the Representation of the People in Parliament* (1884), it was changed to be more inclusive in a statement by US judge William O. Douglas: "The conception of political equality from the Declaration of Independence, to Lincoln's Gettysburg Address, to the Fifteenth, Seventeenth, and Nineteenth Amendments can mean only one thing—one person, one vote" (Shapiro 2006, 138, 211).

Already in his book *Outsider in the House*, Sanders observed that "big money" plays too large a role in American elections, undermining the very idea that in America all people are supposed to be created equal according to the Declaration of Independence and that each and every one of them should have an individual voice in elections: "In recent elections, the concept of 'one person, one vote' has been supplanted by the influence of big money. The more money you have, the more power you have. Some citizens participate by contributing hundreds of thousands of dollars to the politicians and parties of their choice. Most citizens contribute no money and do not vote. To paraphrase Orwell, some citizens are clearly a lot more equal than others" (H, 280).

As expected by now, he quoted the proverbial slogan "one person, one vote" in the opening speech of his presidential campaign on May 26, 2015, stressing the fact that especially in the small state of Vermont, people still for the most part can count on exercising their democratic right of registering their individual vote without outside influence: "In Vermont and at our town meetings we know what American democracy is supposed to be about. It is one person, one vote—with every citizen having an equal say—and no voter suppression. And that's the kind of American political system we have to fight for and will fight for in this campaign" (R, 121; Holschuh 2015, 60).

He repeated this statement quite similarly in his Super Tuesday Speech on March 1, 2016, in Essex Junction, Vermont, quite proud of the direct democratic process in his small rural state. "It is about recognizing that in our state, we have town meetings and people come out, they argue about budgets, and then they vote. One person, one vote" (Sanders 2016b, 73).

The proverb very quickly became yet another leitmotif for Sanders, as can be seen from his campaign speech that he delivered just one day after having announced his presidential candidacy. In this case, he used the proverb as a definition of democracy in contradiction to an oligarchy, in which votes are bought. "Democracy is one person, one vote and a full discussion of the issues that affect us. Oligarchy is billionaires buying elections, voter suppression and a concentrated corporate media determining what we see, hear, and read" (Holschuh 2015, 47).

In his remarks at the Southern Christian Leadership Conference on July 25, 2015, he continued this type of reasoning by emphasizing that it is the individual person's right to vote that makes for a true democracy. "The defining principle of American democracy is one person, one vote—with every citizen having an equal say—and no voter suppression, And that's the kind of American political system we have to fight for" (66).

In his book *Our Revolution*, he hammers home the same point in the four following paragraphs with his "one person, one vote" leitmotif, never tiring of stressing that the electoral influence of wealthy people is undermining the electoral process and thus the foundation of democracy.

> Democracy is about one person, one vote. It's about all of us coming together to determine the future of our country. It is not about a handful of billionaires buying elections, or governors suppressing the vote by denying poor people or people of color the right to vote. Our job is to stand together to defeat the drift toward oligarchy and create a vibrant democracy. (R, 185)

> What, in our day, does democracy mean? To my mind, it should mean one person, one vote. It should mean an equal opportunity for all who wish to seek public office. It should mean that the wealthy don't have undue influence over the election process. (R, 186)

> In America today, instead of one person, one vote, and equal voice for all, we are seeing a small group of extraordinarily wealthy people pump billions of dollars into the political process to buy elections for politicians who will be beholden to them. (R, 189)

> When all 435 seats in the House and 33 or 34 seats in the Senate are up for election every two years, the total amount a single wealthy family can legally

give is truly astounding. And the huge amounts of money these people donate give them disproportionate influence in the political system. It goes against the very idea of equal voice and one person, one vote. (R, 193)

But on these very pages, Sanders also defines what his vision of democracy entails by conjuring up Thomas Jefferson's Declaration of Independence, with its proverb that "all men are created equal" and the proverbial triad of "life, liberty, and the pursuit of happiness" that are part of American cultural literacy (Burrell 1997, 29–32; Aron 2008, 89–96; Mieder 2015a).

Democracy is the right of a free people to control their destiny. Not kings or queens or czars, but ordinary people who come together in a peaceful manner in order to determine the future of their society. Democracy means that the government belongs to all of us and that it is our inherent right to elect people who will represent our interests. After all, this is what our Declaration of Independence proclaims when it profoundly states: "We hold these truths to be self-evident, that all men are created equal, that they are endowed by their Creator with certain unalienable Rights, that among them are Life, Liberty and the pursuit of Happiness. That to secure these rights, Governments are instituted among Men, deriving their just powers from the consent of the governed." *Their just powers from the consent of the governed.* (R, 185–86)

Later in his book, he returns to this proverbial passage by explaining that these ideals are undermined by the economic inequality that is tearing the American society apart. "The idea that all Americans are created equal and that all of us are entitled to life, liberty, and the pursuit of happiness were, according to the founders, supposed to be 'self-evident truths.' But those foundational notions about what this country is supposed to be all about are seriously imperiled by the grotesque level of wealth and income inequality that exists in American today" (R, 277).

It will come as no surprise that Sanders also draws on the proverbial definition of democracy, "government of the people, by the people, for the people." This triad circulated in variants in the first half of the nineteenth century among such renowned Americans as John Adams, John Marshall, Daniel Webster, and Theodore Parker, but it was Abraham Lincoln who gave it this precise formulation at the end of his Gettysburg Address of November 19, 1863 (Mieder 2005a). In his book *Our Revolution*, Sanders recalls a visit to Gettysburg in February 2015, where he was deeply moved by the monuments commemorating this major battle of the Civil War in Pennsylvania. He recalls Lincoln's famous speech with the proverbial triad and then observes that with the Supreme Court having decided to put no limits on campaign donations by corporations, the very basis of American democracy is in jeopardy.

> We also visited the site where Lincoln gave his famous address in 1863. As every schoolchild knows, in his speech Lincoln stated "that we here highly resolve that these dead shall not have died in vain . . . that this nation, under God, shall have a new birth of freedom . . . and that government of the people, by the people, for the people, shall not perish from the earth." As we left Gettysburg, it struck me forcefully that what Lincoln had said in 1863 was as relevant today as it was back then. Especially with the Supreme Court's disastrous 2010 Citizens United decision that opened the floodgates to virtually unlimited corporate spending in campaigns and allowed big money to buy elections, we were still fighting for a government "of the people, by the people, for the people." As a result of that trip to Gettysburg, I often referenced Lincoln, and what he said there on that day in 1863, in my speeches. (R, 81)

And yes, even in this book, he returns twice to Lincoln's wording of the definition of democracy. With honesty and humility, he states America has tried to make its government more inclusive, but clearly the ideal state has by no means been reached: "We also know, however, that the Constitution they drafted, while revolutionary in its day, reflected the values and mores of the 1790s: slavery and racism, rigid class lines, and a deeply rooted sexism. We know that since then, amidst bloodshed, struggle, and turmoil, the American people have sought to expand democracy and make it more inclusive. To quote Lincoln at Gettysburg, our goal has been to create 'a government of the people, by the people and for the people'" (R, 186–87).

Barely another thirty pages later, he cites the pertinent passage from Lincoln's address once again, but this time he expresses his thoughts in an even more drastic and alarming fashion by citing the triad a total of twice. It all amounts to a proverbial warning that America's democratic government is in danger if campaign finance reforms will not be forthcoming to control the influence of big business and wealthy people.

> On November 19, 1863, standing on the bloodstained battlefield of Gettysburg, Pennsylvania, Abraham Lincoln delivered one of the best-remembered speeches in American history. At the conclusion of his Gettysburg Address, Lincoln stated "that we here highly resolve that these dead shall not have died in vain . . . that this nation, under God, shall have a new birth of freedom . . . and that government of the people, by the people, for the people, shall not perish from the earth." In the year 2016, with a political campaign finance system that is corrupt and increasingly controlled by billionaires and special interests, I fear very much that, in fact, "government of the people, by the people, for the people" will perish in the United States of America. . . . The need for real campaign finance reform is not a progressive issue. It is not a conservative issue. It is an American issue. It is an issue that should concern all Americans—regardless of their political point of view—who wish to preserve the essence of

the longest standing democracy in the world, a government that is supposed to represent all of the people and not just a handful of powerful special interests. (R, 203–4)

Among the manipulating corporations are the giant banks that, in Sanders's opinion, have way too much power and influence, not only on elections but on the entire American economy and beyond. In fact, it has been argued that some banks and financial institutions are so big that if they were to fail, the entire economy would collapse if the government were not to step in and bail them out. In other words, such financial powerhouses must not be allowed to fail. All of this brings to mind the major financial crisis of 2008 that led to calls for splitting such large conglomerates up. It was at this time that the slogan "If it is too big to fail, it is too big (to exist)" appeared on the horizon that somewhat indirectly calls for their downsizing. By the time of his mammoth speech of December 10, 2010, Bernie Sanders had alluded to it several times in the truncated form of "too big to fail" (S, 184, 186, 187, 189, 190) and then cited it in its complete form as "If they are too big to fail, they are too big" (S, 192) to stress the absurdity of these developments. As might be expected, this new proverb became a powerful leitmotif in Sanders's anti-big-bank rhetoric. It is already present in his important address of May 26, 2015, with which he opened his presidential campaign back home in Vermont: "It is time to break up the largest financial institutions in the country. Wall Street cannot continue to be an island unto itself, gambling trillions in risky financial instruments while expecting the public to bail it out. If a bank is too big to fail it is too big to exist" (R, 124; Holschuh 2015, 24).

In *Our Revolution* he even creates a telling antiproverb by changing "fail" to "jail" to chastise powerful executives for their wrongdoings for which they did not get punished: "Ending 'Too Big to Jail'" (R, 306; G, 59; varied section title) and: "In other words, not only are Wall Street banks too big to fail, their executives are too big to jail" (R, 306).

In his ever-present fight against Wall Street and big money, the proverbial leitmotif suits Sanders perfectly well to ridicule and attack their questionable practices. As some of the following contextualized references show, this can very effectively be done by employing the adjectival reduction of the proverb to "too-big-to-fail banks":

Ending "Too Big to Fail" (R, 307; section title)

And we must end, once and for all, the scheme that is nothing more than a free insurance policy for Wall Street: the policy of "too big to fail." (R, 307; G, 63)

> Wall Street cannot continue to be an island unto itself, gambling trillions of other people's money on risky derivatives, acting illegally, and making huge profits, all the while assured that if its schemes fail, the taxpayers will be there to bail them out. (R, 307)
>
> We were told these unprecedented actions were necessary because the financial institutions involved were simply "too big to fail." In other words, they were so large and intertwined with all aspects of the economy that if they collapsed, the U.S. economy and maybe the entire global economy would go down with them. (R, 308)
>
> If these banks were too big to fail in 2008, what would happen if any of them were to fail today? The taxpayers would be on the hook again, and almost certainly for more money than in the last bailout. (R, 308; G, 64)
>
> If a bank is too big to fail, it is too big to exist. When it comes to Wall Street reform, that must be our bottom line. (R, 308; G, 64)
>
> The idea of breaking up the too-big-to-fail banks is supported not only by a number of progressive economists, but also by some of the leading figures in the financial community. (R, 309)
>
> While the individuals are much more conservative than I am, all of them understand how dangerous too-big-to-fail banks are to our economy. (R, 309)
>
> While the rich and powerful are "too big to fail" and are worthy of an endless supply of cheap credit, ordinary Americans must fend for themselves. This was a clear case of socialism for the rich and rugged individualism for everyone else. (R, 316; G, 74)

This last reference is of special interest for two reasons. For one, Sanders goes beyond attacking big banks and instead zeros in on the social effects that their extreme capitalistic behavior brings about for normal citizens. But there is also the telling formulation "socialism for the rich," a partial rendering of a statement by Martin Luther King Jr., as Sanders indicates some seventy pages later: "King said: 'This country has socialism for the rich, rugged individualism for the poor'" (R, 384). As Sanders never tires of reiterating, rich people, banks, and giant corporations don't need to be taken care of by the government by way of unnecessary tax breaks and other unnecessary subventions.

In order to chastise them with yet another repeatedly cited proverb, Sanders turned to the limiting proverb "you can't have it all." Once again it is his remarkable speech of May 26, 2015, that gets the proverbial leitmotif rolling. The general proverb starts it off, and employing "you can't" as an anaphora, Sanders enumerates in clear and simple language what in fact needs to stop: "This campaign is going to send a message to the billionaire class. And that is: You can't have it all. You can't get huge tax breaks while children in this country go hungry. You can't continue sending our jobs to China while millions are looking for work. You can't hide your profits in the Cayman Islands and other tax havens while there are massive unmet needs on every corner of this nation. Your greed has got to end. You cannot take advantage of all the benefits of America if you refuse to accept your responsibilities" (R, 124).

In his book *Our Revolution*, Sanders repeats this important message more or less verbatim, and such obvious repetitions should probably have been avoided. But, as has been mentioned, repetitiveness is part of Sanders's authenticity and consistency, always ready to drive home the same point again and again in the hope that his messages will fall on fertile ground.

> In my view, we have got to send a message to the billionaire class: "You can't have it all." You can't have huge tax breaks while children in this country go hungry. You can't continue getting tax breaks by shipping American jobs to China. You can't hide your profits in the Cayman Islands and other tax havens while there are massive unmet needs in every corner of this nation. Your greed has got to end. You cannot take advantage of all the benefits of America if you refuse to accept your responsibilities as Americans. We need a tax system that is fair and progressive. (R, 266–67)

Is there hope at all that the so-called oligarchs will come to their senses, one might ask? In his long Senate speech of December 10, 2010, Bernie Sanders hints at its possibility once by even referring to the Bible and claiming in a nonthreatening way that the wealthy can't have or get it all: "Maybe they [rich people] will understand that they are Americans, part of a great nation which is in trouble today. Maybe they have to go back to the Bible, whatever they believe in, and understand there is virtue in sharing, in reaching out: that you can't get it all" (S, 125–26).

Here Sanders might have employed the proverb "hope springs eternal," albeit with a bit of an ironic touch. But be that as it may, his steadfast hammering away at his sociopolitical messages with a number of proverbial leitmotifs has little room for positive statements concerning the dichotomy between the haves and the have-nots.

Sharing and reaching out could especially help the working class in the United States that is drifting ever more into poverty. As Sanders put it proverbially, unfortunately "some of the more powerful unions, with entrenched bureaucracies and leaders disinclined to rock the boat, have contributed to this malaise" (H, 32) and "working people will continue to get the short end of the stick unless we have a government that represents *their* interests" (H, 33). Employing Herbert Spencer's drastic picture of "the survival of the fittest" from 1865 that was picked up by Charles Dickens four years later (Shapiro 2006, 186, 722), Sanders draws a dire picture of the marginalization of workers by the greed of their corporate employers.

> The law of the jungle, the survival of the fittest. Employers want to pay workers bottom dollar, and workers are too desperate to refuse. Voilà. The "magic of the marketplace" at work, brought to us by people who make $133,000 a year. How very civilized.

> Millions of Americans are now working for starvation wages. To add insult to injury, these low-wage jobs cost *taxpayers* huge amounts of money in corporate welfare. (H, 122)

> I know it is not fashionable to speak of what government is supposed to do for people. We live in an era of "tough love," of the survival of the fittest, when each of us is supposed to do everything for ourselves. Today, a national industrial policy is considered an anachronism by the apologists for corporate America, even though those same apologists never have any quarrel with massive government efforts to assist "free-market capitalism" or establish "free trade" as our industrial policy. (H, 291)

Such accusations lead him to claims that Republicans in particular adhere to this cutthroat behavior: "They believe in a Darwinian style society in which you have the survival of the fittest; that we are not a society which comes together to take care of all of us" (S, 243). Such accusations appear at times to be too inflammatory or certainly overgeneralized, with proverbial expressions like "to add insult to injury" and "to be at each other's throats" adding rhetorical fuel to the fire.

> And then, to add insult to injury, they [Republicans] provide huge tax breaks for the very, very wealthiest families in this country while they raise taxes on working families. (R, 125–26)

> The Republicans of 1996, who undertake massive polling, understand very well the legitimate fears and anxieties that millions of Americans feel. And they are prepared to spend huge sums of money to exploit those anxieties, to divide working people and set them at each other's throats, to blind working people to the fact that instead of justice they are getting scraps from the rich man's table. (H, 158–59)

But Sanders's commitment as a democratic socialist leads him repeatedly to emotional calls for improving the lot of workers, with proverbial expressions underpinning his heartfelt pleas as can be seen from this short statement that incorporates the proverbial expressions "to fight an uphill battle" and "to make ends meet" as well as the somatic phrase "from the bottom of one's heart": "If we don't stand together today, working Americans will continue fighting an uphill battle just to make ends meet at the end of each month. We cannot settle for establishment politics and stale ideas. Now is the time to transform America. That's what I believe from the bottom of my heart" (S, xvi; 2015 ed.).

To add even more emotional power to his call for making certain that workers have jobs that pay them fair wages, he twice draws on another proverbial somatism that stresses the fact that we must not abandon the American workers: "It would be, in my view, immoral and wrong to turn our backs on those workers" (S, 13) and "At a time of deep recession, at a time of terribly high unemployment, it would be absolutely wrong and immoral for us to turn our backs on the millions of workers who are about to lose their unemployment benefits" (S, 239).

Yet another somatic proverbial expression serves Sanders as a leitmotif in his persistent engagement for the welfare of the poor, to wit his repeated use of "to put a roof over one's head."

> There are millions of people in our country, let alone the rest of the world, who are struggling to feed their families. They are struggling to put a roof over their heads, and some of them are sleeping out on the streets. They are struggling to find money in order to go to a doctor when they are sick. (R, 150–51)
>
> And to keep a roof over their heads, many Wal-Mart employees live in subsidized housing—paid for by the taxpayers of America. (R, 223; G, 9)
>
> Of course, the situation is direst for families with the lowest incomes, with 6.6 million families below the poverty line paying at least *half* of their very limited incomes just to put a roof over their heads, leaving precious little for other necessities like food, health care, and transportation. (R, 254)
>
> If you are poor and struggling every day with the stress of putting food on the table and a roof over your head, your health suffers. (R, 333)

Predictably for Sanders, his convictions are not limited to the well-being of American workers. He also champions the fate of foreign or undocumented workers, employing the proverb "a rising tide lifts all boats" as a metaphor for the benefit that results from taking proper and universal care of the entire working force that should include fair and square wages.

> If we start giving undocumented workers legal protections, we can slow down the "race to the bottom." Wages for the lowest-paid workers in the country will rise and, with legal status, they will be able to join unions and negotiate decent pay and working conditions. A rising tide lifts all boats. (R, 395; G, 184)
>
> Too often, guest worker programs are used not to help employers hire labor they couldn't find locally, but to drive down wages with cheap labor from

abroad. Instead of a rising tide lifting all boats, it is a leaky boat sinking slowly to the bottom. (R, 395; G, 185)

It might well be that Sanders picked this proverb up from President Barack Obama, who used it repeatedly in his speeches and writing, to wit, "It has been the ability of working man and women to join together in unions that has allowed our rising tide to lift every boat" or "And when we've succeeded [to be good citizens], it's made America the place where dreams are possible, where freedoms of speech and press and worship are protected, and where the rising tide lifts the boats of the many instead of just the few" (Mieder 2009, 323). Such positive, optimistic statements are, for the most part, not quite Sanders's style, but that is by no means to say that his heart is not in the right place.

Speaking of boats, Sanders is also well aware of the proverbial expression "to be in the same boat" that had its start with Cicero's "in eadem es navi" from 53 BC and has been used over and over again by politicians to express solidarity as they face common concerns (Mieder 2005c). On Sanders's agenda needing serious attention is certainly the worldwide alarm about climate change that affects all nations, and the "boat" metaphor is perfectly suited to give expression to this matter: "Climate change is truly a global problem. . . . The fact of the matter is, we are all in the same boat, together, and solving this unprecedented global challenge will require an unprecedented level of international cooperation. As the most powerful country in the history of the planet, the United States must help lead the effort" (R, 373; G, 147).

Using yet another proverbial phrase, this time "to turn a blind eye to something," Sanders argues powerfully that everything possible must be done to save the environment: "And those who argue that renewable energy has hidden costs conveniently turn a blind eye to the fact that fossil fuels are cooking our planet" (G, 145).

To return to Sanders's commitment to equitable wages, it must be emphasized that the fight for this is definitely part of his social agenda. In fact, in his book *Our Revolution* and its shortened companion *Guide to Political Revolution* (2017), he features sections with the proverbial title "Equal Pay for Equal Work" (R, 228; G, 13; G, 27). He must have been introduced to this slogan while he was a political science student at the University of Chicago, as can be seen from this comment:

> In 1963, President John F. Kennedy signed into law the Equal Pay Act, requiring employers to provide "equal pay for equal work" regardless of gender. . . . A

> year later, the 1964 Civil Rights Act went a step further by prohibiting all wage discrimination on the basis of race, color, religion, gender, or national origin. (R, 228–29)
>
> ...
>
> This means that pay equity is not just a women's issue, it is a family issue. When women do not receive equal pay for equal work, families across America have less money to spend on child care, groceries, food, and housing. (R, 230; G, 15)

Yet it is doubtful that he learned at that time that this feminist slogan turned proverb originated almost one hundred years before President Kennedy made its message a law that unfortunately has still not found general acceptance. Its originator was no less than the early feminist Susan B. Anthony (1820–1906) who, on October 8, 1869, wrote in her journal *The Revolution*: "Join the union, girls, and together say, 'Equal Pay for Equal Work.'" She repeated her formulaic utterance several times, with this statement from her letter of July 6, 1903, showing her fighting spirit still at her advanced age: "Women must have equal pay for equal work, and they must be considered equally eligible to the offices of principal and superintendent, professor and president. The saying that women have equal pay is absurd while they are not allowed to have the highest positions which their qualifications entitle them to; so you [Margaret Haley] must insist that qualifications, not sex, shall govern the appointments to the highest positions" (Mieder 2014a, 99, 100).

Bernie Sanders and Susan B. Anthony would have been quite a fighting team, and it is good that he is carrying the torch forward for her by calling for equal pay for equal work for all as the 1963 Equal Pay Act had established it, at least on paper. Sanders's inclusive social agenda can also be seen from what he does with a powerful statement that Martin Luther King Jr. had made on June 23, 1963, in Detroit and then repeated in his famous "I Have a Dream" speech of August 28, 1963, in front of the Lincoln Memorial in Washington, DC: "I have a dream my four little children will one day live in a nation where they will not be judged by the color of their skin but by the content of their character. I have a dream today" (Mieder 2010a, 193–202). This utterance has become proverbial as "to be judged by the content of one's character and not by the color of one's skin," but while King spoke of African Americans, Sanders takes its message beyond color and race to gender, sexual orientation, nationality, and human beings altogether. "A vision which says that we judge people not by their color, their gender, their sexual orientation, their nation of birth—but by the quality of their character, and that we will never accept sexism, racism, or homophobia" (H, 62).

Elsewhere, he states, "There is no question that in recent decades we have made significant progress in creating a country where we judge people, as Dr. Martin Luther King Jr. urged, not by the color of their skin, not by the language they speak, not by the country they came from, but by the content of their character and their qualities as human beings" (R, 376; G, 156).

Sanders was there when Dr. King gave his "I Have a Dream" speech, and it should not be surprising that as a sincere champion of civil rights, he remembers King's phrase and extends it to all humanity. As a social reformer and humanitarian, Sanders is clearly building on the work of great Americans like Frederick Douglass, Abraham Lincoln, Elisabeth Cady Stanton and Susan B. Anthony, Martin Luther King Jr., John Lewis, Barack Obama, and others (Mieder 2000, 2001, 2009, 2010, 2014a, 2014d).

Sanders's keen understanding of justice and equal rights have motivated him throughout his life as he ran for various elected offices. He often won by just a few votes, as when he became mayor of Burlington for the first time in 1981. Quoting the proverb "every vote counts," he expressed his belief that every person who has the right to vote should exercise this democratic privilege, since just a few votes can make a big difference. "Yet, to my surprise, to Mayor Paquette's shock, to the business community's alarm, and to the deep interest of Vermonters throughout the state, when the absentee votes were tallied in with the rest, I found myself elected mayor of Burlington [in 1981]—by a mere fourteen votes. For once, the old saying was really true: every vote had counted. So stunning was the upset that nine years later the state's largest newspaper would still be referring to it as 'the story of the decade'" (H, 53).

Having been elected by such a minute margin made Sanders very conscious of the electoral process, as well as the serious give-and-take that is necessary even in running a relatively small city like Burlington. Winston Churchill's proverbial triad "blood, sweat, and tears" (Mieder and Bryan 1995, 62–66) served him well to describe the workings of city government. "But the creation of the [city] councils was a major political struggle, complete with blood, sweat, and tears. Almost every funding request was accompanied by vituperative and vicious debate. Everything was partisan. Nothing came easy" (H, 77–78).

Things did, of course, become much more problematic as Sanders began to run for Congress. To run a political campaign for national office is a complex, time-consuming, exhausting effort, and while there might be great ideas on how to do it, the execution of campaign plans is, proverbially speaking, easier said than done. "We have our game plan and must play it out effectively: focus on our issues, respond strongly to inaccurate statements about my positions in either the free or paid media, get around the state as much as we can, motivate our volunteers, be well prepared for the debates, keep raising money, and make certain that our advertising campaign—TV, radio, newspaper, and tabloid—is effective. All this is a lot easier said than done" (H, 240; the proverb also appears in R, 101).

Then there is the money issue! It takes millions of dollars to run major campaign, and it is at this level in particular where big money takes on a manipulative role. There have been numerous attempts to bring fundraising activities under control, and it goes to Sanders's credit that he chose not to accept large amounts of money from wealthy people, Wall Street, and corporations. In fact, his grassroots approach to fundraising resulted in the average donation amounting to a mere $27, with 2.5 million Americans having contributed $232 million during his presidential campaign. He is absolutely correct in claiming proverbially that the modus operandi of political fundraising is best described as a pervasive bad odor: "This whole campaign fundraising situation stinks to high heaven. In the past I have fought hard for campaign finance reform which limits the amount of money that can be spent in an election and which emphasizes public funding of elections and small individual contributions. Ordinary Americans should have a chance to win elections, not just the rich or representatives thereof" (H, 88).

With deserved pride, Sanders could call on the modern American proverb "if you want to talk the talk, you've got to walk the walk" (Doyle, Mieder, Shapiro 2012, 250) to describe his grassroots campaign that relied on small donations—often collected online—by way of the hard work of his staff and hundreds of volunteers: "From the beginning, we knew it was important to fund this campaign differently than most. We weren't going to be receiving a whole lot of support from wealthy donors and we didn't want a super PAC [Political Action Committee]. In the end, 94 percent of our money came in online, and we not only talked the talk about campaign finance reform, we walked the walk" (R, 99).

Speaking of his presidential campaign, his book *Our Revolution*, contains numerous comments on this intriguing process, right from the first thoughts of running for president at all. As he was trying to make up his mind, "testing the waters" was the perfect metaphor to describe the first step. The following three references employ this phrase, with the first one adding the expression "floating a balloon" with a similar meaning to it.

> I did not have to make a definitive decision right away. There was plenty of time to "test the waters" and to determine if there really was the kind interest and support necessary to run a serious [presidential] campaign. What did I have to lose by letting people know that I was "thinking" about running? Jane [his wife], and those politically close to me, reasoned that, at worst, "floating a balloon" would give me the opportunity to get some public attention on issues I felt strongly about. (R, 54)
>
> Testing the Waters (section title)
> In presidential politics, you really hit the campaign trail before you hit the campaign trail. It's called "testing the waters," determining whether there is the kind of support in the real world that you'll need to run a successful campaign. (R, 56)
>
> If one of my goals in "testing the waters" for a presidential run was to attract national media attention, that strategy was working. (R, 69)

Once decided, the problem of making campaign stops in this giant country—sometimes two or even three a day—becomes a major scheduling challenge with staffers having to be keenly aware of the wisdom of the sixteenth-century proverb "you can't be in two places at the same time."

> One of the challenges of a campaign is good scheduling. Don't arrange for the candidate to be in two places at the same time. Make sure the candidate has enough time to go from one event to the other. Schedule events at a time when people are likely to attend. (R, 67)
>
> One of the dilemmas of being on the campaign trail if you are a sitting member of the U.S. Senate is that you can't be in two places at the same time. That means that there are votes you will miss in Washington because you are in some other part of the country, and it also means not being able to attend events in your own state. (R, 136)

There is also the very basic question of how to run a successful major campaign. As is well known, it can fail in an instant, with the candidate falling flat on the face as the proverbial expression would have it: "Well, how do you run an effective national campaign? How do you make sure you don't fall flat on your face and call it quits two months after you begin, which is not uncommon? We hadn't a clue" (R, 86).

Such somatic proverbial phrases are particularly well suited to add emotional expressiveness to Sanders's rhetoric, with his use of the truncated Bible proverb "an eye for an eye, and a tooth for a tooth" (Exodus 21:24) showing his sincere commitment to a fair and humane justice system: "Frankly, we should not be in the company of China (the world's leader in use of the death penalty), Saudi Arabia, Iran, Iraq, Sudan, Yemen, Egypt, and Somalia. Rather, we should be in the company of virtually every other major democratic society that understands that even when confronted with unspeakable violence, we must move beyond ancient concepts of revenge. We must recognize, as Mohandas Gandhi did, that, in the end, an 'eye for an eye' simply makes everybody blind" (R, 384; G, 167).

Here are a few more references containing somatic proverbial expressions that add considerable metaphorical expressiveness to Sanders's rhetoric that engages listeners and readers alike of his serious messages.

> While party liberals [of the Democratic Party] were willing to support my entry into the caucus, the conservatives dug in their heels. (H, 116)
>
> Clearly, we didn't have the votes to defeat the Republicans, but we fought them tooth and nail and in the process helped to illuminate the dirty business behind the high-flying rhetoric. (H, 251)
>
> I know many mayors and Governors would very much like to turn their backs on the infrastructure because it is not a sexy investment. (S, 236)
>
> I want to add the idea that when we think about cutting back on education—whether it is childcare, primary school, or college—we are simply cutting off our noses to spite our faces. (S, 105)
>
> These well-known Americans were willing, sometimes against a great deal of peer pressure, to stick their necks out for the political revolution. (R, 108)
>
> At a time when millions of Americans are struggling to keep their heads above water economically, at a time when senior poverty is increasing, at a time when millions of kids are living in dire poverty, my Republican colleagues, as part of their recently passed budget, are trying to make a terrible situation even worse. (R, 125)

This last reference, with its telling metaphor of keeping one's head above water, is yet another drastic statement by Sanders to show his deep concern for the many poor people in the United States, a sickening disgrace for the richest country in the world. In another comment along these lines, Sanders employs the proverbial comparison "like shooting fish in a barrel," with the meaning of "much too easy," to chastise the Republicans for their economic policies that drive poor people ever deeper into poverty: "Poor people are a good target for the Republicans. Exhausted by an increasingly difficult struggle for survival, they are not organized and can't fight back. Seventy percent of welfare recipients are children, a constituency that cannot vote and has few civil rights. What a target, it's like shooting fish in a barrel. You can't miss" (H, 174–75).

Sanders, the big-city man transplanted to the small city of Burlington and the rural state of Vermont, is perfectly capable of citing proverbial expressions that refer to animals, knowing only too well that these animals—as is the case in fables—stand as metaphors for human beings (Carnes 1988). Here are a few telling contextualized examples for the effective use of animal phrases.

> There are great differences between being a mayor and a congressman. A mayor is a big fish in a little pond. A congressman is one body out of 535 (not to mention the president). But the main difference to me is physical proximity. When you're a mayor, you're *always* home and on the job. In fact, the problem is you can't get away for a minute. (H, 41–42)

> But if he [President Obama] is the Democratic candidate for President and he says: Reelect me to be President because in the future I am going to really get rid of these tax breaks, I am afraid his credibility is not very high because that is what he said last time. I guess there is a limit as to how many times you can cry wolf. (S, 149)

> What we were trying to do was unprecedented in modern American history. We were not just running an insurgent campaign as an underdog, we were taking aim at the nation's entire political and financial establishment. And we were running against the most powerful political machine [Clinton] in the country. (R, 129)

Here are two additional references that include the proverb "don't put the fox to guard the henhouse," to warn people of the ill-conceived political influence of the billionaire brothers Charles and David Koch. The first text is particularly sarcastic in its attack.

> As the owners of a major fossil fuel company, and leading founders of climate change denial groups, they [the Koch brothers] also supported abolishing the Environmental Protection Agency and the Department of Energy. Great idea: Let's just put the fox, a particularly rapacious fox, in charge of the henhouse. (R, 200)

> At least eighteen current and former Fed board members were affiliated with banks and companies that received emergency loans from the Fed during the financial crisis. We can no longer allow foxes to guard the henhouse at the Federal Reserve. (R, 317)

Sanders, as a democratic socialist, returns again and again to the economic pain that wealth in all its forms brings to the poor. But there are, of course, so many more sociopolitical ills that need attention that he never tired of discussing during his presidential campaign. He chastises his fellow members of Congress in particular for having swept these problems under the proverbial rug.

> During the campaign, we forced discussion on issues the establishment had swept under the rug for far too long. We brought attention to the grotesque level of income and wealth inequality in this country and the importance of breaking up the large banks that brought our economy to the brink of collapse. We exposed our horrendous trade policies, our broken criminal justice system, and our people's lack of access to affordable health care and higher education. We addressed the global crisis of climate change, the need for real comprehensive immigration reform, the importance of developing a foreign policy that values diplomacy over war, and so much more. (R, 2)

> We can no longer continue to ignore the tremendous economic pain and anxiety that exists in our country. These problems will not go away by sweeping them under the rug. We have to address them forthrightly, or they will only get worse. We can no longer continue to scapegoat the poor and unemployed. (R, 410)

Speaking to the Kochs and others of that ilk, he accuses them of turning the clock back to former times, a proverbial expression that President Harry S. Truman employed as a leitmotif numerous times in similar fashion (Mieder and Bryan 1997, 103–6). "Even though we have far to go to 'perfect our democracy,' sadly, today, there are people of incredible wealth and power who, instead of moving forward , want to undo the progress we have made and roll back the clock of history. Those oligarchs are threatened by what ordinary people can accomplish through the democratic process" (R, 188).

No matter what people thought about Bernie Sanders, it was high time these issues were openly discussed, and he did this country a great favor in championing a democracy strengthened by socialism in which Republicans and Democrats can work together for the common good. Recalling the proverb "politics makes strange bedfellows," he recalls with a bit of irony how at times he succeeded to get members of both parties to agree on something: "Some strange bedfellows—conservatives and progressives—came together on this issue" (S, 29).

Strange bedfellows or not, Bernie Sanders pursued his sociopolitical goals with refreshing consistency and admirable authenticity. This is perfectly visible in his speeches, many of which are partially cited in his books. In fact, in his book *Our Revolution*, there is a picture of him with a handwritten manuscript in his hands and the caption: "I do write my own speeches" (R, 152). And here is what he says about his rhetorical style that he believes differentiated his presidential campaign from those of his opponents:

> At our rallies I did exactly what the consultants tell you not to do. In each of the speeches, before tens of thousands of people, I spoke for at least an hour and discussed, I some detail, what I believed to be major crises facing our country. I didn't begin with prepared jokes or some other routine, and I didn't shape my remarks around a sound bite for TV. I just laid it out as best I could.
>
> And here is what was remarkable. At all of these rallies, where we were filling up large arenas, people were not walking out during a long speech, they were not (I think) getting bored. They were listening. If there is a lesson I learned from this experience, it was that Americans are hungry for an understanding of what is going on in our country and how we can improve it.
>
> . . .
>
> It is an unbelievable and humbling experience to walk out on a stage and see 25,000 or 30,000 people filling up an arena to hear you speak. The moment not only fills you with awe, but with incredible optimism for the future. There was a microcosm of America in front of me. Black and white, Latino, Asian-American, Native American, men and women, gay and straight, young and old. People who were tired of status quo politics and status quo economics. People who dreamed of a better America. People who wanted real change. To say those experiences "moved" me would be a major understatement. They were some of the most memorable moments in my life, and I am deeply grateful to all who came. (R, 146–47)

One of these memorable campaign speeches was his courageous appearance on September 14, 2015, in front of conservative students at Liberty University, a fundamentalist Christian school in Lynchburg, Virginia. Many a politician would have changed message, but not Bernie Sanders! He simply acknowledged his awareness that he held very different views from those of his audience but that he came to talk to them because "it is vitally important for those of us who hold different views to be able to engage in civil discourse" (R, 14) and try "Finding Common Ground" nevertheless, as the title of the published speech has it (Sanders 2015, partially reprinted in R, 149–52). He told the students at the outset that he was for a woman's right to choose an abortion and that he believes in gay rights and gay marriage, and then, cognizant of where he was speaking, Sanders recalled the Golden Rule (Matthew 7:12) as an appropriate Bible proverb to explain what drives him in his call for equality, justice, and much more.

> Let me take a moment, or a few moments, to tell you what motivates me in the work that I do as a public servant, as a senator from the state of Vermont. And let me tell you that it goes without saying, I am far, far from being a perfect human being, but I am motivated by a vision, which exists in all of the great religions, in Christianity, in Judaism, in Islam and Buddhism, and other religions.

> And that vision is so beautifully and clearly stated in Matthew 7:12, and it states: "So in everything, do to others what you would have them do to you, for this sums up the law and the prophets." That is the golden rule. Do unto others, what you would have them do to you. That is the golden rule, and it is not very complicated. (R, 149–50)

The Golden Rule has been employed by such famous social reformers as Frederick Douglass, Elisabeth Cady Stanton and Susan B. Anthony, and certainly Martin Luther King Jr. as well, and that is also true for various presidents, more recently President Barack Obama's remarks in front of several thousand Egyptian students on June 2, 2009, at Cairo University: "There's one rule that lies at the heart of every religion—that we do unto others as we would have them do unto us. This truth transcends nations and peoples—a belief that isn't new; that isn't black or white or brown; that isn't Christian or Muslim or Jew. It's a belief that pulsed in the cradle of civilization, and that still beats in the hearts of billions around the world. It's a faith in other people, and it's what brought me here today" (Mieder 2014c, 193).

Variants of the Golden Rule are indeed known in the world's religions (Hertzler 193334; Griffin 1991, 67–69; Paczolay 1997, 356–58; Templeton 1997, 9–11), and adherence to this very basic law of life would make the world a better place (Mieder 2011). The universally admired President Abraham Lincoln also asked as early as 1848 in his country of slavery whether "the precept 'Whatsoever ye would that men should do to you, do ye even so to them' is obsolete?—of no force?—of no application?" (Mieder 2000, 80). Thirteen years later, he closed his first inaugural address on March 4, 1861, with the hope that the people of his divided country would someday be touched again "by the better angels of our nature" (Shapiro 2006, 462), probably having the Golden Rule in mind as well. In any case, Sanders combines Lincoln's hopeful proverbial utterance with the Golden Rule in championing the rightful cause of immigrants.

> America has always been a haven for the oppressed. We cannot and must not shirk our historic role as a protector of vulnerable people fleeing persecution. We must, as President Lincoln urged in his first inaugural address, appeal to the better angels of our nature. We must treat others as we would like to be treated.
> Sadly, in 2016, we had a major party candidate for president spending endless hours doing the exact opposite, appealing to our worst human traits—bigotry and racism. It is way past time to stop peddling hatred for political gain. We need real solutions to the real problems facing our country, including immigration. (R, 398)

He does not mention President Donald Trump here in person, but it is clear to readers of *Our Revolution* whom he is referring to in somewhat indirect fashion. There is no need for personal attacks or vendettas, when realistic solution for the multitude of sociopolitical problems facing America are needed. The final page of *Our Revolution* states loud and clear that the country is at a proverbial crossroads.

> The great crisis that we face as a nation is not just objective problems that we face—a rigged economy, a corrupt campaign finance system, a broken criminal justice system, and the extraordinary threat of climate change. The more serious crisis is the limitation of our imaginations. It is falling victim to an incredibly powerful establishment—economic, political, and media—that tells us every day, in a million different ways, that real change is unthinkable and impossible. That we have to think small, not big. That we must be satisfied with the status quo. That there are no alternatives.
>
> The future of our country and, perhaps, the world requires us to break through those limitations. Humanity is at a crossroads. We can continue down the current path of greed, consumerism, oligarchy, poverty, war, racism, and environmental degradation. Or we can lead the world in moving in a very different direction. (R, 447)

The American proverb "think big (big thoughts, big things)" has characterized the forward-looking American worldview since 1907 (Doyle, Mieder, Shapiro 2012, 255; Dundes 1969, 2004), and Bernie Sanders with his vigorous proverbial rhetoric will make sure that it stays that way. As a grassroots democratic socialist, he is committed to continue the upward struggle, mindful of the modern American proverbs "life is not a spectator sport" from 1958 (Doyle, Mieder, Shapiro 2012, 143) and its antiproverb "politics is not a spectator sport" from 1963 (Mieder 2015b). But it speaks for Bernie Sanders that he varies the two proverbs once again by changing their subjects to the all-important word *democracy*. His rhetoric is also enhanced by alluding to Charles A. Tindley's gospel song "I'll Overcome Some Day" (1900) and Pete Seeger's civil rights anthem "We Shall Overcome" (1963), whose hopeful message is part of American cultural literacy (Shapiro 2005, 676, 762): "Yes. We can overcome. . . . We can create a vibrant democracy where knowledgeable citizens actively debate the great challenges we face. . . . No. We will not be able to accomplish those goals if we look at democracy as a spectator sport, assuming others will do it for us. They won't. The future is in *your* hands. Let's go to work" (R, 447).

In his most recent book, *Guide to Political Revolution*, he repeats his newly found proverbial slogan: "In my view, if we are to successfully address the enormous problems now facing our country and planet, we need to understand that democracy is not a spectator sport" (G, xi–xii). Judging by the unexpected success he had during the presidential campaign, he obviously motivated many Americans to jump on his proverbial bandwagon. He put up a remarkable fight as an underdog, and he showed himself to be a serious candidate to be reckoned with. Above all, he touched a nerve that reawakened Americans to the fact that democracy is a work in progress and that it works best by way of active participation on a fair and square playing field.

References

Aron, Paul. 2008. *We Hold These Truths . . . And Other Words that Made America*. Lanham, MD: Rowman & Littlefield.
Burrell, Brian. 1997. *The Words We Live By: The Creeds, Mottoes, and Pledges That Have Shaped America*. New York: Free Press.
Carnes, Pack, ed. 1988. *Proverbia in Fabula: Essays on the Relationship of the Fable and the Proverb*. Bern: Peter Lang.
Conroy, W. J. 1990. *Bernie Sanders and the Boundaries of Reform: Socialism in Burlington*. Philadelphia: Temple University Press (reprinted 2016 with a new preface).
Davis, John. 2015. *Bernie Sanders for President 2016: A Political Revolution*. Cranbury, NJ: Old Town Publishing.
Doyle, Charles Clay, Wolfgang Mieder, and Fred R. Shapiro. 2012. *The Dictionary of Modern Proverbs*. New Haven, CT: Yale University Press.
Dundes, Alan. 1969. "Thinking Ahead: A Folkloristic Reflection of the Future Orientation in American Worldview." *Anthropological Quarterly* 42:53–72.
———. 2004. "'As the Crow Flies': A Straightforward Study of Lineal Worldview in American Folk Speech." In *"What Goes Around Comes Around": The Circulation of Proverbs in Contemporary Life; Essays in Honor of Wolfgang Mieder*, edited by Kimberly J. Lau, Peter Tokofsky, and Stephen D. Winick, 171–87. Logan: Utah State University Press. Also in A. Dundes. 2007. *The Meaning of Folklore: The Analytical Essays of Alan Dundes*, edited by Simon J. Bronner, 196–210. Logan: Utah State University Press. Also in A. Dundes. 2008. *"The Kushmaker" and Other Essays on Folk Speech and Folk Humor*, edited by Wolfgang Mieder, 93–108. Burlington: University of Vermont.
Elliott, Kloa. 2016. *Bernie Sanders: The Essential Guide*. London: Eyewear Publishing.
Griffin, Albert Kirby. 1991. *Religious Proverbs: Over 1,600 Adages from 18 Faiths Worldwide*. Jefferson, NC: McFarland.
Hertzler, Joyce. 1933–34. "On Golden Rules." *International Journal of Ethics* 44:418–36.
Holschuh, Chamois, ed. 2015. *Bernie Sanders in His Own Words: 250 Quotes from America's Political Revolutionary*. New York: Skyhorse Publishing.
Jaffe, Harry. 2015. *Why Bernie Sanders Matters*. New York: Regan Arts.
Lau, Kimberly J. 1996. "'It's about Time': The Ten Proverbs Most Frequently Used in Newspapers and Their Relation to American Values." *Proverbium* 13:135–59. Also in *Cognition, Comprehension, and Communication: A Decade of North American Proverb Studies (1990–2000)*, edited by Wolfgang Mieder, 231–54. Baltmannsweiler: Schneider Verlag Hohengehren, 2003.

Louis, Cameron. 2000. "Proverbs and the Politics of Language." *Proverbium* 17:173–94. Also in *Cognition, Comprehension, and Communication: A Decade of North American Proverb Studies (1990–2000)*, edited by Wolfgang Mieder, 271–92. Baltmannsweiler: Schneider Verlag Hohengehren, 2003.

Manders, Dean Wolfe. 2006. *The Hegemony of Common Sense: Wisdom and Mystification in Everyday Life*. New York: Peter Lang.

Mieder, Wolfgang. 1989. *American Proverbs: A Study of Texts and Contexts*. Bern: Peter Lang.

———. 1992. "Paremiological Minimum and Cultural Literacy." In *Creativity and Tradition in Folklore*, edited by Simon J. Bronner, 185–203. Logan: Utah State University Press. Also in *Proverbs Are Never Out of Season: Popular Wisdom in the Modern Age*, edited by Wolfgang Mieder, 41–57. New York: Oxford University Press, 1993.

———. 1993. *Proverbs Are Never Out of Season: Popular Wisdom in the Modern Age*. New York: Oxford University Press.

———. 1997. *The Politics of Proverbs: From Traditional Wisdom to Proverbial Stereotypes*. Madison: University of Wisconsin Press.

———. 2000. *The Proverbial Abraham Lincoln: An Index to Proverbs in the Works of Abraham Lincoln*. New York: Peter Lang.

———. 2001. *"No Struggle, No Progress": Frederick Douglass and His Proverbial Rhetoric for Civil Rights*. New York: Peter Lang.

———. 2004. *Proverbs: A Handbook*. Westport, CT: Greenwood Press.

———. 2005a. "'Government of the People, by the People, for the People': The Making and Meaning of an American Proverb about Democracy." In *Proverbs Are the Best Policy: Folk Wisdom and American Politics*, edited by Wolfgang Mieder, 15–55, 248–58 (notes). Logan: Utah State University Press.

———. 2005b. *Proverbs Are the Best Policy: Folk Wisdom and American Politics*. Logan: Utah State University Press.

———. 2005c. "'We Are All I the Same Boat Now': Proverbial Discourse in the Churchill-Roosevelt Correspondence." In *Proverbs Are the Best Policy: Folk Wisdom and American Politics*, edited by Wolfgang Mieder, 187–209, 284–87 (notes). Logan: Utah State University Press.

———. 2008a. "'Let Us Have Faith That Right Makes Might': Proverbial Rhetoric in Decisive Moments of American Politics." *Proverbium* 25:319–52.

———. 2008b. *"Proverbs Speak Louder than Words": Folk Wisdom in Art, Culture, Folklore, History, Literature, and Mass Media*. New York: Peter Lang.

———. 2009. *"Yes We Can": Barack Obama's Proverbial Rhetoric*. New York: Peter Lang.

———. 2010. *"Making a Way Out of No Way": Martin Luther King's Sermonic Proverbial Rhetoric*. New York: Peter Lang.

———. 2011. "'It Takes a Village to Change the World': Proverbial Politics and the Ethics of Place." *Journal of American Folklore* 124:4–28.

———. 2014a. *"All Men and Women Are Created Equal": Elizabeth Cady Stanton's and Susan B. Anthony's Proverbial Rhetoric Promoting Women's Rights*. New York: Peter Lang.

———. 2014b. *"Behold the Proverbs of a People": Proverbial Wisdom in Culture, Literature, and Politics*. Jackson: University Press of Mississippi.

———. 2014c. "'The Golden Rule as a Political Imperative': President Barack Obama's Proverbial Worldview." In *"Behold the Proverbs of a People": Proverbial Wisdom in Culture, Literature, and Politics*, edited by Wolfgang Mieder, 172–97. Jackson: University Press of Mississippi.

———. 2014d. "'Keep Your Eyes on the Prize': Congressman John Lewis's Proverbial Odyssey for Civil Rights." *Proverbium* 31:331–93.
———. 2015a. "'All Men Are Created Equal': From Democratic Claim to Proverbial Game." Modern Linguistic and Methodical-and-Didactic Researches series. *Scientific Newsletter*, no. 1: 10–37.
———. 2015b. "'Politics Is Not a Spectator Sport': Proverbs in the Personal and Political Writings of Hillary Rodham Clinton." *Tautosakos Darbai/Folklore Studies* (Vilnius) 50:43–74.
Mieder, Wolfgang, and George B. Bryan. 1995. *The Proverbial Winston S. Churchill: An Index to Proverbs in the Works of Sir Winston Churchill*. Westport, CT: Greenwood Press.
———. 1997. *The Proverbial Harry S. Truman: An Index to Proverbs in the Works of Harry S. Truman*. New York: Peter Lang.
Mieder, Wolfgang, and Alan Dundes. 1981. *The Wisdom of Many: Essays on the Proverb*. New York: Garland Publishing.
Mieder, Wolfgang, Stewart A. Kingsbury, and Kelsie B. Harder. 1992. *A Dictionary of American Proverbs*. New York: Oxford University Press.
Nichols, Ray. 1996. "Maxims, 'Practical Wisdom,' and the Language of Action: Beyond Grand Theory." *Political Theory* 24:687–705.
Paczolay, Gyula. 1997. *European Proverbs in 55 Languages with Equivalents in Arabic, Persian, Sanskrit, Chinese and Japanese*. Veszprém, Hungary: Vesprémi Nyomda.
Raymond, Joseph. 1956. "Tensions in Proverbs: More Light on International Understanding." *Western Folklore* 15:153–58. Also in *The Wisdom of Many: Essays on the Proverb*, edited by Wolfgang Mieder and A. Dundes, 300–308. New York: Garland Publishing, 1981.
Sanders, Bernie. 1997. *Outsider in the House*. With Huck Gutman. New York: Verso. Updated 2015 as *Outsider in the White House*. New York: Verso.
———. 2011. *The Speech: A Historic Filibuster on Corporate Greed and the Decline of the Middle Class*. 2015 edition with a new introduction. New York: Nation Books. All citations are to the 2015 edition.
———. 2015. "Finding Common Ground." In *The Reference Shelf: Representative American Speeches 2014–2015*, edited by H. W. Wilson, 143–48. Amenia, NY: Grey House Publishing. Speech presented at Liberty University, Lynchburg, Virginia, on September 14, 2015.
———. 2016a. *Our Revolution: A Future to Believe In*. New York. St. Martin's Press.
———. 2016b. "Super Tuesday Speech." In *The Reference Shelf: Representative American Speeches 2015–2016*, edited by Betsy Maury, 72–75. Amenia, NY: Grey House Publishing. Speech presented at a Sanders rally, Essex Junction, Vermont, on March 1, 2016.
———. 2017. *Guide to Political Revolution*. New York: Godwin Books (based on Sanders's book *Our Revolution*).
Shapiro, Fred R. 2006. *The Yale Book of Quotations*. New Haven, CT: Yale University Press.
Tasini, Jonathan. 2015. *The Essential Bernie Sanders and His Vision for America*. White River Junction, VT: Chelsea Green Publishing.
Templeton, John Mark. 1997. *Worldwide Laws of Life*. Philadelphia: Templeton Foundation Press.
Titelman, Gregory Y. 1996. *Random House Dictionary of Popular Proverbs and Sayings*. New York: Random House.
Willis, Nathaniel Parker. 1846. *The Complete Works*. New York: J. S. Redfield, Clinton Hall.

9

"M(R)IGHT MAKES R(M)IGHT"

The Sociopolitical History of a Contradictory Proverb Pair

THE RATHER OBVIOUS OBSERVATION THAT PROVERBS ARE CONTRADICTORY has a long history among laypersons and scholars alike. People to this day delight in pointing out that for many proverbs, others can be found that state the opposite wisdom, with such opposing proverb pairs as "absence makes the heart grow fonder" versus "out of sight, out of mind" and "look before you leap" versus "he who hesitates is lost" belonging to the set of frequently cited English examples for this phenomenon. Already in 1616, Nicholas Breton published two small collections of what he called *Crossing of Proverbs* that on just a few pages list debunking reactions to well-known proverbs that include texts that express opposite claims. Other collections followed, including Charles Lamb's "Popular Fallacies" (1850), Dwight Edwards Marvin's "Contradicting Proverbs" (1916, 2:294–321), Rod Evans and Irwin Berent's "Dueling Proverbs" (1993), Ralph Slovenko's "Mixed Messages in Proverbs" (1993), and Mavis Aldridge's "Paradoxical Proverbs" (1997, 87–88). The titles of these popular compilations tell the whole story, so it seems, namely, that proverbs are marked by fallacy, contradiction, and paradox. Apparently, they send mixed messages or duel with each other, leading to the often-heard opinion that proverbs have, in fact, no claim to expressing truth or wisdom (see also Hood 1885, 476–78; Osgood 1985; Richler 2006). The following few examples chosen from these lists at random certainly leave the impression that the two proverbs of each pair cancel each other out.

> Many hands make light work.
> Too many cooks spoil the broth.
>
> Beauty is only skin deep.
> A thing of beauty is a joy forever.

You can't teach an old dog new tricks.
It's never too late to learn.

A little learning is a dangerous thing.
It is better to know something than nothing.

Wisdom comes with age.
There's no fool like an old fool.

Birds of a feather flock together.
Opposites attract.

These few opposing doublets suffice to illustrate that proverbs cannot possibly contain universal truths. After all, they express generalizations about life that are not applicable to every situation. Proverbs are not absolute truths but rather wisdom that mirrors a multitude of experiences and behaviors. It is for this very reason that the adjective *apparent* is of utmost importance in this succinct proverb definition: "Proverbs are concise traditional statements of apparent truths with currency among the folk" (Mieder 2004, 4).

An early but revealing introductory paragraph to yet another list of proverb pairs by an anonymous writer in the *New York Times* of April 29, 1877, makes a similar observation: "Proverbs are never quite true, though they are always plausible. . . . The great trouble with a popular adage, or current phrase of any kind, is, that it is commonly accepted as absolute truth. Hardly any one thinks of examining or questioning it; for has it not already received the approval of thousands, if not generations? It must be sound, especially if it fits our case" (6 [9]). And H. G. Keene, in yet another popular article of a few years later in the *Living Age* magazine of May 24, 1890, continued this train of thought before giving his list of examples:

> Persons must sometimes be puzzled to find that one and the same community is in the habit of using adages which are diametrically opposed to one another. If it were true that "a proverb is the wisdom of many and the wit of one" [Lord John Russell's proverb definition of 1823], we should surely be justified in expecting all accepted proverbs to resemble laws of nature or formulas of mathematics. But we see that this is far from being the case; and no sooner do we think that we have obtained an irrefragable maxim from the crystallization of experience than another, equally authoritative, confronts us with an absolutely opposite direction. (483 [12])

In fact, Keene continues sagaciously toward the end of his article, so appropriately entitled "Conflicts of Experience": "A proverb will usually be merely a compendious expression of some principle, true or false, applicable or non-applicable, as the case may be in which it is employed" (486 [18]; see also Cram 1985; Rogers 1990, 199 [466]; Whaley 1993, 130–31 [559]).

Almost a hundred years later, Nkeonye Otakpor came to the same conclusion: "Proverbs are classifiable but cannot be systematized. Hence they are never deductively valid; neither correct nor incorrect; neither sound nor unsound, but suitable or unsuitable, reasonable or unreasonable, within specific speech contexts" (Otakpor 1987, 267–68). Indeed, proverbs are not absolute laws, with the applicability of their wisdom depending on the context in which they are employed and with what intended purpose. Thus, as linguist David Cram has put it so appropriately, "superficially contradictory proverbs (such as 'Out of sight, out of mind' and 'Absence makes the heart grow fonder') happily coexist within one and the same proverb system" (Cram 1986, 22–23). But speaking of laws, here is a semiscientific law that British critic Richard Boston formulated in his review of the *Oxford Dictionary of English Proverbs* (1970) that hits the proverbial nail on its head: "For every proverb that so confidently asserts its little bit of wisdom, there is usually an equal and opposite proverb that contradicts it" (cited from Dickson 1993, 22 [133–34]).

Turning then to the more scholarly reactions to these contradictory proverb pairs, the predominance of the word *apparent(ly)* should definitely be noted. Thus, in a short section on "The Value of Proverbs as the Expression of Popular Opinion" in his not-at-all-outdated book on *The Influence of Authority in Matters of Opinion* (1849), George Cornewall Lewis makes the following astute observation:

> Proverbs being maxims, in the nature either of observation or of precept, upon human life or conduct, are accredited by the tacit verification which they have undergone in their tradition from one individual and one generation to another. If their truth or soundness had not been recognised by those who used them, and handed them on, they would soon have gone into oblivion.
>
> In general, however, proverbs express only empirical laws of human nature—that is to say, being generalisations from partial experience, they are only true within certain limits, and subject to certain conditions. Before, therefore, a popular proverb can be safely used for philosophical purposes as evidence of a general truth, it must undergo a process of analysis; it must be limited according to mental tendencies which it involves, and the circumstances in which it is applicable. In this manner, proverbs which are apparently contradictory may be reconciled, and the partial truth which they contain will be extracted and rendered profitable. (178–79)

It is a shame that this statement has hitherto not received any notice by paremiologists. Of course, F. Edward Hulme, in his still-useful survey

Proverb Lore (1902), said it shorter and simpler as well: "Proverbial wisdom, it must be borne in mind, deals sometimes with only one aspect of a truth. The necessary brevity often makes the teaching one-sided, as the various limitations and exceptions that may be necessary to a complete statement of a truth are perforce left and unsaid. One proverb therefore is often in direct contradiction to another, and yet each may be equally true" (9–10). It is, however, quite surprising that Archer Taylor in his seminal book *The Proverb* (1931) pushed the intriguing matter of contradictory proverb pairs aside, stating that "a more detailed illustration of such contradictions is unnecessary, and the labor of assembling them may satisfy antiquarian curiosity, but it is not likely to yield useful results" (169). He is, of course, correct in pointing out that collections of such doublets are not necessary, since they would simply exemplify the obvious.

Be that as it may, the significant observation that the great literary scholar Kenneth Burke made ten years later in a book chapter on "Literature [actually Proverbs] as Equipment for Living" (1941) received much attention and has had an immeasurable influence on modern proverb scholarship. Not only did he formulate an extremely important functional and contextual definition of proverbs, but he also succeeded in explaining the phenomenon of proverbial doublets.

> Proverbs are *strategies* for dealing with *situations*. In so far as situations are typical and recurrent in a given social structure, people develop names for them and strategies for handling them. Another name for strategies might be *attitudes*.
>
> People have often commented on the fact that there are *contrary* proverbs. But I believe that the above approach to proverbs suggests a necessary modification of that comment. The apparent contradictions depend upon differences in *attitude*, involving a correspondingly different choice of *strategy*. Consider, for instance, the *apparently* opposite pair: "Repentance comes too late" and "Never too late to mend." The first is admonitory. It says in effect: "You'd better look out, or you'll get yourself too far into this business." The second is consolatory, saying in effect: "Buck up, old man, you can still pull out of this." (256)

More modern scholarship on this issue has picked up on Burke's viewpoint, with Kwesi Yankah answering the titular question of his informed article "Do Proverbs Contradict?" (1984) with a definite "no." Proverbs in collections or paired up without any rhetorical context can be shown to contradict, but "the whole idea of proverbs in opposition seems to be merely a scholarly construct [and also a playful exercise by laypersons], of little or no relevance in the free flow of discourse" (16–17 [139]). Proverbs in contextual usage do not contradict, unless, of course, two speakers are actually engaged in a proverb duel, as they can be found for example in cases of oral sparring in legal proceedings in Africa or in literary dialogues as between Don Quixote and Sancho Panza (see Yankah 1989, 235–43; Mieder 2006, 25–28).

There are also the comments that "a proverb's truth and quality are essentially unrelated. A good proverb need not be generally true, nor will any truth qualify as a good proverb, unless it contains a 'memorable' idea or expression" (Teigen 1986, 44), and "the truthfulness of proverbs depends on the context in which they are placed, or the specific phenomena to which they refer" (Furnham 1987, 51). To repeat, one thing is for certain: "a book of proverbs [and proverbs as such], constituted of opposites, forms as it were the master drama of human relations, in which 'Nothing is certain but uncertainty itself.' . . . It turns out that contradiction isn't the product of conflicting proverbs; contradiction is a product of human experience, in which conflict is inevitable and resilience indispensable. A book of proverbs is like a pharmacy where all varieties of medicine are stored. But medicines that serve as cures for one disease might kill if taken for another" (States 2001, 109–10). It is then high time that contradictory proverbs are seen as proof that individual proverbs are not absolute truths and that they contain only limited wisdom.

> All that such proverb pairs show is that proverbs are but apparent truths about experiences and that each proverb does not have universal applicability. In special situations, let's say where the shoe (the proverb) fits, proverbs do express wisdom of some sort as well as seeming truths. What is of importance is that proverbs are *not* universals. . . . Since proverbs reflect human experiences of all types, they are bound to contradict each other just as life is made up of a multitude of contradictions. Used in a very particular context any proverb will express some short wisdom of sorts that comments or reflects on a given situation, even though the truth of it could be put into question when looked at from a larger philosophical framework. Proverbs are context-bound, and so is their wisdom, no matter how minute that kernel of truth might be (Mieder 1993, 25–26; see also Paczolay 1996, 284–85)

Put another way, "the problem of contradictory proverbs exists primarily because people ignore their social context. If one deals with proverbs only as a concept of a cultural fact or truism, contradictions are easily found in any proverb repertoire. In contextual usage, however, proverbs function effectively as social strategies. Proverbs in normal discourse are not contradictory at all, and they usually make perfect sense to the speaker or listener. After all, people don't normally speak in proverb pairs" (Mieder 2004, 134).

As mentioned, numerous examples of such contradictory proverb pairs have been cited in popular newspaper and magazine articles or in scholarly publications. And yet, one of the truly fascinating doublets has not appeared in any of these compilations or discussions, namely the truly unique proverb pair "might makes right" and "right makes might," with each proverb consisting of merely three words and the contradiction coming about by only changing the order of the two nouns while maintaining the same verb. The multitude of other examples is not based on proverbs with the same structure and same words, with the individual texts usually also having quite different metaphors. Add to this that *might* and *right* are two fundamental aspects of sociopolitical interaction, and it should not be surprising that this proverb pair has a special history in the world of English proverbs.

As is often the case with such basic matters of life, they have long been summarized into sententious remarks or proverbs in classical antiquity before entering the vernacular languages, to wit the following sample from Greek and Roman sources (Benham 1926, 576a; Manser 2002, 160; Pickering 1997, 181; Ramage 1872; Shapiro 2006, 616; Speake 2008, 210; Stevenson 1948, 1,572; Wilson 1970, 530).

> I affirm that might is right, justice the interest of the stronger.
> (Plato, *The Republic*, c. 375 BC)
>
> Right is overcome by might *(Vi verum vincitur)*.
> (Plautus, *Amphitruo*, c. 200 BC)
>
> Right gives way to force, and justice lies conquered beneath the aggressive sword *(Cedit viribus aequum, victaque pugnaci iura sub ense iacent)*.
> (Ovid, *Tristia*, c. AD 10)
>
> Might was the measure of right *(Mensuraque iuris vis erat)*.
> (Lucan, *Pharsalia*, c. AD 60)
>
> Right is in might *(Ius est in armis)*.
> (Seneca, *Hercules Furens*, c. AD 60)

It should be noted, however, that these references do not include the proverbial claim that "right makes might," for even Seneca's statement "Right is in might" does in fact say that "might makes right." The reversal of this original proverb to the idea that it is "right"—in the meaning of lawful or simply appropriate behavior—that makes "might" took time, but both proverbs do appear in European languages. This is not the place to trace these polyglot developments. Suffice it to point out that in German, the proverb variants "Gewalt geht vor Recht" (force goes before right) and "Macht geht vor Recht" (might goes before right) were well established by the early sixteenth century (Wander 1867–80, 1:1,644, nos. 28–29; 3:306, no. 18), with the reversal of "Recht geht vor Gewalt" and "Recht geht vor Macht" gaining currency considerably later (Wander 1867–80: 3:1,528–29, nos. 202–3; see also Benham 1926, 810b).

In the English tradition of both proverbs, it is also "might makes right" that takes the lead regarding historical references. Due to the superb work of Anglo-American paremiographers (see the bibliography), it can be stated that the first recorded instance stems from c. 1311—and not from c. 1325–30, as claimed by others—stating in Middle English that in a land where might rules, there is no place for law (right). In fact, it stems from the lyrics of a political song "On the King's [Edward II] Breaking His Confirmation of Magna Charta" (Wright 1839, 253; see the first text below). But here then is a paremiographical history of this widespread proverb about power politics (Apperson 1929, 416; Benham 1926, 810b; Mieder, Kingsbury, and Harder 1992, 410; Shapiro 2006, 616; Speake 2008, 210; Stevenson 1948, 1,572; Taylor and Whiting 1958, 242; Tilley 1950, 460; Titelman 1996, 232; Whiting 1968, 401; Whiting 1977, 288; Whiting 1989, 409; Wilson 1970, 530–31).

> 1311: For might is riht, / Liht is night, / And fiht is fliht. / For miht is riht, the lond is laweles; / For niht is liht, the lond is loreless; / For fiht is fliht, the lond is nameless.
>
> 1393: For wher that such on[e] is of myht, His will shall stonde in stede of riht.
>
> 1400: Mithgh is Rithgh; lithgh is nithgh; Fithgh is flithgh.
>
> 1475: But strength maykyth right after his owne opynyoun.
>
> 1546: We see many times, might overcometh right.
>
> 1555: Where althynge is there ryght is lost by myght.
>
> 1563: And an olde saying it is, that most tymes myght, Force, strength, power, and colorable subtlete Dothe appresse, debare, ouercum and defeate ryght.
>
> 1573: Considering that the law was now in there [*sic*] own hands, and miht had alreddi overcumd riht.
>
> 1578: I see by proofe, that true the pouerbe is, Myght maisters right.
>
> 1591: Might overcomes right.
>
> 1598: Might overgangs right.
>
> 1616: Might ouerruleth right.

1639: Might overcomes right.

1641: Might, often times overcomes right.

1659: When might overcomes right, the weakest goes to the wall.

1670: Might overcomes right.

1700: For ofttimes might overcomes right, according to the proverb.

1788: Might will overcome right.

1798: Might will overcome Right.

1818: The false maxim that might is right.

1823: Might often makes right here.

1850: But might makes right.

1876: The doctrine "Might makes right" is not popular here.

1933: Might was still right.

1962: The strong prevailed over the weak: Might made right.

1992: Might makes right.

The reference from 1563, albeit cited here without context, indicates by a series of synonyms for "might" that the proverb usually refers to forceful, powerful, unlawful, deceptive, manipulative, and illegitimate might that has little to do with right. This is also strongly suggested by the text from 1818 where the proverb is declared to be false. And yet, it should be pointed out that there is, of course, such a thing as legitimate might, as for example by the majority in a democracy. In other words, there may well be situations in which the proverb is employed in a positive way. But before turning to a series of contextualized examples, here is a list of book and film titles, to continue the minimalistic survey, with the first title commenting on the fallacious power politics of imperial Germany and other titles connecting the proverb with waging wars.

> 1918: Edmonds, Richard H. *Germany, the Super-Fiend: A Nation Gone Mad in Its Lust for Power and World Dominion: A Discussion of the Fallacious Doctrine that "Might Makes Right" and "As the State Can Do No Wrong, if the State Orders Crimes Committed, It Ceases to Be a Crime."* Baltimore: Manufacturers Record Publisher.
>
> 1975: Egbert, Allen L., and Michael H. Luque. *Might Makes Right Among Alaska's Brown Bears.* Washington, DC: National Geographic.

1988: Volk, Steven Saul. *Might Makes Right: US Foreign Policy and International Law in Central America*. Cincinnati: American Historical Association.

2002: Film Media Group. *In the Name of the State: When Might Makes Right*. Princeton, NJ: Films for the Humanities & Sciences.

2005: Gasher, Mike. *Might Makes Right: News Reportage as Discursive Weapon in the War in Iraq*. Lanham, MD: Rowman & Littlefield.

2006: Friday, Karl. *Might Makes Right: Just War and Just Warfare in Early Medieval Japan*. London: Routledge.

2008: Leon, Andrew Michael. *Might Makes Right: The Melian Genocide and the Escalation of Violence During the Peloponnesian War*. Master's thesis, San Diego State University.

2011: Film Media Group. *The Indian Wars: Might Makes Right*. Princeton, NJ: Films for the Humanities & Sciences.

Naturally, more insight into the ambiguous semantics of the proverb "might makes right" can be garnered by looking at least at a few contextualized references over time. At times, authors make a point that they are citing a proverb or a maxim, adding traditional authority to their observation that power politics from wars of all types to slavery and other injustices can unfortunately be summarized under that old truism that "might makes right."

> 1616: It is an old country proverb that might overcomes right; a weak title that wears a strong sword, commonly prevails against a strong title that wears but a weak one. (Sir Walter Raleigh, "The Prerogative of Parliaments," 1829, 8:172)
>
> 1790: Why—that *the Weakest goes to the Wall*—The law is so expensive, and its subterfuges so many, that those who have not sufficient money to support, perhaps a *just* cause, must give it up to another, whose fortune will enable him even to uphold a *bad* one; for *Might* too often *overcomes Right*. To engage, therefore, in litigation under such circumstances, is only *Kicking against the Pricks*, and injuring ourselves. (John Trusler 1790, 78)
>
> 1823: But for my part, although I am a poor man, I can love without the venison [of a shot deer], but I don't love to give up my lawful dues in a free country. Though, for the matter of that, might often makes right here, as well as in the old country, for what I can see. (James Fenimore Cooper 1841, 18)
>
> 1836: These important fruits [of fairness] will not at present be admitted—but it does not less follow that they are true. This is the age of iron, in which might has become right—but the time will come when these truths will be admitted, and your father's name will be more celebrated than that of any philosopher of ancient days. (Captain Marryat 1907, 31)

1843: I believe slavery to be an unrighteous institution, based on the false maxim that Might makes Right. (Henry Wadsworth Longfellow, letter of January 4, 1843, to George Lunt 1891, 2:8)

1846: But now, instead of discussion and argument, brute force rises up to the rescue of discomfited error, and crushes truth and right into the dust. "Might makes right," and hoary folly totters on her mad career escorted by armies and navies. . . . It is practically a war of invasion and conquest, such as has been waged from time immemorial under the barbarous, tyrannical assumption that "might makes right." It puts the nation [United States] into the same category and reduces it to the same plane with the dynasties of the old world. (Adin Ballou 1910, 114, 275)

1846: That often Might has vanquished Right,
   Is now a thrice-told tale.
   But there's a word above the sword
   Shall make the Right prevail.
   'Tis they who think before they strike,
   And strike for Right alone,
   Make good their claim to deathless fame,
   And always hold their own.
   (Travelling Bachelor, "Hold Your Own!"; Sheehan 1876, 22–23)

1854: Nothing is more true than that the whole moral and social atmosphere of Slavery is unfavorable to the growth of common honesty. The cornerstone of its moral is the maxim that "might makes right." (Frederick Douglass, Blassingame 1985–92: 2:482, see Mieder 2001, 361)

1866: The lawyers have always some glaring exceptions to their statements of public equity, some reserves of sovereignty, tantamount to the Rob Roy rule that might makes right. America should affirm & establish that in no instance should the guns go in advance of the perfect right. (Ralph Waldo Emerson, journal entry; Porte 1982, 536)

1891: Society at large, based on the principle that might makes right has in a measure excluded women from the profitable industries of the world, and where she has gained a foothold her labor is at a discount. Man occupies the ground and holds the key to the situation. (Elizabeth Cady Stanton; Gordon 1997–2013, 5:366)

1958: "There is nothing," said the monarch, "except the power which you pretend to seek; power to grind and power to digest, power to seek and power to find, power to await and power to claim, all power and pitilessness springing from the nape of the neck. . . . Love is a trick played on us by the forces of evolution. Pleasure is the bait laid down by the same. There is only power. Power is of the individual mind, but the mind's power is not enough. Power of the body decides everything in the end, and only Might is Right." (T. H. White 1958, 47–48)

1963: In a real sense, Waterloo symbolizes the doom of every Napoleon and is an eternal reminder to a generation drunk with military power that in the long run of history might does not make right and power of the sword cannot conquer the power of the spirit. (Martin Luther King Jr. 1963, 104; see Mieder 2010, 429–30)

1979: By adult examples, pupils are being taught such evil doctrines as "Might is right." (*The Guardian*, May 17, 1979, 24)

2001: As for the House of Lords, what is power if you cannot give your friends their heart's desire, a title and a club? All this means is that in politics, as in war, might is right. (*The Times*, November 7, 2001, 16.)

Martin Luther King Jr., the heroic champion of the nonviolent movement for civil rights in the United States, was absolutely right in stating that "might does not make right" in the struggle for universal equality before the law. Somewhat surprisingly, King, as the masterful user of proverbs and proverbial expressions in his sermonically inspired rhetoric, did not cite the contradictory proverb "right makes might," even though it would have been a fitting slogan for his liberating struggle (see Mieder 2010). Of course, he also did not employ the Middle English proverb variant "right makes the feeble (man) wight (strong)" that seems not to have survived in English folk speech beyond the sixteenth century or so. Here are three references (Whiting 1968, 488):

1375: And rycht mayss oft the feble wycht.

1420: And richt oft makis the febil wicht.

1450: I have the right and he the wrong, Right maketh a feble man strong.

It might well be that the shorter and more powerful "right makes might" helped to replace this proverb variant. But be that as it may, it is also true that the proverb "right makes might" never achieved the frequency of occurrence that its antipode did. In fact, its paremiographical history is rather sparse, to say the least (Mieder, Kingsbury, and Harder 1992, 510; Pickering 1997, 181; Ridout and Witting 1967, 119; Shapiro 2006, 461; Stevenson 1948, 1,572; Taylor and Whiting 1958, 307; Tilley 1950, 460; Titelman 1996, 232; Wilson 1970, 530).

1598: O God, that right should thus overcome might!
    Well, of sufferance comes ease.

1845: Right is stronger than might.

1860: Let us have faith that right makes might.

1967: Right makes might.

1992: Right makes might.

One might well be inclined to draw the conclusion from this dearth of references that the proverb is of little consequence, since most paremiographers refer only to the first text due to Shakespeare's authorship (2 *Henry IV*, V, iv, 24–25). But before presenting several revealing additional references in their context, a small list of book titles featuring the proverb (often as a subtitle) should be added:

> 1884: Optic, Oliver. *Making a Man of Himself, or, Right Makes Might*. Boston: Lothrop, Lee & Shepard.
>
> 1897: Smith, J. Burritt. *Barriers Broken, or, Right Makes Might*. Madison, WI: Busy World Publishing.
>
> 1900: Standish, Burt L. *Frank Merriwell's Power, or, Right Makes Might*. New York: Street & Smith.
>
> 1905: Taylor, Edward C. *Ted Strong's Close Call, or: Right Makes Might*. New York: Street & Smith.
>
> 1956: Begin, Menachem. *Right Makes Might: Address Before the XXIV Zionist Congress, Jerusalem*. Jerusalem: World Union Herut-Hatzohar.
>
> 1998: Gompert, David C. *Right Makes Might: Freedom and Power in the Information Age*. New York: Foreign Policy Association.
>
> 2007: Gaulden, Dorothea E., and Sharon Y. Brown. *Right Makes Might: Reviving Ethics to Improve Your Business*. Austin, TX: Bridgeway Books.

Clearly then, the proverb "right makes might" caught on in the nineteenth century, with William Shakespeare's line for once most likely having had very little if any influence on its dissemination. The honor of having made this proverb first well known in the United States and then throughout the "Englishes" of the world belongs to none other than Abraham Lincoln. In fact, while a Google search (conducted on July 28, 2013) for the proverb "might makes right" yielded 67,900 highly differentiated texts, the result for "right makes might" was but 15,500 items, less than a quarter of the former. It must be noted, an estimated half refer to a statement by Lincoln. Little wonder, then, that at least in the United States, the proverb has been attached to Lincoln, who, to be sure, did not originate it, as will become abundantly clear in the ensuing discussion of contextualized references that include the proverb pair and not just one of the two proverbs.

But what did Lincoln actually say and when? In his celebrated Cooper Union speech held on February 27, 1860, in New York City, Lincoln outlined in very clear and logical terms his solid commitment to maintaining the American Union and to keeping slavery from spreading throughout the country. As he moved toward the final two paragraphs of his speech, the president, with the threat of Civil War before him, rose to an unforgettable oratorical height.

> Can we . . . allow it [slavery] to spread into the National Territories, and to overrun us here in these Free States? If our sense of duty forbids this, then let us stand by our duty, fearlessly and effectively. Let us be diverted by none of those sophistical contrivances wherewith we are so industriously plied and belabored—contrivances such as groping for some middle ground between the right and the wrong, vain as the search for a man who should be neither a living man nor a dead man—such as a policy of "don't care" on a question about which all true men do care . . .
> Neither let us be slandered from our duty by false accusations against us, nor frightened from it by menaces of destruction to the Government nor of dungeons to ourselves. *Let us have faith that right makes might, and in that faith, let us, to the end, dare to do our duty as we understand it.* (Basler 1953, 3:550; see Mieder 2000, 25–27; 2004, 183–85)

It is not surprising that Lincoln, this humble, compassionate, and nonviolent public servant, did not use the proverb "might makes right" in his speeches and writings and that he instead reformulated it to "right makes might" to suit his rhetorical and political purpose. Because it was known that he was an avid reader of Shakespeare, he might have had the Bard's sententious remark in mind, but there is also the possibility that he knew the proverb from oral tradition. If he did not spontaneously come up with this statement on his own, he might also have been influenced by a powerful essay called "The Destiny of the People of Color" (1843, given as a lecture in January 1841) by James McCune Smith (1813–1865), an African American intellectual and abolitionist and clearly Lincoln's contemporary. There is a very good chance that Lincoln had read the following paragraph and that he recalled it when preparing his famed Cooper Union lecture: "But in overcoming the Institution of Slavery, we must by our conduct confute the doctrines on which it is based. One of these doctrines are, that 'Might makes Right': because men have the power, therefore, they have the right to keep other men enslaved.... We are not in possession of physical superiority: yet we must overturn the doctrine 'might makes right,' and we can only do so by demonstrating that 'right makes might'" (Stauffer 2006, 52).

This statement has hitherto not been mentioned by scholars who have carefully analyzed Lincoln's Cooper Union speech (for references, see Mieder 2000, 26–27, notes 59–62), but they have also not referred to the important fact that Abraham Lincoln liked what he had said so much that he repeated the proverb in only very slightly altered contexts in four speeches about a week later (Mieder 2000, 169):

> None of these things should move or intimidate us; but having faith that right makes might, let us to the end, dare to do our duty. (March 2, 1860; Basler 1953, 3:554)

> Let us not be slandered from our duties, or intimidated from preserving our dignity and our rights by any menace; but let us have faith that Right, Eternal Right makes might, and as we understand our duty, so do it! (March 5, 1860; Basler 1953, 4:13)

> Let us not be slandered or intimidated to turn from our duty. Eternal right makes might—as we understand our duty, let us do it! (March 5, 1860; Basler 1953, 4:13)

> Let us have faith that right makes might; and in that faith, let us, to the end, dare to do our duty, as we understand it. (March 6, 1860; Basler 1953, 4:30; identical with his original formulation)

Such repeated use by President Lincoln during a time of crisis must have helped to popularize the proverb "right makes might." But it must be stressed that the following remark can at best be considered to have been attributed to Lincoln: "It has been said of the world's history hitherto that might is (makes) right. It is for us and for our time to reverse the maxim, and to say that right makes might" (Ridout and Witting 1967, 119; Ayres 1992, 130). As far as can be ascertained conclusively, Abraham Lincoln never cited the proverb pair in one statement!

But whether Lincoln was instrumental in making the proverb "right makes might" better known or not, there is no doubt that it continues to compete with the more frequently used "might makes right" in more recent times. For example, there is a humorous postcard showing a large man picking on a smaller one with the caption "Right makes might if you are the biggest" (c. 1900). And there is also the song "Right Makes Might" (1903), written by John Jerome Rooney, with music by Frank Damrosch, that was sung by schoolchildren at the 250th-anniversary celebration of the founding of New York City:

"Right Makes Might"

...

Chorus:
Oh, yes, the city wall is strong, and proud our city's name;
Our lives protect New York from wrong, our deeds defend her fame.

III
But city walls are strong in vain, and wealth itself is poor,
If men seek not a nobler gain in manly hearts secure.
The flag above, with fearless hearts, we'll dare to do the right,
We'll do our great, our humble parts, and right will make the might.
(Anonymous 1903, 26, the entire song text)

Below are a few more modern references, including two from American presidents who most likely had Lincoln's famous words in mind. In the first text, President Kennedy adds a Bible proverb to his interesting variation of the proverb "right makes might," in view of the politics of the Cold War:

> 1961: And while we believe not only in the force of arms but in the force of right and reason, we have learned that reason does not always appeal to unreasonable men—that it is not always true that "a soft answer turneth away wrath" [Proverbs 15:1]—and that right does not always make might. In short, we must face problems which do not lend themselves to easy or quick or permanent solutions. And we must face the fact that the United States is neither omnipotent or omniscient. (John F. Kennedy, November 16, 1961; Kennedy 1962, 725–26)

> 1977: Our hearts and souls and reason have been, in every sense, the most important products of our own evolution. This implies that ultimately, for man, it is true that *right makes might*. (Hermann Joseph Muller 1973, 147–48)

> 1982: For a proper historian of our time, there was only one overtowering beginning—the Year of Victory, 1945. All things flowed from that victory. . . . First, the sense of power which had convinced a peaceful nation that its armed force could and should forever police and reorder the world. Second, the seductive belief that in any contest between good and evil, good always triumphs. We, our soldiers, had proved that Right makes Might. (Theodore White 1982, 3–4)

> 1984: The judicial system in one sense is an attempt to ensure that "right is might" by putting the power of the state behind aggrieved individuals who are suing others for compensation. (Anthony A. D'Amato 1984, 56)

1988: Gerald Ford was not a Lincoln or a Washington or a Roosevelt or a Truman or an Eisenhower. He was and is a regular guy—decent, honest, hardworking, God-fearing, patriotic, and proud American who really believed such shibboleths as "right makes might" and "my country, right or wrong." (Robert T. Hartman; Thompson 1988, 92)

2007: My journey as a freedom lawyer started with naive beliefs that "right makes might," that courts sought only truths, and all judges strove for justice. As I fought for my clients' various rights, I gradually abandoned my King Arthur fantasies for more realistic views. I augmented swords and lances with modern advocacy tools. (Arthur W. Campbell 2007, xv)

2009: America—we are passing through a time of great trial. And the message that we send in the midst of these storms must be clear: that our cause is just, our resolve unwavering. We will go forward with the confidence that right makes might, and with the commitment to forge an America that is safer, a world that is more secure, and a future that represents not the deepest of fears but the highest of hopes. (Obama 2009; see Mieder 2009)

It is hard to believe that President Barack Obama, for whom Abraham Lincoln is a personal hero, did not have Lincoln's "let us have faith that right makes might" in mind when formulating his peroration.

Having thus presented a survey of the individual proverbs "might makes right" and "right makes might" that form a special contradictory proverb pair, the time has come to present a few telling references where both proverbs appear together to illustrate opposite points of view. Here then is a reference in Middle English from 1381, establishing the fact that the proverb pair "Myght goth before ryght" and "Ryght goth before myght" goes back to at least the fourteenth century: "With ryght and with myght, with skyl and with wylle, lat myght helpe ryght, and skyl go before wille and ryght before myght, than goth oure mylne [mill] aryght. And if myght go before ryght, and wylle before skylle; than is oure mylne mys adyght" (Whiting 1968, 401).

The proverbial doublet reappears in an epigram by Robert Hayman in 1628, perhaps also having in mind that there needs to be some give and take between these two extreme points of view and most likely implying also that it is the context that determines which proverb is suitable at a certain moment:

1628: Might overcomes Right. and Right masters Might,
   Yet change one letter, Right makes Might, Might, Right.
   (Hayman 1628, 13)

On a simplistic and perhaps punning level, Hayman points out that just one letter needs to be changed in order to turn these proverbs into their opposites. But even if this is of considerable linguistic interest, the fact that the semantics of the two proverbs are, of course, quite different makes this proverb pair very interesting to this day. There is even the following hair-splitting analysis, trying to argue that the proverb pair is actually not contradictory at all but rather merely the converse of each other.

> 1901: To say that *Right makes* (= implies) *Might* is not in the least to put the contrary of *Might makes* (= implies) *Right*: it is merely the verbal converse, and amounts to saying the very same thing over again; for if all Might is made by Right, and if Right always makes Might, then Might and Right are inseparable, and you cannot have Might without Right, which is exactly what is stated in the phrase *Might makes Right*. The real contrary to that phrase would just be, Might *does not* make Right; you have Might without Right, or Right without Might. (John M. Robertson 1901, 19)

This would be true if the two proverbs were linked by the verb *is*, but the verb *makes* of the proverbs does not just mean *implies* but also *leads to, results in,* and *brings about*. The proverbs don't suggest an equational relationship but rather a developmental relationship. Below are several modern intertextual references that make it abundantly clear that the two proverbs are generally interpreted as two contrary pieces of wisdom. From 1913: "I had supposed that we had advanced along the highways of progress and civilization, until we had finally reached the enlightened state where 'Right Makes Might,' but Colonel [Theodore] Roosevelt wants to carry us back to the barbaric days when the maxim was 'Might Makes Right,' back to the days of the inquisition, the thumb-screw, the instruments of torture and the fagot's flame! Roosevelt calls himself a Progressive. He is progressing more rapidly than the crab, and in the same direction!" (Charles Henry Betts 1913, 89).

Speaking of former presidents, Harry S. Truman also made remarkable employment of the proverb pair to underscore the vast difference between tyrannical and democratic governments. The following paragraph is part of the conclusion to his "Address to the United Nations Conference" on April 25, 1945, in San Francisco. It is Truman's sincere call for a peaceful world at the end of the Second World War.

> 1945: The essence of our problem here [at San Francisco] is to provide sensible machinery for the settlement of disputes among nations. Without this, peace cannot exist. We can no longer permit any nation, or group of nations, to attempt to settle their arguments with bombs and bayonets.
>
> If we continue to abide by such decisions, we will be forced to accept the fundamental concept of our enemies, namely, that "Might makes right." To deny this premise, and we most certainly do deny it, we are obliged to provide the necessary means to refute it. Words are not enough.

> We must, once and for all, reverse the order, and prove by our acts conclusively, that Right Has Might.
> If we do not want to die together in war, we must learn to live together in peace.
> With firm faith in our hearts, to sustain us along the hard road to victory, we will find our way to a secure peace, for the ultimate benefit of all humanity. (Truman 1961, 23; Mieder and Bryan 1997, 42–43)

President Truman obviously was not aware of the fact that the proverb "right makes might" goes back to the fourteenth century and that President Lincoln had used it repeatedly in 1860. He clearly thought that he had come up with his very own antiproverb (Litovkina and Mieder 2006).

Below is a deep philosophical statement from approximately 1950 about the human condition, written by German writer Hermann Broch, cited in English translation in Hannah Arendt's important book, *Men in Dark Times* (1968).

> 1950: The compass card whose function it is to show from which of the four corners of the world the wind of history is blowing; with its inscription "Right Makes Might" points [pointing] toward Paradise, with "Might Makes Wrong" toward Purgatory, with "Wrong Makes Might" toward Hell, but with "Might Makes Right" toward ordinary life on earth; and since again and again what threatens to roar over humanity is the devil's tempest, man usually rests modestly content with the earthly "Might Makes Right," though hoping for the paradisiacal breezes—when there would no longer be any death penalty on all the vast orb of earth—but knowing nevertheless that the miracle will not come unless it is made to come. The miracle of "Right Makes Might" requires first and foremost that Right shall be provided with Might. (Hermann Broch; cited from Arendt 1968, 149–50)

Broch is obviously correct in stating that a world where "right is might" would be paradisiacal, and since he refers to the death penalty falling by the wayside in a more perfect world, he must be including justice in his idea of *right*. This interpretation agrees with Paul Eidelberg's comments on power in the sociopolitical realm, arguing once again for siding with "right is might" over "might is right": "All other things being equal, therefore, power has a claim to rule or to dispense justice. Not that might makes right. It would be truer to say that right makes might. But the truth is complex. Justice without power is less than justice; power without justice is less than powerful" (Eidelberg 1976, 58).

It should be noted, certainly, that Eidelberg does not speak of "absolute" power, realizing that matters are often relative in life. This can also be seen from Richard Brian Miller's comments on war and ethics: "Among men, might not only makes right, but the conviction of being right makes might, and it is impossible to reduce such a conviction to an emotional reaction. However much the power realists may regret the fact, it remains true that in war men do not fight simply for their own interests but make great sacrifices for distant values, for their country, or Poland, or 'democracy,' or 'the new order,' or 'the Four Freedoms'" (Miller 1992, 64).

Finally then, this last intertextual reference with the contradictory proverb pair leads to the question of morality that most assuredly should not be based on extreme interpretations of either proverb. Peter Kreeft in his book *Socrates Meets Kant* (2009) says as much in this paragraph: "Might does not make right for God any more than for man. In morality, right makes might; might does not make right. And the might that right makes is purely moral might, the power to bind the conscience, not the body or the feelings and fears, including the fear of punishment" (Kreeft 2009, 280).

In sum, this historical survey of the sociopolitical significance of the contradictory proverb pair "might makes right" and "right makes might" has shown that both proverbs are no absolute truths and that even their apparent truth value must be taken with a proverbial grain of salt. And yet, applied to certain contexts, they become relevant statements that express the multifaceted human condition. Neither proverb is particularly metaphorical, but they bring to mind the proverbial metaphor "big fish eat little fish" that has survived as a folk proverb since classical times. It certainly could be equated with the proverb "might makes right," with the powerful big fish swallowing up the little ones. But, of course, the reversal is also true in that one small fish organizes all the little fish into one large and powerful "solidarity" fish. They are doubtless justified in doing this, since they are clearly in the "right" to defend themselves against the stronger fish. But what starts as rightful collective action or "right makes might" soon becomes a new power play, for the "wonderful" solidarity fish now pursues the large fish that are no longer a threat. Clearly what is needed is for the large fish and the solidarity fish to get along by calling a truce and thus an end to their uncontrolled power play (Mieder 1987, 2003). The same is true for the struggle between the "might/right" proverb pair. It is impossible to separate might and right completely, since they are interdependent. A check and balance are necessary with both proverbs that reflect the trials and tribulations of the human condition so well. Proverbs like "nothing in excess" and "everything in moderation" come to mind, and there is, of course, also the golden mean of ethical, humane, and fair play. But no matter what, the proverb pair "might makes right" and "right makes might" mirror the dialectics of life, making them, if not absolute, then most certainly apparent truths.

References

This chapter was first published in *Proceedings of the Seventh Interdisciplinary Colloquium on Proverbs, 3rd to 10th November 2013, at Tavira, Portugal*. Edited by Rui J. B. Soares and Outi Lauhakanga, 107–31. Tavira: Tipografia Tavirense, 2014.

Aldridge, Mavis. 1997. *Critical Thinking: Thinking with Proverbs; Reasoning with Analogies*. Dubuque, IA: Kendall/Hunt Publishing.
Anonymous. 1877. "Influence of Proverbs." *New York Times*, April 29, 6. Also in *"Gold Nuggets or Fool's Gold?" Magazine and Newspaper Articles on the (Ir)relevance of Proverbs and Proverbial Phrases*, edited by Wolfgang Mieder and Janet Sobieski, 9–11. Burlington: University of Vermont, 2006.
Anonymous. 1903. "Song for City's Birthday. Stanzas Chosen for School Children to Sing at Two Hundred Fiftieth Anniversary Celebration." *New York Times*, May 10, 26.
Apperson, G. L. 1929. *English Proverbs and Proverbial Phrases: A Historical Dictionary*. London: J. M. Dent.
Arendt, Hannah. 1968. *Men in Dark Times*. New York: Harcourt, Brace & World.
Ayres, Alex, ed. 1992. *The Wit and Wisdom of Abraham Lincoln*. New York: Meridian.
Ballou, Adin. 1910. *Christian Non-Resistance in All Its Important Bearings*. Philadelphia: Philadelphia Universal Peace Union.
Basler, Roy, ed. 1953. *The Collected Works of Abraham Lincoln*. 8 vols. New Brunswick, NJ: Rutgers University Press.
Benham, W. Gurney. 1926. *Putnam's Complete Book of Quotations, Proverbs, and Household Words*. New York: G. P. Putnam's Sons.
Betts, Charles Henry. 1913. *The Naked Truth: Vital Issues Before the Country Clearly Analyzed and Discussed*. Lyons, NY: Lyons Republican Company.
Blassingame, John, ed. 1985–92. *The Frederick Douglass Papers*. 5 vols. New Haven, CT: Yale University Press.
Breton, Nicholas. 1616. *Crossing of Proverbs: Crosse-Answers and Crosse-Humours*. 2 parts. London: John Wright.
Burke, Kenneth. 1941. "Literature [Proverbs] as Equipment for Living." In *The Philosophy of Literary Form: Studies in Symbolic Action*, edited by Kenneth Burke, 253–62. Baton Rouge: Louisiana University Press.
Campbell, Arthur W. 2007. *Trial & Error: The Education of a Freedom Lawyer: Prose Poems*. Madera, CA: Poetic Matrix Press.
Cooper, James Fenimore. 1841. *The Pioneers, or The Sources of the Susquehanna: A Descriptive Tale*. 2 vols. Philadelphia: Lea & Blanchard.
Cram, David. 1985. "A Note on the Logic of Proverbs." *Proverbium* 2:271–72.
———. 1986. "Argumentum ad lunam: On the Folk Fallacy and the Nature of the Proverb." *Proverbium* 3:9–31.
D'Amato, Anthony A. 1984. *Jurisprudence: A Descriptive and Normative Analysis of Law*. Boston: Nijhoff.
Dickson, Paul. 1993. "The Proverbial Dilemma." *Living* (Summer): 21–25. Also in *"Gold Nuggets or Fool's Gold?" Magazine and Newspaper Articles on the (Ir)relevance of Proverbs and Proverbial Phrases*, edited by Wolfgang Mieder and Janet Sobieski, 132–38. Burlington: University of Vermont, 2006.
Eidelberg, Paul. 1976. *On the Silence of the Declaration of Independence*. Amherst: University of Massachusetts Press.

Evans, Rod L., and Irwin M. Berent. 1993. "Dueling Proverbs: A Stitch in Time . . . Probably Doesn't Make Much Difference." *Reader's Digest* (October): 107–8. Also in *"Gold Nuggets or Fool's Gold?" Magazine and Newspaper Articles on the (Ir)relevance of Proverbs and Proverbial Phrases*, edited by Wolfgang Mieder and Janet Sobieski, 142–43. Burlington: University of Vermont, 2006.

Furnham, Adrian. 1987. "The Proverbial Truth: Contextually Reconciling and the Truthfulness of Antonymous Proverbs." *Journal of Language and Social Psychology* 6:49–55.

Gordon, Ann D., ed. 1997–2013. *The Selected Papers of Elizabeth Cady Stanton and Susan B. Anthony*. 6 vols. New Brunswick, NJ: Rutgers University Press.

Hayman, Robert. 1628. *Quodlibets, Lately Come Over from New Britaniola, Old Newfovndland: Epigrams and Other Small Parcels, Both Morall and Diuine*. London: Roger Michell.

Hood, Edwin Paxton. 1885. *The World of Proverb and Parable: With Illustrations from History, Biography, and the Anecdotal Table-Talk of All Ages*. London: Hodder and Stoughton.

Hulme, F. Edward. 1902. *Proverb Lore: Being a Historical Study of the Similarities, Contrasts, Topics, Meanings, and Other Facets of Proverbs, Truisms, and Pithy Sayings, as Expressed by the Peoples of Many Lands and Times: Many Sayings, Wise or Otherwise, on Many Subjects, Gleaned from Many Sources*. London: Elliot Stock. Reprinted with an introduction by Wolfgang Mieder. Burlington: University of Vermont, 2007.

Keene, H. G. 1890. "Conflicts of Experience." *Living Age* 185 (May 24): 483–86. Also in *"Gold Nuggets or Fool's Gold?" Magazine and Newspaper Articles on the (Ir)relevance of Proverbs and Proverbial Phrases*, edited by Wolfgang Mieder and Janet Sobieski, 12–18. Burlington: University of Vermont, 2006.

Kennedy, John F. 1962. *Public Papers of the Presidents of the United States: John F. Kennedy. January 20–December 31, 1961*. Washington, DC: US Government Printing Office.

King, Martin Luther, Jr. 1963. *Strength to Love*. New York: Harper & Row.

Kreeft, Peter. 2009. *Socrates Meets Kant: The Father of Philosophy Meets His Most Influential Modern Child*. San Francisco: Ignatius Press.

Lamb, Charles. 1850. "Popular Fallacies." In *The Works of Charles Lamb*, edited by C. Lamb, 4 vols., 3:346–76. London: Edward Moxon.

Lewis, George Cornewall. 1849. "The Value of Proverbs as the Expression of Popular Opinion." In *An Essay on the Influence of Authority in Matters of Opinion*, edited by G. C. Lewis, 178–80. London: John W. Parker.

Litovkina, Anna T., and Wolfgang Mieder. 2006. *"Old Proverbs Never Die, They Just Diversify": A Collection of Anti-Proverbs*. Burlington: University of Vermont.

Longfellow, Samuel, ed. 1891. *Life of Henry Wadsworth Longfellow with Extracts from His Journals and Correspondence*. 3 vols. Boston: Houghton, Mifflin and Company.

Manser, Martin H. 2002. *The Facts on File Dictionary of Proverbs*. New York: Checkmark Books.

Marryat, Captain. 1907. *Mr. Midshipman Easy*. New York: Century Company.

Marvin, Dwight Edwards. 1916. *Curiosities in Proverbs: A Collection of Unusual Adages, Maxims, Aphorisms, Phrases and Other Popular Dicta from Many Lands*. 2 vols. New York: G. P. Putnam's Sons.

Mieder, Wolfgang, 1987. "'Big Fish Eat Little Fish': History and Meaning of a Proverb About Human Nature." In *Tradition and Innovation in Folk Literature*, edited by Wolfgang Mieder, 178–228. Hanover, NH: University Press of New England.

———. 1993. *Proverbs Are Never Out of Season: Popular Wisdom in the Modern Age*. New York: Oxford University Press. Reprinted New York: Peter Lang, 2012.

———. 2000. *The Proverbial Abraham Lincoln: An Index to Proverbs in the Works of Abraham Lincoln*. New York: Peter Lang.

———. 2001. *"No Struggle, No Progress": Frederick Douglass and His Proverbial Rhetoric for Civil Rights*. New York: Peter Lang.

———. 2003. *"Die großen Fische fressen die kleinen": Ein Sprichwort über die menschliche Natur in Literatur, Medien und Karikaturen*. Vienna: Edition Praesens.

———. 2004. *Proverbs: A Handbook*. Westport, CT: Greenwood Press. Reprinted New York: Peter Lang, 2012.

———. 2006. *"Tilting at Windmills": History and Meaning of a Proverbial Allusion to Cervantes' "Don Quixote."* Burlington: University of Vermont.

———. 2009. *"Yes We Can": Barack Obama's Proverbial Rhetoric*. New York: Peter Lang.

———. 2010. *"Making a Way Out of No Way": Martin Luther King's Sermonic Proverbial Rhetoric*. New York: Peter Lang.

Mieder, Wolfgang, and George B. Bryan. 1997. *The Proverbial Harry S. Truman: An Index to Proverbs in the Works of Harry S. Truman*. New York: Peter Lang.

Mieder, Wolfgang, Stewart A. Kingsbury, and Kelsie B. Harder. 1992. *A Dictionary of American Proverbs*. New York: Oxford University Press.

Mieder, Wolfgang, and Janet Sobieski, eds. 2006. *"Gold Nuggets or Fool's Gold?" Magazine and Newspaper Articles on the (Ir)relevance of Proverbs and Proverbial Phrases*. Burlington: University of Vermont.

Miller, Richard Brian. 1992. *War in the Twentieth Century: Sources in Theological Ethics*. Louisville, KY: Westminster John Knox Press.

Muller, Hermann Joseph. 1973. *Man's Future Birthright: Essays on Science and Humanity*, edited by Elof Axel Carlson. Albany: State University of New York Press.

Obama, Barack. 2009. Remarks by the President in Address to the Nation on the Way Forward in Afghanistan and Pakistan. The White House: Office of the Press Secretary, press release, December 1. https://obamawhitehouse.archives.gov/the-press-office/remarks-president-address-nation-way-forward-afghanistan-and-pakistan.

Osgood, Charles. 1985. "Better Safe Than Sorry When It Comes to Sayings." *USA Weekend* (December 6–8): 22. Also in *"Gold Nuggets or Fool's Gold?" Magazine and Newspaper Articles on the (Ir)relevance of Proverbs and Proverbial Phrases*, edited by Wolfgang Mieder and Janet Sobieski, 79–80. Burlington: University of Vermont, 2006.

Otakpor, Nkeonye. 1987. "A Note on the Logic of Proverbs: A Reply." *Proverbium* 4:263–69.

Paczolay, Gyula. 1996. "Proverbs and Reality." *Proverbium* 13:281–97.

Pickering, David. 1997. *Dictionary of Proverbs*. London: Cassell.

Porte, Joel, ed. 1982. *Emerson in His Journals*. Cambridge, MA: Harvard University Press.

Raleigh, Sir Walter. 1829. *The Works of Sir Walter Raleigh*. 8 vols. Oxford: Oxford University Press.

Ramage, C. T. 1872. "Might Makes Right." *Notes and Queries*, 4th series, 9 (January 27): 81–82.

Richler, Howard. 1995. "Speaking of Language—Proverbs are Pithy Purveyors of Wisdom." *Montreal Gazette*, August 19, G2. Also in *"Gold Nuggets or Fool's Gold?" Magazine and Newspaper Articles on the (Ir)relevance of Proverbs and Proverbial Phrases*, edited by Wolfgang Mieder and Janet Sobieski, 162–64. Burlington: University of Vermont, 2006.

Ridout, Ronald, and Clifford Witting. 1967. *English Proverbs Explained*. London: Pan Books.

Robertson, John M. 1901. *Modern Humanists: Sociological Studies of Carlyle, Mill, Emerson, Arnold, Ruskin, and Spencer*. London: S. Sonnenschein.

Rogers, Tim B. 1990. "Proverbs as Psychological Theories . . . Or Is It the Other Way Around?" *Canadian Psychology/Psychologie Canadienne* 31: 195–207, 215–17 (comments). Also in *Cognition, Comprehension, and Communication: A Decade of North American Proverb Studies (1990–2000)*, edited by Wolfgang Mieder, 459–82. Baltmannsweiler: Schneider Verlag Hohengehren, 2003.

Shapiro, Fred R. 2006. *The Yale Book of Quotations*. New Haven, CT: Yale University Press.

Sheehan, John, ed. 1876. *The Bentley Ballads Comprising the Tipperary Hall Ballads*. London: Richard Bentley.

Slovenko, Ralph. 1993. "Mixed Messages in Proverbs." *Journal of Psychiatry & Law* 21:405–9.

Speake, Jennifer. 2008. *The Oxford Dictionary of Proverbs*. 5th ed. Oxford: Oxford University Press.

States, Bert O. 2001. "Troping through Proverbia." *American Scholar* 70:105–12.

Stauffer, John L., ed. 2006. *The Works of James McCune Smith [1813–1865]. Black Intellectual and Abolitionist*. New York: Oxford University Press.

Stevenson, Burton. 1948. *The Home Book of Proverbs, Maxims, and Familiar Phrases*. New York: Macmillan.

Taylor, Archer. 1931. *The Proverb*. Cambridge, MA: Harvard University Press. Reprinted with an introduction, a bibliography, and a photograph of Archer Taylor by Wolfgang Mieder. Bern: Peter Lang, 1985.

Taylor, Archer, and Bartlett Jere Whiting. 1958. *A Dictionary of American Proverbs and Proverbial Phrases, 1820–1880*. Cambridge, MA: Harvard University Press.

Teigen, Karl Halvor. 1986. "Old Truths or Fresh Insights? A Study of Students' Evaluations of Proverbs." *British Journal of Social Psychology* 25:43–49.

Thompson, Kenneth W., ed. 1988. *The Ford Presidency*. New York: University Press of America.

Tilley, Morris Palmer. 1950. *A Dictionary of the Proverbs in England in the Sixteenth and Seventeenth Centuries*. Ann Arbor: University of Michigan Press.

Titelman, Gregory Y. 1996. *Random House Dictionary of Popular Proverbs and Sayings*. New York: Random House.

Truman, Harry S. 1961: *Public Papers of the Presidents of the United States: Harry S. Truman. April 12–December 31, 1945*. Washington, DC: US Government Printing Office.

Trusler, John. 1790. *Proverbs Exemplified, and Illustrated by Pictures from Real Life*. London: Literary Press.

Wander, Karl Friedrich Wilhelm. 1867–80. *Deutsches Sprichwörter-Lexikon*. 5 vols. Leipzig: F. A. Brockhaus.

Whaley, Bryan B. 1993. "When 'Try, Try Again' Turns to 'You're Beating a Dead Horse.' The Rhetorical Characteristics of Proverbs and Their Potential for Influencing Therapeutic Change." *Metaphor and Symbolic Activity* 8:127–39. Also in *Cognition, Comprehension, and Communication: A Decade of North American Proverb Studies (1990–2000)*, edited by Wolfgang Mieder, 555–70. Baltmannsweiler: Schneider Verlag Hohengehren, 2003.

White, T. H. 1958. *The Once and Future King*. New York: G. P. Putnam's Sons.

White, Theodore. 1982 *America in Our Time*. New York: Harper & Row.

Whiting, Bartlett Jere. 1968. *Proverbs, Sentences, and Proverbial Phrases from English Writings Mainly Before 1500*. Cambridge, MA: Harvard University Press.

———. 1977. *Early American Proverbs and Proverbial Phrases*. Cambridge, MA: Harvard University Press.

———. 1989. *Modern Proverbs and Proverbial Sayings*. Cambridge, MA: Harvard University Press.
Wilson, N. F. P. 1970. *The Oxford Dictionary of English Proverbs*. Oxford: Clarendon Press.
Wright, Thomas, ed. 1839. *The Political Songs of England from the Reign of John to That of Edward II*. London: John Bowyer Nichols.
Yankah, Kwesi. 1984. "Do Proverbs Contradict?" *Folklore Forum* 17:2–19. Also in *Wise Words: Essays on the Proverb*, edited by Wolfgang Mieder, 127–42. New York: Garland Publishing, 1994.
———. 1989. *The Proverb in the Context of Akan Rhetoric: A Theory of Proverb Praxis*. Bern: Peter Lang.

10

"ALL MEN ARE CREATED EQUAL"

From Democratic Claim to Proverbial Game

About eight years ago, I had the fortune of meeting my friend Professor Olga Karpova during the First Interdisciplinary Colloquium on Proverbs, organized by the International Association of Paremiology in November 2007 at Tavira, Portugal. At that time, I was deeply impressed with her fascinating lecture "Dictionaries of Shakespeare Proverbs and Quotations" that was subsequently published in the proceedings of this important meeting of paremiologists and phraseologists (Karpova 2008). After that conference, she sent me her magisterial book *Slovari iazyka pisatelei i tsitat v angliiskoi leksikografii* (2007, together with O. V. Korobeinikova), and subsequently I also received her important book *English Author Dictionaries (the XVIth–XXIst cc.)* (2011) as a much-appreciated present. Of course, as is the custom among scholars, I have mailed her various Anglo-American dictionaries of quotations, proverbs, and idioms in return, and it is exactly this type of international cooperation that results in fruitful scholarship.

By way of Olga Karpova and many of my other Russian paremiological, phraseological, and lexicographical friends like Elena Arsentyeva, Elena Carter, Dmitrij Dobrovol'sky, Sinaida Fomina, Anna Konstantinova, Valerii M. Mokienko, and others, I have become aware of the keen interest that exists in Russia not only about English but also American quotations, proverbs, and idioms. Of course, it has not been easy for paremiographers, phraseographers, and lexicographers in general to create collections or dictionaries that distinguish between British and American texts. After all, for many preformulated statements it would indeed be difficult to ascertain a purely British or American origin. While this is not a problem for quotations with a known authorship, things become quite difficult when proverbs or idioms are involved. To make things even more complex, it must not be forgotten that there are other "Englishes" spoken and written in the world, such as the use of English in Australia, Canada, India, Africa, and many other parts of the world, even if English is employed only as a second language.

There are, of course, excellent standard collections and dictionaries of quotations, proverbs, idioms, and also slang that include texts from all the various Englishes, without necessarily always paying close attention to national or regional origin. Among those volumes that I find most useful in this regard are the following, with Burton Stevenson's massive *The Home Book of Proverbs, Maxims, and Familiar Phrases* (1948) with its 2,957 column-printed pages surpassing all others in lexicographical completeness, including names, dates, contexts, etc. My experience has shown that for references before the 1940s, this compendium is simply the best, and yet it is often not cited as a scholarly source. Some of the even older massive collections are also still of great importance for historical research. In any case, here are a few of those inclusive collections and dictionaries that stand on the bookshelves in my study for quick and reliable reference:

> Adler, Mortimer J., and Charles Van Doren. 1977. *Great Treasury of Western Thought: A Compendium of Important Statements on Man and His Institutions by the Great Thinkers in Western History.* New York: R. R. Bowker Company, 1,771 pp.
>
> Andrews, Robert. 1993. *The Columbia Dictionary of Quotations.* New York: Columbia University Press, 1,092 pp.
>
> Augarde, Tony. 1991. *The Oxford Dictionary of Modern Quotations.* Oxford: Oxford University Press, 371 pp.
>
> Bartlett, John. 2012. *Familiar Quotations: A Collection of Passages, Phrases, and Proverbs Traced to Their Sources in Ancient and Modern Literature.* Edited by Geoffrey O'Brien. 18th ed. Boston: Little, Brown and Company, 1,438 pp. All previous editions from 1855 on are significant for historical research.
>
> Bradley, John P., Leo F. Daniels, and Thomas C. Jones. 1969. *The International Dictionary of Thoughts.* Chicago: J. G. Ferguson, 1,146 pp.
>
> Brewer, Ebenezer Cobham. 1970. *Dictionary of Phrase and Fable.* Revised Centenary Edition. Edited by Ivor H. Evans. New York: Harper & Row, 1,175 pp. The first edition from 1870 is also important.
>
> ———. 1992. *Brewer's Dictionary of 20th-Century Phrase and Fable.* Edited by David Pickering, Alan Isaacs, and Elizabeth Martin. Boston: Houghton Mifflin Co., 662 pp.

———. 2000. *Brewer's Dictionary of Modern Phrase & Fable*. Edited by Adrian Room. London: Cassell, 773 pp.

Browning, D. C. 1982. *Everyman's Dictionary of Quotations and Proverbs*. London: Octopus Books, 745 pp.

Bryan, George B., and Wolfgang Mieder. 2005. *A Dictionary of Anglo-American Proverbs and Proverbial Phrases Found in Literary Sources of the Nineteenth and Twentieth Centuries*. New York: Peter Lang, 871 pp.

Christy, Robert. 1887. *Proverbs, Maxims, and Phrases of All Ages: Classified Subjectively and Arranged Alphabetically*. 2 vols. New York: G. P. Putnam's Sons; reprinted Detroit: Gale Research Company, 1974; reprinted Norwood, PA: Norwood Editions, 1977. 1, 665 pp.; 2, 602 pp. (both volumes bound in one).

Cohen, J. M., and M. J. Cohen. 1960. *The Penguin Dictionary of Quotations*. Middlesex, England: Penguin, 664 pp.

———. 1971. *The Penguin Dictionary of Modern Quotations*. Harmondsworth, England: Penguin, 366 pp. 2nd ed. Middlesex, England: Penguin, 1980, 496 pp.

Daintith, John, Hazel Egerton, Rosalind Fergusson, Anne Stibbs, and Edmund Wright, eds. 1987. *The Macmillan Dictionary of Quotations*. New York: Macmillan, 790 pp.

Douglas, Charles Noel. 1904. *Forty-Thousand Sublime and Beautiful Thoughts*. 2 vols. New York: Christian Herald. Reprinted as *Forty Thousand Quotations, Prose and Poetical*. New York: Halcyon House, 1940, 2,008 pp.

Edwards, Tryon. 1914. *A Dictionary of Thoughts, Being a Cyclopedia of Laconic Quotations from the Best Authors of the World, Both Ancient and Modern*. Detroit: F. B. Dickerson, 678 pp. and 34 pp. (authors' reference index). Also reprinted as *The New Dictionary of Thoughts: A Cyclopedia of Quotations*. New York: Classic Publishing, 1936; reprinted New York: Standard Book Company, 1954, 746 pp. and 34 pp. (authors' reference index).

Evans, Bergen. 1968. *Dictionary of Quotations*. New York: Avenel Books, 832 pp.

Frank, Leonard Roy. 2001. *Random House Webster's Quotationary: The Authoritative Source for over 20,000 Quotations*. New York: Random House, 1,040 pp.

Green, Jonathon. 2010. *Green's Dictionary of Slang*. 3 vols. London: Chambers. 1, 1,884 pp.; 2, 1,997 pp.; 3, 2,204 pp.

Hendrickson, Robert. 1987. *The Facts on File Encyclopedia of Word and Phrase Origins*. New York: Facts on File Publications, 581 pp.

Hoyt, Jehiel Keeler. 1892. *The Cyclopedia of Practical Quotations: English, Latin, and Modern Foreign Languages*. New York: Funk & Wagnalls, 899 pp. Revised ed. New York: Funk & Wagnalls, 1896, 1,178 pp. Revised ed. by Kate Louise Roberts as *Hoyt's New Cyclopedia of Practical Quotations*. New York: Funk & Wagnalls, 1922, 1,343 pp.

Jeffares, A. Norman, and Martin Gray, eds. 1995. *A Dictionary of Quotations*. New York: HarperCollins; reprinted New York: Barnes & Noble, 1997, 1,027 pp.

Kenin, Richard, and Justin Wintle, eds. 1978. *The Dictionary of Biographical Quotation of British and American Subjects*. New York: Alfred A. Knopf, 860 pp.

Knowles, Elizabeth, ed. 1997. *The Oxford Dictionary of Phrase, Saying, & Quotation*. Oxford: Oxford University Press, 694 pp.

———. 1999. *The Oxford Dictionary of Quotations*. 5th ed. Oxford: Oxford University Press, 1,136 pp. (1st ed. 1941), 879 pp.; (2nd ed. 1953), 1,003 pp.; (3rd ed. 1979), 907 pp.; (4th ed. 1992), 1,061 pp.

Mair, James Allan. 1874. *A Handbook of Proverbs, Mottoes, Quotations, and Phrases*. London: Routledge, 505 pp.

Manser, Martin H., and Rosalind Fergusson. 2002. *The Facts on File Dictionary of Proverbs: Meanings, and Origins of More Than 1,500 Popular Sayings*. New York: Checkmark Books, 440 pp.

Mencken, H. L. 1942. *A New Dictionary of Quotations on Historical Principles from Ancient and Modern Times*. New York: Alfred A. Knopf (2nd ed. 1960), 1,347 pp.

Morris, William, and Mary Morris. 1962–1967. *Dictionary of Word and Phrase Origins*. 2 vols. New York: Harper & Row, 1, 376 pp.; 2, 297 pp.

Murphy, Edward F. 1978. *The Crown Treasury of Relevant Quotations*. New York: Crown Publishers. Reprinted as *Webster's Treasury of Relevant Quotations*. New York: Greenwich House, 1983, 658 pp.

Partridge, Eric. 1977. *A Dictionary of Catch Phrases: British and American, from the Sixteenth Century to the Present Day*. New York: Stein and Day, 278 pp. Revised edition edited by Paul Beale. Lanham, MD: Scarborough House, 1992, 384 pp.

Rees, Nigel. 1984. *Sayings of the Century: The Stories Behind the Twentieth Century's Quotable Sayings.* London: George Allen and Unwin, 270 pp.

———. 1995. *Phrases and Sayings.* London: Bloomsbury, 531 pp.

———. 1997. *Cassell Companion to Quotations.* London: Cassell, 640 pp.

———. 2006. *A Word in Your Shell-Like: 6,000 Curious & Everyday Phrases Explained.* London: HarperCollins, 768 pp.

Rogers, James. 1985. *The Dictionary of Clichés.* New York: Facts on File Publications, 305 pp.

Shapiro, Fred R. 2006. *The Yale Book of Quotations.* New Haven, CT: Yale University Press, 1,068 pp.

Simpson, James B. 1964. *Contemporary Quotations.* New York: Galahad Books, 500 pp. Revised edition as *Simpson's Contemporary Quotations.* Boston: Houghton Mifflin, 1988, 495 pp.

Simpson, John A. 1982. *The Concise Oxford Dictionary of Proverbs.* Oxford: Oxford University Press, 256 pp. (2nd ed. 1992), 316 pp. (3rd ed. 1998, with Jennifer Speake), 333 pp.

Speake, Jennifer, ed. 2003. *The Oxford Dictionary of Proverbs.* 4th ed. Oxford: Oxford University Press, 375 pp. (5th ed. 2008), 388 pp. (The designation of "Concise Dictionary" of the first three editions by John A. Simpson and Jennifer Speake was dropped.)

Stevenson, Burton Egbert. 1948. *The Home Book of Proverbs, Maxims, and Familiar Phrases.* New York: Macmillan. Seventh printing as *The Macmillan Book of Proverbs, Maxims, and Familiar Phrases.* New York: Macmillan, 1968, 2,957 pp.

Titelman, Gregory Y. 1996. *Random House Dictionary of Popular Proverbs and Sayings: Over 1,500 Proverbs and Sayings with 10,000 Illustrative Citations.* New York: Random House, 468 pp. (2nd ed. 2000), 480 pp. Reprinted as *Popular Proverbs and Sayings: An A–Z Dictionary of over 1,500 Proverbs and Sayings, with 10,000 Illustrative Examples.* New York: Gramercy Books, 1997, 468 pp.

Tripp, Rhoda Thomas. 1970. *The International Thesaurus of Quotations.* New York: Harper & Row; reprinted New York: Harper & Row, 1987, 1,088 pp.

Urdang, Laurence, and Frank R. Abate. 1983. *Idioms and Phrases Index: An Unrivaled Collection of Idioms, Phrases, Expressions, and Collocutions of Two or More Words which Are Part of the English Lexicon and for which the*

Meaning of the Whole Is Not Transparent from the Sum of the Meanings of the Constituent Parts. 3 vols. Detroit: Gale Research Company, 1,691 pp.

Urdang, Laurence, Walter W. Hunsinger, and Nancy LaRoche. 1985. *Picturesque Expressions: A Thematic Dictionary.* Detroit: Gale Research Company, 770 pp.

Walsh, William. 1908. *The International Encyclopedia of Prose and Poetical Quotations from the Literature of the World.* Philadelphia: John C. Winston, 1,029 pp.

Ward, Anna L. 1883. *A Dictionary of Quotations from English and American Poets.* New York: Thomas Y. Crowell, 761 pp.

———. 1889. *A Dictionary of Quotations in Prose from American and Foreign Authors, including Translations from Ancient Sources.* New York: Thomas Y. Crowell, 701 pp.

Wilson, F. P. 1970. *The Oxford Dictionary of English Proverbs.* 3rd ed. Oxford: Clarendon Press, 930 pp. 1st ed. William George Smith. With an introduction and index by Janet E. Heseltine. Oxford: Clarendon Press, 1935, 644 pp. 2nd ed. revised by Sir Paul Harvey. Oxford: Clarendon Press, 1948, 740 pp.

There are, of course, also collections and dictionaries that deal primarily with British materials, of which I find the following most useful for my diachronic and synchronic studies of fixed phrases of all types. Permit me to single out *The Kenkyusha Dictionary of Current English Idioms* (1964), edited by the Japanese scholars Sanki Ichikawa, Takuji Mine, Ryoichi Inui, Kenzo Kihara, and Shiro Takaha in Tokyo, whose 849 pages, containing many excellent contextualized references, has been unduly ignored.

Apperson, G. L. 1929. *English Proverbs and Proverbial Phrases: A Historical Dictionary.* London: J. M. Dent; reprinted Detroit: Gale Research Co. Reprinted as *The Wordsworth Dictionary of Proverbs.* Ware, Hertfordshire: Wordsworth Editions, 1993, 721 pp.

Bohn, Henry G. 1855. *A Hand-Book of Proverbs Comprising an Entire Republication of Ray's Collection of English Proverbs, with His Additions from Foreign Languages.* London: Henry G. Bohn; reprinted London: Bell & Daldy, 1870; reprinted New York: AMS Press, 1968, 583 pp.

Chiu, Kwong Ki. 1881. *A Dictionary of English Phrases with Illustrative Sentences.* New York: A. S. Barnes; reprinted Detroit: Gale Research Company, 1971, 915 pp.

Cowie, Anthony P., and R. Mackin. 1975. *Oxford Dictionary of Current Idiomatic English*. Vol. 1. *Verbs with Prepositions & Particles*. London: Oxford University Press, 396 pp.

Cowie, Anthony P., R. Mackin, and I. R. McCaig. 1983. *Oxford Dictionary of Current Idiomatic English*. Vol. 2. *Phrase, Clause & Sentence Idioms*. Oxford: Oxford University Press, 685 pp.

Gulland, Daphne M., and David G. Hinds-Howell. 1986. *The Penguin Dictionary of English Idioms*. Harmondsworth, Middlesex: Penguin Books, 300 pp.

Hale, Sarah Josepha. 1854. *A Complete Dictionary of Poetical Quotations: Comprising the Most Excellent and Appropriate Passages in the Old British Poets; with Choice and Copious Selections from the Best Modern British and American Poets*. Philadelphia: Lippincott, Grambo & Co., 576 pp. (primarily British).

Hazlitt, W. Carew. 1869. *English Proverbs and Proverbial Phrases, Collected from the Most Authentic Sources, Alphabetically Arranged and Annotated*. London: J. R. Smith, 505 pp. Rev. ed. London: Reeves and Turner, 1907; reprinted Detroit: Gale Research Company, 1969, 580 pp.

Henderson, B. L. K. 1937. *A Dictionary of English Idioms*. Vol. 1, *Verbal Idioms*. Vol. 2, *Colloquial Phrases*. London: James Blackwood. 1, 352 pp.; 2, 408 pp.

Hyamson, Albert M. 1922. *A Dictionary of English Phrases*. New York: E. P. Dutton; reprinted Detroit: Gale Research Company, 1970, 365 pp.

Ichikawa, Sanki, Takuji Mine, Ryoichi Inui, Kenzo Kihara, and Shiro Takaha. 1964. *The Kenkyusha Dictionary of Current English Idioms*. Tokyo: Kenkyusha, 849 pp.

James, Ewart. 1996. *NTC's Dictionary of British Slang and Colloquial Expressions*. Lincolnwood, IL: National Textbook Company, 573 pp.

Lean, Vincent Stuckey. 1902–1904. *Lean's Collectanea: Collections of Vincent Stuckey Lean of Proverbs (English & Foreign), Folk Lore, and Superstitions, also Compilations towards Dictionaries of Proverbial Phrases and Words, Old and Disused*. Edited by T. W. Williams. 5 vols. Bristol: J. W. Arrowsmith; reprinted Detroit: Gale Research Company, 1969. Reprinted as *Lean's Collectanea: Encyclopedia of Proverbs*. Bristol: Thoemmes Press, 2000. 1, 509 pp,; 2, 1, 477 pp.; 2, 2, 463 pp.; 3, 512 pp.; 4, 481 pp.

Nares, Robert. 1905. *A Glossary of Words, Phrases, Names, and Allusions in the Works of English Authors Particularly of Shakespeare and His Contemporaries*. London: George Routledge; reprinted Detroit: Gale Research Company, 1966, 982 pp.

Partridge, Eric. 1937. *A Dictionary of Slang and Unconventional English.* New York: Macmillan, 999 pp.; (5th ed. 1961) 1,352 pp.; (7th ed. 1970) 1,528 pp.

———. 1940. *A Dictionary of Clichés.* London: George Routledge. (5th ed. 1978), 261 pp.

Skeat, Walter W. 1910. *Early English Proverbs: Chiefly of the Thirteenth and Fourteenth Centuries with Illustrative Quotations.* Oxford: Clarendon Press; reprinted Darby, PA: Folcroft Library Editions, 1974, 147 pp.

Tilley, Morris Palmer. 1950. *A Dictionary of the Proverbs in England in the Sixteenth and Seventeenth Centuries.* Ann Arbor: University of Michigan Press, 854 pp.

Whiting, Bartlett Jere. 1968. *Proverbs, Sentences, and Proverbial Phrases from English Writings Mainly Before 1500.* Cambridge, MA: Harvard University Press, 733 pp.

Wilkinson, P. R. 1993. *Thesaurus of Traditional English Metaphors.* London: George Routledge, 777 pp.

Wood, Frederick T. 1964. *English Verbal Idioms.* New York: St. Martin's, 325 pp. Revised ed. New York: Washington Square Press, 1967, 359 pp.

What I have mentioned thus far is not necessarily unknown to scholars of quotations, proverbs, and other phraseological units, but I would like to make a plea that they be employed especially in historical studies of individual texts.

But let me now turn to a more specific concern, namely the fact that there is an ever-increasing interest among paremiographers, phraseographers, and lexicographers in fixed phrases of the American language—and not only in what texts are being used in the United States but also in what texts are definitely American in origin. Without in any way wanting to be critical—some of the books I am about to mention have simply not been accessible to scholars in Europe and elsewhere—I wish to present a list of major collections and dictionaries that are dedicated more or less exclusively to the American variant of the English language and that certainly need to be consulted. The titles of the following list make this fact rather plain, and I would argue that they should be utilized much more than what can be ascertained from studies concerned with American texts. But to be fair, it must be pointed out that American scholars have also ignored quite a few of these valuable reference works. Perhaps the new generation of scholars goes too quickly to the internet for sources and is at times not even aware of these splendid printed resources. Be that as it may, let me make a plea for the employment of at least some of the reference works presented here.

Ammer, Christine. 1997. *The American Heritage Dictionary of Idioms*. Boston: Houghton Mifflin Company, 729 pp.

Bartlett, John Russell. 1849. *The Dictionary of Americanisms*. New York: Bartlett & Welford; reprinted New York: Crescent Books, 1989, 412 pp.

Boatner, Maxine Tull, and John E. Gates. 1966. *A Dictionary of American Idioms for the Deaf*. West Hartford, CT: American School for the Deaf, 1966. Reprinted as *A Dictionary of American Idioms*. Woodbury, NY: Barron's Educational Series, 1975, 392 pp.

Bohle, Bruce, ed. 1967. *The Home Book of American Quotations*. New York: Dodd, Mead & Company; reprinted New York: Gramercy Publishing Company, 1986, 512 pp.

Burrell, Brian. 1997. *The Words We Live By: The Creeds, Mottoes, and Pledges That Have Shaped America*. New York: The Free Press, 367 pp.

Carruth, Gorton, and Eugene Ehrlich. 1988. *The Harper Book of American Quotations*. New York: Harper & Row, 821 pp.

Cassidy, Frederic G., and Joan Houston Hall. 1985–2013. *Dictionary of American Regional English*. 6 vols. Cambridge, MA: Harvard University Press. 1, A–C, 903 pp.; 2, D–H, 1,175 pp.; 3, S–O, 927 pp.; 4, P–Sk, 1,014 pp.; 5, Sl–Z, 1,244 pp.; 6, Contrastive Maps, Index to Entry Labels, Questionnaire, and Fieldwork Data, 1,053 pp.

Chapman, Robert L. 1989. *Thesaurus of American Slang*. New York: Harper & Row, 489 pp.

Conlin, Joseph R. 1984. *The Morrow Book of Quotations in American History*. New York: William Morrow, 352 pp.

Dalzell, Tom, ed. 2009. *The Routledge Dictionary of Modern American Slang and Unconventional English*. New York: Routledge, 1,104 pp.

Donadio, Stephen, Joan Smith, Susan Mesner, and Rebecca Davison, eds. 1992. *The New York Public Library Book of Twentieth-Century American Quotations*. New York: Warner Books, 622 pp.

Doyle, Charles Clay, Wolfgang Mieder, and Fred R. Shapiro, eds. 2012. *The Dictionary of Modern Proverbs*. New Haven, CT: Yale University Press, 294 pp. (primarily American proverbs).

Federer, William J. 2000. *America's God and Country: Encyclopedia of Quotations*. St. Louis: Amerisearch, 845 pp.

Flexner, Stuart Berg. 1976. *I Hear America Talking: An Illustrated Treasury of American Words and Phrases*. New York: Van Nostrand Reinhold Company, 505 pp. With illustrations.

———. 1982. *Listening to America: An Illustrated History of Words and Phrases from our Lively and Splendid Past.* New York: Simon and Schuster. 591 pp. With illustrations.

Flexner, Stuart Berg, and Anne H. Soukhanov. 1997. *Speaking Freely: A Guided Tour of American English from Plymouth Rock to Silicon Valley.* New York: Oxford University Press, 472 pp. With illustrations.

Foss, William O., ed. 1999. *First Ladies Quotation Book: A Compendium of Provocative, Tender, Witty, and Important Words from the Presidents' Wives.* New York: Barricade Books, 305 pp.

Frost, Elizabeth. 1988. *The Bully Pulpit: Quotations from America's Presidents.* New York: Facts on File, 282 pp.

Harnsberger, Caroline Thomas. 1964. *Treasury of Presidential Quotations.* Chicago: Follett Publishing Co., 419 pp.

Hendrickson, Robert. 2000. *American Regionalisms: Local Expressions from Coast to Coast.* New York: Facts on File, 786 pp.

Hirsch, E. D., Joseph Kett, and James Trefil. 1988. *The Dictionary of Cultural Literacy: What Every American Needs to Know.* Boston: Houghton Mifflin Co., 586 pp. (proverbs, pp. 46–57; idioms, pp. 58–80).

Hurd, Charles. 1964. *A Treasury of Great American Quotations.* New York: Hawthorn Books, 319 pp.

Kieffer, Jarold. 1989. *What Are Those Crazy Americans Saying? An Easy Way to Understand Thousands of American Expressions.* Fairfax, VA: Kieffer Publications. (2nd ed. 1990; 3rd ed. 1998), 472 pp.

Kin, David (pseud. David George Plotkin). 1955. *Dictionary of American Maxims.* New York: Philosophical Library, 597 pp.

———. 1955. *Dictionary of American Proverbs.* New York: Philosophical Library, 286 pp.

Lighter, Jonathan E., ed. 1994–97. *Random House Historical Dictionary of American Slang.* 2 vols. New York: Random House. 1, A–G, 1,006 pp.; 2, H–O, 736 pp. (3rd vol. never appeared).

Mieder, Wolfgang. 1989. *American Proverbs: A Study of Texts and Contexts.* Bern: Peter Lang, 394 pp. With illustrations.

———. 2015. *"Different Strokes for Different Folks": 1,250 authentisch amerikanische Sprichwörter.* Bochum: Norbert Brockmeyer, 313 pp.

Mieder, Wolfgang, Stewart A. Kingsbury, and Kelsie B. Harder, eds. 1992. *A Dictionary of American Proverbs*. New York: Oxford University Press. Paperback edition New York: Oxford University Press, 1996, 726 pp.

Nussbaum, Stan. 2005. *American Cultural [and Proverbial] Baggage: How to Recognize and Deal with It*. Maryknoll, NY: Orbis Books, 160 pp.

Platt, Suzy. 1992. *Respectfully Quoted: A Dictionary of Quotations from the Library of Congress*. Washington, DC: Congressional Quarterly; reprinted as *Respectfully Quoted: A Dictionary of Quotations*. New York: Barnes & Noble, 1993, 520 pp.

Rawson, Hugh, and Margaret Miner. 2006. *The Oxford Dictionary of American Quotations*. New York: Oxford University Press, 898 pp.

Shankle, George Earlie. 1941. *American Mottoes and Slogans*. New York: The H. W. Wilson Company, 183 pp.

Spears, Richard A. 1989. *NTC's Dictionary of American Slang and Colloquial Expressions*. Lincolnwood, IL: National Textbook Company, 528 pp. (2nd ed. 1995), 555 pp.; (3rd ed. 2000), 560 pp.

———. 1990. *Essential American Idioms*. Lincolnwood, IL: National Textbook Company. (2nd ed. 1996), 247 pp.

———. 1995. *NTC's Dictionary of American English Phrases*. Lincolnwood, IL: National Textbook Company, 559 pp.

———. 1998. *Hip and Hot! A Dictionary of 10,000 American Slang Expressions*. New York: Gramercy Books, 555 pp.

Spears, Richard A., and Linda Schinke-Llano, eds. 1987. *NTC's American Idioms Dictionary*. Lincolnwood, IL: National Textbook Company, 463 pp.

Sunners, William, ed. 1949. *American Slogans*. New York: The Paebar Company, 345 pp.

Taylor, Archer, and Bartlett Jere Whiting. 1958. *A Dictionary of American Proverbs and Proverbial Phrases, 1820–1880*. Cambridge, MA: Harvard University Press, 418 pp.

Tuleja, Tad. 1994. *Book of Popular Americana*. New York: Macmillan, 451 pp.

Wentworth, Harold, and Stuart Berg Flexner. 1960. *Dictionary of American Slang*. New York: Thomas Y. Crowell, 669 pp. Revised ed. New York: Thomas Y. Crowell, 1975, 766 pp.

Whiting, Bartlett Jere. 1977. *Early American Proverbs and Proverbial Phrases.* Cambridge, MA: Harvard University Press, 555 pp.

―――. 1989. *Modern Proverbs and Proverbial Sayings.* Cambridge, MA: Harvard University Press, 710 pp. (primarily proverbs and proverbial expressions from American writings).

Woods, Henry F. 1945. *American Sayings: Famous Phrases, Slogans, and Aphorisms.* New York: Duell, Sloan and Pearce, 310 pp. Revised ed. New York: Perma Giants, 1950, 312 pp.

Many of the books enumerated in these three lists will be difficult to obtain outside of Great Britain and the United States, but quite a few of them can be read online. But to be able to do so, they must first of all be known to scholars and students. That is why I have presented the most important publications here, knowing from experience that they have been of great use in my own diachronic research on fixed phrases of all sorts. There are many more reference books for the Englishes of the world and also for other languages. Over the years, I have been able to assemble about four thousand dictionaries and collections worldwide for my International Proverb Archives at the University of Vermont in Burlington; 3,615 are registered in my *International Bibliography of Paremiography: Collections of Proverbs, Proverbial Expressions and Comparisons, Quotations, Graffiti, Slang, and Wellerisms* (2011). The more recent acquisitions are listed in my annually updated "International Bibliography of New and Reprinted Proverb Collections" at the end of *Proverbium: Yearbook of International Proverb Scholarship.*

Having presented the most important collections and dictionaries containing Anglo-American quotations, proverbs, idioms, and to a lesser degree slang, let me now turn to an extremely important American quotation long turned proverb that touches people everywhere in the world, presenting at least a few historical remarks based on a selection of contextualized examples. To be sure, the proverbial quotation "all men are created equal," as one might call this ultimate bit of insight, was, is, and should be a guidepost for humankind, as we are tied together globally in a network of mutuality. There certainly is no American who does not know that this claim of human equality occurs at the beginning of the second paragraph of the Declaration of Independence that was adopted by the Continental Congress as the founding document of the United States of America on the evening of July 4, 1776, at Philadelphia. That day has been immortalized by declaring it Independence Day, which is celebrated every year with readings of the Declaration, parades, concerts, picnics, etc. Two days later, on July 6, the text was printed as an easily distributable and obtainable broadsheet for the residents in the colonies. This was the beginning of it being ingrained in the American mind and heart, and it has remained part of the American cultural literacy ever since (Hirsch, Kett, and Trefil 1988, 241). For those not acquainted with American history, most of the quotation dictionaries listed above will cite the first lines of this paragraph, stating that it was crafted by Thomas Jefferson, who later became the third president of the United States (1801–1809):

> We hold these truths to be self-evident: that all men are created equal; that they are endowed by their Creator with certain unalienable rights; that among these are life, liberty, and the pursuit of happiness; that, to secure these rights, governments are instituted among men, deriving their just powers from the consent of the governed; that whenever any form of government becomes destructive of these ends, it is the right of the people to alter or to abolish it, and to institute new government, laying its foundation on such principles, and organizing its powers in such form, as to them shall seem most likely to effect their safety and happiness.

What an incredible statement Jefferson had crafted that expresses in just a few lines or in one long sentence the very basics of a democracy! John Adams, the second president of the United States (1797–1801), had made but very minor stylistic changes to the original text that is cited here: "We hold these truths to be sacred and undeniable; that all men are created equal and independent, that from that equal creation they derive rights inherent and inalienable, among which are the preservation of life, and liberty, and the pursuit of happiness" (Conlin 1984, 156).

No doubt the changes by Adams improved the text, but it must also be remembered that the final wording was not created in a vacuum, for Jefferson as a Virginian was well acquainted with a draft of Virginia's Declaration of Rights, written by one George Mason, that begins as follows: "That all men are born equally free and independent, and have certain inherent natural rights, of which they cannot, by any compact, deprive or divest their posterity; among which are the enjoyment of life and liberty, with the means of acquiring and possessing property, and pursuing and obtaining happiness and safety" (Aron 2008, 92–93).

Of course, as is so often the case with famous quotations like "all men are created equal," some sort of precursors can be found. Burton Stevenson, in his remarkable *The Home Book of Proverbs, Maxims, and Familiar Phrases* (1948) cites the following:

> We are all born equal, and are distinguished alone by virtue. (Omnes pari sporte nascimur, sola virtute distinguimur.)

> Unknown. A medieval Latin proverb (c. 1350). Related to it is the legal maxim, "Quod ad ius naturale attinet, omnes homines aequales sund" (As far as natural law extends, all men are equal). (Stevenson 1948, 705)

Perhaps Jefferson, who read widely and had one of the largest private libraries of his time, might have come across the Latin legal maxim, but for such a basic assertion as "all men are created equal," no precursor is really necessary. More important is what John Adams, who became a bit jealous of his friend's celebrity status as the writer of the Declaration of Independence, stated three years later in his wording of the Constitution of Massachusetts (1779): "All men are born free and equal" (Stevenson 1948, 705).

The added claim of being "born free" might have been difficult for Jefferson, as a major slaveholder, to write. Adams, on the other hand, was one of the very few Founding Fathers who did not hold slaves.

Stevenson, as a truly superb lexicographer, also adds three later variants by lesser-known writers that show people's preoccupation with the human equality issue:

> We are all equal; nature made you so. Equality is your birthright.
> Robert Southey, *What Tyler.* (1794)

> On the turf and under the turf all men are obliged to be equal.
> R. S. Surtees, *Handley Cross.* (1854)
> An epigram attributed to Lord George Bentinck. (c. 1830) Usually quoted, "All men are equal on the turf and under it."

> It appears that beneath the turf or on it all men are equal.
> Henry Seton Merriman, *The Sowers.* (1896)
> (Stevenson 1948, 705)

In any case, by the 1820s, Jefferson's "all men are created equal"—with its linguistic limitations, as will become clear by 1848—"was well on its way to becoming the premier expression of the American mind [... and] to later generations of Americans, the most important principle pledged in the Declaration was that of equality. Neither the Constitution [of 1789] nor the Bill of Rights [of 1791] asserted that all men were created equal" (Aron 2008, 95). And yet, it took John Bartlett until 1868 to finally include the first part of the second paragraph of the Declaration of Independence in his standard collection of *Familiar Quotations* (nothing in the first to fourth editions between 1855 and 1867): "We hold these truths to be self-evident: that all men are created equal; that they are endowed by their Creator with inalienable [in the original: unalienable] rights; that among these are life, liberty, and the pursuit of happiness" (Bartlett 1868, 376).

The fact that it took Bartlett some years to register this by-now-famous quotation is a clear indication that lexicographers often lag behind in registering quotations, proverbs, and other fixed phrases that are gaining currency during their own time. But this is not the place to review how the quotation dictionaries listed above are handling this particular text. Let me simply state that Gorton Carruth and Eugene Ehrlich, in their well-documented *The Harper Book of American Quotations* (1988), make an exception and include the entire text of the Declaration of Independence to refresh their readers' memory of this democratic document (Carruth and Ehrlich 2008, 61–63).

Naturally, "all men are created equal" started as a quotation by Thomas Jefferson, but over time, it became current, independent of the Declaration, that it could be considered a proverbial quotation, to be sure. However, I would argue that by now it can well be called a bona fide proverb, even though paremiographers, as they are apt to be, have been reluctant or remiss in including it in proverb collections. Most of them do not register it, just as they don't cite the by-now-proverbial triad "life, liberty, and the pursuit of happiness," for which Jefferson was influenced by John Locke, who "had declared that all men had rights to life, liberty, and property. The idea that a good government should promote happiness of the governed was not original with Jefferson, but his substitution of 'pursuit of happiness' for 'property' in the traditional Lockean formulation put a distinctively American imprint on the Declaration—and on the newborn nation itself" (Rawson and Miner 2006, 187). Be that as it may, my coeditors, Stewart A. Kingsbury, Kelsie B. Harder, and I, decided to include "all men are created equal" as well as John Adams's expanded variant "sll men are born free and equal" in our *A Dictionary of American Proverbs* (1992) because they had been recorded numerous times by field researchers during 1945–85 as proverbs and not as quotations (Mieder, Kingsbury, and Harder 1992, 398). And so we were extremely pleased when Gregory Titelman, just four years later, followed suit in his *Random House Dictionary of Popular Proverbs & Sayings* (1996, 7) by including "all men are created equal" as a main proverb entry with eight historical references from the twentieth century. (It is now also cited as a proverb in Manser and Fergusson 2002, 4–5.) Such decisions to include proverbs not registered in other proverb collections is extremely important if paremiography wants to reflect new developments. It is for this reason that Charles Clay Doyle, Fred R. Shapiro, and I published our

Dictionary of Modern Proverbs (2012) that lists only proverbs that were coined after the year 1900.

Many revealing examples of the employment of "all men are created equal" by major political figures abound, of which I would like to cite just a few that I have discovered in my own readings of American social and political history. It will be noted that while the proverb is clearly a claim for equality, the reality of the American nation was a far cry from it. This unfortunate situation forced Frederick Douglass, an escaped slave and then powerful abolitionist, to lash out against American slavery in numerous lectures, arguing that the "equality" proverb is meaningless where slavery is condoned. Here are two short excerpts from 1846 and 1854.

> March 1846. I do speak against an American institution—that institution is American slavery. But I love the Declaration of Independence. I believe it contains a true doctrine—"that all men are created equal." It is, however, because they do not carry out these principles that I am here to speak. I have a right to appeal to . . . people everywhere—I would draw all men's attention to slavery. I would fix the indignant eye of the world on slavery [so it] be swept off the face of the earth. (Mieder 2001, 72)

> August 3, 1854. America stands prominently forth as a land of inconsistencies and contradictions—aspiring to be honest, and yet a nation of liars; for in her Declaration of Independence, and the gateway of her Constitution, she proclaims "all men [are created] equal," while she holds in bondage three millions and a half of her subjects—robbed of every right, deprived of every privilege, and sold and bought like beasts that perish. (Mieder 2001, 74; for many more references citing this proverb, see pp. 353–59)

Abraham Lincoln, who befriended Frederick Douglass, also made repeated use of the proverb in his strong arguments against slavery.

> October 16, 1854: My ancient faith tells me that "all men are created equal;" and that there can be no moral right in connection with one man's making a slave of another. . . . What I do say is, that no man is good enough to govern another man, without that other's consent. I say this is the leading principle—the sheet anchor of American republicanism. Our Declaration of Independence says: "We hold these truths to be self-evident: that all men are created equal; that they are endowed by their Creator with certain inalienable rights; that among these are life, liberty, and the pursuit of happiness. That to secure these rights, governments are instituted among men, deriving their just powers from the consent of the governed." (Mieder 2000, 146)

> July 10, 1858. So I say in relation to the principle that all men are created equal, let it be as nearly reached as we can. . . . Let us . . . unite as one people throughout this land, until we shall once more stand up declaring that all men are created equal. . . . I leave you, hoping that the lamp of liberty will burn in your bosoms until there shall no longer be a doubt that all men are created free and equal. (Mieder 2000, 148)

Like Douglass, he frequently expanded the proverb to John Adams's variant "all men are born free and equal," thereby stressing freedom and equality for the slaves. His most famous utterance of the proverb appears in his noted Gettysburg Address of November 19, 1863, that used to be learned by heart at school (it contains only 272 words) in years gone by (see Wills 1992, 148–73).

> Four score and seven years ago our fathers brought forth, upon this continent, a new nation, conceived in liberty, and dedicated to the proposition that all men are created equal.
> Now we are engaged in a great civil war, testing whether that nation, or any nation, so conceived, and so dedicated, can long endure. We are met on a great battlefield of that war. We have come to dedicate a portion of it as a final resting place for those who gave their lives that that nation might live.
> . . . that we here highly resolve that these dead shall not have died in vain; that this nation shall have a new birth of freedom; and that this government of the people, by the people, for the people, shall not perish from the earth. (Mieder 2000, 150; for many more references citing this proverb, see pp. 146–50)

Of course, both Douglass and Lincoln speak about slavery that resulted in the Civil War, but half the population, at least linguistically, was not addressed in their use of the proverb "all men are created equal." It is a sad fact that the word *women* does not appear in any of the great American documents like the Declaration of Independence, the Constitution of the United States, and the Bill of Rights. Politics and government were a matter of the white male population, while African Americans and women were left out. This lamentable and unfair situation needed correction, ant it took spirited women like Elizabeth Cady Stanton, Susan B. Anthony, and many other early feminists to fight vigorously for women's rights. It all started during a women's rights convention held on July 19–20, 1848, at Seneca Falls, New York, when Elizabeth Cady Stanton presented the magisterially crafted revolutionary manifesto "Declaration of Sentiments," based on the Declaration of Independence. It is here that the well-known proverb is changed to include the female gender.

> We hold these truths to be self-evident: that all men and women are created equal; that they are endowed by their Creator with certain inalienable rights; that among these are life, liberty, and the pursuit of happiness; that to secure these rights governments are instituted, deriving their just powers form the consent of the governed. . . . But when a long train of abuses and usurpations, pursuing invariably the same object, evinces a design to reduce them under absolute despotism, it is their duty to throw off such government, and to provide new guards for their future security. Such has been the patient sufferance of the women under this government, and such is now the necessity which constrains them to demand the equal station to which they are entitled. (Mieder 2014, 68–69; for many more references citing this proverb, see pp. 228–31)

It is a shame that "all men and women are created equal" never caught on, and that is also true for the inclusive "all people are created equal." Of course, it can be argued that *men* stands for humankind in general, and it is to be hoped that this interpretation is the prevailing one today. This was not necessarily the case in the nineteenth century, and it took until 1920 and the passing of the Nineteenth Amendment to give women the right to vote at last. In any case, Stanton's close friend Susan B. Anthony also made use of the proverb in the name of women's rights, as for example in her speech of October 27, 1874.

> Why is it in the face of the utterances of our forefathers relative to all men being born free and equal, taxation without representation, government deriving its just powers from the consent of the governed, that one-half of the people are denied any voice in the workings of the government? Society upholds a false theory relative to woman's place in the world, which thus makes it safe to violate these governmental maxims as regards women, which no one would dare to do in the case of any class of men. The theory is that women are created primarily for man's happiness, and secondarily for her own. (Mieder 2014, 230)

Clearly, the proverb was well established by the turn of the previous century, and there is no doubt that presidents of the United States have relied heavily on its significant claim for freedom and equality, hopefully among all people. At least a few contextualized references will underscore their serious employment of the proverb as an expression of democracy, including President Harry S. Truman's visionary remarks during his inaugural speech on January 20, 1949, in Washington, DC. He certainly employs the plural *men* to stand for people in general.

> The American people stand firm in the faith which has inspired this nation from the beginning. We believe that all men have a right to equal justice under law and equal opportunity to share in the common good. We believe that all men have the right to freedom of thought and expression. We believe that all men are created equal because they are created in the image of God. From this faith we will not be moved. The American people desire, and are determined to work for, a world in which all nations are free to govern themselves as they see fit and to achieve a decent and satisfying life. Above all else, our people desire, and are determined to work for peace on earth—a just and lasting peace—based on genuine agreement freely arrived at by equals. (Mieder 2005, 169–70; for more references, see Mieder and Bryan 1997, 172)

Twenty years later, on January 20, 1969, Richard Nixon also turned to Jefferson's proverbial declaration that "all men are created equal," but he twice changes the verb to *born* as he emphasizes equality among all

Americans after the advances made by the civil rights movement under the leadership of Martin Luther King Jr.

> As we measure what can be done, we shall promise only what we can produce, but as we chart our goals we shall be lifted by our dreams. No man can be fully free while his neighbor is not. To go forward at all is to go forward together. This means black and white together, as one nation, not two. The laws have caught up with our conscience. What remains is to give life to what is in the law: to ensure at last that as all are born equal in dignity before God, all are born equal in dignity before man. As we learn to go forward together at home, let us seek to go forward together with all mankind. Let us take as our goal: where peace is unknown, make it welcome; where peace is fragile, make it strong; where peace is temporary, make it permanent. (Mieder 2005, 175)

Always mindful that citing one of the great American declarations will bring forth an emotional and positive response by listeners, President Jimmy Carter had the following to say in his farewell address to the nation on January 14, 1981:

> Remember these words: "We hold these truths to be self-evident, that all men are created equal, that they are endowed by their Creator with certain inalienable Rights; that among these are Life, Liberty, and the pursuit to Happiness."
> This vision still grips the imagination of the world. But we know that democracy is always an unfinished creation. Each generation must renew its foundations. Each generation must rediscover the meaning of this hallowed vision in the light of its own challenges. For this generation, ours, life is nuclear survival; liberty is human rights; the pursuit of happiness is a planet whose resources are devoted to the physical and spiritual nourishment of its inhabitants. (Whitney 2003, 451)

President Bill Clinton also looked back and forward in his second inaugural address on January 20, 1997, beginning his remarks with a short history lesson in which the proverb is not cited completely but certainly recognizable to his audience.

> The promise of America was born in the eighteenth century out of the bold conviction that we are all created equal. It was extended and preserved in the nineteenth century, when our nation spread across the continent, saved the Union, and abolished the scourge of slavery. Then, in turmoil and triumph, that promise exploded onto the world stage to make this the American century. What a century [i.e., the twentieth century] it has been! America became the world's mightiest industrial power, saved the world from tyranny in two world wars and a long cold war, and time and again reached across the globe to millions who longed for the blessings of liberty. (Mieder 2005, 182)

After this, Clinton moved on to a glance into the challenges of the twenty-first century, declaring that "the future is up to us" (Hunt 1997, 507). This latter statement might well be a shortened version of the longer proverb "the future belongs to those who prepare for it."

Speaking of Clinton, here is what Hillary Rodham Clinton, former first lady, senator, and secretary of state, and would-be president of the United States, wrote in her new book *Hard Choices* (2014) in relation to Eleanor Roosevelt's great achievement of crafting the Universal Declaration of Human Rights for the United Nations. It obviously was a painstaking undertaking, as she led a diverse committee to a document that was approved by the UN General Assembly on December 10, 1948.

> They discussed, they wrote, they revisited, revised, and rewrote. They incorporated suggestions and revisions from governments, organizations, and individuals around the world. It is telling that even in the drafting of the Universal Declaration there was a debate about women's rights. The initial version of the first article stated, "All men are created equal." It took women members of the Commission, led by Hansa Mehta of India, to point out that "all men" might be interpreted to exclude women. Only after long debate was the language changed to say, "All human beings are born free and equal in dignity and rights." (Clinton 2014, 565)

It is interesting to note here how the gender specificity of the proverb "all men are created equal" was overcome not by using Elizabeth Cady Stanton's "all men and women are created equal" but by employing the completely gender-free compound "human beings." Of course, the statement also changes the mere "created equal" to "born free and equal" that John Adams had used.

Speaking of human rights leads to Martin Luther King Jr.'s preoccupation with the proverb "all men are created equal" during his struggle for civil rights in the United States and beyond. This celebrated civil rights leader, defender of nonviolence in the struggle for desegregation, champion for the poor, antiwar proponent, and broad-minded visionary of an interrelated world of free people made the proverbial truth "all men are created equal" and the right for "life, liberty, and the pursuit of happiness" expressed at the beginning of the Declaration of Independence the basis of his engaged and heartfelt fight for freedom, universal suffrage, antiracism, and socioeconomic improvements for minorities. Besides the Bible proverb "love your enemies" (Matthew 5:44), he used "all men are created equal" most often in his sermonic proverbial rhetoric. While King always cites this wisdom with the most positive conviction, it gives him the rhetorical opportunity to show that the ideal expressed in them has not been achieved by far regarding the African American citizens, to wit the following paragraph from his stirring sermon on "The Christian Doctrine of Man" that he delivered on March 12, 1958, in Detroit. Judging by the responses of the audience, people must have been very much taken by King's sermonic stroke of genius of letting God talk to them through their preacher.

> The God of the universe stands there in all of His love and forgiving power saying, "Come home. [*Yeah, Amen, Amen*] Western civilization, you have strayed away into the far country of colonialism and imperialism. You have taken one billion six hundred million of your brothers in Asia and Africa, dominated them politically, exploited them economically, segregated and humiliated them. You have trampled over them. But western civilization, if you will rise up now and come out of this far country of imperialism and colonialism and come on back to your true home, which is freedom and justice, I'll take you in. [*Yeah, Oh amen*] America, I had great intentions for you. I had planned for you to be this great nation where all men would live together as brothers—a nation of religious freedom, a nation of racial freedom. And America, you wrote it in your Declaration of Independence. You meant well, for you cried out, 'All men are created equal and endowed by their creator with certain unalienable rights. [*Yeah*] Among these are life, liberty, and the pursuit of happiness.' [*Preach*] But in the midst of your creed, America, you've strayed away to the far country of segregation and discrimination. [*Say it, Amen*] You've taken sixteen million of your brothers, trampled over them, mistreated them, inflicted them with tragic injustices and indignities. But America, I'm not going to give you up. If you will rise up out of the far country of segregation and discrimination [*Amen*], I will take you in, America. [*Amen, Amen*] And I will bring you back to your true home." (Mieder 2010, 125; for many more references, see pp. 417–29)

Many more powerful and accusatory statements like this could and should be cited, but lack of space does not permit this. Instead, let me give President Barack Obama the last word here as a politician, and it should be remembered that he, by his own admission, has adopted Frederick Douglass, Abraham Lincoln, and Martin Luther King Jr. as his personal heroes and rhetorical teachers par excellence. On the trip to Washington for his first inauguration on January 20, 2009, he stopped in Philadelphia and Baltimore on January 17, 2009, repeating the following words that amount to somewhat of a short history lesson, as Bill Clinton had done twelve years earlier.

> They [the early patriots] were willing to put all they were and all they had on the line—their lives, their fortunes and their sacred honor—for a set of ideals that continue to light the world. That we are equal [All men are created equal]. That our rights to life, liberty and the pursuit of happiness come not from our laws, but from our maker. And that our government of, by and for the people can endure. It was these ideals that led us to declare independence and craft

our constitution, producing documents that were imperfect but had within them, like our nation itself, the capacity to be made more perfect. (Mieder 2009, 262)

The American audience certainly heard the echoes of the Declaration of Independence, the Gettysburg Address, and the Constitution of the United States (making a more perfect union) in these remarks, and there is no doubt that they engendered positive and patriotic feelings. Being well aware of this, Obama said something quite similar in his inaugural speech three days later: "We remain a young country, but in the words of Scripture, the time has come to set aside childish things [1 Corinthians 13:11]. The time has come to reaffirm our enduring spirit; to choose our better history; to carry forward that precious gift, that noble idea, passed on from generation to generation: the God-given promise that all are equal [all men are created equal], all are free, and all deserve a chance to pursue their full measure of happiness. (Mieder 2009, 262; for a few more references, see p. 262)

It has long become customary and expected that presidents of the United States make such uplifting remarks at their inaugurations. But care must be taken with the whole world watching and listening by way of television and radio that such self-praising statements don't deteriorate into the ill-founded claim of American exceptionalism in the world. It was thus good for the brand-new president Barack Obama to temper his praise of American ideals by referring to imperfections and the need for improvement.

As one would expect, not all reactions to the quotation turned proverb "all men are created equal" are so positive and respectful. After all, as the struggle against slavery and the fight for women's rights have shown, the ideals of equality and freedom are one thing, but reality is unfortunately something quite different. Below is a statement from a speech that the early labor leader Seth Luther delivered in 1832 throughout the state of Massachusetts: "Let us no longer be deceived by the cry of those who produce nothing and who enjoy all, and who insultingly term us [the laborers] the lower orders, and exultingly claim our homage for themselves, as the higher orders—while the Declaration of Independence asserts that 'All men are created equal'" (Conlin 1984, 199).

That is a serious indictment of the growing industrialism and capitalism in the young American nation, with its exploitation, greed, and unfortunate belief in the survival of the fittest at the expense of less fortunate fellow citizens.

Gregory Titelman lists a few additional contextualized references from the twentieth century that illustrate the idealism of the proverb "all men are created equal" in light of the harsh reality with plenty of unfortunate shortcomings.

> 1922. All men are not born equal. Some are born blind, some deaf, some lame, and some are born Jews.
> —Harry Austryn Wolfson [the first Jew to hold a chair in Judaic studies at Harvard], quoted by Charles E. Silberman in *A Certain People*.
>
> 1955. Like all other officers at Group Headquarters except Major Darby, Colonel Cathcart was infused with the democratic spirit: he believed that all men were created equal, and therefore spurned all men outside Group Headquarters with equal fervor.
> —Joseph Heller, *Catch-22*.
>
> 1960. "Thomas Jefferson once said that all men are created equal . . . We know all men are not created equal in the sense some people would have us believe—some people are smarter than others, some people have more opportunity because they're born with it. Some men make more money than others, some ladies make better cakes than others—some people are born gifted beyond the normal scope of most men."
> —Harper Lee, *To Kill a Mockingbird*.
>
> 1992. All men are born equal, but some outgrow it.
> —Morris Mandel, *Jewish Press*.
>
> 1993. All financial planners are not created equal.
> —*Modern Maturity*.
> (Titelman 1996, 7)

To be sure, the ultimate parody of "all men are created equal" is George Orwell's "All animals are equal, but some animals are more equal than others" from his famous novel *Animal Farm* (1945) that has become proverbial in its own right, having been registered as such in *Brewer's Dictionary of 20th-Century Phrase and Fable* by David Pickering, Alan Isaacs, and Elizabeth Martin (1992, 179), Gregory Titelman's *Random House Dictionary of Popular Proverbs & Sayings* (1996, 4), and now also Charles Clay Doyle, Wolfgang Mieder, and Fred R. Shapiro, *Dictionary of Modern Proverbs* (2012, 6): "1945. For once Benjamin consented to break his rule, and he read out to her what was written on the wall. There was nothing there now except a single Commandment. It ran: ALL ANIMALS ARE EQUAL BUT SOME ANIMALS ARE MORE EQUAL THAN OTHERS. —George Orwell, *Animal Farm*" (Titelman 1996, 4).

There are plenty of other modern parodies that could well be called anti-proverbs to "all men are created equal". My friend Anna Tothné Litovkina and I have assembled some of them in our book *Old Proverbs Never Die, They Just Diversify: A Collection of Anti-Proverbs* (2006), where they are registered with precise bibliographical information. It should be noted that the texts from 1968 are, for the most part, by Evan Esar, from his edited book *20,000 Quips and Quotes* (1968).

> 1924. All men are born free and equal, but some of them grow up and get married.
> 1945. All animals are equal, but some are more equal than others.
> 1968. All men are born equal, but some of them outgrow it.
> 1968. All men are created equal, but necklines, waistlines and hemlines show that women are not.
> 1968. All men are created equal—especially twins.
> 1968. All men are equal, and the cynic thinks they are all equally bad.
> 1968. All men are equal, but it's what they are equal to that counts.
> 1977. American symbol of democracy: "All men are created eagle."
> 1980. All men are born equal. The tough job is to outgrow it.
> 1980. One of the advantages of nuclear warfare is that all men are cremated equal.
> 1985. In nuclear warfare all men are cremated equal.
> 1992. In a public bath, all men are equal—more or less.
> 1993. Nuclear War: Boom & doom. Where all mean are cremated equal. "Don't blow it. Good planets are hard to find."
> (Litovkina and Mieder 2006, 84–85)

It is well known that any often-repeated quotation or proverb will eventually be parodied in a humorous, ironic, or satirical fashion. While literary authors, journalists, and humorists delight in such linguistic play, it is the world of advertising that relies heavily on creating such antiproverbs for effective marketing slogans (see Mieder 1993, 2004). What follows is an example from Titelman's collection, to precede advertisements that I have collected during the past decades from the mass media: "1993. In his latest sneaker commercial, Dallas running back Emmitt Smith tells listeners, 'All players are created equal, some just work harder in training camp.' —*Times* (Trenton)" (Titelman 1996, 4).

What follow are the antiproverbial advertisement slogans from my International Proverb Archives, which can be divided into two structural types: "All Xs are not created equal" and "Not all Xs are created equal." Please note that while both antiproverbial structures negate the equality claim of the original proverb "all men are created equal," they enable advertisers to create messages that address particular purchasing choices and specific customer groups. Notice that one of the changed texts is the direct negation "all men are not created equal" as an advertisement for different condom sizes.

All Xs are not created equal.

1974. All pickups are not created equal.
Advertisement for Jeep pickup trucks.
(*Playboy*, February 1974, 61)

1974. All glass is not created equal.
Advertisement for PPG Industries.
(*Time*, September 16, 1974, 32–33)

1976. All chemicals are not created equal.
Advertisement for Thetford tank deodorant.
(*Trailer Life*, August 1976, 177)

1976. A smaller condom.
Because all men are not created equal.
Advertisement for Hugger condoms.
(*Penthouse*, November 1976, 20)

1977. All maintenance-free batteries are not created equal.
Advertisement for Delco Remy Batteries.
(*Wall Street Journal*, October 13, 1977, 36)

1977. All Canadians are not created equal.
Advertisement for Seagram's V.O. Whisky.
(*Time*, November 28, 1977, 25)

1978. All food processors are not created equal.
Advertisement for General Electric.
(*Better Homes & Gardens*, April 1978, 182)

1979. All feet are not created equal.
Advertisement for Edwin Case shoe store.
(*Boston Globe*, November 5, 1979, 20)

1980. All hotels are not created equal.
Advertisement for Beverly Wilshire Hotel.
(*The New Yorker*, January 21, 1980, 59)

1980. All beards are not created equal.
Advertisement for Aramis shaving cream.
(*The New Yorker*, October 6, 1980, 21)

1980. All shampoos are not created equal.
Advertisement for Style shampoo.
(*People*, October 6, 1980, 27)

1981. All rates are not created equal.
Advertisement for Burlington Savings Band.
(*Brattleboro Daily Reformer*, January 15, 1981, 8)

1981. All feet are not created equal.
Advertisement for Nike shoes.
(*Scientific American*, October 1981, 20)

1982. All calories are not created equal.
Advertisement for Campbell's soups.
(*Better Homes &* Gardens, November 1982, 121)

1984. All gold is not created equal.
Advertisement for Visa credit card.
(*Time*, September 3, 1984, inside back cover)

The slogan variant "not all Xs are created equal" appears to be a bit less popular, but it basically fulfills the same goal of emphasizing a certain inequality in people or more often in purchasing choices. The first advertising slogan is of special interest again since it negates the original proverb "all men are created equal" directly as "not all men are created equal."

1976. Not all men are created equal.
Advertisement for Pennshire shirts.
(*The New York Times Magazine*, September 19, 1976, 70)

1977. Not all three-head cassette decks are created equal.
Advertisement for Kenwood electronics.
(*Playboy*, November 1977, 254)

1979. Not all stereophones are created equal.
[with the head of Lincoln wearing earphones]
More than a score of years ago, the nation discovered a whole new way to listen to music.
Advertisement for Koss stereophones.
(*Playgirl*, December 1979, 56)

1980. In America, not all television is created equal.
Advertisement for HBO Home Box Office movies.
(*People*, March 3, 1980, 52)

1981. Not all electrical distributors are created equal.
Advertisement for Allied Electric.
(*New England Business*, November 2, 1981, 8)

1982. Not all dads are created equal.
Advertisement for Squire's cashews.
(*The New Yorker*, June 7, 1982, 124)

1991. Not all colleges are created equal.
Advertisement for College for Financial Planning.
(*Registered Representative*, September 1991, 9)

2003. Not all sleeping bags are created equal.
Magazine headline of an article on various types of sleeping bags.
(*Outside Buyer's Guide*, 2003, 98)

A fascinating two-page magazine advertisement for Virginia Slims cigarettes from 1978 deserves special attention. The left page shows a group of four gentlemen standing in a bar several decades ago. On the floor are two women scouring the floor, following their supposed subservient role. The caption reads: "Back then all men were created equal. And all women were created equal."

In other words, each gender had its predestined place, but there certainly was no equality of the genders, as desired by Stanton and other feminists. The right page, in stark contrast, shows a modern, liberated woman, symbolized by smoking a Virginia Slims cigarette. She clearly has freed herself from her subjugated role and made tremendous progress in the male-dominated world. The famous and by now proverbial slogan of the cigarette company says it all: "You've come a long way, baby" (*Family Circle*, March 27, 1978, 84–85).

But there was also this advertisement by the Fruit of the Loom company that traditionally had produced underwear only for men. When the firm decided to enter the market for women, it did well to state that women are created equal but deserve different types of panties. I remember well that I enjoyed this effective play on the old proverb:

> 1986. Fruit of the Loom Ladies' Panties.
> Because woman was created equal . . . but different.
> Fruit of the Loom Ladies' Panties come in
> Feminine styles, fabrics and soft pastel colors
> That are oh, so different from men's briefs.
> But, they're created equal in quality, value,
> Comfort and long-lasting fit.
> Available in briefs, hipsters and bikinis.
> Advertisement for Fruit of the Loom.
> (*Good Housekeeping*, December 6, 1986, 141)

The famous Steinway piano company used its well-known name in the proverb's original structure of "all Xs are created equal" and proclaimed self-assured that their pianos are simply the best: "All Steinways are created equal. Advertisement for Steinway pianos" (*The New Yorker*, December 6, 1976, 141).

Finally, my own University of Vermont placed a unique advertisement about its summer school program in the *Burlington Free Press* that drew on Abraham Lincoln's already-cited use of the proverb in the Gettysburg Address:

> 1999. FOUR SCORE
> AND SEVEN YEARS AGO
> [large image of Abraham Lincoln covering parts of the text]
> our fathers brought forth,
> upon this continent, a new
> nation, conceived in liberty,
> and dedicated to
> the proposition that all
> men are created equal.
> Be there. Hear it, Feel it. Field Experience at Summer University.
> Courses that actually take you to the battlefield at Gettysburg,
> canoeing through Canada, exploring Bali's
> spiritual paths and other intriguing places.
> SPEND SUMMER OUT OF THE ORDINARY.
>   *The*
>   UNIVERSITY OF VERMONT
>   CONTINUING EDUCATION
> Advertisement for the University of Vermont summer school.
> (*Burlington Free Press*, April 4, 1999), 4B)

With this, these deliberations have come full circle, for there is no doubt that the quotation turned proverb "all men are created equal" will forever be associated with Thomas Jefferson's Declaration of Independence from 1776 and Abraham Lincoln's Gettysburg Address from 1863. No matter how much this wisdom of freedom and equality is played with for various immediate purposes, it will remain one of humanity's great principles of fair play. As such, it belongs into quotation dictionaries and proverb collections, and it behooves people everywhere to acknowledge its basic message, no matter how idealistic it might be in the face of human conduct in the world.

References

This chapter was first published in Modern Linguistic and Methodical-and-Didactic Researches series, *Scientific Newsletter* (Voronezh, Russia), no. 1 (2015): 10–37.

Aron, Paul. 2008. *We Hold These Truths . . . And Other Words that Made America*. Lanham, MA: Rowman & Littlefield.
Bartlett, John. 1868. *Familiar Quotations: Being an Attempt to Trace to Their Source Passages and Phrases in Common Use*. 5th ed. Boston: Little, Brown, and Company.

Carruth, Gorton, and Eugene Ehrlich. 1988. *The Harper Book of American Quotations*: New York: Harper & Row.
Clinton, Hillary Rodham. 2014. *Hard Choices*. New York: Simon & Schuster.
Conlin, Joseph R. 1984. *The Morrow Book of Quotations in American History*. New York: William Morrow.
Doyle, Charles Clay, Wolfgang Mieder, and Fred R. Shapiro. 2012. *The Dictionary of Modern Proverbs*. New Haven, CT: Yale University Press.
Esar, Evan. 1968. *20,000 Quips & Quotes*. Garden City, NY: Doubleday.
Hirsch, E. D., Joseph Kett, and James Trefil. 1988. *The Dictionary of Cultural Literacy: What Every American Needs to Know*. Boston: Houghton Mifflin Co.
Hunt, John Gabriel, ed. 1997. *The Inaugural Addresses of the Presidents*. New York: Gramercy Books.
Karpova, Olga M. 2008. "Dictionaries of Shakespeare Proverbs and Quotations." In *Proceedings of the First Interdisciplinary Colloquium on Proverbs, 5th to 12th November 2007, at Tavira, Portugal*, edited by Rui J. B. Soares and Outi Lauhakangas, 271–77. Tavira: Tipografia Tavirense.
——. 2011. *English Author Dictionaries (XVIth—the XXIst cc.)*. Newcastle upon Tyne: Cambridge Scholars Publishing.
Karpova, Olga M., and O. V. Korobeinikova. 2007. *Slovari iazyka pisatelei i tsitat v angliiskoi leksikografii*. Moscow: Moskovskii gosudarstvennyi oblastnoi universitet.
Litovkina, Anna Tothné, and Wolfgang Mieder. 2006. *Old Proverbs Never Die, They Just Diversify: A Collection of Anti-Proverbs*. Burlington: University of Vermont.
Manser, Martin H., and Rosalind Fergusson. 2002. *The Facts on File Dictionary of Proverbs: Meanings and Origins of More Than 1,500 Popular Sayings*. New York: Checkmark Books.
Mieder, Wolfgang. 1993. *Proverbs Are Never Out of Season: Popular Wisdom in the Modern Age*. New York: Oxford University Press; reprinted New York: Peter Lang, 2012.
——. 2000. *The Proverbial Abraham Lincoln: An Index to Proverbs in the Works of Abraham Lincoln*. New York: Peter Lang.
——. 2001. *"No Struggle, No Progress": Frederick Douglass and His Proverbial Rhetoric for Civil Rights*. New York: Peter Lang.
——. 2004. *Proverbs: A Handbook*. Westport, CT: Greenwood Press; reprinted New York: Peter Lang, 2012.
——. 2005. *Proverbs Are the Best Policy: Folk Wisdom and American Proverbs*. Logan: Utah State University Press.
——. 2009. *"Yes We Can": Barack Obama's Proverbial Rhetoric*. New York: Peter Lang.
——. 2010. *"Making a Way Out of No Way": Martin Luther King's Sermonic Proverbial Rhetoric*. New York: Peter Lang.
——. 2011. *International Bibliography of Paremiography: Collections of Proverbs, Proverbial Expressions and Comparisons, Quotations, Graffiti, Slang, and Wellerisms*. Burlington: University of Vermont.
——. 2014. *"All Men and Women Are Created Equal": Elizabeth Cady Stanton's and Susan B. Anthony's Proverbial Rhetoric Promoting Women's Rights*. New York: Peter Lang.
Mieder, Wolfgang, and George B. Bryan. 1997. *The Proverbial Harry S. Truman: An Index to Proverbs in the Works of Harry S. Truman*. New York: Peter Lang.
Mieder, Wolfgang, Stewart A. Kingsbury, and Kelsie B. Harder. 1992. *A Dictionary of American Proverbs*. New York: Oxford University Press.

Pickering, David, Alan Isaacs, and Elizabeth Martin, eds. 1992. *Brewer's Dictionary of 20th-Century Phrase and Fable*. Boston: Houghton Mifflin.
Rawson, Hugh, and Margaret Miner. 2006. *The Oxford Dictionary of American Quotations:* New York: Oxford University Press.
Titelman, Gregory Y. 1996. *Random House Dictionary of Popular Proverbs and Sayings: Over 1,500 Proverbs and Sayings with 10,000 Illustrative Citations*. New York: Random House.
Whitney, Gleaves, ed. 2003. *American Presidents: Farewell Messages to the Nation 1796–2001*. Lanham, MD: Lexington Books.
Wills, Garry. 1992. *Lincoln at Gettysburg: The Words That Remade America*. New York: Touchstone Books.

11

"LAISSEZ FAIRE À GEORGES" AND "LET GEORGE DO IT"

A Case of Paremiological Polygenesis

ABOUT TWENTY YEARS AGO, I MADE THE CURSORY remark that when one considers the origin of any given proverb, painstaking historical and comparative research must be undertaken, and at least in some cases, it should be considered that "polygenesis is possible, that is, proverbs might at times have originated in separate locations at different times" (Mieder 1993, 174). I also have told my students about this possibility, but I must admit that I have hitherto not investigated a proverb that can be shown not to be monogenetic. So, let me present a short case study of a proverb that is identical in wording, albeit in French and English, and which has in fact two origins at quite different times. The older proverb in French is "Laissez faire à Georges," and the much younger English proverb is "Let George do it."

My interest in this proverb pair came about when I read the following short remark by the linguist H.L. Mencken in his celebrated early study on *The American Language* (1921): "It ['Let George do it'] originated in France, as 'laissez faire à Georges,' during the fifteenth century, and at the start had satirical reference to the multiform activities of Cardinal Georges d'Amboise, prime minister to Louis XII" (Mencken 1921, 364).

About ten years later in 1931, Archer Taylor, the renowned American folklorist and paremiologist and obviously a reader of Mencken's classic work, considers this connection of the two proverbs a possibility and adds some important information to it.

> *Let George do it*, which is perhaps a vaudeville phrase, is now less frequently heard than formerly and is perhaps on its way to extinction. [in note 2 Taylor adds:] Possibly we can see a connection with *Laissez faire à George* [sic], *il est homme d'âge*, a historical proverb. We are told that Louis XII expressed his confidence in his minister, George d'Amboise, in these words. The traditional

explanation in America is based on "George" as a name used in addressing Pullman porters. (Taylor 1931, 9)

[*Nota bene*: the spelling of *à*, *Georges*, and *âge* varies in both my French and English sources and will be cited as given throughout.]

Taylor's careful and speculative wording makes it abundantly clear that he was not entirely convinced that there actually is a connection between the two "George" proverbs, although the possibility cannot be denied. Separate origins of such minimalistic texts as proverbs can occur, after all, as Alan Dundes has pointed out: "If one is engaged in citing cognates of a particular proverb, one should be careful to distinguish actual cognates, that is, versions and variants of the proverb in question, assumed to be historically/genetically related to that proverb, from mere structural parallels which may well have arisen independently, that is, through polygenesis" (2000, 298). In fact, the issue of monogenesis vs. polygenesis has been discussed in folklore circles since the Brothers Grimm, and it remains a perplexing scholarly problem to this day (Chesnutt 2002).

The origin of the French proverb, reduced from the longer quotation "Laissez faire à Georges, il est homme d'âge" is well established. In fact, Louis-Pierre Anquetil in his fourteen-volume *Histoire de France depuis les Gaulois jusqu'à la fin de la monarchie* (1805) cites its start in the year 1498, when Cardinal Georges d'Amboise (1460–1510) became the minister of state under King Louis XII, who had been impressed with his administrative abilities: "1498 [in the margin]. Il (Louis XII) avoit une telle confiance en lui que, dans les circonstances embarrassantes, sa solution ordinaire aux difficultés qu'on lui présentoit, étoit, *laissez faire à Georges*, et il se tranquillisoit sur l'événement. Cette sécurité a été souvent funeste. (Anquetil 1805, 5:375–76)

The long version of the proverb appears for the first time in Fleury de Bellingen's early collection *L'Etymologie ou Explication des Proverbes Francois* (1656).

> Le Roy se confioit entierement en sa [Georges d'Amboise] sagesse pour la conduite des affaires de son Royaume, disoit ordinairement en prenant resolution de bien servir le Roy & l'Estat dans les occasions, qui se presentoient, & [l]es choses dont il s'agissoit: *Laissez faire à George, il est homme d'age*. Donnant à entendre par là qu'il se comporteroit prudemment, sagement, & avec toute la consideration, & circonspection necessaire en ce qui concernoit le service de sa Majesté, la gloire de sa coronne, & le bien de ses Peuples; car c'est là agir en homme d'age; comme au contraire proceder inconsiderement, hastivement, & sans meure deliberation, c'est agir temerairement & en jeune estourdi. (1656, 37)

Antoine Oudin also registers the proverb in 1656 with a short explanatory comment, as one would expect it from a dictionary entry: "Laissez faire à George, il est homme d'aage, ne [d]outez point, ne vous mettez point au peine, nous viendrons bien à bout de nos desseins" (Oudin 1656, 194).

The proverb clearly has the meaning of not having any doubts or worries, because everything will work out if George [d'Amboise] is in charge. It is interesting to note here that the minister is actually not mentioned, showing that the proverb has taken on a meaning of its own. In references from proverb collections of later times, the editors have found it necessary to give a more precise historical explanation.

> 1690 and again 1771: *George.*—est un nom propre qui est venu en usage en ce proverbe, Laissez faire à *George*, c'est un homme d'âge. Il s'est fait du temps du Cardinal *George* d'Amboise Ministre d'Estat: quand on parloit des affaires publiques, on disoit, Laissez faire à *George*, il est homme d'âge, pour dire, qu'il s'en falloit rapporter à sa bonne conduitte & à sa grande intelligence. (Furetière 1690, R[3]; almost identical also in Furetière and Souciet 1771, 4:483)

> 1821: *George (laissez faire à), il est homme d'âge.*
> On a tort de dire que ce proverbe a été fait pour le cardinal George d'Amboise, ministre d'état sous Louis XII. A la vérité ce prince lui est redevable du glorieux titre de *Père du peuple*. Le cardinal d'Amboise retrancha le dixième de tous les impôts, et les réduisit aux deux tiers. Sa prudence dans dispensation des derniers publics était si grande, que jamais il ne rétablit ce qu'il avait supprimé; mais comment trouver un homme d'âge dans George d'Amboise qui ne vécut que cinquante ans? (La Mesangère 1821, 207)

> 1826: *George: laissez faire à George, il est homme d'âge.* Ce proverbe est du temps du cardinal George d'Amboise, ministre d'état de Louis XII. Comme ce ministre était extrèmement habile, on disait en parlant des affaires publiques: *laissez faire à George, il est homme d'âge*, pour dire qu'il s'en fallait rapporter à sa bonne conduite et à sa grande intelligence. (Caillot 1826, 333)

> 1842: *Laissez faire à George, il est homme d'âge.*
> Le cardinal Georges d'Amboise, ministre du roi Louis XII, avoit une grande autorité sur l'esprit de son maître. Lorsque l'on estoit embarassé sur quelques affaires importantes, ce cardinal avoit coutume de dire, parlant de luymesme: *laissez faire Georges, il est homme d'aage*; comme s'il eust voulu dire qu'il avoit assez d'expérience pour s'en tirer, parce que l'expérience est le fruit de l'aage. (Le Roux de Lincy 1842 [1996], 471)

> 1842: *George.—Laissez faire à George, il est homme d'âge.*
> On croit que ce proverbe est un mot que répétait souvent Louis XII, pour exprimer sa confiance dans l'habileté du cardinal George d'Amboise son ministre; non que ce ministre fût réellement un homme d'âge, puisqu'il mourut à cinquante ans, mais parce qu'il déployait dans l'administration

des affaires publiques une expérience comparable à celle des plus sages vieillards. *Être homme d'âge* signifiait alors, être homme d'expérience. (Quitard 1842 [1968], 423)

Basically, all of the explanations of the proverb say the same, namely that Georges d'Amboise was indeed a very experienced administrator and that the reference to his age does not refer to longevity (he died at the age of fifty) but rather to his skills based on vast experience. Of much interest and importance is the fact that French lexicographers and paremiographers stopped registering the proverb by the middle of the nineteenth century. I know of only one exception, Claude Duneton's massive *Le Bouquet des expressions imagées* (1990) that registers it as a historical proverb from the seventeenth century but says nothing about its survival in the modern age: "XVIIe 1640 *laissez faire à Georges, c'est un homme d'âge*—proverbe fait du temps du cardinal 'George' d'Amboise, ministre d'Etat: quand on parlait des affaires publiques, on disait: 'laissez faire à George, c'est un homme d'âge': il s'en fallait rapporter à sa bonne conduite et à sa grande intelligence" (Duneton 1990, 228).

Besides this one reference, the proverb is absent in the modern French proverb collections as well as mono- and bilingual (French and English) dictionaries. It also cannot be found in written or oral communication any longer, and it would appear that it never gained much currency in earlier times either—certainly nothing in comparison to the English "let George do it," once it begins to appear at the end of the nineteenth century. This leads me to the informed conclusion that the French proverb had fallen out of use by the middle of the nineteenth century and most likely even earlier, with the paremiographers merely registering it as a historically interesting proverb but not as one in actual use any longer. I have also not found any sign of it in Quebecois or Louisiana French proverb collections or dictionaries (see Boudreaux 1970; DesRuisseaux 1991; Proteau 1982), and so I doubt very much that it was brought to North America by immigrants. I am also quite convinced that the French proverb did not make it to Great Britain.

My major reasons for arguing against a loan translation into English are: 1. The French proverb had currency primarily in its long version of "laissez faire à Georges, c'est un homme d'âge" with its specific reference to the experienced Georges d'Amboise and as such would have made little sense to someone outside of France. 2. The meaning of the French proverb is somewhat different from the English "let George do it," with the French text suggesting that one should or could hand over a difficult task to a more experienced person and the English text usually referring to a situation where someone unwilling to take on a task is pushing it off to another person. 3. The English proverb appears only around 1900, when the French proverb is long out of currency. There is a definite historical, linguistic (long and short texts), and semantic difference that supports the argument for polygenesis.

Yet, it is not to be denied that numerous Anglo-American lexicographers and paremiographers cling to the idea that monogenesis is at play. They argue that the English proverb was translated from the French original, with W. Gurney Benham taking the lead in 1926, most likely taking his cue from H. L. Mencken's claim five years earlier in his widely disseminated *The American Language*. Note by the way that Benham refers to the English text as an American proverb, thereby leaving out the possibility that the French proverb came to North American via Great Britain: "*Let George do it.* —American saying, especially current during the war, 1914–1918. It means 'Let the other fellow do it,' and comes from the French. Laissez faire à George, il est l'homme d'âge. —Leave it to George, he is the man of years. —(Old Fr. saying, said to have been traced to the time of Louis XII (1498–1515)" (Benham 1926, 800b).

What follows is a florilegium of similar references with their insistence on a French-English connection. This does not necessarily devalue such entries that often do include additional information of much use to the development of the English language proverb. Some of the following chronologically arranged paragraphs prove to be a bit repetitive, pointing to the lamentable fact that dictionary makers not only copy a lot from each other but also ignore new findings or neglect to do additional research. This is something that is changing with such modern quotation sleuths as Nigel Rees from Great Britain and Fred R. Shapiro from the United States who make heavy use of the internet to verify and often correct dates of first occurrences of quotations and proverbs alike. The first item also brings the significant variant "leave it to George" into play.

> 1936: "*Let George do it*," or "*Leave it to George*" is another way of expressing buckpassing ["To pass the buck"]. A translation of *Laissez faire à Georges* (Georges d'Amboise, prime minister to Louis XII, c. 1500), the saying was revived in England in reference to [David] Lloyd George. (Holt 1936, 47)

> 1948: *Let George do it, he is the man of years.* (Laissez faire à George, il est l'homme d'âge.)
> Louis XII of France, referring satirically to his prime minister, Cardinal Georges d'Amboise. (c. 1500). Translated into modern slang as meaning "Let the other fellow do it." [And quoting Archer Taylor from 1931, see above:] The traditional explanation in America is based on "George" as a name used in addressing Pullman porters. (Stevenson 1948, 946)

1949: *Let George do it, he is the man of the time.*
Louis XII of France (1462–1515)
[note 2:] *Laissez faire à Georges, il est homme d'âge.*—Referring to his prime minister, Cardinal Georges d'Amboise.
George McManus, American cartoonist, in his comic series, *Let George Do It*, popularized the saying in the early 1900s. (Bartlett 1949, 1218)

1968: *Let George do it.* [Louis XII of France (1462–1515)].
George = Georges d'Amboise (1460–1510), Cardinal, First Minister of State and Lieutenant-General of the Army, one of those incredible Renaissance figures who seemed able to do everything and to do it well.
Louis admired the Cardinal and trusted him, and he was well and faithfully served. But perfection is always slightly annoying and Louis's "Let George do it" was satirically intended. In its original form, it was: "Let George do it; he's the man of the Age." (Evans 1968, 268)

1977: *let George do it!*—roughly. Let someone else do it! A journalistic catch phrase dating from c. 1910 and applied to the enlistment of an unnamed expert or authority and the putting of the writer's own words into his mouth, and probably, as HLM[encken] pointed out in 1922 [i.e., 1921], deriving from the synonymous Fr. *laissez faire à Georges*, which goes back a long way, had an historical source, but 'later became common slang, was translated into English, had a revival during the early days of David Lloyd George's career, was adopted into American without any comprehension of either its first or its latest significance, and enjoyed the brief popularity of a year'. W[entworth] & F[lexner] pinpoint it to c. 1920 and note that it was popular during WW2, when it 'implied a lack of responsibility in helping the war effort': clearly the phrase was general enough during all the intervening US years. Moreover, as Professor John T. Fain wrote to me, on 25 April 1969, it 'can still be heard' in the US. In Britain, it had, by 1950, become very obsolete—and by 1970, I'd say, obsolete. (Partridge 1977, 135)

1994: *Let George do it*: Let someone—anyone—take the responsibility.
Coined at the French court as a derisory remark aimed at Louis XII who was given to passing the buck to Cardinal George, George d'Amboise (1460–1510). The original French '*Laissez faire à George*' became popular throughout France and eventually crossed the channel, reaching peak popularity at the beginning of this century. (Donald 1994, 205)

2001: *Let George Do It.*
If you want to push an unpleasant task upon somebody else, you might say, "Let George do it." The first to use this expression was no less than a king—Louis XII of France.
Louis XII's prime minister was Georges d'Amboise. He was both prime minister and the king's closest confidant, which gave him as much power as the king himself. Louis would not make a move unless it was approved of or urged

by d'Amboise. Whenever the king was asked to do something, his reply was stock: "*Laissez faire à Georges*," which roughly translates to "Let George do it."

So frequently did Louis use this phrase that the court attendants picked it up. Jokingly, at first, they would say "*Laissez faire à Georges*" whenever they wanted to shirk their duties. Through the courtiers, "*Laissez faire à Georges*" circulated throughout France. When it crossed the English Channel, it was translated into its English equivalent, "Let George do it." (Korach and Mordock 2001, 91)

The various references show how lexicographers and paremiographers cling to the idea that the French proverb "laissez faire à Georges" must be the legitimate antecedent to the English proverb "let George do it." To a certain degree, these explanations follow or copy each other, but there is some new information mentioned, specifically the comic strip "Let George Do It" (1909/1912) by George McManus, the association of the proverb with the British statesman and prime minister David Lloyd George, and the association of the proverb with the African American Pullman train porters. But it must be observed that none of the informative paragraphs just cited explain how a French proverb that had long dropped out of use—if in fact it ever was very popular in France at all—crossed the English Channel at about the turn of the twentieth century as a loan translation. It would have had no associative meaning to English speakers—why George and how about this George being a man of age (experience)? The French proverb had long since become obsolete, and it appears that it is Anglo American lexicography and paremiography that is keeping the questionable connection alive. How "dead" the French proverb is can well be seen from a bilingual *Dictionary of French and American Slang* (1965), whose editors know the English proverb but have no idea of the old French version: "George—to let George do it.— laisser à un autre le soin d'accomplir une tâche ou une corvée" (Leitner and Landen 1965, 60). All of this strengthens me in my conjecture that the English proverb had its own origin, and that it was coined in the United States from where it crossed the ocean to become current in England as well.

With this prevalence of associating the English proverb with a French origin, it is surprising that some truly major dictionaries and proverb collections make no mention of this assumed French-English connection. After all, lexicographers and paremiographers do build on earlier reference works, and they must, for the most part, have been aware of this stubborn claim. Could one not have expected a statement to the effect that the supposed French source of the English proverb "let George do it" is no longer tangible? By not stating explicitly that they reject any French claim, I have no definite idea whether these colleagues agree with my decision of a separate origin of the English proverb. In any case, by only consulting the following publications, the serious scholar would remain utterly uninformed of an important part of the whole story. Of course, the major dictionaries and collections listed below—among them the print editions of the *Oxford English Dictionary*—include invaluable contextualized references for the English proverb "let George do it" from the twentieth century, starting with the year 1910. I shall refrain from listing that information.

> 1951: *Let George do it*, let someone (or something) else do the work or take the responsibility. *Colloq.* or *slang*. (Mathews 1951, 690)
>
> 1970: Colloq. phr. *let George do it*: let someone else do the work or take the responsibility. orig. *U.S.* (Burchfield 1972: I, 1218; identical in Simpson and Weiner 1989, 6:464)
>
> 1975: *George do it, let*—Let someone else do it. Said in avoiding responsibility. Common c1920 and during W.W. II when the term implied a lack of responsibility in helping the war effort. (Wentworth and Flexner 1975, 212)
>
> 1980: *let George do it* Let someone else do the work or assume the responsibility; pass the buck. This American colloquial expression dates from the turn of the [nineteenth/twentieth] century. (Urdang and LaRoche 1980, 202)
>
> 1989: Let *George* do it
> [no explanation, just several historical references] (Whiting 1989, 250–51)
>
> 1993: *Let George do it* Find someone else do it; I won't. (Wilkinson 1993, 279)
>
> 1994: *let George do it* let someone else do the task. (Lighter 1994, 1:879)
>
> 1995: *let George do it!* meaning, 'let someone else do it, or take the responsibility', this catchphrase was in use by 1910 and is probably of American origin. (Rees 1995, 121)
>
> 1997: *let George do it* let someone else do the work or take the responsibility. (Knowles 1997, 353)
>
> 2006: *Let George do it.* Anon. referring to the universal nickname of Pullman attendants, who attended to the passengers' every wish; probably from the name of the founder of the company, George Mortimer Pullman. (Dow 2006, 168)
>
> 2012: *let George do it!* on the railways, used as a humorous attempt to delegate an unpleasant task *US*. Pullman porters, low men on the food chain for railway workers, were known as George. (Dalzell and Victor 2012, 1201)
>
> 2012: Let *George* do it.
> [no explanation, but we included it in a list of proverbs that we judged as being older than the year 1900] (Doyle, Mieder, and Shapiro 2012, 288)

All of these references imply or state directly that the proverb "let George do it" is of English or more likely of American origin. This is also true for my friend Nigel Rees, the ingenious phraseological sleuth from London. In one of his more recent comprehensive volumes on phrase origins, he does come in on an American origin of the phrase, even though he mentions the French-origin argument once again.

> 2006: *let George do it!* Meaning 'let someone else do it, or take the responsibility', this catchphrase was in use by the 1900s and is probably of American origin. It appears on a screen title in *Gertie the Dinosaur*, one of the first movie cartoons (US 1909). A bet is placed in an archaeological museum that a dinosaur cannot be made to move. When it does so, a celebratory dinner is held. The question then is, who will pay? 'Let George do it' is the reply. It seems unlikely that this was the origin of the phrase—merely one of the uses that popularized it. Indeed, H. L. Mencken, *The American Language* (1922 [i.e., 1921]), traces it back to the French *laissez faire à Georges*. The phrase received a new lease of life with the invention of the autopilot in the Second World War. Inevitably, the autopilot was dubbed 'George'. (Rees 2006, 407)

This almost-definitely American origin is now being upheld by the up-to-date electronic version of the *Oxford English Dictionary*, as accessed on November 29, 2012:

> N. Amer. colloq. *let George do it*: let someone else do the work or take the responsibility.
> [Origin unknown.
> It has frequently been suggested (e.g., by H.L. Mencken *Amer. Lang.* (1921) xi.) that the phrase is after French *laissez faire à Georges*, said to have been used by King Louis XII (1462–1515, king from 1498) with reference to his prime minister Cardinal Georges d'Amboise (1460–1510), to whom he entrusted much of the day-to-day running of the country. However, this French phrase is apparently not attested before 1805 (in L.-P. Anquetil *Hist. de France* V. 376, which may have been the first source to attribute its use to King Louis XII), although a variant *laisser faire à George, c'est un homme d'âge* is found earlier (1690; apparently last recorded in *Dict. de Trevoux* (1771)). Regardless of the origin of the French phrase, it is very uncertain whether there is any link with the English phrase, since the French phrase (in any form) appears to have been very rare by the date of the first attestation of the English phrase.]
> (www.oed.com)

This incredibly valuable explanatory discussion precedes the earliest reference, dated 1909, found by the staff of the *Oxford English Dictionary* thus far. I can say with a bit of scholarly delight that I cannot only push this date back by seven years to 1902, and I have already shown earlier that the registration of the French proverb begins at least in 1656 (thirty-four years earlier than 1690) and was recorded at least until 1842 (seventy-one years later than what the OED has found). But never mind this expansion of dates. The key issue is that the editors of the *Oxford English Dictionary* agree with me that the proverb "let George do it" is most likely and perhaps definitely of American origin and is not related historically to the French proverb. This does indeed strengthen my claim that all of this is a case of polygenesis.

I believe it is appropriate for a scholar to stick out his proverbial neck on certain occasions. This is one of those cases, for I am convinced that the proverb "let George do it" must have been current before 1900. Sure enough, the earliest printed reference thus far that my friend Charles C. Doyle found stems from 1902, but that basically presupposes that the proverb was in oral use before then. This up-to-now earliest reference makes it clear that the proverb must have been known, for otherwise the occurrence of the name "George" would be senseless.

> I believe about the most aggravating person to come in contact with is the one who, when asked to do a certain kind of work, to which he is not used, will say, "Well, I've never done that before, hadn't you better let George do it!" About this time you want to get out your lecture on self-reliance and confidence and deliver it to that man in such a way that he will not only do the work, but later, in thinking it over, will really feel proud of the fact that he can do something new. (Superintendent 1902, 15–16)

In fact, Doyle also drew my attention to the fact that the variant "leave it to George," with the same meaning of pushing a job off to someone else, was current in the latter part of the nineteenth century, referring me to a short article about the early Quaker George Fox, published anonymously by the "London Society" on September 26, 1886, in the *New York Times*: "Although he [George Fox] was so highly esteemed that when difficult matters arose at the general meetings of the [Quaker] society they were usually shelved with the remark they 'would leave it to George,' individual members who thought he erred did not scruple to tell him so to his face" (London Society 1886, 11).

Yes, Mr. Fox does in fact have "George" as his first name, but I agree with Doyle's comment to me in a letter of November 27, 2012, that included this important reference: "I believe 'Leave it to George' is an authentic variant. In the 1886 article attached, the subject is the early Quaker George Fox—but what's interesting is the enclosure of the phrase 'would leave it to George' in quotation marks, as if the writer is playfully adapting the proverb to the account of the historical figure." In any case, the lexicographer Alfred Holt, it will be recalled, also felt that 'Let George do it' and 'Leave it to George' are two sides of the same proverbial coin" (Holt 1936, 47).

Now comes the sixty-four-thousand-dollar question, to put it proverbially: Who is this George of the English proverb if not Georges d'Amboise of the much earlier French text? The answer has actually already been alluded to by a number of the lexicographical and paremiographical references cited above. The *George* of the American proverb is the generic name that was given to emancipated slaves who were hired by the railroad entrepreneur George Pullman after the Civil War as cheap porters in his famous Pullman sleeping cars. There is plenty of documentation to this stereotypical and degrading name-calling, and it took courageous and powerful labor leaders like Phillip Randolph, the African American founder of The Brotherhood of Sleeping Car Porters, to overcome this infuriating and uncalled-for custom.

> At one time traveling salesmen considered it the acme of wit to call Pullman porters "George," presumably after the paternal founder himself. No one knows precisely when or why Pullman decided that porters must be men of the Negro race; but, for close to a century all porters in the United States have been Negroes. The first was probably a well-trained ex-slave, hired about 1867. Nameless in history, he filled his positions so capably that he established an exclusive field of employment for thousands of other black men, who gained education, mobility, and social status by working for the railroad. (Reinhardt 1970, 298)

True, African American porters were able to carve out a livelihood for themselves and their families, but they were clearly exploited by demanding travel schedules and low pay, resulting in the eventual formation of the Brotherhood union. But travelers clearly depended on the services of the porters, and one wonders why they would have been so condescending as to deindividualize the porters into anonymous Georges. After all, the porters performed a multitude of services to assure a pleasant trip for the Pullman passengers, performing their tasks to such perfection that "In the Pullman Parlor Car of the 1880s, the saying was: 'Let George do it'" (Reinhardt 1970, 304). This statement appears as the caption of a picture of the exquisite interior of one of these Pullman cars, but alas, up till now I have not been able to locate any references of the proverb in the impressive literature dealing with the Pullman porters that actually quote the proverb from the last quarter of the nineteenth century. Most of the extant literature deals only with the name *George*. In fact, Jervis Anderson entitles an entire chapter "George" in his book *A. Philipp Randolph: A Biographical Portrait* (1972), indicating how insulting this generalized naming was to the porters: "'Then, too,' a porter from Jacksonville recalls, 'there was this thing of "George." No matter who you were, or how old, most everybody wanted to call you "George." It meant that you were just George Pullman's boy, same as in slave days when if the owner was called Jones the slave was called Jones. It got so you were scared to go into the office to pick up your check, for fear some little sixteen-year-old office boy would yell out *George*.'" (Anderson 1972, 163).

Jack Santino, in his richly documented book *Miles of Smiles, Years of Struggle: Stories of Black Pullman Porters* (1989), cites numerous interviews with former black porters that illustrate how the generic name *George* rendered them anonymous and subservient to the white passengers. He summarizes his findings in a powerful statement:

> The epithet "George," by which they [the porters] were known generally, did much to create and maintain the stereotypes. The term was associated with the days of slavery, because it identified porters as the property of George Pullman, with all the associated ramifications of inferiority and childlike dependency. As such, A. Philip Randolph insisted there be porters' name cards in each Pullman car, and he recognized that this symbolic change altering the term of address was as important as the more tangible improvements that increased pay and lessened hours. "George" is in many ways the sum total of the stereotype, and porters tried their best to ignore it. (Santino 1989, 125–26)

This change took effect on October 19, 1926, when the Pullman Company officially "announced that thereafter all Pullman cars would have the active porter's name displayed in a prominent place so that the passengers would know how to address him when he was needed. The company instructed porters that they were to answer only to their own names, and that Pullman would take no disciplinary actions against them for refusing to respond to 'George'" (Harris 1977, 83–84).

The African American labor leader and civil rights champion A. Philip Randolph deserves most of the credit for having freed the large number of black porters from their modern enslavement. He brought an end to "the time when all Pullman porters were indiscriminately called 'George', [and] he brought them the respect of the traveling public and confidence in themselves. The value of the union, in Randolph's opinion, lay in its demonstration that blacks indeed possessed a 'spirit of self-help, self-initiative, and self-reliance'" (Pfeffer 1990, 31). It took decades to bring this change about, and with all the "George" name-calling that went on, it should not be surprising that the proverb "let George do it" sprang up in the last decades of the nineteenth century. Clearly, Patricia and Fredrick McKissack must agree with this conjecture, since they employed the proverb as a chapter heading in their book *A Long Hard Journey: The Story of the Pullman*

Porter (1989). The time was ripe for it, and I am thoroughly convinced that the proverb "let George do it" was current in the United States before 1900 and that it came from the questionable treatment that the black Pullman porters received from their white passengers. It is almost inconceivable to me that I have not been able to find it before that date in the many printed and online accounts that I have checked, but, as the proverb states, "Hope springs eternal!"

Be that as it may, the American proverb "let George do it," despite its inauspicious beginnings on the Pullman trains, soon became a generally accepted proverb without being directed in a racially malevolent way against black porters. In other words, the name "George" lost its unfortunate association with George Pullman and his African American porters and took on the meaning of any male person at all. By the end of the first decade of the twentieth century, it was well known in the United States, and it also spread to Great Britain, where it became popularized around 1916–17 in connection with the well-liked prime minister David Lloyd George, whom people trusted to do big things. The proverb appeared in novels, plays, poems (1935 by Ogden Nash), newspapers, magazines, advertisements, cartoons (1909 by George McManus), radio programs, songs (1909 by Ray Zirkel) and popular films with the title "Let George Do It" (1938 and 1940). The proverb became so popular in the United States that linguist Josephine Burnham registered the neologism "let-George-do-it-itis" (1927, 245) referring to the proverb's excessive employment. In its actual contextualized use, the meaning of the proverb is rather ambivalent. On one hand, its wisdom is considered to be ill-advised, and then again other references show that it can be interpreted positively in certain contexts. As is true for most proverbs, their meaning depends on their contextualized use, with this polysituativity resulting in polyfunctionality and polysemanticity (Mieder 2004, 9).

Famed linguist and phraseologist Eric Partridge claimed, as one of my earlier lexicographical references shows, that the English proverb has—somewhat like its French equivalent many years earlier—become obsolete today. When I have undertaken my own field research among friends, colleagues, and students, I have often received the answer that they have never heard of "let George do it." But there is one thing that I have learned over the years when asking native speakers whether they are aware of a certain proverb. They are often surprisingly quick in responding negatively, but upon further probing, it frequently becomes clear that they simply find it difficult to recall proverbs without contexts. In any case, when one checks in Google for "let George do it" or "leave it to George," millions of modern hits occur, and the proverb is surely not extinct in the modern age. Fortunately, its racial beginnings are gone and forgotten, something that becomes wonderfully clear from the popular African American heavyweight boxer George Foreman's delightful children's book, *Let George Do It!* (2005). He certainly would not have given his book this title if he saw any lingering anti-black stereotype in it, and nor would the prestigious Simon & Schuster have published it for children. It is well known that George Foreman (Big George) named all of his five sons "George" and in the humorously illustrated book, Foreman offers some funny insights into his family, where the proverb "let George do it" exhibits a universal applicability. This book remains quite popular to this day, and it surely did its part in keeping the proverb alive.

The fact that the United States had George Washington, George Herbert Walker Bush, and George Walker Bush as presidents with the first name "George" also has helped to keep the proverb current. And when one finds newspaper headlines like "Let George Washington do it" today, it is obvious that it links the complete name of the first president with the idea of the government being located in Washington, DC. In other words, it becomes a somewhat satirical slogan for letting the government take care of things.

I have collected hundreds of references of the American proverb "let George do it" from various types of sources from the twentieth century and today. There is no space here to include them, but let me state categorically that all of those occurrences make it perfectly clear that this American proverb has by no means gone underground or died out. While it might be less frequently heard or read in Great Britain, it is solidly established in the American media and mind, without any connection to the earlier French proverb that has long disappeared and never went beyond France, in any case. Its racially motivated beginning during the last quarter of the nineteenth century is absent from its use and meaning today, but it should not be forgotten that the proverb originated as an insensitive slogan for getting black Pullman porters to be at the beck and call of their white passengers. By now, the proverb is indeed an innocuous statement that can stand next to "pass the buck" in expressing the unfortunately only-too-human tendency of avoiding action or passing responsibility to others. But that is the nature of proverbs in general—they reflect human nature and are used when a ready-made metaphor can hit the proverbial nail on the head better than lengthy prose could. So, even if the American proverb "let George do it" with its independent origin is perhaps less known today (my students claim not to use it), it remains well suited as a concise traditional piece of wisdom to deal with the complexities and ambiguities of modernity.

References

This chapter was first published in *Paremia* 22 (2013): 17–29.

Anderson, J. 1972. *A. Philip Randolph: A Biographical Portrait*. New York: Harcourt, Brace, Jovanovich.
Anquetil, Louis-Pierre. 1805. *Histoire de France depuis les Gaulois jusqu'à la fin de la monarchie*. 14 vols. Paris: Garnery.
Bartlett, John. 1949. *Familiar Quotations*. 12th ed. Edited by Christopher Morley. Boston: Little, Brown, and Company.
Benham, W. Gurney. 1926. *Putnam's Complete Book of Quotations, Proverbs, and Household Words*. New York: G. P. Putnam's Sons.
Boudreaux, Anna Mary. 1970. "[French] Proverbs, Metaphors, and Sayings of the Kaplan Area." *Louisiana Folklore Miscellany* 3: 16–24.
Burchfield, Robert W. 1972. *A Supplement to the Oxford English Dictionary*. Oxford: Clarendon Press.
Burnham, Josephine. 1927. "Three Hard-Worked Suffixes." *American Speech* 2: 244–46.
Caillot, A. 1826. *Nouveau Dictionnaire Proverbial, satirique et burlesque*. Paris: Dauvin.
Chesnutt, Michael. 2002."Polygenese." In *Enzyklopädie des Märchens*, edited by Kurt Ranke and Rolf Wilhelm Brednich, 10:1161–64. Berlin: Walter de Gruyter.
Dalzell, Tom, and Terry Victor. 2012. *The New Partridge Dictionary of Slang and Unconventional English*. 2 vols. New York: Routledge.
DesRuisseaux Pierre. 1991. *Dictionnaire des proverbs québécois*. Québec: Bibliothèque québécoise.
Donald, Graeme. 1994. *The Dictionary of Modern Phrase*. New York: Simon & Schuster.
Dow, Andrew. 2006. *Dictionary of Railway Quotations*. Baltimore: Johns Hopkins University Press.
Doyle, Charles Clay, Wolfgang Mieder, and Fred R. Shapiro. 2012. *The Dictionary of Modern Proverbs*. New Haven, CT: Yale University Press.
Dundes, Alan. 2000. "Paremiological Pet Peeves." In *Folklore in 2000: Voces amicorum Guilhelmo Voigt sexagenario*, edited by Ilona Nagy and Kincső Verebélyi, 291–99. Budapest: Universitas Scientarium de Rolando Eötvös nominata.
Duneton Claude. 1990. *Le Bouquet des expressions imagées: Encyclopédie thématqiue des locutions figurées de la langue française*. Paris: Éditions du Seuil.
Evans, Bergen. 1968. *Dictionary of Quotations*. New York: Avenel Books.
Fleury de Bellingen. 1656. *L'Etymologie ou Explication Des Proverbes Francois*. Paris: Adrian Vlaco.
Foreman, George. 2005. *Let George Do It!* New York: Simon & Schuster.
Furetière, Antoine. 1690. *Dictionnaire universel, Contenant generalement tous les mots françois tant vieux que modernes*. La Haye: Arnout & Reinier Leers; reprinted Paris: Le Robert, 1978.
Furetière, Antoine, and Étienne Souciet. 1771. *Dictionnaire universel françois et latin: vulgairement appelé dictionnaire de Trévoux, contenant la signification & la définition des mots de l'une & de l'autre langue, avec leurs différens usages* . . . . 8 vols. Paris: Avec Appropriation et Privilege du Roi.
Harris, William H. 1977. *Keeping the Faith: A. Philip Randolph, Milton P. Webster, and the Brotherhood of Sleeping Car Porters, 1925–37*. Urbana: University of Illinois Press.
Holt, Alfred H. 1936. *Phrase Origins: A Study of Familiar Expressions*. New York: Thomas Y. Crowell.
Knowles, Elizabeth. 1997. *The Oxford Dictionary of Phrase, Saying, and Quotation*. Oxford: Oxford University Press.

Korach, Myron, and John B. Mordock. 2001. *Common Phrases and Where They Come From.* Guilford, CT: The Lyons Press.

La Mesangère, Pierre de. 1821. *Dictionnaire des proverbes français.* Paris: Treuttel et Würtz.

Le Roux de Lincy, Adrien Jean Victor. 1842. *Le livre des proverbes français.* 2 vols. Paris: Paulin; reprinted Paris: Hachette Livre, 1996.

Leitner, M. J., and J. R. Lanen. 1965. *Dictionary of French and American Slang.* New York: Crown Publishing.

Lighter, J. E. 1994. *Random House Historical Dictionary of American Slang.* 2 vols. New York: Random House.

London Society. 1886. "George Fox." *New York Times*, September 26, 11.

Mathews, Mitford M. 1951. *Dictionary of Americanisms on Historical Principles.* Chicago: University of Chicago Press.

McKissack, Patricia, and Frederick McKissack. 1989. *A Long Hard Journey: The Story of the Pullman Porter.* New York: Walker.

Mencken, H. L. 1921. *The American Language.* New York: Alfred A. Knopf.

Mieder, Wolfgang. 1993. *Proverbs Are Never Out of Season: Popular Wisdom in the Modern Age.* New York: Oxford University Press; reprinted New York: Peter Lang, 2012.

———. 2004. *Proverbs: A Handbook.* Westport, CT: Greenwood Press; reprinted New York: Peter Lang, 2012.

Nash, Ogden. 1981. *A Penny Saved Is Impossible.* Boston: Little, Brown and Company.

Oudin, Antoine. 1656. *Curiositez Francoises, pour Supplément aux Dictionnaires ou Recueil de plusieurs belles proprietez, avec une infinité de Proverbes & Quolibets.* Paris: Antoine Sommaville.

Partridge, Eric. 1977. *A Dictionary of Catch Phrases: British and American, from the Sixteenth Century to the Present Day.* New York: Stein and Day.

Pfeffer, Paula F. 1990. *A. Philip Randolph: Pioneer of the Civil Rights Movement.* Baton Rouge: Louisiana State University Press.

Proteau, Lorenzo. 1982. *La parlure québécoise.* Boucherville, Québec: Les Éditions franco-québécoises.

Quitard, Pierre-Marie. 1842. *Dictionnaire étymologique, historique et anecdotique des proverbes et des locutions proverbiales de la langue française.* Paris: P. Bertrand; reprinted Genève: Slatkine Reprints, 1968.

Rees, Nigel. 1995. *Dictionary of Catchphrases.* London: Cassell.

———. 2006. *A Word in Your Shell-like: 6,000 Curious & Everyday Phrases Explained.* London: HarperCollins.

Reinhardt, Richard. 1970. *Workin' on the Railroad: Reminiscences from the Age of Steam.* Palo Alto, CA: American West Publishing Company.

Santino, Jack. 1989. *Miles of Smiles, Years of Struggle: Stories of Black Pullman Porters.* Urbana: University of Illinois Press.

Shapiro, Fred R. 2006. *The Yale Book of Quotations.* New Haven, CT: Yale University Press.

Simpson, John A., and Ed Weiner. 1989. *The Oxford English Dictionary.* Oxford: Clarendon Press.

Stevenson, Burton. 1948. *The Home Book of Proverbs, Maxims, and Familiar Phrases.* New York: Macmillan.

Superintendent. 1902. "Characteristic of Superintendents and Workmen." *The Wood-Worker* 21, no. 1 (March): 15–16.

Taylor, Archer. 1931. *The Proverb.* Cambridge, MA: Harvard University Press; reprinted with an introduction and bibliography by Wolfgang Mieder as *The Proverb and An Index to "The Proverb."* Bern: Peter Lang, 1985.

Urdang, Laurence, and Nancy La Roche. 1980. *Picturesque Expressions: A Thematic Dictionary*. Detroit: Gale Research Company.
Wentworth, Harold, and Stuart Berg Flexner. 1975. *Dictionary of American Slang*. New York: Thomas Y. Crowell.
Whiting, Bartlett Jere. 1989. *Modern Proverbs and Proverbial Sayings*. Cambridge, MA: Harvard University Press.
Wilkinson, P. R. 1993. *Thesaurus of Traditional English Metaphors*. London: Routledge.
Zirkel, Ray, and Bill Carney. 1909. *Let George Do It*. Columbus, OH: Carney and Zirkel.

12

"TO BE (ALL) GREEK TO SOMEONE"

Origin, History, and Meaning of an English Proverbial Expression

THERE HAVE ALWAYS BEEN FOLK CONCEPTIONS OF WHAT the most difficult languages of the world might be, with linguists also having been interested in this question. As Arnold Rosenberg has shown in his fascinating article on "The Hardest Natural Languages" (1979), Chinese appears to win the prize, with Greek and Hebrew following somewhat behind. It is then not surprising that numerous languages refer to Chinese as a symbol of unintelligibility or incomprehensibility by way of the proverbial expression "to be Chinese to someone." But there are many variants that replace this designation with other difficult languages, notably Arabic, Greek, Hebrew, Latin, and Turkish. A number of European languages prefer "to be Greek to someone," as for example Dutch, English, Norwegian, Portuguese, and Swedish, which does not mean that they might not also have less frequently used proverbial expressions that refer to Hebrew or Latin, for example (Piirainen 2015, see also the impressive list in Wikipedia).

There is no doubt that these varied phraseologisms of expressing the difficulty of understanding someone or something belong to the so-called class of "widespread idioms" (Piirainen 2016, 523–26) with each having its own history. The "Greek" variants might have a common medieval Latin origin, but they might also have been loan translated later from other languages or, perhaps less likely, have their independent origins simply due to the fact that people consider Greek to be a particularly challenging language. In other words, polygenesis could well play into this (Mieder 2014, 34). What follows is an analysis of how the English proverbial phrase "to be Greek to someone" came about and how it has been employed in various ways from the late Middle Ages to the present (see the short notes by

Kulisheck 1952; Williams 1991; Zimmer 2015). Fortunately, there are a number of English collections of proverbs and proverbial expressions based on historical principles, so that a number of contextualized references that will be discussed below were found by consulting them (Apperson 1929, 273; Stevenson 1948, 1,037–38; Tilley 1950, 275; Taylor and Whiting 1958, 161; Wilson 1970, 336; Whiting 1977, 187; Dent 1984, 388; Whiting 1989, 271; Titelman 1996, 184; Bryan and Mieder 2005, 337–38). And, of course, the celebrated *Oxford English Dictionary* (Simpson and Weiner 1989, 6:807) has its ten references, but they are basically included in the proverb dictionaries as well. The present deliberations will go far beyond these lexicographical and paremiographical accomplishments by locating many additional historical references and by grouping them according to variants and providing explanatory comments.

There has been some speculation that the Italian jurist Francesco Accorso (Franciscus Accursius, 1180–1260) might have originated the medieval Latin proverb "Graecum est, non potest legi" (It is Greek, it cannot be read; Anonymous 1798, 393; Moore 1819, 6; Mery 1828, 171; Fumagalli 1911, 100) in his famous legal compilation of *Glossa ordinaria* (c. 1230), an intriguing claim that thus far has not been substantiated. It was also current in the variants "Graecum est, non legitur" (It is Greek, it is not read; Koelb 2008, 78); "Graeca non leguntur (Greek is not read; Liebs 1982, 81; Kasper 1996, 117; Bartels 2008, 77); and "Graeca sunt, non leguntur" (That is Greek and is not read; Oertel 1842, 21; Herhold 1887, 105; Walther and Schmidt 1982, 7:929), with the four statements being employed by monks or notably legal scribes of the late Middle Ages who could not read the Greek passages contained in various types of Latin documents. Greek had been known outside of Greece at a somewhat earlier time among scholars, but Latin had simply become the *lingua franca*, and it took until Erasmus of Rotterdam and his fellow humanists that the interest in the Greek language resurfaced. In fact, in England it took until 1519 for the teaching of the Greek language to become established (Kulisheck 1952, 275; Barta 2010, 1:57–58), and it was above all Sir John Cheke (1514–1557) who as professor of Greek at Cambridge University helped to reestablish the study of Greek in the second quarter of the sixteenth century (Topp 1878, 401–2). His early biographer John Strype in *The Life of the Learned Sir John Cheke* (1705) discusses this in considerable detail and includes the standard variant of the proverb: "This language was little known or understood hitherto in this realm. And if any saw a piece of Greek, they used to say, *Graecum est; non potest legi*, i.e., 'It is Greek, it cannot be read.' And those few that did pretend to some insight into it, read it after a strange corrupt manner, pronouncing the vowels and diphthongs, and several of the consonants, very much amiss.... These errors then Cheke in his lectures plainly discovered, and at length exploded" (Strype 1821, 14).

Yet even though Greek was being taught again, at least somewhat, at the famous universities from then on, the proverb had long become established to signify in a more general way that something is incomprehensible or unintelligible, even if it might be just one or two lines of Greek. This is well illustrated in a tongue-in-cheek passage by Joseph Addison in the British periodical *The Spectator* that he edited together with Sir Richard Steele from 1711 to 1712:

> As for myself, I have had the reputation, ever since I came from school, of being a trusty Trojan, and am resolved never to give quarter to the smallest particle of Greek, wherever I chance to meet it. It is for this reason I take it very ill of you, that you sometimes hang out Greek colours at the head of your paper, and sometimes give a word of the enemy in the body of it. When I meet with anything of this nature I throw down your speculations upon the table; with that form of words which we make use of when we declare war upon an author,
>
> Graecum est, non potest legi.[1]
>
> I give you this hint, that you may for the future abstain from any such hostilities at your peril.
>
> [1]This proverb originated in the jurisconsult Franciscus Accursius, who lived in the thirteenth century. Whenever Accursius, in lecturing on Justinian, met with a quotation from Homer, he said "Graecum est, non potest legi."
>
> (Addison 1711, 369–70)

This is a splendid passage, in that it describes exactly what scholars and students, who do not know even the rudiments of the marvelous Greek language (myself included, unfortunately), do today when they come across a mere Greek word or a phrase: they pass over it without any comprehension. Exciting as the attached footnote is, it is a shame that the precise reference from Accursius was not included. Nevertheless, it reveals that the Latin phrase maintained its proverbial status in the eighteenth century. This can also be seen from a reference from 1742: "Whereas it is being Matter of Fact, that no Greek Copies of this Epistle had that Verse, neither the Author of the Preface, nor any Friend for him, searched for it in any Greek Copy. And its [sic] not altogether improbable, that they could not do it; the Proverb, *Graecum est, non potest Legi*, being remarkably true of those Times. Nay, long before, and longer after the Making of this Preface, the Fathers of the *Latin* Church were generally ignorant of the *Greek* Tongue" (Anonymous 1742, 1:152).

Below is a comment from a letter of March 19, 1788, in which William Cowper describes his frustration about those who might criticize his translation from the Greek when they themselves know barely a word of it: "But alas! 'tis after all a mortifying consideration, that the majority of my judges hereafter will be no judges of this. *Graecum est, non potest legi*, is a motto that would suit nine in ten of those, who will give themselves airs about it, and pretend to like or to dislike it" (Hayley 1812, 3:121–22). It was simply true that "Every passage in Greek, which accidentally occurred in any Writer, was scouted, and consigned to oblivion with the stigma of—'Graecum est; non potest legi'" (Pegge 1814, 89–90). Realizing that the knowledge of Latin was, of course, also waning as time went on and also that someone who knew the Latin proverb had reason to utter it in English for the sake of clear communication, it should not be surprising that it was translated and truncated into the general formulation "to be Greek to someone" in the sense of being incomprehensible. After all, the Greek language had already become synonymous with this connotation in America as well. Thus, Francis Asbury on May 12, 1794, wrote into his journal: "I preached the next day; but it seemed as if my discourse had almost as well have been Greek, such spiritual death prevails among the people" (Clark 1958, 2:14). In a letter of January 4, 1818, American Anne Newport Royall wrote: "I know no more about it than a monkey. I have asked hundreds, and either they, or I, must be fools: Not a soul that I met can explain it [what a gas is] in terms that I can comprehend. They stuff it with such a number of outrageous hard words, that I could understand Greek sooner" (Royall 1818, 125). Little wonder that the English proverbial expression has survived, while the Latin proverb, for the most part, has been erased from common usage.

The earliest recorded reference of the proverbial expression "to be Greek to someone" appears in George Gascoigne's English translation *The Supposes* (1566) of the Italian comedy *I Suppositi* (1509) by Lodovico Ariosto. In the original, a nurse simply says "Either this doesn't make sense or I don't understand. Please speak clearly" (Cunliffe 1969, 1:190) which Gascoigne translated rather freely as "This geare is Greeke to me: either it hangs not well together, or I am very dull of understanding: speake plaine, I pray you" (Gascoigne 1906, 11; Whiting 1938, 347). Since Gascoigne renders this statement so freely into English by way of the "Greek" phrase, it can be assumed that it might already have been current in some circles at that time. And yet, it is perhaps surprising that he did not employ it in his prose work *The Adventures of Master F. J.* (1573): "Gentlewoman (quod he) you speake *Greeke*, the which I have now forgotten, and mine instructers are to farre from mee at this present to expound your words" (Cunliffe 1969, 1:397). This is quite the ironic statement, since the woman is not speaking in Greek but rather utters incomprehensible rubbish. But be that as it may, William Shakespeare is next in line to have used the proverbial expression at least once in his play *Julius Caesar* (1599). Since Gascoigne's play served him as source material for his play *The Taming of the Shrew* (1594), he might have picked it up from him or, as mentioned, it could already have been current in oral use in his circles. In the play, the blunt Casca ridicules the speech of Cicero who is known to have had a good command of the Greek language:

CASSIUS: Did Cicero say any thing?

CASCA: Ay, he spoke Greek.

CASSIUS: To what effect?

CASCA: Nay, and I tell you that, I'll ne'er look you in the face again: but those that understood him smil'd at one another and shook their heads; but, for mine own part, it was Greek to me. *(Act I, scene 3, lines 278–84)*

No matter, due to Shakespeare's fame, who by the way had "small Latine, and lesse Greeke" (Baldwin 1944, 1:1–3), it has become quite customary for lexicographers, paremiographers, and other phrase sleuths to erroneously or unintentionally credit the Bard with the origin of the English proverbial expression (Hyamson 1922, 168; Trevor and Trevor 1985, 214; Knowles 1997, 222; Rees 1997, 486; Knowles 1999, 674). In any case, by 1600 the Latin proverb in its English version must have been well established, as a number of early references from that time from playwrights Thomas Middleton, Thomas Dekker, and John Marston show:

1602: IMPERIA: Nay, nay, nay, 'tis Greek to me, 'tis Greek to me: I never had remnant of his Spanish-leather learning. Here he comes: your ears may now fit themselves out of the whole piece. *(Thomas Middleton, Blurt, Master-Constable (3:3); Bullen 1964, 1:61)*

1603: FAR.: There he grumbles God knows what, but I'll be sworn he knows not so much as one character of the [Greek] tongue.
Rice.: Why, then it's Greek to him. *(Thomas Dekker, Patient Grissil (2:1); Dekker 1841, 17)*

1604: GONZAGO: Of your fair bearing, rest more anxious
(No, anxious is not a good word)—rest more vigilant
Over your passion, both forbear and bear,
Anechou è apechou (that's Greek to you now). *(John Marston, The Fawn (3:1); Marston 1963, 65)*

Established as the phrase might have been at that time, a number of variants ran more or less parallel to it, indicating clearly that it takes time for a new proverbial expression to find its standard form (Mieder 2004, 24–25).

By 1610, in the play *The Alchemist* by none less than the dramatist Ben Jonson, the interesting variant "to be heathen Greek to someone" appeared on the scene. It seems to be an exaggeration, playing off the idea that the ancient Greeks obviously were not Christians. Excerpts from Jonson's play make this quite clear, and it might just be that he came up with the entire idea:

ANANIAS: Heathen Greek, I take it.

SUBTLE: How? Heathen Greek?

ANANIAS: All's heathen but the Hebrew.

SUBTLE: Sirrah, my varlet, stand you forth and speak to him
Like a philosopher; answer i'the language.
Name the vexations, and the martyrizations
Of metals in the work.

FACE: Sir, putrefaction,
Solution, ablution, sublimation,
Cohobation, calcination, ceration, and
Fixation.

SUBTLE: This is heathen Greek to you now?
And when comes vivification?

FACE: After mortification.

SUBTLE: This is heathen Greek to you now?

(JONSON 1995, 254 (ACT II, SCENE 5))

On it goes, with "This's heathen Greek to you?" and "This's heathen Greek to you, still?" also appearing in the same scene. Ten years later, Thomas Shelton made use of it in his early Miguel de Cervantes Saavedra translation with the title *The History of the Valorous and Witty Knight-Errant Don Quixote of the Mancha* (1620), and he might well have picked it up from Jonson: "All this to the husbandmen was heathen Greek or pedlar's French; but not to scholars, who straight perceived the weakness of Don Quixote's brain" (Shelton 1907: 3:200). The expanded version hung on at least into the nineteenth century, as exemplified by the following citations:

1681: GUIL. Friend, what Language can you sing?
PET. Oh, Sir, your Singers speak all Languages.
GUIL. Say'st thou so, prithee than let's have a touch of Heathen *Greek*.
PET. That you shall, Sir, Sol la me fa sol, etc.
FRAN. Hum, I think this is indeed Heathen *Greek*, I'm sure 'tis to me.
(Aphra Behn, *The False Count* (4:1; Summers 1967, 3:146)

> 1688: I should never have known these Worthy Ingenious Gentlemen, my dear Friends, all this fine Language had been Heathen Greek to me. (Thomas Shadwell, *The Squire of Alsatia*; Shadwell 1688, 56)
>
> 1769: Almost as soon as I began [to preach], a large company of quality (as they call them) came, and embarrassed me not a little. I knew this was heathen Greek to them; but I could not then change my subject: however, I diluted my discourse as much as I could, that it might not be quite too strong for their digestion. (John Wesley, journal entry of July 1, 1769; Wesley 1906, 3:377)
>
> 1801: On three subjects he is directed to read and research—corn-laws, finance, tythes, according to their written order. Alas! They are heathen Greek to the scribe! (Robert Southey, letter of November 20, 1801; Southey 1850, 2:175)
>
> 1820: The latter [Master Simon] had a vast deal to say about *casting*, and *imping*, and *gleaming*, and *enseaming*, and giving the hawk the *rangle*, which I saw was all heathen Greek to old Christy; but he maintained his point notwithstanding, and seemed to hold all this technical lore in utter disrespect. (Washington Irving, *Bracebridge Hall*, 1896, 1:22)

As can be seen, this variant also made it to the United States, where the following fascinating dialect adaptation can be reported from Joseph Lincoln's novel *The Depot Master* (1910): "He called most of 'em by their first names and went sasshayin' around, weltin' 'em on the back and tellin' 'em how he'd 'put crimps in the bookies rolls t'other day,' and a lot more stuff that they seemed to understand, but was hog Greek to me and Jonadab" (Lincoln 1910, 262). This is clearly a regional variant without wide distribution, and it appears to have been lost, just as its precursor "to be heathen Greek to someone" has vanquished by now.

The second relatively early variant adds Hebrew as another difficult language to Greek in order to emphasize the claim that something cannot be understood. It appears to have its debut in print in a comedy by the major British author John Dryden.

> 1667: Sir. Mart. This is Hebrew-Greek to me; but I must tell you, sir, I will not suffer my divinity to be prophaned by such a tongue as yours. (John Dryden, *Sir Martin Mar-All, or the Feigned Innocence, a Comedy* (4:1); Dryden 1808, 3:62)

> 1832: *Forlorn Ditty on Red-Riding-Hood*
> Little Red-Riding-Hood! Why won't you speak to me?
> Your cause of offence is all Hebrew and Greek to me!
> I conjure a compassionate smile on your cheek to me,
> By all the salt tears that have scalded my nose!
> (Thomas Campbell, "Forlorn Ditty on Red-Riding-Hood"; Beattie 1850, 3:121)

> 1886: Alexander's French being unintelligible to the person addressed as if it had been Hebrew-Greek (whatever that traditional dialect may be),

> Wightman, strong in black-letter lore, pushed him aside, exclaiming, "be off! Don't you see that he belongs to the good old school, your modern slang is quite thrown away upon him; let me speak to him in the right sort of language, and there will be no further difficulty". (Sir Francis Hastings Doyle, *Reminiscences*, 1886, 239)

> 1892: This was Greek and Hebrew to me; but I had other matters to consider, and the first of these was to get clear of that city on the Leyden road. (Robert Louis Stevenson, *David Balfour*, 1952, 242)

As can be seen by the last reference, this variant once again also made it to the United States, but speaking of Hebrew, it should be remembered that some languages employ the designation *Hebrew* to refer to aspects of incomprehensibility. Regarding these sociolinguistic differences, there appeared a somewhat humorous but also telling essay "Hebrew to Her Is Greek to Me" (1997) in the *Montreal Gazette*.

> "C'est de l'hébreu. It's Hebrew. But in English, we say it's all Greek to me if we don't understand something."
> Her dubious look changed to what-are-you-some-kind-of-a-nut? look.
> Then it occurred to me that maybe she didn't even know the expression c'est de l'hébreu in French, let alone the rest of it, in which case she would not have a clue what I was talking about. Which was funny, because then she could legitimately have used the expression, in French or English, to signify that it was all Greek to her. So I continued my explanation.
> The reason we use that expression is not only that Greek is a foreign language, but it's written in a different alphabet, so we can't decipher it. Presumably, that's why the French use Hebrew in the same context.
> Anyway, this thing was getting out of hand, as I was trying to explain this to the woman in the hospital. Obviously she thought I was a lunatic. (Nick auf der Maur 1997, A4; Mieder and Sobieski 2006, 176–77)

If Hebrew can be connected with Greek in a variant, why not also Yiddish? And sure enough, one reference has been found (1938): "He produced a small dictionary of quotations and laid it metaphorically at Mr. Campion's feet. 'I'm leavin' out the Yiddish,' he remarked as they turned over the pages together. 'See that bit there? And there's another over 'ere.' Campion sighed. 'It may be Yiddish to you, guv'nor,' he murmured, 'but it's Greek to me.' (Margery Allingham, *The Fashion in Shrouds*, Allingham 2008, 58).

But while this is an absolutely isolated occurrence, this is not the case for the association of the also difficult Latin language with Greek. Such a third variant does exist, albeit with merely two references found thus far.

> 1771: My short sack and apron luck [look] as good as new from the shop, and my pumpydoor as fresh as a rose, by the help of turtle-water—But this is all

Greek and Latin to you, Molly. (Tobias Smollett, *The Expedition of Humphrey Clinker*, 2015, 50)

1861: "Is that the name [Manor House] of this house, miss?"
"One of its names, boy."
"It has more than one, then, miss?"
"One more. Its other name was Satis; which is Greek, or Latin, or Hebrew, or all three—or all one to me—for enough."
"Enough House!" said I: "that's a curious name, miss."
(Charles Dickens, *Great Expectations*, 1953, 51)

The second text, by the great wordsmith and stylist Charles Dickens, contains not so much a variant but rather the play with three individual variants of this worldwide and multifaceted idiom. The three major variants discussed here have long been pushed aside in favor of the common proverbial expression "to be Greek to someone" that has conquered the English language worldwide during the past four centuries.

While the variants competed with each other through the seventeenth and eighteenth centuries, the standard form gained ground so that it basically ruled with rare exceptions in the English language by the beginning of the nineteenth century (listed without historical references in Partridge 1970, 352; Ciardi 1980, 160; Spears 1987, 143; Wilkinson 1993, 412). Many contextualized references bear witness to this development, as the following florilegium will show beyond any doubt. The phrase has lost nothing of its appeal, and it remains to be seen whether in a future world in which China gains ever more prominence it might have to compete with the variant "to be Chinese to someone" which is, of course, already the dominant expression in other linguistic cultures. The Chinese language certainly is an enigma to millions of people worldwide, and referring to it in connection with incomprehensibility and unintelligibility might well become the universal worldwide expression in due time. It would help, of course, if speakers of the English lingua franca were to adopt this variant, but this does not appear to be the case thus far to any noticeable extent. In English, it is Greek and not Chinese that comes to mind when things are not understood.

1821: "But this is Greek to you now, honest Lawrence, and in sooth learning is dry work—Hand me the pitcher once more." (Sir Walter Scott, *Kenilworth*, 1893, 165)

1827: "*Nullum simile quod idem est*," replied the boy. "Thy Latin," said Buckingham, "is Greek to me, and to thyself too, I suspect, from the manner thou dost apply it." (Elizabeth Isabella Spence, *Dame Rebecca Berry, or, Court Scenes*, 1827, 2:159)

1841: You are as aghast and disturbed as if I were talking treason against King George. Perhaps you can tell me why, sir, for (as I say) I am a stranger, and this is Greek to me." (Charles Dickens, *Barnaby Rudge*, 1954, 7; Bryan and Mieder 1997, 142)

1852: Tarquin resolved on seeking the aid of foreign talent; and as the omens were worse than Greek to him, he sent to the oracles at Delphi, thinking if the matter was Greek to them they would be able to interpret it. (Gilbert À Beckett, *The Comic History of Rome*, 1852, 37)

1855: What was meant by the "in ox," as against the "off ox," when both were equally fastened to one cart, and one yoke, I could not easily divine; and the difference, implied by the names, and the peculiar duties of each, were alike *Greek* to me. Why was not the "off ox" called the "in ox?" (Frederick Douglass, *My Bondage and My Freedom*, 1994, 261; Mieder 2001, 246)

1887: "I do not understand metaphysics, Mary. Conceptions and executions are Greek to me. (George Bernard Shaw, *Love among the Artists*, 1927, 39; Bryan and Mieder 1994, 133)

1892: But Schubert clothed his melodies in wondrous harmonies, which were "Greek" to his contemporaries; hence he was not appreciated by them. (Anonymous, [a review], 1892, 13)

1894: All these innocent, playful little amenities were couched in a language that was Greek to him—and he felt out of it, jealous and indignant. (George du Maurier, *Trilby*, 1894, 44)

1899: And most pathetic was the melody of his long-forgotten Southern vernacular, as he raved of swimming-holes and coon-huts and watermelon raids. It was a Greek to Ruth, but the Kid understood and felt, —felt as only one can feel who has been shut out for years from all that civilization means. (Jack London, *The White Silence*, 1992, 12–13)

1903: He had tossed me the chart without a thought that I was an ignoramus, to whom it would be Greek, and who would provide him with an admirable subject to drill and lecture. (Erskine Childers, *The Riddle of the Sands*, 1995, 33)

1909: "Oh," she said, this time with an accent of comprehension, though secretly his speech had been so much Greek to her and she was wondering what a *lift* was and what *swatted* meant. (Jack London, *Martin Eden*, 2002, 9)

1913: Now Continentals haven't got that feeling. They are always bothering about ideas, and the result is that every shopkeeper or peasant has a vocabulary in daily use that is simply Greek to the vast majority of Britons. (Edmund C. Bentley, *Trent's Last Case*, 1930, 179)

1913: One man asked me whether I "doubled." I was compelled to ask him for an explanation, for his language was Greek to me. (Weedon Grossmith, *From Studio to Stage*, 1913, 30)

1920: He had been teaching Greek for half a century; yet it was Greek to him that art has been the greatest factor in raising mankind from its old savage state. (John Galsworthy, *Castles in Spain*, 1927, 10–11)

1938: To say that this was Greek to Mr. Uniatz would be misleading. He would not have been quite sure whether a Greek was a guy who kept a chop house, something you got in your neck, a kind of small river, or the noise a door made when the hinges needed oiling. (Leslie Charteris, *Thieves' Picnic*, 1938, 217)

1939: Brother Athanasios thrust an open book into my hand. It was written in Greek, but so dim was the light that I could not read it. In any case, Greek was Greek to me. (Francis Beeding, *The Ten Holy Horrors*, 1939, 294)

1944: The best of the communication an author has to make is to his own generation, and he is wise to let the generation that succeeds his choose its own exponents. They will do it whether he lets them or not. His language will be Greek to them. (W. Somerset Maugham, *A Writer's Notebook*, 1949, 356)

1949: Chaplain. I know I am not
A practical person; legal matters and so forth
Are Greek to me, except, of course,
That I understand Greek. And what may seem nonsensical
To men of affairs like yourselves might not seem so
To me, since everything astonishes me,
Myself most of all.
(Christopher Fry, *The Lady's Not for Burning*, 1977, 46)

1950: If, however, the budding medico is a student of the Latin tongue, his task should not be a particularly formidable one, for some of the medical terminology will make sense, sound familiar, or at least release the right mental associations. On the whole, his "small Latin" is, however, bound to prove inadequate, since most of the medical expressions will remain "Greek" to him. Should he be able to read his Aristotle without difficulty in the original, his worries will be over, and he will feel very much at home in the *lingua medica*. He need merely reap the fruits of his classical labours. If he has no Latin and no Greek, he is compelled parrot-like to learn arbitrary names which, therefore, are mere tags attached to certain structures, physiological conditions, and states. (Victor Grove, *The Language Bar*, 1950, 54)

1962: "It's an angle. And I wouldn't have too much trouble playing dumb. The whole setup's worse than Greek to me. Greek I could learn. But stocks, bonds, puts and calls—it swamps me." (Edna Sherry, *Girl Missing*, 1962, 41)

1964: Miss Sylvia Barrett, the new English teacher, . . . received her B.A. degree with Phi Beta Kappa and Magna Cum Laude (It's Greek to us!) and her M.A. (Miss America?) with highest honors. (Boy! What a record!). (Bel Kaufman, *The Down Staircase*, 1964, 49)

1975: "Some research on the Medes for a collector in Miami. He picked up a cuneiform-Aramaic tablet in an estate—" "One of your 'consultation' deals? Don't bother. Cuneiform's Greek to me. You got something on your mind, or [are] you just running up a phone bill for kicks?" (M. K. Wren, *A Multitude of Sins*, 1975, 26)

With such a plethora of intriguing references attesting to the popularity of the proverbial expression, who could possibly be surprised that it also appears as a title of books. There is first of all Michael Macrone's *It's Greek to Me! Brush Up Your Classics* (1991), a collection of classical Greek and Latin phrases with explanatory comments for the general reader. Almost expectedly, there are also two textbooks for the Greek language with the proverbial title: David Alan Black, *It's Still Greek to Me: An Easy-to-Understand Guide to Intermediate Greek* (1998), and Lyle and Cullen Story, *Greek to Me: Learning New Testament Greek Through Memory Visualization* (2002). These titles are indeed interesting, since they obviously have a double meaning. There is, first of all, the basic idea that the student has by no means mastered the Greek language, but the secondary meaning that the Greek language will come to the student by making good use of these textbooks enters as well. After all, studying Greek is the best way to overcome the frustration that it is Greek to the student.

Correctly noticing that there is a variant that comes close in popularity to the standard form of "to be Greek to someone," lexicographers and paremiographers have at times chosen the closely related "to be all Greek to someone" as the dominant variant, with the earliest lexicographical record dating from the first quarter of the twentieth century (Vizetelly and Bekker 1923, 191; Morris and Morris 1967, 119; Evans 1970, 486; Kirkpatrick and Schwarz 1983, 138; Hendrickson 1987, 233; Manser 1990, 105; Flavell and Flavell 1992, 77; Walter 1998, 163; Oliver 2011, 66–67). It is interesting to note that basically all of their dictionaries include as the only historical reference Shakespeare's line "For mine own part, it was Greek to me," even though it does not include the inclusive "all" particle. Of course, as is usually the case, the dictionary makers were far behind in registering this prevalent variant, which has been recorded since the beginning of the nineteenth century, as the following contextualized examples make clear.

1817: The conversation (which was all Greek to me) was interrupted by the old farmer. (Anne Newport Royall, letter of December 13, 1817, 1969, 87)

1849: This was all Greek to me, and after receiving the order, I stood staring about me, wondering what it was that was to be done. (Herman Melville, *Redburn*, 2002, 34)

1855: "Ah Monsieur," exclaimed the man, and with voluble politeness he ran on with a long string of French, which was all Greek to poor Israel. But what his language failed to convey, his gestures now made very plain. (Herman Melville, *Israel Potter*, 1982, 37)

1869: "Well, if you don't know what that is, give us a champagne cocktail." [A stare and a shrug.] "Well, then, give us a sherry cobbler." The Frenchman was checkmated. This was all Greek to him. "Give us a brandy smash!" (Mark Twain, *The Innocents Abroad*, 1911, 97)

1872: The few Ablishnists we hev, hev gone so far into spellin-books and grammars, that their talk is all Greek to *our* voters, and so they are safe from their contaminatin [sic] appeals. (David Ross Locke, *The Struggles of Petroleum V. Nasby*, 1888, 211)

1873: "That's the regular routine, and it's no trick at all to a New York lawyer. That's the regular routine—everything's red tape and routine in the law, you see; it's all Greek to you, of course, but to a man who is acquainted with those things it's mere—I'll explain it to you sometime. (Mark Twain, *The Gilded Age*, 1884, 514)

1885: All this was Greek to her, and before she could ask Dick to explain he had darted down a passage. (George Moore, *A Mummer's Wife*, 1966, 139)

1895: Your Postal—the other day—alluding to death of some aged person under your roof—was all greek [sic] to me—but so you did what seemed your duty—all is well—each one of us must decide her own work & worship. (Susan B. Anthony, letter of August 26, 1895, Gordon 2009, 5:707)

1911: And if the profane reader ignores all that is either Greek or twaddle to him, there will yet remain for his advantage a vast amount of very sound information and advice. (Arnold Bennett, *The Human Machine*, 1911, 100)

1920: All this to me is Greek, but you, who are familiar with Chicago, may comprehend. (James Branch Cabell, letter of November 8, 1920, Colum and Cabell 1962, 202)

1935: It was all so much Greek to me, but further discussion was cut short by the entrance of Mr. Willis, a typical country landlord, large and stout and perspiring profusely. (Walter S. Masterman, *The Perjured Alibi*, 1935, 5)

1940: He raised his shoulders in almost Gallic gesture. "How about me? This is all classical Greek to *me*." (Ellery Queen, *The "New" Adventures*, 1940, 160)

1958: "What about 'Sans mens sans corpora'?" "That's all Greek to me." Old Meesum had lit a cigar the length of a scepter, which he tended to flourish as such. "I'm a practical man and I say let's ring in the Chamber of Commerce this afternoon." (Peter De Vries, *The Mackerel Plaza*, 1958, 92)

The last reference is especially intriguing, since "Sans mens sans corpora" is obviously a French and Latin macaronic conglomeration based on the classical Latin proverb "Mens sana in corpore sano." No wonder that as such it is all Greek to someone!

Finally then, there is Christine Ammer, who in two of her more popular and well-researched phrase dictionaries realized that due to the popularity of both the variants "to be Greek to someone" and "to be all Greek to someone," it would be best to list them as a combined lemma: "Greek to me, it's all Greek to me" (Ammer 1992, 154; 1997, 272), and that is what the proverbial title "to be (all) Greek to someone" of these deliberations is accomplishing as well. Both variants most certainly deserve equal treatment today, and considering the popularity of this proverbial expression in the modern age, it is utterly mistaken to be included in Steven Price's collection of *Endangered Phrases: Intriguing Idioms Dangerously Close to Extinction* (2011, 99). Judging by the multitude of historical references presented here, one can and must conclude that this English proverbial expression is doing very well and is doubtless here to stay as a generally known and frequently used metaphor for all sorts of incomprehensible or unintelligible matters.

Postscript: Working on this essay as a special tribute to my dear and distinguished friend Professor Minas Al. Alexiadis of the University of Athens brought back the fondest memories of the four days that my wife Barbara and I spent at Athens, where I was awarded the "doctor honoris causa" on December 16, 2014. I am well aware that it was Minas together with our mutual friend Professor Aristeides Doulaveras who initiated the process that made this international recognition of my paremiological work possible and for which I shall forever be thankful. My dear wife and I were, of course, constantly surrounded by the Greek language while in Athens. Regrettably ignorant of this significant language of the world, we would at times teasingly say that what we heard was "all Greek to us." Fondly remembering these utterances and also thinking of the fact that Minas is my dear Greek friend, I chose to investigate the English proverbial expression "to be (all) Greek to someone" to honor him, hoping that he will judge my labors to be worthy of his life's accomplishments as a world-class scholar.

References

À Beckett, Gilbert Abbott. 1852. *The Comic History of Rome*. London: Bradbury, Evans.
Addison, Joseph. 1711. "[Greeks and Trojans]." *The Spectator*, no. 245 (December 11): 369–70.
Allingham, Margery. 2008. *The Fashion in Shrouds*. New York: Felony & Mayhem Press.
Ammer, Christine. 1992. *Have a Nice Day—No Problem! A Dictionary of Clichés*. New York: Dutton.
———. 1997. *The American Heritage Dictionary of Idioms*. Boston: Houghton Mifflin.
Anonymous. 1798. "[A review]." *The Critical Review; or, Annals of Literature* 22:393.

———. 1742. *The History of the Works of the Learned, for the Year 1742*. 2 vols. London: Jacob Robinson.
———. 1892. [A Review]." *The Nation*, 55 (July 7): 12–13.
Apperson, G. L. 1929. *English Proverbs and Proverbial Phrases: A Historical Dictionary*. London: J. M. Dent; reprinted Detroit: Gale Research Co., 1969.
Baldwin, T. W. 1944. *William Shakspere's Small Latine & Lesse Greeke*. 2 vols. Urbana: University of Illinois Press.
Barta, Heinz. 2010. "Graeca non leguntur"? *Zu den Ursprüngen des europäischen Rechts im antiken Griechenland*. 3 vols. Wiesbaden: Otto Harrassowitz.
Bartels, Klaus. 2008. *Veni, Vidi, Vici: Geflügelte Worte aus dem Griechischen und Lateinischen*. Mainz: Philipp von Zabern.
Beattie, William, ed. 1850. *Life and Letters of Thomas Campbell*. 3 vols. London: Hall, Virtue.
Beeding, Francis. 1939. *The Ten Holy Horrors*. New York: Harper.
Bennett, Arnold. 1911. *The Human Machine*. New York: George H. Doran.
Bentley, Edmund C. 1930. *Trent's Last Case*. New York: Alfred A. Knopf.
Black, David Alan. 1998. *It's Still Greek to Me: An Easy-to-Understand Guide to Intermediate Greek*. Grand Rapids, MI: Baker Books.
Bryan, George B., and Wolfgang Mieder. 1994. *The Proverbial Bernard Shaw: An Index to Proverbs in the Works of George Bernard Shaw*. Westport, CT: Greenwood Press.
———. 1997. *The Proverbial Charles Dickens: An Index to Proverbs in the Works of Charles Dickens*. New York: Peter Lang.
———. 2005. *A Dictionary of Anglo-American Proverbs and Proverbial Phrases Found in Literary Sources of the Nineteenth and Twentieth Centuries*. New York: Peter Lang.
Bullen, A. H., ed. 1964. *The Works of Thomas Middleton*. 8 vols. New York: AMS Press.
Charteris, Leslie. 1938. *Thieves' Picnic*. Garden City, NJ: Doubleday, Doran.
Childers, Erskine. 1995. *The Riddle of the Sands: A Record of Secret Service*. Oxford: Oxford University Press.
Ciardi, John. 1980. *A Browser's Dictionary and Native's Guide to the Unknown American Language*. New York: Harper & Row.
Clark, Elmer T., ed. 1958. *The Journal and Letters of Francis Asbury*. 3 vols. Nashville, TN: Abingdon Press.
Colum, Padraic, and Margaret Freeman Cabell, eds. 1962. *Between Friends: Letters of James Branch Cabell and Others*. New York: Harcourt, Brace & World.
Cunliffe, John W., ed. 1969. *The Complete Works of George Gascoigne*. 2 vols. New York: Greenwood Press.
De Vries, Peter. 1958. *The Mackerel Plaza*. Boston: Little, Brown.
Dekker, Thomas. 1841. *Patient Grissil: A Comedy*. London: Shakespeare Society.
Dent, Robert W. 1984. *Proverbial Language in English Drama Exclusive of Shakespeare, 1495–1616: An Index*. Berkeley: University of California Press.
Dickens, Charles. 1953. *Great Expectations*. Oxford: Oxford University Press.
———. 1954. *Barnaby Rudge*. Oxford: Oxford University Press.
Douglass, Frederick. 1994. *Autobiographies*. New York: Library of America.
Doyle, Francis Hastings. 1886. *Reminiscences and Opinions of Sir Francis Hastings Doyle*. London: Longmans, Green.
Dryden, John. 1808. *The Works of John Dryden*. 18 vols. London: William Miller.
Evans, Ivor H. 1970. *Brewer's Dictionary of Phrase and Fable*. New York: Harper & Row.
Flavell, Linda, and Roger Flavell. 1992. *Dictionary of Idioms and Their Origins*. London: Kyle Cathie.

Fry, Christopher. 1977. *The Lady's Not for Burning*. Oxford: Oxford University Press.
Fumagalli, Giuseppe. 1911. *L'ape latina: Dizionarietto di 2948 sentenze, proverbi, motti, divise frasi e locuzioni latine*. Milano: Hoepli.
Galsworthy, John. 1927. *Castles in Spain and Other Screeds*. New York: Charles Scribner's Sons.
Gascoigne, George. 1906. *Supposes and Jocasta: Two Plays Translated from the Italian*. Edited by John W. Cunliffe. Boston: D. C. Heath.
Gordon, Ann D. 1997–2013. *The Selected Papers of Elizabeth Cady Stanton and Susan B. Anthony*. 6 vols. New Brunswick, NJ: Rutgers University Press, 1997–2013.
"Greek to Me." 2016. Wikipedia. https://en.wikipedia.org/wiki/Greek_to_me.
Grossmith, Weedon. 1913. *From Studio to Stage: Reminiscences*. New York: John Lane.
Grove, Victor. 1950. *The Language Bar*. New York: Philosophical Library.
Hayley, William, ed. 1812. *The Life and Letters of William Cowper*. 3 vols. London: J. Johnson.
Hendrickson, Robert. 1987. *Encyclopedia of Word and Phrase Origins*. New York: Facts on File Publications.
Herhold, Ludwig. 1887. *Lateinischer Wort- und Gedankenschatz*. Hannover: Hahn.
Hyamson, Albert M. 1922. *A Dictionary of English Phrases*. New York: E. P. Dutton.
Irving, Washington. 1896. *Bracebridge Hall*. 2 vols. New York: G. P. Putnam's Sons.
Jonson, Ben. 1995. *Volpone, or The Fox, Epicene, or The Silent Woman, The Alchemist, Bartholomew Fair*. Edited by Gordon Campbell. Oxford: Clarendon Press.
Kasper, Muriel. 1996. *Lateinisches Zitaten-Lexikon*. Stuttgart: Philipp Reclam.
Kaufman, Bel. 1964. *The Down Staircase*. Englewood Cliffs, NJ: Prentice-Hall.
Kirkpatrick, E. M., and C. M. Schwarz, eds. 1983. *Dictionary of Idioms*. Edinburgh: Chambers.
Knowles, Elizabeth, ed. 1997. *The Oxford Dictionary of Phrase, Saying, and Quotation*. Oxford: Oxford University Press.
———. 1999. *The Oxford Dictionary of Quotations*. 5th ed. Oxford: Oxford University Press.
Koelb, Clayton. 2008. "'Graecum Est, Non Legitur.' Hugo's *Notre-Dame de Paris*." In *The Revivifying Word: Literature, Philosophy, and the Theory of Life in Europe's Romantic Age*, edited by Clayton Koelb, 78–96. Rochester, NY: Camden House.
Kulisheck, Clarence L. 1952. "Christopher Fry and 'It's Greek to Me.'" *Notes and Queries* 197: 274–75.
Liebs, Detlef. 1982. *Lateinische Rechtsregeln und Rechtssprichwörter*. München: C. H. Beck.
Lincoln, Joseph C. 1910. *The Depot Master*. New York: A. L. Burt.
Locke, David Ross. 1888. *The Struggles of Petroleum V: Nasby*. Boston: Lee and Shepard.
London, Jack. 1992. *Short Stories*. Edited by Earle Labor, Robert Leitz, and Milo Shepard. New York: Macmillan.
London, Jack. 2002. *Martin Eden*. New York: Modern Library.
Macrone, Michael. 1991. *It's Greek to Me! Brush Up Your Classics*. New York: HarperCollins.
Manser, Martin H. 1990. *Get to the Roots: A Dictionary of Word & Phrase Origins*. New York: Avon Books.
Marston, John. 1963. *The Fawn*. Edited by Gerald A. Smith. Lincoln: University of Nebraska Press.
Masterman, Walter S. 1935. *The Perjured Alibi*. New York: E. P. Dutton.
Maugham, W. Somerset. *A Writer's Notebook*. Garden City, NJ: Doubleday, 1949.
Maur, Nick auf der. 1997. "Hebrew to Her Is Greek to Me." *Montreal Gazette*, December 10, A4. Also in *"Gold Nuggets or Fool's Gold?" Magazine and Newspaper Articles on the (Ir)relevance of Proverbs and Proverbial Phrases*, edited by Wolfgang Mieder and Janet Sobieski, 176–78. Burlington: University of Vermont, 2006.

Maurier, George du. 1894. *Trilby: A Novel.* New York: Harper.
Melville, Herman. 1982. *Israel Potter: His Fifty Years of Exile.* Evanston, IL: Northwestern University Press.
———. 2002. *Redburn.* New York: Modern Library.
Mery, M. C. de. 1828. *Histoire générale des proverbs, adages, sentences apophthegmes.* Paris: Delongchamps.
Mieder, Wolfgang. 2001. *"No Struggle, No Progress": Frederick Douglass and His Proverbial Rhetoric for Civil Rights.* New York: Peter Lang.
———. 2004. *Proverbs: A Handbook.* Westport, CT. Greenwood Press.
———. 2014. "Origin of Proverbs." In *Introduction of Paremiology: A Comprehensive Guide to Proverb Studies,* edited by Hrisztalina Hrisztova-Gotthardt and Melita Aleksa Varga, 28–48. Berlin: Walter de Gruyter.
Mieder, Wolfgang, and Janet Sobieski. 2006. *"Gold Nuggets or Fool's Gold?" Magazine and Newspaper Articles on the (Ir)relevance of Proverbs and Proverbial Expressions.* Burlington: University of Vermont.
Moore, George. 1966. *A Mummer's Wife.* New York: Liveright.
Moore, N. F. 1819. *Remarks on the Pronunciation of the Greek Language.* New York: James Eastburn.
Morris, William, and Mary Morris. 1967. *Dictionary of Word and Phrase Origins.* 2 vols. New York: Harper & Row.
Oertel, Eucharius. 1842. *Auswahl der schönsten Denk- und Sittensprüche, Sprüchwörter etc: Aus lateinischen Dichtern und Prosaikern.* Nürnberg: F. Campe.
Oliver, Harry. 2011. *Flying by the Seat of Your Pants: Surprising Origins of Everyday Expressions.* New York: Perigee Books.
Partridge, Eric. 1970. *A Dictionary of Slang and Unconventional English.* 7th ed. New York: Macmillan.
Pegge, Samuel. 1814. *Anecdotes of the English Language.* London: J. Nichols.
Piirainen, Elisabeth. 2015. "Dat ass Chineesch fir mech—é grego para min—to mi je turško; Fremde Sprachen in einer verbreiteten Redensart," *"Bis dat, qui cito dat":"Gegengabe" in Paremiology, Folklore, Language, and Literature: Honoring Wolfgang Mieder on His Seventieth Birthday,* edited by Christian Grandl and Kevin J. McKenna, 319–30. Frankfurt am Main: Peter Lang.
———. 2016. *Lexicon of Common Figurative Units: Widespread Idioms in Europe and Beyond.* New York: Peter Lang.
Price, Steven D. 2011. *Endangered Phrases: Intriguing Idioms Dangerously Close to Extinction.* New York: Skyhorse Publishing.
Queen, Ellery. 1940. *The "New" Adventures.* New York: Frederick A. Stokes.
Rees, Nigel. 1997. *Cassell Companion to Quotations.* London: Cassell.
Rosenberg, Arnold L. 1979. "The Hardest Natural Languages," *Lingvisticae Investigationes* 3: 323–39.
Royall, Anne Newport. 1969. *Letters from Alabama 1817–1822.* Tuscaloosa: University of Alabama Press.
Scott, Sir Walter. 1893. *Kenilworth.* Boston: Dana Estes.
Shadwell, Thomas. 1688. *The Squire of Alsatia: A Comedy.* London: James Knapton.
Shaw, George Bernard. 1927. *Love among the Artists.* New York: Brentano's.
Shelton, Thomas, trans. 1907. *The History of the Valorous and Witty Knight-Errant Don Quixote of the Mancha by Miguel de Cervantes.* 4 vols. New York: Charles Scribner's Sons.

Sherry, Enda. 1962. *Girl Missing*. New York: Dodd, Mead.
Simpson, John A., and Ed Weiner, eds. 1989. *The Oxford English Dictionary*. 2nd ed. Oxford: Clarendon Press.
Smollett, Tobias. 2015. *The Expedition of Humphrey Clinker*. New York: W. W. Norton.
Southey, Charles Cuthbert, ed. 1850. *The Life and Correspondence of Robert Southey*. 6 vols. London: Longman, Brown, Green.
Spears, Richard A. 1987. *NTC's American Idioms Dictionary*. Lincolnwood, IL: National Textbook Company.
Spence, Elizabeth Isabelle. 1827. *Dame Rebecca Berry, or, Court Scenes*. 3 vols. London: Longman, Reese.
Stevenson, Burton Egbert. 1948. *The Home Book of Proverbs, Maxims, and Familiar Phrases*. New York: Macmillan.
Stevenson, Robert Louis. 1952. *David Balfour*. New York: Charles Scribner's Sons.
Story, Lyle, and Cullen Story. 2002. *Greek to Me: Learning New Testament Greek through Memory Visualization*. Fairfax, VA: Xulon Press.
Strype, John. 1821. *The Life of the Learned Sir John Cheke*. Oxford: Clarendon Press.
Summers, Montague, ed. 1967. *The Works of Aphra Behn*. 6 vols. New York: Benjamin Blom.
Taylor, Archer, and Bartlett Jere Whiting. 1958. *A Dictionary of American Proverbs and Proverbial Phrases, 1820–1880*. Cambridge, MA: Harvard University Press.
Tilley, Morris Palmer. 1950. *A Dictionary of the Proverbs in England in the Sixteenth and Seventeenth Centuries*. Ann Arbor: University of Michigan Press.
Titelman, Gregory Y. 1996. *Random House Dictionary of Popular Proverbs and Sayings: Over 1,500 Proverbs and Sayings with 10,000 Illustrative Citations*. New York: Random House.
Topp, John. 1878. "Shakespeare's Knowledge of the Classics," *Melbourne Review* 3: 391–417.
Trevor, Griffiths, and Joscelyne Trevor. 1985. *Longman Guide to Shakespeare Quotations*. Harlow, Essex: Longman.
Twain, Mark. 1884. *The Gilded Age*. Hartford, CT: American Publishing Company.
———. 1911. *The Innocents Abroad*. New York: Grosset & Dunlap.
Vizetelly, Frank H., and Leander J. de Bekker. 1923. *Idioms and Idiomatic Phrases in English Speech and Literature*. New York: Grosset & Dunlap.
Walter, Elizabeth, ed. 1998. *International Dictionary of Idioms*. Cambridge: Cambridge University Press.
Walther, Hans, and Paul Gerhard Schmidt. 1963–86. *Lateinische Sprichwörter und Sentenzen des Mittelalters un der frühen Neuzeit*. 9 vols. Göttingen: Vandenhoeck & Ruprecht.
Wesley, John. 1906. *The Journal of the Rev. John Wesley*. 4 vols. London: J. M. Dent.
Whiting, Bartlett Jere. 1938. *Proverbs in the Earlier English Drama*. Cambridge, MA: Harvard University Press.
———. 1977. *Early American Proverbs and Proverbial Phrases*. Cambridge, MA: Harvard University Press.
———. 1989. *Modern Proverbs and Proverbial Sayings*. Cambridge, MA: Harvard University Press.
Wilkinson, P. R. 1993. *Thesaurus of Traditional English Metaphors*. London: Routledge.
Williams, Fionnuala. 1991. "Survey of 'It's All Double-Dutch to Me.'" *Proverbium* 8:203.
Wilson, F. P. 1970. *The Oxford Dictionary of English Proverbs*. 3rd ed. Oxford: Clarendon Press.
Wren, M. K. 1975. *A Multitude of Sins*. Garden City, NY: Doubleday.
Zimmer, Ben. 2015. "If It's 'All Greek to You,' Blame Monks and Shakespeare." Vocabulary.com. https://www.vocabulary.com/articles/wordroutes/if-its-all-greek-to-you-blame-monks-and-shakespeare/.

INDEX

"absence makes the heart grow fonder," 16, 263, 265
"absence makes the heart grow wander" (antiproverb), 16
"accidents will happen in the best-regulated families," 5
Accorso, Francesco (Franciscus Accursius), 335, 336
Across That Bridge (Lewis)
  "all men are created equal," 162
  "to be a voice crying in the wilderness," 161
  on "beloved community," 172–73
  "caught between a rock and a hard place," 155
  "an eye for an eye, a tooth for a tooth," 157–58
  general use of proverbs and proverbial phrases in, 154
  "to have the scales fall from one's eyes," 160–61
  "keep your eyes on the prize," 147
  "life, liberty, and the pursuit of happiness," 163
  on "making a way out of no way," 176–78
  nonviolence emphasized in, 157–58
  rhetorical style of, xi
  on taking action, 165
action/inaction
  "actions speak louder than words," 165
  "all talk, no action," 11

"to be at the crossroads," 117
"deeds, not words," 188
"example is better than precept," 82
"God helps those who help themselves," 36–37, 111–12, 178
"to hit the ground running," 173
"if you want to talk the talk, you've got to walk the walk," 166–67
"to keep a lamp burning, we have to keep putting oil in it," 164–65
"making a way out of no way," viii, x, xvi, 23, 136–38, 140, 151
"the mountain labored and brought forth a mouse," 67
"practice what you preach," x, 108–109
"when you pray, move your feet," 165
Adams, Abigail, viii, 18, 36–38, 64
Adams, John
  and "born free and equal" wording, 300, 301, 303, 306
  edits made to Jefferson's Declaration of Independence, 299
  "government of the people, by the people, and for the people," 222
  proverbs in correspondence of, viii, 36, 37
Adams, John Quincy, 16
Addison, Joseph, 336
advertising field, 21, 310–14

affirmative action, 164
African Americans
  "different strokes for different folks," viii, 23–24
  and "George" stereotype, xv, 327–29
  and "making a way out of no way," 136–38, 141
  as Pullman porters, 318, 323, 327–29
  voting rights, 52, 79
African tribal languages, proverbs of, 8
"aid is a bridge to trade," 211
"aim for the stars," 12
"aim small, miss small," 11
"the air is still as death," 166
Alexiadis, Minas Al., 347
"all animals are equal, but some animals are more equal than others," 308
"all men and women are created equal," 16, 66, 84, 222, 303–304
"all men are created equal," xiv, 298–314
  Anthony's citation of, 304
  and antiproverbs, 310–14
  born included in, 300, 301, 303, 304–305, 306
  Carter's citation of, 305
  H. Clinton's citation of, 221
  B. Clinton's citation of, 305–6
  contradictory references to, 308–9
  disagreement on proverbial status of, 301
  Douglass's citation of, xiv, 183, 302
  included in recent references, 301–2

353

all men *(cont.)*
   and Jefferson's Declaration of Independence, xiv, 16, 242, 298–300, 301, 314
   King's citation of, x, 52, 123, 132, 139, 306–7
   Lewis's citation of, 149, 162
   Lincoln's citation of, xiv, 104, 302–303, 314
   and Marshall, 104
   Nixon's citation of, 304–305
   Obama's citation of, 187, 307–308
   parodies of, 309–10
   precursors to, 299–300
   Sanders's citation of, 242
   and slavery, 302–303
   and Sly and the Family Stone's "Everyday People," 24
   Truman's citation of, 304
   and Universal Declaration of Human Rights, 221–22, 306
   variants of, 300
   "women" omitted from, 303
"all roads lead to Rome," 3–4
"all talk, no action," 11
"all that glitters is not gold," 3
"all the world's a stage," 165
"all work and no play makes Jack a dull boy," 87
Amboise, Georges d', xv, 317–23, 325
The American Language (Mencken), 317, 321, 325
American proverbs, viii, 1–24
   about American values, viii, 23–24
   about automobiles, 21
   about life, 22–23
   about money/finance, 22
   about sports, 21
   about success, 22
   about time, 22
   from advertising, 21
   antiproverbs, 15–16
   authorship of, 16–20
   average length of, 10–12
   collections of, 1–2
   and English proverbs, 4–5
   from films, 20
   Franklin's contributions to, 17–18
   and German loan proverbs, 7–9
   misattributed proverbs, 5–6
   origins of proverbs, 3–5
   scatology/sexuality in, 12–13
   from songs, 20
   structural patterns in, 13–15
   US-specific proverbs, 9
   variants in, 11–12
   See also other specific proverbs, including "all men are created equal" *and* "government of the people, by the people, and for the people"
Ammer, Christine, 347
ancient proverbs, 16
Anderson, Jervis, 327
Animal Farm (Orwell), xiv, 308
animal-related metaphors and proverbs, xiv, 72, 81, 255, 308
"another day, another dollar," 22
Anthony, Susan B.
   "all men are created equal," 304
   animal metaphors used by, 72
   and Clinton, 222
   on education, 86
   on employment of women, 88–91
   "equal pay for equal work," 16, 90–91, 250
   and feminist rhetoric, 63–66
   general use of proverbs and proverbial phrases, ix
   and Golden Rule, 91–92, 93
   lectures and speeches of, 74–75, 77–80
   on motherhood, 81, 87–88, 205
   "mother knows best," 205
   "plain English" emphasized by, 75
   as proverbial giant, 182
   scholarship on, 63–64
   Stanton's relationship with, 66
   "these are the times that try women's souls," 65
   "in union there is strength," 43
   on voting rights, 42–43, 90–91
antiproverbs, 15–16
   "absence makes the heart grow wander," 16
   for "all men are created equal," 310–14
   Anthony's creation of, 65
   "beauty is only skin," 15
   "child care is not a spectator sport," 225
   Clinton's citation of, xii, 216, 225
   "do unto others before they do unto you," 16
   and "do unto others before they do unto you" antiproverb, 16
   "expedience is the best teacher," 15
   "high expectations begin at home," 225
   "if at first you don't succeed, try, try reading the instructions," 16
   "love thy neighbor, but do not get caught," 16
   for "might makes right" (*see* "right makes might")
   of modern feminists, 91
   "mother knows best," 205
   "no body is perfect," 16
   "no family is an island," 225
   "an ounce of prevention is worth a pound of intensive care," 225

"politics is not a spectator sport," xvi, 259
"the rich get richer, and the poor get children," 235
"time flies when you are having fun," 16
"too big to jail," 244
for "a woman's place is in the home," 91
"any port in a storm," 5
"anything goes," 157
A. Philipp Randolph (Anderson), 327
"appearances are deceptive," 4
"an apple a day keeps the doctor away," 7
"the arc of the moral universe is long, but it bends toward justice," 16, 52, 134, 137, 161–62
"as American as apple pie," 157
Asbury, Francis, 337
"ask not what your country can do for you, ask what you can do for your country," 17, 50–51
AT&T phone company, 21
"at a crossroads," 259
atomic weapons utilized in World War II, 49–50
The Audacity of Hope (Obama)
  on democracy, 196–97
  on economic opportunity, 190–91
  on faith, 191–92
  general use of proverbs and folk speech in, xii, 189–90, 197
  on international diplomacy and world affairs, 195–96
  on "making a way out of no way," 175–76
  on partisan politics, 185–87
  on race, 192–95
  reviews of, 184, 189
  and rhetorical style/skills of Obama, 183, 184–85, 189–90

on US Constitution, 188–89
on values, 187–88
authority of proverbs, 263–65

"back on their feet," 109
Bacon, Francis, 46
"bad sex is better than no sex," 13
Baker, Ella, 168
Baldwin, Lewis V., 124
"banks have no heart," 22
banks "too big to fail," 244–45
Bartlett, John, 300–301
baseball, 9
Basler, Roy P., 40
Beard, Charles A., 131
beauty
  "beauty is in the eye of the beholder," 5
  "beauty is only skin" (antiproverb), 15
  "beauty is only skin deep," 15, 85, 263
  Stanton on, 85–86
  "a thing of beauty is a joy forever," 263
Beecher, Henry Ward, 18
"been there, done that," 183
"beggars can't be choosers," 4, 88
"behind the clouds the sun is shining," 18
Benham, W. Gurney, 321
Berlin, Germany, 6
Berra, Yogi, 18
"the best-laid plans of mice and men often go astray," 186
"the best tool you can give a child is a shovel," 205
"the best way to kill time is to work it to death," 22
"be sure you are right, then go ahead," 18
"a bet is a bet," 14
"better is not good enough," 183, 193
"between the cradle and the grave," 156
biblical proverbs and passages

Abigail Adams's citation of, 37
"am I my brother's keeper?" 95, 194
Anthony's citation of, 67
and antiproverbs, 16
"to be a thorn in the flesh," 160
"to be a voice crying in the wilderness," 161
"blessed are the meek, for they shall inherit the earth," 159
"blood asks for blood," 158
Clinton's citation of, 206–7
"don't put your lamp under a bushel basket," 206
Douglass's citation of, 41–42
"eat, drink, and be merry," 85–86
"an eye for an eye, a tooth for a tooth," 156, 157–58, 253–54
"faith, hope, and love," 160
"faith can remove mountains," 191
"give us this day our daily bread," 110
"to have the scales fall from one's eyes," 160
"he who is not with me is against me," 186
"he who lives by the sword shall perish by the sword," 128, 133
"a house divided against itself cannot stand," viii, xii, 5–6, 38–39, 53, 54, 174–75, 183
Kennedy's citation of, 277
King's citation of, x, 52, 126, 127, 128, 133–34, 161
"let judgment run down like waters and righteousness like a mighty stream," 133
"let the dead bury their dead," 70, 71
Lewis's citation of, xi, 155

biblical proverbs *(cont.)*
  "love thy neighbor as thyself," 37, 158, 206
  "love your enemies," x, 126, 127, 133, 206, 306
  "man does not live by bread alone," x, 3, 115, 127
  Marshall's citation of, x
  Obama's citation of, xii, 95, 183, 186, 191–92, 194, 308
  and origins of proverbs, 3
  "the prophet is not without honor, save in his own country," 3
  Sanders's citation of, 246, 253–54
  Sermon on the Mount, 192
  "a soft answer turneth away wrath," 277
  "sour grapes will set teeth on edge," 67
  "straight is the gate, and narrow is the way which leadeth unto life," 155
  "in the sweat of thy brow shalt thou eat bread," 88
  "there is nothing new under the sun," 3, 88
  "to wash one's hands of something," 71
  "woman is the weaker vessel," 76
  and women's rights, 64
  "to worship the golden calf," 73
  "you reap what you sow," 52, 137, 161–62
  See also Golden Rule
"big fish eat little fish," 3, 37, 281
"big fish in a small pond," 255
"bigger fish to fry," 66
"the bigger they are, the harder they fall," 18
Bill of Rights, 300, 303
"a bird may love a fish, but where would they live?" 14

"a bird needs two wings to fly," 168–69
"birds of a feather flock together," 4, 264
Bismarck, Otto von, 35
"the blacker [skin color] the berry, the sweeter the juice," 13
Bland, Larry I., 101, 114
"blessed are the meek, for they shall inherit the earth," 159
"blood, sweat, and tears," 251
"blood asks for blood," 158
"body and (or) soul," 77
Bond, Julian, 170–72
"bosses are bosses," 14
Boston, Richard, 265
"Boston folks are full of notions," 9
"bottom line," 190
Brandt, Willy, 5–6
brevity in proverbs, 10–11
"brevity is the soul of wit," 3
Broch, Hermann, 280
"broken eggs cannot be mended," 16
"brother's/sister's keeper," 95, 194
Brown, Hubert "Rap," 156–57
"the buck stops here," 19, 48–50, 224
"build a better mousetrap, and the world will beat a path to your door," 20
Burke, Kenneth, 266
Burnham, Josephine, 329
"a burnt child dreads the fire," 80
Bush, George W., 53
"business goes where it is invited and stays where it is treated well," 22
"the business of America is business," 17
Butch Cassidy and the Sundance Kid (film), 20
"but does thou love life, then do not squander life, for that is the stuff life is made of," 36

"buy low, sell high," 22
"by diligence and patience the mouse bit in two the cable," 18

Campbell, Karlyn Kohrs, 64
"a candle loses nothing of its light by lighting another candle," 223
"candy is dandy, but liquor is quicker," 19
"can't never could," 11
Carnegie, Andrew, 20
Carruth, Gorton, 301
Carter, Jimmy, 305
Carville, James, 208
"caught between a rock and a hard place," 155
Chafe, William, 153
"changing course," 185
"charity begins at home," 82, 225
"the chase is better than the kill," 14
Cheke, Sir John, 335–36
"chicken today, feathers tomorrow," 11
children
  "the best tool you can give a child is a shovel," 205
  "a burnt child dreads the fire," 80
  "child care is not a spectator sport," 225
  "children are our future," 13, 207, 208
  "every child needs a champion," 211
  "high expectations begin at home," 225
  "it takes a village to raise a child," 214–17
  "late children, early orphans," 11
  "the rich get richer, and the poor get children" (antiproverb), 235
  "security takes more than a blanket," 211, 220

"a strong mind in a strong body" (*mens sana in corpore sano*), 218
"there is no such thing as other peoples' children," 211
Chinese language, 334, 342
"the chips are down," 116
Churchill, Winston S.
"to be in the same boat," 54–55
"blood, sweat, and tears," 251
"deeds, not words," 188
general use of proverbs and proverbial phrases, 35, 46
rhetorical skills of, 65, 108
on Soviets' "iron curtain," 103
Cicero, 34, 54, 55
"a civilization flourishes when people plant trees under whose shade they will never sit," 217
civil rights movement, 51–52
battle hymn of, 145–47
"Bloody Sunday" march on Edmund Pettus Bridge, 149
and "faith, hope, and love" triad, 160
and Golden Rule, 42
internal difficulties, 170
King's leadership of, x (*see also* King, Martin Luther, Jr.)
Lewis's leadership of, xi, 147, 148–49, 150–51, 166, 169–70 (*see also* Lewis, John)
"making a way out of no way," 177–78
and Malcolm X's militancy, 156
nonviolence emphasized in, 126, 128, 129, 147, 150, 156–58, 167–68
and progress in race relations, 134–36, 161–62, 172

"cleanliness is next to godliness," 4
"clear as crystal," 117
Cleveland, Grover, 17
climate change, 249
Clinton, Bill, 164, 202, 223, 305–6
Clinton, Chelsea, 216, 219
Clinton, Hillary Rodham, xii–xiii, 200–226
and antiproverbs, xii, 216, 225
on criticism, 221
Dear Socks, Dear Buddy, 203
favorite proverb of, 219
general use of proverbs and proverbial phrases, 202, 207–8, 226
and "glass ceiling" metaphor, 213, 214
introductory formulas used by, 217, 219–20, 223
An Invitation to the White House, 203, 222–23
"it takes a village to raise a child," 214–17
modern proverbs cited by, 223–25
parents of, 203–205
phrases and passages collected by, 206, 208
phrases/pseudoproverbs crafted by, 211–13
presidential campaigns of, 200, 204, 213–14
and proverbs from other languages, 217–18
public servant career of, 200–201
quoting well-known figures, 208–11
religious faith of, 206–7
rhetorical style of, 201–3, 213
and E. Roosevelt, 201, 209–11, 214, 306
women's rights advocacy of, 211–14, 221–22
youth of, 203–5

See also *Hard Choices*; *It Takes a Village and Other Lessons Children Teach Us*; *Living History*
"a cluttered desk is a sign of a messy person," 12
"the coldest peace is better than the warmest war," 209
Cold War, 106, 277
Common Sense (Paine), 38
"competition is the life of trade," 22
"consistency is a jewel," 11
contexts of proverbs, 265, 266, 267, 281
contradictory proverbial pairs, 263–67
about, 263–64
and authority/validity of proverbs, 263–65
and context-bound nature of proverbs, 265, 266, 267, 281
"nothing is certain but uncertainty itself," 267
scholarship on, 263
See also "m(r)ight makes r(m)ight" proverbial pair
Coolidge, Calvin, 17
Cooper, James Fenimore, 18
counter proverbs, 15
Cowper, William, 337
Cracked but Not Shattered (Sheckels), 213
Cram, David, 265
"cream will rise to the top," 207
"crime does not pay," 11
Crockett, David, 18
"crying wolf," 255
"crystal clear," 117
"culture wars," 185
"curiosity killed the cat," 5
"the customer is always right," 22
"cutthroat politics," 185
"cutting off one's nose to spite one's face," 254

Daniel, Jack L., 136
"the darkest hour is just before dawn," 137, 176
Davis, Bette, 20
"dead as doornails," 70, 71
"a deadline is a deadline," 14
Dear Socks, Dear Buddy (Clinton), 203
Declaration of Independence, US
  Adams's edits to, 299, 300, 303
  celebrated on Independence Day, 298–99
  Clinton's citation of, 223
  Jefferson's composition of, 298–300
  King's citation of, 123, 132
  Lewis's citation of, 162
  Marshall's citation of, 103–4
  Sanders's citation of, 242
  See also "all men are created equal"; "life, liberty, and the pursuit of happiness"
"Declaration of Sentiments," 222, 303
"deeds, not words," 188
"deficit reduction can't take place on the backs of the poor," 186
definitions of proverbs, 264, 266
democracy
  "democracy is not a spectator sport," 259–60
  and elections, 237–38
  "government of the people, by the people, and for the people," 23, 57–58, 104, 222, 242–43
  Marshall on, 103–4
  and "might makes right," 270
  "one man, one vote," 240–42
  "the voice of the people is the voice of God" (*vox populi, vox dei*), 196

democratic socialism, 230–32, 234–35, 237–38, 255–56, 259
"denial ain't just a river in Egypt," 219
"the devil is in the details," 223–24
"diamonds are a girl's best friend," 8
Dickens, Charles, xv–xvi
A Dictionary of American Proverbs (Mieder, Kingsbury, and Harder), 1, 301–2
A Dictionary of Modern Proverbs (Doyle, Mieder, and Shapiro), 301–2
"different strokes for different folks," viii, 23–24
"Different Strokes for Different Folks": 1250 authentisch amerikanische Sprichwörter (Mieder), 2, 12, 16, 17, 21, 22
"digging in one's heels," 254
"dogs do not bark at parked cars," 21
Dolman, Joseph, 153
"do not advertise what you can't fulfill," 21
"do not throw the baby out with the bathwater," 1, 164
"don't ask, don't tell," 223
"don't bite off more than you can chew," 13
"don't change horses midstream," 6
"don't give up the ship," 74
"don't judge someone till you have walked a mile in his shoes," 12
"don't kick a fellow when he is down," 13, 207
"don't mess with Texas," 9
"don't put all your eggs into one basket," 4
"don't put the fox to guard the hen house," 255

"don't put your lamp under a bushel basket," 206
"don't rock the boat," 13
"don't sell America short," 9
don't structural pattern, 13
"don't worry, be happy," 224
Douglas, William O., 240
Douglass, Frederick
  "all men are created equal," 183, 302
  general use of proverbs and proverbial phrases, viii, 41–42
  and Golden Rule, 41–42, 94, 188
  "if there is no struggle, there is no progress," 16, 41, 163
  Lewis's quotation of, 163
  and Obama, 56, 58, 183, 185, 192, 307
  as proverbial giant, 182
  rhetorical style of, 41–42
Doulaveras, Aristeides, 347
"do unto others." *See* Golden Rule
"do unto others before they do unto you" (antiproverb), 16
Dowdy, Zachary, 153
Doyle, Charles Clay, 15, 211, 301–2, 326
The Dream (Hansen), 139
Dreams from My Father (Obama), 182–83, 189
"drinking from a fire hose," 189
"drive thy business, or it will drive thee," 18, 36
"a drowning man will clutch at a straw," 88
Dundes, Alan, 318

"each generation is better than the last," 19
"the early bird catches the work," 4
"early to bed, and early to rise, makes a man healthy, wealthy, and wise," 36, 82

"easier said than done," 221, 252
"eat, drink, and be merry," 85–86
economics
   "deficit reduction can't take place on the backs of the poor," 186
   effect of income inequality on political ideals, 242
   "it's the economy, stupid," 208
   Obama on economic opportunity, 190–91
   and plight of the working class, 246–49
   "the rich get richer, and the poor get poorer," xiii, 235
   and Sanders's political ideology, 232, 233, 254
   "socialism for the rich," 245
   "too big to fail," 244–45
   and wealth inequality, 242, 256
   "what is good for Main Street is good for Wall Street," 208
   "where women prosper, countries prosper," 211
   See also money
Edison, Thomas Alva, 18
education
   Anthony on, 86
   "education is a journey, not a destination," 14
   Stanton on, 84–85
Ehrlich, Eugene, 301
Eidelberg, Paul, 280
Einstein, Albert, 19, 20
elections in the United States
   and campaign finance reform, 243–44
   and campaign fundraising, 252
   "every vote counts," 251
   influence of "big money" on, 237–38, 240–44
   "one person, one vote," 240–42
   and political campaigns, 252–53, 255–57
Emancipation Proclamation, 39
Emerson, Ralph Waldo, 18, 20, 47
empathy, 187–88
employment, 88–90
English language, 1, 4–5, 7, 287–88
"enough is enough," xiii, 232–34
"*e pluribus unum*" (out of many, one), 57, 194
"equal pay for equal work," 16, 90–91, 249–50
Erasmus of Rotterdam, 34
Esar, Evan, 310
"eternal vigilance is the price of liberty," 16
Europe, proverbs originating in, 3–5
European Proverbs in 55 Languages with Equivalents in Arabic, Persian, Sanskrit, Chinese and Japanese (Paczolay), 4
"everybody shits," 10
"everybody wants to go to heaven, but nobody wants to die," 20
"everybody will be famous for fifteen minutes," 19
"every business is a family business," 211
"every child needs a champion," 211
"every cloud has a silver lining," 208
"every game has a winner and a loser," 21
"every girl is born into the world with a stone on her head," 44
"every man for himself," 45, 174
"every pig will burn its nose in the hot swill," 72
"everything in moderation," 59

"every vote counts," 251
"the evil that has come with the good," 45
"example is better than precept," 82
"expedience is the best teacher" (antiproverb), 15
"experience is the beat teacher," 15
"experience keeps a dear school, but fools learn in no other," 18
"extend a hand if you are willing to unclench your fist," 209
"an eye for an eye, a tooth for a tooth," 156, 157–58, 253–54

"facts are facts," 14
"facts don't lie," 11
"faith, hope, and love" triad, 141, 160
"faith can remove mountains," 191
"falling flat on your face," 253
"familiarity breeds contempt," 164
Familiar Quotations (Bartlett), 300–301
"father knows best," 87, 88, 183, 205
fear, 46–47
Feinman, Barbara, 203
"fighting tooth and nail," 254
films, proverbs from, 20
finance, world of, 22
Fitzsimmons, Robert, 18
"flattery will get you everywhere"/"flattery will get you nowhere," 15
Fleer, David, 125
Fletcher, Jane Cowen, 216
"floating a balloon," 252–53
folk speech, 70, 80–81
"follow your own bliss," 23
"fool them and forget them," 12
Ford, Henry, 18
foreign-language proverbs, 1

Foreman, George, 330
"for every drop of rain that falls, a flower grows," 20
"forewarned is forearmed," 4
Forrest Gump (film), 20
Fox, George, 326
Franklin, Benjamin
  Poor Richard's Almanack series, viii, 17, 35
  as proverbial giant, 17, 35–36, 182
  "time is money," 7
  The Way to Wealth, viii, 17, 36–37
"freedom is not for sale," viii, 23
"freedom is not given, it is won," 17
"a friend nearby is better than a brother far off," 14
"from shirtsleeves to shirtsleeves in three generations," 20
"from the bottom of one's heart," 247–48
Frost, Robert, 19
Fruit of the Loom, 313
"fuck them and forget them," 12
"the future belongs to those who prepare for it," 306

Gandhi, Mohandas, 159, 254
"garbage in, garbage out," 5
"genius is 1 percent inspiration and 99 percent perspiration," 18
"gentlemen prefer blondes," 18
George, David Lloyd, 323, 329
George C. Marshall (Stoler), 100
Germany and German language
  division of, 5–6, 112, 116
  English language proverbs circulating in, 4–5
  "a house divided against itself cannot stand," 5–6
  "it takes two to tango," 7
  loan translations of American proverbs, viii, 6–9
  proverbs originating from, 1
Gersen, Michael, 53
"get its house in order," 116
"getting it right," 203
"getting their money's worth," 190
Gettysburg Address of Lincoln
  "all men are created equal," 303, 314
  Chinese Premier's recitation of, 223
  "government of the people, by the people, and for the people," 23, 57, 104, 222, 242–43
  Sanders on, 242–43
  and University of Vermont's summer program, 314
"give an inch, take an ell," 76
"give me liberty, or give me death," 16
"give us this day our daily bread," 110
"glass ceiling" metaphor, 213, 214
"the glass is either half empty or half full," 8
"God doesn't make junk," 12
"God helps those who help themselves," 36–37, 111–12, 178
"God will make a way out of no way," 136, 137, 175
Golden Rule
  Clinton's citation of, 206–7
  Douglass's citation of, 41–42, 94, 188
  and "do unto others before they do unto you" antiproverb, 16
  and human rights, 95
  and immigration policies, 258–59
  King's citation of, 94–95, 183
  and Lewis, 159–60
  Lincoln's citation of, 94, 188, 258
  Obama's citation of, xii, 58, 95, 187–88, 192, 194, 206, 258
  Sanders's citation of, xiii, 257–59
  and slavery, 41–42
  social reformers' citation of, 91–96
  Stanton's citation of, ix, 95
  universal relevance of, 165, 206–207
  and women's rights movement, ix, 91–93, 95
"golf is a good walk spoiled," 209
"good Americans, when they die go to Paris," 9
"good enough is not good enough"/"good enough is good enough," 15
"good fences make good neighbors," 7, 19
"Good Morning, America" (Sandburg), 196
"goodness is the only investment that never fails," 120
Gordon, Ann D., 74
"Gospel Plow" (American folk song), 145
"government of the people, by the people, and for the people," 23, 57–58, 104, 222, 242–43
"go with the flow," 23
graecum est, no potest legi ("it is Greek, it cannot be read"), 335, 336–37
"the grass is always greener on the other side of the fence," 8
"great minds think alike," 13
Greek antiquity, proverbs originating in, 3, 268

"Greek to me." *See* "to be (all) Greek to someone"
Griffin, Albert, 95
Guide to Political Revolution (Sanders), 249–50, 259–60

Haliburton, Thomas Chandler, 18
Hamlet (Shakespeare), 3
"the hand that rocks the cradle is the hand that moves the world," 81
"happiness is a journey, not a destination," 14
"happy is the country which has no history," 16
"hardball tactics," 186
Hard Choices (Clinton), xii, 203, 204, 212–13, 226, 306
Harder, Kelsie B., 301
The Harper Book of American Quotations (Carruth and Ehrlich), 301
"hate begets hate," 126
"having to pay the price," 188
Hayman, Robert, 278–79
"a healthy mind in a healthy body," 82
"hear before you blame," 18
"hearts are filled with joy," 69
"heavy-handed approach," 190
Hebrew language, 340–41
"a hedge between keeps friendship green," 5
helping, proverbs on
　"God helps those who help themselves," 36–37, 111–12, 178
　"help others as they help you," 111–12
　"to lend a helping hand," 107
　"you always help yourself by helping others," 111–12
Henry, Patrick, 16
"herculean labor," 73–74

"here today and gone tomorrow," 169
"he that riseth late must trot all day, and shall scarce overtake his business at night," 36
"he who hesitates is lost," 263
"he who is not with me is against me," 186
"he who lives by the sword shall perish by the sword," x, 128, 133
"he who sups with the devil should have a long spoon," 4
"high expectations begin at home" (antiproverb), 225
"history is bunk," 18
Hitchens, Christopher, 184
"hitch your wagon to a star," 18
Hitler, Adolf, 35, 46
"hoe your own row," 23
Holmes, Oliver Wendell, 51
Holt, Alfred, 326
The Home Book of Proverbs, Maxims, and Familiar Phrases (Stevenson), 288, 299–300
"honor lies in honest toil," 17
"honor the past, imagine the future," 211
"hope for the best, plan for the worst," 220
"hope springs eternal," 84, 246
"a house divided against itself cannot stand"
　A. Adams's citation of, 38
　biblical origins of, 5
　Bush's citation of, 53
　and division of Berlin, 5–6
　and Lewis, 174
　Lincoln's citation of, viii, 5–6, 38–39, 54, 56, 174–75, 183, 189
　Obama's citation of, xii, 56
　Perot's citation of, 54
"the houses hope builds are castles in the air," 18

Houston, Sam, 38
Howell, Dorothy Emma, 204–5
Hulme, F. Edward, 265–66
human rights
　and "all men are created equal," 221, 306–7
　Carter's advocacy of, 305
　H. Clinton's advocacy of, 211–13
　and Golden Rule, 95
　"human rights are women's rights and women's rights are human rights," 211–13
　King's advocacy of, 134, 138, 140, 177, 306–7
　Lewis's advocacy of, 150, 154, 173–74, 178
　"life, liberty, and the pursuit of happiness," 222
　"making a way out of no way," 138
　E. Roosevelt's advocacy of, 210, 221–22, 306
　Universal Declaration of Human Rights, 221–22, 306
"hurry and wait," 11

Ibrahim, Hafez, 209
"ideological deadlock," 186
"idle hands are the devil's workshop," 219
"if at first you don't succeed, try, try again," 16
"if at first you don't succeed, try, try reading the instructions" (antiproverb), 16
"if it looks like a duck, walks like a duck, and quacks like a duck, it's a duck," 12, 171
"if life gives you a bag of hammers, build something," 23
"if life hands you lemons, make lemonade," 23, 208

"if passion drives, let reason hold the reins," 18
"if there is grass [female pubic hair] on the field, you can play ball," 13
"if there is no struggle, there is no progress," 16, 41, 163
"if they are too big to fail, they are too big," 244–45
"if time be of all things the most precious, wasting time must be the greatest prodigality," 36
"if wishes were horses, beggars would ride," 126
"if women and girls don't flourish, families won't flourish; and if families don't flourish, communities and nations won't flourish," 211
"if you can't beat them, join them," 14
"if you can't be good, be careful," 14
"if you can't dazzle them with brilliance, baffle them with bullshit," 15
"if you can't run with the big dogs, stay on the porch," 15
"if you can't stand the heat, get out of the kitchen," 19
if you can't X, Y structural pattern, 14–15
"if you have to ask the price, you can't afford it," 22
"if you invest in America, America will invest in you," 9
"if you've got it, flaunt it," 13
"if you want to talk the talk, you've got to walk the walk," 166–67
"I have a dream. . . .," 51–52, 138–41, 149–50, 250
"an ill wind that blows nobody good," 80

immigrants, 108–109, 258–59
"in a nutshell," 67
inclusivity in proverbs, 194–95
"industry need not wish," 18
The Influence of Authority in Matters of Opinion (Lewis), 265
"injustice anywhere is a threat to justice everywhere," 17
"in order to get where you want to go, you have to start from where you are now," 12
"in politics, perception is reality," 200
"International Bibliography of New and Reprinted Proverb Collections" (Mieder), 298
International Bibliography of Paremiography (Mieder), 298
International Proverb Archives, University of Vermont, 298
interrogatives, parables as, 14
"in the long run," 154, 162
"in the middle of difficulty lies opportunity," 20
"in the sweat of thy brow shalt thou eat bread," 88
"in union there is strength," 43, 71
An Invitation to the White House (Clinton), 203, 222–23
Irving, Washington, xvi
"Is It a Crime for a US Citizen to Vote?" (Anthony), 77–78
Islam, 56–57
isolationism, 47
"it is a poor rule that will not work both ways," 18
"it is better to know something than nothing," 264
"it is difference of opinion that makes horseraces," 18

"it is Greek, it cannot be read" (*graecum est, no potest legi*), 335, 336–37
"it is harder to use victory than to get it," 5
"it is hard to miss what you have never known," 166
"it is not the trumpeters that fight the battles," 18
"it is no use crying over spilled milk," 4
"it pays to advertise," 21
"it's never too late to learn," 264
"it's not easy to be green," 13
"it's not over till it's over," 18
"it's not the meat [penis], it's the motion," 13
"it's not the size of the dog in the fight that matters; it's the size of the fight in the dog," 11
"it's not what you've got [penis size], it's what you do with it," 13
"it's the economy, stupid," 208
"it's the hit dog that howls," 219
It Takes a Village (Fletcher), 216
It Takes a Village and Other Lessons Children Teach Us (Clinton)
  on building character in children, 205
  chapter titles in, 220, 225
  on Clinton's youth, 204
  general use of proverbs and proverbial phrases, xii, 226
  "it takes a village to raise a child," 214–16, 217
  scope and success of, 203
  "it takes a village to raise a child," 214–17
"It Takes a Village to Win" (Spiker), 201–202
"it takes money to make money," 239

"it takes two to quarrel," 53
"it takes two to tango," 6–7, 53

Jackson, Andrew, 16
Jackson, Jesse, 192
Jefferson, Thomas, xiv, 16, 23, 183, 298–300. *See also* "all men are created equal"
Jeremiah, Milford A., 136
Johnson, Samuel, 209
Jonson, Ben, xv, 339
"judge not from appearances," 76
"justice too long delayed is justice denied," 51

Kakutani, Michiko, 184
Karabegović, Dženeta, 124
Karpova, Olga, 287
Keene, H. G., 264
"keeping one's head above water," 254
"keep it real," 168
"keep your eyes on the prize," 147, 150, 165
"Keep Your Eyes on the Prize" (battle hymn of civil rights movement), 145–47
The Kenkyusha Dictionary of Current English Idioms (Ichikawa, et al., eds.), 292
Kennedy, John F.
  "ask not what your country can do for you, ask what you can do for your country," 17, 50–51
  and Equal Pay Act, 249–50
  general use of proverbs and proverbial phrases, ix, 35, 50
  "let us never negotiate out of fear; but let us never fear to negotiate," 50, 209
  "right makes might," 277
Kennedy, Joseph P., 20
Keyes, Ralph, 211
Khrushchev, Nikita, 35
King, Martin Luther, Jr., 123–41

"all men are created equal," 306–307
"the arc of the moral universe is long, but it bends toward justice," 52, 134, 137, 161–62
"to be judged by the content of one's character....," 139, 250
civil rights work of, 130, 305
on economic disparities, 245
general use of proverbs and proverbial phrases, ix, x–xi, 123, 125–26, 128, 132, 138, 139–40
and Golden Rule, 94–95, 183
"I have a dream....," 51–52, 138–41, 149–50, 250
"injustice anywhere is a threat to justice everywhere," 17
on interrelationship with the world, 130–31
"justice too long delayed is justice denied," 51
and Lewis, 134, 148, 149–50, 154, 158–59
"life, liberty, and the pursuit of happiness," 132, 306, 307
"love your enemies," x, 126, 127, 133, 306
"making a way out of no way," 136–38, 141, 176
on "maladjustment," 132–33
"man does not live by bread alone," x, 127
"might does not make right," 273
"no lie can live forever," x, 52, 134, 161
nonviolence emphasized by, 126, 128, 157–58, 159, 273
and Obama, 56, 58, 183, 185, 192, 193, 197, 307
on poverty, 127

on progress in race relations, 134–36, 161–62, 172
as proverbial giant, 182
rhetorical style of, x–xi, 124–28, 134, 139, 152
and Sanders, 250–51
scholarship on rhetoric of, 123–25, 139
on segregation, 129
Strength to Love, 126
Stride toward Freedom, 176
"truth crushed to earth will rise again," 134, 137, 161
use of word *way*, 134–36
Where Do We Go from Here, 131
"you reap what you sow," 52, 137, 161–62
Kingsbury, Stewart A., 301
King's Dream (Sundquist), 139, 140
Klein, Michael, 184
knowledge
  "it is better to know something than nothing," 264
  "it's never too late to learn," 264
  "a little learning is a dangerous thing," 264
  "what you don't learn from your mother, you learn from the world," 217
  "you can't teach an old dog new tricks," 264
knowledge of proverbs, 220
Koran, proverbial wisdom from, 56–57
Kreeft, Peter, 281

"the laborer is worthy of his hire," 89
"laissez faire à Georges," xv
  case against loan translation, 320–21
  historical explanations of, 319–20
  longer version of, 318
  obsolescence of, 320, 323
  origin of, 318, 325–26

"last hired, first fired," x, 129
"late children, early orphans," 11
Latin, medieval, 3
"laziness travels so slowly, that poverty soon overtakes it," 18, 36
length of proverbs, 10–11
Lenin, Vladimir, 35
"let George do it," xv
  contemporary use of, 329–30
  earliest print references to, 326
  and identity of "George," 327–28
  popularity of, 329
  and Prime Minister George of Great Britain, 323, 329
  and Pullman porters, 327–28, 330
  references citing English/American origins of, 323–25
  references citing French origins of, 321–23
  variants of, 326
"Let George Do It" comic strip (McManus), 323
"let judgment run down like waters and righteousness like a mighty stream," 133
"Letter from a Birmingham Jail" (King), 51
"let the dead bury their dead," 70, 71
"let the past be the past," 66
"let us never negotiate out of fear; but let us never fear to negotiate," 50, 209
Lewis, George Cornewall, 265
Lewis, John, 145–78
  on affirmative action, 164
  and Biblical proverbs, 155, 160
  biographies on, 148
  and Bond, 170–72
  book dedicated to, 151–52
  on church leaders, 156

family life of, 155–56, 165–66
general use of proverbs and proverbial phrases, 154
and Golden Rule, 159–60
and King, 134, 148, 149–50, 154, 158–59
leadership of civil rights movement, xi, 147, 148–49, 150–51, 166, 169–70
on "making a way out of no way," 175, 176–78
and Malcolm X's militancy, 156
nonviolence emphasized by, 149, 150, 156–58, 167–68
and Obama, 192
and parents' perspectives, 155–56
political career of, 150, 167, 171–73
on progress in race relations, 172–73
on public attention, 169
rhetorical style of, 153–54, 174
on segregation/separation, 164
on social awareness/activism, 160–61
on solidarity in human rights struggle, 173–74
on youth activism, 162–63
youth of, 155–56, 166, 177–78
See also *Across That Bridge*; *March*; *Walking with the Wind*
"a lie can be twice around the world before the truth gets its boots on," 11, 219
life
  American proverbs about, 22–23
  "but does thou love life, then do not squander life, for that is the stuff life is made of," 36
  "if life gives you a bag of hammers, build something," 23

"if life hands you lemons, make lemonade," 23, 208
"life comes at you fast," 23
"life has its ups and downs," 23
"life is a bitch, and then you die," 23
"life is a bowl of cherries," 23
"life is like a box of chocolates," 20, 224–25
"life is not a spectator sport," 23, 225, 259
"life is too short to drink bad wine," 225
"life is too short to wait for someday," 225
"life is too short to waste sleeping," 23, 225
"life is what you make it," 125
"nobody ever said life is easy," 23
"you get out of life what you put into it," 23
"life, liberty, and the pursuit of happiness"
  as American ideal, 23
  Carter's citation of, 305
  Clinton's citation of, 222
  disagreement on proverbial status of, 301
  King's citation of, 51, 123, 132, 306, 307
  Lewis's citation of, 162
  Lincoln's citation of, 302
  Marshall's citation of, 103–104
  Obama's citation of, 187
  Sanders's citation of, 242
The Life of the Learned Sir John Cheke (Strype), 335–36
Lincoln, Abraham
  "all men are created equal," xiv, 104, 302–3
  "broken eggs cannot be mended," 16
  general use of proverbs and proverbial phrases, 35

and Golden Rule, 94, 188, 258
"government of the people, by the people, and for the people," 23, 57–58, 104, 222, 242–43
"a house divided against itself cannot stand," viii, 5–6, 38–39, 54, 56, 174–75, 183, 189
and misattributed quotes, 19
and Obama, 56, 58, 183, 185, 189–90, 192, 197, 278, 307
proverbs falsely attributed to, 5–6
"right makes might," vii–viii, xiv, 40–41, 48, 274–76
See also Gettysburg Address of Lincoln
Lindbergh, Charles A., 18
"the line of progress is never straight," 17
Litovkina, Anna Tothné, 310
"a little knowledge is a dangerous thing," x, 105
"a little learning is a dangerous thing," 264
"a live trout is better than a dead whale," 14
Living History (Clinton)
on Clinton's youth, 204
general use of proverbs and proverbial phrases, xii, 220, 226
"it takes a village to raise a child," 216–17
on religious faith, 206
scope and success of, 203
Locke, John, 301
Lombardi, Vince, 20
Longfellow, Henry Wadsworth, 18
A Long Hard Journey (McKissack and McKissack), 328–29
"a long shot is better than no shot," 14

"look before you leap," 183, 196, 263
Loos, Anita, 18
"lost time is never found again," 22, 36
Louis, Joe, 19
"love is blind," 3
"love thy neighbor, but do not get caught" (antiproverb), 16
"love thy neighbor as thyself," 16, 37, 158, 206
"love your enemies," x, 126, 127, 133, 206, 306
Luther, Martin, 5, 19, 34
Luther, Seth, 308

"Makin' a Way out of No Way" (Daniel, Smitherman-Donaldson, and Jeremiah), 136
"making a way out of no way"
as American ideal, 23
as American proverb, viii
and "God will make a way out of no way" variant, 137, 175
King's citation of, x, 136–38, 140, 141, 176
Lewis's citation of, 151, 175, 176–78
"Making a Way Out of No Way" (Mieder), 151–52
"making ends meet," 74, 178, 247–48
Man Cannot Speak for Her (Campbell), 64
Mandela, Nelson, 209
"man does not live by bread alone," x, 3, 115, 127
"manners matter," 10
"man proposes, God disposes," 112
"many hands make light work," 263
March (Lewis), 154, 168
marriage, 88–89
"marriage is a journey, not a destination," 14
Marshall, George C., x

brevity of, 106–7, 108
and Churchill, 108
on democracy, 103–4
on East/West division, 116
on European refugees, 108–9
honors, 100
impact of, 119–20
on language skills, 108
"man does not live by bread alone," x, 115
retirement of, 119
and Roosevelt, 107, 119
on small/interconnected nature of world, 102–3
and Soviets, 103–4, 106
and Truman, 119
Marshall, John, 222
Marshall Plan, x, 100–120
approval and enactment of, 118
and author's childhood, 101
criticized as imperialistic, 107–8
and "equivalent to the Marshall Plan" proverb, 119
and European refugees, 108–9
humanitarian aspects of, 105–6, 110–11, 115, 117, 118, 120
Marshall's advocacy for, 105–18, 120
name of, 111, 118
Soviets' rejection of, 106
and Truman, 101, 103, 114, 115, 118, 119
Mason, George, 299
Mather, Cotton, 18
McClintock, Elizabeth W., 92
McGrory, Mary, 153
McKissack, Fredrick, 328
McKissack, Patricia, 328
Meacham, Jon, 153
media, parables from, 20–21
Meis, Morgan, 189
Melville, Herman, xvi
Mencken, H. L., 317, 321, 325

Men in Dark Times (Arendt), 280
mens sana in corpore sano ("a strong mind in a strong body"), 218
mens sana in corpore sano ("the coming girl is to have health"), 43
"a messy desk is a sign of a messy mind," 12
Middleton, Thomas, xv
Mieder, Horst, 109
"might makes right," vii, xiii–xiv
  antiproverb of (*see* "right makes might")
  in authors' commentaries on power politics, 271–73
  book and film titles featuring, 270–71
  European language variants of, 268
  and "m(r)ight makes r(m)ight" proverbial pair, xiii–xiv, 48, 268, 276, 278–81
  paremiographical history of, 269–70
  in sources from classical antiquity, 268
  Stanton's citation of, 43, 83
Miles of Smiles, Years of Struggle (Santino), 328
Miller, Keith D., 124, 125
Miller, Mike, 153
Miller, Richard Brian, 280–81
"the mills of the gods grind slowly, but they grind exceedingly fine," 114
"mind your own business," 102, 103
minorities, 8–9. *See also* African Americans
misattributed quotes, 19, 210
money
  "getting their money's worth," 190
  "it takes money to make money," 239
  "making ends meet," 74, 178, 247–48
  "money begets money," 167
  "money doesn't grow on trees," 205
  "money has no memory," 22
  "money is power," 22, 78
  "money is the sinews of love and war," 73
  "a penny saved is a penny earned," 4
  "penny wise, pound foolish," 231
  "time is money," 7
  See also economics
Montaigne, Michel Eyquem de, 46
Morgan, J. P., 20
Morrison, Toni, 216
Morton Salt company, 21
motherhood
  "denial ain't just a river in Egypt," 219
  "the hand that rocks the cradle is the hand that moves the world," 81
  "late children, early orphans," 11
  "a mother is a school; empower her and you empower a nation," 209
  "the mother is the queen of the home," 87–88
  "mother knows best," 205
  "what you don't learn from your mother, you learn from the world," 217
"the mountain labored and brought forth a mouse," 67
"m(r)ight makes r(m)ight" proverbial pair, xiii–xiv, 278–81
  early references to, 278–79
  interpreted as contrary pieces of wisdom, 279–81
  and Lincoln, 276
  Truman's citation of, 48, 279–80
  See also "might makes right"; "right makes might"
"my country, right or wrong," 16
my X, my/your Y structural pattern, 11

Nash, Ogden, 19
Native Americans, 8–9, 44
"nature abhors a vacuum," 67, 79
nature-nurture question, 207
"nature passes nurture," 207
"need to push and push and not stop pushing," 169
Nelson, Jack, 153
"never bring a knife to a gunfight," 12
"never give a sucker an even break," 14
"never play leapfrog with a unicorn," 14
"never say die," 14
never structural pattern, 14
"never try to teach a pig to sing; it wastes your time, and it annoys the pig," 14
"new brooms sweep clean," 3
Nichols, Ray, 58
Nixon, Richard, 304–305
"nobody bats a thousand," 9
"nobody ever said life is easy," 23
"nobody is perfect," 16, 112
"no body is perfect" (antiproverb), 16
"nobody washes a rental car," 21
"no family is an island" (antiproverb), 225
"no gain without pain," x, 130
"no glove, no love," 13, 20
"no just government can be formed without the consent of the governed," 163–64
"no lie can live forever," x, 52, 134, 161
"'No Lie Can Live Forever'" (Karabegović), 124

"no man is an island," x, 130–31
"no matter how long the night, the day is sure to come," 218
"no one ever went bankrupt taking a profit," 20
"no pain, no gain," x, 130
No Struggle, No Progress (Mieder), 163
"not all publicity is good publicity"/"all publicity is good publicity," 15
"nothing in excess," 59
"nothing is certain but uncertainty itself," 266
"nothing is more precious than time, yet nothing is less valued," 22
"nothing is perfect," 118
"nothing succeeds like success," 22
"not holding up their end of the bargain," 190
no X, no Y structural pattern, 14

Obama, Barack, xi–xii, 182–97
  "all men are created equal," 307–8
  on the black church, 175–76
  and Clinton, 202–3, 209, 213
  and Constitution of United States, 188–89
  and economic opportunity, 190–91
  on empathy, 187–88
  faith of, 191–92
  general use of proverbs and proverbial phrases, ix, 35, 183–84
  Golden Rule cited by, xii, 58, 95, 187–88, 192, 194, 206, 258
  "government of the people, by the people, and for the people," 57–58
  "a house divided against itself cannot stand," 55–56
  "if you invest in America, America will invest in you," 9
  on international diplomacy and world affairs, 195–96
  and King's rhetorical style, 134–35
  and Lincoln, 56, 58, 183, 185, 189–90, 278
  and partisan politics, 185–87
  and proverbial wisdom of Koran, 56–57
  and race, 192–95
  rhetorical style/skills of, 183–85, 189–90
  "right makes might," 278
  "a rising tide lifts all boats," xii, 183, 190, 193, 249
  and Sanders' political ideology, 233
  sources of rhetorical inspiration for, 56, 58, 183, 192, 197, 307
  values of, 187–88
  "what is good for Main Street is good for Wall Street," 17, 208
  See also *Dreams from My Father*; *The Audacity of Hope*
"old age is not for sissies," 20
"old enough to bleed, old enough to breed," 13
Old Proverbs Never Die, They Just Diversify (Litovkina and Mieder), 310
Olive, David, 184
"one hand (person) cannot bring up (nurse) a child," 216
"one hand washes the other," 3
"one man/person, one vote," 240–42
"one picture is worth a thousand words," 7
"one swallow does not make a summer," 3
"the one who smelt it dealt it," 13
"the only good Indian is a dead Indian," 8–9, 44
the only good X is a dead X structural pattern, 8–9
"the only place where success comes before work is in a dictionary," 22
"the only thing we have to fear is fear itself," 17, 46–47
"the only way to have a friend is to be one," 47
"opposites attract," 264
Otakpor, Nkeonye, 265
Otis, James, 19
Oudin, Antoine, 319
"an ounce of prevention is worth a pound of cure," 225
"an ounce of prevention is worth a pound of intensive care," 225
"Our Boys" (Stanton), 85
"our choices define us," 23
"Our Girls" (Stanton), 82, 84–86
Our Revolution (Sanders), xiii
  on "big money" influencing elections, 242–44
  on democratic socialism, 232
  on economic disparities, 246
  on equal pay, 249–50
  "government of the people, by the people, and for the people," 242–43
  "one person, one vote," 241–42
  on presidential campaign, 252–53
  "the rich get richer, and the poor get poorer," 238–39
  on speech writing, 256
  "too big to fail," 244–45
  and Trump's immigration policies, 258–59
  on universal health care, 231
"out of many, one" (*e pluribus unum*), 57, 194

"out of sight, out of mind," 171, 263, 265
Outsider in the House (Sanders), xiii, 235–36, 240
"over the long term," 190
Oxford Dictionary of English Proverbs (Boston), 265
Oxford English Dictionary, 324, 325–26

Paczolay, Gyula, 4
"paddle your own canoe," viii, 23
Paine, Thomas, 5, 16, 38, 65
The Papers of George Catlett Marshall (Stoler and Bland), 101–2, 114
parallel structure in proverbs, 11
Parker, Theodore, 16, 222
Parks, Rosa, 192
partisan politics, 185–87
Partridge, Eric, 329
"a penny saved is a penny earned," 4
"penny wise, pound foolish," 231
The People, Yes (Sandburg), 196
"the perfect is the enemy of the good," 208
Perot, Ross, 53–54
phraseology, 123
Phraseology (Bulger), 123
"pie in the sky," 156
"the pitcher goes so often to the well that it is broken at last," 3
"play hard," 205
"play to win or don't play at all," 21
political discourse, proverbs used in, 34–59
of A. Adams, 36–38
"ask not what your country can do for you, ask what you can do for your country," 50–51
"the buck stops here," 48–50
of G. W. Bush, 53
"*e pluribus unum*" (out of many, one), 57
on fear, 46–47
"government of the people, by the people, and for the people," 23, 57–58
on imperialistic policies/threats, 44–45
on isolationism, 47
of Kennedy, 50–51
of King, 51–52
"might makes right," 43
and "m(r)ight makes r(m)ight" proverbial pair, 48
on Native Americans, 44
of Obama, 55–56
of Perot, 53–54
potential ambivalence in, 35
of Reagan, 52–53
"right makes might," 39–41
of F. D. Roosevelt, 45–47
of T. Roosevelt, 44–45
on slavery, 5, 39–42
"taxation without representation is tyranny," 42–43
of Truman, 47–50
"in union there is strength," 43
on unity and common purpose, 54–58
of Wilson, 45
on women's rights, 42–44
See also "a house divided against itself cannot stand"
"politics is a contact sport," 200
"politics is not a spectator sport" (antiproverb), xvi, 259
"politics make strange bedfellows," 200, 256
polygenesis of "laissez faire à Georges" and "let George do it," xv, 317–30. *See also* "laissez faire à Georges"; "let George do it"
Poor Richard's Almanack series, viii, 17, 35
poverty
"deficit reduction can't take place on the backs of the poor," 186
"it takes money to make money," 239
"laziness travels so slowly, that poverty soon overtakes it," 18, 36
"man does not live by bread alone," 127
"the rich get richer, and the poor get children" (antiproverb), 235
"the rich get richer, and the poor get poorer," xiii, 235–40
and Sanders's political ideology, 232, 233, 254
"you can't get blood out of a stone," 239
"practice what you preach," x, 108–9
"prevention is better than cure," 225
The Princess (Tennyson), 91
productivity
"idle hands are the devil's workshop," 219
"many hands make light work," 263
"too many cooks spoil the broth," 263
"you can't roll up your sleeves and get to work if you're still wringing your hands," 219
"the proof of the pudding is in the eating," x, 107, 220
"the prophet is not without honor, save in his own country," 3
Protestant work ethic, viii, 36
The Proverb (Taylor), 266
Proverb Lore (Hulme), 266
"the public debate has been deadlocked," 190
Pullman porters, 318, 323, 327–29, 330
"put their heads together," 68

quotations turned to proverbs, x

Rabin, Yitzhak, 209, 219–20
Race Grit (Hayne), 175
racial minorities, 192–95.
  See also civil rights
  movement
racial stereotypes and slurs,
  8–9
*Random House Dictionary
  of Popular Proverbs
  & Sayings* (Titelman),
  301
"the rank and file," 154
"the rats are leaving the
  sinking ship," 72
"reach out and touch
  someone," 21
Reagan, Nancy, 210
Reagan, Ronald, ix, 6–7, 20,
  52–53, 224
"Reconstruction begins at
  home," 82
Rees, Nigel, 321, 325
refugees of Europe, 108–9
Religious Proverbs (Griffin), 95
Reynolds, Barbara, 207
"the rich get richer, and the
  poor get children"
  (antiproverb), 235
"the rich get richer, and the
  poor get poorer," xiii,
  235–40
Rieder, Jonathan, 124, 134
"right makes might"
  book titles featuring, 274
  European language
    variants of, 269
  frequency of citation, 274,
    276
  Kennedy's citation of, 277
  and King, 273
  Lincoln's citation of,
    vii–viii, xiv, 40–41, 48,
    274–76
  Lincoln's role in
    establishing, xiv, 274–76
  Middle English variants
    of, 273
  modern citations of, 277–78

and "m(r)ight makes r(m)
  ight" proverbial pair,
  xiii–xiv, 48, 268, 276,
  278–81
Obama's citation of, 278
paremiographical history
  of, 273–74
and "Right Makes Might"
  (song), 276–77
Sanders's citation of, xiii
Shakespeare's citation of,
  274, 275
Truman's citation of, 48,
  280
"Right Makes Might" (song),
  276–77
Rigsby, Enrique, 153
"a rising tide lifts all boats"
  Obama's citation of, xii, 183,
    190, 193, 249
  Sanders's citation of,
    248–49
Rodham, Hugh Ellsworth,
  204, 205
Roman antiquity, proverbs
  originating in, 3, 268
Roosevelt, Eleanor
  and H. Clinton, 201, 209–11,
    214, 306
  "each generation is better
    than the last," 19
  and Universal Declaration
    of Human Rights,
    221–22, 306
  and "a woman is like a
    teabag" proverb, 209–11
  on women serving as
    president, 214
Roosevelt, Franklin D.
  "to be in the same boat,"
    54–55
  general use of proverbs and
    proverbial phrases, ix, 35
  and Marshall, 107, 119
  "the only thing we have
    to fear is fear itself," 17,
    46–47
  rhetorical power of, 45–46
Roosevelt, Theodore, 17, 35,
  44–45, 279

Rosenberg, Arnold, 334
"a rose would smell just as
  sweet by any other
  name," 78
Roughing It (Twain), 48
"rules of the road," 195–96
Russian interest in English/
  American quotations,
  proverbs, and idioms,
  287

"safety first," 10
Salmond, John, 153
Sandburg, Carl, 39, 196
Sanders, Bernie, xiii, 230–60
  and animal-related
    metaphors/proverbs, 255
  background of, 230
  on "big money" influencing
    elections, 237–38,
    240–44
  on climate change, 249
  "enough is enough," 232–34
  equal rights advocacy of,
    250–51, 257–58
  filibuster speech of 2010,
    233–34, 239, 246
  and Golden Rule, xiii, 257–59
  "government of the people,
    by the people, and for
    the people," 232, 242–43
  on greed of the rich, 245–46
  *Guide to Political
    Revolution*, 249–50,
    259–60
  and health care debate, 231
  on immigration policies,
    258–59
  and King, 250–51
  Outsider in the House, xiii,
    235–36, 240
  on plight of the working
    class, 246–49
  political ideology of,
    230–35, 237–38, 255–56,
    259
  presidential campaign of,
    232, 234, 237–38, 240–41,
    245–46, 252–53, 255–57,
    260

Sanders, Bernie *(cont.)*
　public service career of,
　　230, 251–52
　rhetorical style of, 231–32,
　　249, 253–54, 256–57, 259
　"the rich get richer, and the
　　poor get poorer," xiii,
　　235–40
　"too big to fail," 244–45
　See also *Our Revolution*
Santino, Jack, 328
scatology, 12–13. *See also* shit
scholarly texts on proverbs
　and proverbial
　expressions, 288–98
Scott, Sir Walter, xvi
"security takes more than a
　blanket," 211, 220
"see America first," 9
"seeing is believing," 220
"seeking to chip away
　at the very idea of
　government," 186
Sermon on the Mount, 192
service
　"[service is] the rent we pay
　　for life," 219
　"service is not a one-way
　　street," 211
sexuality in proverbs, 12–13
Shakespeare, William
　"all the world's a stage," 165
　"brevity is the soul of wit," 3
　"it was Greek to me," xv,
　　338, 345
　"m(r)ight makes r(m)ight"
　　proverbial pair, xiv, 274
"shaking in their boots," 66
Shapiro, Fred R., 301–2, 321
Shaw, George Bernard, xvi
Sheckels, Theodore, 213
Shelton, Thomas, 339
Sherman, William Tecumseh,
　20
shit
　"everybody shits," 10
　"shit happens," 12
　"shit in one hand and hope
　　in the other; see which
　　one fills up first," 13

"shit or get off the pot," 13
"you can't kill shit," 13
"you can't make a chicken
　salad out of chicken
　shit," 13
"shoot for the stars," 12
"shooting fish in a barrel," 254
"shop till you drop," 21
"the show must go on," 7
"sick and tired," 233
"silence is not spoken here,"
　211
"situational normal—all
　fucked up," 13
"size doesn't matter"/"size
　does matter," 15
slavery and abolitionism
　and "all men are created
　　equal," 302–3, 308
　Anthony on, 93–94
　and Declaration of
　　Independence, 300
　Douglass on, 41–42
　and Golden Rule, 93–94
　and Lincoln's "house
　　divided" speech, 5, 39–41
　and "right makes might,"
　　275–76
　Stanton on, 93
　See also Douglass,
　　Frederick
"the sleeping fox catches no
　poultry," 36
"slicing the pie rather than
　growing the pie," 190
"sloth, like rust, consumes
　faster than labor wears,
　while the used key is
　always bright," 36
"sloth makes all things
　difficult, but industry all
　easy," 18, 36
Sly and the Family Stone,
　viii, 24
Smith, Emmitt, 310
Smith, James McCune, 275
Smitherman-Donaldson,
　Geneva, 136
socialism, 230–31
"socialism for the rich," 245

Socrates Meets Kant (Kreeft),
　281
"a soft answer turneth away
　wrath," 277
solidarity, 174
"some are weatherwise, some
　are otherwise," 18
"someday they will give a
　war and nobody will
　come," 8
Sommer, Theo, 7
songs, proverbs from, 20
"sounds often terrify more
　than realities," 16
"sour grapes will set teeth on
　edge," 67
Soviet Union
　and Iron Curtain, 103
　and Marshall, 103–4
　and Marshall Plan, 106
　and Reagan's "trust but
　　verify" perspective, 224
　US relations with, 53
"speak softly and carry a big
　stick," 17, 44–45
"speed kills," 10
Spiker, Julia A., 201–2
sports, 9
Stalin, Joseph, 103, 106
Stanton, Elizabeth Cady
　abolitionist stance of, 93
　"all men and women and
　　created equal," 16, 66, 84,
　　222, 303–4, 306
　animal metaphors used by,
　　72, 81
　Anthony's relationship
　　with, 66
　and Clinton, 222
　death of, 69
　"Declaration of
　　Sentiments," 222, 303
　and feminist rhetoric,
　　63–66
　general use of proverbs
　　and proverbial phrases,
　　viii–ix
　and Golden Rule, 91–93, 95
　lectures and speeches of,
　　74–77, 80–86

on marriage, 88–89
and "m(r)ight makes r(m)ight" proverbial pair, 43, 83
"Our Boys," 85
"Our Girls," 82, 84–86
"plain English" emphasized by, 75
as proverbial giant, 182
scholarship on, 63–64
"Woman's Rights" speech, 75–77
Steele, Sir Richard, 336
Steinem, Gloria, 20
"step up to the plate," 9
Stevenson, Burton, 288, 299–300
"sticking one's neck out," 254
"sticks and stones may break my bones, but words will never hurt me," 204
"stinks to high heaven," 252
Stoler, Mark A., 100, 101, 114
"stoop low and it will save you many a bump through life," 18
"straight is the gate, and narrow is the way which leadeth unto life," 155
Strange, Lisa, 86
strategies, proverbs' role as, 266
"the straw that breaks the camel's back," 78–79
Strength to Love (King), 126
Stride toward Freedom (King), 176
"strike while the iron is hot," 3
"a strong mind in a strong body" (*mens sana in corpore sano*), 218
structural patterns in proverbs, 13–15
Strype, John, 335–36
"stuff happens," 12
success
 "if wishes were horses, beggars would ride," 126
 "nothing succeeds like success," 22
 "the only place where success comes before work is in a dictionary," 22
 "success comes in *cans*, failure in *can'ts*," 22
 "success is a journey, not a destination," 14, 22
 "success is always preceded by preparation," 22
 "success is never final," 22
"survival of the fittest," 247
"swimming against the prevailing tide," 190

"take a deep breath and count to ten," 204
"Taking Possession of the Country" (Gordon), 74
"talk is cheap," xii, 11, 188
"taxation without representation is tyranny," 19, 42–43, 78
Taylor, Archer, 266, 317–18
technology, influence of, 21
Tennyson, Alfred, Lord, 91
Teresa, Mother, 164–65
"testing the waters," 252–53
"there are no atheists in foxholes," 8
"there are no bad dogs, only bad owners," 15
"there are no bad students, only bad teachers," 15
"there are no dull subjects, just dull writers," 15
"there are no problems, only opportunities," 15
"there are no rules in a knife fight," 20
there are no X, only (just) Y structural pattern, 15
"there is an app for everything," 5
"there is no 'I' in team," 21
"there is no such thing as other peoples' children," 211
"there is nothing new under the sun," 3, 88

"there is room enough at the top," 19
"there must be pioneers, and some of them get killed," 18
Theresa of Avila, Saint, 46
"there's more than one way to beat the devil around the bush," 15
"there's more than one way to cook a goose," 15
"there's more than one way to peel an orange," 15
"there's more than one way to skin a cat," 15
there's more than one way to X structural pattern, 15
"there's no fool like an old fool," 264
"there's no place like home," 220
"there's nothing like family," 166
"there will be sleeping enough in the grave," 18, 36
"these are the times that try men's souls," 16
"these are the times that try women's souls," 65
"a thing of beauty is a joy forever," 263
"think big," 10, 259
"think globally, act locally," 8
"think outside the box," viii, 23
"this is a free country," viii, 23
Thoreau, Henry David, 47
"a threat to justice anywhere is a threat to justice everywhere," 149
"three removes is as bad as a fire," 18
"three strikes and you're out," 9, 223
"tightening their belts," 110
time
 "the best way to kill time is to work it to death," 22
 "if time be of all things the most precious, wasting time must be the greatest prodigality," 36

time (cont.)
  "lost time is never found again," 22, 36
  "nothing is more precious than time, yet nothing is less valued," 22
  "over the long term," 190
  "time and chance happen to all men," 22
  "time and tide wait for no man," x, 130
  "time flies," 16, 74
  "time flies when you are having fun," 16
  "time heals all wounds," 130
  "the time is always right to do what is right," 17
  "time is money," 7
  "the time to shoot bears is when they are out," 22
  "time wasted is time lost," 22
  "time will tell," 67
  "turning back the clock," 256
  "a watched pot never boils," 5
  "a week is a long time in politics," 200
  "what we call time enough, always proves little enough," 36
Titelman, Gregory, 301
"to add insult to injury," 247
"to be (all) Greek to someone," xv–xvi, 334–47
  and Accorso's *graecum est, no potest legi* ("it is Greek, it cannot be read"), 335, 336–37
  book titles featuring, 345
  and decline/resurgence of Greek language, 335–36
  early recorded references of, 337–38
  and English translation, 337–38
  florilegium of, 342–44, 345–46
  popularity of, 346–47
  variants of, 338–42, 345–46
  and waning knowledge of Latin, 337
"to be a dark hour," 46
"to be a dog in the manger," 47, 72, 73
"to be a flash in the pan," 169
"to be all together in something," 173–74
"to be an ostrich," 47
"to be at each other's throats," 247
"to be a team player," 154
"to be a thorn in the flesh," 160
"to be at the crossroads," 117
"to be at the heart of something," 187
"to be at the helm," 108
"to be a voice crying in the wilderness," 161
"to be dead set against somebody or something," 154
"to be in something together," 191
"to be in the air," 154
"to be in the middle of nowhere," 154
"to be in the same boat," 54–55, 174, 249
"to be judged by the content of one's character and not by the color of one's skin," 139, 250
"to be on one's own," 191
"to be the last straw," 154
"to break the bottleneck," 114, 115
"to break through the glass ceiling," 213, 214
"to burn one's bridges," 70
"to circle the wagons," 174
"to cross the Jordan," 87
"to draw a line in the sand," 234
"to draw the line," 154
"to egg someone on," 167–68
"to fight an uphill battle," 247–48
"to get back on one's feet," 114, 115
"to get between two millstones," 72–73
"to get down to business," 114, 115, 154
"to get in the way of something," 149, 150, 151
"to get the ball rolling," 114, 115
"to get the short end of the stick," 246
"to hang in the balance," x, 113–14
"to hang like (have) a millstone around one's neck," 80
"to hang on a thin thread," 178
"to have a long way to go," 134–35, 172–73
"to have a stake in something," 113, 174
"to have come a long way," 134–35, 172–73
"to have egg on one's face," 168
"to have fair play," 45
"to have the scales fall from one's eyes," 160
"to hit the ground running," 173
"to join hands with someone," 139
"to jump like parched peas on a hot shovel," 70
"to keep a lamp burning, we have to keep putting oil in it," 164–65
"to keep the pot boiling," 67
"to know where the shoe pinches," 87, 88
"to lend a helping hand," 107
"to let it all out," 157
"to look someone square in the eyes," 187
"to make ends meet", 74, 178, 247–48
"to make up one's mind," 45
"to not give (change, yield) an iota," 78
"too big to fail," 244–45

"too big to jail" (antiproverb), 244
"too many cooks spoil the broth," 263
"to open someone's eyes," 154, 159
"to pay the price for something," 148
"to play by the rules," 154
"to play cat and mouse," 70
"to pull a string," 76–77
"to put a roof over one's head," 248
"to put one's best foot forward," 68
"to put on the line," 154
"to put something in a nutshell," 67
"to rise to the occasion," 114
"to rock the boat," 246
"to roll up one's sleeves," 154
"to rub someone the wrong way," 154
"to see eye to eye," 71
"to see something through someone else's eyes," 187
"to see the bad with the good," 45
"to see the big picture," 154
"to sell the same horse twice," x
"to set the wolf to keep, care for the sheep (lamb)," 76
"to shake in one's boots," 70
"to sink or swim," 80
"to sit on the fence," 80
"to speak the truth, the whole truth, and nothing but the truth," 46
"to stand in somebody else's shoes," 187
"to stand one's ground," 154
"to stand on the shoulders of giants," 170
"to strike a chord," 154
"to take into one's own hands," 154
"to take someone to task," 154
"to throw down the gauntlet," x, 154

"to throw overboard," 72–73
"to throw the baby out with the bathwater," 1, 164
"to throw to the wind(s)," 77
"to tighten one's belt," x
"to turn a blind eye," 249
"to turn one's back on somebody or something," 174
"to wash one's hands of something," 71–72
"to work behind the scene," 154
"to worship the golden calf," 73
translations of proverbs, 1, 4, 217–18
trends in proverbs, 10
"a true friend is the best possession," 13
Truman, Harry S.
  "all men are created equal," 304
  "the buck stops here," 19, 48–50, 224
  on difficulty of presidency, 209
  general use of proverbs and proverbial phrases, ix, 35, 47–48
  "if you can't stand the heat, get out of the kitchen," 19
  and Marshall Plan, 47, 101, 103, 114, 115, 118, 119
  and Marshall's retirement, 119
  and "m(r)ight makes r(m)ight" proverbial pair, 48, 279–80
  rhetorical style of, 47–48
Trump, Donald, 259
"trust but verify," 20, 224
"trust in God, but lock your door/car," 21
truth
  "a lie can be twice around the world before the truth gets its boots on," 11, 219

"to speak the truth, the whole truth, and nothing but the truth," 46
"truth crushed to earth will rise again," 134, 137, 161
"the truth is marching on," 161
"turning back the clock," 256
"turning one's back," 254
"turning over in their graves," 66
Twain, Mark, xvi, 18, 48, 209
20,000 Quips and Quotes (Esar), 310
Twitter, 238
"two dogs over one bone seldom agree," 81
"two wrongs don't make a right," 79

United States, proverbs specific to, 9
United We Stand (Perot), 54
unity and common purpose, proverbs about, 54–58
Universal Declaration of Human Rights, 221–22, 306
University of Vermont, 314
unproven attributions, 19–20
US Constitution, 188–89, 300, 303
"use it or lose it," 221

validity of proverbs, 263–65
values, 187–88
variants in proverbs, 12
"violence begets violence," 166–67
"violence is a dead end," 57
Virginia Slims, 313
vision
  "a civilization flourishes when people plant trees under whose shade they will never sit," 217
  "honor the past, imagine the future," 211

vision (cont.)
  and King's "I have a dream," 138–41, 250
  "think big," 259
  think globally, act locally," 8
  "think outside the box," viii, 23
The Voice of Black Rhetoric (Smith and Robb), 135
"the voice of the people is the voice of God" (*vox populi, vox dei*), 196
Volkswagen, 21
Voss, Johann Heinrich, 19
"*vox populi, vox dei*" (the voice of the people is the voice of God), 196

Walking with the Wind (Lewis)
  autobiographical scope of, 148
  on community and human rights, 173–74
  general use of proverbs and proverbial phrases in, 154
  on King, 159, 161–62
  nonviolence emphasized in, 156–57
  on public attention, 169
  rhetorical style of, xi, 152–53, 169
  on solidarity in human rights struggle, 173–74
  on taking action, 165
"walk with the wind," 150, 151
war
  "the coldest peace is better than the warmest war," 209
  "money is the sinews of love and war," 73
  "someday they will give a war and nobody will come," 8
  "war is hell," xii, 20, 186
  "war will cease when men refuse to fight," 19

Warhol, Andy, 19
Warren, Mervyn A., 124
Washington, George, 16
"waste not, want not," 5
"a watched pot never boils," 5
The Way to Wealth (Franklin), viii, 17, 36–37
Webster, Daniel, 5, 19, 38, 182, 222
"a week is a long time in politics," 200
Wellesley, Arthur, 47
"we must learn to live together as brothers and sisters or perish together as fools," 149
"we rise and fall together," 191
"what gets measured gets done," 220
"what happens in Las Vegas stays in Las Vegas," 9
"what is good for General Motors is good for America," 9, 208
"what is good for Main Street is good for Wall Street," 17, 208
"what we call time enough, always proves little enough," 36
"what you don't learn from your mother, you learn from the world," 217
"when all is said done," 190
"when it gets dark enough you can see the stars," 131–32
"when it rains, collect water," 218
"when it rains, it pours," 21
"when the going gets tough, the tough get going," 20
"when you are in a common boat, cross the river peacefully together," 218
"when you pray, move your feet," 165
"when you're up to your ass in alligators, it's hard to remember you're there to drain the swamp," 12
Where Do We Go from Here (King), 131
"where's the beef?" 14
"where women prosper, countries prosper," 211
"while the cat's away, the mice will play," 170
Whiting, Bartlett Jere, 2
"the whole world hangs in the balance," 101
"why buy milk when you've got a cow at home?" 14
"why go out for hamburger when you can eat steak at home?" 14
Willis, Nathaniel Parker, 235
Wilson, Woodrow, 45
Wine, Alice, 145–46
"winning isn't everything," 186–87
"winning isn't everything; it's the only thing," 20, 187
"wisdom comes with age," 264
Wolfe, Thomas, 19
"Woman's Rights" (Stanton), 75–77
women
  and America's founding documents, 303
  and "glass ceiling" metaphor, 213, 214
  "if women and girls don't flourish, families won't flourish; and if families don't flourish, communities and nations won't flourish," 211
  "these are the times that try women's souls," 65
  "where women prosper, countries prosper," 211
  "a woman is like a teabag; you never know how strong she is until she's in hot water," 209–11
  "woman is the weaker vessel," 76

"a woman preaching is like a dog's walking on its hind legs," 209
"a woman's place is in the home" and modern antiproverbs, 91
"a woman without a man is like a fish without a bicycle," 20, 91
"women hold up half the sky," 217–18
women's rights movement, 63–96
  "all men and women are created equal," 16, 66, 84, 222
  and "all men are created equal," 308
  animal metaphors used in, 72
  and antiproverbs of modern feminists, 91
  Clinton's advocacy of, 211–14, 221–22
  Douglass's championing of, 41, 42
  and education of women, 84–85
  "equal pay for equal work," 16, 90–91, 249–50
  and feminist rhetoric, 63–65
  and Golden Rule, ix, 91–93, 95
  "human rights are women's rights and women's rights are human rights," 211–13
  and marriage, 88–89
  and motherhood, 87–88
  and passage of the Nineteenth Amendment, 69
  voting rights, 42–43, 69–71, 79, 81, 82–83, 90–91, 304
  and work outside the home, 88–90
  See also Anthony, Susan B.; Stanton, Elizabeth Cady
"work before play," 11

"work hard," 205
working class Americans, 246–50
The World According to Garp (film), 20
"the world is a place," 20
"the world is a small place," 102, 103
"world jogs on," 74
"would go a long way," 190
Wright, Jeremiah, 194

X, Malcolm, 156
X breeds Y structural pattern, 164
X is (are) X structural pattern, 14
X is a journey, not a destination structural pattern, 14
X is better than Y structural pattern, 14

Yankah, Kwesi, 266
"years bring wisdom," 84
"you always help yourself by helping others," 111–12
"you are slower than molasses running uphill in winter," 206
"you can fool all of the people some of the time; you can fool some of the people all of the time; but you can't fool all of the people all of the time," 19
"you cannot have two bites of a cherry," 68
"you can run, but you can't hide," 19
"you can't be a little pregnant," 13
"you can't be in two places at one time," 253
"you can't ever tell what a lousy calf will come to be," 13
"you can't fight city hall," 13

"you can't get blood out of a stone," 239
"you can't go home again," 19, 207, 208
"you can't have everything/it all," 11, 245–46
"you can't hit the ball if you don't swing," 9
"you can't judge a book by its cover," 21
"you can't judge a car by its paint job," 21
"you can't kill shit," 13
"you can't make a chicken salad out of chicken shit," 13
"you can't ride a man's back unless it is bent," 129
"you can't roll up your sleeves and get to work if you're still wringing your hands," 219
"you can't score if you don't shoot," 21
"you can't steal first base," 9
you can't structural pattern, 13
"you can't teach an old dog new tricks," 264
"you can't unscramble eggs," 7
"you can't win them all," 21
"you could have cut it with a knife," 171
"you don't take a knife to a gunfight," 12
"you get out of life what you put into it," 23
"you have to kiss a lot of frogs to find a prince," 8
"you have to live with yourself," 204
"you have to pull your own wagon," 23
"you never accumulate if you don't speculate," 22
"you reap what you sow," 52, 134, 137, 161–62
"you're on your own," 191

WOLFGANG MIEDER is University Distinguished Professor of German and Folklore at the University of Vermont. He is the founding editor of *Proverbium: Yearbook of International Proverb Scholarship*. His most recent books include *"Behold the Proverbs of a People": Proverbial Wisdom in Culture, Literature, and Politics* and *"Entkernte Weisheiten": Sprichwörter in Literatur, Medien und Karikaturen*.

www.ingramcontent.com/pod-product-compliance
Lightning Source LLC
Chambersburg PA
CBHW031845220426
43663CB00006B/499